The Fourteenth
Chronicle

The Fourteenth Chronicle

LETTERS AND DIARIES OF JOHN DOS PASSOS

Edited and with a
biographical narrative by
Townsend Ludington

Gambit
INCORPORATED
Boston
1973

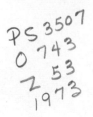
First printing
Copyright © 1973 by Elizabeth H. Dos Passos and Townsend Ludington

All rights reserved including the rights to reproduce this
book or parts thereof in any form

Library of Congress Catalog Card Number: 72-94006

International Standard Book Number: 0-87645-073-7

Printed in the United States of America

A Pushchart at the Curb, Copyright 1922 by John Dos Passos
Copyright renewed 1950 by John Dos Passos

Preface

In the 1960's John Dos Passos began calling his novels "contemporary chronicles," and to his last piece of fiction he gave the working title *The Thirteenth Chronicle*. These letters and diaries make a chronicle too; the fiction is primarily about the United States and other nations; *The Fourteenth Chronicle* is chiefly about him and his constant journeying during a life that began January 14, 1896, and ended September 28, 1970. Dos Passos' travels started in his early youth, and everything he saw gave him a perspective on what interested him most: the U.S.A.

In these letters and diaries, extending from 1910 until two months before his death, he tells of what he is doing, describes vividly the scenes before him, and tries to explain his stands on the social issues he felt compelled to confront. He also talks about writing. His diaries and particularly the early letters to Walter Rumsey Marvin reveal how much he worked to create a distinctive style out of the literature, art, drama, and music he was absorbing. Much more, I think, than in his previously published work, one finds in this collection Dos Passos talking personally, revealing a man of humor, intensely loyal to his friends, be they famous like Ernest Hemingway, Edmund Wilson, and F. Scott Fitzgerald, or unknown to the general public like Walter Rumsey Marvin and Dudley Poore.

The letters, postcards, and one telegram included here were chosen from among the several thousand papers I examined. Dos Passos was a prolific letter writer, and I make no claim to having located all his correspondence. This selection was made in an attempt to present his life. It is then, if successful, a kind of autobiography, with my biographical narrative intended to fill in gaps and clarify references. One collection of letters, those to his college friend Arthur McComb, I could not include because of publication restrictions. The diary selections are a representative sampling of those he kept from as early as his days at the Choate School until after World War I. I did not include excerpts from later notebooks and journals, because at about the same time as he began publishing novels, his entries became less the sort of personal comment that seemed to fit the autobiographical pattern of this book. Also at about this time he made more friends to whom he could pour out his thoughts, and, perhaps most important, he gained confidence.

These letters and diaries should enhance Dos Passos' reputation. They show a complex person few but his friends knew, an intelligent man, remarkably well read, sensitive and shy, who struggled constantly with his own preconceptions and those of his nation as he tried to make sense of the change and disorder he saw about him. It is my hope that the book will be of interest to people who have known little or nothing of Dos Passos or who may only know him because of his satiric chronicles like *Manhattan Transfer* and *U.S.A.* I hope further that the edition will be of value to students of Dos Passos, providing them with some of the materials they need as they set about assessing his contributions to American literature.

A project of this sort requires the aid and cooperation of many people. Mentioning those to whom I am indebted does not tell in how many ways their efforts have enriched the volume. To everyone who had some part in making *The Fourteenth Chronicle* I mean to express my appreciation.

First, I should like to thank Elizabeth Dos Passos. Her permission, patience, and gracious goodwill made the book possible. Her son Christopher, daughter Lucy, and son-in-law Rodney Coggin helped me, particularly because they gave me confidence that my approach to the material was satisfactory.

Surely it was their admiration for Dos Passos that caused his friends to treat me so kindly. The chance to see his papers was important, but beyond that, talking and corresponding with people who knew him was immensely valuable to get a sense of what he was like. For their patience in answering many questions and letting me pour over their papers—and in some cases for their room and board—I am particularly indebted to Mr. and Mrs. Brodnax Cameron, Mr. and Mrs. Thomas P. Cope, Mr. and Mrs. William M. Donnelly, Dr. and Mrs. W. Horsley Gantt, Lois Sprigg Hazell, John Howard Lawson, Marion Lowndes, Mr. and Mrs. Frank MacDermot, Mr. and Mrs. Walter Rumsey Marvin, Dudley Poore, Mr. and Mrs. Daniel Rice, Erico Verissimo, Mr. and Mrs. Harold Weston, William L. White, and C. Dickerman Williams.

Dudley Poore undertook the task of reading the entire manuscript when it was first completed. The inaccuracies he caught and the changes he suggested were invaluable. What errors remain in the text are mine. Professor James T. Patterson, Jr., read my biographical narrative in detail and offered valuable criticism; Professor Max Steele helped me with my preface. Professor Carlos Baker's generous assistance enabled me to decipher and date the correspondence with Ernest Hemingway. Further, his biography, *Ernest Hemingway: A Life Story,* was a kind of guidebook along with Dos Passos' memoir, *The Best Times,* as I tried to piece together his life.

For sensible advice and oft needed encouragement I thank my colleagues Professor Joseph Blotner, Professor Lewis Leary, and Professor Louis Rubin, and three true professionals, Carol Brandt, Mark Saxton, and Lovell Thompson. Professor Bernard Duffey's guidance when I first began learning about John Dos Passos was essential, as was a summer study grant from the University of North Carolina. Special thanks go to Donald Gallup, Curator of the Collection of American Literature, the Beinecke Library, Yale University; and to Edmund Berkeley, Jr., Curator; Anne Freudenberg, Assistant Curator; William G. Ray, formerly Field Representative; and the staff of the Manuscripts Division of the Alderman Library, University of Virginia, for their interest, aid, and friendship.

Seymour and Merloyd Lawrence and Seymour and Alyce Auerbach offered assistance and hospitality repeatedly. Patricia B. McIntyre and the staff of the Reference Division at the Wilson Library, University of North Carolina, Chapel Hill, aided me with many editorial problems. Nancy Sorkin, Kathleen Cain, and especially Martha Cohn endured nobly the pressures I placed upon them to compile information, type the manuscript, and then assist with proofreading. Alice Chludzinski by her intelligent editing brought order to my manuscript.

A special word of thanks should go to "Chantegrillet," an idyllic *grande propriété* in Ecully, France, whose ambience made work a pleasure.

For help of several kinds—by supplying letters, pictures, facts, and encouragement—my thanks go to all the following: Professor Daniel Aaron, Mr. and Mrs. Oliver Austin, Ellen S. Barry, Alfred M. Bingham, Professor Jonathan Bishop, William H. Bond, William F. Buckley, Jr., Myra Champion, Alexander P. Clark, Winifred Collins, Malcolm Cowley, Rodney Dennis, Cyril F. Dos Passos, Clive E. Driver, Professor F. W. Dupee, Professor Robert H. Elias, Mrs. Arthur D. Ficke, Richard Friedman, Andrew H. Gantt II, Roswell Garst,

Adelaide L. Gaylor, Arnold Gingrich, Mr. and Mrs. Eben Given, Marguerite Tjader Harris, Granville Hicks, Professor Hugh Holman, John Jay Iselin, Oliver Jensen, Matthew Josephson, William Jovanovich, John G. Kerr, Carlos Lacerda, Elfrieda Lang, Kate Drain Lawson, Joanne LeGoff, Helen Taylor Lindley, Virginia Lowell Mauck, Senator John L. McClellan, W. B. McDaniel II, Archibald MacLeish, John S. Mayfield, Alyce Nash, Robert Nathan, Anna Peirce, Milo R. Perkins, Mrs. M. K. Pershing, Professor William Phillips, John B. Pierce, Charles H. Ryland, Professor Arthur Schlesinger, Jr., Marian Seldes, Mr. and Mrs. William B. Smith, James S. Sprigg, Jr., Donald Ogden Stewart, Lee Sylvester, Rayner Unwin, Rita Vaughan, Charles R. Walker, Dr. J. S. Watson, Neda M. Westlake, Walter Muir Whitehill, Rosalind Baker Wilson, Elena Wilson, Craig Wylie.

Most important of all was my wife Jane. Her assistance, advice, and good humor were continuous. Her companionship—like that of David, Chad, Jamie, and Sarah, who understood their father's task far better than I had a right to expect of them—made this a thoroughly satisfying endeavor.

T. L.

Chapel Hill, North Carolina
May 1973

Acknowledgments

Publication of these letters and diaries and quotations from other writings of John Dos Passos are with the permission of Elizabeth Dos Passos, who retains copyright. Permission to publish letters, postcards, and a telegram from John Dos Passos, as well as quotations from letters to him, has kindly been granted by the following individuals and libraries: the letter to Professor Daniel Aaron, by him; those to Allen and Unwin, and their reader's reports, by Rayner Unwin; to the American Committee on Spanish Democracy and to Cabell Greet, by the Libraries, Columbia University; to Sherwood Anderson, by the Newberry Library; to Maurice Becker and to John Wilstach, by the Manuscripts and Archives Division, New York Public Library, Astor, Lenox and Tilden Foundations; to William Rose Benét, by the American Academy of Arts and Letters; to John Peale Bishop, by Professor Jonathan Bishop and the Princeton University Library; to Professor Joseph Blotner, by him; to William H. Bond, to Fredericka Field, to Eugene Saxton, and to Alexander Woollcott, by the Harvard College Library; to Dr. Israel Bram, by the Library of the College of Physicians of Philadelphia; to Van Wyck Brooks, to Theodore Dreiser, to James T. Farrell, and to Carl H. Milam, by the Van Pelt Library, University of Pennsylvania; to Mr. and Mrs. Brodnax Cameron, by them; to Robert Cantwell, by the University of Oregon Library; to Myra Champion, by her; to William L. White and to the Committee on Admissions, the Century Club, by him; the open letter while Dos Passos was serving on the Committee to Aid Striking Miners, by the Humanities Research Center, University of Texas; those to Thomas P. Cope, by him and the Alderman Library, University of Virginia; to Malcolm Cowley, and the excerpts of two letters from him, by him, the Poetry Collection of the Lockwood Memorial Library, State University of New York at Buffalo, and the Newberry Library; to Mrs. Edward Cummings, to Dos Passos' father John R. Dos Passos, to his mother Lucy Madison Dos Passos, to Katy Dos Passos, to Ernest Hemingway, to Robert Hillyer, to the House Un-American Activities Committee, to Professor Arthur Schlesinger, Jr., to Edward Grant Taylor, to the editor, New York *Times* Book Review Section, and to

Abbott Washburn, by the Alderman Library, University of Virginia.

Permission to publish letters to E. E. Cummings has kindly been granted by the Harvard College Library, the Alderman Library, University of Virginia, and the New American Library, for the use of an excerpt of a letter to Cummings which first appeared in *The Best Times;* to Dos Passos' daughter Lucy, by her; to Max Eastman and to Upton Sinclair, by the Lilly Library, Indiana University; to John Farrar, by him, the Harvard College Library, and the Collection of American Literature, Beinecke Rare Book and Manuscript Library, Yale University; to Arthur D. Ficke, by Mrs. Ficke and the Collection of American Literature, Beinecke Library, Yale University; to F. Scott Fitzgerald, by the Princeton University Library and the New Directions Publishing Corporation, for the use of a letter to Fitzgerald which first appeared in F. Scott Fitzgerald, *The Crack Up,* copyright 1945; to Dr. W. Horsley Gantt, by him; to Lois Sprigg Hazell, by her; to Josephine Herbst, by Hilton Kramer and the Collection of American Literature, Beinecke Library, Yale University; to Bernard Knollenberg, by the Collection of American Literature, Beinecke Library, Yale University; to John Howard Lawson and to José Giner Pantoja, by the Morris Library, Southern Illinois University, and Professor S. B. Liljegren, editor of the series *Essays and Studies on American Language and Literature,* in which appeared *John Dos Passos and the Revolting Playwrights,* written by George A. Knox and Herbert M. Stahl. In that book Dos Passos' letter to Lawson and Francis Faragoh was published in its entirety; two letters to Lawson were quoted extensively.

Further, permission to publish letters to Lloyd and Marion Lowndes has kindly been granted by Mrs. Lowndes and the Alderman Library, University of Virginia; to Dwight Macdonald and to Philip Rahv, by Professor William Phillips, editor of the *Partisan Review;* to Walter Rumsey Marvin, by him; to Stewart Mitchell, by the Boston Athenaeum; to Gerald and Sara Murphy, by Mrs. William M. Donnelly; to Charles Norman, by the Humanities Research Center, University of Texas, and Hawthorn Books, Inc., who presently control Norman's book, *E. E. Cummings: The Magic Maker,* in which appeared a portion of the letter to Norman; to Charles A. Pearce and to Helen Taylor, by Harcourt Brace Jovanovich, Inc.; to Dudley Poore, by him; to George St. John, by the Choate School; to Mark Schorer, by the Director of the Bancroft Library, University of California, Berkeley; to Theodore Stanton, by the Douglass College Library,

Rutgers University; to Lovell Thompson, by him, the Harvard College Library, and Houghton Mifflin Company; to Mr. and Mrs. Harold Weston, by them; and the letters to Edmund Wilson and the excerpt of one letter from him, by Elena Wilson and the Collection of American Literature, Beinecke Library, Yale University.

The estate of John Dos Passos now controls the rights to much of the material used in this volume. In cases where it does not, thanks are gratefully acknowledged to the following for permission to quote: *Antioch Review,* for the·quotation from Granville Hicks, "The Politics of John Dos Passos"; Cornell University Press, for diary excerpts reprinted from John Dos Passos, *One Man's Initiation: 1917.* First published in 1920 by George Allen and Unwin Ltd. and copyrighted by them under the Berne Convention. This edition copyright © 1969 by John Dos Passos; *Esquire Magazine,* for the quotation from John Dos Passos, "Facing a Bitter World: A Portfolio of Etchings, by Luis Quintanilla," copyright © 1935 (renewed 1963) by Esquire, Inc.; *National Review,* for quotations from John Dos Passos, "On the Way to the Moon Shot"; New American Library, for quotations from John Dos Passos, *The Best Times,* copyright © 1966; *Twentieth Century Literature,* for the quotation from Martin Kallich, "John Dos Passos Fellow-Traveler: A Dossier with Commentary"; and Frederick B. Wells, for the quotation from a letter by Thomas B. Wells.

Contents

List of Illustrations

Between pages 354–355

Between pages 532–533

Note: Unless stated otherwise, photographs are courtesy of Elizabeth H. Dos Passos.
Sketches following chapter headings by John Dos Passos

A Note About Editing

The hardest decision to be made about editing these letters and diaries was what to do with Dos Passos' spelling and punctuation. He was not an accurate speller; and he punctuated as he saw fit, often omitting apostrophes, commas, and periods, then sometimes substituting a dash. Partly this was because he wrote fast, partly because he saw no need for conventional punctuation.

Eventually the publishers and I decided to try to render the punctuation as close to the way Dos Passos had it as we could, but to correct spelling. We made corrections because this is a reading edition; spelling errors and the repeated use of [sic] we felt would lessen the flow of the text. Further, when I reread the original manuscripts, again and again I found that what I first thought to have been spelling errors were not, but simply my misreadings of Dos Passos' handwriting.

The kinds of changes made were matters like omitting one "the" when Dos Passos in his haste would write "the the"; changing "ackwaintance" to "acquaintance"; correcting names like "Dostoieffski" to "Dostoevski"; and in a poem omitting "reveration"—as he wrote in a manuscript—and substituting "reverberance," as it appears in the published poem. A point of interest for some readers may be to compare the early versions of his poems which appear here with those published in *A Pushcart at the Curb,* Dos Passos' volume of verse. In a few instances I inserted a needed word where he had left one out; and in cases where it was not absolutely clear that he meant to run words together, I separated them if they were joined because of his fast writing.

Where it seemed helpful to clarity, I corrected foreign languages, but left Dos Passos' particular punctuation, his spelling of slang or colloquial phrases, and interesting idiosyncrasies like "La chere est triste," where one would expect "la chair." After much discussion we left foreign languages unitalicized—except where Dos Passos underlined them—and rendered titles as he had written them, believing this would give the reader a better sense of the writer's use of languages and informal style.

I hope that readers will not think such changes detract from the value of the edition. These letters and diaries are as close to the originals as I could bring them, save for such alterations as I have mentioned.

"My heart rebels against my generation,
  That talks of freedom and is slave to riches,
  And, toiling 'neath each day's ignoble burden,
        Boasts of the morrow."

                    George Santayana, "Ode"

"I cannot rest from travel; I will drink
  Life to the lees. All times I have enjoyed
  Greatly, have suffered greatly, both with those
  That loved me, and alone . . ."

                    Alfred Tennyson, "Ulysses"

"A HOTEL CHILDHOOD"

January 14, 1896–June 1917

When the twentieth century began, John Roderigo Madison was a lonely child living abroad with his mother and knowing little about the United States. Born on January 14, 1896, in a hotel in Chicago, he was the illegitimate son of John Randolph Dos Passos and Lucy Addison Sprigg Madison. "John R.," or "The Commodore," as his father liked to be called—though his family also called him "Didi"—was in every sense a self-made man. Born in 1844 in Philadelphia, he early tried to run away to sea, then next worked as office boy in a law firm before serving as a drummer in a Pennsylvania regiment for part of the Civil War. Afterward he studied law and in 1867 began his own practice in New York. Successfully defending Edward S. Stokes—the man accused of shooting Jim Fisk—made him a prominent lawyer at the age of twenty-seven. He moved into brokerage and then corporation law and was known for his successes in establishing several of the large commercial trusts.

He was a man of many interests and genuine tenderness. "The story of Cupid and Psyche," he began one of his many letters to Lucy, "is one of the most beautiful and chaste in mythological history. Cupid is the personification yea the very embodiment of love. He is the son of Venus, and how could he be otherwise than filled with love from top to toe? Psyche is the personification of the Soul—She is the Soul—Cupid is love—Psyche the Soul! The man the animal! The woman the ethereal—the former physical the latter spiritual! Beautiful is it not? Let us work it out. Let us put the light of analysis upon their lives." He applied the tale of Cupid and Psyche to his and Lucy's own love affair, and the letter became—while insistent—less didactic and even a touch frivolous. In subsequent letters to Lucy, John R. developed his ideas about the two mythical figures, often seriously, sometimes lightheartedly, and frequently romantically. The tone was always warm but assertive; he enjoyed playing the teacher.

The Commodore was, according to all accounts, a strong, athletic man, a touch mercurial of temper, a lavish spender, and an affectionate if imposing parent. Immensely energetic, he tended to control situations and friendships, it seems, while nonetheless desiring companionship. Surely he intimidated his shy, near-sighted son Jack, and Lucy too, though perhaps he did not intimidate her so much as dominate her. One of his nieces, while admiring him, thought him cocky, conceited, and self-centered.

Despite the press of his practice, he found time to write several books about the law and a study in 1903 entitled *The Anglo-Saxon Century and the Unification of the English Speaking People,* in which he championed Anglo-Saxon culture. He was also involved in public affairs, as late in his life as 1912, for example, appealing through a circular to the delegates at the Democratic National Convention in Baltimore for a plank which would promise "the reformation of the legal system." John R. declared that the present system discriminated against the poor because they could not pay for lawyers and all the steps necessary in litigation. A humanitarian, he had been attuned to business and government during the growth of the great trusts, but was out of touch with the Progressive Era. In his memoir *The Best Times,* Dos, as Jack came to be called, remembered that when he went off to Harvard in September 1912, he noticed his father's loneliness— "the loneliness of a man who has outlived his generation. More and more he found himself on the unpopular side of political questions. He opposed votes for women and President Wilson's putting through legislation for an eight-hour day."

As if his affairs did not keep him busy enough, he wrote Lucy and Jack long letters—often in French—almost daily during his long absences. Those to Lucy often read like sermons in which he interpreted the Bible or discussed their love or some contemporary situation. This intelligent, complex man had room for many emotions. He fascinated his son, who, when later he seemed to be denying his parents in fiction like *Streets of Night, Manhattan Transfer,* or *U.S.A.,* was not so much denying them as he was challenging the validity of the social milieu of which they—and he until his manhood—were a part. John R. enjoyed life and people; and he tried to impart his vitality to those around him, as a letter he wrote to Lucy from New York in July 1912 suggests as well as anything can:

> I love to dwell upon the happiness of the past. One can draw both physical and mental pleasure from such a retrospection! The year hath passed and yet bringing it up before us again the contemplation of it produces a certain sweetness. Let us to-night in our minds eye make a photograph of our lives from the fourth of 1911 to the fourth of July 1912! Let us hold it before us. It makes a beautiful landscape does it

not? Look at the lovely sky undermined by a single cloud—how bright the tableau is with an effulgent sunshine? On the one side of the picture is Sandy Point and Cintra the Yacht and the White House with the shaded lawn and exquisite moonlight. On the other is our Washington Home— quiet but bright—made joyous and funny by our readings, songs and recitations! And how many little by-plays and side shows! Surely we must baptize it the blessed year! The serene year! The tranquil year! How we can appreciate the feelings of Othello when in the fullness of his joy he exclaimed if it were now to die t'were now to be most happy for I fear my soul hath her content so absolute that not another comfort like to this succeeds in unknown fate.

But we must multiply the pleasures of life—One never surfeits and new avenues of enjoyment are always opening. We think we have reached the sublimity of life when lo! we discover some new delight. Riches wear out—society and fashionable life fade fast, but the pleasures of the soul are inexhaustible—they are always opening up new visions and fresh pastures to dwell in. The soul! Let us cultivate it—and multitudinous joys await us!

Born February 9, 1854, Lucy Madison was from a Maryland family of some social standing. When she met John R. in the early 1890's, she was a widow. He was already married to Mary Hays Dos Passos, but she was mentally ill, and divorce in such a case was illegal. Hence it was only after her death on March 20, 1910, that he and Lucy were married that June 21 in Wilmington, Delaware. The marriage was not made public until 1912. Lucy was a gentle, mildly poetic person with firm religious convictions. As a girl she composed conventional poems, such as a lengthy one she penned in her scrapbook for 1869, beginning thus:

> I dreamt *Thee* in the shadow,
> I saw *Thee,* in the light,
> I heard Thee in the thunder's peal,
> And worshipped in the night.
> All beauty, while it spoke of *Thee,*
> Still made my heart rejoice,
> And my spirit bow'd within itself,
> To hear thy "still, small voice!"
> I have not felt myself a thing,
> Far from thy presence driven,
> By flaming sword or marriage ring,
> Shut out from *Thee,* and heaven!

She and John R. had each had a child by their first marriages. Nevertheless, one can imagine that she was a lonely woman when she met him in her thirties. She sought companionship and, one suspects, needed the support a man like John R. wanted to give her. Theirs was a romantic love always. He was kind and paid her as much attention as he could. Lucy adored him in turn but sometimes felt remorseful about their long affair. A year before they were married she wrote him a note from her New York hotel after he had telephoned her:

> The telephone rang a few moments ago—I felt dead, lifeless—I recognized your voice—in an instant—my heart beat to suffocation, every artery throbbed, my whole nature is alive, filled with intense excitement —sleep has left—fled—I must write—My sweetheart—I love you as intensely as ever in my life, yet—I must leave you—you cannot make up your mind to leave the woman who has been the bane of your existence, and I cannot *live,* and see the decay the torture of nerve and body, of the one, who has been the sunlight of my life—God will not let me live, to *know* you again, will gratify her vanity by living under the same roof— long years ago—you said, "Lucy if I had to save one or the other—I would save you"—I *know* now it can never be—God knows I have tried, because of my great love, every thing on earth to save you—all the nature, the Great-God has given me has been lavished on you—I have suffered torture, with a face lighted by the ecstasy of suffering for you—Yes, I loved you so madly, every pain was bliss—I must go away *at once*— Jack wrote me, L

At the moment she wrote this she was near distraction. The affair caused her at least as much pain as happiness, for she didn't really have John R. as long as his first wife lived, and the clandestine nature of their life together disturbed her. Then, shortly before they were married heart trouble invalided her. She and the Commodore could not have the life together they had hoped for; and she, increasingly helpless, relied heavily on young Jack as well as his father.

The unconventional relationship of Dos' parents made his life unusual indeed. As he put it in *The Best Times,* "Since [my father's] tenderly affectionate relations with my mother remained technically irregular so long as his first wife lived, it was only in Europe that they could travel openly together." Thus while he was a small boy, he traveled about Europe, lived for a time in Brussels, and boarded during school semesters in London with a lady named Mrs. Gee while his parents were off by themselves. It was a lonely existence—"a hotel childhood" he called it in the novel *Chosen Country*. He saw relatively little of his father during those years; his mother—whom he sometimes called "the Princess" and "the Baby"—was nearly forty-two years old at his birth and though affectionate could not take the place of friends his own age.

His first schooling was in England, "at Peterborough Lodge in Hampstead in the northern suburbs of London." At least until he was ten he continued there part of the time, because a report card mailed to "Mrs. Gee, 2 Springfield Abbey Road. N.W." tells of his grades for the term ending July 31, 1906. Of a class of ten, he stood first in Latin, second in French, third in algebra, only sixth in English, ninth in arithmetic, and, among twelve students, sixth in geometry. His Latin teacher commented, "Has worked extremely well & will do well in the future"; his English teacher noted only "Good."

It is not clear exactly when he and his mother moved back to Washington, D.C. Whenever they did he went to Sidwell Friends School until in January 1907 he began four and one-half years at Choate School in Wallingford, Connecticut. While he was there, he kept the name Madison, still referring to his father as "my guardian."

A good student, he liked George St. John, the young headmaster of Choate, but did not like boarding school, even though his record was excellent. He was literary editor of the school paper and a member of the Dramatic Club, acting in several plays, one of them William Gillette's *The Private Secretary*. It was presented in February of Dos' last year, and the Choate School *News* reported his playing an Eva Webster "as pretty as one could desire to meet," but Dos was displeased because the part was very small. When he left Choate he received a prize for his work in English and ended up being voted the best student in his class. But his mother's illness and subsequent dependence worried him. Choate's restrictions and the harassment he got there were disagreeable; in *The Best Times* he remembered "being called Frenchy and Foureyes and the class grind." He had only two close friends, and because of his accent and mannerisms he seemed "different" and as a result was subjected to such painful hazing as being hung out a window by his hands. In addition, his poor eyesight kept him from being a good athlete, so the years of boarding school were often extremely lonely.

Eager to be out, after leaving Choate in June 1911, he went up to Harvard, where he took and passed the entrance exams. Thus, he was finished with boarding school at the age of fifteen, but his parents decided he should wait a year before entering college. With a tutor nicknamed "Uncle Virgil" Jones, he sailed in November 1911 aboard the *Baltic* for a long tour to study art, architecture, and to absorb old world culture. As he told it in *The Best Times,* he "quoted Gibbon in the Roman Forum, read Thucydides (from the trot) in Athens and evoked Julius Caesar and Napoleon while brushing off the baksheesh-seekers in front of the Sphinx." This offhanded account does not reveal how much he saw and noted. Dos kept a diary of the trip in which he revealed a fast-developing eye for details, as well as a mind for facts. For instance, when he and Uncle Virgil were in Avignon on December 8, he noted:

> Had our *"Petit déjeuner"* at the Hotel and then took our things to the station, and having left them *"en depôt"* went out to see the town First we went to the ancient Palace of the Popes, which was begun in 1336 and finished in 1364. Jean XXII the second Pope to live there was one of its chief constructors. The style is sombre gothic and the buildings are being restored by the government, as they were very much mutilated at the time of the Revolution, when the Palace was turned into a fort. There are some very interesting frescoes, which have just been uncovered by removing several coats of whitewash, in several of the rooms, and more will undoubtedly be found later. We saw, among other things, the prison in which Rienzi was confined during the 11 months which he was a prisoner of the Popes.
>
> After leaving the Palace we went into the cathedral for a moment and then crossed the bridge to Villeneuve-lès-Avignon, on the other side of the Rhône. The old walls are well preserved all around the city and are especially interesting on this side of the city. Villeneuve is one of the *dirtiest* and most picturesque little places I have been in for a long while. There, we visited the Cathedral, which was very interesting, more so than the finer one at Avignon. It was originally the chapel to a monastery of Franciscans, and there are the remains of old cloisters near it. In the vestry, we saw a very interesting and well executed statue of the Virgin in ivory.

He went on to describe more of Villeneuve, and throughout the rest of the tour his diary continued to be this complete.

Returning to the United States in early May 1912, he spent a hot, lazy summer caring for his mother—now thoroughly invalided from a series of heart attacks—in Washington and at Cintra, the site of his

father's farm near the mouth of the Potomac River in rural Westmoreland County, Virginia.

At some point during his adolescence, Dos had wanted to go to the
U.S. Naval Academy, but his poor eyesight quickly ended that idea,
and in September 1912, he began at Harvard four years of what would
be an important and for the most part happy experience for him. Here
he was freerer than he had been of his parents' domination or the
domination of the "clean young American Rover Boys" at prep school,
as he referred to them in "Camera Eye 7" of *U.S.A.* Choate's restrictions, its isolation, and its insistence that all partake of the robust life
had not sat well with him, and Harvard was a stimulating change. He
thrived on the literary life, became close friends with, among others,
E. E. Cummings, Robert Hillyer, and Stewart Mitchell, and was a consistent contributor to the *Harvard Monthly,* of which he was an editor
his senior year. Dos had time for friendships and writing; he also was
an omnivorous reader, keeping literary diaries in which he noted what
he had read and jotting down some critical comment about each bit of
writing as he finished it. For example, in his "Literary Diary" for
September 1914, he commented about Fielding, Stendhal's *La Chartreuse de Parme,* Goldsmith's *The Vicar of Wakefield,* de Quincey's
"Reminiscences of the Lake Poets," some of Chekhov's stories, and
writing by O. Henry, Lafcadio Hearn, Henry James, Robert Louis
Stevenson, George Sand, Turgenev, and William Morris. In addition
he read Shelley's "Queen Mab" and "The Devil's Garden," by W. B.
Maxwell—an amazing but for him typical amount of reading during
one of these months at college.

His lifelong friend Dudley Poore, who met him in Charles Townsend Copeland's composition class in the spring of 1915, remembers
Dos as always a happy companion who was constantly inventing
delightful ventures—long walks; dinners at Young's Hotel in Boston,
where the cook would make a punch from John R.'s recipe; or gather-
ings in one or another of the friends' rooms to praise the virtues of
poets like Masefield, Amy Lowell, Eliot, Verlaine and Verhaeren, or
novelists like Compton Mackenzie, D. H. Lawrence, Tolstoi, Gogol,
Dostoevski, Turgenev, and Chekhov. Opera, particularly Diaghilev's
modern ballets, and art, particularly the Armory Show of 1913, powerfully affected him. In short, he immersed himself in art and literature.

His summers, a great part of them spent at Cintra, were times for
more reading and attempts at writing amid the tasks of helping the

nurse, Mrs. Harris, to care for his mother. Her death on May 15, 1915 meant he was less bound to home and family, though he did become closer to his father for the year and one half more that John R. lived.

In the summer of 1915 Dos went west to see some cousins in San Diego. From there he took the Shasta Limited to San Francisco, and during this trip he met Walter Rumsey Marvin, four years his junior, but someone with whom he had much in common. The two met again at the World's Fair in San Francisco, and still a third time at the Grand Canyon. Marvin, at the time a student at St. Paul's School in Concord, New Hampshire, had a lively mind, enjoyed literature, and was trying his hand at poetry. The two quickly became close friends; and on August 28, returning east, Dos began what would become perhaps the most extensive correspondence he would have with any-one. Marvin was an ideal friend; Dos relished the chance to pour out his thoughts to the younger man. There is something of the tutor-pupil relationship in the early correspondence, particularly in the letters he wrote during his senior year at Harvard, when he was shaping his own ideas about language, subject matter, and style in literature.

Though the college years were pleasant, he began to chafe at the scholastic life. After his mother's death he was not anxious to return for his last year, but his father insisted he do so. Then too there was the excitement of the war in Europe. More aware of that continent than most young Americans, he wanted to see the action. But he stayed to finish his degree work and was graduated in June 1916, although he did not remain around Cambridge to receive his diploma.

He found the summer of 1916 a languid time filled with reading, arranging with the help of his father for the publication of a small anthology entitled *Eight Harvard Poets,* and generally, as he described it in *The Best Times,* "mounting my fiery steed and riding off in all directions." He planned definitely to go abroad in the fall, but in what capacity he did not know. He wanted to join Herbert Hoover's Belgian Relief but was turned down, and his father disapproved of his joining the Norton-Harjes volunteer ambulance unit that was then forming. The compromise they worked out was for him to go to Madrid to learn Spanish and study architecture.

On October 14 he sailed aboard the *Espagne* for Bordeaux. Coinci-dentally, it was the day the *New Republic* published "Against Ameri-can Literature," the first bit of writing for which Dos received money. From France he traveled soon to Madrid, where he quickly settled into study but still had ample time to venture about the countryside with his Spanish acquaintances and with two college friends, Lowell Downes and Roland Jackson, who arrived later that fall. He saw as much of that part of Spain as he could and had hopes of going to Paris in the spring, there to join the Norton-Harjes ambulance unit; but his plans were shattered when John R. died of pneumonia on January 27, 1917. Initially Dos thought not to return to the United States. There were no immediate relatives to console, and he dreaded the sentimental ceremony that surrounded a death. But by February 10 he was in Bordeaux trying to arrange passage home, and ten days later he wrote Marvin from aboard the *Touraine* as she sailed through the now dangerous Atlantic for New York.

Once there he found himself involved with family affairs. He told Marvin that "I am doing personal business about my father's estate, attending to the publication of the Anthology, trying to find a studio-place or a cheap apartment to live in—all at once and the result is I have to fit my days together like a jig-saw."

The settlement of John R.'s estate did not produce much working capital for Dos. John R.'s law practice had brought in large sums, but his expenses were heavy and he was a lavish spender, some years, according to Dos, ending up in debt. John R. told Dos and his older half-brother Louis that all they would receive at his death would be land in Virginia. Such was the case, so, although Dos also received some money after his mother's death from the sale of a house in Washington, D.C., that had been in her name, he had only a small income. Because he knew he would be traveling and did not want to bother with finances, in the spring of 1917 he turned over in trust his interest in the family land to his Aunt Mamie, his mother's sister Mrs. James Riely Gordon. Although from then until 1940 she did pay him sums totaling about $15,000, most of the money that came from timber-cutting and farming on the land during those years never came to Dos. When he began in the late 1930's to take an interest in family and land affairs, he discovered that James Gordon and Gordon's son-in-law had been getting, but not passing on, income from the land amounting to $100,000. Thus for the two decades after John R.'s death, Dos had to rely almost entirely on what he could earn from his writing.

New York in the spring of 1917 Dos thought a nightmare, so even while he got an apartment of his own he sought to return to Europe to see the war firsthand. Eventually his choice narrowed to the Norton-

Harjes group—in a letter to Dudley Poore written May 8, he said he was "going to take a course at an auto-school in N.Y. & then in about a month sail for France with the Norton-Harjes Ambulance." As he eagerly anticipated the prospect of new experiences, he threw himself with a kind of adolescent glee into political causes, apparently never sensing that there might be something paradoxical about a self-pro-claimed rebel and pacifist being anxious to see the war. *The Masses* offered "the word"; Woodrow Wilson became a villain; conscription and the declaration of war were betrayals; Robert Lafollette, Eugene Debs, and Max Eastman became idols. By the time he sailed aboard the *Chicago* for France on June 20, 1917, innocently excited by what was in store, he believed himself a confirmed socialist.

To George St. John (1877–1966), *who became Headmaster of the Choate School in 1908 and remained so until 1947. He was responsible for Choate's growth into one of the prominent New England prepara-tory schools.*

Annisquam, Mass.
Aug. 16th 1910

Dear Mr. St John,

I want to beg forgiveness for not having written you before, but . . . I am afraid that there is no excuse. We have finally landed here on Cape Ann near Gloucester and will stay here for the rest of the summer I have just received the report of my examinations. I am very sorry to say that I failed Greek. I do not know why I did but I did. I do not think I ought to have failed as I certainly was perfectly well prepared for it. I got an "E" in it—a "C" in Elementary Latin—a "C" in Advanced French—a "P.P." in English—a "B" in Algebra and an "A" in Elementary French. Do you think that I can prepare for college in one more year? I think that my guardian wishes me to do it and then perhaps to travel for a year before entering Harvard. I think that I can do it as I have now ten points to the good. I only need 16 more—Elementary Greek would be four (I hope that I will pass that next year), English—four, Elementary History—two, Geometry—two, Advanced Greek—two and Advanced Latin—two, that would make 26. It certainly is a lovely place here. We have rented a cottage for the rest of the summer and are enjoying it very much although we dont know a soul. I hope that you are all well and that the Baby is learning to talk.

Give my best regards to Mrs. St John—   Yrs. very sincerely,
John R Madison

[Diary]
Jan 9th [1911]
I have finally determined to keep a diary which I will try to make as interesting as possible to myself. I wish to make it a greater success than any of my former attempts and will try to write it up each evening before I go to bed—

So hail, thou patron divinity of diaries—whichever of the muses thou art—look propitiously upon my attempts to keep a diary & instill me with a desire for literary fame—. May this diary be as interesting as that of Pepys, as historical as that of "Everett?", as useful as Franklin's—So once again "Hail, Muse of diaries, all hail"

Monday Jan 9th [1911]
Suffered with Ennui most of the day. Rehearsal of 2nd Act of the play [*The Private Secretary*] in the afternoon. Alas, I have a very secondary & small part in the play! I expected that I could easily get the part of "Miss Ashford" but I was superseded by Handley and given the part of Eva. It's the smallest part in the play—except that of John & Knox—and I feel very badly about not getting a better one.

The sixth form have received their privileges entire today—hereafter we can go down town whenever we want to—and go into each others rooms after bells.

	Cash Account	
	Balance	5.00
pd.	Hull for glasses	.50
	Scissors	.50
	Andy	.20
rd.	from Walcott	.05
	In pocket	.02
	Total	3.87

February 15th [1911]
Alas! What resolutions have been broken! For a whole month I have
scarcely thought of my diary but hereafter I will try to do better.

February 16th [1911]
My purse has been restored today from a state of almost total bankruptcy. Have received a pound of candy from mother etc. and feel
quite jubilant. The play is not going along as well as it might be but I
hope that it will be all right next week.—Snow on the ground—

April 5th [1911]
Alas! Alas! Alas! I have done no better in keeping my diary—will try
hard, however this time. Am again in a state of bankruptcy—It is only
when I am in that condition that I write my diary at all
    First day after vacation. Mr. St John called meeting of sixth form &
all athletic officers at the old workshop.
    Decided:—
        1. Should not play Cheshire next year in foot-ball.
        2. Should try track practice as an experiment
        3. Should have sixth form table.
Stayed in meeting all after-noon which was very rainy & disagreeable.
The weather is really very bad this Spring & everything is extremely
backward. Am now seated next to Miss Clark at Mr. Temple's table I
like this much better than sitting at Mrs Beale's. Oh, her lady-like airs
really disgust me! I must try to keep a diary this term as it is quite
amusing & also a cash account as Didi always wants me to do so, so
much. It seems very hard to get into the habit of doing it, but I suppose
that it will come easier later on. I am writing Miss Pearse tonight and
must write Aunt Kate soon.

Cash Account

April 5	on hand	$ .04
April 5	Stamps	.04
	Total	0

Bankrupt Again!

April 6 [1911]
I forgot to write my diary for this day and am getting cold this evening. I do hope that we are not going to have another cold spell. I have

quite a bad sore throat this evening which is very disagreeable. I hope, though, that it will be gone in the morning. I *must* write my diary tomorrow—will try hard to.

May 5th [1911]
Well, "tomorrow" has just come! I will not try any more to write my diary regularly; if I do it, I'll do it, but if I don't, I wont and that is all. Didi does not send very encouraging reports from mother, I hate to think of it, but I am afraid that she will never get well—He and I long to have her well and to do the countless things which we have always planned to do

May 13th [1911]
Had the class dinner this evening at Oakdale Tavern. Mr. St. John was invited, and, in turn, invited all of us to be back to dinner with him a year from today. Had rather dull time at banquet as everyone was rather embarrassed and stiff. I wonder where I will be a year from tonight!* I really must economize somehow but it is very hard as there are many things that I need. I have not money enough now to pay for my photos which I had taken the other day, as I only have $3.75, counting what John owes me left. I must get a pair of shoes and several other things before the thirtieth. I ought to write Lois [Hazell] this morning but I am afraid I shall not have time. I am finishing yester-day's diary this morning from the place where the asterisk is.

May 17th [1911]
We played Kent School today and beat them in a very interesting game 5-2 Made out the dummy for the Fiction Supplement. The 'News' will be very late this issue, I fear, as there is a lot more stuff to be written up. The weather has been very fine lately; nearly like summer and the trees etc. are all out in fine shape. Mother is going down to the farm soon I think—so she says through the nurse's letters. I should very much like to go with her.

May 15th—Lent John	1.00
May 16—Received ¢ 50 back	.50
May 17th Balance	¢.50
Soda	.20
Total	.30

June 17th [1911]
Today I spent my last hours as a pupil at the Choate School. I left for
Boston, with Walcott at 10.25 A.M. Mr. St. John said goodbye rather
coldly, but I must expect that, as I have lost favor with him greatly,
lately. I did not get a diploma, either, which surprised me a good deal;
for I really think that I deserved one. I am staying now at Young's
Hotel in Boston and have a fairly good room.

Postcard to his father (1844–1917)

[Rome
December 14, 1911]

Nous sommes arrivés ici de Paris, il y a quelques minutes. Nous sommes
à la ville Eternelle! Where Caesar ruled, where Cicero thundered
against Calatine, where Virgil read the Aeneid to Great Augustus!
    J'espère que vous excuserez la carte mais je n'ai pas temps
d'écrire une lettre, comme il fait tard, Jack—

Postcard to his mother (1854–1915)

[Rome
December 14, 1911]

Imperial Rome!
Conqueror of the world!
Enlightener of the ages!
We are within thine ancient walls!
From the Imperial City to the Royal Princess love and greeting
I will write to Her sublime, serene and celestial majesty tomorrow.
With much love from her

Jack—

To his father

[Athens]
Feb. 19th 1912

My dear Didi,
    We took the trip to the Temple of the Eleusian Mysteries at
Eleusis today by carriage along the Sacred Way over which the yearly
procession travelled from Athens. The ruins were not very imposing
but very interesting from their association. We had a picnic lunch

among the ruins near the cave in the Acropolis of Eleusis which was dedicated to Pluto. After dinner we entered this and I being weary stretched myself out on the stones and lo, in a moment, I slept.

Of a sudden, it seemed to me that I waked, but it could not have been so; for I seemed to be in a place exceeding dark. I started up; for I noticed that the moonlight gave a subdued radiance to the grotto, and went out, but as I reached the threshold, lo a hand seemed to hold me and I stood still. As I gazed towards the ruins I was surprised to see that they had nearly vanished and as I looked they disappeared entirely. A great altar was raised before my awestruck eyes, and behold, it seemed that a white bird hovered over it. But I could scarcely see the bird for it was covered with a thick veil. And it spake in a voice of silver, and at that voice I grew faint from the beauty of it, my knees grew weak, I fell upon the ground. For the voice said "I am *Truth*" But the strong hand that held me raised me again from the ground and I saw that before me stood a savage, and he came to the great altar and made offerings thereon and prostrated himself before it; but soon he vanished. In his place stood a great chieftain with Mycenaean armor, and he placed goblets of gold and silver upon the altar, which increased greatly in beauty and was covered by a rude temple while he stood there. But soon he too vanished, and after him came many others and with each one the Bird's veil grew lighter and the temple grew larger and finer.

Suddenly I recognized a shade that stood before the altar and I said "He is Solon"; and, straight way, the veil of the Bird grew much lighter; but when he went, it thickened again. And now the shadows flitted to the altar in quick succession and I recognized the faces of the early philosophers and with each the veil grew lighter. At last I saw Pericles stand in the temple which was now a magnificent structure of Pentalic marble, and with him entered the great sculptors and artists. And at that time one could almost see the outlines of the beautiful Bird through the veil. The great tragedians entered, and the Bird shone with beauty. They vanished and there stood alone a small man of ugly countenance. And lo, the veil became as thinnest gauze. That man was Socrates. Next followed Aristotle, preceded by his tutor, Plato, and the Bird could be seen most plainly through the veil. They vanished and the veil darkened, many philosophers entered and loaded the altar with gifts, but with each the veil grew thicker. At last, Cicero stood before the Bird and the outlines could be seen through the veil. Virgil poured his gifts on the altar and the Bird fluttered with joy. After them came many others but the veil grew thicker with each. Finally Marcus Aurelius stood in the temple; the veil became lighter than the morning mist on the mountains, but did not vanish. After that last sage had gone, there came a great wave of Barbarism and the Truth could barely be seen the veil was so thick and so black. It became so dark that the Bird took fright and fled and left Eleusis for ever. "Since then," so a voice seemed to say, "Truth has flitted over the world, now in a dark veil now in a light one; but few have seen behind that veil."

Then, with a start, I awoke, and realized what I had seen. I had seen the results of the Eleusian Mysteries; though the Mysteries themselves are lost in the depths of time they had brought the scholars, philosophers and poets and all the initiated in Greece and Rome nearer the snow-white Bird and had lightened ever so slightly the veil that hung about it. Perhaps the lawyer or the Doctor or the Minister has found the Bird, without its veil by this time, if the spots in the lights of their souls have vanished!

But to return to base mundane matters—

We enjoyed the excursion very much and expect to go to Marathon tomorrow.

I am afraid that we have calculated a little too closely in our finances and the trip generally is costing more than we expected. I am afraid that we will not be able to stay more than a very short time in Italy on leaving Greece and will have to leave everything except Rome for another time as I do not think that our money will carry us much more than across Italy to Paris and London and then to the steamer. This is partly due to the fact that we went to Constantinople, but as that trip did not cost more than $70 altogether I am very glad we took it, though I shall be sorry to miss Florence and Venice. I am not quite sure yet how far it will go, of course, but I fear that we will have a rather hard time to make it cover much more than the stay in Rome, Paris, and London of a few days and the travelling expenses, especially as this is the season in Italy and everything will be expensive.

With much love,
Jack
(mimic of Señor Cornida in
first part of letter)
Monsieur Singe

To his father

Florence
March 28th 1912

My dear Didi,

I have just received your letter of March 13th, although I did not expect anything more until we reached Rome. I think that we will leave here on the 30th and after spending a day in Perugia, go on to Rome.

You ask me what I think of Alcibiades. He is certainly a very interesting character. It seems to me that he must have been in early life a proud, ambitious, but indolent young man about town in Athens. He had a great deal of magnetism and talent but had no principle except the desire for his own happiness. He evidently loved Athens, but he did not love her enough to bear penury and hardship for her. In fact, it was not in his nature to put his ideals before his pleasures. When he was young, he evidently took the popular fancy by his witty and cultured speeches and popularity turned his head. His ambition urged him to propose the expedition against Syracuse, and his pride forbade his giving in, to the advice of wiser if less brilliant men. Then came his recall to Athens from the command. His friends were all with the army and he knew that if he went back he would be condemned for impiety, for he had made many enemies by his pride, his unscrupulous ambition and many other great men thought him an extremely dangerous demagogue and thought it best to get him out of the way if possible. If he did not go back, he must either lose his pleasures and business and spend the precarious life of an *honest* exile or turn traitor to his city and join the Spartans. He was very likely also driven on by a foolish spite against those who had illtreated him, as he thought, and by the pangs of hurt pride and disappointed ambition. It cost him a pang but he did it—and Athens was ruined. Soon after, however, when he saw the evil he had done, remorse must have come over him for he fled from Sparta to Hellespont. Later, when Athens had recovered from the terrible blow that had been inflicted on her by the loss of the Sicilian expedition, he was called back and for some time manfully tried to repair the evil he had wrought. He won several battles but things began to go against him, so he fled again for he had not the moral courage to face the angry citizens, who suspected him, this time unjustly, of a second treason. He still tried to help his city, however, and sent a warning to the admiral in charge before the fatal battle of Aegospotami warning him of the Spartan ambush. No notice was taken of it and the Athenian fleet was entirely captured with the exception of three or four ships. After this Alcibiades gave himself over entirely to pleasure and was killed a little later in a small skirmish in Phygia, I think. He seems to me to have been one of the most danger-ous men possible. If he had been totally bad, he could have done no harm, but it was his great good qualities, which if united with a moral courage and a disinterested patriotism would have made him a great man, that gave him his immense power to do evil. Of course, every historian has a different opinion of Alcibiades, but that is the light in which he appears to me.

Avec beaucoup d'amour,
Jack

To his mother

22 Matthews
[Cambridge, Massachusetts]
Oct 8th 1912

My dearest Mother,
   The dear Princess complains that I do not tell her what I am doing so I will try to do so in this letter. My time is chiefly taken up with:—

$$\text{ὅνἐφ'ἡμετέρᾳ γῆ Π·ολυνείκης}$$
$$\text{ἀρθεὶς νείκωνἐξ ἀμριλόγων}$$
$$\text{ὀξέα κλάξων}$$

also with:—
   Eulenspiegel wurde in dem Dorfe Kneitlingen in Sachsen geboren etc.
   or:—
   Namque Proculus Julus sollicita civitate desiderio regis et infensa etc.
   and other equally interesting things. However, as a side issue, I went to the Boston art museum on Sunday with some boys and spent part of the afternoon there. There are some quite interesting collections in different parts of the building which is new and very fine. We also went to the public library here the other day.

Saturday is Columbus day and a holiday, so I am going down to spend it and Sunday with the commodore in New York.

I should love to be able to take a flying trip down to the dear Baby at the farm. How is she? And how is her nurse? and the garden? You have not told me anything about it or whether the bulbs have arrived yet. I am very eager to hear.

With much love to the dear Baby & best regards to Mrs. Harris—

Jack

P.S. I have just received a letter from James [Madison, Lucy Madison's first child]. Please tell him that I will answer in a day or two.

To his father

[Cintra, Westmoreland Co. Virginia
June 1913]

My dear Didi,

I forgot to tell you lots of things in my last letter. The little landing for boats at Sandy Point is lovely as is the carriage House, which is nearly finished.

I went up into the vegetable garden today. It is a dreary waste,—a regular Sahara,—chiefly weeds & cabbages. What has happened to all the seed we sent down I can't imagine.

The gardener Rhode will not do at all. He does moderately well when I am over him, but he does not know how to attend to the garden. Moreover he is stupid and unreliable, and I don't think over honest in little things. I should be much relieved if you started looking out for another. Joe can see some of the applicants. We need not hurry but we might be able to pick some one up. Scott says that the old man, David, is not worth much and I agree with him from what I have seen.

I hope that you will take my advice in this as the present people are most unsatisfactory.

Avec beaucoup d'amour,

Jack

[Literary Diary]
Oct 30th [1914]
Finished "The Europeans" Henry James—a delightful, entertaining little story, in which a pair of Europeans are transported into the midst of a puritanic Boston family of the '50s. The characterization is won-

derfully careful & delicate & the satire exquisite. The strokes of James'
portraits are so fine, so miniature. They remind me of the delicacy of
The Angelico, or better, of some of the more refined Dutch portrait
painters.

Oct 31st [1914]
"Daisy Miller" an interesting character study by Henry James. Very
subtle, almost too subtle and minute description of a certain kind of
woman. Minute, almost microscopic, but hardly very vivid; still a most
excellent piece of work of its kind. James 'secondary characters' are so
delightful—his ladies like the aunt in this. Every here & there is a
delightfully "chucklesome" phrase, or little bit of satire. The dialogue
in places almost reminds me of Oscar Wilde, although intensely more
restrained and realistic.

Nov 1st [1914]
Finished at last "Vanity Fair"—have been rereading it off and on since
September. The more often I read it the more delightful it seems. It is
certainly one of the great books of the world—the inimitable characters, the satire, the wit, the humorous descriptions, the universality of
the book is overwhelming! I am anxious to start reading it all over
again!

Nov 2nd [1914]
"An International Episode" Henry James—a delicately written story of
the familiar type—entertaining, lacking in power and vividness, in deep
emotion; but preeminent in its fine drawing & truth to life, and delicate
subtlety.

Nov 3rd [1914]
Essay on Stevenson in Henry James' "Notes on Novelists"—Excellent
despite involved style—far more so than in the Daisy Miller volume—
but rather unsatisfactory there is not enough red-bloodedness & feeling
to the essay to properly express Stevenson.
   Finished Ibsen's "The Enemy of the People"—play of good technique & interest & excellent character drawing, notwithstanding lack of
finish in minor parts, but rather lacking in power, in 'entertainment'.
One's reaction to it is entirely intellectual; it does not really grasp the
feelings. Still is fully worth reading, as is everything Ibsen ever wrote.

Nov 5th [1914]
Finished "Elle et Lui" George Sand—The account of her love adventure with de Musset. A most interesting chapter of autobiography thinly disguised as a novel—Sincerely, earnestly written, in beautiful French. There is a great deal of pathos a great deal of true emotion in the story—and the characterization of de Musset is most enlightening. Really a very powerful book, though redolent with 1830.

Nov 10th [1914]
Turgenev's "Fathers and Sons"—a most disappointing novel. I have always thought of it as something radical, incendiary. Characterization is excellent, although construction is rather lacking. There is a sort of pointlessness to the book which is quite unexpected. It seems, moreover, to be a book whose day is departed—lacking in universality—lacking in significance for our generation.

Nov 15th [1914]
Henry James "Portrait of a Lady"—a most remarkable miniature study of a fascinating character. H. J.'s women are marvellous!

To Rumsey Marvin (1900–   ), *whom Dos met during the summer of 1915, when both were traveling out west. After graduating from St. Paul's School in Concord, New Hampshire, Marvin went to Yale. He was graduated in 1922, worked for the family business in Pittsburgh in 1922 and the winter of 1923, then began writing for the Pittsburgh* Gazette. *In January 1924 he headed south, working subsequently in Salisbury, Goldsboro, and finally Wilmington, North Carolina.*

From 1930–1935 he was the town clerk of Mamaroneck, New York, during which period he saw Dos frequently in New York City. Then he worked for the Knickerbocker Federal Savings and Loan Association in the city, and later served in the U.S. Navy during World War II.

In 1946 he and his wife Beatrice moved to Columbus, Ohio, where they were joint heads of the Columbus School for Girls. Marvin became executive director of the Martha Kinney Cooper Ohioana Library Association from 1954–1965, when he retired. In 1961 he married Beulah Hoagland Cosler, after the death of Beatrice in 1957.

[On board train returning east]
Aug 28th 1915

Dear Rummy,

When our roads divided the other morning I had quite reconciled myself to not meeting any of you people again—because, you know, you never do meet people again that you want to—; but since then I have waked up to the fact that Uncle Sam's mails are a golden road. We may be able to keep track of each other over them, and then again we may not. I, for one am an abominable correspondent—but I could make an effort.

But it's so rarely I meet anyone who's interested in the same things I am, that I don't like to let him slip through my fingers. There is a good deal in common—food, first & foremost is a splendid subject for letters; next to that literature, reading is useful; then there is always travel—I think we both have the disease—. Italy's another thing to chat about—all lovers of Italy have something in common, and that a good deal, for once you fall in love with Italy, there's no cure. You always have the Grand Canal in the back of your brain, and Vesuvius always smokes from its purple cone somewhere inside you.

Talking of smoke, I nearly passed out cold (or rather hot) crossing the desert to Salt Lake. I tossed around in my berth like a fish out on the deck of a boat in the hot sun. And I expect I went through about the same sensations. C'était horrible.

Still, all that was wiped away by the joyful coolness of Colorado Springs. I got in a delightful walk there, through the Garden of the Gods and across the mesa to Manitou. I seemed to be the only one who had ever attempted anything so bold, by the way every one stared when I asked the way. Scornful automobiles packed with the petite bourgeoisie, on sight seeing bent, purred past me every now and then. I can't say that I envied them.

I have just finished Byron's "Childe Harold." You have probably read parts. It was rather a task, and I am going to wash the taste away with a draught of Stevenson. You must read The *Inland Journey* & The *Travels with a Donkey*—They are two of the books one can read forever, and still want to read again.

If you feel like dropping me a line my address will be

Cintra, P.O.
Westmoreland Co.
Virginia

for some time.

I'd really be awfully glad to hear from you, and should try to reply in due time.

Au Revoir,

J. R. Dos Passos Jr.

These hieroglyphics are probably rather hard to deciphre but the train makes my pen dance a jig over the page.

29 Thayer Hall

Cambridge, Mass.

Oct 5th [1915]

Dear Rummy!

Awfully glad to get your letter. Yes we certainly must keep it up. It'll be great fun—and Uncle Sam's mails'll fairly groan.

How do you like my beloved *Inland Voyage?* I dont suppose you get so very much time for reading at school, still there are always times when all the world bores you or irritates you, and you have a "Nobody loves me. I'm going into the garden to eat worms", feeling when some book you're fond of acts like magic. It's like diving out of everything bothersome and plunging in a new comforting world where you have adventures and drink canary sack, and live a dozen people's lives instead of your own puny little one. It must be like that to write books, only nicer. How people get along without reading all the glorious things there are to read, I don't see, but most of them seem to be able to exist very comfortably without it. I suppose the fact that most people dont live at all, merely vegetate, like cabbages, accounts for it.

I've been rushing about without doing much of anything intellectual for the last week. Mainly I've been trying to find window curtains for my room. I dote on shopping; don't you? That is when you are on the war path for interesting things—rugs and tea cups and gay window curtains.

Why that should make me think of our glorious swim at Ocean Beach, I don't know, but it pops up in my mind. Do you remember our mountain climbing in bathing suits? On that nice red sandstone, too. That's one of the two or three *red-letter* swims of my life. Another one was up in Newfoundland. I'll tell you about it some day.

But I must stop scrawling and get to work at a fat tome on *The Religion of the Greek Poets*.

Do write me soon, Rummy.

[Cambridge]
Wednesday [*Fall 1915*]

Dear Rummy,

Again I delay—abjectly beg forgiveness—

But, young man, I am also a New Yorker (as much as I am anything) have lived there, & there possess a paternal roof—18 East 56th Street, which is nearer the Heart of the City (that has no heart—vide the popular song—) than New Rochelle! Furthermore—'twas I that invited you to be my guest, my convive; so, the party's mine—all this to obviate squabbling at the time.

But, this I'll grant, if you are obdurate, we'll organize a sort of return treat another time when you shall pay & furnish the cash & play host.

Now for more important matters—

Your poem worries me. It has charm and delightful sincerity, and a nice lilt—and I really quite love it. Still, I can't help feeling that it'ld be better more restrained, more concrete. The great trouble with that meter is that for some reason it is very easy to slop over in it. You have to be on your guard against so many things in writing verse—and that is one of them. What I mean to say is that an idea or emotion has usually to be tied up in a picture, a figure of speech or something like that, before it is really available for poetry—in the highest sense—

I'm afraid this preachment is stupid, but it is, with limitations, true.—Yet O there is something awfully nice about your little poem. vraiment!

I'll keep it unless you want it back.

By all the gods of Flaubert, of Homer, of modern realism and the new poetry, I conjure you, Oh Rummy, to take back them words. Prize fights are every bit as good a subject for poetry as fine ladies and illicit love affairs. What is the *Iliad* but a succession of rather sweary & infinitely bombastic prize fights? Admitted that excessive & artificial use of "sweat and swear" to make poems seem manly and modern is abominable and heinous and in every way to be brought up before the tribunals of good taste and good sense—still, I insist that every subject under the sun which has any thing to do with human beings—man, woman or child—is susceptible of poetic treatment.

There's an outburst for you.

And, moreover, one of the prime reasons why American literature *isn't* is that we as a nation have not that feeling of the infinite beauty and infinite poetry underlying things—love, war, sunsets, tin pans, lawnmowers, etc etc—. . . .

(You should hear me when I get really started on the subject of American literature etc—due for three hours steady!)

Don't be bored—it is so darned unpleasant, worse than having an uncomfortable collar on. . . . listen to me preaching—when I am parching for a rampage of some sort myself. The trouble is, Rummy, that the modern world is made for people of forty or over—Actually, the only resort of people who feel aggressively young and adventurous is literature—or walking—Have you tried the walking cure?

It proceeds thus: When you have reached the last stage of boredom and are surrounded on all sides by blue devils, take your hat, or leave it behind which is better, and with in one hand your favorite poet, march out. Go in any direction, not noticing where you are going, if possible chanting your poet (or your own works, according to taste) to the May breezes as you walk.

At the end of two hours you'll be rather hoarse, tired and generally contented with life, and if the cure is a success, temporarily lost! Then find your way home in great content, with nary a blue devil in sight—

But perhaps you have *bounds* at school—inventions of the evil one—

Am in the midst of Jean Christophe—

'Daffodil Fields' is not one of my favorite Masefields—you'll love "Dauber"—but there are delightful passages—

Au Revoir
Jack

We'll have to rampage together someday in search of adventure with a capital *A*.

For the Lord's sake don't have scarlet fever—I had it once—shut up for eight weeks & read Polish novelists & Swedenborg very unpleasant, take my word for it.

[Cambridge
Fall 1915]

Dear Rummy,

I really think that if we keep the pot of our correspondence boiling, we'll end by furbishing ourselves to the point of being decent letter-writers—So "on with the dance, let joy be unrefined—no, unconfined"—

You must send me the whole of your sea poem. The stanza has lots of descriptive gumption—Incidentally, I consider "glee" a dangerous word, sort of newspaper-poetry I don't know why. The 'swirled' & 'curled' give a very good "internal rhyme" & the verse has a nice tinkle; too, it really makes you see the white spume-water swirling on the beach—that's the important thing.

So glad you like my Brussels sketch-thing. I am going to try & write a little batch of things of the sort in the next couple of months. It is such fun to do.

My story is a longish collection of sketches dealing with the life of a young man rather boy ('young man' is a horrid phrase—'young men' are what fashionable clothes are made for) in New York: Very psychological & lots of description and I fear very dull—but it amuses me to write it. Sometime, when it's finished, I shall send it you & you'll nearly turn up your toes to the daisies from boredom reading it. I'll tell you the plot etc—in my next letter—I've about half finished it.

The verse affair in the last [Harvard] Monthly is pretty ragged & 'modern' & I fear very bad. It is an attempt to combine "free verse" with rhyme.

I haven't read "Les Possedés." 'Crime & Punishment' of Dostoevski—is a wonderful novel, hideously unpleasant—to read it is like a night-mare, it grips you so—about a murderer.

I am so glad you liked "Kim"—I've read it several times and always enjoy it, particularly the scenes on the road and in the Himalayas. And the wonderful lama!

Rummy, we're *going* to meet next summer. The only question is how—That must be decided later.

Do you know? we could have lots of fun walking through the Berkshires if we could only manage it. I, too, find that things of that sort always fall through. However, I intend to turn over a new leaf and be free from "the slings & arrows of outrageous fortune" in future, if it is humanly possible. So a determined effort must be made to Berkshirize.

However that may be, we must try to meet in June.

Don't hurry about sending back Housman's poems—I'm in no hurry. Talking of sea poems, here's a sonnet of Andrew Lang I think you'll like—

["The Odyssey"]
"As one that for a weary space has lain
Lulled by the song of Circe, and her wine
In gardens near the pale of Proserpine,
Where that Aegean Isle forgets the main,
And only the low lutes of love complain,
And only shadows of wan lovers pine—
As such an one were glad to know the brine
Salt on his lips, and the large air again—
So gladly from the songs of modern speech
Men turn, and see the stars, and feel the free
Shrill wind beyond the close of heavy flowers,
And through the music of the languid hours
They hear like ocean on a western beach
The surge & thunder of the Odyssey."

I think the last line's a wonder.

Here's another water poem called "The Water Nymph" that may interest you—by a man named Noel I think:

I flung me round him,
I drew him under;
I clung, I drowned him,
My own white wonder. . . .

Father and mother,
Weeping and wild,
Came to the forest,
Calling the child,
Came from the Palace
Down to the pool
Calling my darling,
My beautiful!

Under the water
Cold and so pale,
Could it be love made
Beauty so frail?
Ah me for mortals,
In a few moons,
If I had left him,
After some Junes,
He would have faded,
Faded away,
He the young monarch, whom

All would obey,
Fairer than day,
Alien to Springtime,
Joyless and grey,
He would have faded,
Faded away,
Moving a mockery,
Scorned of the day!
Now I have taken him
All in his prime
Saved from slow poisoning
Pitiless time,
Filled with his happiness,
One with the prime
Saved from the cruel
Dishonor of time.

Laid him, my beautiful
Laid him to rest,
Loving adorable
Softly to rest
Here in my crystalline,
Here in my breast.

Its sort of wishy washy but I thought it might amuse you & it has clever rhymes—

So long—
Jack

[Cambridge]
Dec 6th [*1915*]

Dear Rummy,

Your letter was delightfully long—

I meant to write after the Yale Game to crow over you—but it's so late now that I shall resist the temptation. Should have loved to have jaunted up to see you—maybe I shall some day—but I have been too horridly busy to think of such a thing.

Are you reading Cicero now? That gentleman, in small doses, is rather fun I think—the ones where he calls poor Cataline every name in the calendar are particularly amusing.

I admire you for reading Molière—haven't read any of him for ages—At present I am indulging in an orgy of two modern French poets—Verlaine & Verhaeren. The latter's a Belgian and very wonderful.

What do you think about the war? It is fearfully wearing to have so little happen—If they could only get one victory, we'd all be so much more comfortable. My gay yellow paper is exhausted and here I have to write on a banal white pad.

Oh, I must tell you about that swim in Newfoundland. There was a wonderful bay, without a house or a town on it, that had a wide white beach backed up by pine forests. We were absolutely the only living things about except white cawing sea gulls. The water was pale green, and simply stung when you got in—but it was like a bath in champagne! After it we danced about the beach like Greek fauns or nymphs. You can imagine what fun it was. You'ld have loved it I know.

My main amusement of late has been wandering about Boston streets at night. You see the most interesting little incidents and types— types enough to keep any painter busy a century. Then there are little Italian restaurants way down town, where you can get spaghetti and Orvieto wine and little slimy Italian herrings.

You must be getting hugely husky with football practice & other athletic doings. Don't get too husky, please; husky people invariably have a brain the size of a pea & are awful bores. At least I find them so at college here.

Suppose you're preparing for the Xmas vacation & similar joys— Has the term gone quickly?—For me it's been like lightning. How long a vacation do you get?

We—poor things—get about ten days. Is'nt it sad?

I am hoping to get lots of letters from you—you see, I refuse to be discouraged by your pleading studies etc. By the way, you might tell me what they are—if you want padding for a letter. But as long as you write messily & say the first thing that comes into your head I'll be satisfied.

I hate formal letters like sin—anything else is a joy & a relief—particularly if one says all sorts of mad things most people would'nt dream of putting in letters—

But you've probably had enough of my scrawl for one day—

Jack

My writing's a good preparation for a study of hieroglyphics! Isn't it?

[Cambridge
February 13, 1916]

Look here Rummy!

Even if you are winter sporting and skiing in this gay blizzard—I insist on correspondence. Here is my ultimatum: If one Rumsey Marvin does not see fit to write, send postal or otherwise communicate within thirty days with, one, J.R.D.P.Jr, said R.M., alias Rummy, shall incur unheard of penalties of all sorts, better *imagined than described*. Thereunto, I, J.R.D.P.Jr, being in full use of my faculties, do hereby set my hand and seal, on this 13th of February, in the year of Our Lord's Grace 1916.

Signed, J.R.D.P.Jr.

There now, young man!
Am reading Don Quixote.

Au Revoir

Écrivez, écrivez, ou, foi de gentilhomme, parbleu, sacré tripes, as they say in Dumas, je—like the witches in Macbeth—"I'll do, I'll do, I'll do".

Jack

[Cambridge
Spring 1916]

Rummy!

Your stuff interested me a lot.

Now you're in for theory, criticism and other horrors—Don't believe it all, but bits may help you.

First I am going to copy down a verse or two from my beloved Verlaine—

Art Poétique
De la musique avant toute chose

. . . .

Il faut aussi que tu n'ailles point
Choisir les mots sans quelque méprise:
Rien de plus cher que la chanson grise
Ou l'indécis au précis se joint.

. . . .

Now for the poems. Really, the "sonnet's" darn good.

A rimeless sonnet is certainly a novelty, Rummy; but I'm the last one to object to that—I am more likely to cry—"originality before anything else!"

There's a lot of thought in it a good solid rhythm and the wording isn't too trite, though it has tendencies in that direction.

I don't think "Mundane lights appear as blanks" is exactly successful.

By the way "joys" are always "trivial"—also words like "mundane", "puny", "petty" etc are a little high falutin' for poetry in my opinion. Try to run down the simple (not the hackneyed) and colorful words.

Now for some general advice—I'll try not to sound priggish; forgive me if I do—Why don't you try for a little more description—not in vague worn-out terms but in concrete images—? See what I mean? It seems to me you can express emotion much better through a novel-*colored* descriptive bit than through "black despair" or some other phrase of that sort.

There now! Really, Rummy, I think your stuff is worth plugging at—I think you'll be able to go something darn good if you make sure to say what you feel and see in your own way & not to moan out poetic palpitations in the mode of the newspaper poets—

You must read lots of verse, though; that's one of the best ways of learning how to write it—Old friend Tennyson is always there & Rudyard, and R.L.S. & Browning . . .

How do you like "A Shropshire Lad"? You may not like them at first—but read them over a couple of times and they'll grow on you terrifically.

Do forgive this preachy letter—Maybe parts'll be useful—

Dont fail to send me your stuff as you write it—So long—

Jack

[Diary]
[March 1916]
"In Quest of Bohemia"
New & revised version

Young man who buys flowers for "sick friend"—wants them for himself but ashamed. Sympathetic flower shop girl. Sick friend gets elaborated—Young man a pale poet—No, this can be a story of its own; not In Quest of Bohemia at all—When she learns at last that sick friend is non existent snorts—more so when thinks of flowers—for some girl? no for himself—The memory, switches off in disgust—

Le Grand Roman

Atmosphere of streets at night Supper tables & garish restaurants Youth in the city.

1. Friendship—the strong unsympathetic character, the weak boy who adores him. Man of white hot burning idealism, of huge power & desire for self expression—The scene in the run-away.

2. Love—a woman—The strong man has wild passions love affair absolutely subdues character of girl to him. Hideous jealousy on the part of the boy. Life to him turns to dust and ashes.

3. The hero strides on—he progresses—his mores cannot they are too wrapped up in the old man. Might even become evangelist or something of that sort—He grows older—the others are weak & miserable & destroyed but they keep their youth. At last he utterly breaks with them. They drift away into the sea of faces that you pass in the streets at night

At the Bourse—*March 26th '16*
Hokku

Comme des moineaux dénichés
Est la voix de la dame
Au chapeau rouge.

La dame au chapeau rouge
Dans le restaurant,—
Elle danse, elle bouge,
Elle nous regarde avec vivace,
Son ris âcre nous agace.
Est elle la reine du printemps,
Aimée de Zephyr, le doux vent,
Ou, simplement
Une gouge?

To Rumsey Marvin

[Cambridge]
April 23rd [1916]

Right-O-Mr Rummy,

rapid fire let it be. But first let me explain—the reason I didn't answer your bubblesome patriotic & otherwise delightful letter was that I was in Virginia gaily vacationing, riding, & digging in mi garden, among the cabbages, à la Diocletian! Moreover I was reading Marcus Aurelius, "The Brothers Karamazov" (by Dostoevski), "Elizabeth and Her German Garden" [by Mary Annette, Countess von Arnim], two anthologies of contemporary verse, on which I wrote a labored essay; and a couple of mildly philosophical textbooks—*3rd*ly I wrote said essay & a couple of chapters of a novel-thing ie: story (longish) I am trying to do; *4th*ly and most difficult, I tried to think—*logically*— on divers important subjects; (that nearly killed me, as you may imagine.) There, doesn't my list of activities pretty near match yours? To be sure, my veins did not glow with patriotism, but, what's better, I got *sunburned*—beat you there! Ha Ha!

Now, although it is in the wee hours of the morning and I just got in from New York, I propose to write you a mighty letter, the which you must answer instanter, young man—at great length.

I quite admire your Plattsburgette idea, although I abhor the militarists and all their works. I too feel a crying need to look less like a bean pole and more like a human being—I have vowed that I shall disappear somewhere for a space of time and come back a New Hercules in an affrighted world; but, darn it all, I never get time to do it.

Tell me what you saw *les belles Russes* [probably the Russian Ballet] do—

Gee! you have a list of books—do tell me how you liked "Kim". I am glad you've embarked on G.B.S.—I have most of his plays—If you want I'll send them to you, but you must send them back fairly soon as I read him when I reach a certain stage of boredom, and can't exist long without some of him.

Look here Rummy, don't you go getting down at the mouth about your poetry. It's damnably good for a beginning, and you must keep it up. It's only by making a frightful lot of messes that one gets anywhere at all. If you aren't careful I'll send you some of my stuff to show you what bad verse *can* exist. And I'm quite chipper about it,—when I'm not so blue I can't see straight!

I'm glad you've also achieved the New Republic—I read it muchly —I think it's the only live magazine in the country—though its not so radical as I should like it to be. I'm dying to get them to accept some stuff of mine—they nearly did once, *nearly*. Ugh!

I'd love to meet Leary—he sounds delightful—Do you know? it's funny, but my best friend is Irish too—

More yet, I want to meet you—Now look, if we have to kill

ourselves doing it, we've got to meet somewhere next summer if only for a day or two. That is decided, isn't it? Ways & means must be considered later—because however well one can converse by letter, the only way to 'really' get to know a person is to walk with them through nice hilly country (not too hilly) for at least five hours.

I do envy you people your trolley jaunt—It'll be great fun. When is it coming off? I am dying to take a walking trip up through the Berkshires. In fact I think I'll do it, if I have to go alone: I have been planning it with different people for ages, but it never comes off.

But I'll tell you what I am going to do. At Nahant on the North Shore are some delightful cliffs from which a fledgeling poet of my acquaintance and myself have vowed to see the sun rise over the grey Atlantic—We're going to start at midnight and walk there—It will be great fun going through the streets in the dawn-gloaming.

Rummy, do you remember the race we had for the train when I scattered the silver dollars?

By the way, I am enclosing this in a Monthly that has some stuff of mine which may amuse you—Then I am sending you later a little green volume of the poems of one Dick Aldington, an Englishman—and it seems to me the best of the Imagists. Do tell me what you think of him—au grand sérieux, because I am planning a "monumental" essay on the subject & a fresh point of view will be most illuminating.

Au Revoir—
Jack

[Cambridge]
May 29 [1916]

Dear Rummy,

Although I am awfully busy—exams are coming so soon—my *last* exams, pensez à ça—that is if I don't go to Oxford or somewhere absurd, which is possible.

About Masefield, you go and read 'The Widow in the Bye Street,' young man, and see if you don't think it has really tragic beauty. Of course bits of it, taken by themselves are ugly and disgusting, but, *as a whole,* it seems to me to have a peculiar sort of pathetic beauty—and a marvellous feeling of life—

Your long letter was a joy, really, and *I don't get bored,* 'cep'n with myself and with magazines and periodical literature in general—

One minute—I must go back to my muttons, What in the name of Heaven are "life's meaner things"? To me they are stockbrokers and hypocritical clergymen far more often than they are women of the streets or prize fighters or any of Masefield's riff-raff, not that I prefer them in literature to "decent" people—but I think that one's ideas as to what decent people are can't go according to conventional lines, if they are going to be ideas at all—

Nevertheless you must read 'Dauber' you'll like that and it isn't "slummy"—

Before I forget, listen what I did the other afternoon. In company with several friends, a cold roast chicken, cheeses, jellies etc, I went out in to the country and we had a most delightful souper sur l'herbe on a hillside that fronted the sunset. I've never known anything so delightful—It was a wonderful red-orange sunset, fading gradually through rosy-purple and violet to a sort of dim lavender with a yellow sheen—

We climbed into a big oak tree—as if we were Bonnie Prince Charlie being pursued by the King's men, and watched it (when we'd demolished the eatables) and then walked back to Cambridge through the gloaming.

'My muttons' is an English expression, I fear; that comes, I suppose from the horrid habit of serving up a cold joint of mutton again and again—till Fido gets the bone!

Poor Kitchener! Still I suppose one can't have a better death than to go down at the height of your achievement with band playing, and colors flying.

Were'nt you excited over the great sea battle?

I'd like to have been there.

The little poem is in a delightful cadence

"And went away" is rather a smash—could you get it more into tune?

Don't you love "A Night Among the Pines" in *Travels with a Donkey?*—I knew you'ld like it. You make me feel like reading it over again—out of sympathy!

Plus plus tard
Jack

But Rummy, to come again to our muttons—(I argue in chorus—with interludes of description!) there isn't so much really distasteful—if you get the right point of view to it—on the breast of the teeming earth. You can find a sort of mad splendor in things, the ugliest, the filthiest things, if you really look for it—if you don't, as most people do, put up stone walls and bar the gate on it.

There's a wonderful religious poem ["The Hound of Heaven"] of Francis Thompson I like to apply to beauty—

> "I fled him down the nights and down the days;
> I fled him down the arches of the years
> I fled him down the labyrinthine ways
> Of my own mind; . . . .
>
> From those strong feet that followed,
> But with unhurrying chase,
> And unperturbèd pace,
> Deliberate speed, majestic instancy,
> They beat". . . .

It is a queer strangely fascinating poem which you'll have to read soon.

Speaking of rhythm in Masefield, can anything be more rhythmic than this:

> "I heard a partridge covey call;
> The morning sun was bright on all.
> Down the long slope the plow team drove
> The tossing rooks rose and hove.
> A stone struck on the share. A word
> Came to the team. The red earth stirred" . . .

in a strange rather harsh way, to be sure, but still rhymic. However, I agree with you completely on the subject. All the poetry I love best is intensely musical.

By the way—speaking in un-realistic mood—do you read Maeterlinck? If not you must tackle "Pelléas and Mélisande" and some of his other plays—you'll like them—perhaps you've seen Debussy's opera—

I should at this moment be reading a very dull book for a philosophy course on the Neoplatonists. Speaking of them, I've also been reading a novel of Merezhkovski called "The Death of the Gods"— about Julian the Apostate—Do you like him—from earliest infancy, he's been one of my pet Roman emperors.

But this letter's degenerating (ink has given out) into a literary causerie—which is dull—so let's change the subject to baseball—

No let's not—

We must & we shall arrange our grand New York spree for before July *3rd*—I dont know many queer restaurants in New York, but I can hunt for one. Now if it were Boston I could take you to a dozen—

I jabber Spanish a little & read it a little—have read "Don Quixote" vol 1 & 2 in original and I intend to study it violently in the near future—So you have the linguistic bug too? I've always been mad to know a lot of languages—it's so humanizing, don't you think so?

Have heard of, but never read "The Anvil of Chance"—I envy your English teacher his story in *Scribners*.

Gosh, but I envy you your five months at Capri—it must have been wonderful. It's rather funny but I have never achieved Capri— Three times I have tried and each time a storm has come up, or been up and the boat has had to turn back—isn't that maddening? Once we tossed about for five hours in the Bay of Naples—I sitting on the cabin floor with a very sick Italian baby's head in my lap. C'était gai je vous assure

And how I long to stretch my legs on a good piece of road and set off, like Gil Blas or Don Quixote and everyone amusing who's ever lived—videre mundum.

I always envied Satan in 'Job' who was coming "from going up and down the earth"—

Don't you want to go up and down the earth?

Adios
Jack

[Cambridge
Spring 1916]

Dear Rummy,

I've just been on a tremendously long ramble through Boston—I love cities on a rainy night—The reflections of the orange and yellow lights are so gay on the wet streets—Particularly Saturday night— there's a wonderful atmosphere of gaiety & a sort of paganism about which always delights me—I mean in the cheaper parts of the city— those are the only parts of any city that are ever alive—The market was wonderful—all old women, young women, boys, old grizzled men, flashing eyed Italians buying vegetables and meats—and the reds and greens and yellows were so fresh in the rainy atmosphere—It is won- derful what beautiful faces you sometimes see at such times—ugly

gargoyle-grotesques too, to be sure—Still it is all very alive and exciting—when not done up in stays like the life of us cotton-wool
plutocrats—because we are plutocrats compared to those people—But
enough romantic sociology!

Congratulations! Once long ago I got fourth in a hundred yard
dash—but——You know I've spent my entire existence vowing that
sometime in the future I should develop my body and become a young
Hercules. You make me quite envious with your blue ribbons.

Gee, but I used to hate to be made to exercise when I was at
school!

I'll be awfully interested to see McLane's poem—hope to meet him
someday.

By the way—I like your smash in "And went away" but somehow
it might smash a little more successfully—You must write more. It
doesn't hurt a bit to imitate form in poetry—so long as you have your
own ideas—you'll find, too, that squashing an idea into a given form so
transforms it (no pun!) that it ends up by being yours anyway.

Next week I am going to take a little walking trip up Cape Cod
with a couple of friends. We'll start from inland and walk out to
Provincetown. It'll be great fun I think, particularly as we know
nothing about roads or inns or anything. I'll write you all about it.

Do you know, Rummy? I think the pair of us ought to under-
study Stevenson sometime—and go on a ramble with some volumes of
verse & an indefinite objective. We'll have to try to manage it.

Au Revoir
Jack

[Cambridge]
June 20th [*1916*]

Dear Rummy—

Your letters are a delight—

Wrong—hurrah—your guess was 'most an insult—; you know I
haven't any grey hairs yet! I am just twenty—only a little more than
four years older than you are—so there, young man. I'm so accustomed
to being taken for a greybeard myself that I could guess pretty well how
much younger *you* were than you seemed.

This is Class Day—I've marched & counter marched in processions—and heard endless orations. Now it is dark and the Yard is hung
with Japanese lanterns, is lilting with the music of three bands and two

fountains—and I have a pink in my buttonhole—You know their wistful far away odor—all conduces to a mood of pleasant aloofness. I've been wandering among the crowd and listening to their footsteps and feeling a strange half-melancholy.

What little family I have I would not let come—so I feel like Virgil and Dante in a pleasant Purgatorio—interested but aloof—(N.B. will probably end in a shocking attack of the blue devils.)

Wish you were here—It is very fascinating—glow of lanterns and ripple of voices above a low grind of footsteps—through it all runs like a gilt thread, the brazen sound of the band—Then the occasional militia uniform gives it a

> 'There was a sound of revelry by night
> And Belgium's capital had gathered then
> Her beauty & her chivalry, and bright
> The lamps shone o'er fair women & brave men'

atmosphere—Let's hope "the cannon's opening roar" won't follow—

Lord! I have the same trouble with my poetry—I find it awfully hard to correct things that I know are out of tone—but I find the trick is, if possible, to mellow a verse in your mind a good deal before writing it down—

I've been out wandering about again—a heavy wind has come up and set all the lanterns jigging and all the ladies' dresses a-flutter

To come back to your poem, I didn't mind the 'rim' line because there was a sort of emphasis about it, and it made you see what you wanted it to.

Your singing propensities fill me with awe—it must have been the German food you ate in Switzerland—Know then that I have two permanent grudges against Providence—(Improvidence in this case!) I can make no form of music—vocal or instrumental; I cannot draw. If I ever enter another incarnation, and am consulted about my status, I shall be a combination between Whistler and Debussy!

Is there anything more wonderful than the sniff of meadow land in the warm sun, when your body is all tingling from a long walk?

Don't be afraid that I'll forget our engagement next week—I'm only afraid that our time to jabble will be so limited that we'll be absolutely tongue-tied from pure need of talking.

Au Revoir—

Jack

[Cambridge
June 1916]

Dear Rummy,

Rejoicing in my large and examless freedom I have been making vows. Firstly I am going to start educating myself—it's wonderful how much college interferes with ones education. Secondly I am going to write huge amounts each day—Thirdly I am going to wander far and wide over the face of the globe. Small order!

As to wandering: I begin tomorrow by setting out with two friends on a Conquest of Cape Cod—Never having been out there and knowing nothing about the whereabouts of inns etc. it will be interesting to see where we turn up. Shall write you en route—

Am taking a toothbrush, razor and a volume of Merediths poems, so you see, it will be a very vagabondy affair.

By the way, I received the Horae [St. Paul's School literary magazine]—Tell McLane his poem is damnably good—particulaly the first line and the descriptive bits. Of course the diction was a bit flabby in places—unoriginal, unalive—but on the whole its one of the decentest poems I've ever seen in a school paper.

About your verse—do you know? I think the line about "huddled clouds" before snow in one of your winter things is the best you have done. It had real gumption Try some more stuff on that order—The game is to get musical-picture words and pack them with the desired emotion——Comprenez? Of course the best results come when they appear of themselves and when your poem comes as easily as sausage from a sausage machine—Even then—it takes a shocking lot of work—

This summer I expect "Rhymes of a Plattsburg Volunteer"—or "Callings from the Canteen"—marches militaires in great quantity.

A bientôt
Jack

How about June 20th or so for meeting in NY?

To Dudley Poore (1893–   ), *who met Dos at Harvard during the spring of 1915. Poore was graduated from college in 1917 and went immediately into the American Field Service. He ran into Dos in Paris that October, then joined the ambulance group in Bassano early in 1918. Later he and Dos were together in Spain in 1919 and New York in the early 1920's. Poore was a freelance writer during the twenties, publishing often in the* Dial. *From 1930–1939 he taught at Harvard and*

Radcliffe, then freelanced for the next five years before joining the Department of State in 1944. He served as a Cultural Affairs Officer until 1961, when he retired. Poore visited Dos and Katy frequently at Provincetown during the summers in the thirties and forties and remained a close friend until Dos' death.

Cintra—Westmoreland Co. Va.
July 5 [*1916*]

Pobrecito!

Here I am ecstasizing—to the surprise & mild shockdom of certain cousins visiting us—over poppies, gooseberries, currents immense Shasta Daisies and other glories more or less indiscriminately—

It's a wonderful blowy day and the hollyhocks are nodding and bowing like tall ladies at a country dance—the poppies are all a-flutter and the lavender comes in puffs of glorious fragrance through the window— Soon I shall bathe in the river and read "Pierre Nozière" of the beloved Anatole in a bathtowel dressing gown—En effet je suis étourdi—crackbrained with rusticity & divers delights.

To come earthwards, I enjoyed "London Visions" a lot. There are bits in it that are surprisingly good—in fact I think his [Laurence Binyon's] poetry rather a glorious failure—

The odor of lavender from the garden is simply maddening

Do write me often, Dudley, from your northern fastness ('Tennysonian, n'est-ce pas?)

And for the Lord's sake send me some verse—you won't, I fear—being a *Clam* as far as your productions are concerned. Now you'll have to send some—to un-clam your soul—

Saw the Auk [Stewart Mitchell] in Stamford & the delightfullest aunt, who plays Bach raptly and with charm—pensez—speaks with a French accent and is full of the old régime—The Chopin, Liszt (?) old age—you know the time I mean—Also she's an occultist and has the tiniest little feet I ever saw on mortal—She ought to be a marquise—

Shall try to write sanely later in the week—

Really you must write for I already have an emptiness for Cambridge & literary jibber-jabber—Don't think that I'm "casting asparagus" at your letter, as yet unborn—

Au Revoir
Dos

Pobrecito—you must come down here—The garden is joyfully disheveled and tangled—

To Rumsey Marvin

Cintra,
Westmoreland Co Va.
July 30th [*1916*]

Well, ye spalpeen, Rummy,

Notwithstanding church yard silence on your part, here's a log to raise the almost extinct blaze of our correspondence. The fact is that I have in my time been the killer of so many correspondences through pure laziness, that, as a sort of penance, I have vowed not to let this one languish—so long as yellow paper holds out—

And then, darn it all, I should really like to hear what you are doing with yourself—the results of Plum Island, etc.

As for me, I am vegetating, reading a little, writing a little, sailing an impromptu sailing canoe, which is great sport, but rather inefficient, gardening, and riding horseback, and bathing. You'd love the bathing here. We are right where the Potomac joins the Chesapeake and have mild surf or still water according to the wind, and a nice little beach. At night it is often phosphorescent, and wildly exciting to swim in. Your arms and legs are as if they had flaming draperies and you trail jewelled bubbles behind you through the water. Then there is a sort of jelly fish which lights up like a milky star when you hit it.—I don't know anything more gorgeous—

What have you been reading? I have been having a scrumptious time with Benvenuto Cellini's Autobiography—you know, he was the chap who did the Perseus in Florence—You must read it—It gives you the most wonderful picture of the High Renaissance and is full of screamingly funny incidents, and with hardly a word of description, simply shrieks Italy; Italy at her best, golden sun, cypresses almost black against the extreme blue of sky, and all the enthusiasm and vigor and wonderful livingness of it. Why, the book is a tonic to one living in our sea-green, twaddling, ranting little agelet of greedy capitalists and sallow humanitarians! (Isn't the lad fierce? for a pacifist too!)

For the Lord's sake and in the name of numerous things, such as red sandstone cliffs etc, write—

Adiós
Jack

[Cintra, Virginia]
Aug 24th [1916]

Rummy, I like you for liking Plum Island—It must have been great
fun—I quite envy you rubbing shoulders with such a lot of fellows of
all sorts and conditions. My main moan has always been the lack of it.
At school I was a most unsocial friendless little beast—and it has been
hard to shake off the habit of solitude—Something like Plum Island
would have been awfully good for me—although you know there are
people who sort of have solitude in their blood, who are just as lonely
in a crowd or on a mountain top—I may be one of them: quien
sabe?

However, I assure you that its damned unpleasant, particularly
when you have instincts that desire the extremest sociability—From
that point of view I approve heartily of military service—because it
would make young men rub shoulders more, get to know people outside of their class—be actually instead of theoretically democratic.

But the devil of it is that military affairs lead the other way—Just
think of the insufferable snobbery of army officers, of the swagger
everything in uniform puts on when it runs up against a poor civilian
(why I expect to be shoved off the very pavement by the breadth of
your shoulders—your chestiness when I see you again)—and the messy
picture of a military democracy—poet and peasant, doctor and butcher,
arm in arm, sweating together, marching together, heroizing together,
to the tune of a patriotic song—sort of fades away. Et plus when you
have an army you immediately want to use it—and a military population in a government like ours would be absolutely at the mercy of any
corrupt politician who got into the White House, of any millionaire
who could buy enough newspapers——mais je vous ennuie mon
pauvre Rummy—

But look! I have a idee—you really must agree to it—by Mars and
the Star Spangled Banner—

I shall be in New York for a couple of weeks in early september—
Now attention, my plan is thus: I have never been in the Catskills—
they are near—a couple of hours I guess—Have you?—Now supposing
we go to some place there and say walk for two days and then come
back to N.Y.—What do you think of it?—We may hit godforsaken
holes but we can always get a train or car or something and move on.

And we could do wonders in two days. We'd learn all each others
absurdities and would quarrel madly at every cross roads—as a result

we'd know each other better than by four thousand letters—Write at once what you think of it. All we'll need to take is a toothbrush comb and clean socks and books of verse—of course—Dont you dare say you can't do it—because I am going abroad—where as yet undecided—at the end of the month, and may not be back for an age—You see I shall vow not to come back until I've come to grips with old lady adventure—sort of a search for the Holy Grail.

I quite envy your hangings on the edge of love—Good God, though, if one is feeling well and properly in tune with earth and sky—one is already in love with every man woman and child in sight—except for those few repulsive mummified corpses of people that freeze the very name of love—Eros is a great god—I like his beautiful Greek name better than his Roman one that makes you think of St Valentine's and Baroque interiors—But how few votaries he has compared to the banal gigglesome Cupid. And so few girls have any idea of him—of his supreme human dignity.

But I'm probably talking rot—If you really fall I shall send you Swinburne

Ecrivez bientôt
Jack

For the Lord's Sake remember that neatness is a minor virtue—often a vice, and that hesitation delay and worry (+ alcohol) are what high art feeds on— Finally, Rummy, man *is a thinking* animal—
Describe *her* or them

Fair?
Fat?
Thin?
Dark?
Languid?
Vivacious?
Frank?
Piquante?
Mysterious?
Seductive?
Miscellaneous?

[New York
September 28, 1916]

Thanks awfully Rummy dear but I possess a French Oxford Book—it has lots of nice things in it, hasn't it?

Was awfully glad to get your delightfully long letter—It carried me all through breakfast this morning—I wish you could have enclosed yourself in the envelope with it, though, as I am still in this beastly New York—all alone in our dark sepulchral house—You see I can't get out of here until Oct 14th when I sail on the 'Espagne' for Bordeaux. That's more than two weeks to wait and nothing particular to do ('ceptin my everlasting reading & writing which is part of the day—sort of like cleaning my teeth.)

I'm awfully glad you like the Swinburne you've read so far. How about 'The Garden of Proserpine'? I also particularly like the Sonnet to "Mlle. De Maupin"—a strangely exotic book you must read someday, by Gautier—a combination of rather decadent beauty and real passion and smut of a very low order. I think the sonnet's one of the most beautiful in English.

The account of the analytical amours delighted me—and as I said before, I love the name of Peggy—Don't think that I am utterly unsusceptible. I often fall in love with a face or a glint of light on hair or an intonation of the voice . . . Rather hard too. I admit that the idea of marriages and engagements and all the conventional fluffiness of respectable mating doesn't attract me particularly—It rather spoils things—And two of my best friends are getting married this fall—awful thought—for a friend married is a friend lost—and when the commodity is so rare—so damnably rare—I like to hold onto them.

Facilis decensus est—the descent into limbo of writing is easy—but the ascent into print! . . . But you can't begin too soon—as the mere fact of writing improves ones outlook and sharpens ones style—and so much is a question of dexterity acquired by practice—that is if you've got the stuff internally—and most of us have—I believe—the trouble is in finding a medium of outlet.

Apropos of scenario—make flirtatious lady a German spy trying to blow up a shipment of chipped beef or something; hero disentangles himself—convoys chipped beef to France—is met by French Girl in a nurse's uniform—and you have done the trick—

Send it to the Vitagraph or the Famous Players Co. 57th Street (bet. 6th & 7th Ave) & *maybe* you'll get back the desired $25 . . . and maybe not!

I really am interested in architecture—and I think the grinding study necessary will be good for my lazy & undisciplined soul—The plan is this: I shall go right to Madrid where I have letters to a number of rather interesting people learn Spanish & meanwhile take architecture courses in the University—unfortunately I'll have to take some Math too, since architecture is not possible without it—horrid thought —then in the spring I shall go to Paris and try to get an Ambulance job of some sort. Après? Let us hope Berlin on General Joffre's sight-seeing tour—I fear though that there will be nothing as exciting—For some reason I confidently expect peace next year—

Look here Rummy—you and I must take a trip together or something before long—We might go to Iceland or Montevideo or Clapham Junction—

About the Man on the Street: Collectively he's the forces of darkness—but taken one by one . . . You know, I rather divide people into those who see, and those who drift. There are people—you and I and Swinburne—who analyse, who observe, who think, and then there are people who merely follow the bandwagon—The people who are free, who are in revolt, and the people who are shackled by all convention—But the illuminati are not to be found in any one class of society—Lower than the stupidity of the uneducated is the stupidity of the educated whose education is nothing but a wall that keeps him from seeing the world—And most of our schools and college do that merely—Then there are so many other sorts of education—a farmer's boy who has never been to school may be beautifully deeply educated— again he may not But a stupid farmer is no lower on the scale than a stupid Harvard graduate—one who can't see beyond wealth and clubs and that abominable coverer up of things—niceness—See what I mean?—It is so hard to get away from the lingo, from the little habits of speech and action, from the petty snobberies of ones own class that it takes a distinct effort to see real 'illumination' and appreciate it, regardless of garlic or lavender water.

Undoubtedly the worst abomination and the commonest is snobbery——its so blinding to the human beauty that everything is warm with, that touches you like a friend's hand when you are walking through the dirtiest, slummiest streets or sitting in the most corsetted drawing room—

Forgive this young essay—this conte morale—(on second thoughts, it is about a third true)

But the greatest truths are thoroughly honey combed with lies, so I should worry—

I'd love to meet *your* Irishman—Do you like Irish legends? I quite dote on them

I see you have your emotional thermometer in good working order—You'll be ready for a course of Russian novels in no time—I admit that I have the same disease and if I ever were to fall in love with a whole person—instead of with part of one—I should probably make out graphs of myself on ruled paper; like the statistics of an epidemic—

Write me again before I leave &
I'll send you my address—
Jack

Bordeaux
Oct 24th [*1916*]

Rummy, Rummy, I meant to write you tons on the boat, but honestly I was in a state of complete coma—you've never seen anything like. I just lay around and looked at the sea and felt the damp caressing breath of it and sort of melted into it—gee it was wonderful!

But its result was nothing in particular—As for excitement—temps de guerre etc. There was unfortunately none—

I met a couple of people who confessed to having slept in their clothes, and was told of a man who slept in a life preserver—but everyone was astoundingly placid. Of course, there was nothing to make anybody anything else but placid, as not one thing happened and we only saw three cargo boats and a few lights all the time we were crossing. And under sea—nothing, not even a porpoise.

Still, at both ends of the trip we ran without lights and with portholes muffled, and the trip up the Gironde at midnight was very interesting as there were said to be floating mines there, and the captain would'nt let anyone go to bed until we were safe in the channel to Bordeaux.

Have you ever been here? It's an awfully nice city, with a couple of charming old churches and very many beautiful houses in High Renaissance style, very simply and charmingly built. Oh it's so nice to get to France again—so sort of cosy and homelike—the long windows, the donkey carts full of vegetables, the odor of café au lait and fresh-baked bread in the early morning, the nice little écoliers with their bare legs and their black capes, the horse chestnut trees . . . if I had something with me to bubble over to I should be quite contented—as it is I am highly delighted and trying, as I wander about the cobbled streets, with the grass growing bright green in the chinks of the grey stone, to lash my poor brain into a state of productivity.

Its remarkable how soon, if I let myself, I relapse into a state of complete cabbagism without thought of any sort, with merely sensual joy in the colors and scents of the world, or unreasoning discomfort in physical—not exactly physical either—rather in emotional disabilities of my own—Its so darn hard to get outside of oneself enough really to see clearly and to follow frankly your ideas to whatever rocky ground or shaky rope ladder they lead you.

By the way read by all means Hugh Walpole's "Fortitude"—I read it coming over on the boat. Most of it is simply ripping. One of the vividest—most forceful—novels I've read for an age——

How about your muse?

Verse?

Prose?

I leave here for Madrid tomorrow

Jack

c/o Banco Hispano Americano
  1 Calle de Sevilla
  Madrid Espagne

[Madrid]
Oct. 30th [1916]

Dear Rummy

Madrid! The chocolate they give one for breakfast is divine, there is a lovely view from some parts of town of the mountain chain of the Sierra Guadarrama, the streets abound in donkeys & mules with lovely jingly harness inlaid with brass and red enamel, there are lots of Goya's little ragamuffins about, and people actually use pottery water bottles of the most divine shape,—apart from all that and the Prado Museum, Madrid is not awfully interesting in itself. The country of Castile is brown and rolling with dry arroyos and irrigated patches much like California only the brown of the hills is a pale nankeen instead of the rich sienna of the California slopes.

Although Madrid's modern and not awfully interesting—I think I'll stay here a trimestre at the Centro de Studios Historicos—(three months), where I am taking two courses in Spanish language and one in Spanish literature as I think listening to a Spanish lecturer will be good for my un-Iberian ears—As usual I'm already counting the days before I shall be at liberty again to roam—But I hope to get a tremendous amount of work done in the three months.

By the way, did I tell you that some of my poetry was coming out in a volume called Eight Harvard Poets, some of us are bringing out this winter? (publisher Lawrence Gomme, New York) I shall have the thing sent you as soon as it comes out—I'm afraid my stuffs awfully bad, but there are, in the volume, some real poems by friends of mine; so I think we ought to 'trouble the waters' a little bit:—in any case it'll be pleasant to see oneself in print.

Later: Having tramped about and done some errands I return to try to lash myself into a state of work—I am a lazy beggar and it always takes me an age to get started, particularly when I haven't written for some little time.

Its rather funny; the Madrileños seem to have a deathly fear of the night air and just as I came in everyone was appearing like this [refers to a sketch], muffled to the eyes—Some of them wear the gayest colored ones, red and green, purple and yellow—its something splendid. Another amusing feature of Madrid is the hours it keeps: One has déjeuner à la fourchette—almuerzo—at about one or two and then dinner between nine and ten at night. No one seems to get up in the morning and as late as I have ever been up the cafés and things seem to be in full blast. My Spanish is almost nil & I have the gayest time making myself understood

Look Rummy you must send me any stuff you produce—Don't send anything you haven't a copy of as the Spanish mails are said to be famous for losing things. Whats going on at school this year? Honestly I shall miss being within such easy writing distance of you.

I wish you'ld wrap yourself up in a jacket of poems or a box of candy or something and come along too, as "foreign travel" gains immensely by company

Au Revoir
Jack

[Madrid]
Nov. 12th [*1916*]

Rummy!

At last a letter from you—The mails are damnably slow—Your letter took very nearly a month—First, the poetry—its the best you've done & is very charming & unpretentious I think your 'scrambling' is better than 'toiling', even if it does make you think of eggs—and I think I like 'choking' better than 'gasping' for a flower. "On a wood nymph's bower" is better than o'er. The last line of all I like immensely —why not write it? "That's where I'm going." Could you find something else for the next to the last? "Where the winding footpaths lead—/ That's where I'm going" How about that? Between 'polar' & 'purple' is a matter for you to decide—Did you *see* them polar or purple? As for me, I think I see them polar. "Peeping thru the hedges" is lovely. The music of it on the whole's delightful—Sort of "over the hills & far away" piping. As for plains, I like them neither sun-parched or sun-baked—a perfectly simple or else a recondite adjective—me parece—is needed there. Send me a copy in your next letter, as I'm returning this one with marks. I want a copy so don't forget—

Do tell me what you didn't like in the N.R. [*New Republic*] article—there are many things I don't like in it.

Do write more—& read Keats' Eve of St. Agnes, Shelley's Adonaïs —there you will learn something about words.—I wish I were there as there's lots of stuff to the point I'd like to read you—The main thing is to write what you see as simply as possible No, not exactly, the main thing is to keep the proper average between the music of the thing, the meter and the words—& don't be afraid of any word if it seems to fit—sincerely. What I mean is, if you never sit down to *write a poem,* but always to *express a mood,* or *a picture* or anything—You won't go far away. Of course you always have to look out for wornout words. The piano, you see, is out of tune and there are certain notes that strike dully. A great poet is a sort of piano tuner—He cleans the dusty keys, avoids the strings that are worn to a frazzle and plays his tune. The great thing is to play your tune & not set pieces . . .

Do tell me the story plot.

Honestly, I've never been in such a musical city as Madrid, everything jingles and rings. . . .

Nov 13th

My room, as I think I've told you is hung over the Puerta del Sol, the biggest & noisiest square in the city, and the noises are really fascinating they are so constant and jumbled into long jangling chords, or something of the sort—

Oh dear, I have so much to tell you that—it brings on a sort of paralysis. Things to be said jostle and tread on each other's heels—I am sleepy tonight, so I shall put it off till tomorrow when I shall be, I hope, more intelligent. A Mañana.

Nov 15

I've been trying unsuccessfully to write all the morning—and have got into a most irritated state. It always makes me furious how slowly I turn out things. I must somehow learn to work quicker if I'm ever going to get anything done at all.

I had the most wonderful day yesterday. With two college friends of mine who turned up most unexpectedly here in Spain I walked out from Madrid to a little royal Hunting Lodge, El Pardo—A most beautiful morning's walk through a misty river valley with long yellow slopes dotted with evergreen oaks—a bit like California—under a wonderful burning blue sky with the Guadarrama mountains rising to meet us as we advanced. At El Pardo we lunched at a little table in the village square under yellow autumnal poplar trees, that dropped their leaves with a little rustling sound through the perfect glowing sun-drugged stillness of the afternoon. The Vino de Jerez cast a wonderful flare of light on the table where the sun shone through it. We ate omelettes and jambon and fruit all sprinkled with gold dust by the sun and watched the leaves fall rustling down through the yellow poplar trees . . . Then we walked back to Madrid through the afternoon, the autumn air, full of the tang of raked leaves being burned and climbed a hill in face of a marvellous sunset and saw Madrid sparkle below us with its rows of yellow lights in the blue grey dusk and heard a squeaky organ playing and saw people dancing, whirling under a red gasflare, while the organ ground out its jerky little tune—Mon enfant—it was a day—

I am quite settled in Madrid now, feel as if I'd lived here all my life—Am taking three courses and one in drawing and studying Spanish and jabbering at every chance a confused tongue of my own invention which people sometimes understand. I am also reading considerably and going to the theatre as much as possible. I find I can understand spoken Spanish, if not rattled too fast, fairly well.

You talk about pressed for time—I never have a moment—it is strange; with nothing to do but things I want to extremely badly, I have an awful time getting anything actually completed—I find myself frittering frightfully—I guess I shall have to turn over some new leaves or bust, from sheer desperation. The idea of writing down youthful

memories is awfully good—I do it quite a lot as it is such fun—I'd love
to see yours. It is wonderful how your earliest memories become simply
golden as you look back on them—Why one of my greatest joys is
going back and wandering in those quaint dark, dimly fragrant
rooms—You find so much—it's like rummaging in an attic. Except you
are wild to go back sometimes—just to step into the picture you're
drawing. There was so much charm and wonder—and one never had
the cold—all alone in the gloaming feeling or the great Boyg—that are
my bugbears *today*. The Great Boyg happens in Ibsen's play "Peer
Gynt"—you know the music for it—grieg's—It is something that Peer,
wandering in the mountains, finds coiled about him, a sort of snake
that makes no resistance to his blows—Whichever way he goes, he runs
into the passive motionless Boyg——Comprennez?

I admit my sins apropos of fever in Nicaragua—But isn't there
something a little romantic in quinine cocktails?

Apropos of learning, I'm much in the same boat, except that I
think I hate to study worse than you do and am probably lazier. Still I
have something internal which gnaws like hell when I'm not busy at
something—so I exhibit a battleground—between the worm of action
and the torpor of inertia—It's damned unpleasant. And when the
weather's fine I absolutely can do nothing but look at it, and when it
rains the same—The world's so darned interesting in every conceivable
aspect that it's frightfully hard to shut your doors & windows and sit in
the dark of your own intelligence & spin. The trouble is that I want
both to spin in the attic & to gape at the dance on the green and maybe
even dance too—but most of all to spin——

You have the misfortune of receiving a letter written before
lunch—and you know how introspective one is on an empty stomach—
so please forgive and think of the nice exotic Spanish things I shall eat
for almuerzo.

Why can't people proceed through the air?—You might come over
here on Sundays then & take walks with me through Castile

                                                    Adiós écrivez bientôt
                                                              Jack

[Diary]
Monday Nov 13 [1916]
   Where the week has gone the Lord only knows—
   Downes & Jackson have turned up & the excitement of finding

myself not all alone in the gloaming seems to have put the quietus on all forms of reading or writing. This sort of thing must stop.

Yesterday I had a most delectable day—took with Señor Rosada the morning train for Cercedilla—It's funny, but all Madrid seems to deck itself out in Alpine costume of a Sunday and betake itself to the Sierra. A morning of burning greenish blue sky—Well, walked to the "Twenty Club" where almuerzoed pleasantly—Well at twelve Señor R & his brother-in-law & little me in my beloved palegreen boots—started for the puerto (whose name, with incredible stupidity, I have forgotten) Well, when we got to the puerto we broke off to the left up the first peak of the mountain of the Siete Picos—a long range that waltzes all about you as the train takes its devious course from Madrid through the foothills. A long grind up through pine woods, lovely gnarled pines shaped like appletrees with the younger trunks of a pale brown, creamy color that contrasted wonderfully with the warming, purpling blue sky and the blackgreen needles in tight bunches. And the odor! A charming twittering little bird a bit like a sparrow kept hopping about us—When we got to the bald rockstrewn first summit a lovely view of the mountains and the bounding plain the warm yellow-reddish Plain of Castella la V. & the colder tinted Castella la N. We could see Madrid—Segovia, La Granja, Escurial & all this section of Spain as far as the Mountains of Toledo in the South, that hung in long stripes above a grey mist. Then on to the second peak where the end of the climb was up a rock-chimney and great fun. The north side was covered with snow frozen & blown into feather shapes by the wind as you scrambled up the snow on the tiers of feathers, above you was something—whiz! On the top we ate naranjas and nanzanas & chocolate and bananas and had a glorious time. Right up against the blue, with all the world shadowed and misty, streaked with rich sienna of bracken and black of pinares below us. As we were going, by the devil's own luck, we saw two boys climbing up the vertical south face. As it was very hot, one of them had taken off all his clothes except boots & stockings and little drawers—and what did he do when we got down from the chimney and were on the next peak, but silhouetted himself, a marvellous brown figure, against the sky? All of which gave a finishing touch to the beauty of the mountains. Then we skirted the north side of the other peaks—walking at times in rather deep snow and came down through a puerto into a southward sloping valley full of lovely pines noisy with streams—Beside a most nymphaic fountain

we ate more bread & chocolate and then trundled back to the train
through a beautiful, lucid—Peruginesque—evening——

Whee!

To Rumsey Marvin

[Madrid]
Dec 4 [*1916*]

Dear Rummy—Here are two letters from you within a week—most
joyful—You ask why I talked to you in California on the numerous
trains where—by the Devil's own luck—I ran into you—Lord, I don't
know exactly—except that your "all together" sort of pleased me & then
once started . . . Do you know, I sometimes think one can tell congenial people a mile off—rather like Masons with highsigns!—the
trouble with me usually is that they stay a mile off—You see in
California the luck was with me——

Is there anything on earth more wonderful than the 'silent on a
peak in Darien' feeling? You say in your first letter you felt it about
Walter L.'s book—I'm feeling it now about Spain—and afterwards
always comes the chilly mud-case sensation of complete ignorance—
which I am also feeling now about everything in general.

Hurrah for the touchdown! (I once caught a fly in a baseball
game—that's the beginning & end of my athletic record).

You ask me to talk architecture—I'll try to be learned about
Spanish cathedrals someday—at present my architecture consists of
drawing plaster casts in a man's studio for two hours daily, and a jolly
mess I make of it so far.

Oh—I must run to my lecture in Spanish phonetics—which is at
the other end of town—

A bientôt

Imagine me seated in a smallish room with pink shiny walls on
which I have plastered numerous photographs of my pet Velasquezes
& El Grecos—wrapped, as it is extremely cold & heating is unknown, in
a large woolen manta I have bought—The peasants wear them, the
women as shawls, the men as togas.

The wonderful thing about Spain, speaking of togas, is that it is a
sort of temple of anachronisms. I've never been any where where you
so felt the *strata* of civilization—Celt-Iberians, Phoenicians, Greeks,
Romans, Moors and French have each passed through Spain and left

something there—alive. Roman Italy is a sepulchre—Roman Spain is living—actuality—in the way a peasant wears his manta, in the queer wooden plows they use, in the way they sacrifice to the dead—not consciously of course, but with a thin veil of Catholicism. The pottery you see in the markets is absolutely Greek in shape. The music and the dances are strangely Semitic & Phoenician Moorish—Even the little cakes in the pastry shops are Moorish—oriental—the sort of things odalesques with henna stained fingers eat in the Arabian Nights. Its the most wonderful jumble—the peaceful Roman world; the sadness of the semitic nations, their mysticism; the grace—a little provincialized, a little barbarized, of a Greek colony; the sensuous dream of Moorish Spain; and little yellow French trains and American automobiles and German locomotives——all in a tangle together!

Oh but Rummy you mustn't stop talking about yourself—to me at anyrate—and what is English between friends? Then, too, my letters are as full of 'I's as yours are and the paper actually blushes at some of the grammar—If people got all the letters I composed to them, if all the plots I thought up in bed & then promptly forgot got turned into literature, if all the phrases that came bubbling up to the waterlevel of consciousness got written down. . . . well I don't know what would happen. Indeed I have often had the experience of composing letters to people or holding conversations with them (sort of subconsciously at first) while walking about—

Some day get hold of William James' 'Shorter Psychology' or his 'Varieties of Religious Experience' and I think you will have an awfully interesting time, as they are wonderfully fascinating books and not a bit dry. And they are the most interesting books on psychology I know. I suppose you haven't much time for them—but the time may some day be found—The question of getting time to do anything in is constantly acute with me—I always have a feeling of running after a bus and never catching it. It is so hard to get half the desired things done—and particularly if, as I do, you waste time wandering about—

I'm quite settled in Madrid now, and shall probably be here until quite long after Christmas—when I shall go South and wander about Andalusia and Granada—but I really have no plans;—indeed, I still have a vague hope the Belgian Relief may produce something yet. Here enclosed are a couple of strange poetic sketches I'd like your opinion on—They are part of a running series of things on Spain—As you see they are very wild and irregular—Please write me what you think as

I'm anxious to know—& do try & remember what it was you didn't like
in the article.

V

Green against a livid sky
In their square dun-tinted towers
Hang the bronze bells of Castile.
In their square light brown towers
Rising from the furrowed hills,
Clang the bells of all the churches
The dust-brown churches of Castile.

How they swing the green bronze bells
Athwart olive twilights of Castile
Till their fierce insistent clangour
Rings down the long plowed slopes
Breaks against the leaden hills,
Fades amid the trembling poplars
Beside the silent swift green river.

Oh you bronze bells of Castile
That commanding clang your creed
Over treeless fields and villages
That huddle in arroyos, gleaming
With orange of lights in the greenish dusk,
Can it be, Bells of Castile,
Can it be that you remember?

Lurks there in your bronze green curves
In your imperious evocation,
Stench of burnings; ringing screams,
Quenched amid the crackling flames!
The crowd, the pile of faggots in the square,
The yellow robes . . . Is it that,
Bells of Castile, that you remember?

IX

"Die shöne Tage in Aranjuez sind nun zu Ende"
                                   Schiller 'Don Carlos'
The Tagus flows with a noise of wiers through Aranjuez.
The speeding dark-green water mirrors the old red walls,
And the balustrades and close-barred windows of the palace,
And on the other bank, three stooping washer women,
Whose reddish shawls & piles of linen gleam in the green,
The swift dark green where shimmer the walls of Aranjuez.

There's smoke in the gardens of Aranjuez,
Smoke of the burning of the year's dead leaves;
The damp paths rustle underfoot,
Thick with the crisp broad leaves of the planes.

The tang of the smoke, and the scent of the box,
And the savour of the year's decay
Are soft in the gardens of Aranjuez,
Where the fountains fill silently with leaves
And the moss grows over the statues and busts,
Clothing the simpering cupids & fauns,
Whose stone eyes search the empty paths
For the rustling silk brocaded gowns,
And the neat silk calves of the halcyon past.

The Tagus flows with a noise of wiers through Aranjuez
And, slipping by, mirrors the brown silver trunks of the planes and the hedges
Of box, and the spires of cypress and alleys of yellowing elms,
And, on the other bank, three grey mules pulling a cart,
Piled with turnips, driven by a boy in a blue woolen sash,
Who strides along whistling, and does not look towards Aranjuez.

and another

IV

Difuntos (All Souls' Day)
Women are selling tuberoses in the square,
And sombre-tinted wreaths,
Stiffly twined and crinkly;
For this is the day of the dead.

Women are selling tuberoses in the square;
Their velvet odor fills the street,
Somehow stills the tramp of feet;
For this is the day of the dead

Their presence is heavy about us
Like the velvet scent of the flowers—
Incense of pompous interments,
Patter of monastic feet,
Drone of masses drowsily said
For the thronging dead . . .

Women are selling tuberoses in the square,
To cover the tombs of the envious dead
And shroud them again in the Lethean scent,
Lest they should remember . . .

Aranjuez is a sort of Spanish Versailles not far from Madrid with a lovely palace of red brick & grey granite and most wonderful gardens. (I mean the *outside* of the palace—The inside is as usual, a thing of horror).

Well I must stop this scrawly letter & get to work on a story—

Au Revoir or rather
à la prochaine lettre
Jack

[Madrid]
Dec 12th [*1916*]

At the same time Rummy dear as you were writing your plaint of the passage of time and the not getting of anything done ever, I was scrawling the same thing to you—Isn't it a joke? Indeed I can sympathize—For my life is a mad scramble after a bus that I never can catch, and juggling oranges the while! Some day we ought both of us to go and live in an abandoned monastery after having left fictitious addresses for all the world, and try to make up for lost time. Or else a voyage round the Horn on a sailing ship with a box of books & a ream of paper, might help—When I sailed for Spain I certainly thought that, away from distractions and boredoms, I could get a pile of work done and also amuse myself immensely—and yet—here I am moaning the old moan—stealing time from this to do that, and finding that I absolutely can't loaf about as much as I'd like to—I mean, wander about the streets and sit outside cafés and watch the people and let Spain soak in.

Then there is something frightfully paralysing to me in the war— Everything I do, everything I write seems so cheap and futile—If Europe is to senselessly destroy itself—Its as if a crevasse had opened and all the fair things, all the mellow things, all the things that were to teach us in America how to live, were slipping in—a sort of tidal wave and blood and fire—I can't grasp the idea of conflict any more—it seems more some thing immense and malignant and living that is grinding the helpless nations—Oh those boys in Bordeaux—limping in and out of the hospitals— . . . It is the sort of feeling it gave me when

I was awfully small and read somewhere of human sacrifices—The senseless grin of the brass idol—the stench and sizzle of the bodies in the flames—the cold, the blackness, the nauseous hideousness of it. I remember how I closed the history book feeling cold and sick all over—Would to God I could close this one. I sort of lose my nerve when I think of it. . . .

Rummy—I stopped your letter to write a poem & it's now one o'clock so as we say in Spain hasta mañana——P.S. The poem is damnably bad.

Its very cold in my room and I am anxiously awaiting the arrival of my coffee & roll—Enter said coffee & roll—Promptly to be engulfed—

The story of the pirate fight of the Italian Gardener ought to be fine—particularly as you'll be able to ring in a lot of local color Capri blues etc. Don't swab it on too thick though. In fact at this moment, when I ought to be doing other things I am reading a book about Arab pirates in the Mediterranean. Fancy your reading Le Cid—it's such a silly play—though of course beautiful velvety verse—the French classic tragedy does so amuse me—I don't think such boresome ranting was ever put into such perfect language—Still a little goes a long way— Poor Don Rodrigue—Imagine Mio Cid Campeodor, the champion of the Faith, the cruel sinister warrior—turned into a china shepherd!

Oh such a funny thing happened the other night. I was on my doorstep clapping for the sereno—a most medieval watchman with lantern and pike who keeps the keys to the outer doors of the houses— and when the door is closed you stand outside and clap lustily till he comes—when a rather passé painted lady in a shawl came up and said 'oiga, estoy muy simpatica' "Look, I'm awfully congenial!"—in the most coaxing tone. Poor woman. To get to the point where she had to be congenial! Fortunately the sereno came at that moment and let me in—but afterwards I couldn't help thinking how often I, like the Madrid dama, had wanted to go up to people and say "oiga, estoy muy simpatica"—

For the Lord's Sake, Rummy, don't complain of the frequency of ideas—You see the thing is that it takes a pound of internal idea to produce an ounce of really proper stuff, or at least I find it so—probably according to the law of degeneration of energy or something more complex still. But don't let school stand too much in the way of your education—though it's most meritorious to achieve marks etc, your real education is what you plug out for yourself—'tween times, don't you think so? And the atmosphere of the American school is numbing to the intelligence—at least so it seemed to me—I think one reason is that everything is so pleasant and well managed and healthy and godly that no one has a moment's time in which to think out a darn thing for himself. Everything is so predigested that the mental gastric juices disappear through pure inaction.

Sunday I went up to the mountains—the Sierra Guadarrama— with some Spanish friends and watched the winter sports! Skiing and the like. Moreover we went for a long walk and in one of the passes got into snow up to our thighs—it was wonderful, though bitterly cold with driving snow that nearly put your eyes out—Spain is indeed different than I had expected and Oh Rummy! so fascinating—Castile, all I know anything about (and that just a radius of thirty miles about Madrid)—is a dry dun-brown land of rolling hills—deep arroyos like in California and dry lead-grey mesas. Now the long slopes are powdered with delightful green of the sprouting wheat, and in the distance to the north, sometimes faint as clouds, sometimes sparkling like lumps of nibbled sugar is the Sierra Guadarrama—In the mountains it's very cold and even here in Madrid it goes down to freezing very often—is always chilly—And I had expected to lie in orange-gardens!

Have I told you about Toledo? Oh but that'll have to take a letter to itself. Suffice it that the entrance is over one of the most beautifully proportioned fortified bridges, old as the Moors and the rest of the city is the most wonderful conglomeration of gothic walls, Moorish palaces, Christian churches—all built of stone & brick in different shades of warm brown——

but I mustn't get started

Adiós
Jack

Madrid
[*December 25, 1916*]

Rummy! It's after three Christmas morning, Noche buena—they call it here, and I have been having a most wonderful time—You see, the entire population turns out into the streets with drums and horns and tambourines and sings and dances and shouts—Its a perfect Saturnalia—Men women and boys run about the streets in a sort of Dionysian drunkenness, a little from the noise and rhythm and songs, a little from wine, and everybody is wonderfully happy and boisterous and not a bit disgusting—Well, I've spent the night marching about with a great big tambourine—the which I have beaten and shaken and banged against my knees and elbows until I'm stiff. The people have a wonderful sense of rhythm and some of the drum beats you hear are wonderful—Then the songs they sing would send you wild with delight, they have so much music and strangeness in them—

Nóche bú-éna

Nóche d'Alegrí-á

Is one of the most common—I wish I could render the tune——

But you can't imagine how wonderful it is to skip down the street beating a drum when everyone else is beating and singing and dancing——it has the emotional pull that I imagine Indian wardances have——

But more tomorrow——I must go to bed although a tremendous racket is still going on below my window.

A most wonderful warm day—quite different from most of Madrid's winter weather—Oh before I forget it, I must tell you about the Huélga—the strike—That was last week: the government was, for some reason inordinately frightened because the labor party declared a general strike—fairly well carried out too—all over Spain. Well—we awoke in the morning to find the streets of Madrid all heavily sanded—That's a gentle hint the government makes to the populace when trouble is expected—you see the sand is so the horses won't slip when the cavalry charges—

Nothing really happened, but there was a wonderfully tense ante-revolutionary atmosphere—Cannon were placed outside of the barracks, patrols of cavalry clattered about through the town—and the big square—the Puerta del Sol—where revolutions always happen—was very crowded with all sorts of people and dozens of horse guards—who charged the crowd now and then, to keep their hand in as it were, thwacking people on the back with the flat of their swords. The clatter of hoofs and crunch of gravel and growl of the crowd—was tremendously exciting; but nothing came of it—probably on account of the rain which poured now and then in buckets—and a wet revolutionist isn't worth a hill o' beans.

Then—the walk to Torrejon: After the theatre one night a friend—a fellow from Harvard I ran across here and myself were taking a bite in a café when we decided we wanted to go to Toledo, so we each took a handful of malted milk tablets (God save the mark) and at 3AM set out from the Puerta de Toledo, crossed the bridge over the Manzanares and were off along the old road to Toledo.

Do you know the wonderful feel of old old roads which have been worn to a sort of velvet softness by the feet of generations and generations and generations? And at night they all seem to get up and follow you in a crowd—the Romans and the Carthaginians and the Moors and the mitred bishops going towards Toledo, and the mule drivers with skins of wine from the south. They sort of follow you and troop about you as you walk and keep time with your step—

Oh but it was a wonderful night—a cold metallic moon, and stars—and we passed every now and then, long strings of mule-teams, with little tinkly bells and the drivers, wrapped like Romans in their mantas striding along behind—We went through lots of little sleeping villages, whose church towers stood out against the stars and at last a dawn broke—found ourselves in the brink of a wide shallow valley—so filled with mist it looked like a lake—with the mountains of Toledo ahead in the distance—You can't imagine the wonderfulness of a little village we passed just at dawn—with a big buttressed church and a tall leaning church tower and everything pearl-blue and purple and lemon yellow——

Well at Torrejon, a couple of hours later, I remembered I had an engagement in Madrid that night—& my friends' feet began to expire—so we took the train home for Madrid after having done about half the distance—about twenty four miles of it. You can imagine I slept well that day in Madrid.

But I must get to work—

Write when you get a chance——

Jack

I am going to Valencia & Murcia for a few weeks, so my next letter'll be from the shores of the Mediterranean

Hasta luego

To Rumsey Marvin

Játiba [Spain]
Jan 8th [*1917*]

Well—I saw Gandia & this morning pulled out *on top* of the train for Cartagena—a delightful journey through orange groves so thick that the little train brushed against them as it chugged through and knocked off great fat golden oranges that fell with a plunk onto the red exuberant earth—then up into the dry hills and down into more orange groves—then a couple of hours wandering about Cartagena that smelt of ripe olives and had rich-cream-brown colored houses and several old places that rather reminded one of Italy—built like this [refers to a sketch] with a loggia along the top story—the loveliest way of building a house ever invented—Unfortunately, as you find in Italy, later brutes had come and walled up the graceful arches. Then to Játiba which I have only seen by the very scanty lamplight its municipality affords—

But I am in the most wonderful Fonda! In a regular Don Quixote-Gil Blas Fonda—It is in a great palace-place with an entrance that must be twenty-five feet square & great oak gates—Then an immense arch lets you in from the hall to the patio & a tiny tiled staircase climbs to the upper rooms. My room is quite vast & has a bed—two chairs a table & a little combination wash thing—& looks out on the patio where a fountain splatters gaily and will lull me to sleep & to dream of the Alhambra & Moorish princesses & Provence roses or perhaps only of the bathroom at home when somebody left on the tap and it over flowed, ie the tub,—or of the wonderful time in London—when I was 'young & charming' (like Buttercup) when a schoolboy friend & I played the taking of Port Arthur with my battleships in the bathtub above a luncheon Mother was giving, & in our terrific excitement didn't notice that the floor was awash—The guests below in the dining room did; & part of the ceiling fell—c'était un jour pénible.

In a week or so—after Valencia, The City of Joys, as the Moors called it—and Sagrunto where there are a lot of Roman ruins—I shall to Madrid once again & try to really do some hard work, to get rid of a little of the "lofts to let" sensation which has been troubling me of late—There I shall get a ton of letters—I hope—several weeks accumulation.

I'll tell you later about Játiba which promises to be fascinating—
Hasta mañana ó pormañana
Jack

Residencia de Estudiantes
Madrid
Jan 31st 1917

Dear Rummy—

In times of crisis there are just two things to do—sit on the stairs and weep, or send cablegrams. I have been doing the latter and feel—I suppose—comforted—

It gives you a queer catching of the breath to find yourself suddenly alone in the world—You see, my father died yesterday [in fact he died January 27] in New York.

It is silly to make a fuss about anything as obvious and humdrum as death,—except perhaps to be glad when people you love die suddenly, without the long sordidness of disease.

Only—one feels as if all one's protection against the knocks and pains of life had been pulled away—for one hasn't much except the love of others to retire into—It's like a man who has been walking hours and hours through a blizzard trying to reach a tiny light that promises warmth and food and rest from the straining exertion—and suddenly the light has gone.

My plans are at present—to say the least vague—I think I shall stay here a few months longer—Though I suppose the conventional thing to do'ld be to go home—I don't know exactly why—I have no one to console. Still I dread too much the condolences of people and all the sentimental flutter that clutters up the great stark events of life—to go back yet, although I may have to.

Then too I am so fascinated by Spain. I am just beginning to fathom a little, to understand a little . . .

But I don't know—There's a certain exhilaration about being absolutely untrammelled and having no idea what one is going to do next

Don't condole.

Thanks for the book—which appeared.

Do let me hear from you

I'll write again in a day or two and announce my where abouts.

Love
Jack

On board the S.S. *Touraine*
Feb 20th [*1917*]

Hello Rummy!

We have just started out of the Gironde—after having waited two days on the river between Bordeaux and the mouth.

Great excitement—You see, the Touraine is the first ship to sail since the closing down of the blockade—

Last night we lay with all lights out—and tonight passengers are not to be allowed to go to bed—and must sit with clothes and life-preservers on all ready to take to the boats—But we are to be convoyed—and it is blowing a little gale to boot—so I doubt if we have any trouble—still it is most interesting—The mouth of the Gironde is full of shipping—steamers, sailing vessels, waiting, I suppose, to get up their courage to go out—

The Touraine is an old slow and rather uncomfortable steamer—and I imagine will roll like a log—Strange to say, she is full up—first class, second class and steerage——2. PM.

21st

I *did* go to bed—and slept undisturbed by mines or submarines—And today I believe we are out of danger—

You can't imagine how amusing it was to see all the passengers roaming about with life-belts on—in the dark

About college—Don't go to Williams I beg—it is the home and original abiding place of the Y.M.C.A. young man—I'm rather cynical about American colleges anyway—Yale and Harvard are about even in my estimation—both having many faults and I suppose, virtues. Chicago is supposed to be good and Columbia They have the merit of having no "college life", and I imagine U of California and that other Californian college,—I cant think of its name at the moment—are good.

Of course I am personally tremendously fond of Harvard and Cambridge—and the Harvard kind of snobbery does not irritate me so much as the Yale kind—I mean the sort of thing those sacred 'frats' breed—

But the intellectual life in any of them is slim enough;—and they are all pleasant in their way and—if one doesn't take them too seriously—one can chug very happily through four years and emerge without having ones intellect utterly mossed over.

But, as I say, I am cynical about American colleges.

Do you know, Rummy, we must try and get together for a week or so somewhere sometime very soon—There are so many things to talk about and to do together. I want to read you all my favorite poems, make you read my favorite books, expound my favorite ideas—my favorite foods—and Heaven knows what besides. And all that'll take time you know.

I have not an idea in the world what my plans are, and shall not know until I have been some time in New York—

We are having a very mild and smooth passage for this time of the year—that is—so far—Off the Banks we shall probably strike dirty weather—as this is the worst part of the year on our coast.

Friday—Dear Rummy! Fire Island Light is now astern of us and, after a trip of 13 days we are pretty nearly in. I suppose we will dock tonight. Everything must be in wild excitement about War—The latest rumor that I've received is that a secret treaty has been made between Mexico and Germany deeding Mexico "the three southern provinces of the United States", whatever that means. But it's too absurd even for Germany Diplomacy; so it probably springs from the fecund brain of a New York reporter.

Drop me a line to 18 East 56th Street. It'll get to me even if I have gone to Washington, which I shall have to do before very long.

Oh, Rummy, I dread the arrival in New York and the sympatheticness of certain relatives I shall have to see. I wish people wouldn't make such a fuss about the most ordinary things like death and birth and marriage. There is enough incidental pain connected with them anyway, without cumbering them with conventions and childish trivialities—

If people would only look at life straight and sincerely without having to dim their sight—faulty enough, God knows——with colored glass of different sorts—with church windows and shop windows and the old grimy glass of outworn customs.

But I suppose ones own individuality is so much of a distortion of clear reality (and one can't see except with ones own eyes, can one?) that other little distortions don't matter much. And the glittering wonderfulness of it all bursts through somehow.

I've been reading Flaubert's "Tentation De Saint Antoine" coming over—it is a marvellous nightmare of religion and philosophy, a book positively seething with life and beauty and bitterness. As vivid as Salammbô and much deeper.

I'm having the bank in Madrid hold my letters—Eventually I suppose I shall collect quite a little budget of yours from there. Perhaps I'll go back.

But I really haven't a plan in the world——

Love—
Jack

214 Riverside Drive
New York NY
March 10 [*1917*]

Dear Rummy,

Apollonius of Tyana used to pray on entering a city that the wise might remain poor. There is something to be said for the idea. In fact I agree with him so much that it is with a certain joy and much amusement that I am watching the rapid evaporation of The Estate.

It's rather grisly, isnt it, how soon a living man becomes nothing more than a collection of stocks and bonds and debts and real estate?

Eventually I shall scrape up enough of the debris to keep the wolf from the door etc etc—The annoying thing is that I cant do anything until the estate is settled and I am wasting a lot of time when I might be writing. At present I am living up here at my aunt's—but before long I shall find a room somewhere where I can stack my books and retire into monastic seclusion in order to try and finish that famous novel-thing. How long I shall be able to stand New York I don't know, but I want to finish the stuff I'm at present writing before doing anything else. And it is much more convenient to be here for peddling stuff around to publishers and sech—

By the way—I think that my Times Irishman has met your Times Irishman—Mine's name is Wright McCormick.

But Rummy, whether you are in New Rochelle or in New York we must see each other when you get down for your vacation—Drop me a note here at 214 (Telephone 7979 Riverside) and we can go to the theatre and ride up and down in a bus—or perhaps I shall have my diggings and shall be able to offer you a hospitable ceiling up fourteen flights of stairs in an odorous neighborhood.

I can at least take you to the Italian restaurant we tried to find on our last expedition—which I have located only recently.

It's tough luck about your exams. Still

> A little flunking now and then
> Is healthy in the best of men—

etc

And one ought to flunk once in a while to see what it feels like to be the under dog. Still you probably wont do it again.

From your sample of the dialectics of a church school I shall expect to hear that you've been arguing the famous case of how many angels can dance on the point of a needle—You see; if angels are

infinite, an infinite number can dance on the point of a needle,—etc etc
involving the whole of the cosmos and the celestial Hierarchy,—
Thrones, Domination, Powers, etc etc.

But let me know your plans at once—I mean as soon as they
exist—because I may have to go up to Washington on business and I
want to arrange so that I can have a day with you—or something of
the sort—

So long

Jack

[New York]

April 10 [*1917*]

Dear Rummy——

Forgive me for not writing sooner but I've been very busy boring
myself to death with barren business details. I hate money more than
ever—I feel like taking a cockle & script, giving my goods to the poor &
my body to be burned, and making a pilgrimage to Jerusalem—And
more than ever do I believe that to achieve freedom from utter asininity you have to do something very like it. Oh the triviality that people
fritter their lives away in—when the great untrivial—the essential
glamour encompasses them about. And all the forces of life seem to be
occupied in swaddling one up in inessential absurdities, so that a constant stripping process is needed before one can live naked and clean—
in the full blast of experience. Maybe I'm preaching bosh—a not unfre-
quent happening in my correspondence.

Alas I am not yet settled in the Labyrinth—the official name of 15
East 33rd Street, top floor—but, next week the happy event, the install-
ing of the Minotaur—will take place. You must visit me there at the
first opportunity. No excuses—family orders, space, time, war, or high
cost of living,—will be accepted.

Why Rummy, about book reviewing: they are usually done to
order, but there is always a chance—with the N.R. particularly, that a
good one will be accepted.

I approve of your manual labor scheme. How does one do it? I
have for years been wanting to do something of the sort, but have
never got to anything more strenuous than gardening.

But remember that a week or two of your summer—come what
will—must be spent walking & talking with me. Are you game? How

we'll manage it Heaven and the Celestial Host only know, but manage it we must if we are ever to know each other except via paper & ink.

On my side the only drawback will be that I may be doing something military. I am trying to do three things at once—enlist in the mosquito fleet, be an ambulance attendant, and get a job as an interpreter or something of the sort with the first expeditionary force. Out of those something *must* pan out. Don't think that I've gone militarist or believe in conscription—far from it. I merely want to see a little of the war personally—and, then too, I rather believe that the deeper we Americans go into it, the harder we put our shoulders to the muskets and our breasts to the bayonets, the sooner the butchery will stop.

I am not yet sure of getting anything at all, because my eyes are very much below par and my general physical condition a little unprepossessing to an army doctor.

Write me until I let you know—
At 214 Riverside Drive——
Until later

Jack

You must read lots of Maupassant. A certain sort of thing—like 'La Parure'—he does supremely.
Read 'Le Morceau de Ficelle' 'L' Heritage'—'Une Vie'
Have not found you a female co-respondent yet.

[New York]
April 28 [*1917*]

Dear Rummy—
I am still hesitating on the edge of—on one hand—the Ambulance, and on the other the Naval Reserve. The scale is sinking in favor of the Ambulance. But before I do anything I must settle down and get some real work done—I've been leading a terrifically uninteresting and unprofitable existence since I got back from Spain. Puttering about money matters, and arranging my apartment—weird place—the furniture for which has not yet arrived; so we sit on the floor on cushions & stretch out on Turkish rugs of which I fortunately possess some few. My Irishman—Wright McCormick—is taking one of the rooms of my floor, which has been officially named and christened the *Labyrinth*.

I sympathize with your school paper agonies. Mine—at Choate—nearly bored me into my grave.

I feel very much bound to the wheel of Karma at present: before long I shall up and shake myself and send my trivial annoyances scuttling to hell

Right at this moment I'm going out for a walk—a good long one—by Jehosophat I wish you were here to go with me. You could probably assist in the process of discobwebbing my brain——

Au Revoir——

Jack

Bored & Blue

To George St. John

214 Riverside Drive
NY
May 5th [*1917*]

My dear Mr. St. John,

I hope you will forgive my long delay in answering your very kind letter—as I have been very busy doing all sorts of uninteresting things. But don't think that I haven't thought of you and of Choate.

And we too have entered the dance of death. It was inevitable—I suppose it would have been better had we done so earlier—but I can't quite reconcile myself to the thought yet. The whole condition is so hopeless. It seems as if all our energy—all this complicated civilization the European races have labored and murdered and cheated for during so many evolving centuries were frittering itself away in this senseless agony of destruction. Germany seems to me rather a symptom than the cause.

Oh but it is wonderful to live amid the downfall—and perhaps it is the birth-pangs too—

I really dont know why I should take up your most valuable time by disburdening myself of my half-baked ideas—please excuse them.

In three or four weeks I expect to sail for France—either as an Ambulance Driver with the Norton-Harjes people, or in some other capacity with the Red Cross.

I have been for a long while very anxious to see things at first hand—but circumstances have in every case interfered This time, however, along with the rest of America—I think I shall get my taste of the war.

Please remember me to Mrs St. John and tell her that my Greek
has, alas, improved very little since the days when she used to coach me
in it in the parlor of the then "Horne House"—also to the other
masters that date back to those prehistoric days—

Very sincerely yours
Jack Dos Passos

To Rumsey Marvin

June 5th [1917]
15 E. 33rd Street

Dear Rummy—

You poor child—I thought that something of the sort had been
up . . . I wonder if you hate to be sick as much as I do—that is, if they
won't let you read.

Speaking of sickness, our correspondence is awfully ill and in need
of a tonic. It'll pull through all right, but I fear it's temperature is low
and that it is suffering from anemia and debility. But I miss it—an' I
hope you do. Of course I've been as much to blame as you. I've been
very busy, and a strange lethargic state has brooded over me—so that I
haven't wanted to do anything. I have been darn depressed about the
war and myself and everything.

Moreover I've been trying to pound out an article on Spain for the
Seven Arts—I think they are going to publish it during the summer.

The loss of the chance to have a hike and a ramble with you—you
damn lazy correspondent—has annoyed me amazingly.

When does your school close?

I sail the sixteenth for France as a driver with the Norton-Harjes
Ambulance—I'll send you my Paris address later—

For God's sake write & cheer me up—and I'll try to answer with a
little pep.

My only amusement has been going to anarchist and pacifists
meetings and riots—Emma Goldman etc. Lots of fun I assure you. I
am thinking of becoming a revolutionist!

For the love of Mike

Write on the first mail

Jack

[New York
June 1917]

Honest I was delighted to get your letter—Rummy one——Is this your last year at St. Pauls? As I remember, ones last year at school is a strangely important performance while it is going on—which suddenly waxes big and bursts in the strange and chilly newness of being almost in college.

Shall it be Harvard or Yale? It really doesn't matter—if you dont take either of them seriously. If it weren't for the existence of President Lowell and other annoyances, I would urge my beloved Harvard more strenuously, and I wouldn't mind Yale a bit if it weren't for Tap Day.

But, mon ami, apropos of free verse—it's *meant* to have rhythm— its not the same rhythm as so-called metrical verse; but it's a perfectly definite and sometimes quite *regular* cadence. I'd like to read some of my stuff and other people's aloud to you to show you what I mean. Of course I very often don't succeed in getting any effect at all—but that's ofter the case with the regularest of verse!

Your suggestion of the swim is splendid. I've found another preventative of blues, however. An artist friend of mine here has found way down in the lower East Side a strange little restaurant—where are Arabs and Spanish Jews and a weird Arab orchestra and women in ordinary street-walkers' clothes who dance the most amazing half-Spanish, half-Egyptian dances, while Spanish Jews, Lascars and Turks sit about smoking hookahs and drinking bad beer—It's really too good to be true and reminds one more than anything of bits of the Port Said part of "The Light that Failed." The East Side is a wonderfully fascinating place anyway. After much wandering I've decided that the only nice and human parts of New York are the East Side and Greenwich Village.

But, darn it man, glory or no I refuse to be killed until I've hiked somewhere with you—I warn you that my ghost'ld haunt you and refuse to be exorcized except by being walked for days through soothing scenery.

From the mouth of the Ambulance, and from the jaws of Hell (ie War-vide Mr Sherman) I cry to you one word apropos of God and man and all things on the teeming earth. Don't believe the New York Times. You see I live with a man who's on it and knows its inner workings. Believe rather the Call or Masses or the New Republic or the

Ladies Home Journal—I vow before Jehovah that half the ills of the country are caused by the fact that all educated and intelligent Americans believe the New York Times as if it were Direct Revelation—or Tablets found on a Mountain by a reputable Brigham Young.

I'm sure that by the time I get back from the war you'll disown me entirely, I'll be so red, radical and revolutionary.

I've decided that the thigh or the ear are the two nicest places to get wounded. You should see the delightful equipment I have to get— wonderful big boots and duffle-bag and bed roll and hurricane lantern and pins and needles and a cake of soap and other wonders besides.

Did I tell you about sitting next to Emma Goldman's table in the café at the Brevort some time ago. It was wonderful—the people I was with knew lots of her myrmidons and we were the outer circle of her glory—She's a Bronxy fattish little old woman who looks like a rather good cook. She has a charmingly munchy fashion of eating sandwiches and pats her myrmidons on the head and kisses them in a motherly fashion.

I'm not leaving till Wednesday so Write—

Jack

On board the S.S. *Chicago*
June 20, 1917

Dear Rummy—

I'm awfully cut up about leaving without a glimpse of you—you old bigoted militarist—

You must write often—as I shall need cheering up I expect.

You see I dont believe in the "spiritual good" of war and I expect to have one hell of a time until I get accustomed to taking ambulance loads of pulverized people about—

I'll write as often as I can—

Do tell me what's going on with you—Why don't you learn to drive a car and come on over? You're not too young if you could get your parents to consent and you are certainly as efficient as I am—— aren't you?

Hurrah—the whistle's blowing and the old tub is starting to move—Your letters'll be food and drink and ice cream sodas—to my dusty imagination.

My address is

c/o The American Red Cross Ambulance
7 Rue François Premier
Paris—
Gee the river's glorious, pink and grey and pale orange with
lights—

Love
Jack

ONE MAN'S INITIATION

June 1917–August 1918

Aug 27 [1917]
By candle light in
a dug out —
Outside it is raining
& German shells falling
Sound like infinities of
heavy chains dropped
all at once

The trip across the Atlantic on the *Chicago* added to Dos' anticipation. He thought the ship's company a "three ring circus," felt a touch nervous because of the threat of submarine attack, and scorned what he considered the virulent militarism of Teddy Roosevelt's sons Theodore, Jr., and Archie, whom he overheard discussing the United States' growing military might. Not only was the voyage exciting because he was seeing another side of life, but he met John Howard Lawson, a gregarious, lively man who like him was in the ambulance group. The two became friends immediately; politically they thought alike, and Lawson was also a writer, but of plays. He, in fact, had a considerable influence on Dos Passos; without doubt the latter's own experimental dramas and adaptions of expressionistic technique owed much to Lawson. Further, Dos' involvement with the New Playwrights Theatre in 1927–1929 was directly due to him.

Having arrived in Bordeaux to the cheers of friendly people, the ambulance drivers took a slow train to Paris through the magnificent countryside of summertime France. Before being sent to a training base, they had several days to poke around Paris. The day after arriving Dos ran into his college friends Robert Hillyer and Frederick van den Arend, who were with Norton-Harjes, and Dudley Poore, who was with the American Field Service. The camaraderie and the beauty of the city seemed highly incongruous with the gruesome fighting and an oppressive wartime government of which Dos was increasingly aware.

The next stop was Sandricourt training camp, 25 miles to the northeast of Paris. After several weeks of drilling Dos received orders to Châlons-sur-Marne, so returned to Paris to form up with Section Sanitaire 60 of the ambulance corps. To his delight he found himself again in the company of Hillyer and van den Arend. As the Verdun offensive was about to begin, his group was sent in convoy into that sector, and by August 2 it had reached Erize-la-Petite, a small village on the Voie Sacrée above Bar-le-Duc.

Action was not long in coming. On August 16 his section went to the front; by August 21 the allies had claimed the offensive successful. In those five days Dos had seen, heard, and smelled the horrors of real warfare; his initiation had begun, and it is perhaps not too extravagant to claim that these days of actual combat had more effect on him than would any other single experience. Certainly it was one of the two or three pivotal moments in his eventful life. The war destroyed what vestiges of romantic aestheticism remained from his Harvard days; it heightened his belief in the importance of individual liberties and his respect for the common man, and it deepened his hatred of the cant, even the inhumanity, of officialdom.

Three weeks after it had begun, the big offensive was over, and the drivers were moved back from the front lines. Soon the Medical Corps of the A.E.F. took charge of Section 60, and Dos, still serving as a driver, had to mull over what he might do next.

While he and van den Arend enjoyed a placid time in a small village named Remicourt in the Argonne, Robert Hillyer departed for home, leaving with Dos the manuscript of a novel—they referred to it as the Great Novel—which they had been jointly writing when off duty. Dos would continue to work on it later; in fact the climactic fourth part became *One Man's Inititation—1917,* about the lies and cant of governments at war. The earlier sections became a novel entitled *Seven Times Round the Walls of Jericho.* Part one is about the childhood and adolescence of Martin Howe, "Fibbie" as he is called in the manuscript. The second part is about his Harvard days, and part three, about his days in New York City prior to leaving for the war. Dos' first attempt to put into fiction the themes, emotions, and ideas emerging from his experiences in 1917–1918 was in *Seven Times.* Both *One Man's Inititation—1917* and *Three Soldiers* are in many ways but extensions of it, and it even contains hints of his first drama, *The Garbage Man,* and also of the city themes of *Manhattan Transfer.*

Dos first tried to publish *Seven Times* in 1920. He sent the novel to George Allen and Unwin in London, who were at that time publishing *One Man's Initiation—1917.* They declined it, because their reader said, "He is only in the making yet but he has real powers of emotion and expression, though, as a novel, this is inconclusive, aimless, almost chaotic." The reader praised it in many ways, but uncertainty about the pertinence of the American material for an English audience and the risk of losing money on an unknown author made Allen and Unwin reluctant to publish. Later the manuscript made the rounds in the United States but nothing ever came of it.

Eventually the Norton-Harjes drivers ended their temporary duty with the Medical Corps. Dos and van den Arend returned to Paris where, before leaving for Italy with the American Red Cross in mid-November, they were joined by Dudley Poore and again reveled in that city's life. Morgan-Harjes, a bank then at 31 Boulevard Haussmann and later on the Place Vendôme, was Dos' mailing address. A new friend, Tom Cope, joined the group and together they wandered about Paris, feeling the strange contradictions of contentment, dislike for the war, and yet a fascination for its exciting moments.

When the time arrived to depart for Italy, Dudley Poore stayed behind, though he would rejoin the others at Bassano later. But Jack Lawson was among the drivers of Section 1 of the Red Cross, so it was a friendly band who began the pleasant, slow convoy down through France into Italy. They arrived in Milan December 6. The rest of the convoy left December 13 toward Dolo, a small town near Padua, but because of a sick Fiat ambulance Dos and his fellow driver, Sidney Fairbanks, had to remain behind until after December 20. The section believed it was going to the Piave, but as 1917 ended, it was halted in Dolo.

It was not until January 16, 1918, that Dos and Fairbanks could coax their Fiat 4 to Bassano. This town in northern Italy became their base, although they made constant ambulance runs, day and night, to other towns and villages in the region. Amid the duties of ambulance service the friends had time for amusements. When in February Dudley Poore read a news clipping about the death of Empress Tai-Tou of Abyssinia, they held a wake for her. The group made an effigy with large white eyes and laid it out in Lawson's bed. Then they cooked a great feast on their stove "Fafner," or "Hope Deferred Maketh the Heart Grow Fonder." That during the ceremonies the Germans were bombing Bassano did not daunt them; the air raid added to the occasion. In *A Pushcart at the Curb* Dos parodied a high literary style when he described the mock dirge:

And when the news of the Death of the Empress of that Far Country did come to them, they fashioned of her an Image in doleful wise and poured out Rum and Marsala Sack and divers Liquors such as were procurable in that place into Cannikins to do her Honor and did wake and keen and make moan most piteously to hear. And that Night were there many Marvels and Prodigies observed; the Welkin was near consumed with fire and Spirits and Banshees grumbled and wailed above the roof and many that were in that place hid themselves in Dens and Burrows in the ground.

But this sort of behavior irritated the Red Cross authorities. Also, Dos made no secret of his distaste for the war and, to an extent, for the Italians. At about this time he wrote a Spanish friend, José Giner Pantoja, discussing the war and introducing Arthur McComb, who had arrived in Madrid. The letter, however, was intercepted by a Red Cross officer named Bates, and on the basis of it and Dos' general comportment, Bates recommended that he be dishonorably discharged. While Dos was on leave during the last two weeks of March, the issue grew, so that when he returned he knew he was under suspicion, but nothing more developed, and it would only be when he got to Rome in June after his enlistment expired that he would face the charge of being pro-German. In some manner—he doesn't remember how—Jack Lawson got a copy of Dos' letter with Bates' comments on it.

The March leave—a glorious trip down through Italy—was a high point of that or any other time. Dos, van den Arend, Poore, and Lawson headed off from Bassano. After stopping at Bologna, they saw Rome, then Naples, and afterward began a walk to Pompeii, Lawson—according to Dos—remaining behind to be with the ladies of Naples a bit longer. They finally took a small train that ran around the base of Vesuvius to go the last part of the way to Pompeii; getting there late, they had a magnificent setting all to themselves. So engrossed were they that they got locked in when the gates to the ruins were closed, and after dark they had to climb out, but this simply added to the romantic adventure. Dudley Poore, who enjoyed the trip as much as did Dos, recalled that after they extricated themselves from the ruins, they found a *trattoria,* "Albergo del Sole," where they had supper outdoors in a small arbor. Poore remembered van den Arend and Dos, as they drank a rich, red wine, having an intense discussion about enlisting in the army. Both felt ardently against it.

From Pompeii the three walked to Castellammare, took the Sorrento trolley to Meta, then hiked across the ridge of the Sorrentine peninsula and onward, by what is now called the Amalfi Drive, to Positano, where they spent the night. The next morning they headed off, passing along the edge of the sea to Amalfi and Ravello, and eventually stopping at Cetara, a small village in a cove where they found a house in which an aged couple lived. The woman cooked them at least twenty-four eggs, as Poore remembered it, and served them bread and wine. The couple took so to Dos that he and they enchanged cards for years. Then the three Americans went on to Vietri, getting there exhausted around midnight. But they found a café full of *les jeunesses,* began to drink coffee, and only later took a room. Overtired, full of coffee and the excitement of the trip, they could not sleep, and to add to their discomfort, there were hard straw mattresses and an ample supply of chickens sharing the quarters.

At dawn the next morning they took a train to Paestum, passing through Salerno on the way. The ruins at Paestum were deserted, so once more they had a magnificent setting all to themselves. After swimming in the bright, clear Mediterranean, they spent the day tramping through the ruins, made the more picturesque by rich grass and weeds full of fragrant violets. Toward the end of the day they came on a house, whose occupant, an old woman, they found sitting dignified and sybil-like in the front door. She gave them spicy, hard cheese, wine and bread, and asked if they knew her son, who lived in Brooklyn. Just as they were leaving, up drove Lawson, who had taken a horse cab all the way from Salerno. After more exploring of the ruins, they headed back to Salerno, and, as Poore recalled, took the train for Rome the same night, arriving on Palm Sunday. The next week they spent in Florence and then returned to Bassano, all agreeing that Paestum was the most glorious moment of a glorious, carefree leave.

For Dos as well as the others the importance of this period was not only being able to travel about France or Italy. They talked and argued, developing their ideas about politics—as Dos' diaries show— and about art. Early in April Dudley Poore recorded in his diary a discussion between Tom Wharton, another of the drivers, and Dos:

At table. Dos, Wharton, & I. Must one know how to draw in order to paint well?

The use of color one step beyond drawing.

A different affair altogether rather than a higher. . . . Whistler couldn't draw. His people are always out of drawing. After you've looked at them for a while you begin to wonder which arm it is coming out from under the drapery.

But I don't see that it matters, if the picture means something

But when you see an arm coming out of the small of a back it disturbs you

Only if the picture means nothing anyway. There's nothing makes me so crazy as the people who come to you when you're looking at something by Verocchio and tell you that the arm is four times as long as it ought to be. Why, just the other day in Florence

Well, its rather different with the primitives

But Verocchio isn't primitive. And there is El Greco. They come and say to you: His people are green! And once in a painting of his somebody discovered a hand with six fingers. . . . What difference does it make if a foot has three toes or five?

But with El Greco it's different, too. It's intentional, or it's part of his effect. But when a man is trying to draw correctly and fails. . . .

Then he's impossible. If he were trying to draw an arm as if for an anatomist, with every muscle arranged so that you could name it, and if he failed in doing that, then he would be not worth bothering about. As he would be if he succeeded But I can image a man intending to draw a figure quite correctly and in the excitement of genius getting the head turned round hind *side* before. But then the intelligent person looking at the picture would be so excited by what the painter had to say that he'd not notice whether the head were on straight or crooked.

April and May passed without incident, and on June 1, having been released from their units, Dos, van den Arend, Poore, and Lawson left Bassano, taking their time traveling down to Rome, where they hoped to secure new enlistments in the Red Cross. But once there Dos found himself again facing the Red Cross officer, Guy Lowell, the Boston architect whom he had disliked from the days at Dolo. While the other three had no problems with charges of disloyalty, Dos did, so on Lowell's advice he headed to Paris by himself to try to rectify matters with higher authorities.

Though the living was pleasant in Paris, his affair could not be cleared up. The authorities ultimately gave him the choice of returning to America or being deported; so, after nearly two months in France, and having asked his Aunt Mamie, Mrs. James R. Gordon, to intercede with Washington on his behalf, he boarded the *Espagne* in Bordeaux and by August 12 was headed back to the United States.

Just before he sailed he saw the gruesomeness of war once again. After an offensive—probably Château-Thierry—the wounded were brought into Paris, and he volunteered his services. The night he remembered most vividly, he wrote in *The Best Times:* "it was my job to carry off buckets full of amputated arms and hands and legs from an operating room." With this episode his first initiation ended. During the placid trip home on the *Espagne,* he read—*The Duchess of Malfi, The White Devil,* the *Confessions* of Jean Jacques Rousseau—and wrote. In the year he had served in Europe he had accumulated a wealth of material—scenes, emotions, and the like. So to tell what he had seen and felt, he took what was to have been part four of the Great Novel and finished it hastily during the voyage. The tale of Martin Howe's experiences at war became *One Man's Initiation—1917,* his first published novel.

[Diary]
Sailed June 20th 1917
Band playing hula hula on the wharf people dancing in and out among the luggage—

Man who wanted paper as a souvenir—"cause you see sir I'm seein' off my son. I don't reckon they'll mind do you, sir?"

"I don't reckon they'd mind" goes off mumbling.

La traversée—uniforms—smoking room crap games. Singing. champagne—

"For we're bound for the Hamburg show to see the elephant and the wild kangaroo"

"God help Kaiser Bill
God help Kaiser Bill
Oh old Uncle Sam,
He's got the infantry
He's got the cavalry
He's got artillery . . .
Then by God we'll all go to Germany
And God help Kaiser Bill"

General atmosphere of expectation of raising hell in Paris.

June 26th [*1917*]
Where' we going boys?
"Oh we're bound for the Hamburg show

To see the elephant and the wild kangaroo
   And we'll all stick together
   In fair or foul weather
For we're going to see the damn show through"

               At Sea June 27th 1917
        I have no more memories.
        Before,
        My memories with various strands
        Had spun me many misty-colored towns,
        Full of gleams of halfheard music,
        Full of sudden throbbing scents,
        And rustle of unseen passers-by—
        Vague streets rainbow glowing
        For me to wander in . . .

        Today,
        As if a gritty stinking sponge
        Had smeared the slate of my pale memories,
        I stand aghast in a grey world,
        Waiting . . .
        I have no more memories.
        Sea and the grey brooding sky—
        Two halves of a flameless opal—
        Glow soft and sullenly
        In a vast sphere about me
        As I, very drowsy, lie
        On the deck; by the rise and fall
        Of the sound of spumed water
        Lulled into dreaminess,
        Into a passionless mood
        Of utter lassitude,
        A dull Nirvana where stir
        Negations without stress.

        As the petals are stripped from a rose,
        Faded to grey by the rain
        Of a sere autumnal day;
        So, shrivelled, grey
        The pale veils of pain
        And pleasure skip from the morose
        And bitter emptiness
        Of the core of lives and deaths

But gently through the deck beneath my back
Pounds the rhythm
Of engines urging the ship on her track.
In the stoke hole
Shoveling coal, shoveling coal
Stokers are striving
And sweating in the heat and dust
Their hard bodies writhing
With the weight of great shovels of coal
While the sweat runs in white streaks
Through the black coal-dust
On their bare heat-singed flesh . . .

Pain, a dagger plunging
Tears the misty veil.
Strife, a red sword, lunging
Forward out of the pale
Blankness of despair,
Rings its tocsin-flare
Of life through the grey charnel air—

June 27

Old man rushes out to put a hat on the head of a fellow who has none while the ambulance section is walking through Bordeaux.

Whores—protection etc—Champagne

Poitiers—July *2nd*
Wide grey-green fields,
Dappled with swaying vermillion,
 . Everywhere glowing with stains of poppies,
Poppies sprung from old sad fields
Of a battle long fought out . . .

How many years, oh God,
Before the blood of battles springs up
Into the arrogant glowing youth
Of poppies?

Grey-green fields,
Wide dappled with swaying vermillion,
Everywhere stained with a glow of poppies—
Bleeding with poppies,
Poppies sprung from old sad fields

Of a battle forgotten . . .
How many years oh God
How many rains and suns,
Before the blood of battles springs
Into the arrogant glowing Youth
Of poppies?

To Rumsey Marvin

[Sandricourt Training Camp]
July 12 [*1917*]

Dear Rummy—

I wonder where you are—and I hope you've been wondering where I am—But America seems infinitely far off now—I can hardly imagine it exists at all. I've never experienced anything quite like the strange break with everything past that has seemed to come over me since that sleepy quiet trip—of which I remember nothing but sleeping in the sun on the hard friendly deck.

Life since then has been a grotesque—a jumble of swooningly pleasant and strangely sinister despairing times. A sort of Alice in wonderland with the world at stake instead of the March Hare's watch.

(I'm a fiercer pacifist-at-any-price than ever)

I'm still in training at a camp in the middle of heavenly French hills within distant hearing distance of the big guns to the north—and of course I am nearly bursting with impatience to get to work—but I must wait for a new section to be made up—an affair of ten days or two weeks.

In Paris, by the wildest good luck—I ran into three of my best friends. We had a lovely time wandering about dark silent Paris, quite forgetting war and discipline and duty in our excitement at meeting.

Tell me what you're reading—and for God's sake don't believe what your prep-school teachers tell you. With this St Paul to the Thessalonians sort of an exhortation, I close

Love
Jack

To E. E. Cummings (1894–1962), *the noted poet and artist, of whom Dos was a close friend from their Harvard days. The two traveled to-*

I   John Randolph Dos Passos.

Kets Keméthy, WASHINGTON, D. C.

II Lucy Addison Sprigg Madison.

III

Dos, June 14, 1896, age five months.

IV

Dos and his parents at Niagara Falls,
circa 1908.

V

Dos, while in England as a child.

VI   Dos costumed for a play at Choate School, circa 1910.

Dos in front of "The White House," Cintra,
Virginia, circa 1912.

VIII   John R., Dos, and his half-brother James Madison, circa
1914.

IX Dos in his Ambulance Corps uniform, 1917–1918.

gether in the twenties and remained in touch always. Dos' techniques were undoubtedly influenced by Cummings' experiments with language in his poetry, prose, and dramas.

Sandricourt
[*July 13, 1917*]

Hello Estlin!

I hear you are with section twenty-two, wherever that is. I got over here a little over a week ago on the Chicago, and am now in the training camp of Sandricourt—hoping to be sent out in a couple of weeks—somewhere—and meanwhile drilling, eating watery soup, and listening with vague interest to the casual tomtoming of guns that you can barely hear to the North. The scenery, however, is delightful and most soothing. Of course there's no chance that we'll land in the same section, but perhaps we might get together on leave sometime—

Drop me a note as soon as you can—addressed 7 Rue François I

I've met already—Bobby Hillyer & Van den Arend, both of Norton's gang—and Dudley Poore—on the American Ambulance Field Service—

Au Revoir
Dos

Written on a hillside with larks.

[Diary]

July 31st [1917] St. Martin-les Prés—Definitely I must start jotting things down——

Paris—A strange Paris of whores and tragically sad widows—The abandon of complete misery—My God—how ridiculous it all is—I think in gargoyles

The men of the Middle Ages had the right idea in their rollicking grotesque dance of Death—I want to write a novel called the Dance of Death—or some such title—though I fear it'll be much used and abused by the time I come to do it—

I'm dying to write—but all my methods of doing things in the past merely disgust me now, all former methods are damned inadequate— The stream of sensation flows by—I suck it up like a sponge—my reactions are a constant weather vane—a little whimsical impish— giggling—sneering at tragedy—Horror is so piled on horror that there can be no more—Despair gives place to delirious laughter—

How damned ridiculous it all is! The long generations toiling—
skimping, lashing themselves screwing higher and higher the tension
of their minds, polishing brighter and brighter the mirror of intelligence to end in this—My God what a time—All the cant and hypocrisy, all the damnable survivals, all the vestiges of old truths now
putrid and false infect the air, choke you worse than German gas—The
ministers from their damn smug pulpits, the business men—the heroics
about war—my country right or wrong—oh infinities of them! Oh the
tragic farce of the world. Hardy's Arch satirist is more a bungling
clown than an astute and sinister humorist.

Châlons—
    We left Paris early, and arrived there, marching from the station
through grilling hot streets full of powdery dust to a big arid "park" of
automobiles & camions—there we were put up in a barracks—very
hot—and "fraternized" with many poilus—all told the same story of
utter boredom—and desolation—Hate of the Germans is rung in now
and then, conventionally, without convictions—one is too tired to be
anything but bored. Oh the dull infinity of dead. Occasional flashes of
the most charming and graceful spirit of comradeship liven the dry
dustiness of it all.

Bobby & Van & I had a delightful time in Châlons—going in swimming in the Marne, arrayed in the delightfully abbreviated & striped
French tights, finding things to eat and drink, nosing about the rather
unimpressive cathedral & the lovely church of Notre Dame & the
lovelier church of St Alpin—that has one of the loveliest square Gothic
towers I've ever seen—over the crossing.
    I'm enjoying myself vastly, though I have a dusty unfruitful feel-
ing—shall I ever produce anything? I wonder. I'm so damned lazy—so
damnably lacking in conviction. Perhaps I shall—
    One thing I know however—all my past attempts are on the wrong
tack—I've closed the book of them, thank goodness,—and I've cleared
the space for the new edifice. At least I think I have—but I know in
my heart that whatever I do will be along the old lines—I want these
notes to really begin something—I wonder if they will.

    I'm sitting in the old beer garden of the erstwhile inn we're using as
a barracks—in an arbor—how many pleasant drinks have been drunk

here! how many wedding parties flushed with champagne have giggled and blushed and felt the world soft and warm with the phallic glow!

Behind me the French cooks are assiduously preparing our supper with an inimitable air of Savarins cooking for Henry Quatre. The French have such a wonderful relish for simple eternal things—food, women, music, soft undulating scenery . . .

It's raining pleasantly and lucid pensive drops fall one by one from the smallish horsechestnut trees, falling with a faint kiss on the puddley gravel. A rather seedy arbor vitae in front of me has its lower branches fringed with the gleam of the raindrops.

How ridiculous that Bobby—Van and I should be here—Its so very pleasant in the sloppy untidy garden—with the Frenchmen preparing dinner in such a charmingly noisy manner, and the children in dirty blue pinafores crunching about in wooden shoes.

Then, too, I've had my hair all clipped off and it's wonderfully amusing to explore with my fingers the hills and valleys and bristling tablelands of my skull.

The fellows on the section are frightfully decent—all young men are frightfully decent. If we only governed the world instead of the swag-bellied old fogies in frock-coats that do! oh what a God-damned mess they have made of organized society, the bankers and brokers and meat-packers—and business men. Better any tyranny than theirs. Down with the middle aged!

Aug 15 [1917]—Have been amusing myself in three ways
  1. Writing a novel in collaboration with Bobs
  2. Eating & drinking omelets & white wine
  3. Having wonderful naval fights with fleets of paper boats on the brook—
Tomorrow we go to the Front to a devilish hot section
Don't forget Athos, Porthos & d'Artagnan—

To Rumsey Marvin

[Near Verdun]
Aug 23 [*1917*]

Dear Rummy
  I've been meaning to write you again & again—but I've been so vastly bitter that I can produce nothing but gall and wormwood

The war is utter damn nonsense—a vast cancer fed by lies and self seeking malignity on the part of those who don't do the fighting.

Of all the things in this world a government is the thing least worth fighting for.

None of the poor devils whose mangled dirty bodies I take to the hospital in my ambulance really give a damn about any of the aims of this ridiculous affair—They fight because they are too cowardly & too unimaginative not to see which way they ought to turn their guns—

For God's sake, Rummy boy, put this in your pipe and smoke it—everything said & written & thought in America about the war is lies—God! They choke one like poison gas—

I am sitting, my gas mask over my shoulder, my tin helmet on my head—in a poste de secours—(down underground) near a battery of 220s which hit one over the head with their infernal barking as I write.

Apart from the utter bitterness I feel about the whole thing, I've been enjoying my work immensely—We've been for a week in what they say is the hottest sector an ambulance ever worked—All the time—ever since our section of twenty Fiat cars climbed down the long hill into the shot-to-hell valley back of this wood that most of our work is in, we've been under intermittent bombardment.

My first night of work I spent five hours in a poste de secours under poison gas—Of course we had our masks—but I can't imagine a more hellish experience. Every night we get gassed in this sector—which is right behind the two points where the great advance of the 21st of August was made—look it up & you'll see that we were kept busy—we evacuated from between the two *big hills*.

It's remarkable how many shells can explode round you without hitting you.

Our ambulance however is simply peppered with *holes*—how the old bus holds together is more than I can make out—

Do send news of yourself—and think about the war—and don't believe anything people tell you—'ceptin tis me—or anyone else whose really been here.

Incidentally Jane Addams account that the soldiers were fed *rum* & ether before attacks is true. No human being can stand the performance without constant stimulants—

It's queer how much happier I am here in the midst of it than in

America, where the air was stinking with lies & hypocritical patriotic gibber—

The only German atrocity I've heard of was that they sent warning to a certain town three days before they dropped aero bombs on it so that the wounded might be evacuated from the hospitals—

Even French atrocities that you hear more of—slitting the throats of prisoners etc.—sort of fade away in reality—We've carried tons of wounded Germans and have found them very pleasant & grateful & given just as much care as the French. The prisoners & their captors laugh & chat & kid each other along at a great rate.

In fact there is less bitterness about the war—*at the front*—than there is over an ordinary Harvard-Yale baseball game.

It's damned remarkable how universally decent people are if you'll only leave them to themselves——

I could write on for hours, but I'm rather sleepy—so I think I'll take a nap among the friendly fleas——

Love
Jack

SS.Ane 60
7 Rue François I
Paris France
Here's another page—

You should have seen the dive I took out of the front seat of the car the other day when a shell exploded about twenty feet to one side of us—We were trying to turn on a narrow & much bombarded road——C'était rigolo, mon vieux! The brancardiers in the dugout are practicing their German on a prisoner——So long—Write at once.

[Diary]

August 24th [1917]

Seated in the garden, where I've been sleeping all the afternoon en repos—It is the most charming of gardens with what was once a pool of water with a fountain, at one end in front of the shell of the little pink stuccoed house the garden belonged to. We use it now as a dug out and dive into it when the shells the Germans persist in tossing into this blessed village get too close. It is just the sort of garden a pensive little French boy with large brown eyes & premature scepticisms should play in, a garden full of such plaisance with its white

roses and its fat-juiced pears and its white blotches of phlox-flowers
among evergreens that it makes one hate still more all the foolishnesses
with which men try to disturb the rich ease of life—The soul of it is in
the faint breath of box, musty with generations of tranquil closes,
shutting out the turbid asininity of life about us, or of death & dullness.

Death, that should come tranquilly, like the dropping of an over ripe
pear, brimming with sweetness, why should it come in the evil shriek
of a shell? And what's it for, What's it for? Governments are only
makeshifts—like patent toothpaste—less important perhaps—and who
would die for toothpaste, or kill for it.

The gas waves of stupidity!

I wish I could write verses, but I cant concentrate my mind enough
on any one rhythm or mood—My ideas come in little hesitant showers,
like flower petals when a wind blows after rain.

I'm sitting in the garden amid the aroma of it, soothed by the
pathetic ruined soul of it—and over across the river in our dusty barracks, the rest of the fellows—alas Americans have so little tea—are
probably quarrelling over their food.

Why can't they learn the lesson of perfect camaraderie from the
French?

At present America is to me utter anathema—I cant think of it
without belching disgust at the noisiness of it, the meaningless chatter
of its lying tongues.

I've been trying to read a copy of the New Republic that has come
over—honestly I could'nt get through it. Its smug phraseology, hiding
utter meaninglessness—was nauseous.

And away off the guns roar & fart & spit their venom & here I lie
spitting my venom in my fashion—

A bottle of white wine & a jar of gooseberry jam & an evil memory
of canned goods on your stomach—such is war.

For some reason one falls back constantly on profanity. I've never in
my life sworn so many swears or thought so many swears or thought so many swears as since I
have been "doing my bit" in France.

The utter goddamned ridiculousness of things so takes your breath
away that you have no other recourse than the lame one of profanity—

And then of course when artillery trains get in ones way & camions
run amuck in gas-soaked valleys—there is nothing to do but swear.

Aug 26th [1917] Out of sheer desperation of laziness I have been trying to sleep—but as the flies & the fleas and the biting & nipping & crawling things that I have acquired in postes de secours are equally desperate in their resolution to bite & itch

The little doctor at PJ gauche bending interestedly over a piece of cheese—mais il y a des petites bêtes dedans—regardez donc les petites bêtes—Qu'elles sont grandes—

Meanwhile the shells fall snort snort all round & the brancardiers from the door of the abris shout in vain for him to come in

Also the doctor & the aumonier at PJ right—seated at dinner with the inimitable air of a function the blessed French give every meal while shells burst all round & spray them with small stones go on drinking from their petites verres (conserved heaven knows how and looking utterly fantastic among the tin mess kits) continue with perfect calm to discuss linguistics, I think—

Later, the delightful aumonier out looking for his glasses—without his helmet, chased by a brancardier who pops it on his head—

How wonderful they are those nonchalant priests who wander about under shellfire, never a bit preachy, always quiet and absent minded and mildly amused—They make things go marvellously smoothly & well. Imagine a troop of heroic American clergymen in their place—

The marvellous part of the French is how unheroic they are The despair of them is absolutely Greek in its calm beauty——

Curious how impossible it is for me to write any verse—prose comes rather well—but verse simply wont

I wish I'd kept this beastly diary up—as things slide by so far they lose their impressiveness—except those that outstand, which of course gain.

But, gosh, I want to be able to express, later—all of this—all the tragedy and hideous excitement of it. I have seen so very little. I must experience more of it, & more—The grey crooked fingers of the dead, the dark look of dirty mangled bodies, their groans & joltings in the ambulances, the vast tomtom of the guns, the ripping tear shells make when they explode, the song of shells outgoing, like vast woodcocks— their contented whirr as they near their mark—the twang of fragments like a harp broken in the air—& the rattle of stones & mud on your helmet—

And through everything the vast despair of unavoidable death of lives wrenched out of their channels—of all the ludicrous tomfoolery of governments.

To Rumsey Marvin

[Near Verdun]
Aug 27 [1917]

By candlelight in a dug out—Outside it is raining & German shells falling sound like infinities of heavy chain dropped all at once

Dear Rummy—

I've wanted time after time to write you & have produced many unwritten letters—you know the kind—Also two delightful letters from you have spurred me on—

But I've had so much to say & so much of it will be so hostile to your ears, you old militarist, that I haven't known where to begin.

Let's see When did I last write? It seems that it was in Sandricourt, when I was enduring the sorrows of training camp—After that we formed our section, S.S. 060 in Paris & jaunted by easy & unwarlike stages to a town on the Sacred Way, a little above Bar le Duc of blessed reputation——Ah but I'll continue in the morning—Imagine me stretched out on a stretcher on the floor of the dugout listening to the German shells whistling overhead & wondering if a chance one'll hit our roof—

Aug 29th [1917]

I am sitting in the charming weedgrown garden of a little pink stucco house whose shell only remains & if fortune favors I shall finish this letter. It is a delightful day of little sparkling showers out of thistledown clouds that the autumn-nipped wind speeds at a great rate across the sky. I've not been on duty today—so I've been engaged in washing off to the best of my ability the grime and fleas of two nights in a dugout. Nos amis les boches have been keeping us excessively busy too, dropping large calibre shells into this town; as if the poor little place were not smashed up enough as it was.

We stayed for two weeks with our feet in the mud at Erize la Petite—a puny & ungracious hole—There the only interest was watching the troops, loaded on huge trucks—*camions*—go by towards the front where an attack was prophesied.

For some reason nothing I've seen since has affected me nearly as much as the camion loads of dusty men grinding through the white dust clouds of the road to the front. In the dusk always, in convoys of twenty or more escorted by autos full of officers, they would rumble through the one street of the ruined village.

The first night we were sitting in a tiny garden—the sort of miniature garden that a stroke of a sorcerer's wand would transmute into a Versailles without changing any of its main features—talking to the schoolmaster and his wife; who were feeding us white wine & apologizing for the fact that they had no cake. The garden was just beside the road, and through the railing we began to see them pass. For some reason we were all so excited we could hardly speak—Imagine the tumbrils in the Great Revolution—The men were drunk & desperate, shouting screaming jokes, spilling wine over each other—or else asleep with ghoulish dust-powdered faces. The old schoolmaster kept saying in his precise voice—"Ah, ce n'était pas comme ça en 1916 . . . Il y avait du discipline. Il y avait du discipline."

And his wife—a charming redfaced old lady with a kitten under her arm kept crying out

"Mais que voulez vous? Les pauvres petits, Ils savent qu'ils vont à la mort"——I shall never forget that "ils savent qu'ils vont à la mort"— You see later, after the "victory", we brought them back in our ambulances, or else saw them piled on little two wheeled carts, tangles of bodies with grey crooked fingers and dirty protruding feet, to be trundled to the cemeteries, where they are always busy making their orderly little grey wooden crosses——

Its curious. Do you remember Jane Addams statement that everyone in America jeered at, about the French soldiers—all the soldiers in fact, being doped with rum? Its absolutely true—Of course anyone with imagination could have guessed anyway—(there went a shell— near our cantonment, too) that people couldn't stand the frightful strain of deathly—literally so—dullness without some stimulant—In fact strong tobacco very strong red wine, known to the poilus as Pinard, and a composition of rum & ether—in argot, agnol, are combined with the charming camaraderie you find everywhere—the only things that make life endurable at the front—

Having our headquarters in the much bombarded remnants of a village, we do our business in a fantastic wood, once part of the forests of Argonne—now a "ghoul haunted woodland"; smelling of poison gas, tangled with broken telephone wires, with ripped pieces of camouflage—(the green cheesecloth that everything is swathed in to hide it from aeroplanes), filled in every hollow with guns that crouch and spit like the poisonous toads of the fairytales. In the early dawn after a night's bombardment on both sides it is the weirdest thing imaginable to drive through the woodland roads, with the guns of the batteries tomtomming about you & the whistle of departing shell & the occasional rattling snort of an arrivée. A great labor it is to get through, too, through the smashed artillery trains, past piles of splintered camions and commissariat wagons. The wood before and since the attack—the victory of August 21st look it up & you'll know where I was—has been one vast battery—a constant succession of ranks of guns hidden in foliage, and dugouts, from which people crawl like gnomes when the firing ceases and to which you scoot when you hear a shell that sounds as if it had your calling card on it—

The thing is that we, on our first service, landed in the hottest sector ambulance ever ambled in. My first night out I was five hours under gas—of course with a mask, or I shouldn't be here to tell the tale——

But the whole performance is such a ridiculous farce. Everyone wants to go home, to get away at any cost from the hell of the front. The French soldiers I talk to all realize the utter uselessness of it all; they know that it is only the greed and stubbornness and sheer stupidity of the allied governments &, if you will, of the German government, that keeps it going at all——Oh but why talk?——its so useless—There is one thing one learns in France today, the resignation of despair—

Still, I'm much happier here, really in it than I've been for an age. People don't hate much at the front; there's no one to hate, except the poor devils across the way, whom they know to be as miserable as themselves. They don't talk hypocritical bosh about the beauty & manliness of war: they feel in their souls that if they weren't cowards they would have ended the thing long ago—by going home, where they want to be. And lastly and best, they don't jabber about atrocities—of course, everyone commits them—though about one story in a million that reaches our blessed Benighted States is true.

But I really must shut up. More later—

Love—
Jack

[Remicourt
September 12, 1917]

Dear Rummy—

The ever blessed and ever intelligent government has seen fit to take over the Volunteer ambulance service. We have the choice of enlisting in the army or retiring——

So I am out of a job—that is will be in a couple of months.

Plans depend—

The war looks as if it would never end and the net of slavery to it grows tighter and tighter about all of us——

If people could only realize the inanity of it—or if they had the courage to stop being dupes . . . I am convinced that it is through pure cowardice that the war continues—

The only thing it has proved to me is the necessity of alcohol and tobacco to the human race—American sentimental gibberish not withstanding—

Yet curiously enough, I enjoy the life vastly, from a purely personal point of view

love,
Jack

The usual Argonne village
Oct 2—[*1917*]

Dear Rummy

On detached duty in a most placid village behind our sector—we are "at the disposition of the Médecin Divisionaire" and alternately act as a sort of taxi for him and carry wounded and malades between hospitals. The sector is very quiet except for aero-attacks in the rear and we have very little to do; so I sit all day at a table in front of the little yellow limestone church and write, now and then looking up to see a general in a staff car go scooting down the street, raising a terrific dust, as is the custom of generals, and sending the fairhaired children scuttling into the doorways. Then too long artillery trains pass, artillery trains disguised by ingenious—"protective coloration" camouflage—we call it—as oak trees and flowerbeds and cabbage patches—all of which is highly diverting. A charming woman cooks us our meals and watches us eat them with meditative interest in her smoky-beamed, red-tile-floored kitchen. At night our sleep is sortied by the *distant* explosions of aeroplane bombs or by the rumble—like carts incessantly crossing a wooden bridge—of an artillery scrap somewhere on the lines.

In the evening one goes to little wineshops where soldiers gather and sing songs—many of them very charming and all significant in a thick atmosphere of beer and unwashed clothes and camaraderie.

It seems ages, by the way, since I've had a letter from you, Rummy, and I am sure it's ages since I've written—so lets forgive and not forget but remember to write.

How's school this year?

Love
Jack

Paris—
Oct 26 [*1917*]

Dear Rummy—

I was delighted to get a letter from you—as the aforesaid have been rare articles——Still, we'll blame the submarines.

I am in Paris writing in a small chilly room (8 francs a week!) on a certain delightful Rue Descartes behind the Pantheon on the Rive Gauche. The reason is that our everblesséd Uncle Samuel has decided he will have none of the aid of volunteers, and has replaced all the volunteer ambulance sections with "trained" American army ambulance drivers. One was offered the privilege of enlisting, which one rejected. The result is that I am a gentleman of leisure in Paris—for the time being. Probably I shall get into one of the few volunteer unmilitary organizations remaining—the Exchange of prisoners service—or a rear line ambulance service, or something of the sort.

I'm amusing myself going to many concerts, eating many delightful meals in miscellaneous restaurants, snooping about bookshops—& being as unmilitary as possible. Moreover I'm writing a wild sort of novel I started at the front in collaboration with a friend of mine.

To a certain extent I'm eating the lotos——and a delightful lotos— the wistfulness of russet fall in the Luxembourg gardens, cold twilights walking up Montmartre to get escargots in a certain little restaurant in a certain little square that is the tip top of Paris, the refined gluttony of patisseries, concerts with lots of César Franck——oh many are the seeds of my autumnal lotoses.

But one has moments when the bile rises and chokes and even the sweet languid flavored lotos seeds dont take the taste out of your mouth

So you've been to Toronto—don't you think its a beastly place? Toronto on a Sunday morning . . . A very dear friend of mine—he's just been drafted, poor devil—went to school there—and his description of the utter middle-class gracelessness of it has perhaps tinged my ideas. But I have been there—and I admit, that I loathe it.

Man alive, you seem to be constantly giving lectures—What an awful thing to teach the young! What can you find to lecture about nowadays that isn't unpatriotic?

School without masters must be rather nice though—schoolmasters are such a desiccated lot as a rule——

Paris is full of American uniforms and of Serbian generals.

Do write often——

Jack

Write care

Morgan & Harjes

31 Boulevard Haussmann for the time being——

Gosh I wish you were over here, young man,—we could have a wonderful time wandering about Paris together—There are so many places I'd like to take you to——if this thrice & fourtimes damned war would only stop——

But it wont—people haven't been killed——oh fudge—je m'en fiche——

The new motor ambulance service that's being formed—which I shall possibly be in—is going to recruit in the States from people *under age* & people maimed halt & blind—

I'll write you about it later.

It'll be painfully safe—which might soothe parents——

Quantum suffisit

[Diary]

> This is a garden
> Where through the russet mist of clustered trees
> And strewn November leaves
> They crunch with vainglorious heels
> Of ancient vermillion,
> The dried dead greens of summer
> And stalk with mincing sceptic steps,
> And sound of snuff-boxes snapping
> To the capping of an epigram,
> In nodding fluffy scented wigs
> —The exquisite Augustans
>
> Nov 3 [1917]

To Rumsey Marvin

                                                                    Paris
                                                        Nov 12th [*1917*]

Dear Rummy—
    "In that part of the book of my memory, before which little could
be said, may be found a rubrick, reading: Incipit Vita Nova"——and so
begins Dante's Vita Nuova & my excursion into Italian——
    For know that many things have been happening—The Volunteer
Service on the French front has been, as was threatened, taken over by
the American army. I gracefully retired and have been lazing in Paris
ever since—an atrociously delightful month of wandering through
autumn gardens and down grey misty colonaded streets, of poring over
bookshops and dining at little tables in back streets, of going to concerts, and riding in squeaky voitures with skeleton horses, of wandering constantly through dimly-seen crowds and peeping in on orgies of
drink and women, of vague incomplete adventures——All in a constant sensual drowse at the mellow beauty of the colors & forms of
Paris, of old houses overhanging the Seine and damp streets smelling
of the dead and old half-forgotten histories.
    And now, mon enfant, I'm going to Italy——
    Therefore a Dante, panoplied with Italian grammars and dic-
tionaries.
    You see in view of the recent excitements, a hurry call has been
sent out for more ambulances. A lot of the remnants of the old service
have volunteered—and here we are, off day after tomorrow in a convoy
of Fords for the Italian front—
    God knows where it'll be by the time we get there!
    Write voluminously & often—
c/o Morgan, Harjes & Cie
31 Boulevard Haussmann

                                                        Lots of love——Jack

[Diary]
Nov 14th [1917]
    In Cope's room waiting for him to awake & arise & dine. Have spent
the afternoon reading Petronius & Dante's Vita Nuova—strange combination!
    Then I wrapped my head in Dudley's "this-colored" comforter &

went to sleep—a light charming sleep in which—as in a frieze in
Livia's house on the Palatine, moved the little contorted episodes, the
Priapus—figures, and the little flashing pictures are scenes of the
Satiricon—all curiously illumined by the white liturgical light of the
Vita Nuova—

Then to awaken & to leave Dudley who wanted to ruminate over
solitary herbs—& to walk at a mad rate through the fog & the glaring
lights & the little groups seen & lost again—all the while thinking of
the marvellous life of the Satiricon—how far away they are in their
unreformed joy of the flesh——how it brings out the tragedy of lust—
all the yearnings & risings of the penis & phallic flashings—

The more you fan the flame of your desire—the more frothings of
the lard there are—

Nov 17 [1917]

> The present is an unmasticated thing
> The digested in the future.
> The past is the blood in your veins
> The harp the future plays upon

[November 28, 1917]

The marvelous Moulin à Vent dinner with Fairbanks

The cafe of the acrobatic waitresses oh god oh Montreal what a
spectacle (pron. à la boche)

The way they histed up their skirts & seized the pennies—all with
the expression of a Boston Child's lady sympathetically bringing a fine
cut piece out of her apron—

and the unshockingness of the performance—the utter casuality of
it—Waitresses, bar maids picking up pennies in their cunts!

bah one has seen it every day of ones life——

[December 7, 1917]

I am writing this in a very bad musical show. I am too far away to
hope to understand and I am sleepy and its dull and I wish I had the
sense to amuse myself with literature—The people I'm with want to go
whoring, I wish I did. It is such a simple naive way of amusing
oneself—Why people think it is worth the trouble I can't imagine. Of
course love, attraction, the most temporary sort of affair of that sort is
different—a barrel with a bunghole in it seems to be their only idea of

women. It isn't worth the trouble. I suppose its only by going out &
getting them that one makes adventures—but good God—why not
wait? Things do turn up in time—vide Cope's letter

Also the guide who came up to us in the Square—in very bad
English almost singing this

> Nice girls
> Naked girls
> Open all the time
> Dancing

What a fine chorus for a troop of pandars in a mask of love

To Rumsey Marvin

Hôtel Cavour
Milan
Dec 9th [*1917*]

Darn your hide Rummy—

I want to hear from you and a letter persistently refuses to come—
For some reason Italy keeps making me think of you—and its the very
devil not to have you around or at least an eidolon (an image of your
soul) in the shape of a letter——Gawd, what a soul I must have if this
letter's an eidolon of mine. But I feel irrepressibly writative tonight so
you'll suffer for it. But first I am going out into the cold and clammy
streets of the ponderously dull city of Milan, a city of bankers that
might be Denver, Colo., for any charm or beauty—Still Italia and the
south and the ancient dream does creep in. In one of the rawest streets
there rises the solemn series of a Roman Colonade. In Sant' Ambrogio
are exposed three brown skeletons of Saints, in gold crowns and with
embroidered slippers on their feet. On the coldest days women go
about the streets selling yellow Solferino roses and chrysanthemums
and carnations that have split with their fatness the spathes of their
calyxes.

I have been out & have eaten pasta al sugo and pesce frito and
salata and violent formaggio in a small and mournful restaurant. It is
snowing, and I am wondering where we will go at the front. If they
send us into the Alps—it'll be the frozen hell of the inner circle of
Dante's Inferno, how frozen you'll know if you try to crank a recalcitrant automobile on a cold day when the crank handle bites your
fingers and every piece of metal you touch is colder than ice—But there

is a chance that we shall go to the western Piave—where it'll be warmish and rainy, and far pleasanter. At any rate we are leaving Milan in four days for some unknown point on the front.

The trip up here was great sport. From Paris and across to the Loire through the Forêt de Fontainebleau, a marvel of faint color in the ashen greyness of winter; then up the Loire to the uplands at its source and down through the mountains into Mâcon in the valley of the Soâne; then down the Soâne to Lyon and Vienne and out into the warmth and sunlight of the valley of the Rhone, where the roads were dusty with the white dust of the Midi and where cypresses rise in solemn exclamation marks among the vines.

In Montélimar, a white town full of plane trees above Orange, I met one of the most charming people I ever hope to run into—a boy of about thirteen whose passion was to faire le piano, and who was an amazingly vivid and fiery young person. We talked while I was ministering to the wants of my car and later walked together about the little town, he pointing out the interesting things with a wonderful contemptuous familiarity. He was one of those people who leave a glow in your memory for ever. I dont think there is anything on earth more wonderful than those wistful incomplete friendships one makes now and then in an hour's talk. You never see the people again, but the lingering sense of their presence in the world is like the glow of an unseen city at night—makes you feel the teemingness of it all.

Then we went on to Marseille where we stopped a few days to repair cars. There, in the glittering comic opera atmosphere of a city full of a scent of voyages to distant places, full of exotic vistas through the ages, I nearly fell in love with a girl I saw in the promenoir of a Variety, the very temporary love of a friend of mine—again one of those fervid people from whom life glows in a sort of halo. Probably fortunately the section was leaving the next morning, so she remains a dazzling memory. Then we passed through the post card colored Côte d'Azur, Nice and Cannes and the rest of them—meaningless places after the crude jingling color of Marseille. The Italian Riviera was a different story; a wonderfully dangerous road winding among brown cliffs and through steep olive gardens and terraced gardens where white pergolas held up the vines arching paths that led to the doors of preposterous pink and mauve and ochre-colored villas with pea green shutters,—a road that dove into villages through ancient machicolated gates and gave you glimpses of court yards and dark doorways where old women sat and shelled beans and where corn hung to dry in bright orange clusters of ears——a road that lasted for two solid days, during which we wound with the sea at our feet and the hills at our left hand and the sky at our right hand.

The convoy turned north outside of Genoa and stopped in a cold and miserable village—Pontedesimo. That night I escaped with another fellow and took a car into Genoa. The glimpse we had of Genoa by night is one of the most fascinating things I've ever done. An oilship was burning in the harbor and lit up the tips of towers and the broad facades of the houses on the citadel with a pearly pink glow. The dark streets near the harbor were the very middle ages made manifest, full of shrines and oaths and meaningful whistles and women leaning seductively from high balconies, and footsteps lost about sudden dark turns. There were drunken sailors there bawling bawdy songs in all sorts of languages, pursuing savage looking women with frowsy hair. We found a café where the orchestra was playing wonderfully noisy Offenbach, where we drank strega and ate ices. Then we wandered about on the smooth mosaic pavements of the main streets of the city, which are very wide and edged with sumptuous colonades. We looked for a long while at the two great marble lions in front of the Cathedral and then came away through harbor streets now dark and sinister and round the point where the great square lighthouse is. From there we got a last view of the city—dark moulded hills holding pools of lights, like stones in the palms of a negro's hands, and the bay still glowing with the burning oil ship. Then we walked back to the place where the cars were parked—fifteen very weary miles. We got past the Italian sentry who was guarding the cars from the natives and then found Gouverneur Morris, our correspondent, a little drunk & reeling about in the moonlight. It was nearly dawn and he couldnt get into the hotel and nor could we—so we all camped in a doorway at the foot of a flight of stone steps in a great mass of army blankets and were stepped on in the morning by the people in the house——altogether an awfully funny affair.

Hah—another break in your letter during which I took a bath & now I am going to bed—I also read some Rabelais and yawned over an Italian grammar——

Love
Jack

By the way what are you reading nowadays? For the Lord's sake
don't get the idea that your school work is educating you—'taint—All
the education one gets comes from ones own reading or ones own
living and you really have to have the reading to have a standard to test
the living by——

School & college interfere with ones education most horribly
anyway

Addio

[Diary]
Dec 9 [1917]
     Still Milano—
By the way—

An oil ship was burning in the harbor the night we were in
Genoa; a pearly rose glow lit up the pedimented facades of the houses
on the hill and the square pointed church tower that rose above them,
etching them curiously against the dark hills behind the town where
the lights along streets dotted out new constellations to match those in
the brilliant night sky—

This sentence has haunted me for days, I used to think it was
good; now I know it's bad—It is now Dec 10. I am in Milan at the
Hotel Cavour—sitting beside Van, who in a bearish mood is trying to
compress himself into letters & send himself off to America. The most
amiable thing about that curious person is his love for his friends in
America.

Have I the faculty for making friends? I wonder—I seem in my
life to have made exactly two—which is little for one so greedy as I.

I've just been dining with Fairbanks & his whore, Nita at Com-
pari's—a curious rather sad meal in elaborate surroundings that constantly made me think of *La Dame aux Camélias*—The poor girl had a
bad cold and a cough and could eat nothing and was as miserable as
only a lady of pleasure can be. We heard the usual story—How universal it is, and, stranger still, how universally true. She was a dancer—
balleto classico—before the war took away her trade—did the oriental
dance in Aida as première danseuse at the Della Verona Theatre. Then
she lived with an American for three years, who finally left her in a
furnished apartment with a child, he going off ostensibly to the front

but really with a cocotte from Covu's. She had never heard from him since; the child had died.

Her tale of keeping up appearances, for one who knew her lover had deserted her—was pathetic. And now she was in the streets with a certain Nida, a boisterous friend.

After the war she would take a dancing contract for vaudeville & tour America. The high comedy of their hiding from the waiter & chambermaid and director of the Hotel Diana. Jack's sudden leaving of Nida was worthy of a cleverer Congreve, was actually Shakespearian

What marvellously brutal people are the clever & radical young like Jack & Van! I suppose I'm as bad in my supercilious way—Youth is a hideous period—from some aspects—C'est un horrible gâchis, la vie des hommes.

To E. E. Cummings' mother

> Milan
> *Dec 16th 1917*

My dear Mrs Cummings,

Can you tell me anything new about Estlin? Ever since his arrest last Fall I've been trying to find out about him—but have been unable to get at anything definite, either through Mr Norton, or members of section XXI, or French army people I've talked to about it. Everyone agrees, however, that nothing serious could happen to him—They think he'll be held for sometime at a concentration camp and then sent back to America. If that has happened—everything is probably over by this time.

I sympathized with him so thoroughly, and my letters being anything but prudent, that I expected I'd be in the same boat but the censor evidently didn't notice me—so I'm still "at large", as the blood and thunder militarists would say of us. I'm in the Italian Ambulance Service of the American Red Cross (address c/o American Consul, Milan)

I hope it won't be too much trouble to drop me a line—as I'm awfully anxious to get in touch with him again.

Please remember me to Dr Cummings and to your sister—

> Very sincerely yours
> John R. Dos Passos

By the way, Mr. Gannett is also trying to find out about Estlin—I got a letter from him on the subject sometime ago from the American Red Cross, Paris.

To Rumsey Marvin

Hôtel Cavour
Milan
Dec 20th [*1917*]

Well Sergeant Marvin, You Rummy—
　　Your letter brought great delight into the camp of the unorthodox. Here is my tale in the worst of verse——

The Bad Ballad of Milan
One chanteth merrilie

Oh I have come out of the North countree
On roads that climb from the mist of the Loire
To heights from which to the South you see
Among the hills the Soâne wind far.

And I have slept in Mâcon, Vienne,
Passed Orange of the Arch and come
Through white rows of planes to the South again
To the air spiced with garlic & roses and sun.

There have I sung of my mystic South,
Of olive gardens, and the olive skin
Of the girl whose classic laughing mouth
Waits under the dark lace of the whin.

Then lounging among the opera
Comique of Marseille crowds, I've been
Spectator of sights improperer
Than Rabelais;—exotic sin

That lurked in every secret street
And dark café, whose exit way
Was loud with memories unmeet
For the making of poem or novel or play.

I've seen a burning oil ship flare
In the bay of Genoa—flushing rose
The tall towers of Genoa; there
Drunk Strega romantically.—Froze

On the footsore fifteen kilo' walk
Back to the convoy's dingy square,
Where the sound of our nocturnal talk
Made the moonlit sentries glare.

But the congealed evil of one day
Frowned as we entered the ponderous gate
Of bankers built in a bankers' way,
Of the bankers city desolate.

(It was as unexpected, I can swear,
As if turning from an intimate chat
To open my door with welcoming air
I should find what's below a drill sergeant's hat.)

Incipit the Dirge of Milan to be dolefully chanted or keened

"Fiat 4, Fiat 4,
Oh mecanician of Milano;
When will she roll my Fiat 4?"
"Piano, signore, va piano."

Oh the days blow long and the days blow cold,
And the hours drag on and the hours drag by,
And my heart and my soul are cold and old.
I sit in cafés and slump and sigh.

The days drag by and the days drag on,
The dreadfully desperate days of Milan;
In lonely cafés I groan and moan,
At the wasting of days in chilly Milan.

"Fiat 4, Fiat 4,
Oh mecanician of Milano,
When will she roll my Fiat 4?"
"Piano, signore, va piano."

Oh the days blow long, and the days blow cold
In the ponderous chill of the streets of Milan—
And lo! in the name of Milan is told
A tale of days as long as the span

Of a thousand years where every year
Is bored to tears, indeed to wails,
And squeezed all dry to its last bored tear.
The spinster Hours carry pails

To gather the tears of the ennuiés.
The streets are bored with the blank facade
Of rows of palazzios where no ray
Of life or humor ever strayed.

"Fiat 4, Fiat 4;
Oh mecanician of Milano,
When will she roll my Fiat 4?"
"Piano, signore, va piano."

For I might be waiting in Marseille
Or under Avignon's southern wall
Dreaming of Nicolette or Mireille;
Or I might be in Portugal,

Leading a grey mule loaded with porto
Up the steep road to Cintra, to feed
The new deputies and stir as it ought to
Their revolutionary speed;—

"Fiat 4, Fiat 4;
Oh mecanician of Milan
When will she roll my Fiat 4?"
"Piano, signore, va piano"

—Or sitting with a quiet mind
Beneath the palms in Timbuctu,
I might wait while they relined
The seventh stomachs of my new

Splendidly tan-colored dromedaries
That they might bear me without stop
To Samarand and the saffron prairies
That towards the Yogi [Gobi] Desert drop

Fast from the laurel-covered hills
And Himalaya's tantalizing chain.—
Or might be in Devon picking squills,
Or in the tingling London rain.

"Fiat, 4, Fiat 4"
Oh mecanician of Milano
When will she roll my Fiat 4?"
"Piano, signore, va piano."

Here endeth the Dirge of Milan

There upon shall it be sung boisterously with merrie music—thus:

There's one braw sight in the streets of Milan
However hard the bankers toil
And deny its joy no Christian can
Who has stood in front of the stone turmoil,

Of the Duomo's vast ineptitude,
And seen how high in the square there stands
A horse of taste, a horse of mood,
Champing against the bridle bands.

The brazen horse is sat by a man
As brazen as he, and more solemnly dressed,
Who holds him still in the square of Milan,
Against his will for the horse is distressed . . .

To be spoken with great solempnetie
He has seen the cathedral.

Envoi
"When will she roll my Fiat 4
Oh mecanician of Milano?"
"When the horse in the square takes time by the hair—
And shies and refuses to stand still any more
In the brava piazza del Duomo,
The Fiat will run both night and day;
The facade will have scared the horse away.

And now you're probably as bored as I am——
The sad fact of this mournful Glee is its truth—My section has left
for the front, and I am left to languish in Milan, waiting for my car to
get repaired. I expect to be grey haired from impatience when I get it.

[Dolo]
Dec. 30th [1917]

Rummy!
I write you in the midst of reading Shelley's Lines—written among
the Euganean Hills. I am sitting in the upstairs room of a villa on the
Venetian plain behind the Piave. The room contains two beds, three
camp cots, piles of blankets and kitbags and miscellaneous confusion.
The table is satin covered and was once in a lady's boudoir. There is an

evil odor of pipes, and the sound of a gasoline stove cooking water later to be used for tea. Tea, in default of sugar and cream, will be drunk with a certain cordial Campari in it.

This afternoon I walked over to the end of the causeway that connects Venice with the marshy mainland. You can't go any farther without special and complicated permessos—so I stood and looked at the flat straggle of the city a mile away across the lagoon, with the campanile tall and rose in the late afternoon light, and the domes of St. Marks' and San Giorgio Maggiore rising a little above the flat roofs. The lagoon was very still, though every now and then the detonating of guns in the distance shook the windows of the café at the end of the wharf. When I turned away, the snowcovered mountains rising from shadowy foothills to clusters of brilliant peaks to the north and west were stained wine-rose from the sunset.

All this is why I'm reading Shelley so ecstatically. Then Shelley is a wonderful change from Dante and Rabelais, that have been alternately depressing and cheering me lately.

The reason for all this literary stimulation is that we are stuck, rusticated, in the said countryhouse in the Venetian plain without any hope of escaping. Section 4 is still waiting to get to the front—we've been within the sound of guns and of aeroplane bombs—but nothing more—nary a blessée, a ferito, rather, have we carried. Of course it'll all come in due time—and waiting is the main thing one does in the war—Alternations of excitements, of dull work, of parties, and of waiting for something to turn up—comprises every phase of the military life. . . .

The fellow opposite me at the table is reading de Musset's *Confession D'un Enfant Du Siècle* and looks up every four minutes, crying "God what a fool"—and then we fall to and argue for a half hour—From this comes the chaos of this letter—I'm trying to defend de Musset's sanity—you see, unsuccessfully to be sure, for he's the darndest ass in literature.

Well, this stupid of 1917 is nearly frazzled out—I hope to God its successor'll be fuller of hope—Curious, but I have to admit—that I never had a more interesting year—

Write:——

Jack

[Diary—"Dolo Bassano"]

The Lotus

The fruit of the lotus is wet with rain
Aslant subtle misted colonades
Whispering down polished streets
That stoop through resonant arcades
Into grey squares where the day's wane
Lingers in kiosks and faint trees

The fruit of the lotus is russet of leaves
That flutter in wistful curves through the mist
And swirl in their rustling dance of death

Dec 31st [1917]

The Italians are hopeless. They trouble me vastly—because I fear that my reluctance to be American & Anglo Saxon and unsympathetic (not that anyone else is sympathetic with foreigners, God knows) is a hopeless bar to any real estimate, as if anyone could form a real estimate on any country living in it for three weeks in the peculiar parasitic way we do.

I'm fed up with the whole business anyway—now the thing is to retire into that famous shell of mine & open the door ajar, and gird on butterfly wings in the large lands behind it—absolute fantasy is the only escape—the drunkenness of the imagination. . . . .

Meanwhile—as I write—Jack and I are discussing America in a vague way—Its the motto "Be good & you'll have money"—or "have money & you'll be good"—

I wonder—

I'm at the moment terrifically taken with [Shelley's] *Julian and Maddalo*—& shall probably write huge amounts in imitation of it.

11:30 The last minutes of the seventeenth abortion of an abortive century are flying and the obstetrics of the New Year are at hand. Funny—Last New Year I was in Cartagena—dark Phoenician streets with latticed bays & big bird cages and shrill whistling of birds—and the ruined castle on the hill where the Gypsies lived—. Since then rather a lot has happened—Didi—those beastly months in New York—and the Rabelaisian roister of the summer on the fringes of death's dull carmagnole.

12:30—Why wont they let a year die without bringing in a new one on the instant, cant they use birth control on time? I want an interregnum. The stupid years patter on with unrelenting feet, never stopping—rising to little monotonous peaks in our imaginations at festivals like New Year's and Easter and Christmas—But, goodness, why need they do it?

Damn it—I shall read Shelley

I've lost the key to my famous door—

Yes the coming of the new year is certainly a gloom—New Years always are—but never so much as this one—I am filled at the moment with a mad desire for poetry—to write it. As a poor substitute I can read it—As an illustration of my pitiful state,—I feel like copying down the entire of Shelley's Westwind, part to feel my fingers forming poetic lines—

Jan 1–1918

> The future has become the present
> A fact for love to resent

as Blake would have written.—Anyway the constant pour of futurity is a bally bore—The present's all right in its way—if only it weren't formed out of the dust of the future's rainbowings.

To call the war a carmagnole is an unpardonable preciosity. Stupidity has more of the exhilaration of madness.

The New Year—celebration—oh God I hate to write about it: Two majors—the Guy Lowell man who built Emerson Hall and a certain effeminate Wilkins-creature—also a major—came in rather drunk to wish us, out of the real kindness of their hearts—a Happy New York—God! the things they said. We are here for propaganda it seems—more than for ambulance work—we will be used in the most conspicuous way possible—We must show Italy that America is behind them. That is to say—America has entered—with England & France into the publicity contest as to who shall save Italy—

The soldiers, they said, were so stupid and ignorant that if you gave them two packages at once they would look from one to another stupidly like an ass between two bundles of hay or a bally Figian—but, that, with cajoling, he thought they'd be induced to remain in the trenches they had tenacity and fought with the courage of devils when fully aroused—and properly manipulated—God, it made you want to vomit to hear it. So we are here to help cajole the poor devils of Italians into fighting—they dont know why, they dont care why——

Probably—from a coldly intellectual viewpoint—the most interesting feature of the Italian situation will be that here, owing to the simple-mindedness and ignorance of the Italians all the issues are vastly simplified. The machinery of how governments are run and controlled into war is more obvious—to a citizen of fairly sophisticated countries the wires will seem plain as day

Jan 2 [1918]
a cold day of blank fog—read, amid much suffering from ailments, Antony & Cleopatra & Measure for Measure——

Great enthusiasm thereat

Drank much tea with figs & lemon in it——

Van & Jack & I sat all day amid the Russian novel atmosphere of our disorderly room.

On account of my thorn in the hand I cant write

Jan 3rd [1918]
To write or not to write—fafreddo e umido e oscuro—I shall write Mickey—inspiration——

I am sitting in the upper room of our cheerless villa at the table that has the pink lace skirt-thing on it, a table at which the lady of the house once sat to do up her hair—now, alas, fallen & stained with tea and ink and candlegrease—In the center of the table is the peacock blue flame of the famous & trusty gasoline stove—"Hope-Deferred-Maketh-the-Heart-Sick". Around it are Van & Jack & me; Van in a dirty tea shirt with a blanket round him so that he looks like lo the poor Indian, Jack scrawling large on foolscap, and meeself, cold & minished.

We live in a sort of Russian novel atmosphere—cold, dinginess, dirty nails, untidy beds, lack of washing appliances—idleness punctuated by tempestuous arguments & bitches personal squabbles over small irrele-vancies. All day long we sit about and drink tea with figs in it, glanc-ing out now and then at the dreary winter of the Venetian Plain, where rows of pollarded trees make dreary processions of hunchbacks, black & gnarled in the mist, and where Italian soldiers tramp meaning-lessly back & forth through the cold.

On some days the Euganean Hills and the mountains behind lie in dazzling white and rose above the plains to the North, then there are airraids at night, and in the day the sun shines and we walk through the mud and go to look at the campaniles of Venice across the lagoons, rising commonplacely above the railway track and freight-yards, and smoking factory chimneys of the landward side—a denial of Romance.

Afternoon—walked with Van & Bragg—They seem to be making a line of defense from Padua to the sea along the canal—Barbed wire stretches in long blue strips across the wheatfields and vineyards looking like some obscure crop sprung up in a nights growth—behind the road this side of the canal trenches are being dug and machine gun emplacements made. The whole defenses show a completeness that seems to mean business rather than insurance against emergency.

I suppose that if the Germans break through at Asiago—the Italians will thus fall back from the line of the Piave to the line of the Brenta Canals & Padua—abandoning Venice & this entire strip of land.

Lets hope they retreat before we leave.

Jan 4th [1918]
Breakfasted this morning off huova all'burro at the little trattoria—Sat watching the grey warmish half light of the dark wooden tables coming out from the two walls, regularly, like pews, and the brilliant white light on the walk across the street against which anyone coming in was silhouetted, as he opened the glass door—All the time a string of soldiers marched down the road outside—helmets and guns and blanketrolls showing out strangely against the brilliant light—Exactly that arrangement would make a wonderful stage set——
Note:

At college Fibbie's finding of Suzanne's letter written him a couple of years before about his Uncle James' death—telling about the long summer after his illness when he lay languidly, dying, pouring out all his life into her—Thus Suzanne in future will be the result of those two summers spent with James Clough. They will be the gold by which she tests the tinniness of the world's standards.

Night of Jan 4th [1918]
Coles Seeley's room at the hospital in Mestre—watching to keep him from getting out of bed in his delirium.

A cold uncomfortable vigil whiled away by reading Flaubert—Un Coeur Simple, St. Julien l'Hospitalier, & Herodias

At four two big snorting explosions shook the windows and the glasses on the table—air bombs. Then the electric light snapped off and the fun commenced. I stood on the balcony of Seeley's room & watched the searchlights ineffectual in the glare of the moon & the red flashes of guns & the spit of machineguns as everything let loose at the sky. Once I imagined I saw a shadow like a plane across the beam of the searchlight—but it is unlikely—The main effect of the roughhouse was the whimpering sound and the menacing rattle as they hit, of pieces of shrapnel falling.

It's quieted down now, so I suppose the Austriaci have done their damnedest & left.

To Rumsey Marvin

[*Mestre*]
Jan 4th [*1918*]

Dear Rummy—
First let me light into your poem—There'll be hacking & hewing I warn you, so prepare: I have blood in my eyeteeth.
You, Sir, have writ a poem.
Honest to gawd you have, But—(the fight is on!)
In what language, except that of certain dead gentlemen, appears the word 'smooth'st'? For heavens sake man—write live language not dead Keats & Shelley—Read Masefield Read Chaucer,—(thunder & lightning!)
The first two lines might perfectly well read, 'smoothing' and 'stroking'. Then, too, I object that the thought & images are awfully reminiscent—not too much so though—

> That I may have a dream of silver wrought
> Think in thy dreamy mind a silver thought

is as good as Rossetti—it's amazing—
The next two lines are not so good—but good—
Then the 'azure heavens wide' & the 'lordly eagle' stuff is infantilely expressed.
The third stanza's excellent, except, what exactly is a 'stricken coast'? I fear it is an adjective for the sake of an adjective—not for the sake of any meaning

The fourth stanza's a little too abstract—(one thinks of capital letters Strife, War, etc) but its noise is awfully good.

I object to the " 'st's" in the last stanza—. . . .

The electric light's just gone out and the church bells have rung an air raid warning. We all piled out to see anything to be seen—but there was nothing but a cold empty sky, still flushed with sunset—and a few tiny bright stars—. . . .

But as I was saying, I object to the "s't's"—in the last stanza and to the rather lame "slumber sweet"

Apart from that the poem's a damn fine piece of work. It has all the nice directness that I like so much about your stuff—I mean, I don't feel that you wrote a poem for the sake of five stanzas of verse.

Do send me some more stuff

I've probably been much too harsh—but I think a good fire eating criticism is the best thing in the world. I wish I could get some out of you on my stuff.

I haven't written any verse, except for abortive fragments, in a dog's age. Not from blueness—but from lack of conviction. I write copious notes of all sorts & work intermittently on a diary & on the novel affair I started with another fellow.

The first book is finished.

Infancy of Martin Howe—a sensitive child—nicknamed Fibbie from his habit of telling steep & impossible yarns—

At school—friendship with a young fellow of sceptical turn of mind & the regular revolt & moral adventures of people of their age

Through it all runs the influence of a literary Uncle & of a little French girl, Fibbie's nurse's daughter—whom the uncle finally has a liaison with.

The *uncle* dies—Of course that doesnt mean anything, any more than bald descriptions of events ever do. There's a general undercurrent of the feeling that instead of Fibbie being the liar—it is Society——& the uncle is the sensitive soul which the world ends by killing—Then through the rest of the book—his influence is supreme over the two chief people, Suzanne and Fibbie during the rest of the book—I dont know if they meet again after the first part—but they both buckle against the incomparable asininity of things in general—conventions, social ordinances, the lies of a civilization, living in the shell of a totally different way of life—now dead a hundred years or more.

Stated that way it all sounds like sublime rubbish—but I don't think it is, quite. It's awfully crude & abrupt and jerky—but it tries to state my present point of view towards things as vividly and frankly as possible. You'll have to read it some day.

Any poetry I write—or find lying about—I'll send you.

Jan 5th

In the hospital at Mestre. I've been spending the night with a man from our section who is down awfully badly with pneumonia. It was rather harrowing as he was frightfully delirious—So I sat up beside him all night reading Flaubert. Do you know those three wonderful stories that for some unknown reason always turn round together in one volume? Herodias, Un Coeur Simple & La Légende de Saint Julien l'Hospitalier—Flaubert is, anyway, one of my Olympian gods, even the Cloud-Compeller himself.

But to continue: The night was enlivened by the jolliest airraid I've been through yet—two huge k-plunks that rattled the window panes and shook the medicine bottles on the table, jerked me out of the little provincial town on the Channel Coast of Un Coeur Simple—I stood on the balcony and looked over the roofs of the town and at the sky streaked with search lights. The guns going off all round gave a constant sound of preternaturally large rockets, the shrapnel exploding high in the air with the same sort of dull paff—rockets make. Then machine guns started tap-tapping & a couple more bombs were dropped —and the sky was full of the whimper of falling shrapnel pieces.

That's the beauty of air-raids: on the principle that all that goes up comes down the shrapnel fired at the enemy comes pottering about your own ears—Of course it does about as much damage as the aeroplane does.

Now I'm very cold and waiting to be relieved. The fellow I've been watching with is sleeping heavily.

Why in the name of Heaven isn't [Ibsen's] "Ghosts" a play one might like altogether? Because it deals with flesh and blood instead of with the sugar coated sentimentalities of the higher things according to Ella Wheeler Wilcox or the Lady's *Home Companion?*

Send me the learned essay and I'll tear it limb from limb.

For the Lords sake Rummy, don't enter the Flying Corps. You know that I'm not a person to council an excessive care of ones skin— But the R.F.C. is such awfully certain death. This is about how the matter stands. You enter the Corps and have six or eight month's training, much of which is mere waiting round for a chance to fly at all. During that time you have good pay, Kudos & you faites la bombe, generally with the wine-woman & song accompaniment. Having raised hell in a feverish *moratori* te saluant manner for six months you are either accepted as a pilot or observer—or, if you're not a success, are removed to the infantry—

Say you're a pilot—your life may be a day, or it may be six months, but they are almost sure to get you in the end. If you are an observer your chances are much better, I believe—

Of course that is all very well in its way—but there is too much interesting on the orb of the world—for any such speeding up of existence to be necessary except for the very jaded.

Then too, the war is awfully poor sport—in any branch of the service. There are moments of excitement—but even about the excitement there is a sameness.

Nothing like being pursued across the Gobi desert by Tatar horsemen in flamingo-colored coats.

By the way, I want you to get Stendhal's *La Chartreuse de Parme* & read the first part of it, about the romantic youth who went to the battle of Waterloo—It applies.

Of course, I'm not saying that he wasn't glad afterwards that scepticism had followed experience, instead of preceding it——

If you must get into something, why not the Italian Ambulance Service—which, I think is now recruiting in America——There is no age limit in particular & you could easily learn to drive a car. Even I who am actually feebleminded, mechanically, can do it . . .

Do you like O'Henry's Cabbages & Kings? It pleased me very much.

But I'm afraid I've strung out a dull & chilly letter—

love
Jack

[Diary]
Jan 5th [1918]
Flaubert was the most wonderful company in the world last night, and read in their strange context the family warmth of the three stories stamped itself strongly on my mind—I feel as if I had lived them.

After the air raid things quieted down and at about five Coles fell into a heavy sleep. I slept too till half after eight—then thankfully drank some coffee & a mouth full of wine & feel awfully chipper.

God, how beastly it is when our bodies go back on us and betray us to a nest of microbes. Yet there is a certain romance about illness in the Mediaeval manner that makes you almost desire it; Arthur, faint unto death, carried away by the queens on a barge to Avilion . . .

Jan 6 [1918]

Again in Seeley's room in the hospital. He is vastly better this time & I merely sit about & wish I were a chatty conversationalist. It is villainously cold in this room & the light is barely good enough to write by: I try to display my inchoate Italian for the benefit of the very pleasant orderlies—but it is hardly a success—Reading Villon—but I feel too dopy & cold to concentrate on anything except the hope of food. And people say that cold is stimulating, bosh—

The section left today for Bassano—under Monto Grappa—said to be a villainously cold town—but lively with what liveliness the Italian front can produce——As usual S. F. [Sidney Fairbanks] & I are left behind on account of the repairs to our blessed bus—We are to rejoin the section in three days.

I still sit rigid writing cold—waiting for pranzo.

Jan 8th [1918]

Women & the war—The new feminism—And the more women who get mixed up in it the better. Its an education in gall & wormwood and flesh and hate and the varied hideousnesses and beauties of life. The idea that a woman is a high fallutin' uncarnal creature, that, if she has any mind she must keep it resolutely fixed on the Ideal, whatever that is, refusing to look at things as they are. Out of things as they are are ideals made, worthwhile ones, not out of the waxwork figures that stand about on clouds of pink sentimentality in the woman's world. The sad part of it is that its from the women of a generation that the next generation gets its all-important things—life, attitudes, sensibilities & revulsions—The men make a great jabber, but they are awfully incidental parts of the machine of reproduction. Its on the women, that the men to come, as well as the women to come, depend. That's why it seems to me so infernally necessary for women to be mixed up in the holocaust. American women, especially, for in America lies the future, the menace & the hope—At present more of menace than of hope. Our whole life is a childish failure—our inane attitudes towards the war, our ignorance & stupidity, our womanish sentimentality stored up like a vat of dye, ready to be poured over whatever those who pull the strings of our ideas & emotions want disguised.

And on this question of wars & nations the future depends— Whether it shall be the old round of greedy miseries—of sacrifices to ancient blood tainted tribal gods—or something new—with hope in it.

Jan 10th [1918]

Sitting in the "palatial Villa" occupied by Section III beside a man who looks the image—God save him—of the typical Schubert Chorus man in a Broadway show—in the next room, the billiard room—the Section is playing craps—wonderful ejaculations & a primeval clink of the bones—come in to me, mixed with the crinkle of notes—A phonograph plays sentimental pieces fed to it by the Schubert-man.

Yesterday—was the great offensive on Venice—F [Fairbanks] & I started out suddenlike on the car & came—following the canal, deep puttey-green through plains covered with snow, to Fusina, where the little steamer leaves for Venice. It was a grey day with a faint rosiness of sunlight that brought out most wonderfully the colors of the houses along the canal—pink with pale blue shutters—greenish ochre, peeling to pink of old bricks, magenta covered with black and green lichen. ("My dice") (He-ow, ten")—and all the roof tiles snow-covered—a little like some of the brilliantly colored snowy Christmases imagined by early painters—who felt they must have orient color & winteriness as well—There was something about the grey light & the greenish reflecting canal—that raised all the little houses above the commonplace picturesque—into an amazing patchwork of beauty. Then came the blank marshes & flocks of sea birds & the utter classic borediness of a gull poising over a black stake—& on the boat a little man was informing us—between salutes—that really we could not get into Venice without the written permit of someone—he didn't care whom—As a favor, he said we could go over with the boat so long as we remained on board until she came back—

So there we were standing, ruefully enough, in the bows, with the feeling of people under taboo in a fairy tale—The boat slithered through the cold lagoon water & we watched the factory chimneys & commonplace greyness of the city on the horizon become Venice. We passed an island with brick fortalice walls against which were moored black barges & where the houses stood over the water on black vaults— with watergates—Then the Hoboken grey became touched with red— Venetian red—and we were sailing up a wide road with a row of torpedo boats to the left & an island to the right covered with long houses, off which the stucco peeled in green & orange leprosy. Then the little boat was coming up to the shore just beyond a bridge spanning a canal—up which we peeped into the intricacy & charm of Venice—For some reason one was impressed—One thought Byronically, de Mus- setly—one hung out of balconies & threw roses to imperious gondolas— the threadbare garment of a century's romanticizing was for a moment whole cloth—nay it was the embroidered garment of an ancient courtesan of Venice, a mistress of Spinello, whom Titian painted—and who went on a spring day to wander with Giorgione along the hedge- rows of the Euganean Hills——One joined the vast company whom Venice had for a moment drugged out of the sordidness of life—— little Germans schoolteachers, fat Jewish bankers, elderly Englishmen full of gout & decorum——all the imitative of the Shelleys & Byrons——

——Venice makes one feel a little like a person impressed by a Coney Island side show—there's a vast & beautiful & varied vulgarity about it—and yet in Venice there is the Byzantine the concentrated Oriental that thrills one immeasurably——

Julian & Maddalo—with its color, its touches of pomposity, & its sentimental psychology—is the soul of Venice.

Then the barges alongside, black—held to the wharf by ropes of brilliant ochre, and then on their decks what a comic opera crew—But, damn it, man genuine—the woman in blue with a great apron & a magenta rose shawl crossed on her breast—she was genuine——And the lion of St. Mark up on his column & the St. George standing on his column astride his dragon that looks like a tunny-fish. And the lace fruit of the Ducal Palace with its frillings & flutings bricked up for fear of aero-bombs—and the string grooved Campanile——

> Doges coming down to the sea
> To inspect wharves & cargoes
> To sniff with the noses of merchant princes
> The quality of pepper and spicebales
> That negro slaves are unloading
> Marmosets pulling at their velvet gowns

> Parrots shrieking on chrome yellow bales
> Heat and a smell of ships
> And the sweat of galley slaves
> And the rinds of fruits of the orient
> That drift in the greentide towards the Lido
>
> Venice rises like a dream
> Sharpening dull brains to the brilliance
> Of the varied color of earth
> Out of the sluggish lagoon
> Of the popular imagination

Jan 10 [1918]

A foot sore walk over slippery kilometers—twenty three of them or twenty seven of them to Padua—there the severe coldness of one of its restaurants & a little excitement over a German plane that calmly sailed to & fro in the azure above the city. Cold.

Venice achieved Jan 11 [1918]—Color—Cold—rosy sunlight across a pale blue lagoon—faintly covered with purple "purpurato haze"—and the little steamboat crunching through the ice that skidded ahead & swirled in white chunks astern—St. Marks—a gilded parchment of the middle ages—St. Mark's. The usual gondola ride between the beautiful facades of the palaces of families with old sounding names—Then the ducal palace the huge halls full of the romance of dead pomposities, of past injustices—from which the canvases that told with such gaudy braggadocio the wealth & the arms of Venice have been moved to Firenze for fear of the Tedeschi aeroplanes.

Venice is totally dead—swathed in sandbags—shops & shutters closed, windows boarded up—inhabited by soldiers on permission & by sailors & a few scared civilians—yet there was enough life left in it to excite me considerable—

> The doge goes down in state to the sea
> To inspect with beady traders eyes
> New cargoes from Crete, Mytilene,
> Cyprus and Joppa, galleys piled
> With bales off which in all the days
> Of sailing, the seawind has not blown
> The dust of Arabian caravans.

In velvet the doge goes down to the sea
And sniffs the dusty bales of spice:
Pepper from Cathay, nard and musk,
Strange marbles from ruined cities, packed
In unfamiliar-scented straw.
Black slaves sweat and grin in the sun
Marmosets pull at the pompous gowns
Of burgesses—scuttle in sudden fear
To hide in crimson sails or climb
In gibbering on the naked back
Of a lash scarred galley slave. Parrots scream
And swaying clinging to ochre bales—

Dazzle of the rising dust of trade—
Smell of pitch & straining slaves
And out on the green tide towards
Drifts the rinds of orient fruits the sea
Strange to the lips, and bitter, and sweet . . .

Venice, a drugged summer dream
A waking drum, a bewildered momentary life
Rises, thrilling with color sheen
Of the sluggish lagoon
Of popular imagination

O I must go out alone

In velvet state the doge goes down to the sea,
To inspect with sharp beady eyes of a trader the three
Laden galleys from Mytilene, Crete
And Joppa

My verse is no upholstered chariot,
Gliding oil-smooth on oiled wheels,
No swift and shining limousine
But a pushcart, rather . . .

A crazy creaking pushcart, hard to push
Round corners, slung on shaky patchwork wheels,
That jolts & jumbles over the cobblestones
Its very various lading:

A lading of Spanish oranges, Smyrnian figs
Flyspecked apples—perhaps of the Hesperides,

Curious fruits of the Indies, pepper-sweet——
Stranger—choose & taste

Jan 11—1918

Jan 14 [1918]

Solitary birthday dole-feast in Venice—where I went to buy condensed milk for section 1—I'd describe the marvellous beauty of the lagoon at sunset, the Alps to the north the domes & campaniles and flat intricate facades of Venice—but I've already done so in letters to Dudley & Auk—& my thin ingenuity is completely worked out—
Dolo We are still here—piano—domani—I'd gladly skin alive to a slow fire those bastardly dastards of mechanics at the auto park—

I'm sleepy & have a contented sponge feeling—What's the use though? Sopping up color-impressions is as meaningless as sopping up alcohol if you dont follow it up by any reactive process—I fear I'm a mere sponge.—Sometimes I show stains on the outside—but thats not creation—When one's spirit wants to plunge head down into the abyss & with huge arms measure off——like Blake's drawing——Damn—I'll go to bed!——

Jan 15th [1918]

Went up to the garage: the car will be ready domani—as usual. While there I somehow tumbled into a discussion of the war & the world in general … Everybody joined in; it was great fun—the corporal and the sergeant and the bystanders. I made my usual little speedrifications, thinly spreading the butter with words like militarismo—capitalismo—socialismo—and though now & then I got out of my depth & nearly choked in a flood of Italian—The sergeant was disgusted with all civiltá; he wanted to get away from war and government—and hide in Asia or Africa somewhere, where he could live off the fruits of his toil & till the ground in peace. "Life's a short & painful process at the best—let us for God's sake, live it out untroubled by your greeds & wars and sanctimonious laws—you people who govern—if not we'll eventually show our teeth—à la lanterne!"

God! If people were not so damnably adaptable to any form of misery——

But it gave a glow of delight & comfort to feel that they were not entirely dupes. Universal disbelief in anything is what the dear bourgeoisie are bringing on us with their wars & creeds & cants——

O for a revolution of laughter—couldn't all the world at once see the gigantic humor of the situation—and laughter shall untune the sky.

Midnight Jan 15th [1918]
Reading Butler. Someone is playing the *Seraphina* on the phonograph—There's a festival brass in it that makes me think of health resorts—a continental watering place on a warm summer's night with lights & crowds walking about & sharing cafés and a ship—a long string of lights—coming into the harbor from the sea.

Jan 18th [1918]
Bassano at last—Day before yesterday—after much desperate waiting about at the garage—we finally dragged the famous Fiat 4, odds curse it, out of the clutches of the automobile park and late in a foggy afternoon—set out for Bassano, giving farewell to Dolo & Mira very joyfully. At Padova we picked up a young English officer who wanted to go to Cittadella. It got very dark and very foggy, and our acetylene headlight wouldn't work. The Englishman got politely nervous and we ended, after fruitless efforts at lighting the acetylene which only made a bad smell—by sticking two candles in our headlight. Even that was unsatisfactory as it was raining & the road was muddy—a notto louta—as Touda, our Sardinian mechanic, said. The Englishman was good enough to have us to dinner—an Italian farmhouse room with four Englishmen, one the Padre & F [Fairbanks] & I, & an English soldier who waited on us like a butler—and English food & all the appurtenances of a truly British dinnertime . . . How wonderfully true to type the British are! fantastically so. We ended by spending the night there with them—awfully nice young fellows they were, the officers of a trench mortar battery, most courteous & amiably simpleminded, disliking the war yet seeing nothing to do but keep on. Their greatest passion was the fear of being unEnglish. With them we went in the evening to a wonderfully futile cinema entertainment given by the padre to the men of the battery—also a marvelously English affair.

Then we had a very English breakfast—porridge—bacon & eggs & tea & toast—How marvellously they manage to take their isle with them wherever they go!

Run up along the main road to Cittadella, a fortress with huge red brick walls in ponderous decay—a wonderfully fine place, and thence by the muddly main road, since so familiar, in its crowdidness & general excitement & badness, to Bassano.

Bassano's an awfully fine place completely empty—with frescoed house faces & arcades & beautiful towers. There is, too, a wooden bridge across the Brenta—a red covered bridge—that is a braw thing to see—The town stands about on an irregular hill & there are fine views of the gap through which the Brenta breaks through the mountains & of the high hills in front of Grappa.

There are batteries not very far away that make a great racket every day at about dawn. We have evacuation work at present & have so far done considerable. We sit about in a room that smells vilely of gasoline vapor from Fafner & Hope-Differed-Maketh-the-Heart-Sick—and we overeat God! how we overeat!

I am reading with great amusement Don Juan—a pleasant but it seems to me a marvellously unimportant poem—cheap cynicism, cheap sensuality, cheap romantic claptrap—all suffused by a warmth of color & at the same time by a colloquial smartness that is vastly annoying. Its the sincere fervor of coloring that saves it though; and one can't deny moments of acid cynicism that bring up the end of certain stanzas with the snap of a whip.

Jan 20th [1918]
Walk with Van up the Brenta Valley—How great the mountains are!

Jan 21st [1918]
Last night read my chapters to Jack & Van—their sum of criticism was that things are too jerky, not elaborated enough and that too much is left unsaid, so that the unfortunate reader wallows desperately in a slough of constant misunderstandings. My retort was that happenings meant nothing in themselves, anyway—& that I tried to give that impression—by the recurrence of words & phrases etc—but I rather agree with them that it isn't done successful—still. . . .

I'm sitting in the window feeling a bit chilled—looking at the slender campanile whose dome is shaped like a hare bell—Then there's the wide bed of the Brenta silvery green though sheenless in this light—In the center is the fine covered bridge that crosses the narrow part of the river further down—and to the left the dark green hill of Bassano with towers coming up out of the foliage One can hear just a little sh-sh from the river and now and then a gun shot reverberates in the mountains behind us. I'm as usual hoping for lunch—Belly is a tiresome god—unapt to any purpose—but he does pass the time particularly as worship at his shrine is sublimely easy, compared to the toiling needed by other divinities—

Jan 24th [1918]
Sitting up in bed with a belly ache due to the hellbrew of rum punch last night—a fair grey morning tipped with rose & faint salmon color— I am still struggling to find chapter to write about what ??—in beginning of Book II—

and evening & morning were another day——Zabaglione is a genuinely champagne-tinted drink, thick & velvety, scented of rum & vanilla, oversweet, oversoft, overstrong—but full of a fascination—To be drunk by fat Isoldes on deep champagne colored couches while Tristans with rosy round cheeks & fair flowing hair let their great slow tears plash in the huge cold cup—A vision of a—what's the name of the sad baritone in whose arms Tristan dies? (Jack shouts 'call him James')——beating the posset behind the scenes with his sleeves rolled up——
Red-nosed gnomes roll & tumble in the rosy firelight—roll on their backs and drink out of earthen pots, wriggling their huge round bellies—and the air of the cave is heavy with a smell of crushed vanilla and of hot punches cooking.
One lies in a velvetiness of yellow moths stirring faintly tickling wings—One is heavy & full of sleep and tingling langor—until later one goes and pukes beautifully under the moon.

Jan 25th [1918]
Asolo—at the end of a long road—
Bragg to Jack—"You can talk about your soul all you want and all that, but—when I've gone to bed you might moderate your voice"— —

Asolo appears in the hills, a squarehold, gray against the sky, and lower hills covered with houses, with towers and tiled roofs—then one climbs and sees no more of Asolo, toiling up a most painful road—and at last you find yourself in a street climbing up much like a street in

Dunsany's town at the edge of the world.—O it's a splendid town and after walking through it you come to the Scuola Meletti Browning on the Via Roberto Browning and things are made manifest in the flesh.

Tonight is bright moonlight & a cold keen wind and a sound of a German avion overhead—

> Oh get away from that window
> My light & My life
> Get away from that window
> Wont you please?
> For there's going to be a fe-ight
> In the middle of the ne-ight
> An' the razors come flying through the air.

Sitting on the edge of my bunk—above my watch's ticking, people talking in the next room, Jack & Van snoring—I can hear the tease of an avion overhead—

An the razors come flying through the air
Book II of the novelthing is underway—or is it? It wants—1. To give a number of pictures of Harvard—*only such* however as lead up to the point—the merry mountain of lies—2. There must be swagger and rattle and the chorus of the Marvells every four chapters. . . .

(By the way—Suzanne is going on the stage—and there is going to be a rousing echo of her success in the distance—)

3. the People are Fibbie, & John Andrews, new friend—& Weston Nichols & James L. Bridge, & Joseph di Castello, musician, & Weber the wealthy one & a great swarm at Mem. from the Middle West. Then there's Suzanne & the young manager, Epstein, the man who made her. . . .

4. then there's the occasional chorus of the servants at the Marvell's Lizzie, Newman & Bertha.

5. Through it all interwoven—more consciously than ever—in a merry confident—swaggering tune the merry mountain of lies motif & the little & growing tune of the personality of James Clough—

Damn. What on earth is the use of making lists of things—it's like making lists of things you want to do or be in life—You just chugg along without regarding them at all anyway:—so you might just as well not tabulate them. All they do is give you a vaguely satisfied feeling—in itself of canker badness.

Jan 25th [1918]
Reading Lorenzo de Medici's Apologia—& conceiving wonderful
scene in play or story Ecco! Someone has killed the Tyrant and no one
will believe that he is dead—He goes about the dark street with the
dripping head under his arm—& even to the eye & feel people think it's
a tete de veau, vinaigrette—And so are slaves slaves unto the last day—

Jan 28th [1918]
Yesterday went Again to Asolo—Van & I took a call early in the
morning—at 4 AM, to be exact & after a wild ride to Cittadella in
which he ran into some horses and I blew out all the electric lights &
the exhaust became red hot & parted in the middle, leaving tongues of
blue & red flame squirting about at our feet, getting vastly near the
gasoline line—anyway we deposited our blessés & fled away—under a
very wonderful moon—Then we started walking along paths &
across the fields ghostly with hoarfrost under the moon. We struggled
much with barbed wire entanglements prepared for the inevitable
retreat—why anyone should retreat God knows, but they are preparing
as if it were inevitable——At dawn we were coming down a steep wide
avenue that dipped from a high hill into the blue valley. The red
sunrise & the yellow trunks of the planes—& then to turn around
suddenly & see the mountains, coming out in procession beside us as
we went down the hill, rose with violet shadow—and the sky clear
green above them. Then over hills & valleys with the changing colors
of the mountains on our left, and in front of us the sunrise brightening
into obvious light—Then Asolo—and there a breakfast of eggs and red
wine & a climbing up to the square hold on the hill from which one
can see everything—Mountains—strange regular knobs & welts of foothills—& the mist covered plain——
   Every glimpse of Asolo composes into a view of full delight—
through every arch—the whole world seems to open up—lost in the
mist of conjecture.
   And there is a tavern in the town—Where in a fantastic room which
you reach by stairs from the street is a stove—a stove as fine as the
kitchen stove in Jack's play—At the head of the stairs stands stuffed the
last specimen of the Dodo—On the stove are many pans & pots steaming mingled & fragrant steams—
   One sits down and asks for food—and then the strange thing strikes
one—all the peoples of the world, are walking about the room, craning

their necks at the food & stirring it with large copper ladles. But when one wonders what is in the pots & pans, when one asks for risolto, one is told niente. When one asks for salata, one is told niente, when one asks for potate, one is told niente, when one asks for verdura, one is told niente. And all the while old old men, and youths with the o fortunate adolescens expression, and all the seventeen little girls carefully gradated in size, all looking exactly the same and with faces like fishes & stringy yellow hair, go back and forth into the rooms beyond—stand over the stove and stir—but when one asks what is in them, the chorus thunders niente.

At last, after much waiting & moaning they very grudgingly dole out of the smallest saucepan the soup the demiurges eat when they are about to create worlds and one eats & is glad and there come throngs bearing big copperpails of water which they pour into the pots and steam rises and the seventeen with fishy faces & yellow hair go back and forth doing miracles & feeding all the people in the rooms beyond with loaves & minestra—But when one asks for more or for any other thing, they answer in their self-possessed way—Niente.

And all the while there bends over the stove, chuckling, an old woman with a face like Clytemnestra or Clotho. But the patrons of the place go and wrest their food from her in person & peer boldly into the pots and pans and carry away bowls piled with salad & many other things, fragrant to the smell and taste——

The soup being the soup of the Demiurge is filling—and having paid ones tithe one goes forth refreshed—

The name of the Tavern is the Trattoria dell'Paraiso & it is on the little streets that lead towards where the mist cuts off the plains from view

Teatime—Trying to write—God! I have a brain like a peanut. . . . "Found a peanut, found a peanut"—echoes in my head the insane song the section sings at meals—& I am trying madly (Idea! Let Asolo—be the first letter of the Letters of an Embusqué) to be on the shore of the Charles River, marching along with John Andrews & Martin Howe & talking about the horror of existence—The Abbatoir "Thronging generations tread me down"—Yet I must not be there too much, as I am now—I must be there as I was in my Sophomore year at college— In the first throes of elaborating my own particular sort of pantheism, a mushy sort, rather sentimental about the oneness of the protoplasm

etc—Just beginning to be sure that the ingrained taboos were taboos &
not fast in the core of things—suspicious of the decalogue, etc—over-
full, however of morbidities & fastidious barriers, with that infantile
feeling of being cut off from all the world—not being en rapport——
Now I feel much stodgier & sturdier—I realize there is no all the world
to be en rapport with. I suppose I must thank the war for some of it—In
fact I'm a much heartier son of a bitch than I used to be much readier
to slap my cock against the rocks of fact. But the play's the thing, as is
writ in the heart of theatrical managers and on the proscenium of
cheap theatres in the provinces—

After dinner   At dinner people talked war & Y.M.C.A. two topics that
always give me the deepest dyed darkblues——

One thing comes out clear the one thing that enslaves people more
than any other to the servitude of war is nationalism—the patriotic
cant—Religious cant is feeble; its on a down slope fighting to hold
territory—but the patriotism——all the noxious influences of the world
seem to have thrown their tentacles about it—Its the mask of all the
trade-greed & the glory-breed—and the asininity that makes people
insist on sacrificing themselves on the nearest altar—no matter how
brazen the God above it.

I got a sort of hallucination while the people were talking—Apple-
yard & Kohn & Walderspirel & Fairbanks a hallucination whether for
good or bad I know not—of all the fanaticism and cant & sacrifice &
sincere endeavor suddenly turned against the nations. The Y.M.C.A.
becoming a Revolutionary society——and for a minute I felt in me a
little of the hard fanatic fire . . . God—someone must come with a
single mind and a single purpose and the hard fire of fanaticism in him
and batter his life away against it . . . hundreds must batter their lives
away . . . and to what good?—to have the baaing sheep fly to worship
some other false god. Oh the hopelessness of it. Yet one is dragged
helpless to join in the silly processes of time.

We make a funny ménage—I must write it up someday—a rather
matrimonial sort of one—as we are thrown too constantly together
forwards with the result that personalities clash & wrangle—not so
much as Fairbanks thinks—but a good deal. At this moment I am
sitting at the table—on the other side of two candles is Van, looking
picturesque in his Russiany blouse, typewriting as noisily as possible
because he knows it annoys me. Jack is reading Jean Christophe
moodily on the bed—Bragg has just gone out but was annoying the

company mightily making unusual & unnecessary noises etc. The trouble with me is that I've been trying all day to write—without the least success—which is frazzling to the nerves of the best of men— What smithering idiocy.

Jan 29th [1918]

The Heyne Affair—a young fellow of German parentage had to leave the section today because the Italian censorship had intercepted a letter speaking slightingly of the Italians. The Red Cross was asked to have him arrested and court martialed; but it was finally smoothed over to the point of allowing him to resign. His resignation was asked for on three counts—Because he had divulged military information (the nature of which the Italian officials refused to divulge) 2. unfavorable criticism. 3. for what Lowell called low language—low moral tone of his letters.

I've never known the man at all personally, but the affair seems all put up on account of his parentage—God! how filthy—And the final ungentlemanliness & utter indecency of Major Lowell's adding the third charge . . . It's maddening. And how much of just this sort of sheer meanness & small mindedness is going on everywhere! It makes you long for a desert island or an ivory tower—somewhere you'd never see anything so small as a man again.

And there's nothing one can do about it—no more than one slave can protest when another slave is whipped.

Jan. 31st [1918]

The section held high festival. Partly to propagand among the Italians, partly to express a perfectly sincere fondness for the French. The chasseurs' band came down to play to us—also officers & miscellaneous Italians, colonels, majors, captains a great horde—

The fanfare played and one talked & the French expressed in different ways subtle & unsubtle, their dislike for the Italians—As Jack remarked, when the Italians showed a liking for the punch, the French called loudly for beer . . . It was all a great success.

Feb 2nd [1918]

Perched on the wall of the Campo Santo—being gazed at with wonder by an Italian who his chin rested on the world—in every sense of the world—admires us—perched on the wall as I said—with the sun wonderful on my right cheek and Bassano piling up its towers against the sky in front. It's a very bright day—given an unbalanced mournful-ness by the fact that it's winter and that the trees and vines are bare and the grass olive-grey—("the fact that" cut it out for God's sake—man alive—you have the beastliest phrases in the wide world.)

Yesterday Van & I did a splendid walk up the valley of the Brenta, that wound up between great drab deep shadowed hills, with rosy rock faces & then snow shoulders towering behind them. There was no one in the towns, that, although whole for the most part, had a bleak air with their big bare houses and dispirited churches. We passed many batteries, variously disguised, and endless amounts of barbed wire strung across the narrowing valley. The road became more and more camouflaged—and we kept thinking we were getting near the front lines. At last we turned across a bridge in a rather smashed up town and went up a road on the left side of the valley that had an uncom-fortably shelled look, full of holes and covered with splinters of rock, until, passing numerous machinegun batteries & various sorts of entrenchments, we were motioned by a sentry into a boyau. All the time we were expecting to be arrested; still we pushed forward and at last found ourselves in a narrow trench skirting a steep hill above the valley, where there once had been a railroad track, well made & pro-tected by sandbags & with a tunnel gouged out of the rock along side it, in case of bombardment. That abutted in some machine gun batteries and a tunnel, the old railway tunnel blocked up and made into a huge abri where the people live—The further end was defended by several walls of sand bags and a great lighted fire gun & generator. The gun looked absurdly like a large blunderbuss & the tanks of the generator had a very peaceful air. We stood in front of the vedette for sometime looking at the rockpiles and little white houses that marked the Austrian outpost. Meanwhile we talked to a tragic face man with good natured gorilla face, who spoke very bad English.

There's no real fighting in the valley. In that post they just lie round and shoot off machine guns now and then: the Italians and Austrians play tattoos to each other on them. The men are badly fed and no one seems to take any interest in them. The man we talked to was a Calabrian: he wouldnt be there if he could help it, bet yer goddamn life he wouldnt, his home was in Calabria, and the Germans'ld never get that far; anyway—He had not had a permission for eighteen months and so he hadn't been with his wife and had had to screw other women, which pained him.

Then he led us back through the smoking tunnel, full of people sleeping and lying about listlessly, lighting us with a little oil lamp made from an old hand grenade.

At a machine gun battery some good looking young fellows were amusing themselves throwing hand grenades into the Brenta.

Van took many unhindered photographs, one particularly of a dirty pleasant man with a black beard who appeared suddenly, speaking excellent English, out of a small hole in the ground.

We didn't see an officer all the time we were near the front. 40 kilometers pulled off.

Last night and night before we had rip-roaring airraids over Bassano, three or four a night—one stands shivering in the window and watches the *searchlights* & the electric sparkle of machine guns and the great red flare of bombs that explode with a thunderous snarl that rips the horizon—and the shrapnel bullets and cases simply rain about our heads.

The joke is that you get up in the morning and go about Bassano, just nose in the air for horrors, and try eagerly to find where the bombs exploded, where the widows were made & the orphans bereaved and, nothing,—streets placidly empty—the famous bridge that they are aiming at—arid and untroubled as ever . . . Of course you do find things smashed up a bit here & there, a couple of roofs mashed in or a room turned inside out, or somebody's garden given a new conformation, but it's nothing at all to compare with the wild brilliance of the airraid the night before that makes you expect smoking ruins & entrails smeared about the paving stones.

Finished *Bouvard & Pécuchet*—a rather desperate book which so exposes people's idiocies & the cult of the great gods that it ceases to be funny—It leaves you with a feeling of miserable futility, partly because it's unfinished and partly because it is so brutally bitter—so utterly illusionless . . . of course that's the fault of my own cowardly soul not of Flaubert. Nothing ever more effectual took the wind out of the sails of the fine ship of ones thoughts than Bouvard & Pécuchet.

Dont forget the type of man that must at all costs hold the center of the stage—one could write a wonderful high comedy performance of some sort—with three or four of that unpleasant sort of beast all brought together. There'd be a wonderful battle royal.

[February 5, 1918]

A most excellent day of walking with Van. Started up the Brenta Valley with Jack & Bragg—let them go up to the tunnel that was our last objective & turned off to the left at Valstagna up a cañon road. In the bed of the stream, as the road climbed, were lots and lots of small alpine guns, sitting on their tails and pointing their muzzles up like dogs howling. A few miles up we came to a road that spiralled straight up, a road, literally plastered onto the face of the mountain that rose almost sheer, with frequent slides, from the cañon. We walked up the road for pretty nearly ten miles, finding it surprisingly littered with shrapnel bullets and éclats from Austrian shells. Van went rhapsodic over the beautiful workmanship of the fragments of round polished steel. The valley disappeared below us as we climbed—and at last we reached a group of soldiers working, boys of seventeen and eighteen most of them who looked like Sicilians. They produced for our examination a great paper manifesto dropped from an aeroplane, written in Slovack on the one side and in Czechish—ungodly language that they in their simplicity expected us to read off. Then we climbed up on a road obstructed by piles of sand bags & lots of stone fragments & splinters where shells had exploded until we came to a soft voiced man, very dirty, a cook I suppose, who spoke excellent English. He had been in West Australia. Then we kept on up and were produced by a sentry before a bunch of officers. Everybody was very pleasant and wondered who we were. American Red Cross had an exotic flavor to them that was quite entrancing. Among them was a Roumanian, a lieutenant in the medical corps, who spoke very good English which he had learned, it came out, in Bucharest. He fed us Marsala and water in the tunnel where his quarters were—which was to us like a drop of water on the tongue of the rich man burning in hell, for we'd walked all morning unfed & un-wetted. In the conversation it came out that the road we had come on was right under the nose of the Austrians, who held the ridge to the left and could pick anyone off on it they wanted. As we had been climbing the road calmly & puffily for about two hours, the fact was amusing.

The Roumanian was an awfully pleasant man with a beautiful Roman nose and those vaguely liberal ideas always held by travelled

Europeans. One thing interesting he did say, sincerely too—'An educated man cannot hate'—Anyway, his conversation gave that balm to the soul that perfect manners only can give.

He piloted us up the steep path, introducing us to all manner of officers, tenantes, capitanos, Majores, that popped out of holes in the ground, as numerous in the mountains, as they'd been scarce in the valley. After much labor & panting, we reached the abode of the commandante, who inside of a little shack in a crevice in the cliff, sat like Old King Cole with his capitanos & tenantes about him, drinking amid a great array of bottles—. We drank white wine with him in solempne splendour; He out of a special glass—a sort of curved beaker—while one stood by who continually wiped glasses. On the table was the apparatus of a dictaphone with which they listened to what the Austriacos were doing.

Then we climbed on up until we came to a cliff-ledge that bulged out overhead, leaving a sort of cave underneath. Until three days ago this was the position the Italians held—The Austrians being on the slope right on top of them. Then one afternoon, the Italians put ladders up in a cleft in the rockwall, hoisted up a machine gun, popped it over the edge and let fly. They took about eighty prisoners and remained masters of about four feet of the slopes above the cliff. There a company hangs on by its eyelashes, with a row of sandbags in front of them, dangling their feet near the mountains and valleys, and getting their supplies up by means of a pulley.

Then we climbed down the ladders again, and stopped to drink Vermouth with the Commandante and to have tea with our Roumanian friend—tea with real milk in it——and then down by a mulepath to the Valley at Valstagna through the twilight purpling the mountains that had already faded to dim in the smoke of brushfires.

Then home by road with long loose strides and that feeling of being euzooné that comes from great exercise. Followed by a most delicious dinner of rice & cauliflower and by a reading of poetry in bed afterwards and a sleep of marvellous comfort, punctuated by the usual airraid.

Feb 6th [1918]
Dragged by S.F. to be a social luminary—funny & marvellously delicious dinner with officers—colonel, major, captains & lieuts.—funny jolly easily amused people. Much food & much drink—

The phallic method of drinking toasts.

Then a funny walk up a hill to view the pan-ora-a-a-m-a, as they called it & much photography & jokosifying & divers cordial asininity— a *solempne processioun* back, colonel in the lead. The colonel deplores the growth of socialism in the north of Italy—tells how when the Principe of something his brother in law visits his estates in the south the peasants kiss his hand. He's a walrusey & jovial man with a broad waistband & he's fond of animals——

A springy day—with Catkins on a beech tree—or something of the sort (elm probably) & the hill where the great searchlight & the great dog were & the pleasant unshaven man who tended it & who, when he patted the dog had the soft look of a faun.

Now the novelthing Bk II Chap V

Nicholas Murray Butler's address to students of Columbia

At this Christmas season when the good cheer & good will that should mark it are so sadly absent from the lives & hearts of millions of human beings, Alma Mater has a special word of greeting and encouragement for those of her brave and stalwart sons who have given themselves to the service of the nation, even though their lives be the sacrifice. No contest in which you could possibly engage can equal this one in moral significance. Everything which distinguishes right from wrong in public conduct, everything which marks off principle from expediency in national life, everything which draws a line between liberty and despotism, everything which removes human opportunity from the grasping hand of cruel privilege, waits for its safety, and perhaps, for its very existence upon your success and that of the noble men of allied nations who are fighting by your side on land and sea.

When this war shall have been righteously won there will be peace on earth for all men of good will.

Feb 7th [1918]
An absurd ride on Fiat 4, to Cittadella, Jack Lawson accompanying. Coming back at least fifteen chasseurs piled into the back of the car and a stoutish Italian lieutenant, from Naples, sat in front with us. The Chasseurs kept passing about wine in bidons and the lieut. enlivened

matters by passing about hideous pictures of naked women and making one invariable joke asking in very bad French, if one could buy at the coöperative these same pictures of Parisiennes. Each time it caused a riot and the Chasseurs piled three deep inside slapped each other on the back and produced new bidons, which they poked out through the front window. It was a wild ride.

Read Bk. II, chap I to Chap V to assembled quinquumvirate—seems to go fairly well with less jerkiness than before.

Feb 8th [1918]

I wonder what day it is—Maybe its the eighth—Anyway it is signalized by the arrival of Dudley & Fred Bird.

We went into Bassano to buy vast amounts of food & drink to celebrate. While paying for some condensed milk I noticed the clerk begin to get flustered. He even refused to put paper round the cans—the shutters came down with a bang & Bragg said "they're shelling the town." Whereupon we went out and found the streets full of scurrying people and bang of shutters being pulled down by nervous store-keepers.

Sh-sh-Sh-Sh-ssss——broom!—overhead and off in the corner of town where the big cement bridge is! We went, laden with bottles & packages to the big piazza—passing the spot where someone had just dropped a Chianti bottle in their flight. In the middle of the square a big staff car was being hurriedly piled with French generals, who were still pulling their caps down on their heads as it scooted into a side street. There was a great scuttle of civilians up arcades and away—as more shells squealed overhead & snorted in among the houses——

The old women who have the fruit stand at one end of the piazza started packing their goods into a cart, and spilt a great lot of oranges, that rolled one by one, out from under the arcade and down the steps and solemnly out over the flag stones—people pursuing them the while—

And we, waving our bottles, shrieked with laughter.

Other shells

A big French camion full of soldiers passing hurriedly through, stalled in front of us, the driver calling out wildly 'vite—vite'—

Another shell

A man jumping out from the back to crank the car slipped on the flagstones and took the most wonderful cropper ever seen of mortal man—Laughter drowned out the next shell—

The camion got started at last & scuttled away and the square was empty—except for four foolish ambulance drivers waving bottles & laughing, with their mouths full of chocolate

But by that time the shelling had stopped.

Today we heard of the first case—in America—of a man sentenced to death by court martial for refusing to undertake military duty, when drafted and assigned. This is probably rather important. Won't it be strange if it comes to that in my case? Might happen pretty soon too—It'll just be luck if it doesn't, as I see it. God! they'll probably even do their best to take the dignity out of death for a conscientious objector.

Feb 10th [1918]
Long walk with Dudley over little intimate hills that rise to a great crest that breaks into rock like a wave breaking into foam at the foot of the mountains. Wonderful villages perched among high terraced valleys full of vineyards whose grapes must grow right on the floor of heaven. We climbed along a great ridge, and down the end of it, a valley opening out in either side and a view of Monte Grappa and the great cliffs that stand above the Brenta Valley on the right. Coming down we found heaths blooming on the sunny slopes & on one bank bright purple blue hepaticas, one white violet and yellow primroses . . . Then later, down in the valley, snow drops in the hedgerows and one plant of hellebore in flower.

I wish I could sing spring songs innumerable—feel the sap rising fragrant in the branches and everything droning with life. . . . Perhaps I could if I could be alone enough—I used to feel myself full of rhythms and cadences of words—so many that I could not express them—Now I feel none—except things as banal as The minstrel boy to the War has gone. For poetry one needs a certain resiliency of soul. I have none—why hatred and disgust—How can one sing in slavery?

Note Feb 13th What asininity

[February 15, 1918]
Eggs! Who shall sing their epic? Mightn't it have been an egg that Eve

divided in the garden with Adam—an egg laid by the clucking hen of science?

Days of egg-orgy, airraids & calls to Cittadella & Carmagnona at all hours of the morning—cold & miserie

In the intervals read Boccaccio & rejoice—most wonderful stuff!

> Rondel to our Lady of Abyssinia
> Our Lady lies on a brave high bed—
> On pillows of gold with gold baboons
> On red silk deftly embroidered—
> *Oranges & eggs & candlelight.—*
> Her gold specked eyes have little sight.
>
> Our lady cries on a high brave bed
> The golden light of the candles lights

The crown of gold on her frizzly head—
O candles and angry eggs so white!—
Her gold specked eyes are sharp with fright

Our lady sighs till the high bed creaks
The golden candles gutter and sway
In the swirling dark the dark priest speaks—
O his eyes are white as eggs with fright—!
"Our lady's to die twixt night and night"

Our lady lies on a brave high bed
The golden crown has slipped from her head
Only the pillows crimson embroidered
O baboons writhing in the candlelight!—
Her gold-specked soul has taken flight.

Subjoineth the attendant and unhallowed Crew
The omelet's done
The bombing's begun
O we'll eat five thousand eggs
Till we can't stand on our legs
Bombarding's fun
If you don't run
But sit in your abri of omelets & wine
While outside the shrapnel-splinters whine
And the big bombs snort;
But they are naught
If you drink muscato, piano,
While the Germans bomb Bassano

And you may be sure you'll grow no skinnier
Although there be mickle grief within yer
For the late deceased empress of free Abyssinia

Feb 18th [1918]

A Makeronick Dirge to the Late Deceased Empress of Abyssinia
L'Impératrice vient de mourir—
Anger and eggs and the candles gleaming—
Once again the planes are here
Hear the sirens screaming.

Fut la reine d'outre-mer—
Eat we toast in holy sorrow
Shrapnel whining down the air
Early trips tomorrow.

Où le Christ encore est doux
Add the kindly milk for token;
Feast as Eastern mourners do
All the eggs are broken.

Vous qui aimiez la reine—
The silly searchlights end their riot
Marquez lentement votre peine—
Now the guns are quiet.

L'âme errante dans la nuit—
Sick we cause for laughing, wearily
Dont le vent fait morne bruit
God but the game goes drearily!

To Rumsey Marvin

[Bassano]
Feb 18th [*1918*]

Rummy—

A longish letter from you written just after the beginning of the winter term—delighted me extremely and destroyed the bluedom of a long cold afternoon, spent trying to write and eat tangerines all at the same time—with fingers absolutely blue & stiff.

We are in a small town, much bombarded by aeroplanes on moonlight nights, a small town with brown square towers and an old wall, and a covered bridge spanning the Brenta. The front, where the two armies play hide and seek among the mountains and hang to the edges of cliffs, is behind the range of mountains, the first row of the Alps, that rise from our back-door on either side of the valley. There's a little rather futile artillery action—at night we can see the shrapnel bursting along the ridges—and the Austrians now and then shell our town, so that the shopkeepers have taken fright and fled and there are no cafés open, which is annoying.

We get spurts of active duty, long cold night rides, but a great deal of the time you are free. I'm acquiring Italian slowly. I speak it with un-believable badness, but I can read it without great difficulty. I'm at present reading Boccaccio, who is wonderful sport. The stories and particularly the little passages in the Decameron at the beginning and end of each day, before the people start their tales give you the most exciting vivid pictures of Italy in the early Renaissance. Then I do a little writing and read Villon and Rabelais and the Note Books of Samuel Butler—a wonderful Victorian Englishman whom you must know. If you find his *The Way of All Flesh,* a novel, anywhere about, read it by all means.

How do you like Vergil? His amiable pomposity and his wonderful sounding lines used to please me a lot.

I hope your magazine scheme came to fruit. Nothing is more fun to play with than a school or college paper. You can have a wonderful time and get yourself into the allfiredest scrapes . . . at least we used to. It'll be a wonderful way of getting over being too serious minded— as you put it (100 in Physics & that sort of monstrosity!)—not that I think you are, for a moment. The only thing I dont think you ought to do is let your studies interfere with your education——I mean reading. I found that school and college interfered most damnably—and all real education you get yourself anyway. The things people try to teach you in order that you shan't flunk exams—are most of them terrifically perfunctory and shouldn't be taken too much to heart.

The thing is to read good literature and cultivate things you're interested in and let the rest go hang, don't you think so?

Ha—I hear a Mercedes motor in the air—our friends the Austriaci are coming to visit us. There's something wonderfully exciting about the quiet sing song of an aeroplane overhead with all the guns in creation lighting out at it, and searchlights feeling their way across the sky like antennae, and the earth shaking snort of the bombs and the whimper of shrapnel pieces when they come down to patter on the roof. Almost as good as your skiing, which must be ripping.

About plans—I don't know in the slightest I never do. And, anyway, we're all galley-slaves now—No one has the slightest iota of liberty. Je m'en fous——

By the way get, in French if possible, Barbusses *Le Feu*—"Under Fire" in English translation. Its the only good book the war has produced—as I see it—the only book that has any frankness or fervor of portrayal.

Love—
Jack

I wish you were over here. I've been to Asolo-Browning's place. You'ld have loved it, I know Remember me to your mother.

[Diary]

[February 20, 1918]

A splendid ride yesterday—with light assis to some place miles beyond Carmignano—nearly to Vicenza. The rosy and the dust of the road with camions booming sudden & dark out of a smear of rosy, ash color sky clear blue, darkening overhead, and ground clear grey beneath. Then with the moonlight to Carmignano and on the avenue of great trees that runs from Cittadella to Vicenza. At Lisura the hospital had a great courtyard and a square machicolated tower, wonderful in the moonlight. After having delivered our wounded, we went to a small *trattoria* for dinner. All they had was eggs and cheese. There they served us with ceremonious white linen on a dark oak table, a slab of yellowish cheese & four eggs sur le plat in olive oil. There was a great and merry crowd of villagers and soldiers *in reposo* that enquired and wondered and applauded until we thought ourselves a seven day's marvel. Fairbanks made a great impression by producing his two knives. At the long dark table opposite us was a wonderful group of peasants two men with reddish nobbly faces—as if hastily made out of clay and between them a radiantly beautiful boy who looked like a St. John in a Last Supper—He had exactly the Lord's Supper way of talking, leaning far towards the man he was talking to and showing us his clear profile—just as the apostles do—as he talked he made fine excited gestures with his hands. The girls who waited on us were rosy large-breasted creatures, handsome and healthy like clean white cows with huge udders, Hathors of women—The whole place was so wonderfully clean and lively and happy——After the mesquine misery of the front, the shitten, lousy, filthy smelling barracks, the tired illfed soldiers . . . God it was a window thrown open upon the possibilities of life!

Coming home, in my elation at the moonlight and the straight road between trees and the astringent red wine and the joyousness of the tavern—I ran the unfortunate Fiat 4 plunk into the back of a wagon —result a much bent mudguard—a feeling of annoyed shame, despite the consolations of F. joyous at their being proved superior—car!—you not F—We ran home, running like a Ford instead of like a Fiat . . . this morning the faithful Tonda is taking off the steering gear to straighten it.

Feb 22nd [1918]

Trips by day and night to many distant places—Carmignano, San Pietro de Gre, Brasanvido and all manner of small hospitals in great country houses, beautiful spacious places with loggias and courtyards. Those that aren't overornamented are positively stunning.

So much service that for days I've done no writing and not even read my portion of Boccaccio or gone to talk Italian with the pleasant major down in the Hospedaletto.

Letters have taken up my little spare time & sleep and great egg-parties. The food has finally become unbearable and we make up by having huge feeds of eggs—fried, boiled, shirred, scrambled and indeterminate. The egg is undoubtedly the rex and imperator of foods.

Even the sight of the Galleries Lafayette would delight me, so nostalgic am I for Paris.

Volupta in Zabaglione

Champagne-colored,
Deepening to tawnyness,
As the throats of nightingales,
Strangled for Nero's supper

Champagne colored
Like the Coverlet of Dudloysha
At the Hotel Continental.

Thick to the lips and velvety,
Scented of rum and vanilla,
Oversweet, oversoft, overstrong,
Fall of a froth of fascination . . .

Drink the drink of Isoldes,
Globular recumbent Isoldes,
Sunk in champagne colored couches
While Tristans with fairflowing hair
And round cheeks rosy as cherubs
Stand and stretch their arms
And let their great slow tears
Roll and fall
And plash in the huge gold cups.

And behind the scenes, with his sleeves rolled up
Kurwenal beats the eggs
Grandeloquently

Into spuming symphonic splendor
Champagne colored . . .

Red nosed gnomes roll and tumble
Tussle & jumble in the firelight.
Roll on their backs
Spinning rotundly
And drink out of earthen jars
Gurgling gloriously
Wriggling their huge round bellies—
And the air of the cave is heavy
With steaming Marsala and rum
And hot bruised vanilla . . .

Champagne colored, one lies in a velvetiness
Of yellow moths stirring faintly tickling wings
One is heavy and full of languor, champagne colored
And sleep is a champagne colored coverlet,
The champagne colored stockings of Venus . . .

And later
One goes
And pukes beautifully beneath the moon,
Champagne-colored.

from Jan 24*th*
recopied

Feb 24th, 25, or is it 26th? [1918]
Again am I fallen on evil days—sitting in a dirty courtyard in the front of my car because there is no where else to sit—with a smell of bad pipes, of gasoline, of mule dung and of the Italian army—Then the noises are all unpleasant, sounds of tin cans full of oil, of motors running, of tools jingling, of people hammering iron things . . . and, oh God—we are here for three days—Its a day of brilliant sunshine and azure and the mountains are a dry dun color—a rather tiresome high noon sort of a dun color.

The only thing to do is to watch the camions climbing Grappa—like black cockroaches—

To José Giner Pantoja, *whom Dos apparently first met in Spain in the fall of 1916. Dudley Poore, who met Giner when he was in Spain after World War I, thought Giner to be somewhat older than he and Dos and remembered him as belonging to "a family with a long tradition of liberal sympathies—liberal in the 19th century English sense of parliamentary government." Giner was a devout Catholic, had a great interest in architecture and painting, and knew most of the distinguished Spanish artists and scholars of the period. He supported the Republic, so when that fell he escaped to France, where he lived in exile. Dos lost track of him in 1949.*

[Bassano
February–March 1918]

Mon cher ami:

Pardonnez moi une autre lettre mal et hativement ecrite. Encore j'aurais voulu ecrire en espagnole, mais l'idee me donne une peur bleu, car j'aime tant votre belle langue, que ca me ferait bien de peine de l'ecrire a l'italienne. Lisant et parlant l'italian tout le temps que je suis ici, je crois que si j'avais ecrit en espagnole, je ne reussirais a faire qu'un melange funeste.

Ici, sur ce point calme, ou l'on a tant de temps, en attendant dans la pluie, dans les cours des hopitaux, ou dans les ambulances sentant de carbolique, je pense tres souvent a vous et aux belles plaines de Castille. Deloin, ca doit apparaitre un peu theorique la guerre, mais ici, ou n'importe ou sur le front, je vous assure que c'est tout autre chose. C'est l'ennui, l'esclavege a toutes les stupidites militaires, la misere la plus interessante, le besoin de chaleur, de pain, de proprete. Il n'y a rien de beau dans la guerre moderne, je vous assure. J'y ai vecu pour un an maintenant, et bien des illusions se sont alles vers le fleuve du Styx. Ce n'est plus qu'un digression enorme, tragique dans la vie des peuples.

C'est plutot a vous autres, dans les pays qui sont au dessus de la melee, c'est a vous qui rests l'oeuvredu progres de cette pauvre civilization tourmentee de nos jours. Pour toutes les choses d'intelligence pour l'art et pour tout ce qu'il faut dans le monde, la guerre—une guerre moderne je veux dire—c'est la mort. Et au dela de ces choses la, qu'est ce qu'il y a qui vaut dans le monde? Non, c'est a vous, qui faites tranquillement et tumultueusement des revolutions, qui essayez, vainement peutetre, d'envolververs un but la vie de nos jours, c'est a vous qui rest de saufguarder toutes les belles choses de l'humanite, pendant que nous autres, nous luttons brutalement, avec un acharnement de suicide. Pourquoi? Pour des mensonges, meme pour des verites, pour les nations lites avares d'un monde ivre de commerce

J'ai bien peur que vous autre Espagnoles idealisent un peu ce vilain monde de l'Europe et de l'Amerique-monde en . . . . . . peutetre, mais, Grand Dieu, vers quel but? Partout il me pariat, on ne trouve que l'esclavage, a l'industrie, a l'argent, au mommon de business, le grand dieu de nos jours—chez les riches et les pauvres. Et ou dans tout cela, se trovent les bells choses? les choses qui font de la vie quelque chose de plus qui transcendent la lutte pour le ventre, pour l'existance.

C'est seulement chez vous en Espagne et en Russie, il me parait, que la conquete n'est pas tous a fait accomplie—c'est un peu pour cela que j'adore tant l'Espagne.

Et mon pauvre pays . . . il me parait qu'avec la guerre, et avec le passage de la loi de service militaire, la liberte y est eteinte pour long-temps, et le jour de triomphe de la plutacratie est venu.

A propos il y a maintenant a Madris un de mes meilleurs amis— Arthur McComb—qui etant antimilitariste im . . able, a fallu quitter les Etats Unis, et qui restera, je pense, longtemps en Espagne. C'est un garcon tres intelligent et tres aimable, et j'ai pris la liberte de lui dire d'aller vous voir, parce que je savais qu'il n'y avait personne en Espagne qui pouvait lui donner tant de renseignments que vous. Par-donnez masans-facon, qu'on peut attribuer a l'impolitesse americains, d'ailleurs je n'ai jamais pu m'habituer aux convenances, meme en Amerique.

Je scrai enormement content de recevoir une de vos lettres si charmantes. Mon address est soins Consolato Americano, C.R.A. Sezione l. Au revoir, votre tres bon ami.

[This is the letter, transcribed with Bates' errors and omissions, which caused Dos Passos to be threatened with a dishonorable dis-charge from the Red Cross. Appended to the letter is the notation of "Bates to Lowell," both Red Cross officers:

Bates to Lowell.
My own strong opinion is that the writer should be dishonorably dis-charged. He belonged in the Section to a group of Pacifists, some of whom are now in Rome. In spite of my repeated warnings, a general notice on the subject, the example of Heine who was discharged from their section, this man has still endangered the cordial relations existing between us and the Italians. I have no sympathy for him. It is about time we had another object lesson. If circumstances had demanded my action, I should have discharged him.

Of course we have no reason for action in the cases of the men with him, except that knowing their pacificist ideas we need not give them further employment in the American Red Cross.]

[Translation of Dos' letter to Pantoja]
My Dear Friend,

Forgive me for another badly and hastily written letter. Again I would rather have written in Spanish, but the idea puts me in a blue funk because I love your beautiful language so much it would be very painful to make it read like Italian. Having been reading and speaking Italian all the time I've been here, I know that if I had written in Spanish I would have succeeded only in producing a miserable mélange.

Here, in this quiet place, where one has so much time, while waiting in the rain, in the yards of hospitals, or in ambulances smelling of carbolic, I think often of you and the lovely plains of Castile. From a distance the war must seem a little theoretical, but here, or anywhere at the front, I assure you it is a wholly different matter. It is boredom, slavery to all the military stupidities, the most fascinating misery, the need for warmth, bread, and cleanliness. I assure you there is nothing beautiful about modern war. I have lived in it for a year now, and many illusions have crossed the river Styx. It is nothing but an enormous, tragic digression in the lives of these people.

Rather it is for you people, you who inhabit those countries that are above the battle, to assume the struggle for progress on behalf of this wretched and tormented civilization of ours. For all the things of the mind, for art, and for everything that is needed in the world, war—I mean modern war—is death. And beyond those things, what is there on earth that is worth anything? No, it's up to you, who can make revolutions either quietly or violently, who are trying vainly, perhaps, to evolve a purpose for the life of our times, it is up to you to safeguard all the finest human things, while the rest of us struggle on brutally with suicidal madness. Why? For lies, even for some truths, for greedy nations in a world drunk on commercialism.

I am very much afraid that you Spaniards are a little idealistic about this evil European world and about America, in . . . perhaps, but Great God, to what end? Everywhere it seems to me there is nothing, either for the rich or the poor, but slavery; to industry, to money, to the mammon of business, the great God of our times. And where in all that are the good things to be found? The things that give life an added dimension, that go beyond the struggle to fill the belly, for mere existence.

It seems to me that only in your Spain and in Russia is the conquest not quite complete—it is in part because of that I love Spain so much.

And my own poor country—it seems to me that with the war, with the military service law, liberty there is extinguished for a long time to come, and the day of triumph for plutocracy has arrived.

In this connection, one of my best friends is now in Madrid—Arthur McComb—who, being an unshakable anti-militarist, has had to leave the United States and will stay in Spain, I think, for a long time. He is an intelligent fellow and very likable, and I have taken the liberty of telling him to go to see you, because I knew that there was no one in Spain who could give him as much information as you. Excuse my informality, which you may credit to American rudeness. Besides, I have never been able to get used to convention, even in America.

I would be extremely pleased to get one of your charming letters. My address is care of Consolato Americano, C.R.A. Sezione I. Au revoir, your very good friend.

Diary—"Inaugurated Feb. 26th at Romano Alto"
[Borso, March 4, 1918]
By the way last night I, ass that I am, took a dare of Fairbanks's & having already drunk considerable Marsala without eating anything—on returning miserably cold and wet from one of those damned evacuations to Carmignano—said dare being to drink a full bottle of Marsala unaided—The litre bottle was sent for and I guzzled it—rather unwillingly—It gave me a feeling of being padded with velvet all over—I read Cope's letter to the assembled multitude. The Marsala gave it the depth and color of stained glass—a slight kaleidoscope effect was noticeable in the swirl of sensation. Then I read Hertha tumultuously—*Heap cassia buds*. Then as one started to go to bed, suddenly like releasing a spring—everything whirled, and it went on whirling, particularly the bed . . . Bassano whirled and the campanile bobbed like a minuet eructairt . . . Then Fairbanks to prove he was sober—crawled into the room like an Indian scout—wriggling on his belly among the debris of a jampot I'd upset in my evolutions—laughter dissolved into sleep with a sensation like going down a shoot the chute.

Its awfully funny the way I was seized at times with feelings of utter blankness. At this moment I very much want to write a poem—to draw, to do something—but a certain deadness—perhaps the deadness of cold and damp—muffles everything—I'll read Cellini and try to lose myself there—Or shall I walk down to the car and get my Leopardi—

For two solid hours I've been mooning about trying to decide—what puddingheadedness—Why not write some verse though? I'm sure I'd write excellent verse at this moment—wouldn't I?

> Like a dream I'll beat a tune
> On the belly of the moon

Smoke rising.
Blue of the peace of the faded day . . .

Black smoke and brown,
That turbulent swirls
From dark lines of chimney-pots,
Blocks and rows and clusters of chimney-pots,
Chimney-pots hooded, angled, fantastic.

Smoke settling,
Black, sootladen,
About the roofs of the city
That jut out of the pool of night
Into the warm purpurate gloaming;
About the towers and steeples and great girdered bridges
And tall factory chimneys flaunting smoke gaudily,
Smoke spreading in huge blood-tinged spirals,
Grasping with shadowy coils, and claws
Spread like dragons' claws
Against the red sky
Over the city.

Lamps are strings of amber beads,
Intricately twined,
Gold thread of a net,
In which wither the great caught dragon
Of brown darkness

On the streets,
The loud resounding streets,
Footsteps of people marching,
Of men and women and children,

With clatter of worn-out boots
And dragging rustle of rags,
Mud spattered, crowded, advancing . . .
Hoarse whispers rise in the streets,
Grow loud and shout in a tumult of talk
And wail away
Into the continuous tramp
Of feet marching, advancing . . .

In the dark loft the bats stir,
And flutter away, squeaking faintly,
Into the brown smoke-soaked darkness.

A stroke,
And the dark air quivers
With reeling clangor of bells,
The steeples sway,
And the great square towers.
Bells sound the tocsin,
Jangle and throb,
Wide mouths of bronze
Swing and wheel.
The bell-jangle whirls in huge coils,
Quivering scarlet dragons in coils,
That fill the sky and the streets
And writhe among the people,—
Agony of clanging tongues of bronze.

They murmur in the great squares of the city,
They march with the feet in the thoroughfares,
They jangle with shattering of glass and of street lamps
And are lost in the rise of flames
That mocking, roar
And lick the brown dark away
Disclosing cornices, smashed doors, blank windows
Windows steaming reflection of fire and crowds,
And faces,
Packed like graves,
Dappled with flare and shadow,
Round like coins spread on a gambling table,
Upturned amazed white faces . . .
In their eyes the red tongues lick and glitter,
In their ears the roar
And the bronze agony of bells,

The tramp of those marching,
The chant domineering,
   of trumpets

White frightened faces,
Footsteps ringing down the empty streets
Terror of silence and dark
Under the red bronze sky.
Dragons of flame leap
Sear the sky with wide yellow wings
Beat scarlet tongues
Against the vaulted dark
And in the streets and houses
And the packed squares where the people troop
Aimlessly to and fro
The great form of the darkness
Writhers and shivers
Brooding under the fear.
People trooping
In lines like ants to and fro
Under the hard bronze sky
Between black houses.

People in terror
Of footsteps down the clanging streets
Scuttle like cockroaches
And slink into the cellars
Cuddling into the ancient dark

The bells hang silent,
Quivering still,
And the bats flutter back to their places.
The grey inevitable dawn
Thins to nothing
The swirling dragons of smoke,
Smother the turbid sky to blue.

                                        Borso—March 4

And lick the brown dark away,
Disclosing tottering cornices
Eyeless blank of windows
Doors that gape like snarled mouths—
Everywhere windows

Glaring reflection of fire and crowds
And faces
                              etc—
Les p'tites marionnettes
Font, font, font
Trois petit tours
Et puis s'en vont

March 6th [1918]
Borso again rain again—Damn all condensed milk—I ate it in chocolate last night and as a result have a feeling of having a very tinny can
of it in the middle of my gullet—

   The gleaming putty color of the roads—with yellow twigs straight &
stiff with rising spring on either side—drenched mules black—hooked
shoes dripping gleaming putty colored mud at every step—

To Rumsey Marvin

                                                        [Borso]
                                                  March 6 [*1918*]

                      Le Jour de Gloire est Arrivée
         Smoke rising
         Blue of the peace of the faded day . . .

         Black smoke and brown
         That turbulent swirls
         From dark lines of chimney pots
         Blocks and rows and clusters of chimney pots,
         Chimney-pots hooded, angled, fantastic.

         Smoke settling,
         Black, soot laden,
         About the roofs of the city
         That jut out of the pool of night
         Into the warm purpurate gloaming;
         About the towers and steeples and great girdered bridges
         And tall factory chimneys flaunting smoke gaudily,
         Smoke, spreading in huge blood-tinged spirals,
         Grasping with shadowy coils, and claws
         Spread like dragons' claws
         Against the red sky
         Over the city.

Lamps are strings of amber beads,
Intricately twined,
Gold thread of a net
In which writhes the great caught dragon
Of brown darkness.

On the streets,
The loud resounding streets,
Footsteps of people marching,
Of men and women and children,
With clatter of worn-out boots
And dragging rustle of rags,
Mud spattered, crowded, advancing . . .

Hoarse whispers rise in the streets,
Grow loud and shout in a tumult of talking,
And wail away
Into the continuous tramp
Of feet marching, advancing . . .

In the dark loft the bats stir,
And flutter away, squeaking faintly,
Into the brown smoke-soaked darkness.

A stroke,
And the dark air quivers
With reeling clangor of bells.
The steeples sway,
And the great square towers.
Bells sound the tocsin,
Jangle and throb,
Wide mouths of bronze
Swing and wheel
The bell-jangle whirls in huge coils
Quivering scarlet dragon coils
That fill the sky and the streets
And writhe among the people—
Agony of clanging tongues of bronze.

They murmur in the great squares of the city,
They march with the feet in the thoroughfares,
They jangle with shattering of glass and of street lamps,
And are lost in the rise of flames,
That mocking, roar
And lick the brown dark away

Disclosing tottering cornices,
And eyeless blank of windows
And doors gaping like smashed mouths——
Everywhere windows
Glaring reflection of fire and clouds,
And faces,
Packed like gravel,
Dappled with flare and shadow,
Round like coins spread on a gambling table,
Upturned amazed white faces—
In their eyes the red tongues lick and glitter,
In their ears the roar,
And the bronze agony of hills,
The tramp of those marching
And the chant domineering
Of trumpets.

White frightened faces,
Footsteps ringing down the empty streets,
Terror of silence and dark
Under the red bronze sky.

Dragons of flame leap,
Sear the sky with wide yellow wings,
Beat scarlet tongues
Against the vaulted dark.

And, in the streets and houses
And the packed squares where the people troop
Aimlessly to and fro,
The great form of the darkness
Writhes and shivers,
Brooding under the fear.

People trooping
In lines like ants to and fro
Under the hard bronze sky
Between the black houses

People in terror
Of footsteps down the clanging streets
Scuttle like cockroaches
And slink into cellars,
Cuddling into the ancient dark.

The bells hang silent,
Quivering still,
And the bats flutter back to their places . . .
The grey inevitable dawn
Thins to nothing
The swirling dragons of smoke,
Smooths the turbid sky to blue.

Ecco! Master Rummy—here's a poem for you—It may be good and it may be bad. God rest its soul in peace.

You poor chump, Rummy, why in hells name take a course in military tactics or whatever the blooming thing is. You dont think the Goddamned war is going to last forever do you?

College courses were inane enough in the old days—but—God! Military Tactics—for three years! Imagine anything staler, flatter, more unprofitable.

I admit that it doesn't matter much what you take; you do your own educating outside—but, Holy Jerusalem, Sacred Swine of St Anthony! Military tactics! Be sensible—even if every one else in that godforsaken country has lost his head completely—Just imagine—Fortifications 1, Rape 4b, Poison Gas 11, History of Bayonets 6—Imagine anything more stale flat and unprofitable! Why go to college at all—if not to study the humanities?

Three years military training at Yale——damn it man, America's not Prussia (Or is it?). Come over and see the war if you want too—but in a—darn, what's the use of talking?

You dont know how utterly desperate the idea makes me of having every bit of America militarized—If you knew the boredom and brutality and stupid dirtiness of military life——

Forgive the tirade——

love
Jack

[Diary]
March 10th [1918]
Again a day in view of the Brenta and the Piave, above Borso—Climbed up in the Campanile at Borso where the clock ticks away—a beautiful piece of beaten ironwork—simple and with a sure dignity—like the law of gravitation or one of those simple rigorous thoughts of men like Galileo or Archimedes.

At Cánolo—where the little Tempio de Canova is—we took a walk
about with the Torenese Captain—an intelligent man with a large nose
and sensitive impatient features. He says that three nations will win the
war, while all the rest are beaten = England, Germany and the United
States—He denies that the 10 socialist deputies were arrested before
war was declared—He has no illusions of alliedship—By the way what
particularly annoyed him was that the British artillery had been unnec-
essarily destroying Italian villages held by the Austrians. Its funny, to
us he's awfully pleasant and polite, yet as soon as he talks to an inferior
he becomes a regular Tartar—His ideas of Puccini are interesting. He
and a sentimental little dark lieutenant had a wild argument about
him—Puccini—he says should be heard with a large cigar in your
mouth, a newspaper to read in the dull moments and an armchair to
go to sleep in. Then he said that Italy was famous for three things
D'Annunzio because he was immoral, Caruso because he was a bad
singer, Marinetti because he was mad.

Lucenza—March 16th [1918]
Just out of Bologna—a smoky train—frightfully crowded—outside one
can see vague outlines of the Apennines and a few stars—
    Bologna—orange houses and green shutters—great smooth wall-
places of orange and umber and pale yellow and grey—and brick
arcades and carved windows—and in the midst the drunken leaning
towers—The red tower of the Asinelli shooting heavenwards with a
wonderful soar—leaning confidentially towards its neighbor as Anteus
hung over Hercules—says Dante
    Then the Duomo and the Palace where Enzio was imprisoned—and
the church of Santo Stepano—The little round temple of brick—inlaid
with beautiful marble mosaic outside—with old columns of pagan
temples and a great old marble altar under which is the sarcophagus of
Santo Petronio—
    A most wonderful little old woman—a little old woman with a black
shawl and a slow priestly walk and a wonderful way of talking French
& Italian with an occasional popped English word—all spiced with the
most thickly rolled 'r's imaginable—she told us everything in a little
drawling voice with comical sceptical undertones. Santo Petronio came
from Constantinople: 'fu un turco' and she stuck out her tongue
quickly as a lizard—Later in the crypt showing us the gilded sarcophagus on the altar into which the remains of San Vitale and Sant'

Agricola had been transferred from the two great stone sarcophagi—
the basilica of Peter and Paul next door—Mais dedans il n'y a pas
grand' chose. Then later in the crypt of the church there was a little
marble pillar supposed to be the exact height of our savior Jesus
Christ—mais vous savez on dit beaucoup de choses.

2nd day
Cramped, cabined, cribbed, confined in uncomfortable & unholy slum-
bers on the packedest train ever invented—

The black outlines of the Apennines slipping by in a night of sparse
stars . . .

Awoke near Rome. Walked about vaguely in the morning—In the
afternoon went in a cab to the casale Rotunda on the Appian Way—A
wonderfully soothing afternoon with the shadowy mellowness of the
Campagna and the procession of tombs on either hand, huge cores of
gone pomposity, bits of vault and cornice, remnants of stiff Roman
ladies and gentlemen—in grey stone—every now and then the carriage
pitched and jolted out some of the old stones of the Roman road—

Tea at Latours—(memory of the last time I was in Rome & the
deBeers)

And a hasty planning of escape from the incubi.

3rd day
Piazza di Spagna with the flowermarket and the house of Keats &
Shelley—

The Pantheon

Escape to Naples—long afternoon sitting on our bags in the corridor of
the railway carriage, crowded, as usual. First through the shadowy
Alban hills and the faint green and tan landscape of Romagna, then
through a wide flat valley in the Apennines, the mountains getting
rougher and bleaker all the time. Past Monte Cassino—out on to the
lower Campagne of Capua. Then a craning at Vesuvius who was
sending up big puffs of white smoke—and Naples—in time to walk
hurriedly through town—go up in the Posilipo lift and pop into a
marvellous sunset view of dark mountains and the sea and of gleaming
silver-lavender.

4th day
A walk about Naples in the early morning—ugly lively streets and
flowers and a breakfast of coffee and something very like churros

Museum—alas.

Van Dudley & I leave for Sorrento—Jack refusing to be dragged
away from Napoli. No boat—We go to Pompeii instead and wander
delightfully about the ruins in a sparkling wind full of the odor of
almond blossoms.

5th day March 21?
Pompeii—The rinae of the Forum—The statue of Artemus in the
temple of Apollo
    The house of the Vettii Puery Roman taste—apropos of the man
weighing his penis against a money bag in the vestibule of the house of
the Vettii?
    The Villa of Diomede
    The House of the Amorini
    Then the beautiful tomb outside the Vesuvius gate with the four
sculptures on the sides—
    Walk hungrily to Castellammare—There had lunch & trolley very
slowly & squeakingly to Meta—from there one of the most glorious
walks in my life to Positano.
    Indescribable
    Positano is as beautiful as Denia
    There the best dinner ever with wine like liquid rubies

Some things are too fine to write about——

To Rumsey Marvin

Albergo del Sole-Pompeii
March 21 [*1918*]

Dear Rummy——
    What do you think of that? And of Vesuvius outside the window,
steaming hugely through a rain cloud——
    I'm on leave—and am crowding as much galivanting about Italy
as possible into fourteen days.
    We came out from Naples yesterday—and after wandering about
the ruins a little more—we are going to walk to Castellammare—there
take the train for Sorrento and then walk again to Amalfi. At present
matters are held up by a slight rain storm—
    Rummy you ought to be here
    Positano—night after dinner Oh Rummy—one of the most glori-

ous days I've ever spent—Morning in Pompeii—Then we walked to
Castellammare for lunch—from there to Sorrento by trolley then
walked to Positano on the way to Amalfi, along a road that hung on the
cliffs above the sea—Almond blossoms, anemones—oh I can't describe
things—They were too marvellously beautiful

I dont think—except Denia that I must have told you about—that
I've ever been in a town so beautiful as Positano. I'm overwhelmed and
smothered in beauty—sight and smell and the soft wind off the sea in
your ears——Also I have had one of the best dinners ever invented—
risotto, omelet, cheese & such oranges as I think the "apples" of the
Hesperides must have been—and wine——a light red wine—a wine
full of the brisk hills and the great exhilarating spaces of the sea, and
the smell of thyme and gorse and almond blossom and rosemary and
basil and lavender from the fields that make little ribbons of velvet
among the shaggy rocks.

Cetara

Rummy—

Waiting for a dinner to cook itself after a huge day's walking—We
walked from Positano to Amalfi—Then up to Ravello—then from
Ravello round Capo d'brio to Cetara and Vietri. Then we took the
train next morning for Paestum—where there are the remains of
three very early Greek temples from the ancient Poseidonia, a colony of
Sybaris—The huge doric temple of Poseidon, a glorious burnt orange—
with all the cinnamon richness of thousands of suns——The temples
lie in the middle of a solitary plain near the sea—(where we bathed on
a wonderful beach) with the mountains behind them. We spent the
whole day there—I in the state of prostrate worship Greek things
always put me into. Then we went back to Naples and now I am
writing in the Hotel Continental in Rome.

Love
Jack

[Diary]
March 31st [1918]
The sad day—the day of our homing like good little pigeons, the
fourteenth day having elapsed, we return to the sectional roost—

Florence—drab olive grey with bright green shutters and the preposterous icing of the Duomo—green, pink and white in the center and

Brunelleschi beautiful red dome—dominating the roofs and the dainty tower and the castellated squares of the Barjello and the Signoria

The Pollainolo fresco in the cloisters of Santa Maria Novella—of the Deluge and of people sacking a city
The Judith of Donatello
All San Marco & particularly Christ being received as a pilgrim—
And the Ponte Vecchio on a rainy night

The ceremony of the dove that propells it self by emitting fire from its rear end—After a miracle there must be the same fascinating odor of fireworks—

News of the Death of Claude Debussy

Rome—The Appian Way and the funny stiff Roman ladies and gentlemen and the tombs along the Road——

The golden honey of the sun——
The fritturas one eats
The little streets and the pleasant people and the indolence of infinite age——

San Clemente—the Apse—
The basilicas & their mutilated mosaics.
The joyful liveliness of early Christian painting.

Contrast with the awful pomposity of the Roman Empire—
The Pantheon—the rayed arches in the Roman brickwork—

The wonderful leisure of Rome—never shoving forward into your vision effortlessly impressing you with the seal of its ancient power—
On the way to Naples we looked up wistfully at the monastery of Monte Cassino——

Naples——

Pompeii—The newly discovered tomb outside the city—The Louis XV atmosphere of Pompeiian decoration——
But golly the beauty of incidental decoration and of small bronzes—

The Albergo del Sole & the first Lyric Meal since Paris——

The phalluses & the whore houses—The copulations the best drawn things in Pompeii

The penis lamp tripod in the Naples Museum——
The magic wine at the hilltop above Sorrento and the subsequent enchanted coast——
The Arabian nights and the hotel reached by climbing streets and stairs and steep vineyards and at last a spiral staircase with a dog on it.
Come back at once to America. Horrid thought giving me cold *shivers* I'll be damned if I'll do it though—it seems that Cyril [Dos Passos, a cousin] & Louis [Dos Passos, Dos' half brother] & Co refuse to renew *the agreement*—The joke is that I can't for the life of me remember what the agreement is—its something about the administering of the Estate goddamn it—but what I have no idea——

To Rumsey Marvin

[Bassano
April 1918]

Harlequinade
*Par le chemin des aventures
Ils vont, haillonneux et hagards.*
[from "Grotesques," by Paul Verlaine]

Shrilly whispering down the lanes
that serpent through the ancient night,
they, the scoffers, the scornful of chains,
stride their turbulent flight.

The stars spin steel above their heads
In the shut irrevocable sky.—
Gnarled thorn-branches tear to shreds
their cloaks of pageantry.

A wind blows bitter in the grey,
chills the sweat on throbbing cheeks,
and tugs the gaudy rags away
from their lean bleeding knees.

Their laughter startles the scarlet dawn
among a tangled spiderwork

of girdered steel, and shrills forlorn
and dies in the rasp of wheels.

Whirling amazed, like gay prints that whirl
in tatters of squalid gaudiness,
borne with dung and dust in the swirl
of wind down the endless street,

with their lips laughing bitterly,
through the day smeared in sooty smoke
that pours from each red chimney,
they speed unseemily.

Bent women with thin unlustered hair,
men with huge ugly hands of toil,
children, impudently stare
and point derisive hands.

Only—where a barrel organ thrills
two small thin-chested girls to dance,
and among the iron clatter spills
a swiftening rhythmy song,

they march in velvet, silk slashed hose,
strumming guitars and mellow lutes,
strutting pointed Spanish toes,
a stately company. . . .

The cold wind shrills down the screaming
discord of toiling wheels and dank street
of harness strained and tramp of feet,
dragged on pavement-stones,

and bears them off in jumbled flight
with cries of children and laughter of dance
to merge in the shout of triumphing might
that rumbles down the roads . . .

Roads which with untired stride
and turbulent laughter the scorners spurn,
and journey across the country-side,
breaking the fences down.

Till the laughter dies on each white lip;
they shiver prone on the grassless bank,
and through their frippery the whip
of the winter northwind stings.

Before them in the dun dry path
frozen the pale gold primroses fade
that inopportune have burst the spathe
remembering balmier springs . . .

Their frail warm yellow fades to grey
beneath the shut irrevocable sky
that ironcold crushes out the day
grey of a dead man's eye.

Rummy! *W*hile trying to get my nerve up to do some writing I shall write something to you with the enclosed poem—by the way, what do you think of it?

An awfully nice letter from you was waiting for me when I got back from licenza—

The Harder Part: A Question of Sacrifice—sounds dangerously like the Y.M.C.A.—they do pump so much twaddle into one at American schools—so much watery heroics—that I doubt if even an essay of yours with that title can escape getting sloppy—

I'm awfully glad you've decided to get educated—(if you think college'll do that for you, you've got another guess coming, but, still . . .) For God's sake take a decent unpractical course and there'll be plenty of time to get into the war afterwards—Take everything unwarlike & unbusinesslike you can lay your paws on—you'll get the other stuff packed into you with force pumps as it is.—Gee this is a regular sermon—do forgive me, but voices have to be raised in the wilderness against the Babylonish asininity of everything in the blooming country of ours.

Apropos of Macaulay—have you read Swift—he's the person for style—according to my way of thinking—not that you ought to imitate anybody—the only way to get style is, I vow, to try to avoid it, to take no thought for it, to try to express what you have to say as richly and meaningfully and briefly as possible and let luck do the rest——Still hobnobbing with good style in your reading does help—and the daily papers and current literature shows you about everything you ought not to do.

What the devil d'you want such a bloody lot of training for anyway? I swear—you people in America are daft on the subject— Training does nothing but eradicate original ideas and stultify the mind to the state of a drill-sergeant.

I've gone quite dippy about early Italian fresco painting—God I've never seen such gorgeous, unimaginably interesting decoration as those people—even the rather poor ones could do—from Giotto to Botticelli—with Raphael all Italian painting seems to go to smash in vapid banality and a coloratura sort of ease. Then the sculpture in Florence of Donatello & Verrocchio is as great as anything Greek—in Michelangelo—in sculpture—is supreme—O my permission was a riot of it all and of large dinners and good wines and scents of Italian spring.

The coast from Sorrento to Salerno—down which we walked—is so plumb beautiful one cant talk of it. A changing peacock sea—splendid as the Odyssey, mountains, towns like strange adventures in the Arabian Nights, ruined churches and palaces of the Normans—— Amalfi, and Ravello far up among the azure, and then at the end, the plain and hills of Hellenic blue and the temple of Poseidon at Paestum. The temple—on a plain, near a wide beach where the galleys used to be drawn up in double rows—is quite the most beautiful building I've ever seen. We bathed on the beach and spent all day jus' lookin'

And now I'm back at my usual window looking down the swollen river at the towers and the covered bridge and the huge scroll-like clouds piled above the town——

By the way—after April 20—send letters to Morgan Harjes again—

Love
Jack

Thanks immensely for the W.S. Gilbert—Its just come and it's a joy—I've always loved the Mikado & the Pirates as much as nursery rhymes—You cant imagine what fun it is to have in this humorless part of the world——

[Diary]
April 7th [1918]
Ecco! Here am I, bored at Borso—Have finished my books, got disgusted with my novel—

April 8th [1918]
At Gherla—we were told to appear there early this morning & did—result—we wait in boredom for something to turn up—a rainy-blue grey & green day—The mountains are splendidly dark with ragged steamy clouds over them. There's a rather chilly wind in which the engine of the teleferica puffs and chugs amid a sound of steel cables. Have been

talking to a poor devil of a Genoese—who seems to have had a lot of brothers killed in the war, and whose mother died while he was on licenza—(The Italians do hold by family affection like the devil)—He had the usual sad story—the war—the officers were all bought—everything came by graft—camossa—He seemed quite borne down by the injustice of everything; he was a little drunk too, which helped. He'd deserted once but had been dragged back to the front—The army wasn't an army, it was a scandalo—Italy was a casino—a whore house—everything was bought and sold and the poor devils of soldiers died.

The war would only end when they'd killed everybody—everybody—he swayed drunkenly and waved his head towards the wide plain in which the green darkened into blue and blue grey on the horizon—quando tutt saranno morti, finirà la guerra—

Serable meglio un terremoto an earthquake, to kill us all outright—

He was going to get an English uniform & get into the English army—anywhere out of this misery—and the humiliation of being kicked and beaten by the officers—They didn't dare kick him though. He was dangerous.

In Genoa he'd seen lots of English they'd drunk together—He'd sold boots and clothes for them—stolen money—he said, opening his pocket book all stolen—from the govreno inglese—Then he showed me the usual little array of cards and photographs of dead brothers and scraps of ordini de movimento—

God it was pitiful.

Some day—soon—he said—I shall shoot an officer—Then it'll be all over—It'll be finished—he said rather in the tone of the end of Pagliacci—

A band's marching and playing along the road below and you can hear the sounds of camions bubbling along—and near at hand the cling-clang of the engine of the teleferica—

Gloire & Servitude Militaire

This is a rather suitable place to have read that curious little book—telling of the hollowness of old wars—O what a different word—de Vigny speaks of the military as a race apart—a race of gladiators hated and feared by the people of the country—And now the people are their own executioners, their own gladiators. The spectacle of the whole world lashed to war in dirty greyish uniforms——ordered about by the middle classes—the shape of petty officers, by the high financier spheres in the shape of generals & such canaille—would have nearly killed de Vigny—with his quaintly stiff ideas of the honor and shame of arms, with his ancient dragoons uniforms, so carefully brushed—and his monastic conception of the army—And where are gone his poor hopes of a warless future? The future is full of wars—of brutalizing slavery for all the young men in the world—and brutalizing dominance for the rich and the cunning and the well-convicted—

The strange little sentimental stories in de Vigny's book—with their curiously exciting frames of the retreat from Paris of Louis XVIII and the 1830 Revolution—really cover all of the Napoleonic sort of wars, where people fought for Kudos and for personal devotion and for strange outworn stupidities, but stupidities that had a charm and a halo of belief about them. The modern war for butchers and bakers and candlestick makers in which the trader has dressed himself up in the old outworn armor would be to the men of those days inconceivable.

At the bottom of all our nationalities—under the royal robes and the polished imperial helmets and the abstract talk of domination—are hidden the murky factory chimneys that are our world's God—

Boccaccio—I've just finished the fifth day—It is wonderful what a picture he gives you of his time, of the life of the merchants riding forth from the walled towns of Italy, of sea travel with its amusing interludes of Barbary pirates—of the cultured, Saracen-leaning courts of Frederick, and the Rogers in South Italy—heat and gardens and flowers, and lovely women in Kiosks—escaping through shuttered windows into the silk clad arms of their lovers while the shutter creaks in the scented night breeze and there comes on the wind a sound of breakers—a swift galley is waiting on the shore and the lovers lie naked in each others arms on piles of carpets in the stern, cooled by the faint spray borne on the hot breathing night wind—and the rowers row towards a dark orient city where they will land in pomp and all magnificence, and wander and lose themselves in strange streets, full of throat gripping odors, pale scents of flowers, cloying incense smoke and smell of secret lives behind latticed balconies—There they will have stranger adventures with robbers and princes—and return in the end to silken ease on some distant islands where they pass their last contented years to the sound of flutes and fountains, or else, come to violent gorgeous deaths, by flames or stabbing with an emerald handled dagger—

Of course people have always called out against the servitude of their lives, but we, today, do seem particularly enslaved.

Anything you read of or think of—seems to have had some escape in it, some escape from the humdrumness those in charge of the world would infect life with. There has never been a time when a person who despised & detested the world's phrases and turpitudes and heroisms was so utterly bound—for the slaves it's not a bad age; they live fast, have much kudos, and die in the miserable mud of the table lines. But for those who had thought to weave out of their lives something more delicate. . . .

4PM at Gherla—bored, mon ami, bored to tears—Oh God I want to go to sea, or to Greece or to Spain, or to glory—anywhere away from the Italian rear—I've been trying to draw—I cant draw—I want to novelize—I cant novelize—

I want exotic ultrathings—freedom—Home life—the right spirit

Search for the phrases of Americanism triumphant.

April 9th [1918]
Stuck in the damn mud hole of Borso—again the noise of wailing goeth up to heaven—I have no books and I'm bored—I'm bored and I have no books—was ever a creature more dependent on literature for life & stimulus—I can't live passively—God—I must be either on the move externally or internally via literature—I'm like a dope-fiend about it.

And here am I in Borso without a book—and we seem stuck here for an indefinite period. The lack of reading matter has induced me to peep inside the covers of magazines—always a bad thing to do—for it leaves you with a miserable mental nausea—Even for purposes of satire & collection of phrases—such utter mediocrity, such asinine revamping of conventional phrases—is absolutely sickening——I shall climb up the Campanile to write—

In Muselente, waiting for our captain to finish his business with the corpo d'armata, in a courtyard made delightful & noisy by a big mill-wheel—I am reading an asinine pamphlet by some mouthy French-man—on the great words of Napoleon.

La religion chrétienne sera toujours l'appui le plus solide de tout gouvernement assez habile pour savoir s'en servir. The old whited sepulchre God Bonaparte must have smiled when he said that—

In fact many of N's sayings resemble strikingly those of Barnum—the other great showman of a philosophic trend.

Apropos—in the de Vigny book—Napoleon's interview with Pope Benedict VII is marvellously well done—I think it was Benedict VII—

Afternoon
Seated at the top of my campanile at Borso with the clouds, grey marbled clouds of spring rain—and the silver thread of the Brenta flowing through the distance among blue grey hills——There's the plain green with purple gashes, then purple, then silver grey and far away opposite the Euganean Hills, the Hills that Shelley looked at from Venice—. All of which for some reason makes me think of the Auk—I shall write him—

Sacré mille cochons—in the middle of my letter a soldier's head appeared above the trap door in the floor and informed me that one wasn't allowed to climb up the campanile without a permesso—Damn their asinine rules—So I, cursing the military with a new curse with every rung of the ladder, climbed down—and finished the letter in our cantonment amid the noise of soldiers and soup kettles and the smell of the greasy soldier's food cooking outside and of their poor filthy bodies—

God the nastiness of the petty tyranny the war has plunged the world in—Everywhere in Europe—America—little bumptious sergeants are chasing poor devils off the steeples that afford them the only spots in a crowded world where they can think and look at their poor stock of dreams, the way a soldier pulls out and looks over lovingly the few grimy cards and passes and state papers he carries in his pocket book——

I wonder whether shooting an officer and finishing it as the man told me the other day he was going to do—isn't about the only Solution. It's humiliating to be alive . . . Nous sommes tous des poires, and God! What pityfully taken in, cowardly dupes we are. We half know we're being fooled, yet we haven't the courage to admit it to ourselves—so we follow the merry parade that is stifling in brutishness all the fair things of the world.

This is the feast of death
When we worship the drawn out agony
And the blood and pain of our gods'
            last breath

Good Friday 1918

This is the feast of death
When we make agony God
And pain's last choking breath
When we worship the nails and the rod
And the bleeding rack of the cross

Good Friday—in Florence
                at hearing of the death of Claude Debussy

This is the feast of death.
We make of our pain God.
We worship the nails and the rod,
and pain's last choking breath,
and the bleeding rack of the cross.
The women have wept away their tears;
With red eyes turned on death, and loss
of friends and kindred, have left the biers
flowerless, and bound their heads in their
                blank veils,
and climbed the steep slope of Golgotha; fails
at last the wail of their bereavement,
and all the jagged world of rocks and desert places
stands before their racked sightless faces
as any ice-sea silent.

This is the feast of conquering Death.
The beaten flesh worships the swishing rod.
The lacerated body bows to its God,
adores the last agonies of breath,
And one more has joined the unnumbered
death-struck multitudes,
who with the loved of old have slumbered
ages long where broods
the ultimate queen of quietness,
Earth the beneficient Goddess,
Taking all tired souls and bodies
back into her womb of the first nothingness.

But ours who in the iron night remain
Ours the need, the pain
Of your departing.
You had lived on out of a happier age
Into our strident torture cage
You still could sing
Of quiet gardens under rain
And clouds and the huge sky
And pale deliciousness that is nearly pain.
Yours was a new minstrelsy
Strange plaints brought home out of the rich east
Twanging songs from Tartar caravans
Hints of the sounds that ceased
With the casual dawn—wailings of the night
Echoes of the web of mystery that joins
The world between the failing of the hot day and the rising of the night
Of the sea and of a womans hair
Hanging gorgeous down a dungeon wall
love in the mist of old despair . . .

They were so few and one by one they go
leave us to our ongoing captivity
To our blank age of shame and agony
Death is a river in flood carrying all in its flow

But ours, who in the iron night remain,
Ours the loss, the pain
of his departing.
He had lived on out of a happier age
into our strident torture cage.
He still could sing
of quiet gardens under rain
and clouds and the huge sky,
and pale deliciousness that is nearly pain.
All to the tune of a new minstrelsy,
Strange plaints brought home out of the rich East,
Twanging songs from Tartar caravans;
hints of the sounds that ceased
with the stilling dawn, wailings of the night
Echoes of the web of mystery that spans
the world between the failing and rising of daylight;
of the sea and of a woman's hair
hanging gorgeous down a dungeon wall,

evening falling on Tintagel,
love lost in the mist of old despair . . .

Against the bars of our torture cage
We beat out our poor lives in vain
We live on cramped in an iron age
Like prisoners of old
High on the world's battlements
Exposed until we die to the chilling rain,
crowded and chattering from cold
For all men to stare at—
And we watch one by one the great,
Those who have spread some splendor round their lives
Stroll leisurely out of the western gate
And without a backward look at the strident city
Drink down the stirrup cup of fate
without solemnity
And ride the road of nothingness,
We worship the nails and the rod,
And pain's last choking breath
We make of our pain God
This is the feast of death

                                        April 10

April 16th [1918]
Have been reading Crime and Punishment. It is curious how reading it extinguishes ones proper life and makes one live only in the novel—I am trying to decide to start Part III of my affair. Virtually I only have three weeks to do it in—I must hurry—as yet I don't know how to start—I should like to gabble endlessly about my usual asininities . . .

The passage about the tiny black dots of the nomads' tents in the steppe in the end of Crime and Punishment . . .

Svidrigailov's talk with *Rodya Raskolnikov* about eternity

Part III
The agony of suffering of Crime & Punishment & The sudden whiff of the miseries of the world—Fibbie reads in the place where Rodya kisses the feet of Sonia—

The red haired girl at the cakeshop—what is her name by the way— He reads the passage to her, translating as he goes along—

The Lusitania

The slow realization of the oppression of government—

Begin Chap I with a talk with someone on the subject. The third way of looking at the world. Marx—the battle of the classes—The laughter Weston Nichols comes in quite a lot at first—goes home to England—Letter from him

Chap   I The oppression
"   II The War
"   III Crime & Punishment & the Red haired girl at the cake shop
"   IV The War—Conscription in England—
      V The Last Boredom of College
      VI New York

                      Fifth Avenue with flags on it—the glorious April Conscription
      VII The realization of slavery
      VIII the slave drivers—the Riot in the Bronx etc.
      IX Suzanne—her friend Revolt revolt & still revolt.

        The Laughter Police raid

        The Vita nova feeling—on the boat—the dock with uniform and a band playing and people dancing about among the luggage and everyone getting drunk—

                   Second Avenue

The idolization of action

Then on through growing cloud of depression—broken by boisterous joyous excitement—

                Pictures of the war front

                Opposing all the strident ugliness of life glimpses of Paris—talks with soldiers—the man from Bordeaux with the long whiskers.

The old woman who had lived for a year on potatoes

Man's description of running a bayonet into somebody—The drunken party in the cart—Revolution

Pinard—cigarettes

                                    La ginolle

The man who sang at Givry—

Night under gas—

The shelled roads

The incident of the drunken drivers . . . He has come to die with us.

The talk at the little village near Givry—over champagne.
Atrocities—the mountain of lies—

Part III
Beginning with the first realizings of human slavery—via Crime & Punishment & the red haired woman—
Works up gradually to an overwhelming sense of the slavery of our time—2nd Avenue—Conscription Riots—Salvation Army—a man talking in a whining voice of the wrongs of India.
Then the war—enters with Weston Nichols' death.

joins the slavery-motif—becomes the great experiment of the mountain of lies.
The depression culminates in it—and in the little glimpses through the overwhelming darkness of his world as it might be—even of other's world—were they just a little less slaves

Suzanne in New York—has 'gone red'—is working in a milliners—
Aretino's motto was Veritas odium parit.

April 17th [1918]
Finished a nasty little life of Pietro Aretino—written by some prudish French flubdub of a professorial prig.
Aretino seems to have been a truly wonderful sort of a person—blackmailer of the first order, satirist with a blunt fury, a sort of literary pirate who loved his friends but had few, played his game supremely without hypocrisy, took the world by the throat and lived free—But the little curs bark and snarl, and every pride that sees fit to handle with gloved prurient hands the shocking life of the cynic, the voluptuary
The maligner of kings and princes thinks himself required to soil his memory, turning his every good action into filth, persecuting every sincerity of clearseeing intellect, putting his image in the pillory of their outraged conventions to appease the furies of the moral gods——
Now—as Jack says I'm about to take up Leopardi—in a serious way

Van says the Colorado Springs High Schools are much troubled by an epidemic of German measles. They were undecided what to call the ailment, but at last decided that liberty measles would be a patriotic name——

The authorizations to wear red white & green service ribbons have just come—that a wonderful joke—They denote us by the title *Il Gentleman*—so the gentlemen volunteers—are still in the running— How does one indicate shrieks of laughter on paper?

Captain Pietra at Borso shot himself in the head today. He was a curious man—the sort of person who crosses the back of the stage in a Dostoevski novel now and then. He was the only embusqué in his family, he would tell you. 'Today I shall go within thirty meters of the Austrians' he would say, *sono il solo emboscato de mia famiglia. He* must have been a coward for he had a sort of nervous mania for taking risks—a hectic anxiety to show you he was not afraid. He had a certain nerve though—he must have had to shoot himself so cleanly. I can imagine him looking down the barrel of the revolver and saying to himself "I am the only embusqué in my family—I'm not a coward

But maybe he did it out of spite—He always used to get into frightful tempers.

All the Americans hated him.

April 20th [1918]
Last night I had an awfully interesting talk with Charley A. and Rieser and Tom Wharton about the war and pacifism. C.A. it came out is a believer in the individual, put himself down as a conscientious objector on the draft—He's going—he says—to refuse to serve.

Talk with Tom Wharton & Carolt and even Rieser, who although a violent anti German and in favor of the war in every way and in suppressing antiwar opinion during the war—is sincerely down on militarism——for some reason I suddenly became tremendously hopeful—Here were three people—Americans out of totally different environments all absolutely determinedly against the machine that has been crushing us all—Even if we are slaves we are unwilling ones. When you think of these people and our friends—and of Baldwin and that sort of man, who believes but who is carried along in the swirl out of our natural American easygoingness. Oh I cant write straight this morning, but I am anxious to get this down—

God if I could see clearly what to do—

I suppose one should do something conspicuous if possible—I hate conspicuousness—We have so much to do—it will take generations to leaven the great stupid mass of America—we are in the position of the first Russian revolutionists who struggled and died in despair and sordidness—we have no chance of success, but we must struggle— live—I dont know why—I hardly believe in it—yet

The world as it is at present hardening into organization seems to be a worse place for humanity than it has almost ever been before—too—it has possibilities—It is better to be dead than living

Now is the time when the effort has got to come—perhaps out of the great stupid mass of America—from under the crushing weight of industry—there must be so many of us—yet so few—

Perhaps being in France will teach some of the people

That quotation from Aeschylus about the evil that slunk down the rope that moored the ship to the shore——

> Place in the shrine a last offering
> Of huge red poppies from the field
> Below the vineyard where this spring
> The yokes of old white oxen feed.
> And stand in the gloaming a little time
> Clinking the smoothe age-fingered heads,
> To madonna at our own old shrine
> A few last prayers, tear soaked seeds
> To spring before her throne and gods

To Rumsey Marvin

[Bassano]
April 26 [1918]

Rummy—Just back from Milan, where I had 48 hour leave—delighted by a letter from you——

Lis Flaubert mon vieux, lis Flaubert, lis Flaubert si tu veux le style, lis donc Flaubert, si tu veux la vie, lis Flaubert——Absolutely I beat my forehead on the ground before him——

But Name of God, the idea of mentioning Carry On in the same breath with Le Feu: What the devil does it mean to call a book *unpleasant?* Of course it does not conform with the hallelujah-breathing standards of the Y.M.C.A. Life according to those standards, according to the Anglo-American Grundy ruling an expurgated earth in behalf of a Heaven too dull to need expurgating, is a pretty poor business.

About style—I think that reading people in order to get 'style' from them is rather soft-headed. Your style is like the color of your hair or the cut of your pants—half accident, half act of God—to take thought to change or improve it results usually in rank affectation.

Of course I dont mean that you should not read and read and reread all the well written things you ever laid your paws upon. Reading Pater "for his style" is like going to a restaurant and ordering a dinner in order to admire the crockery it is served up on.

You don't want to write for style—you want to write—and god knows you will have a hard enough time cudgelling the British language into saying what you want it to—without needing to waste any hours on the trimmin's—The only way of getting the command of English needed to express ideas is by reading & reading a damn lot. English instructors have an idea that 'style' is a subtle art to be practiced for its own sake—a sort of parlor gymnastics of literature that makes people "cultured." O they are a benighted lot.

Paradise Lost is wonderful stuff to read aloud. It says absolutely nothing, but its sound is a symphony—and O the gorgeous jewel-work of names——I think the names in Paradise Lost are almost the most wonderful in English.

I'm awfully interested to hear about your "little group of serious thinkers"—God save the mark. My prep-school was the aridest place on God's earth in that way.

Do tell me more about them.

Poor old America needs so people of brains and courage and art—for the revolt that must come against the stupid moloch we all immolate our lives before——

By the way—on your French Revolution affair—Carlyle's book [*The French Revolution*] is wonderfully exciting.

I'm awfully glad you didn't debate—it may be an evil memory of debating at college—but for some reason the very name of debating shocks & grieves me beyond words.

Really I dont think you ought to worry about writing. If you want to do it badly enough—nothing on earth except want of conviction can stop you. Honestly I really think that a person of your lively imagination & general awakeness and gusto for things can do about anything he wants in literature. But he must *want* and damn hard too. He must give up his father and his mother and take no thought for the morrow, or for what he shall wear or what shoes shall be on his feet. Of course one must do all that to do anything worth while—Anyway taking up letters as a career isnt committing oneself for ever & ever amen—It's merely the most convenient way of saving oneself from the chaingang of offices & from the petty thievery of a business career—That we must all do at all costs——If one wants to stop writing one can always become a blacksmith or a cobbler or a peanut vendor or-a tramp—all honorable occupations.

O Rummy—I wonder when we will pull off one of our famous plans—We must manage it——But god knows when I'll be in America again—or under what conditions——But manage it we will—if the spheres split——

Love Jack

A cold rainy day in the mountains in a little dirty village full of a smell of wet troops and latrines and soup cooking. It'll be awful when we do meet again—We'll have to talk for 40 days and 40 nights and will probably be found swooning from exhaustion, feebly moving our jaws, after the fourteenth day of solid conversation.

I've been reading Boccaccio a lot and Leopardi in Italian—Then I have got hold of Swinburne's Poems & Ballads & the Rossetti poems—all of which give me great solace & joy—

As you love me—Read in *Poems & Ballads* Swinburne's Song in Time of Order & Song in Time of Revolution

Do you read Walt Whitman?

[Diary]
April 27th [1918]
Borso again—cold wet rain—a smell of soggy soup and shitten hillsides and miserable soldiers.

1.

Place in the shrine a last offering
Of huge red poppies from the field

Below the vineyard where this Spring
The yokes of old white oxen feed.
And stand in the gloaming a little time
Clinking the smooth age fingered heads.
To Madonna at our own old shrine
A few last prayers, tearsoaked seeds
To spring before her, throned with God,
To bear us, distant, flowers of grace
And fortune in turning the unturned sod
That's sown with gold in the new far place.
There's gold in the sod of the new far place.

2.

Purple in the star-sown purple night
The house is shut against the rustlings
and the rare whirl of a bat's flight
and all the night-stirrings mingling
like faint sounds of flutes or voices calling
in the long drawn strummings of the breeze in the house

May 14th [1918]

Another nastily typical affair of officers—Dudley tells the story from Rova—a cousine of the farmhouse where the officers are quartered appears—causes violent rumpus of sex & smut in the conversation. Is led into the mess room for lunch & tickled and poked and made jokes at . . . she is obdurate and behaves in a quiet rather dignified manner. The stewards look as if they wanted to shoot the officers—wish they had—At dinner the affair is repeated—the girl is forced to drink Strega and wine and is kissed and Ellsworth much annoyed and not knowing what to do is made to put his arm round her—The girl finally gets away, by one of the men of the farm appearing and raising hell Dudley thought she was going to be raped before his eyes. The light comedy kidding is worth remembering. The next day at lunch the officers are in a storm of indignation at hearing the rumor that the girl slept that night with a corporal.

But it does illustrate the swinish uppishness of the Italian officers— God they are a nasty crew . . . When some spoons were not well washed they threw them at the steward's head.

Even the rather decent ones have the same disease—their overbearing nastiness to anyone they dont lick the boots of is disgusting.

May 17 [1918]
at Rova with Dudley—we each of us have a broken down Ford that won't run; fortunately there is no work to do.

We have an enormously pleasant little room, whitewashed with blue woodwork in the windows and a pale red tiled floor. There is a stove of which the pipe goes up into the wall with the poise of the neck of a startled ostrich—outside is a pleasant jumbled little farmyard with roosters cockadoodledoing and soldiers, rather clean comfortable orderlies of the sanitary section—people who never have anything to do except screw the neighboring women and grumble about their food

The officers here are a nasty illbred arrogant set—the food, however is very good.

The fields round about are simply packed with flowers . . . But to the novel—noteably wonderful great single dandelions of a fine clouded yellow—to the novel—

At lunch the tall Sardinian lieutenant gave us an exhibition—There was some talk of a bella ragazza with a very servile red faced sergeant—after a moment the Sardinian jumped up from his chair half seriously and half in earnest and started kicking the sergeant, chased him round the room kicking him in the tail with a long thin leg and finally out of the messroom, slamming the door behind him——

May 22nd [1918]
At dinner—our pleasant Bourgeois captain with his air of bonhommie —the little lieutenant a woosy looking young fellow with a clever aquiline nose—the flaccid red lieutenant and the curious ecclesiastic, Dom Pietro—who is the image of Velasquez's first portrait of Philip IV—all talked about the Madonnina de Grappa—the little shrine of Madonna on Grappa summit—

—After the war, said the captain—there would be a restaurant there

After the war, said the chaplain—the broken bronze Madonna would be mended and set up again and a tumulus made of all the bones of the dead per la patria on Grappa and a chapel with a crypt built there to commemorate——

After the war, said I timidly, perhaps people would not want to remember——

In the evening we went down to see the canteen man—a flabby pink goodnatured object.

We fortunately tumbled into the general's mess hall and found ourselves, all of a sudden being introduced to a fair youngish general, with fair—Kronprinz moustaches and a conceited boyish air that made him rather attractive. We were sat and fed coffee and cognac and felt lost and embarrassed and the gramophone covered our gêne.

I talked to a pleasant Italian from Tunis, who said that the only good thing the war had brought had been—that people in the allied countries had travelled about and got to know and like each other— That is probably true—for though as a mass the allies hate each other worse than poison—individually—countless bonds have been struck up—between people of different nations. They've learnt to a certain degree that everything and everybody's human, 'cept the government.

Fairbanks indulged his base passions in an endless game of chess— with a young Italian lieutenant who had an enormously pleasant & intelligent face—

Then we went home & I for one vowed never again to commit the politeness of calling on someone—One always tumbles into embarrassing situations and one barely escapes death by boredom—Never again.

This morning is wonderfully fine—the bluest of blue skies, a brilliant white sunshine—and many aeroplanes, flashing in the dark sky like mica in a piece of granite—Sparano un po'—Shrapnel has exploded quite near and there's a good deal of artillery activity on both sides.

May 25 [1918]
Period of loafing about The Walls of Jericho—I wonder if that's a good title
at Rova—
Yesterday day of great excitement—In the morning an English aeroplane fell into Brenta right outside our windows and in the excitement two poor Italians were drowned, Bayard Wharton did the hero & saved the drowning aviator just in the nick of time. And there were all sorts of complications——

Rova May 27 [1918]
A rainy day—Ellsworth has gone up the mountain to see a captain of his acquaintance I am absolutely crevé de faim waiting for lunch, as I

have had nothing except a tiny cup of coffee very early this morning—
hunger is not suitable to literature either, alas, at least this stage isnt—

A wonderful scandal is going on at the Mensa at Rova now—a
squabble between the white worm captain—who looks like a woodlouse I think more than a white worm—but Dudley insists on the
white worm—and the tall Sardinian lieutenant. The captain ordered
the lieutenant to go about the yard and quarters of the 67 Ambulanza
and pick up the rubbish—the lieutenant refused. (It was hardly an
officer's job). The captain put him under arrest—He retorted by sending in a complaint to headquarters on various counts. Yesterday
depositions were made against him—large quantities—And at night it
was awfully funny—because he sits in his room drawing and playing
the mandolin—He has composed a pleasant laughing little march—to
show the captain, he says, that he is still allegre—and all through
dinner the sound of it came drifting down from his room—which
annoyed the worm woodlouse captain like hell.

May 28 [1918]
Have been talking literature with Randaccio—and music. He's a
futurista—an awfully interesting chap—rather instructive as I think he
is more or less typical of new Italy—How sublimely self satisfied is
their attitude—Italy is, has been, and ever shall be the home of art,
literature music—Yet it may be only the Latin bragadoccio—A great
hullabaloo of the new and explosive and not awfully much fire—but I
may wrong them—Still as a figure with his handsome rather spanish
face and his small beard on the chin and his tall spongy stature
Randaccio is a pretty fine fellow.

Smoke: talk, talk, talk, & never anything coming of it.

Conversation with the Young Spanish Anarchist
The Russian Jew

June 1st [1918] Lucca
Ecco! Who'd a thought it? Day before yesterday I was just sitting
down to sketch the Bassano mountains when news came that Utany's
Millions [?] were on hand and that we were to go into Vicenza that
afternoon. We were joyful at the idea of going and the general staff
was joyous at the idea of getting rid of us—so the incident was closed.

We left Fairbanks, who had also left—on the platform—somehow we induced him to go to Milan; wicked.

But of that tale makéd Chaucer namore——

We got off the train at Bologna—rather late & the next morning—took train for Pistoja—of the joys of Bologna . . .

Pistoja—a cheerful beggarwoman drowsing in her rags—amid a swirl of dust and sunlight.

In Pistoja there is a wonderful Ospedale del Ceppo a grey-green-mustard colored building with a loggia like that of the Innocenti in Florence—and a gorgeous frieze—della Robbia work—making a wonderful band of blue and white and warm reds and browns. In the places between the arches, too, there are rather beautiful medallions—There is a wonderful deadness and a frail charm of very faded things about Pistoja—There we met a funny little lavender lady—who nearly broke one's heart she so felt the war—We saw her again getting off the train at some watering place or other—The last thing she said was six thousand refugees——

Lucca—Where we got very late gave us a great air of gaiety as we walked to our hotel. A remarkably delightful town—full of bustle and business and clean narrow streets—The churches are wonderful alive and beautiful—San Michêle with its trees of colonades like the carved prop of a galleon, San Frediano Irlandese, with a huge mosaic like a painted sail and one the most beautiful interiors in Italy—almost coming up to San Zeno at Verona—Frescoes rather charmingly done—by one Asperetini pupil of Francia—Then the Duomo and the church beside it—are from the outside marvellously lovely—full of sculpture and liveliness—dragons gentleman being swallowed by dragons, graffiti medallions of faces—all the surge and life of a Gothic cathedral——

All about Lucca there is a life and merriness of the sea—you feel that the Lucchese lived by it——

Herein is a sad tale of our pesterment by a well meaning gentleman who pursued us after having talked to us on the train—asked us to lunch and all sorts of things—and finally went to Pisa with us—but he certainly was a weight on our proceedings—We finally got him into a cab and rustled him to the station where we deposited him just in time to take the train back to Lucca—which, to our horror, he had threatened to miss.

Pisa—The wonderful Coney Island affair of the Baptistry, the Duomo

and the campanile Pendente—were full of life Sunday morning when
some sort of festival affair was going on, and there were great numbers
of people in different costumes with gay parasols. A man selling ice
cream cones completed the picture—and O how the buildings livened
up under it. The Leaning Tower was as exciting as one of those
complicated spiral shoots they have at Revere Beach—The Battistero
was like a merry-go-round—the sound of a calliope should have come
out it. The Campo Santo at Pisa is a marvellous place—a different
world from the rather tasteless town and the care free merryment of
the Cathedral buildings—

June 6 [1918]
Seated at an awful place a large arcade—a bare cement Cafe à liquori—
Tea Room place—where they feed you coffee in coffee machines—
Later in the square—front of the wolf statue—Van has been making
him self annoying—damn his hide—
                    The Letters of an Embusqué
   Freedom of speech has never been established—it must be—All that
religious toleration means is that religion is no longer considered
important.

To Rumsey Marvin

                                                    [Rome–Paris
                                                    June 1918]
Dear Rummy—
   It is a dog's age since I either wrote or got a letter—I am in
Rome—my term with the Red Cross in Italy has expired and I am
going to France to see what else I can get to do.
   Meanwhile I have a little time to myself—and all sorts of things I
have wanted to do——so many that I sit and do virtually nothing—in
one of those nasty flat moods one gets in now and then—where everything suddenly loses its vividness for some reason.
   Rome is a rather wonderful place. There is an almost unbelievable
mellowness about it—It's nothing definite—really, but a feeling of
endless age, a mellowness of disillusion in which all crude bright things
have burned themselves away in a wonderful selfpossession of pale
eternity. The sunlight rests softly and with an intimacy of agelong
comradeship on the old walls of Roman brick and on the obelisks and

the mosscovered fountains—Everything is through a haze of pale gold light——

A wonderful shining day like a glass of white wine—pale sun and clouds that pile in great white masses over the buildings—the orange and faun colored buildings—and over the roofs covered with rusty golden moss.

Paris

For some reason this letter got stuck in Rome and never got on any farther—I heard some awfully good opera in Rome—Bellini's Norma most beautifully sung, and L'Elisir d'Amore a charming little thing by Donizetti—as well as the vapid "grandness" of Aida—Verdi was an excessively bad composer—One doesn't realize it until one hears other earlier operas of the Italian school, like Norma—

In Torino I heard a splendid performance of Tosca—

Now I am in Paris a Paris emptier and sadder than ever—But—for some reason I have more hope of the war's ending soon than I have ever had before—

By the way—it is days later—this letter'll never get off—

About 'free verse'—I think your last letter was fatheaded—What the devil does it matter what one calls it?——I'm perfectly willing to have it called syncopated prose of hypersulphate of magnesium. I break it into lines because I want the pauses to come in certain places and ordinary punctuation will not quite do—That is virtually why "regular" poetry is broken up into lines—Of course I realize that in most "regular" poetry since Elisabeth's time the line breaks mean nothing. You'll find that Milton is written in paragraphs. Swinburne is one of the few poets I know who keeps the value of the break at the end of the line.

By the time you get this letter you'll have emerged from the stupid drillhouse of boarding-school more or less permanently. I wonder if you'll be as delighted as I was to get out. I wish you'd come over to Europe with the Red Cross or something instead of going in Yale—It would be far more educational. You could drive a car in one of their ambulance services. But I imagine your parents would dislike the idea—Still there is a dreadful need for people who have minds of their own—and they are rare God knows—to come over to Europe and see exactly what sort of a party this is in which Europe is so merrily suiciding. Just so that they can understand the next war—when it comes.

What are you going to do this summer? Not military training I hope——O but—Je m'en fiche—perhaps you enjoy it—perhaps people enjoy the war—

Au Revoir

By the way there's a chance I may be sent to Palestine—an ambulance service of some sort is being started there.

Love
Jack

Saint Germain

The shadows make strange streaks and mottled arabesques
of violet on the apricot—tinged walks
where the thin sunlight lies
like flower petals.

On the cool wind
there is a fragrance
indefinably sweet;
as of strawberries crushed in deep woods
as of flowers passed unaware
on a long dusty city street;
as of your hands when you have, all the pale morning in a garden
been picking flowers.

The fragrance and the flushed sunlight
and the wistful patterns of shadow
on gravel walks between tall elms
and broad leaved silver lindens;
the stretch of country
yellow and green,
full of little particolored houses;
and the faint intangible sky
have taken my soggy misery,
like clay in the brown deft hands of a potter,
and moulded a song of it.

Tivoli

The ropes of the litter creak and groan
as the bearers turn down the steep path.

Pebbles scuttle under slipping feet . . .
But the Roman poet lies back confidently
Among his magenta cushions and mattresses,
thinks of Greek bronzes
at the sight of the straining backs of his slaves.

The slaves' backs shine with sweat
and they breathe deep of the cooler air
as they lurch through tunnel after tunnel of leaves,
leaves that tremulously dance
in the roar of the glen.
At last where the spray swirls like smoke
and the river roars in a cauldron of green,
he stops the litter, and standing by the white water's edge
feels his fat arms poetically quiver,
and every sense of him drowned and exalted
In the reverberance of the fall.

The ropes of the litter creak and groan
the embroidered curtains, moist with spray
flutter in the poet's face.
Pebbles scuttle under slipping feet,
as the slaves strain up the path again.
The Roman poet leans confidently back
Among silk cushions of gold and magenta
his hands, with their rings and Assyrian seals
clasped across his mountainous belly,
thinking of the Sibyll and fate,
of gorgeous and garlanded death,
mouthing hexameters . . .

And I, my belly full and burning as the sun
with the good white wine of the Alban Hills,
Stumble down the path
into the cool green and the roar
and am abashed and wonder . . .

[Paris]
July 17 [*1918*]

Dear Rummy—
  Delighted to get a letter from you saying you'ld won the essay
prize. I'm most anxious to see the essay—By the way—you have a

volume of Eight Harvard Poets, haven't you?—It came out about a year ago and I seem to be the only person who hasn't been able to secure a copy—Lawrence Gomme, NY. is the publisher—

I fear I sha'nt get the famous essay, as I never seem to get things sent me—I'll have to read it on that distant day when we have a grand walking and talking party somewhere, somehow.

At present I'm in Paris fussing and squabbling and trying to clear myself of charges—a hell of a nasty business, though I don't think my sense of humor has entirely deserted the ship. Paris is wonderfully beautiful in its emptiness; when not fussing and fuming—I have a gorgeous time writing in a little room on the Ile St. Louis—or sketching along the Quais—Go and hear Louise [opera by Gustave Charpentier set in Paris] when you want to find out what I feel about Paris—

Rummy—about the Temptations of St. Anthony—I'm afraid that at the school they've been filling you up with the Y.M.C.A. idea of the period of storm and stress in a young man's life when etc etc. Honestly I think that is an awfully dirty way of looking at it. The storms of desire to reproduce the species are such a jolly natural sort of thing—that instead of torturing oneself about them I think one should accept them—at their cash value. Not that I mean that you should run to the first scarlet woman on the town Main Street or anything of the sort—but you should realize that life is a sweaty, semeny business and that one shouldn't be shocked by its commonplace mechanism any more than by the digestive juices. I think one should look all one's desires straight in the face and have it out with them by force of argument rather than shut them up in boxes. And any manifestation of vigor and vividness is worth something—The water under the ice is perfectly good flowing water—a trifle muddy if you stir the bottom—but its good reproductive mud—If one only realizes that skating becomes much surer business, and holes in the ice dont bother you in the least. Of course you have to keep your wits about you—But that is necessary in everything.

I honestly think all the purity gag, mixed up with facts of scientific misinformation about venereal diseases that American youth has its mind polluted with is simply disgusting. The facts they ought to know—but why in God's name not tell them straight forwardly like an account of a track meet, without leering hints of filth on the one hand

and sentimental slush on the other. Never be afraid of anything in God's name—the muddiest monster and the most cream and white damosel show themselves good average companionable clay if you only dont let them hypnotize you into looking at them askew——

Forgive this disquisition—but I think its a most interesting subject.

Love
Jack

[Diary]
July 21st [*1918*]
Finished for the second time James Joyce's Portrait of the Artist—pray God I shant start imitating it off the face of the earth, Cuthbert-like [reference to Cuthbert Wright, a Harvard acquaintance]—I admire it hugely—It is so wonderfully succinct and follows such curious by-ways of expression—old abandoned roads that are overgrown but where the air is cleaner than in the modern dusty thoroughfares—constantly churned by people's footsteps.
note—How about the parallel between modern industrial overorganization—crushing the soul and mind and ancient savage overorganization, crushing the savage clan and tribe—and getting away from any chance of progress.

In these terms—might not civilization be the crowding of order by the critical intelligence of man.

To Rumsey Marvin

Paris
July 27 [1918]
in a nasty fancy little patisserie
drinking cold chocolate.

O mirabile puer—insigne homo!

Nothing but bad latin can express the fervor of my admiration. You've pulled off something that I've never had the guts to do more than theorize about. I've all my life wanted to work in a shipyard— They are the most wonderful places in the world, and doing 'unskilled' labor must make one lay hold on the elementary facts of existence in a wonderful way. I've always found it so when I've done work on our erstwhile farm in Virginia—I've found it so very recently working as a volunteer stretcher bearer in one of the hospitals here.

You see I have to marshal my little puny stock of labor to be able even to write to a horny handed son of toil like yourself.

For de lord's sake chile, write me all about it. Your letter make me hugely anxious to hear more. I'm still hanging about in Paris trying to clear myself of the charges I wrote you about. The complete lack of human decency people exhibit at times staggers you—I'll tell you all about it when I can.

I live on the Ile St Louis, in the Seine, a beautifully old seedy part of Paris that I love—I spend my spare time writing and sketching up and down the river. For the first time my drawing is emerging from primal chaos a little and a few of the crayon things I've done seem to exhibit a faint hope—faint as unheard ditties!—of improvement. Après la guerre . . . I shall take a whack at the graphic arts—poor dears—I wander about and go to little restaurants and outlandish little cafés and frequent the few café dansants that are still open, and manage to have an awfully good time in a quiet mournful sort of way.

There is a chance that I can get into an expedition going to Palestine—or maybe I can get into the American or French army as a stretcher bearer—My eyes and my rep are a nuisance wherever I go.

I'll write you as soon as things materialize one way or the other— For God's Sake write as often as you can—as I assure you I need cheering often—studying the Spanish Inquisition from the underside must have been amusing to look back on—like hanging——

> In a jolly little restaurant,
> at a table on the pavement, peeping
> at the world through a fence of bay-
> bushes. Drinking Dubonnet—a not
> unpleasant mahogany colored apéritif.

Someday I want to teach you Paris. The Butte de Montmartre, where I often go to have dinner is I believe firmly the most exciting place in any city in the world. (Apropos—see [the opera] Louise) The gayest and shabbiest and the most unalloyed people in the world stroll about the little treeshaded squares and the steep streets that become steps every now and then . . . and the views of Paris darkening in the sunset—One reason the people up there are so nice is that it takes so much climbing to get up there that none except the jolliest people ever seem to succeed, the others roll back and eat greasy dinners on the Boulevard de Clichy.

Look—some day very soon after the war has finished, if I'm still above ground and you—let's start out from anywhere in Europe and wander towards no where in particular, on foot, working at grape harvests, and wheat thrashings and pig killings and other rustic joys for our bread and bacon—I shall never have enough of walking down country roads away from places and towards places till the feet wear off my legs. I shall take fat notebooks and make weird sketches of things on the road and you must take a mouth organ or other musical instrument so that if all else fails we can tootle and sing in taverns on the roadside. Look will you do it? . . I'll guarantee to drop anything I'm doing, be it novel or marriage or a sentence in jail and do it too, when you give the word. Among other places—Id like to go to Algiers and Budapest.

But à plus tard—

love
Jack

To John Howard Lawson (1895–   ), *a playwright, who graduated from Williams College in 1914. After two attempts to produce his dramas, he went to Europe as an ambulance driver in 1917. His close friendship with Dos extended from then until the late 1930's. Dos was deeply impressed by Lawson's manuscript for the expressionist play* Roger Bloomer, *and wrote an introduction to it when it was published in 1923.* The Garbage Man, *the first of Dos' own plays, was a direct result of his and Lawson's talks.*

Both men served as directors of the New Playwrights Theatre from 1927–1929. Afterward, Lawson moved to Hollywood, where he became a successful screenwriter until he found himself challenged by the House Un-American Activities Committee in 1947. Refusing to answer whether or not he was a Communist, he received a one-year sentence for contempt of Congress.

Among Lawson's produced plays, in addition to Roger Bloomer, *are* Marching Song, Success Story, The International, Loud Speaker, Nirvana, *and* Processional. *He has taught drama and film. He continues to live and work in California with his second wife, Susan Edmond.*

Bordeaux
Aug 11 [1918]
In a most gorgeous cafe with large
painted ladies in green and gold
and the sunlight scrumptiously hot
and white outside . . . Not so hot
and white as the sunlight in Rome,
though.

Jack—My bitching, my twilight, my soucis proceed. Nothing was of avail and followed by a cortège of curses I am going to America. I'm not trying Antonio Spagoni or Lope de la Vega, perhaps asininely perhaps wisely, and am in hopes that having thrown myself at the feet of Washington, I shall arise whiter and more patriotic than the lily and with the same attributes as to toiling and spinning.

It will be interesting, though nasty, in God's country and I shall at once undertake démarches not to remain there.

I tried to enlist in the U.S. Ambulance Service, but they fainted at the sight of my eyes; you see I couldn't even see the top letter.

The full tale of my procés would take four volumes of fine print— it will probably appear in a new J'Accuse in the great by and by.

Glorious—Dudley and Van are, I think for six months, or maybe forever, enrolled in the Quaker reconstruction.

C'est moi l'agneau noir.

Write me to 214 Riverside Drive—New York City—how is the Lake of Nemi?

I shall signify my misfortunes, one by one, as they occur—and remember the tryst thirty days after the millennium.

Bobby's a lieut. and joy rides with a colonel round about Tours.

Love
Dos

Imagine me in the stern of the S.S. Espagne in a Napoleon in the Bellephon attitude . . . Dirges where dismal will rhyme with abysmal, and howl with Lowell and hates with Bates and fetter with letter.

To John Howard Lawson

On board the *Espagne*
August 17 1918

Jack—

Go to the front of the Pantheon under the *Arippa Fecit* and pour a libation to my manes in gold wine of Frascati. I am about to enter the Land of Promise. If you go to the eighteenth turning to the left on the fourteenth passage of the third series of the catacombs of St. Domitilla, you will probably find there a new grave in an elaborate and very lovely niche; there in white stone will be inscribed a letter. The censor will have deleted the inscription but you will know that my Ka is buried there. Later, like Robert Bruce or somebody, I shall send my heart to be preserved in a pichet of Vin de Beaujolais in the restaurant in the place du Tertre on the summit of Montmartre. In the grey eventual year when three mumbling and toothless greybeards will assemble thirty days after the millennium to gird up their lean loins towards Baghdad, it can be taken out with appropriate ceremonies, sprinkled with the juice of escargots, and adored by the faithful.

When I get to America I shall probably be deleted too—But if any of me escapes erasure it will take itself up and walk to some distant course of the sphere and and thence trek eastward. At Bordeaux I didn't try to commit Antonio Spagoni, because I was seized with a sudden and violent interest in the said land of Promise. Morbid, n'est-ce pas? But remember the desire of the moth for the arclight.

It's heavy moist gulfstream weather and I love it—I have all but finished part four and last of the Roman Comique—Have been reading the Confessions of Jean Jacques, which are lots of fun.

By the way write me what you think of Seven Times Round the Walls of Jericho for a title or Seven Times Round Jericho? Is it too silly. One could prefix it by the quotation where the children of Israel march round the walls with trumpets and things and the walls fall down on their bally heads and suffix it by the same quotation, with an addition to the effect that the walls of Jericho still stand. But maybe that's all asinine.

Dudley has the MS and I shall send him the end—it was not thought safe to transport the poor thing. If you happen to be in Paris and want to try to read it, get it from him.

My address is still and shall remain By God Morgan Harjes—30 Boulevard Haussmann Paris—France.

I like your Sunday breakfasts in the Villa Borghese—Do they continue? Write of the Lago di Nemi.

Love
Dos

"THE WORLD OUTSIDE"

August 1918–December 1921

Dos' recollection much later was that he polished the manuscript for *One Man's Initiation—1917* back in New York while he was striving to get into the Medical Corps. Enlistment seemed a great struggle. Not only because of his poor eyesight but because of his "scandal" in the Red Cross the army was reluctant to have him. His Aunt Mamie worked particularly hard contacting James Brown Scott, at that time president of the Carnegie Peace Foundation. Scott, serving as a major in the Judge Advocate Corps, apparently helped Dos to enlist and then to get the waiver necessary because of his bad eyes.

Before he reported to Camp Crane in Allentown, Pennsylvania, where there was a casuals company of the Medical Corps, he had some time to himself which he passed with relatives at Bay Head, New Jersey, and with friends like Rumsey Marvin. Marvin recalled in particular a walk the two of them took in early September from Stamford, Connecticut, up the Housatonic River to the Massachusetts line. They spent a night in Danbury, where Dos with his beret and a "foreign accent" had trouble getting a lodging.

Camp Crane quickly became "Queen Ennui." He reported there September 27, and though he tried to see the bright side of the experience—discovery of another sort of life, of the American common soldier, and so forth—nothing could prevent him from intense boredom. The time seemed an eternity; it was in fact little more than one month. On October 31 Acting Quarter Master Sergeant Dos Passos and his section 541 left Camp Crane for Camp Merritt, New Jersey, there to await embarkation. On November 11, 1918, the Allies signed an armistice with Germany; on November 12 section 541 boarded the *Cedric* for a slow voyage in convoy to England.

After a few days in Camp Winnal Downs, Dos' group crossed the channel to France and went to Ferrières-en-Gâtinais, a small town some fifty miles south of Paris, there to endure more army boredom. He enjoyed Ferrières, however, and was free to spend time in places like Strasbourg and Saussheim in the department of Alsace. When he got the freedom to visit these places, he would write long descriptive letters to his friends, like that from Sens to Dudley Poore shortly before Christmas. He commiserated with Poore about the death of an acquaintance, Mlle. Racine, whom Dudley had introduced him to in Paris. She had taught Poore French in 1910 but during the war had grown increasingly despondent and finally committed suicide in 1918, in her way a victim of the conflict.

By March 1919 Dos had been released from the medical section to attend classes at the Sorbonne, which gave him a chance to get back to his beloved Paris and to begin work in earnest on his numerous literary projects—he recalled in *The Best Times* that, sharing a room on the Quai de la Tournelle with Jack Lawson, he could "write [his] head off every morning." He stayed mainly in Paris until mid-June, writing, attending concerts, operas, and thoroughly enjoying himself. When Lawson left for the United States, Dos planned to take over the room with Robert Hillyer, he wrote Poore in early April. Poore was studying at Emmanuel College, Cambridge, after having been released from his regular duties in the army as a courier, most of the time carrying dispatches between Bordeaux and Brest. Dos continued to work on a novel, probably the last half of *Seven Times Round the Walls of Jericho*, Lawson having taken the first half with him to New York where he was going to try to find a publisher. Although the Sorbonne did not excite Dos, the life was good, and he was happy, cheerfully asking Dudley for news of the "Nymph of Newnham," Jane Harrison, an author and scholar who had written *Prolegomena to the Study of Greek Religion* in 1903.

Hillyer left for the United States the end of April; Dos had to remain because he was still technically in the Medical Corps. He took short leaves to Rouen and Chartres, all the while working to arrange his discharge so he could be off to Spain for the summer. But before he could finally manage this, he was sent for several weeks to Gièvres, a mustering-out point where in a casuals company he had to move heavy scrap iron back and forth across some railroad tracks. Feeling desperate, he sneaked out of camp, made his way to Tours, got a friendly top sergeant to make out discharge orders, and got back to Gièvres in time the next morning to avoid being caught. With that he was free of the military, and after quick stops in Tours, Blois, and Vendôme, he got to Paris by Bastille Day, July 14, feeling very much unburdened in his new civilian attire.

He remained in Paris but four days, then headed for Brest, where, he told Rumsey Marvin, he hoped to help a friend who was "languishing in a camp also waiting for discharge." The friend was Dudley

Poore, who at that time may have been en route to Gièvres himself. He
and Dos did not meet up, at any rate, and he was discharged a few
days later, on July 18. By July 22 Dos was at Boulogne, on board a boat
waiting to leave for Folkestone, England, on his way to London to
arrange for the publication of *One Man's Initiation—1917* before going
to Spain.

"London's the same old smoky chaos," he wrote Marvin on July 25,
"a little more interesting than ever before, I expect; the feeling of
impending doom is always interesting. I spend my time looking up
publishers, having tea with little old ladies who knew me when I was a
nasty quarrelsome brat of eight, and going to the Ballet Russe." The
publishers, Allen and Unwin, were interested in the story of Martin
Howe after their reader commented that "Mr. Dos Passos is an impres-
sionist. His technique is good; his method powerful, economical,
brutally sincere. As a revelation of the insanity & sordid horror of war
this book has really very great merit. . . . I recommend you to secure
this. It is good." Cautiously Allen and Unwin agreed in August to
publish if Dos would guarantee a part of the cost. After thinking about
the proposal for several months he decided he would because he was
understandably anxious to get his novel into print.

With the novel tentatively placed, he returned to Paris before traveling down to Biarritz on the Spanish border to meet Dudley Poore.
Poore recalled much later that they found the Spanish border had
suddenly been closed temporarily as it often was whenever there were
student or labor riots in Spain. Dos, who had gotten a visa in Paris,
was anxious to meet Arthur McComb in Santander on the date they
had set, so he went ahead, taking Poore's suitcase and leaving him in
St. Jean de Luz to follow when he could. Because the border was not
opened quickly, Poore got into Spain without his visa by wading across
the Bidassoa River. Only after he reached Madrid did he legalize his
presence.

Poore found the other two in Santander. From there, while McComb
apparently headed off separately, he and Dos began a journey through
the Basque country and across the Picos de Europa that would
eventually take them by the end of August to Madrid, where they lived
in a fonda on a "rollicking back street" for most of September.
Although Dos wrote Stewart Mitchell that McComb was with them,
Poore insists he was not. Probably Dos meant that McComb intended
to get to Madrid; but he never did before Dos headed off to Granada.

It was there he met up again with McComb, and the two rented a summer house at a pension called *Carmen de Matamoros,* belonging to a Scottish woman named Miss Laird.

Dos had arranged a job as correspondent for a British labor paper, so when there was word of a plot to overthrow the Portuguese republic he immediately went to Lisbon for eight days in October. But the revolt never materialized. He returned to Granada, where soon after rheumatic fever laid him low with high temperatures and even delirium, and for a month Dudley Poore, who had come from Madrid, cared for him at the pension. Cured, he and Poore returned to Madrid, Dos to work on the manuscript for *Three Soldiers* in the early months of 1920, writing every day at the Ateneo, a library and club for literati to which José Giner had gotten him a card.

By January 1920 Allen and Unwin had had *One Man's Initiation—1917* cast off by the printers and were concerned because the book made only 128 pages. They agreed to go ahead and publish if Dos would contribute 75 pounds, but they warned that "we think it fair to warn you to be prepared to lose a considerable part of your outlay." The book moved ahead until April, when Allen and Unwin insisted that Dos alter parts of it. The proofs he received were marked up, calling for paraphrases and omissions. He held out for the inclusion of a scene in which Martin Howe mocked some believers in Christianity. Allen and Unwin thought in the scene "the words 'old boy' and 'romantic' are needlessly offensive. Possibly you wish to show that Martin was contemptuous of the behavior of followers of Christianity in the War, but you can do this without making him indulge in cheap gibes at the founder of that religion." They included a suggested paraphrase, which Dos refused to permit, though he agreed to omissions if the publishers insisted. The printers—who in England are held liable for the language in a book—still balked at some passages, so though the publishers said that "we object to dictation from printers, we strongly advise you, in this case, to heed their objection." Dos agreed, the cuts were made and finally *One Man's Initiation—1917* appeared in October 1920.

Despite long weekend walks—such as he described in a March letter to Marvin—with Poore, José Giner, and sometimes a friend of Giner's named León, who would be shot in the Spanish Civil War, Dos had been getting restless in Madrid. Shortly before mid-March he moved to Barcelona, where McComb was also, and met Lawson's wife Kate

Drain, son Alan, and sister Adelaide there late in the month. Dos, strapped for money, borrowed some from a Mr. Sweeney, an older man whom he had known for some time, and from Kate. In early April he saw Kate, Alan, and Adelaide off at Palma, and then the middle of that month met Lawson in Carcassonne, France, arriving back in Paris by May 1.

He finished the manuscript of *Three Soldiers* quickly and had it typed so he could go in June to England to talk with Allen and Unwin, whose reader had mixed feelings after seeing the manuscript. The novel is, he said, "a consistently realistic account of life in the American Army, hung round the person of a young musician who is drafted into the infantry." Certain words like "friggin" and "bugger" and scenes with French whores he doubted would pass. "The book is able," he continued, "a fine piece of realism, and a powerful antimilitarist document. But there is no getting away from the fact that its very realism produces an effect of monotony." And he confessed, "I hardly know what to advise. It is a long book—would be costly to produce. It is truthful, so would probably not appeal to a large public. . . . I am afraid you will decide that you can't risk the book, and you will probably be right, though as propaganda one would like to see it printed." Dos' editor at Allen and Unwin decided against the risk, and the author had his first of fourteen rejections for the novel which would make him famous when it saw the light of day in America.

It was at this time that Dos also gave Allen and Unwin the manuscript for *Seven Times Round the Walls of Jericho,* which they also declined, although the reader said he would like to see it published. "It has vitality without vulgarity. If it repaid expenses it would be time enough to think of 'Three Soldiers', which is vaguely a sequel. . . . 'Three Soldiers' is more mature and less varied. It is a fine picture of revolt against brutalizing discipline and unmeaning work. This is a picture of revolt against an old man's—and old lady's—civilization." If they had not already committed themselves to the shortest of Dos' manuscripts, *One Man's Initiation—1917,* they might have chosen one of the others. As it was, they couldn't have picked a work that was less profitable for them both. Dos' first published novel sold 63 copies in the first six months.

Luckily for his own self-confidence in the face of these rejections, he was busy with other projects. Back in France in July, he met Rumsey

Marvin for a week's walk in the Auvergne; then on August 7, 1920, he sailed for the United States aboard the *Espagne,* enjoying a leisurely voyage that took him via Spain and Cuba to New York.

The big city amused and appalled him. He settled into a "large room off Stuyvesant Square," he told Marvin, while he tried to market his two novels and to write a play, "a historical pastoral comical realistical fantastic lyrical tragical farcical morality." It was a creative time; he saw much of the group who ran the *Dial;* ate, drank, and observed with E. E. Cummings—had his first real taste, that is, of the post-war American arts.

After making the rounds of publishing houses, *Three Soldiers* found a home with the publisher George H. Doran, but the editor's wish to cut out some language caused Dos consternation. He argued with Eugene Saxton; some changes were made, and by then he was anxious to get out of New York and travel again so he and Cummings took passage on the *Mormugão.* They departed around mid-March 1921 and had a slow, delightful trip to Lisbon. They poked around Spain, but Cummings grumbled for France, so it was that by late April they arrived in Paris, where Dos put the finishing touches on *Rosinante to the Road Again,* his first book of essays which Doran was also to bring out. He corresponded with his editors about the two books and found out that the publication of *Three Soldiers* had been put off at least until August, to get "good support" for it, John Farrar said, adding that he thought they should go easy on Dos' ideas about dropping apostrophes and using dashes instead of quotation marks. Doing so might antagonize readers as too novel, when the text otherwise was in familiar English.

But by this time Dos wanted to leave such problems in the hands of the publishers, because he did not intend to remain long in Paris. Before leaving New York he had arranged to write some pieces for the *Tribune* and *Metropolitan Magazine,* and in Paris he met Paxton Hibben, then secretary of a Near East Relief mission. In Constantinople Hibben could arrange for Dos' travel with the mission, so he headed there in July to begin the adventurous trip through Asia Minor that would take him until the end of December. It was exciting, and he would chronicle it with great relish in *Orient Express* and much later in *The Best Times.* So exhilarated was he by the adventures he had no sympathy for more mundane enterprises. When Dudley Poore re-

turned to the U.S. in October to go to graduate school, Dos sent him a
card which said simply, "SHAME."

[Diary "Summer 1918"]
Bay Head—Aug 24 [1918]
Could anything be stranger than the contrast between Bay Head—the
little square houses in rows, the drugstores, the board walks, the gawky
angular smiling existence of an American summerresort—and my life
for the last year. Hurrah for contrast. Americans honestly carry innocence to a vice!

The strange innocuousness of a place like Bay Head. And the
dollars—Nom de dieu—the dollars—I am already drowned in dollars—

Still I love America—
O but the Hun-gabbling.

on the beach—Bay Head
Have found a refuge in an old boat in the shade of the boardwalk—
There by God's grace I shall make much literature—

But with the sound of the waves and the wind and the scent of the
sea—and a box of chocolates to nibble on, and wish later I hadn't eaten,
how in God's name can one write

I keep thinking of that poor little Swiss on the boat, his funny little
face with its sparse grey hair and his little eyes so close together, as
pitiful as a monkey's. His wife was so charming with her pop eyes and
her brown skin and her Zut alors! and he doted on her so foolishly—It
was as unnecessary to have her die, to extinguish so wantonly such a
harmless existence. Poor little man landing in New York with his
wife's body—What a hell——

There is something almost beautiful in the harmlessness of a place like Bay Head—It is so completely innocuous—and therefore dead in every sense of the world—and that is one aspect of American life—the external.

Innocence—hiding what?

Aug 25 [1918]
Still Bay Head
Notes from The Family
  The grotesque, the farce—quality of American life.
  A woman wrestling with the stairs to climb
  The Turn of the cycle from Prosperous—Cousin Sally Carroll to legendary prosperity and misery and back to prosperity again.

It is not until the last cycle that the *grotesque* comes in—

Aug 30th [1918]
Washington—
  The idea of individual liberty does not exist any where—There are inklings of it in the conversations of Englishmen and Frenchmen—but in all my long talk with Major Scott—an unusually intelligent man—a man of unusually deep sympathies—but a governor through and through—not a ripple of it broke the calm of his oligarchic way of looking at things. That is what must be developed in the new Contract Social. The balance sheet between the power over the individual of a national government and the good to the individual of a national government must be drawn.
  Something must come out explaining in terms that the simplest person will understand that all the rights so many centuries have bled or struggled for, the rights of the governed against the governors—at the present day are so non-existent as to leave no inkling in the mind of anyone—and yet they have existed and they shall exist—The incubus the old man of the sea of national government must be thrown off, as the incubus of feudalism and the incubus of religion have been thrown off—But God, have they? Haven't they merely appeared in new form? O it is an unended and unending battle that of man to free himself from the monsters of his own creation——Now and then—for a second

he stands free and then with a rush he is downed again and is struggling for breath in coils of the Bogg—

Sept 2nd [1918] *Labor Day*
The reason people of the stomach of my uncles so hate the Bolsheviki is not because they are traitors to Russia but because they're social revolutionists. Socialist with them is a vague term of horror. For a socialist no punishment can be too great, no death too painful—Socialist, Pacifist, Anarchist, these three are the horror and terror—words that make the mouths of my uncles curdle with loathing The funny thing is that they never seem interested in the object of their righteous hatred enough to ever try to conceive what the words mean—Oh what series and generations of words there must be in the Family Connection——Changing every ten years—I must show how the horror of one generation is the joy of the next and how the same people proudly accept with a sense of ownership even of I told you so—the things that terrified them not long before.

On the central thread of the Money—from the French Spoliation claims must be woven the changing ideology of the family the phrases and the terrors and the revolts—all marching time when necessity arises to money—money money. Aristocracy, seedy gentility, plutocracy with occasional revolters.

Sept 15 [1918]
> 9
> The great discussion
>   Jean Chénier jesuit
>   André Dubois revolutionist
>   Sully anarchist
>   Tom Randolph
>   Fibbie
>   Merrier socialist

The first part was Fibbie's getting of freedom—from the family—its religion—its way of looking at things its success—worship—its sex ideas
Then New York and freedom and the gradual feeling of being caught up in the net of the nations. Flags—The world—Governments

must go in There must be only the church triumph revolutionary—taking all the men the all mother—the great civilizer that will rescue men forever from savagery—All the church's faults come from the need to struggle with Governments. What other Government does man need but his mind? and his soul?

You're right there says Sully—but why for a multiform tyranny substitute a single one—Though that is better let us raise God and we will find that we've been raising our own image all the while—God is man's shadow in the clouds. Give us liberty—think of the cost of governments through the ages——are they worth it? Give man a chance for once. Government does not accomplish what it sets out to do even if what it sets out to do is necessary——It results in the strong having overwhelming power over the weak. Abolish the idea of property—the great central evil in the world—the cancer that has made life a hell until now civilization has been spurred on by it to suicide. Then what use would there be in fighting, what use in anything but life and love and creation of beauty—People dont commit crimes for the sake of committing them—Abolish property and you'll need no Government to protect it. Disorganization not organization is the aim of life——Merrier

It is partial organization that is bad——a partial organization abused by a piratical few. I have not faith enough in human nature to be an anarchist what we must have is by sensible organization organization from the bottom not from the top—democratic organization—a state of affairs in which things are more evenly distributed so that economic war can gradually be supplanted—That will be the first step in civilizing man—individual war economically of every man against his neighbor will be supplanted by cooperation in the great war against nature. The tyranny of the feudal money lords is driving the lower classes together into a cooperative fraternal existence—The lower classes are therefore what the new society must be founded on—There is nothing for the rich but extinction. There exists no possible reconciliation, no point of agreement between a rich man and a poor man.

Yes said Andre Dubois, but why talk—we are slaves—we are blind we are deaf—First we must burst our bonds, open our eyes, clear our ears We know nothing but what we are told by interested parties everything is distorted to use—oh the lies the lies—the lies We must make another strike for freedom—O how many times have we men

tried and failed—once more, blind, we must strike at our oppressors—
hopelessly cynically—ruthlessly. We must indicate the dignity of
man——O the lies—the lies they kill us with—all society all is a structure of lies—of lies for self interest by those in power who work on the
cowardice of men. O if men were not cowards—if men trusted themselves instead of their lying governors there would be none of this
supreme asininity of war. We are all cowards and God we believe what
we're told—*Nous sommes tous despoirs.*

> *Cease: drain not to its dregs the urn*
> *Of bitter prophecy*
> *The world is weary of its past*
> *O might it die or*
> *rest at last.*

Camp Crane—Allentown
Sept 27th [1918]
The little man who made out my papers at the local board spoke
feelingly, lyrically even, of the excitements of war and the thrill of
thinking you might be potted at any minute and wrang my hand with
considerable effusion as I left to go to Allentown. The next morning I
went early to the camp, a converted fair ground with a race course and
a lovely grove of trees where the grackles made a pleasant cheering
racket last evening. There I spent the day with a sergeant and his
assistant in a large bare gymnasium-like room, drowsy and over
heated. The sergeant sat at a desk and arranged little stacks of papers
in piles, then pursed up his lips, cleared his throat, took up the papers
and glanced over them with hurried care and rearranged them. His
assistant with great difficulty copied the account of the case of a man
who had been discharged for imbecility. He could not typewrite and he
could not read the writing of the doctor who had made the diagnosis
so he went tick tap click, damn, tick tap click damn and erased every
other word. In the course of proceedings numerous papers were made
out about me, I was examined physically and my eyes were found
wanting. I telegraphed the miraculous Major to get me a waiver. Now
there is nothing to do but wait to see what forthcomes. A waiver or a
return to my local board with thanks.
    Come ennui——

Sunday 30th Sept—[1918]

The band plays in the pale blue stand under the tall oak grove of the fair ground . . . The instruments glitter—silver facets of sun—in the mottled varying shadow of the tall oak-trees and men and women walk to and fro—and soldiers—mostly soldiers—changing patterns like the bits of a picture puzzle cut into scraps by the alternation of sun and shade—shifting and forming into pictures—purple and blue, drab yellow and lilac against a background of khaki—mostly khaki—Questing faces of homely young women—questing faces of brown reddish healthy youth—glances meeting comprehending—and behind the glances the invariable picture of skirts lifted and clothes undone—of white legs and hair between them and the necessity of junction of body strain to body. The band plays.

Monday—Oct 1 [1918]

I might have known it would be like this.

This is the fourth day:

I just looked at my watch, expecting it to be say five o'clock—It is just ten past two!

I might have known I should get like this—

It drives me mad to think of losing any of my precious hours—hovering this way in an agony of boredom.

It's so stupidly unintelligent—so emptyheaded—If I took the trouble I could get into conversation with any number of men—I could sit on this bench and think—I could make up verses I could plan novels—I could draw. Why let this beastly paling fence frighten you out of your wits into this strangulation of boredom?

At least I can sit and meditate upon the great excellence of Queen Ennui

I've read a terruful lot in the thrice blessed Y.M.C.A.

      Tamburlane

      The Red Badge of Courage

      Vachel Lindsay's Congo Volume

      A book by an ambulance driver that made me terribly

      homesick for the front.

O Ennui dangle your squirming jumping jacks in front of my eyes——

There is something enormously nice about southern and western American voices.

You wanted to be in America—well here you are—drowned in it.

Marlowe has a wonderful trick of repeating a line at regular inter-vals—The Second Part of Tamburlane is really a superb piece of bombast——The lament for Zenocrate The diction of Tamburlane

O the railing and the three strands of barbed wire—o the closed in dullness of army life—I'm drinking to the dregs that dusty ennui I've always felt hung round garrisons and garrison towns.

Organization kills.

To John Howard Lawson

Camp Crane
Allentown Pa
[*October 1918*]

The Greeks and Romans with their glorious sense of the necessity for platitude spent all their lives making up suitable mottos for just this sort of thing; so you can pick one out for yourself—But know my dear Jack that I'm in it—in a condition known as Casuals—in it—and done of my own accord. The moth will fly into the candle flame, so why worry—

By the aid of my Aunt of course I got specially inducted into the Ambulance Service and here I am. I hope before long to be packed on a transport and unloaded in France—but who knows, who cares—I have given myself wholly up into the keeping of a grey symbolical paramour Boredom. The depth and the height of my boredom is an inspiration. Its a state that approaches Nirvana.

I might have struggled and squirmed into the Red Cross and perhaps to Palestine—but my lady Ennui had already her arm around my neck—

The after accounts of my scandal are funny. It seems that my aunt mobilized battalions of senators, armies of congressmen who marched with banners and countermarched, who sent telegrams and made promises—but the telegrams didn't get to the telegramees and the thing fell rather flat. If there ever was a funnier tempest in a teapot—and the result is that I am persona non grata in a variety of quarters—As I say and sing

Sinbad was in bad all around

But now I am lost—buried in Khaki.

I should not have imagined that demon Detweiler would have lasted so long. Great and wonderful are the works of Allah—and notably the Red Cross.

There's a green paling fence and three strands of barbed wire all round the camp. One can't go out without a pass and we are under quarantine for Spanish Influenza—

Bulgaria has seen the light—Hurray! When the vultures and the buzzards start wheeling round in the sky there's a hope of an end.

How well the high collar fits American necks! O no we will never unsheathe until the purposes for which it was drawn are accomplished.

You can't imagine the good nature and blundering willingness to be human of the American privates. It gives an idyllic low comedy quality to things—

We have movies every night—on Sundays gentlemen in black hold prayer meetings in the YMCA and preach the Huns to Hell.

I am glad I'm here. I have always been curious about America—now my curiosity is being rapidly—o so rapidly satisfied—

But I am safe in such a mantle of Ennui as the world never saw; it's warm and comfy though and conducive to sleep and dreams—

As to the Schmelkes—I shall certainly go to see them if I get into New York before I am shipped over. I should have gone before but I knew neither their names or their addresses—

As I write—at the other end of the YM.C.A. room a gentleman is lecturing a great many young lieutenants on the subject of court martial—to make the punishment fit the crime, the punishment fit the crime—

Love
Dos

My address later—its
   214 Riverside Drive
   New York City

To Rumsey Marvin

What Ho Rumsey!

I am in the Y.M.C.A. at a board table where people are playing
checkers. At the other end a prayer-meeting is vainly attempting to be,
succeeding only in making a doleful noise.

A secretary is just going round nudging people to take off their
hats.

Somebody's had an inspiration. They are singing the battle hymn
of the Republic—which livens people up . . .

What a nuisance; I've just been handed a hymnbook—I wish I
didn't feel twinges of good manners. I shall have to go and make
doleful noises too.

God—I hate the nasal moaning of hymns.

It's funny how American life is always pitched in the key comedy—low comedy—farce—sometimes for a moment exulted into the
high comedy that makes the spheres laugh. Never tragic

Exult ye generations of psalm-droning puritans! The whole room
is humming and moaning to your tunes, sitting in rows on the hard
unpolished benches of your faith—sending up a thin incense of song to
the evangelical God who straightens the ends of his white necktie and
smooths his frock coat at the sound of it.

For some reason there is something in preachifying that makes me
profoundly miserable; I feel like howling like a dog when you play the
piano.

I ought to be accustomed to it by this time; with an American
education, but I am not—

By the way—I'm not sure yet if I am going to stay here. They
turned me down on my eye examination and I have to wait for a
waiver of physical requirements to come from Washington. Meanwhile I linger in a vague limbo known as Casuals, unknown, ununi-
formed—where I dally with my paramour, Queen Ennui, the most
powerful of all goddesses. She wraps her sleepy shawls round me and
dangles before my eyes her toys and jumping jacks, her teasings and
itchings, desires that die before they are born, yearnings after music
and wandering and work, after unknown cities and friends and desert

isles and sun mottled rivers to bathe away all restraints in. 'Tis a good wench.

The food might be very much worse—one receives it in huge splashes in a complicated mess apparatus that it would take a juggler to handle with ease—

By the way what is your address?

Write me to 214 Riverside Drive until I let you know what happens to me—

Love
Jack

[Diary]
Oct 2nd [1918]
And here am I waiting waiting—the length of the days is simply phenomenal—I am beginning to enjoy them just for themselves—and then once one has embraced Queen Ennui boldly, kissed her square on the mouth—she's not a bad mistress and she lulls you to waking sleep with her strange nostalgic songs.

Durance Vile—I have been finishing The Confessions of Jean-Jacques—poor Jean Jacques—Like him I long for an Island Avalon where I may go and sleep and dream and build my soul a garlanded altar; white, implacable, where I may place as sacrifices all my past and all my future O to get away from all troubling things from war and governments and the entrenched stupidity of people—to get away and breathe and find myself and them come back to strive and love and hate and blow my little trumpets and unfurl my little flags until I can slip away on my last exile to Avalon or St Helena or Ellis Island—who cares—so long as it is an island where one can be alone with the dawn and the sunset.

I want to write a poem about the coming of The Queen of Cypris and Jerusalem to Asolo—

It is I, the Cyprian—might be a sort of refrain to it.

The Sixth Day of my captivity—Swept 6:30 to 9:30—The Gospel of the army is cunning, as of all other human activities. The wisdom of the snake under the meekness of the sheep is what wins out.

The first Commandment is—never let them get anything on you—

The second: Graft—get privileges others haven't got—worm yourself into confidence

The Third—seem neat and prosperous—as if you had money in the bank——

To Rumsey Marvin

> [Camp Crane
> Allentown
> *Oct 4* [*1918*]

Dear Rummy

Hast ever washed windows? It's a merry sport

It has a philosophic aloofness from the world: ie one is perched on an incredible high and rickety stepladder. It has the philosophic concept of eternity: for to the washing of windows there is no end. I calculate that in the course of the day I've washed 7,898,976,432,148,264,-312,800 windows and a few more. First one daubs them disdainfully with soap: "dreams breathed by the everliving on the polished mirror of the world"—"a dome of many-colored glass stains the white radiance of Eternity." Then one comes with a cloth and rubs them clear and shiny—Nirvana burning through the mist of Karma—"and there was a great ironic god, above all gods, who gave unto each of the souls a life to polish"——

Now I feel like the unfortunate Huguenots in the Wars of Religion in France that the followers of the Duke de Guise made dig up Catholics they had killed out of the ground where they had buried them—and with their bare fingers—Then I think they popped the Huguenots in and buried them alive——

Above all things humans love torturing one another—or seem to——

But I meant to say that my fingers were too tired to write.

We are under quarantine on account of the 'flu.

Write when you can——

> Love
> Jack

I look most baroque in a high collar—Notice the Pershing chin——Ecris mon vieux même si tu n'a pas le temps.

[Diary]
The Seventh Day of Captivity

Noon—The camp is Quarantined—we shall never get out—The world outside the green paling fence and the three strands of barbed wire may have come to an end entirely for all I know—Last night I met a man named Johnson who had been in Section 7—

Evening—Have in the course of the day cleaned a million windows —with each window I scrubbed my mind got murkier so now I have no mind at all though the windows shine resplendently—Why number the days of my Ennui?—This is

Oct. 5 [1918]
I am still in Casuals, have been, as usual sweeping floors—as usual I wait frustrate in Casuals.

My first encounter today with unpleasantness in high places—I hate to get to that blood-boiling state—it takes so long to get over it. That furious foiled anger drives everything out of one's head—O bitter is the fruit of slavery——

There's comradeship in it though—and one learns—o may it all some day sprout into green shoots of vengeance—my sort of vengeance——

A green picket fence and three strands of barbed wire—does the world outside still exist——

People tell one confidentially the most amusing things about how to get on—Be nice to corporal so and so . . . Smile at sergeant so and so—he has charge of the transfers—Sergeant so and so likes to talk about the weather—He might get you into the garage—He likes Melachrinos

Luck or Cunning—which is the evolutionary factor in the army?

The Grove—Camp Crane Sunday—the band is playing tinnily but with brio—

For the *Sack of Corinth*—just told me this afternoon by a little raucous-voiced Californian named Fuselli. Family went over on the ferry to Oakland—much weeping—In a shop window he spied a service flag with a gilt stripe round it and one star embroidered with the caduceus—the emblem of the Medical Corps—"I didn't give a shit how much it cost"—bought it and as was going into the station gave it to his girl—"Here don't you forget me"—The girl produced with great promptness a large box of candy—"How the devil she got hold of it I dont know"—

Other sexual adventures of the same youngster—Girl named Mabel he got to write love-letters to but real girl found out about it and he stopped—Portugie girl, but she was a toughee—Wants to marry the girl who gave the box of candy when he goes back. Tough street corner lounging crap shooting past——

But why should I make a pseudo-medical diagnosis of the poor kid?

O for a bumper full of the warm south——

Monday Oct 7 [1918]

Last night a particularly inept movie was presented for the edification of young America seated in the grandstand. Yet as German soldiers marched by and were very clumsily atrocious—I could feel a wave of hatred go through the men. Muttered oaths and shouted imprecations—God-damned bastards—cocksuckers every one of them—were sincere. The men were furious with war—kill kill kill. For the fellow beside me I gathered that he had a notion that in The War he would be engaged in constantly snatching halfraped Belgian women from the bloody claws of Huns; that all the Germans spent their time in atrocities and that the American soldiery marching on—actually would step in every few minutes and cry, 'Shoot not this old grey head' etc.

What he saw was a village in an over picturesque country with local color plastered on very thick, donkey carts, dog carts, milk carts with much shell fire and Germans rushing about with cans of kerosene setting things on fire—Germans whom the brave Americans chase out of towns, thereby saving crowds of young girls in peasant costume a la musical comedy—and battalions of dear old ladies in lace caps from being raped and ruined and cut up into small pieces, or toasted in fires by the Horrible Huns.

A cold rainy day—no news as yet—oh the infinite boredom of army camps. This is the eleventh day now since I came inside of the green picket fence with its three strands of barbed wire. What matter? You are safe in the arms of Ennui, your paramour—nothing can break you from her embrace.

I can see the room now that I had in the upper school—with mustard colored burlap on the walls—The bed was under a slant in the roof so that the ceiling rose over it like the side of a tent. There only did I feel secure from teasing and harassing and from games. How loath I was to leave its warm protection in the morning. When I think back at the misery of those years at school—I rejoice that I have at least got hold of *things* a little better in the six years that have gone by—But I'm much the same, by golly——

'I dont fuck women but I'm going to—God—I'd give anything to rape some of those German women. I hate them—men women children and unborn children—They're either Jackasses or full of the lust for power just like their rulers are—to let themselves be ruled by a bunch of warlords like that'—This after saying that he realized that after this peace move the Germans would legitimately feel that they were fighting for their homes and to protect themselves against foreign aggression.—Oct 7 1918—This I should say is the typical American spirit with regards to the war.

Indeed indeed the country is warmad——

Damn that sense of expectation—it drives you stark crazy—Hope deferred—The name brings up memory of much boredom—
Italy in company of the famous Fairbanks—
O if it were only mess time—Then after it, one thinks o if it were only mess time—not that there is anything particularly pleasant about mess—but it is an *event*. This morning I found myself hoping prayerfully that a slight squabble between Mirabella and the tall man who gives out the mail would end in a fight. I pictured the little Italian drawing a dagger and great pistol-shooting.
The other Event is the movies—every night out in the open air in the grand stand—they show most excellent ones. The great indicator of the pathetic state into which I am fallen is that I gurgle and chortle with delight over them.
As usual people's cowardice surprises me. The attitude of the papers over the German peace proposal and the speeches in the Senate all seem to me to show the most abject terror of saying the wrong thing. There's in America no inkling of the conception that a man has a right

to his opinion no matter what it is—Therefore there is no honesty in America.

One could make a very decent volume out of the frustrated people in such a limbo as casuals. The war from the point of view of those who merely pace in time with the military machine, but never get to the front.

Girls, letter writing, fortune telling (murder of brother by sister-in-law)—oh the thousands of photos of smirking young women that go through the mails! Of young men too—It's a comfort to be somewhere where sex performances are frank. In the army everyone wears a phallus on his sleeve.

oh what dullness What rot! O Bored, bored bored—lets go and read

Incidentally one is constantly making the mistake of confusing liberty with democracy—They have nothing in common at all—In America the one means "every man as good as his neighbor—liberty means nothing, except possibly political autonomy. I mean that the idea of liberty being the expression of the right of the individual to the freedom of thought and expression and to "the pursuit of happiness" in his own way—does not exist. In England liberty calls to mind successive charters of the rights of man contested by various uprisings of various classes from oppressive privilege.

To Rumsey Marvin

> [Camp Crane
> Allentown
> *October 11, 1918*]

Dear Rummy

What is the Reedy Mirror?

Public's a single tax magazine started by George some years ago. It's half-human and timid as a snail.

By the way about being mentally lazy. It seems to be the prevailing disease of our generation. I have it dreadfully. You cant imagine the battle I have with myself everytime I sit down to write. Sometimes Lazybones wins, sometimes I. And every victory makes the next a little easier, or maybe it does. The first couple of years I was in college I think I was as diffident as you are about writing—and God! how bad the stuff was. If I hadn't been so damn lazy then I'd be further ahead now.

Of course I did have my moments of inspiration—the sort of drunk feeling you get over an idea—but I really can't say if the result was any better than that of the sober struggles. One thing I do know—to this day it takes all the will I possess and more to get down to write and I'm subject to paralysis at any time. Of course I'm always happiest when I'm dizzy with work—and the ominous emptiness that comes from a long period of do-nothing manages to scare me into working eventually.

One thing I cant get to learn is the very simple—'never let a chance go by'—a chance for an adventure, a story, a dinner. There's a sluggishness somewhere in me that has left me many a time philosophically gaping on the bank while the enchanted bard drifted away into the mists of surmise. Life doesn't often hold out her hand to you—I think one should take it when she does and let the consequences take care of themselves, rather than stop to ask if she wears gloves or not.

Your Training Camp sounds interesting—lucky it encloses the library—I was sure you'ld find time to read—My experience with the army is that it leaves you hanging round a large part of the time—with nothing to do and no chance to do anything you want to do. I've got into the habit of always having a book in my pocket and relapsing into it at every occasion. At present I'm reading and re reading the first two sestiads of Marlowe's Hero and Leander—rich and flowing and full of over wrought opulence of life as an Italian marriage coffre of the Quinque-cento——

I'm still in a suspended state——

Addio
Jack

I'm sitting in the only pleasant part of our wretched compound, a grove of spindly oaks where the grackles chuckle mightily every evening, presumably discussing the silliness of that plucked and wingless fowl—man, and hawhawing over it.

You cant imagine the awfulness of quarantine But maybe you are quarantined too——

> The autumn leaves that danced this morning with the wind
> Curtseying slow in minuettes

Giddily whirling in bacchanals
Balancing in tiptoe contre-dances,
While the wind whispered of distant hills
And clouds like white sail, sailing
In limpid green frost-sparkled skies
Sailing beyond the horizon—
Have crossed the green picket fence
And the three strands of barbed wire.
They have kept the green picket fence
Despite the sentries' bayonets.

Under the direction of a corporal
Three soldiers are sweeping them up,
Sweeping up the autumn leaves,
Crimson maple leaves, splotched with saffron,
Ochre and cream,
brown leaves of horsechestnuts—
And the leaves dance and curtsey round the brooms
Full of mirth,
Wistful of the journey the wind promised them.

This morning the leaves fluttered gaudily,
Reckless, giddy from the wind's dances,
Over the green picket fence
And the three strands of barbed wire.
Now they are swept up
And put in a garbage can
With cigarette-butts
And chewed-out quids of tobacco,
Burnt matches and torn daily papers,
Old socks and the dusty shattered glass
From the multitudinous blind windows of barracks.

And the wind blows tauntingly
Over the mouth of the garbage can
Whispering—up and away,
Mockingly—far away.

I too am swept up
And put in a garbage can
With smoked cigarette ash
And chewed out quids of tobacco.
I am fallen into the kingdom
Of the great dusty queen . . .

Ennui, iron goddess, cobweb-clothed
Goddess of all useless things
Of cluttered rooms and sewed up rags
Of strong legs writhing on office stools,
Of camps bound tight with barbed wire
And green picket fences—
Blind my eyes with your close dust,
Choke up my ears with your cobwebs
That I may not see the clouds
That sail away across the sky
Far away, tauntingly;
That I may not hear the wind
That mocks and whispers and is gone
In pursuit of the horizon.

                                                        JRD. P.

[Diary]
Oct 14 [1918]
Have just been talking to a man who has been in camp here for
eighteen months. Was going across as sergeant, but went on a joy ride;
goggle eyed drunk, up Fifth Avenue and was found out. From every
hand as usual in these beastly army camps rises the moan of the
leftovers. Oh the incalculable waste of energy—the waste of years and
months of young manhood in these armies.

God! how can one write in captivity in quarantine?
The man who loved Service—I must see more of him. Service, with
all his rather colorless diction, his banal imitation of Kipling Masefield
and Co—must have things to be said for him. He is genuine I think
and he expresses things in terms that are exactly those of the untrained
who love him. He is expressive, I swear, he's a good example of the sort
of poetry that lasts its generation and dies—perhaps this is the background, the loam from which real poetry draws its power to grow into
eternity. In music—probably in all art we have the same thing it is no
use sneering at it. Jack London, Zane Grey and such people are other
examples of the same school.
Here's an idea for the plaything that has thrust itself so obtrusively
into my consciousness—
The scene in the garden in Greenwich Village with skyscrapers in
the background and garbage cans in the foreground—

Enter the *Garbage Man*—

How about this?

Act I—the first act of James Clough's play—Death in a respectable family

Act II The garbage man in the Greenwich Village garden—gets the fruit and things—the girl who escaped in Act I escapes again in Act II by climbing to the top of the highest building and striking the gong of the moon—at least her lover does it.

Act III Success—The lover has succeeded—the girl has succeeded—a very scantily furnished but beautiful room with a landscape with cedar trees outside Death strolls in at the door—They are middle aged—they talk faintly dismally—Success is death.

In Act I Death is a lousy little man rather like a doctor, with a black bag.

In Act II he is the garbage man

In Act III he is a very gorgeous person—a Wall Street broker's idea of a King

> The Cyprian
> The air is drenched to the stars
> With fragrance of flowering grape
> Where the hills hunch up from the plain
> Till they blot out half the golden grain
> Of stars scattered on the threshing floor
> The road winds faint up the hills
> So full of the tinkle of bells
> Of the climbing track of mules

Oct 17 [1918]

Yesterday I was tremendously excited by the prospect of the end of the war—Today all seems cucumber-calm. The allied press talks bigger and bigger as time goes by and the prospect of a democratic Germany fighting for life against the oligarchic allies becomes more and more likely. O Lord how wild it makes me to be stuck in this damn camp—I lay awake last night thinking up complicated swearing to express the situation. I could find nothing strong enough. O for a Jew's wailing place.

The end of the third week of waiting—Jehosophat.

It took me a half hour in doping out how to spell scissors—In yer medical pouch you've got stuff to bring yer to and bandages and scissors—now how the divil do you spell scissors

O mutter take in yer service flag yer boy's in the medical corps

All this saith the marvellous Kipling O. Flarrety—

I'll open a Irish house in Berlin, I will—and there'll be O Casey and O Brien and Flannagan and Flinnigan, and begad the King of England'll be there.

To Rumsey Marvin

[Camp Crane
Allentown]
Oct 20 [1918]

Rummy—

Still stationary—foaming at the mouth, gnashing my teeth, swearing, squirming, raging, pacing up and down in the cadenced monotony of utter boredom—bored as a polar bear in a cage—Golly.

They seem to be keeping you busy—at least they give you the illusion of activity—I wish I had it. I wonder that the U.S. army hasn't yet found a way of polishing the moon—they will soon, don't worry.

They are sane about sex in the army, aren't they? It is a comfort not to have the sacred phallus surrounded by an aura of mystery and cant, but one sometimes wonders if man is a selective animal at all in matters of sex. Yet I think he is. The fact remains though that the majority of men—allowing for the fact that they talk bigger than they act—, think rather of a piece of tail than of a woman. It means to them the frequent stimulation of a certain part of the anatomy and nothing else. Perhaps I overrate the mating instinct, but I think it is susceptible of slightly higher development. Maybe it isn't. Still I think that the piece of tail attitude is partly caused by the stupid conventional morality that makes copulation wrong in itself, and only licenses it grudgingly through a marriage ceremony. The result is that people degrade their everyday habits to a sexual stupidity hardly shared by animals.

I *almost* think that Europeans have a higher—less promiscuous view of sex than Anglo Saxons. The Frenchmen goes out pour faire l'amour instead of to have a piece of tail. Maybe the difference is mainly in superior phraseology, but I think not. Amour postulates reciprocity, a human relation. A piece of tail might be got off the bunghole of a cider barrel—And the American hates with a righteous hatred born only of outraged morality the goddam' whore who gives him his piece of tail—or rather sells it.

Excuse me for inflicting this ethical disquisition, but it is a subject that interests me hugely—almost in a scientific way. One has no data to go on, as the moralizers have falsified everything; so one has to find out for oneself—and it is so shrouded in the mists of conflicting conventions that research is fascinatingly difficult.

One peels off layers of conventions like skins off an onion.

First there is the family convention that man is a monogamous animal swiving few times a year for the production of offspring.

Then there is the sporty young man convention that a man should want to swive everything in skirts.

Then there is the convention of the god dam' whore as opposed to the real nice girl who'll go just so far but no further—and how many others?

It does seem to me that we of the present day have managed to bring sex to a pitch of ugliness never before reached. We have so muddied the waters that it is hardly possible to see clearly even with the greatest effort.

(To be continued)

The departing of a section for Hoboken and the front is nearly killing me. I had counted on getting into it, but Headquarters refuses to hurry itself in deciding my status. I'd like to dynamite them from Colonels to office boys——

And we are still under quarantine for the floo——

Write lots to the Prisoner of Camp Crane

Talk about the Bastille!

love
Jack

[Diary]
Oct 29th [1918]
now Acting Q.M. Sergeant sect 541 Rumor that we leave tonight for France. The above is a joke——

Nov 1st [1918]—Camp Merritt
Am in charge of a barracks full of men with the dull job of keeping anyone from going out. Yesterday after two days and nights of inspec-

tions and waiting round without any particular food or sleep—we marched out of Camp Crane—Section 541 USAAS—with much laboring and people falling out of ranks on account of ill arranged packs—entrained and jolted about and waited on sidings for the rest of the day with very little food except for half an apple no an apricot pie—But this existence wipes ideas off ones mind as a damp rag wipes pictures off the blackboard before class——What's the use of writing?

To Rumsey Marvin

                                                        Camp Merritt N.J.
                                                        [*November 1918*]

Rummy—

Its a great life. Three times we have been ready to pile on a transport and be desperately seasick and louseaten for two weeks of convoy travel. Three times we have been held up. Great is the hand of Allah. Now I wonder if I shall ever see the A.E.F. at all.

A pack is great fun, a regular Noah's Ark on your back. I'm still "acting" sergeant, a nasty, neither flesh, fowl, or good red herring position; but things amuse me much. People are very pleasant and reveal new amusing features daily. Our top sergeant is a delight: a regular New York Irish politician always ready to do a friend a good turn and play a mean trick on an enemy, a darn nice fellow. One of the corporals is an ex-taxi driver, another used to drive a motor hearse. Then there are cowpunchers and railroad men and farmers and bakers and butchers and candlestick makers.

I may leave for France anytime and I may never leave——

                                                                  love
                                                                  Jack

[Diary]
Nov 4th [1918]
Still Camp Merritt & still about to sail for France; nearly crazy with waiting and with the fear that we wont go. O the maddening uncertainty of the damned army.

Four coons singing in and dancing in a barrack—black shiny coons amid the pinkish faces and khaki of the soldiers crowded round One coon sings with a guitar

O dis is de song ob the Titanic
Sailin' on de sea

How de Titanic ran into dat cold iceberg
How de etc.

O de Titanic's a sinking in the deep blue
She's sinking in de deep blue
Sinking in de deep blue
Sinking in de deep blue sea
O de women an de chilren a floatin in de sea
Round dat cold ice-berg
Sung near-er ma gawd to thee
Nearer ma gawd to thee
    Nearer to thee
O de women an de children
a floating and a sinkin in de cold blue sea

Nov 11 [1918]

or is it 12th anyway its two AM and we are leaving Camp Merritt at once presumably for the boat—the transport which will take us to France or Siberia or somewhere else.

Rumors float back and forth. Everytime anyone comes back from that great council chamber the can, a new flock appears. Talk is mainly of seasickness and the possibility of French jazz—The married men are sore as they expected to be mustered out and dont want to go overseas to 'clean up shit,' as the war's over they say. Single men on the whole rather excited at the prospect of new lands.

Everything——

Nov 15 [1918]

A convoy day—Our ship, the Cedric; the Adriatic; the Empress of Britain; the US warship Nebraska, three anonymous cargo-carriers, a converted German liner and a big destroyer make up the convoy, and roll along lazily with a stiff Northwest wind in the quarter. The convoy is greatly delayed by a zebra-striped cargoboat that keeps lagging behind so that the battleship has constantly to go back and pick it up. Imagine: the war has been over for three days. Nov 12, the morning we left Camp Merritt the Armistice was signed. It takes sometime to realize it. The years of that particular sort of darkness are over.

How about collecting my verse and calling it Sketches of the Dark Years Letters of an Embusqué might be called that, but God, with so much on hand how shall I ever get started—The Sack of Corinth isn't started yet and that will take months and months Golly!

I am in charge of the mess hall in the bowels of the ship, where I have to coerce unwilling and half seasick soldiers to sling the hash in an atmosphere unbelievably sordid. How I keep from puking at the thought I dont know—It is fantastic how much more one can stand than one thinks one can——

A troopship is a remarkable place—miserable seasick unwashed with officers stalking about looking for trouble as hens look for worms in a barnyard—eyes steely necks outstretched—Yet that is not absolutely true in my experience—of course always in the medical corps the officers are kindly and gentlemanly and really interested in the welfare of the men. The sergeants etc are pretty blustery and enjoy inordinately showing their authority—but the army, the army, the democratic army—is about as much so as the French army.

As the men troop in and out of the messhall I notice the sheeplike look army life gives them—a dumb submissive look about the eyes. They usually submit cowedly to my shoutings to move on with the hurt look of dogs that have been illtreated. Yet some are quizzical some stupidly truculent—I have more hopes of the U.S.A. since I've been in their damned army than I ever had before—

Nov 17 [1918]
Ordering people about—habitually—as a daily occupation—is the most remarkable experience I ever had. It is so curious bawling people out—

Nov 18 [1918]
Oh the sordidness. They call the garbage cans Rosies—that's the only redeeming feature of my frightful K.P. sergeancy—

Nov 19 [1918]
Free at last from the abominations of K.P.

A sergeant's is a comical sort of existence—sick call—Qualification cards—record boxes—and much amiable rot—

I carry about boxes of CC pills for constipated members of my gang. I get them books and writing papers from the Y.M.C.A. room. I advise them to eat a lot to cure their seasickness—I bandage their vaccination scars—It's a curious existence. That is not so bad but being a mess sergeant—was a sordid hell—stuffy stinking of grease and dishwater—enough to keep you from ever eating anything again—

The poking of fingers into the corners of dishpans to see if they were clean and dry—the shouting with the sweat—sweat! I sweat enough in the week in that mess hall to fill the sources of the Nile—shouting at the steward with the sweat rolling off my face, quarrelling about sugar and jam and numbers of oranges and when the K.P.s shall be fed—I shall never forget the stench and the squabble and the gluttonous seasick sordidness of it—But one thing: I can never be seasick again after having lasted out in that mess hall for—let's see—for seven days—Nine meals a day most of the time. It is remarkable what the human organism can stand.

But a troop ship is no place to try to write or read or think——

O if I could have painted the sea as it was yesterday with a great steaming of coppery saffron clouds over it. Or the peacock brilliance of the rainbow the other day over a hazel green sea—one of the few rainbows—by the way that have not seemed to me sentimental—

                    The Sack of Corinth
              Camp & lives
          On emerging there
            stories
            Backgrounds
            Tail
            Food
            ———

            Transport
              Foreigners
              Petulency   l'esprit
              Conceit   National
            ———

Prologue

Nov 22 [1918]
Still chugging along in convoy—a seasick homesick rather blue bunch

of troops except a few who assert the educational value of foreign travel—

The conversation with a man in the dark—a pitch black moonless rainy night—and the terror of submarines and loneliness and strange unaccustomed things—Can be the climax of a series—The feeling of the frightfulness of the unknown—sea cold, sea dark—the little comfortable soul born out of its groove and shivering in the great shaggy world.

In a dream in Verdun as I looked the sun was filmed over like a bloodshot eye and began to sway and wabble in the sky as a spent top sways and wabbles and whirling rolled into the seas vermillion ways so that pitblackness covered me.

Nov. 27 [1918]
After four days of miscellaneous and most grievous disease I feel well enough to start to scribble notes again I think I've had symptoms of all known diseases: pneumonia, T.B., diphtheria, diarrhea, dispepsia, sore throat, whooping cough, scarlet fever and beri-beri, whatever that is.

Americans crab so—I wonder if all people do when you get them in unusual positions. Hell I cant write with every body singing crabbing mainly crabbing

Nov. 29 [1918]
Le Havre This is the most miserable existence imaginable—From camp to camp one wanders weighed down by that beastly heavy pack that gets one into a state of sullen rage so that one can't even talk to new found people for amusement.

This is the beginning of the third month of my servitude. In all that time I haven't once been outside of fences and barbed wire—oh why talk about it all. I have never sunk into such complete sordid misery.

And it's hardly any use marking down names of towns

Nov. 30 [1918] Never mind—
O' Reilly's Travelling Circus is rather amusing when those two old Teutons Schultz and Wiendieck get drunk on beer at the canteen and when Yoat has to be carried in to bed— The Beer Canteen is a great improvement over the YMCA as a hanging-out place.

A sergeant is really rather a cheese in a British Camp—the B.E.F. seems a strangely ineffective affair, as I had always thought. Spends all of its time polishing brass buttons and kowtowing to rank.

At this moment the King of England is having Hallelujah festivals in Paris—who the hell wants to see him?

It must infuriate the socialists

Dec 2 [1918]

At Ferrières—a charming little town in Loire et something at the USAAS base camp. The monotonous army routine drums on round me. I have really nothing to do. An occasional job to attend to as Q.M. Sgt. helps to pass a small part of the interminable days. I have an utterly desperate feeling of helplessness. If we had work to keep us busy it would be different—but this way it is a sullen black dullness all the time, bitter, bitter, bitter.

To Dudley Poore

Ferrières
Dec 2 [*1918*]

Tenebrae, tenebrae—the slaves in the clay pits of Babylon could not see because of the red dust in their eyes. There is no more sordid misery than blindness. I know nothing of what is going on in the curious farcical world outside. I know nothing but routine and waiting about and insufferable dullness. I suppose I am in France. In the Army all countries are the same. They mean merely drink and tail and M.P's driving you back to camp and sudden alluring glimpses through fences.

This would be a delightful spot—an old abbey piled upon a hill muddled unexpectedly at the edge of a little town full of steep roofs and beetling chimney pots. In a day or two I'll let you know my address. Then please write me about yourself. How soon do you expect to be free? You and I and Tom must galivant if the skies fall for it. I'll have money and perhaps the novel'll publish. O there will be so many things to do, time to be made up, miseries boredoms to be atoned for. One must be revenged on the order of things for the ridiculous boredoms endured in these years.

Tell me about Lieut Bobby and the Auk and John Wolcott and later when we meet I shall want to hear about what has been happening in the last months.

But probably I shall be shipped back to America before any chance of seeing you. Then I shall bob back at once—Or will you go back to the U.S. for awhile? I must know the probabilities.

O God how long? Still it is funny, in a way—many things are very funny. The Sack of Corinth will be mainly farce, I think. Adieu D

[Diary]
Dec 3 [1918]
Things look better—leisurely French dinners in the Hotel du Cheval Blanc and the smell of the French winter and the ancient pillars of the Abbey, founded the postcards say, by Clovis. Ferrières-en-Gâtinais is a pleasant rambling little town—with a bakery where one gets delicious bread and wine shops where the beer and red wine are good and where the Americans crowd wonderingly, sneeringly, drunkenly. There are many streams and I suspect millwheels. I have not had a chance yet to wander round the town, as one cant leave the camp till half past four when its dark.

Sunday—Dec 8 [1918]
Still at Ferrières-en-Gâtinais—at the Base Camp—for the first time since I've been here—or in the army, for that matter, I've been really busy, writing innumerable reports, which I count out with two fingers on a lame Corona. The all pervading red tape of the army is something stupendous.

Things are pretty dull and the high collar galls frightfully—

The Americans trooping about the old Abbey church—founded by Clovis where Carloman, Clodimir are buried—Et la musique de ton nom Mérovingien—a strange sight—

Every now and then one gets a glimpse of the farce and the deformed enormities of war—

The man talking of the mad house where they choked the noisy insane man—

The tale of the man under sentence of court martial—of the wild ride from St Nazaire to Paris with a drunken convoy Wanderings behind the front of an unattached soldier.

Drunk Drunk Drunk—

The men hang about the pretty girls with red cheeks in the epicerie like flies on a damp day round a plate of cakes.

Ferrières is a charming old town full of all old memories of Mérovingians and Franks of Clovis and Clodimir and Clothilde.

Charlemagne frequented the Abbey which was said to have been founded by three of the Disciples Altian Politian and Hermatian— some such names—

Alcuin was Prior and learning and holiness went hand in hand

A family de Blanchefort seems to have had lots to do with the rebuilding of the church in the fifteenth century—

There is a cupola over the crossing on beautiful high stepped pillars

The pleasant sound of rooks on a winter morning and the green and lilac colored boughs of trees against the dove grey sky.

To John Howard Lawson

Private J. R. Dos Passos
S.S.U. 541. USAAS
Convois Automobile
Par B.C.M. Paris
Dec 8 [*1918*]
Ferrières—en—Gâtinais
(Loiret) France

Jack!

Wo bist du? In the words of Monsieur le général Pershing in those immortal words—Lafayette nous sommes voilà—

Ferrières is an excellent and ancient town that reeks of sounding Mérovingian names, Clovis and Clothilde Carloman and Clodimir, Pepin le Bref and Charles le Chauve. The base camp of the USAAS is in the remnants of an old abbey; stove pipes stick out coquettishly under crumbling cusps; the click of typewriters reeling up red tape echoes in gothic vaulting and disturbs the rooks in the mossgreened trees.

There are many little cafes—all choked with khaki and one can get good dinners and cheap at the Cheval Blanc, and good golden Barsac—but I am at the moment broke, penniless, and flat. The army never seems to pay one and frantic letters to Morgan Harjes only induce silence stony as the Sphinx's smile. So I wander hungrily through the dark streets of the village and peer at diners and winers through the smoked panes—or else I most barefacedly bum food and drink off the first comer.

For heaven's sake let me know where you are, why and when; and what is going on in the world. I know nothing of anything. Ears and eyes are sealed by the omnipotent khaki

I am frantic for mail—

Figurez-vous I am only fifty miles from Paris It must be a frantically exciting place now. How's Rome? Or where are you?

You may be in America—

There's a chance that one may be allowed to muster out of the army over here on condition that one signs up in the Red Cross in Serbia. So I may be back at the old touring business again. Anything to wriggle one's neck out of the collar.

Still it has been well worthwhile—

Addio
Dos

[Diary]
Dec. 12 [1918]
The days succeed one another sordid, without a jot of variety. O the unexpressible sordidness of army life—the filth and greasiness of it.

The only interest is getting money. I have not had a cent since I landed in France and neither has that remarkable Irishman Sergeant O Reilly and yet we manage by hook or by crook to get a meal at the Cheval Blanc every night and much drink at different cafés scattered about town

The unforgettable scene with the whore in the back room of the Cheval Blanc—a page out of Artzibasheff. That must go in the Sack of Corinth word for word.

Also the partie Madeleine, at the other café. . . .

Dec 18 [1918]
The days drag by.

Madeleine and the girl with the red cheeks when the boys cluster like

flies on a wet day, loitering hungrily like dogs round a back door
where they half expect to be fed, and the whores and the man who is
going to marry the French girl.

The artist who left yesterday for Belfast, a funny rather maudlin
little man.

I am sitting in the little inner room at the cafe de Madeleine, while
they talk about death at the table. The sergeant says what a little thing
it is to die—in the generations a man is nothing. Tout est bien fait dans
la nature. Dans la mort il n'y a rien de terrible.

Quant on va mourir on pense à tout—mais vite

To Dudley Poore

Sens
12/22 [*1918*]

Dudloysha

Out of the dark that covers me etc I escaped for the day to Sens. I
have tasted of the divine one of the movable mansion, I have eaten of
escargots—great juicy squirming escargots. Therefore I am strength-
ened to write one more appeal for news. I don't care if your mouth and
both hands are constantly full of letters, or if you never have a moment
in which you are not couriering after something—you must write with
your toes or by telepathy or somehow—

We must stop drifting, we must take the bit in our teeth (as you
see the escargots are mighty within me) What is your future? I'd cast a
horoscope if you'd give me any data to go on—but all I know is that
you have acquired a certain Mme Lecomte and that the little silver
shekels don't dance as merrily as they might. All this from Tom whom
I saw on a hasty scramble through the MP haunted woodland of Wier
where gloom rhymed with Ullalume as far as I was concerned.

Sens is a delightful holy little town where the dank streets drip
holy water and the rain sprinkles like a hyssop out of a benitier. Aged
abbés shuffle goutily along irregular pavements and dart into doorways whence come greasy religious smells of déjeuners being cooked
by wrinkled housekeepers. Nuns with butterfly hats convoy trains of
little girls out of dark doors hurriedly to the nearest gate of the cathedral, letting none linger in the polluted air outside. At mass there is
much sniffing and coughing and a shuffle of the slippers of two very
old suisses in crimson who now and then let their canes rattle impa-

tiently on the pavement—the voice of the Lord in the ears of sinners. There are lots of beautiful half-timbered houses and several carved wooden facades from the moyen age. Sens expresses its yearning for the modern and for speed by means of an exquisitely ugly Hotel de Ville built right under the wrinkled aged nose of the cathedral, tweaking it, pour ainsi dire.

Some of the glass is superb. There's a furious futuristic rose window in crude orange and lilac and yellow and a window of which the center is a broad band of interlaced scarlet between blues and purples—the most beautiful I think I've ever seen.

O but M. le Duc, Violet le Duc, what have you done? Everywhere new noses and toeses—Or worse yet whole acres of wall space replaced with neat new nicely cut stone identical with that in the Hotel de Ville. And in a sort of dungeon under the Archbishops palace is a tas of the rejected ones, disgruntled ladies and gentlemen and leaves and arabesques that all have the resentful air of those captains and colonels and generals in the U.S. Army, boys at eighty, who were chucked out by some law or other and raised a great clamor in the newspapers about it, refusing to be retired except by force.

It has been a pleasant misty day and all the gargoyles have dripped as they ought and the moss has been vivid as emeralds on the roofs of the houses, and my face has the pleasant flushed feeling of having been rained on all day—but the hour is striking. The coach is a pumpkin again, the horses are mice with the mange and Cinderella must run back to her ashes and her scrubbing brushes and her typewriter.

Adieu D

Just as I was starting to call on her Tom told me of Mlle. Racine's death. I shall never forget her. Her pale sacrificed life somehow sums up all that is tragic in the world. It is my loss that I did not know her sooner. It is a great gap in our Paris.

I must add another sheet for the censorship to hold my lieut's initials. Have you heard the rumor that members of the A.E.F. qualified to study in foreign universities who desire to do so may (may alas) be allowed to muster out over here? I am a candidate for a doctorat at the Sorbonne in anything that may be pleasing to official ears, from Icthyology to Hermetic languages. In case you need it I enclose a cheque on the blessed M and H.

To Rumsey Marvin

Pvt. J. R. Dos Passos
SSU 541
Convoy Auto
par B.C.M. France
December 29, 1918

Rummy!

A letter from you has turned up with a wonderful project—cocoa-beans and Spanish and poetry and wandering—but mon cher I have no granpère to come across with the dough! And I have a frightful lot of work to do as soon as I can wriggle my neck from out of the collar. Look at this.

1. Rewrite Seven Times Round the Walls of Jericho and get it published, if that is possible.

2. Write a certain Sack of Corinth—a monumental work on America Militant.

3. Write a certain play of which the scenario has been gradually cooking for the longest time.

4. Write a certain The Family Connection an opus a novel of the exegi monumentum aere perennius type

5. Collect numerous fragments into a series of essays.

6. Study the Anthropology of religions or religious anthropology, possibly in some university

7. Learn to paint

8. Paint

9. Visit Abyssinia

and so on ad infinitum.

Now what is one to do with such a program? And here I am wasting days and weeks and months in the state of servitude you so admire. I'll make their ears tingle though, by God, if I die in the attempt. I'll dust their coats with a clanking of printing presses. O things are not what they seem. I wish you had got a larger dose of what you love so. You would have come to know it better, I warrant you.

Don't worry about not having an aim. I felt the same way when I first went to college. It took me a good three years to get rid of family bred inhibitions before I realized exactly what I wanted to do. When I think how far I am from doing it I become terrified. Then too I suffer from a multiplicity of desires. I want to swallow the oyster of the world. I want to peel the rind of the orange. I want to drink the cup to the dregs—no—I want to swallow it and still have it to look at. I want to peel off the rind in patterns of my own making. I want to paint with the dregs pictures of gods and demons on the great white curtains of eternity.

And I do nothing. I blame the army, the weather, the food—O if I could wrench myself out of the blankness of inertia.

Like you I believe in frugal living, unwasteful—Like you I abhor the puppyish lying about of college life, the basking in the sun with a full belly. Life is too gorgeous to waste a second of it in drabness or open-mouthed stupidity. One must work and riot and throw oneself into the whirl. Boredom and denseness are the two unforgivable sins. We'll have plenty of time to be bored when the little white worms crawl about our bones in the crescent putrifying earth. While we live we must make the torch burn ever brighter until it flares out in the socket. Let's have no smelly smouldering.

I wish I could get to South America with you Rummy. Maybe it can be worked. Or couldn't you let cocoa wait a year and come to Spain. That would be cheaper for me and I vow you'll gain as much.

But who knows? Spain, or Peru, Abyssinia or the Yalu River we must go somewhere together very soon—

There's a chance that I'll be able to get a furlough to try for an A.M. in an European University—so a couple of months may find me at Cambridge or the Sorbonne. Then work! work! Gods how the dust'll fly.

I have been bitterly disappointed by the defeat of the British Labor Party—The world has not yet seen an end of its backsliding. Old Bogey is Lord God. Mumbo Jumbo reigns supreme—Hurrah for the dark ages!

Love
Jack
Write Morgan Harjes

To Dudley Poore

Montargis
4 Janvier [1919]

'Loysha—I have had a very warm lingering bath and a dinner in a crowded table d'Hôte near the market, and a mouthful of very expensive caramels and have taken refuge from the pleasant insinuating eternal gentle rain in this café. Your letters from Bordeaux are most exciting: they are full of the smells of wine casks from the quais and garlic and oil and mandarines from the bistreaux that seem to be your abiding place. They make me want to cour too. So much that I wrote Bobby to find out what my chances of transferring to the P.E.S. were and what were the means of accomplishing it.

In the USAAS Base Camp I die of dust and gray mould. Not even the tall town or the Abbaye or its flèche, which the tailor told me was made that way to imitate the scales of a fish, or the little tortuous streets of Ferrières suffice to revive me from the dismals. But I've made demarches.

You must too

I have written the Army Overseas Education Commission 10 Rue des Elysées, Paris, telling them that I am A.B. of Harvard etc and that I desire to pursue an A.M. in Anthropology in Continental Universities, needing therefore an immediate release from the Legions of Maman Liberté.

You see things are brewing. Plans are being matured to allow properly qualified members of the A.E.F. to study in foreign universities on a sort of scholarship system. It is highly probable that a HQ order will be out on the subject before long. Meanwhile the thing to do according to the University Union is to file an application with your Commanding Officer, and to write stating your pedigree at length and your desires in the Groves of Academe to the address I just gave you.

While we're on a rather dull subject don't you think that Anthropology is rather chic as a profession? One's papa was always telling one a young man should have a profession. Ergo it has suddenly dawned upon me that a profession I must have.

And Anthropology connotes Abyssinia and the New Hebrides and the Gobi Desert and the Moon and the mountains thereof.

Qu'en penses-tu?

I've written Bobby to discover things about the P.O.2.C. which is I believe a branch of the YMCA.

Jack writes that he is in Rome, anxiously awaiting the arrival of M. le President Veelson whose advent it seems the Croce Rossa is going to celebrate with song and dance. Then if he doesn't go to Constantinople he is coming to Paris and to Ferrières to put the slug horn to his lips and blow a call to the Place du Tertre.

Van thinks of going to Russia with the Friends.

I was awfully grateful for the autobiographical fragments you vouchsafed. I was tingling with curiosity to know how you had become a member of the P.E.S. But must one go to Tours to perform that ceremony to receive the chrysm and the collar?

Adieu D

To Rumsey Marvin

[Strassburg]
Jan 22–25 [1919]

In Strassburg is the first continuous vaudeville on record. It consists of a clock, constructed by some intricate-minded person, in which little figures walk about and ring bells and cocks crow and all sorts of joyous things happen, minor events on the quarter hour and half hour, full acts on the hour and the great drama twice a day at twelve when the twelve apostles walk out and bow elaborately to the Lord and the cock crows thrice and the figure of the day of the week rolls out—All of which is great fun. Strassburg is a glorious place, full of preposterous peaked gables and old carved wooden houses that hang story after ornamented story over the street going up to roofs unbelievably steep and whimsical, ending in little gilded peaks and weather cocks—a city out of Grimm; over all rises the featherwork tower of the Munster—high and ornate a slender filigree of reddish stone—

Joy—I am in curious little dive of a café where a negro in French uniform is dancing with a faded blonde Alsatian to the raucous music of the strangest music box man ever saw—a contraption with dancing negros and a cuckoo, cousin to the clock in the cathedral.

O Rummy why aren't you here? We could dash about the little zigzag streets and listen to fat Teutonic waltzes in noisy cafés, and watch the snow-flakes die in the polished surface of the canal where a few lamps trouble the dark peacock blue reflections of the huddled roofs of houses . . .

This is the wildest little café ever discovered—a sort of frantic spirit of farce seems to emanate from the silly music box—making everything like those curved mirrors at Coney Island. But I must go out and find dinner—and then I shall become farcical myself if I stay too long within earshot of this insane music box.

Jan 25 [1919]

Saussheim again—It's very cold and the German tiled stoves are the greatest comfort in the world.

By the way when you write be sure to address letters to Morgan Harjes—always—as I keep them advised of all changes of address and letters get to me much quicker through them than any other way.

When shall we walk thirty-six miles again together and where?

There are many roads in the world—and they are all waiting, long and winding, climbing hills to the sky, stretching sheer across plains to the sunset—

> Jack
> Pvt J. R. Dos Passos
> SSU 523
> Convois Auto
> par B.C.M. France

To Dudley Poore

> [Paris]
> *March 6* [*1919*]

It was with extraordinary dismay that—upon jauntily bouncing into Mme. Lecomte's with my papers condemning me to the Sorbonne in my pocket—I learned that you had disappeared to England. Dismay that refuses to wear off. I have tried and shall try to be transferred, but I am sure it is impossible.

I have been dolefully wandering about the long corridors of the Sorbonne trying in vain to find anyone who knows anything about anything. I hang my hopes on meeting you . .

This broke off to eat coquilles and merlan and beignets and Mme. Lecomte says to tell you On fait mieux Quai d'Anjou qu'en Angleterre.

Have seen a little man with skyrocket eyelashes and heard part of a lecture on Vertumnus. Am advised to go and wait on the mighty Reinach at St. Germain en Laye.

Look Dudley—you must keep me copiously informed of things— do be garrulous as I am very curious as to things in England. Later I'll send the addresses of my little old ladies and you must go down to London to see them.

And for God's sake keep your eye peeled for publishers. If you see one in a hedge or balancing on a clover head net him. At all cost publishers must be caught. You can tell them by their whiskers—

To Rumsey Marvin

Paris—*March 17/19*
A little estaminet—rue St. Honoré

Rummy—

I have been dreadfully mum in the last months—forgive and prepare to receive penitent avalanches.

I am free—at least provisionally

Libertad libertad! As Walt would have cried, tearing another button off his undershirt.

I loll in the groves of Academe. I am at the Sorbonne—a large monumental place that has up to the writing given me no other impression but that of massy dullness—but I live in a pleasant little room on the Montagne St. Geneviève, near the Pantheon, where I typewrite from morning till night with intervals for food—delicious sizzly Paris food and concerts, preparing the M.S. of Seven Times Round the Walls of Jericho for a journey to London and a promenade in publishers' wastebaskets. Furthermore another novel and a play are clamouring for a hearing and I hope that the dear things will be able to see the light before long. There is alas, so remarkably little time in twenty four hours. Why don't days have forty eight?

I am enclosing a couple of poems in case the magazine scheme comes through. Do write me more about it—I'm tremendously interested. Why go out for the business end of the Record? You'ld much better get in by writing comic verses about the Peace Conference or the American Public or God or Joan of Arc, or serious sonnets about the sadness of a beerless Hofbrau.

I saw last night at the Adevil de Musset's most exquisite play On ne Badine pas avec l'Amour—one of the loveliest things I've ever seen on the stage—though it was acted in a heavy classic manner—It shows you what really happens to a romance of syrup and mintleaves and moonlight if you leave it alone—written in a superb futuristic casual style.

Then the other day I heard a whole Debussy concert——delight of delights—though I was so crowded in with other people that I had to stand for four hours on one leg with the elbow of a very Katisha in my tummy and a gentleman's beard tickling the back of my neck—the whole bunch of us hanging precariously from a brass rail in the highest balcony the while That is the way to hear music.

Later: I seem to have strayed away from my usual paths into a nasty little restaurant into which I was lured by a pleasant odor of fried fish—it turns out to be full of RedCrossworkers whose conversations are very annoying. They say such madly asinine things about France and always the same things.

Here are more: Y.M.C.A. workers this time; much worse than Red Crossworkers—mealymouthed. They talk about how expensive food is, and about Y.M.C.A. prizefights and how immoral Paris is——

What about coming to Europe next summer? I rather hope to be in Spain—if I can get out of the Army as soon as the University closes at the end of June. Though everything depends on the possibilities of publishing the novel. Why cant you come and galivant about Spain? You could learn Spanish and increase your leg-muscles walking over stony mountain paths and if you want to be "practical" study treatises on quadruple entry bookkeeping under the shade of olivetrees while I sketch the antiquities. Wont you try the project on the family?

I may be trying to collect material for a treatise on Spanish Folklore or something of the sort for a Doctorat or a Licenciat at the Sorbonne

But, as I said, everything depends on the possibility of getting a publisher. I expect to go back to America in the fall to write for my bread and butter, or something of the sort—though there is a vague chance that I may teach out in Roberts College—Constantinople—I've been recommended by a friend of mine. It would be rather fun to be out there for a year I think. One would have a chance to travel all over everywhere in the vacations. But I doubt very much if anything materializes.

If I go utterly broke I shall try to get a job with the Red Cross.

Do write me all about Yale—I suppose it's gradually changing back into an institution of learning—getting out of its degraded state of last year.

A bientôt
Jack—

Spain—Spain—garlic and roses and mountains tawny as panthers.

To Dudley Poore

[Paris]
April 6 [*1919*]

Dudloysha,

I write abed in the last stages of recovery from a remarkable disease, during which my head swelled into a large revolving lighthouse in which a gong rang continually and I coughed in a manner to turn my throat inside out and then outside in again. From the warm and stormy altitude of my revolving tower, I lay and regarded my past with much discontent and my present with more. Can you conceive it: I am still frittering about that ridiculous novel. On reading Part Two to Jack Lawson and a friend of his—the sort of person who knows—named Barry—a very delightful man, a friend, not of the Lippmann sort, of Compton Mackenzie, who has spent the year in Russia necessary to enlightenment, it seems—on reading Part Two to them I suddenly discovered that it would never do. It's positively horrid. So I promptly went home and took to my bed, where I have remained ever since, Part One, however, went like a dream.

So now Part Two has got to be fussed at and fidgeted over and cut down—you can't imagine how horrid it is.

Parts iii and iv come up to trial today, if I have enough voice to les gazouiller as they say at the Chat Noir.

And all this time I ought to be advancing to new pastures.

Kate Drain [Lawson's wife to be] left for America day before yesterday. Jack is going back to fuss at his plays Wednesday, swearing to return in July.

Robert is at the Hotel Méditerranée. He and I are going to occupy Jack's apartment Quai Tournelle.

In the belle science I have discovered little, except that the Quiché of Guatemala thought it High Heaven's pleasure that they perforate their tongues and draw through the hole a little string adorned with aloe-slivers and that the Most Holy Umbilical of Christ was a popular relic in the ~~Moyen Age~~ Middle Ages—(I am getting the most dreadful habit of interlarding asinine French words perfectly unconsciously with the English—something that must at all costs be stopped)

I have managed to get twice to a pleasant little life class, Boulevard Montparnasse, where by paying a franc one can contemplate a lady's nude contortions from 7.30 till ten every evening. All I have produced have been strangely celluloid-looking. With them I am befouling that very beautiful book of yours that has the Tours drawings in it.

But I am dying for news of the Nymph of Newnham and of Granchester where the church clock stands at ten to three.

If you run into any entertaining books please send me their names and addresses.

Au revoir

This is what my attempts at the nude are like—only worse [refers to a sketch]

To Rumsey Marvin

Rouen
29 avril [*1919*]

Rummy:

Having walked an hour about dark streets looking for the night life of Rouen, I have decided that there is no night life of Rouen.

Still Rouen is a delightful town, full of flamboyant gothic churches with as many spires as a hedge hog has quills, and old peaked houses of plaster and timber with the ends of the beams carved into faces and crouching men and dragons. I came down here on two days leave to have a change of air and water, to write letters, to sketch and to talk confidentially with Psyche my soul as Poe would have put it. I've done nothing so far but climb among the gargoyles and the little timid greystone saints, miraculously untouched by vertigo, that cluster about the roofs of Gothic Churches. Rouen is wonderfully unchanged since the sixteenth century—it has the charm of being almost a seaport; and further—for me—the sentimental interest having been more or less the center of Flaubert's life. I even passed the hotel where the lovers met in Mme Bovary and the cab—I am sure its the same cab—It was leading a wedding this time—in which Léon and Emma had their amazing journey. I shall write you soon What of Spain?

Love
Jack

45 Quai de la Tournelle
[Paris
Spring 1919]

Rummy——

Where are you hiding yourself—or rather your letters? Up and at
'em! stand and deliver! For God's sake dont wait till you see the whites
of their eyes to shoot!

Frankly—I, though I may seem a rather solemn serious bespec-
tacled person, though I am a registered and accepted candidate for a
doctorat at the University of Paris, though I am head and shoulders
deep in dusty tomes on dry dead dusty divinities, I—am going crazy,
spring-struck, moon-struck . . . I feel like an entire pompeian frieze of
little red naked people dancing, I feel like a room full of orgiastic and
rather indecent Greek vases. I feel like an election parade that's forgotten the names of the candidates. I feel as a horse chestnut tree in bloom
would feel if everyone of the little mouths that form the tiers of the
white pagodas of the flowers should start singing the Internationale in
falsetto voices.

I feel like standing on my head on top of a taxi-cab, like making a
proposal of marriage to eighteen elderly spinsters, like jumping into the
Seine. I probably have suddenly and accidentally become an incarnation of Dionysus by some crossing of the celestial wires of fate. This
morning I sat down in a barber chair to have my hair cut and the chair
fell to pieces under the mightiness of my sitting. At any moment I
expect the fourteen volumes in dark green cloth of Mr. Frazer to turn
into maenads, arms stained to the elbows with wine, or the chair to
start singing like a lark, or the roof of the house to open like the corolla
of a flower, or the gutters of the Quai de la Tournalle to run ~~amythest~~
amethysts—How d'you spell them?

And all this caused by six fine days and the prospect of demobili-
zation.

Hell no! I'm not going to a lecture on the very complicated
calendar of the early Americans. I'm going to do brun sketches along
the Quais.

But Rummy how about Spain? Is there any chance? I am going to
have such a galavant there, such a climbing of mountains, such an
examining of churches such a hallelujah of Roman viaducts and prehistoric remains and modern harvest festivals that nothing like it will
have been seen before or after—And you are, I swear, the only person I

know, who's lively enough and jolly enough and unfretful enough to be a halfway decent companion on such an expedition.

If any drawback arises I'll let you know at once.

But I must go out—

Lots of love
Jack

To Dudley Poore

[Paris]
May 4 [*1919*]

Dudloysha—

I've been rather worried about you. Do you need money? If so, let me know at once. I'd send it, but the exchange is so ruinous that it seems foolish to risk your not needing it.

But probably you are having a high time in Devonshire. What sort of people have you run into at Emmanuel?

I just got back from a Saturday and Sunday in Chartres. Though the glass is not all back yet by any means it is a marvelously beautiful place. The sculpture is superb and the town a lovely quiet little place full of nuns in starched butterfly hats and red faced abbés and little old women in white caps or in strange toque-like bonnets. And the fervor with which the black virgin is invoked by hordes of these same tiny black women! For it seems that she is a very useful as well as a very ancient virgin. In fact, on dit that she had a scandalous connection with an ancient well and druids and gallo-Roman figurines and all that sort of thing but at any rate O Vierge toute puissante mère de dieu, priez pour nous maintenant at à l'heure de notre mort is the moan of all the little old women and of the youthful fervent seminarists and of the abbés whose eyes remain forever glued to their breviaries.

A propos—some evil genius made me buy La Cathédral of M. Huysmans—the nastiest, snivelingest dribblingest, measliest droolingest collection of lukewarm belly washes for the soul I've ever had the ill-luck to come into contact with. It is with great difficulty that I re-strained myself from doing violence to the wretched thing—Dos.

To Dudley Poore

45 Quai de la Tournelle
[Paris]
May 14 [*1919*]

Dudloysha

It is a desperately beautiful afternoon. I am staying in, trying to work, to scribble, to scrawl over pages—but I can't manage it! The day is too gorgeously hot and green and white and vigorous. The carts rattle so along the quais and the little boats shriek on the river with such demoniac glee and the people who are unloading the barges shout so jollily and the warm wind tugs so at my paper. How do people manage to live through the spring? I have never felt it more insanely.

Dudley, you don't vouchsafe the slightest information about yourself. Have you punted yourself into the Styx via the Cam? Or are you lost in the blandishments of the attendant nymphs eating lotus somewhere in the groves of Newnham to the dulcet sounds of the works chanted out loud of the departed Sybil?

Please write me about the people at Cambridge. Do they eat, and what? Do they think and what? Why in both cases? Whence? Whither? and you bandit, have you money enough?

Tom is up on the Somme for a few days inspecting the proposed sites for movable houses or something of the sort.

I dwell at Jack's old apartment 45 Quai de la Tournelle and am gradually going crazy under the influence of a fortnight, each day of which is more beautiful than the last.

Can no incantation evoke you?

My application for discharge in France is in. Also I've been accepted as candidate for a doctorat.

To Dudley Poore

[Paris]
May 21 [*1919*]

Dudloysha—

I shall enclose five pounds and register this and by the grace of God you will receive it. When you were in London you ought to have gone to see my little old ladies, wretch! Your letter made me rather angry anyway. It implied a threat of not writing again: which was not nice.

And what in the name of Heaven does it matter whether you

know anything about Iowa or not? You're not trying to write a scientific description of Iowa for the Royal Anthropological Society. You are trying to make up something purely fictitious and imaginary that is meant to amuse and excite some person or persons unknown, as the coroner puts it. If you want to call it Iowa you can—but you might just as well call it Matabulu—and obviously as you create it you know everything about it that there is to be known from the number of hairs in the beard of the oldest inhabitant to the color of the stamens of the petunias that grow in the grocer's back yard.

O your letter made me furious. . . . Mme Lecomte says she's going to vous tirer les oreilles when you come back to Paris. I'll do it too, till they are long as the ears of King Midas (who according to M. Reinach was not a king at all but merely the anthropomorphized donkey totem of a Lydian clan, who got mixed up with a Cretan-Lydian-Etruscan navigator named Midocrates who brought tin from Cornwall and was not a Phoenician—But all that is hardly to the point, and M. Reinach is, it must be admitted, a trifle morbid about totems, he sees them under every bush, as one with the DTs sees snakes).

But Dudley, it is time that you acquired from somewhere a little healthy conceit. You know perfectly well that what you have been writing is probably damnably good, and that you can't put pen to paper without writing well, even in this abominable letter, which I hasten to say I was delighted to receive. You know perfectly that I'd enjoy your letters even if you took up New Thought or Theosophy or Pelmanism—and if you feel that way about it, much better to write it and get rid of it than to chew it all day like spearmint gum.

But I've probably scolded you too much. But I vow that it's enough to make the blessed Sainte Geneviève turn in her tomb to have you claiming to be unable to write.

The fourth part of Fibbie never was part of him at all. I merely pretended that it was, and as soon as it was read aloud my pretense collapsed. That's all. I'm going to enlarge it and put in steam heat and enameled bath tubs and call it France 1917 or something of the sort and try to publish it that way. Really it's rather fun suddenly having two children instead of one. I've got a discharge application in, but doubt if anything will come of it. Moreover I am sure to get leave June thirtieth for ten days in England.

About the P.E.S. Is there anything I can do? I'm afraid not. Really you must get the money out of them. It's a scandalous performance.

Why not write each week the same letter? It may at least get noticed. Can't your C.O. at Emmanuel College do something? Do try him. Of course it's almost impossible for one of the downtrodden to get anything done. People just refuse to notice one.

I'm awfully anxious to see you.

Have you met any pleasant people?

Addio.

To Rumsey Marvin

[Paris
June 1919]

Rummy—

For some reason your letter made me angry as the devil—Why can't you come to Spain? You profess to be ready for anything, yet you refuse even to entertain the hope that you may be whizzed off to Spain in a whirlwind, like a minor prophet. I vow that you need Spain and Spain needs you, and I need you, and you need me.

Have you read Marius the Epicurean? It may be all sheer rot, but its a sort of rot that is at times beneficial. As you love me read at once, furthermore, Anatole France's La Revolte des Anges, L'Ile des Penguins and La Rotisserie de la Reine Pédanque. Also read all the Elizabethan lyrics you can find lying round. Add thereto Shakespeare's Sonnets, Tom Jones, Rabelais and even, possibly the Satyricon. Then cap the whole by Renan's Vie de Jesus and George Moore's The Brook Kerith. All of which means that I feel that you need to be confronted with the eternal verities

This sort of statement is indefensible even on the grounds that your typewriter ran away with you: . . . *as we certainly seem to have come out on top in this war, and we undoubtedly live saner, happier lives than better educated and underdeveloped people with nervous and mental troubles which vigorous bodies etc* Because it very simply isn't so. Any fair minded person will admit that the average Frenchman at the front showed greater powers of endurance than the average American, and that life in Europe is saner, healthier, and happier than in America. I admit that America is more dear to me than Europe—probably its colossal hideousness, its febrile insanity are evolving towards a better life for man. But none of that's to the point. The thing I object to is the mental attitude involved—And at this moment I cant quite explain why I object to it.

O but Rummy will you—for me—plant a little grain of the mustard seed of doubt before your great steel idol of success.

But I'm talking even worse rot than you are. In fact I'm not at all sure that you are wrong. Still something in your letter got my bile up.

By this time you will have received bunches of letters from me all imploring you to try to get to Spain—Constant wearing will——O I'm crazy this afternoon—What I mean is—little drops of water, little grains of sand, make the mighty etc——

I'm in a horrid mood today—and I feel like lecturing so you are getting the brunt of it—But Rummy my love, I hope you read something else in Freshman English than Shakespeare Ruskin Carlyle and Tennyson—Carlyle I'll admit as a good old brute of a minor prophet, and of course Shakespeare is enough to counteract all ills—but why in Gods name Tennyson and Ruskin?—Why is a mouse when it spins?

While I'm still in the pnyx or the pynx or the pyx or the xyp or whatever the thing was that Athenian orators stood in when they talked—and I must be quick for the pallium is falling fast from my shoulders, let me beg you to read a lot of classical stuff.

You know that I hate Nothing worse than old fogyism and looking backward out of the sordid present into the glories of the past sort of bombast, but still I solemnly aver, that the only education in the world that is worth calling an education comes from the stimulation of the spirit that contact with the two great flowerings of our race brings: The Renaissance and the Age of Athens. The Renaissance for us, who speak English is best expressed by the plays and poems and prose of Elizabeth's time. And Greece . . . Do you know G. Lowes Dickinson's *Greek Civilization* (that's not the title, but you can easily find it in the library catalogue)? Then Pater's *Greek Studies* open certain doors—Then there is Andrew Lang's Odyssey and the Gilbert Murray translations of Euripides.

Why don't you—even if you do go to a summer resort—shut yourself up like a hermit and do oodles of reading this summer? You almost make me want to go back to America to do it too.

Forgive this rotten illtempered carping letter, Rummy. It's a boresome irritating sort of afternoon and the vast stupidity of man—my own—my own too—seems to rise in a drowning wave about me.

O we must up and at 'em: we are too lively, we have too much curiosity, too many desperate desires for unimaginable things to let ourselves be driven down into the mud of common life. You and I and a few others and thousands of others we do not know—O it is so much harder than it has ever been before to lead a good life, to dominate life instead of being driven in the herd. Intellect, vigor have more to struggle against than ever before, except perhaps in the darkest of feudal times, when religion held the world crouched in gibbering fear. This all pervading spirit of commerce—this new religion of steel and stamped paper! O it is time for Roland to blow his horn that the last fight may start. To think clearly and piteously, to love without stint, to feel in ones veins the throbbing of all the life of all the world——is that not better than to succeed and to be tapped on tap day and to make ΦBK and grow a paunch on the income from slavelabor?

Forgive much rot, Rummy out of which you may be able to sift a little sense—

Love
Jack

Vendôme
July 13th [*1919*]

Rummy—

I am a free man.

After days of waiting in a dreadful hole named Gièvres, in which I fell into the most ridiculous despair, where life seemed absolutely unliveable, I received my discharge. In Tours I bought a shirt and neck tie and socks, emblems of freedom, and a hat, a large and pompous brown felt hat. So equipped I went to a public bath, stripped off my ancient smelly galley-slaves' garments; dressed in a borrowed civilian suit and strode out into the world.

But though Tours was a most beautiful place, it was full of memories of despair. So I fled from there on the first train to Blois where, in the Chateau built at the moment of the highest vigor of the Renaissance, I hoped to forget old slaveries. Blois a city of gardens and balustrades from which you lean to look down the lazy windings of the slate-colored Loire, was too gaudy; so again I fled to this pinched little provincial town of Vendome, where I am caught for an afternoon while waiting for the train for Paris. It is a green, tree-shaded town, built on islands in the bed of a green solemn little river. There is a flamboyant gothic church, anciently part of a monastery, and one of the most beautiful bell towers in France. As I write the bells make a wonderful weary ceaseless clamour. Over the town brood the ruins of a castle of the Dukes of Vendome. At the moment I am waiting very hungrily for lunch, wishing I had someone to talk to.

I was awfully disappointed you couldn't get to Spain. I see that I'll have to come back and carry you away by the scruff of the neck. To travel nowadays it takes a marvellous amount of lying. I am hoping eventually to collect enough letters to enable me to go anywhere— letters from cotton firms directing me to buy beans in Chili, and from hardware merchants sending me to Abyssinia to discover the reason for the rise in price of Boston garters and beeswax—I'm going to Spain as correspondent for the London Daily Herald; but that's real. So real that I lay great stock by it, as an avenue of entrance into free lance journalism. But one cant tell yet what will come of it.

Really Rummy I feel so happy to be free I'm almost solemn about it.

I've been getting solemn of late about things. It's a horrid habit, a habit I must get rid of at all costs. But those three old ladies who sit knitting somewhere behind the curtain of conjecture have played me sorry tricks of late.

I must have six weeks of walking—O damn the government and everything else! Never mind next summer! The old plum tree of time has other fruit on it, even if we cant reach this one——On with the dance.

Write me to Morgan Harjes until I let you know——

Ill let you hear from England my news——

Jack

I really was most dreadfully disappointed. If I could only have got to Spain sooner, I could have got some business firm to cable for you—but now I suppose its too late—

To Stewart Mitchell (1892–1957), *whom Dos met in 1914 or 1915, when Mitchell was editing the* Harvard Monthly. *Writing about him in the* New England Quarterly *in 1957, Dos recalled his "half-comic, half-pompous way" and his "unique collection of information about American politics. . . . In politics he was a congenital Democrat, but his judgments of men's sayings and acts remained very much his own. As prejudice became more and more the substitute for thought in the minds of our contemporaries, Stewart Mitchell remained one of the few men with whom it was possible to talk about political principles freely and entertainingly."*

*Mitchell served in the army in France during World War I, then
in 1919–1920 was managing editor of the* Dial. *He did graduate work
at Harvard from 1925–1928, became managing editor of the* New England Quarterly *in 1928, and earned his Ph.D. at Harvard in 1933.
From 1929–1939 he was an editor for the Massachusetts Historical Society, then served as its director from 1947 until the year of his death.*

Saint-Malo
July 19 [*1919*]

Stewart:

Hearing from you was a great joy. I had given you up entirely;
and to have the Phoenix arise from his ashes is as pleasant as knowing
you all over again.

I too am arising from the Tenebrae. Hell has belched its victims
forth into the ambrosial day again. A week ago I was under the yoke.
Today—Libertad—camerado! as Walt Whitman would have cried.

It's funny—I am staying in the hotel where Chateaubriand was
born—It seems that for eighty francs you can sleep in the very bed he
was born in. Dead and turned to clay he not only keeps the wind away,
but lines the pockets of a Swiss hotel proprietor. Progress indeed since
Shakespeare's time! O resurrected Auk!

I am in London peddling manuscript, without much success so
far. At the end of the week Dudley and I go to Spain.

If wishing were ocean liners I assure you that the resurrected Auk
would be with us.

Never fear—now that the chains have ceased clanking about all
our necks—we shall have many a revel.

In your letter to Dudley you spoke as if it might be possible to do
something about our old scheme of starting some manner of periodical
into which to unburden our souls. Do let me know what comes of the
idea. I should love to have a finger in the pie. I assure you that I should
come flying from the antipodes at the first note of the horn, at the first
melodious clank of the presses.

Of course we'd all land in jail at the end of a week—in this age of
liberty, but, what of it?

But Stewart, don't accuse me of Olympus. If I ever abode there,—I
have fallen headlong into the abyss long since—and it was no Lemnos
that I landed on, no island full of worshippers and dancing maids.

I have been very low for a very long time. I have been abject. It is only recently that I have begun to lift myself from my dungheap.

But now by the grace of the sea and sky, I shall start carving a destiny out of the dull clay. It's been thumped enough, God knows, to be ready for the most fastidious potter.

O Auk I am anxious to see you. Give my love to Sibley and to any other of the faithful you happen to see

Auk, please don't flee into any deserts, because I shan't have enough money to ride and its so far to walk to Ohio or Wisconsin. Do write me care Morgan Harjes—14 Place Vendome—Paris. I shall probably be in America in the Autumn—unless something very lucky turns up in the correspondent way. I am anxious to break in to the so called free lance business.

Love
Dos

Tell Bobby to write.

To Rumsey Marvin

Paris
Aug 2. [*1919*]

Rummy,

Just got in from London.

Am wandering about the Boulevards in one of those moods of isolation where I seem utterly left out of the gaudy stream of life that throbs and thunders about my ears with a sound of kisses and fighting, a tenseness of muscles taut with love and hate.

It comes, I suppose, of expecting too much of life, of wanting to live more than ever man lived before. There is such an endless welter of experience to untangle, Beauty and misery are so unutterably manifold that there is no time for triviality The strangest thing of all is how, in spite of the fury of my desires, I seem to remain for ever rigid in the straightjacket of my inhibitions . . . M'en fous!

I'm off to Spain, by the grace of San Jaime de Compostella and Don Quixote de la Mancha and all the other Iberian divinities, in a day or two.

Even if you are not with me this time, we'll get back at the envious hags, at those nasty old women with needle and thread that are forever putting the wrong patches side by side in the crazy quilt of destiny——

We'll pull off such a royal party under their very noses before long that they wont know what to make of it.

When two men hold together, the Kingdoms are less by two! Do you know that splendid song in Time of order of Swinburne's.

O Rummy we must keep our heads above water, our feet out of the ruts and make up a few times for the glory of man in this age of dullness and dissolution.

love

Jack

By god it's not dull. I take that back—But it's damned distressing at times.

Postcard to Stewart Mitchell

[Avilés

August 24, 1919]

O Auk you should be with us. For two days first on a great jaunty coach out of Rabelais then on foot on winding powdering roads, we have been following a river up towards the high wall of mountains they call the Picos de Europa. Tomorrow we cross them.

Dos

To Rumsey Marvin

[Avilés-Granada]

Aug 24 [September 20, 1919]

Dear Rummy;

I have just come down from some mountains very justly called Los Picos de Europa, where I have been walking about. We got into wonderful lost valleys where no one ever seemed to have seen a foreigner before, and managed to get right through the range down the wildest and most superb gorge I have ever seen. We ended by scrambling over a pass that nearly did for us, and eventually got to Oviedo, a Rembrandt brown city full of convents that look like palaces and palaces that look like convents. Today I am going on to Leon, on the way to Madrid, where, among other things, I hope to find mail from you.

Avilés is a windy dusty glary little market town, one of those places one gets to by mistake and goes away from on the first train.

However, I saw some excellently red and mammoth lobsters in the kitchen of the place where I expect to have lunch, So it may hold good things to eat.

To lose the habit of writing is the worst thing on earth that can befall one. It is exactly a year since I really wrote anything—though I have worked over lots of stuff—and I am finding it intensely difficult to get into the creative way of thinking. I am trying to finish up a novel I began ages ago in Alsace last winter. At present it calls itself The Sack of Corinth, though I fear the title will have to be changed. I want to express somehow my utter . . . Its not exactly that though. The feeling of revolt against army affairs has long crystalized itself into the stories of three people, a clerk in an optician's in San Francisco, a farmer's son from Indiana and a musical person who appears in S.T.R.W.J.—so much so that I cant get a word down on paper. The story's all ready to be written—but it wont come. A maddening state of affairs.

The first part is at training camp in America, the second part at the front, the third in that strange underground world of deserters and AWOL's, the underside of the pomp of war. There is going to be rather a lot of murder and sudden death in it, I fear. I am rather excited about it, and it is just agony being unable to put it on paper.

on the train St. Malo to Mt. St. Michel
My desires have a-hunting gone.
They circle through the fields and sniff along the ridges,
Like hounds that have lost the scent.
Outside, behind the white swirling patterns of coal smoke
Hunched fruit-trees slide by
Slowly pirouetting,
And poplars and aspens on tiptoe
Peer over each others' shoulders
At the long black rattling train;
Colts sniff and fling their heels in air
Across the rusty meadows;
And the sun; now and then,
Looks with vague interest through the clouds
At the blonde harvest mottled with poppies,
At the Joseph's cloak of fields, neatly sewn together with hedges
That hides the grim skeleton
Of the earth.

My desires have taken ship.
In rain-drenched velvets and brocades
They huddle on the lurching deck
Of a lost galleon.

Out of the mist and the galloping waves
Into the infinite stillness of the bay
Where the pale sea's streaked grey and green
And there lie long reaches of violet sands
like the long clouds in the violet sky.

To be continued in our next

Granada Sept 20.

Dear Rummy,

As you see nearly a month has gone by since I started this letter to you. At present I am living in a charming little domed summer house in a garden that overlooks Granada. I write all the morning and most of the afternoon and then sally forth and wander in the frivolous courts and halls of the pastry palace the moors built among the superb red towers of their fortress on the hill. I've got the first part of my new novel done, thank heaven. So I feel quite come to life again after a long sojourn in the blue infernal regions.

I never seem to be able to get this letter finished. I don't know why. I had another wonderful walk, along the coast of the province of Malaga, between the Sierra Nevada and the sea. Superb burnt hills and irrigated valleys full of banana trees and sugar cane and of the sound of water running through irrigation ditches. A wonderful part of the world. The people in the towns hire a fig tree for the summer and go out under it with their pigs and goats and cats and chickens and eat the figs and enjoy the shade. Life has no problems under those conditions.

I am awfully glad that you enjoyed Tom Jones. To me it is one of the rocks upon which English literature is built. And James Stephens, along with broiled live lobster, is one of the reasons why I shall never commit suicide.

About Joyce. I'm not sure that you're not right. Yet I think its a very expressive book and the hero doesn't seem to me remarkable particularly—a hypersensitive person the like of which abound in our asinine modern society.

One might write a very pretty psychopathic essay entitled "The age of seduction". But I think that you'll find that in America the age of seduction is later among our class than in any other and that in most other countries fifteen or sixteen is a perfectly good average date.

Isn't it curious how completely ignorant we all are of the most important part of our bodily mechanism. It is really criminal. Yet there is no nation in the world that doesnt surround sex with fantastic walls. Of course ours are sillier than any—but not much.

The army's the only place I know where people are frank about it—and there their point of view is strictly limited and offers neither variety nor interest.

A bientôt—

Jack

To Rayner Unwin *of George Allen & Unwin, Ltd., the British publishers of Dos' first book,* One Man's Initiation—1917.

Credit Lyonnais
Alcalá 8 Madrid
August 29, 1919

Dear Mr. Unwin,

I telegraphed you as soon as I received word from the lady who was kind enough to discuss the matter of my book [*One Man's Initiation—1917*] with you.

I am afraid that I am not quite in the position to take part of the risk of publication, but I shall be very glad if you will act as my agent in the matter on your usual terms.

I think I may as well authorize you to accept any offer that does not necessitate my taking part of the risk of publication, as I am rather anxious to bring it out and the chances seem to grow slimmer daily.

Yours Very Sincerely

John R. Dos Passos

To Thomas Pym Cope (1897–   ), *who met Dos in France in 1917, probably at Sandricourt Training Base. During that summer Cope served for two months at the front. Then when the U.S. Army took over the Norton-Harjes group, he joined the American Red Cross and the British and American Friends War Victims Relief, doing hospital work, evacuating refugees, and building prefabricated houses while serving as Paris representative of the Friends Housing Department.*

In 1919 he returned to the United States; after six months at the

Pennsylvania Academy of Fine Arts he joined the Eastern and Gulf Sailors' Union and spent eighteen months as ordinary seaman on coastwise and overseas freighters. The next two years he lived in New York, writing, painting, and doing odd jobs, before going to work for his father's architectural firm in Philadelphia in 1924. After more architecture in New York, marriage in 1929, and a long trip abroad, he lived in Philadelphia until 1943. That year he went to work for the Department of State, aiding displaced persons while stationed in Europe and the Far East. In 1953 he became Director of the Unitarian Service Committee in Boston, but soon moved to Chicago to practice architecture again. In 1956 he returned to Lincoln Center, Massachusetts, where he and his family have lived since.

To Thomas P. Cope

[Madrid
September 1919]

Shivermetimbers Captain Tom (as I was walking down Paradise Street) your shipowning proposition seems to me marvellous. May I make immediate application for the job of cook and cabin boy. I'll even polish brass (a practice which frankly I disapprove of on the high or low seas) in order to be allowed to come aboard—I may even be discovered to have stowed away. What is the name and lineage of this famous yawl—?

Splendid anyway—because I need a rigorous apprenticeship under a sterling tar like yourself (and so do his sisters and his cousins and his aunts, his sisters and his cousins, whom he reckons by the dozens, and his *aunts*) before I embark on my own maritime ventures.

I'm at this moment in Madrid waiting (as usual) for a flight of buttered quails to drop into my mouth—said buttered quails are not flowing as freely as in the good old days—In fact I think very soon I shall reach such a pinnacle of brokeness as has been attained by few even in the latitudes of Bedford Street.

Have come from the finest month of my life almost in a little fishing town named Motrico on the coast of Guipuzcoa—where everybody speaks basque and drinks the noblest hard cider ever moulded to the lips and gullet—One of the few places where they still dance the Auresku—like living in the first act of Tristan performed by the Russian ballet—for 10 pesetas a day there we reserved enormities of such delicious food that I've grown a paunch worse than a polichimelle—

Saw your brother Oliver in Paris, had just arrived on a Danish boat—I was on my way to catch a train, so I didn't quite gather all his adventures. Everybody 'xcept me seems to do the most extraordinary things—one finds oneself saying—

I'm now on my way, when my moneys come into port, to Nerja on the coast of Malaga where I shall sit in a garden full of fig trees on the edge of the cliff and eat a wonderful cold soup made of almond-milk and garlic with grapes in it and look towards Africa

Love to Esther and Canby—

Yrs
Dos

To Stewart Mitchell

Lisbon
Oct 8th/19

Dear Auk—

What is going on in that curious country of ours? It seems as if those who sowed the wind were about to reap the whirlwind; but who knows. Man seems to be an animal whose capacity for lies is only equalled by his credulity; it does no good to let battalions of cats out of bags, to produce whole harems of naked facts, people eat the same three meals daily deception, and are always ready to turn with fury upon the purveyors of bagless cats and facts undraped. Probably their instinct is wise. Who knows?

Whether this sudden unburdening is the result of trying to read a long Latin inscription on Fielding's Tomb, to which I paid a senti-mental visit just now, an inscription in good pompous style which the moss had partly succeeded in effacing—or whether is it the result of talking to Portuguese journalists, I do not know.

Anyway, here I sit upon the soil of my ancestors, drinking coffee in solitary grandeur at a small white table on the Avenida da Liber-tade. I have been in Lisbon a week, journalizing—The Portuguese, I find, are a good people, somewhat dirty, somewhat thievish, somewhat humble, lacking that superb haughtiness which seems to be the heri-tage of the Arabs to Spain, but a people full of goodness. Their main vice is their language, of which I disapprove entirely. It jibes in no way of my ideas of what a language should be. I utter with a feeling of pain the few sounds I have been able to master in it. They are not a pictorial people, but they have a certain charm, and express their goodness by a mild jollity. I imagine if I stayed long among them I should be taken with a sentimental fondness for them, and weep large republican tears upon leaving. But that shall not be. Leave for Spain tomorrow. How can you stay in a country where they call your name Dsh Pass-sh. Think of it! My honorable ancestors called themselves Dsh Passs-sh. Do you wonder that I don't believe in God?

The other day in a trolley-car I sneezed violently into my handkerchief. The man opposite answered in Portuguese.

I am beginning to be interested in settling down for a while somewhere. Do you realize that I've been on the move more or less constantly for the last three years? And the fever is not yet out of my blood. I look with lustful eyes towards Abyssinia, Russia, Siam—

But Auk, what paths are you following with your slow meditative stride, in what groves are you flaunting your velvet dressing-gown? In the only letter I have had from you, you let drop something about collecting poems, which interested me hugely. Are you, like the children of Israel, going to sing psalms of your captivity? Or have you a sonnet sequence d'outre tombe to spring on us? I hope that you were like the young syndicalists in the Lisbon jail, who have recently given much trouble to the free and republican government, because even behind the bars they would sing the Internationale. They turned the hose on them, they turned the republican guard on them, they beat them with the flats of swords, but nothing stopped their singing of the Internationale. Did you, under the pounding of artillery and the shrieking of sergeants still find time for the measured cadences of your verses? If you did they will certainly be worth hearing.

When shall we see each other, and while the cups of soda water flow fast, recount in Homeric style the history of our trials and heroic strife?

I left Dudley surrounded by much paper and a bottle of thick black ink—in a garden overlooking Granada—

What of Sibley Watson?

Estlin?

Greetings to any of the faithful who may be about—

Love
Dos

To Rumsey Marvin

Granada
Oct 15 [*1919*]

Dear Rummy:

It's raining; from my window I can look over a garden wall at a big clump of pink and white cosmos and at an orange tree where the green of the oranges is just beginning to fade into gold. It is a soft autumnal rain. Through a gap in the trees beside a big funereal cypress I can see the Sierra Nevada and a bit of the tawny foot hills. Il Pleure dans mon coeur

Comme il pleut sur la ville—I am thinking of how quickly the days slip by and thinking of all the roses I have left ungathered. Verlaine's language monotone!——Silly.

I've been getting letters from America—a darn good one from you too——and it makes me blue to think of the strange lack of energy that young Americans of attainments and sensibilities seem to have. I know so many who are really brilliant people who seem to be drifting into meaningless boredom. I cant understand it. It would be better if they took to drink or religion or patience. Anything taken up hard is better than that vague dissent from the inelegance of life today which is the main quality of the people who ought for good or bad to be getting into the turmoil. You must know lots of them too, fellows who are too intelligent and too alive and have too much poetry in them to take to the regular balderdash of the average sheep, but who just hang about in the world. If they didn't have enough money to be comfortably off, their bellies would push them to something—but as it is, there they are, sheer waste.

I'm not thinking of you, Rummy. You've got too much gumption for that. Though why you should want to expend that gumption on "business" is beyond me, I admit. Of course everyone has to do a certain amount of business to keep alive—but its a means not an end. That's the tragic fundamental fallacy in the minds of Americans—not Americans only, god knows—Everywhere they—take the means for the end. It's inconceivable to me—Just look at their faces, those business men. Talk to them. Can't you see that their sense of values is pathetically wrong?—That they dont know why they're working, that they get to be mules in the tread mill in order that their wives may spend thousands boring themselves elaborately in "society".

A man can't live without a trade. That sounds dogmatic, but I swear that its true. A man to give and enjoy any sort of happiness in this shaggy old world has got to have something that preoccupies him supremely above anything else. You certainly don't want extracting money from other people to be your supreme preoccupation. A man's mind is moulded by his occupation, willy nilly. The ideas of a shoemaker are those which are useful in shoemaking, the ideas of a banker those useful in banking. Think what your mind will be like after forty years of exploiting other people.

If you want to take up manufacturing, for gods sake take up the scientific end of it. You want to be a brain that creates; not a parasite living off other peoples brains, off other people's work. And there's enough work to be done. There are endless possibilities in almost anything anyone takes up; but ones got to sell one's soul for them. To save ones life one must lose it, and lose it hard.

My father who had the best brain I've ever known was a tragic example. He was poor and energetic and lively, and in his day the only thing for a poor boy to do was to make a fortune. He did. But he got so entangled in that famous "business" that interests you so that when he wanted to start being a person instead of a business man he couldn't disentangle himself, and all through his life he could only really live— use his brain (not his wits) creatively in odd moments. He never had time. That was the tragedy of his generation. But the problem of being wealthy is already out of date; what was rather splendid in 1860 becomes mesquine and sordid in 1920——Dont be an anachronism. But Rummy, think of the endless trades from bootcleaning to mathematics. There must be something in all that gamut that suits you better than making a trade of exploitation. Just in science alone think of all there is to do. Why throw in your lot with the old regime, at the last minute. You may think you can keep your mind clean of your occupation—but I swear you cant—a shoemaker has the mind of a shoemaker, a college professor of a college professor, a painter of a painter, a businessman of a bandit—within the law.

Theoretically you are perfectly right about Marxian socialism, of which I am intensely suspicious. [Part of letter missing] There is an interesting account of the Kansas jails going about which is illuminating—It's a question of *existence not of theories.*

I've just come back from Portugal—and I am thinking of walking from here to Cadiz—if I can get some articles finished I've got to write.

If I can scrape up the money I am going to Tetuan in Morocco—I am curious to see the process of spreading civilization at the hands of the Spanish army.

love
Jack

I may turn up in America during the winter.

To George Allen & Unwin, Ltd.

c/o Credit Lyonnais
Alcala 8 Madrid
Granada, Nov 15 [1919]

Dear Sirs,

As I have not heard from you, I presume that an American publisher did not materialize for *One Man's Initiation.*

In August, as I remember you were willing to publish it yourselves if I would stand part of the risk. At that time I was not prepared to do this, but I think now that if you care to renew your offer I can see my way to defray part of the expenses. Will you be so kind as to notify me at your earliest convenience what you think of the matter.

Very sincerely yours,
John R. Dos Passos

To Rumsey Marvin

Credit Lyonnais—Alcala 8, Madrid
Granada—Nov 17 [1919]

Dear Rummy—

I have just finished wasting a month in a very foolish business. On my way back from Portugal, just at the moment when I had about fifty articles to write, I had the bad taste to go to bed with a damn fool rheumatic fever. Just the day too that I was to start out from Granada to walk to Cadiz! And here I've been ever since, within four walls till yesterday when I first got out to sniff the crisp autumnal air. A most miserable waste of time. And even now I toddle about more or less like a scare crow.

But it was almost worth it for the keenness with which I breathed the tang of drying leaves and overripe fruits, the wonderful fullness and richness that is in the air in autumn. It was as if I'd just been born. The poplars in the valley are all bright yellow like candle flames, and the Sierra Nevada is blue white with snow, and one eats huge squashy

Japanese persimmons, that burst with sweetness when you bite into them and drip in orange juice over your fingers. And the custard-apples, full of a flavor of resin, are like a bite taken out of the sparkling cold air itself and the streets of Granada are full of a smell of roasting chestnuts and in the evenings a faint blue haze goes up where the people are lighting their charcoal brasiros in front of the houses, and the little ruddy pile of embers at each doorstep glows through the purpling dusk.

This wretched disease has muddled up everything and all my affairs are bubbling gleefully in the soup. M'en fous!

While in bed I read stories out of a splended unexpurgated Spanish edition of the Arabian Nights—so different from that sickly Lane-Poole affair doled out to Anglo-Saxons—packed with life and color and giving one a splendid idea of that second flowering of Rome that was Arab civilization. Burton's translation must be as good.

As soon as I dare I shall trek for Madrid, as this absurd illness caught me in a dreadful English pension into which I had been inveigled by a friend.

And in the midst of jolly preposterous Spain to be caught in an atmosphere of moral malignancy and Scotch parsimony is too awful for words. My friend and I have our meals with three old hags who sit and hate the Huns and make moral judgements on the Spaniards. I swear it takes many a Byron, many a Marlowe and many a Shelley to expiate the sins of the Anglo Saxon race. They have been able to conquer the world, but they have never been able to understand, which means I suppose to love—probably thats why they were able to conquer it—Brrr—Dont generalize—

Do write me more often—Your letters are as rare as good deeds—again the moral note! I abdicate—

love
Jack

To George Allen & Unwin, Ltd.

Credit Lyonnais
Alcala 8 Madrid
12/4/19

Dear Sirs—

In receipt of your letter of Nov. 24.

I have sent word to have the manuscript returned to you. I have come to think that it may be worth while to risk fifty pounds or so on publishing One Man's Initiation—I am afraid, however, that I should not be able to go much further than that.

Still—I await your opinion in the matter—

Very sincerely yours
John R. Dos Passos

To Rumsey Marvin

Madrid
Dec 6-19[19]

Rummy—you wretch; one never gets letters from you any more. I hope you aren't plying the oar so hard that you've forgotten how to ply the pen—or perhaps your tail is so sore that you cant sit down to write . . . Odd's fish! lad, write standing up.

I'm in the nasty period of convalescence—when one has to be careful. There's nothing in God's earth more annoying than being careful. It takes all the poetry out of existence.

News from America is rather two edged. At the same time as we seem to be shutting ourselves out for ever from the esteem of civilized peoples—if there are any—by the recrudescence of the Inquisition and by acts of the filthiest barbarity, there seems to be growing a realization, among honest people who aren't fools or cowards, of what is going on. At least the period of tame acquiescence seems to be coming to an end. Yet liberty—civilization—have in all ages hung on such a tenuous thread—that one can not but fear for the outcome of the struggle. The trick has been played before—many times—in the gory tortured history of peoples (I can hear the cymbals of your optimism clanging objections even from here) I dont deny that you can never quite trample out the things worth while—but you can crush out the spark in ten generations—and the poor little individual objects to being under the heel—to feel it slowly crushing the life out of him——One doesnt want to belong to one of the submerged generations, does one? If this keeps up you and I will be damn near it, that's all.

Madrid is a chilly jolly town—I have a rather good time here always, although I wish I could be walking across the tawny plains of Castile

Love
Jack

To Stewart Mitchell

[Credit Lyonnais
Alcala 8] Madrid
Dec 8/19

Dearest of Auks—

Again I cast a pinch of incense into the wind with the hope of
being rewarded by direct communication with your Aukship. I am not
sure that it is exactly your fault that you have not answered my letters
as a recent discussion with Dudley has led me to believe that I have
sent letters and cards in your honor to Sherwood, Ohio—wherever—if
anywhere that may be.

Still, O Auk the milk of human kindness should have flowed out
from you in the form of letters. One doesn't want to make the business
a base barter, does one?

Dudley and I at present inhabit in Madrid a rather sepulchral little
chamber which we try to heat by an apparatus which would best be
called an asphyxiatorium—its charcoal fumes fill the air and dim one's
eyes that strain to guide the cold fingers to flymarkings on paper. We
tea with one of the mystic M's as you used to call them—with Arthur
McComb—who has taken stride after stride to the right and laments
the good old times before the war. He's a positive Jaimist for conserva-
tism, a partisan of Noske. He has washed his hands and feet for ever of
the U.S., for which one can hardly blame him; and is going soon to
dwell among the chaste shades of departed liberals in Geneva.

I, on the other hand, like Walt Whitman still cry Allons Democracy, I have not deserted you ma femme—up camerados! Even am I
moved to attempt to live there for a while. For riotous absurdity surely
no country can beat us. Whether riotous absurdity, interspersed with a
brutal cruelty that makes the witch toasting and the Inquisition seem
tender hearted, is an ambiente, that stimulates to anything more fertile
than horror and despair is another matter. But is there anywhere a
civilized person can live at this moment? France, where three fourths
of the people have just deliberately approved of Clemenceau's slave-
trade, is hardly possible. In England the food is soggy and depressing,
to say nothing of the intellectual atmosphere. In the rest of Europe
there isn't any food at all. Italy is the exception. It really seems that one
country at least is awaking to realities, and riots are always fun in latin
countries; they are so well stage managed. There remains only Spain
and Italy. Down with the barbarian North!

I cant describe to you the delight of crossing the border, of coming from out of the fetid cloud of the Entente, of breathing free air. The Bidassoa has become a Rubicon and the Pyrenees, thank God, are marvellously high. From across them one can hear the final death rattle of Europe.

But Stewart when I think how long it is since I saw you, it gives me the blind staggers. If we are not careful we'll only meet to clasp our hands once before we sink into our respective graves, finally overcome by the utterness of the asininity. But no—Tonnerre de dieu!—we'll wrench many a jolly time yet from the niggardly fates. This business makes ones blood boil—where has all the joy and the frankness in the world gone to. The early part of the war was jolly as hell—literally— diabolically jolly—but since the end of nineteen seventeen the joy and recklessness have gradually ceded before the poison gas. These sallow leavings of capitalism that govern us that poison us and starve us—can it be that they have downed the world? Where are the hearty sons of bitches who will laugh away this cowardice, this wave of poltroonery? There aren't even any anarchists to blow us up—trembling crowd that is afraid to live.

But Auk—Dudley and I have things to show you in Spain.

A little bird with a yellow bill and green eyes—yea his eyes were green—told me that a volume of yours was about . . . O what is the name of the hippopotamus-headed goddess of childbirth? She should be invoked and a plover and two larded quails should be sacrificed upon her obstetrical altar and a libation made of apricot brandy! . . . to see the light. You must send a copy at once if its already out. I cant wait to see it. Did your muse put on olive drab and carry a fucking pack? Or did she remain at home? News! news! You may be writing Pindaric odes in Esthonian for all I know.

Rumor hath it also—unconfirmed—as unreliable as a Stockholm report—that a work of mine—'One Man's Initiation: 1917'—will be brought out by Allen and Unwin in London—Its fairly rotten and I know nobody'll read it, but having it in my background may help on others of the unborn. More probably it'll bitch them altogether, as its not very nice. The novel still hangs on tenterhooks in the hands of an agent in New York. It is said that people are quite terrified by unre- spectful references to the flag and to the glories of war in the last part, so I fear it is forever shelved. Probably it deserves no better fate.

I hasten to announce to you that my ship of state is sinking fast. Every time I plumb the hold I find the balance lower. I shall soon be struggling in the waters of the mundane with the usual problem of sell your soul or starve. This so that you may not be surprised if when next we meet I wear the uniform of a crossing sweeper, or the white apron of a baker. I'd rather like to be a baker. Wright McCormick is editing the Garment News or something of the sort in New York—so I may get a job under him writing little verses in which ecru will rhyme with fichu, and chic with electric. But who knows what the urn of the future holds—there may be golden beans and satin dressing gowns for all of us.

Love
Dos

Are you really coming to Paris in the Spring?

To George Allen and Unwin, Ltd.

c/o Credit Lyonnais
Alcala 8 Madrid
December 15-[19]19

Dear Sirs—

In receipt of your letter of Dec. 10.

As soon as you say the word I can have the £75 sent you from America, as it seems to me worth while to get *One Man's Initiation* out even at a loss; and I imagine that the sooner the book appears, the more chance there is of diminishing that loss.

I shall await with interest your statement as regards Royalties.

It had better be published under the name of John Dos Passos, which I have just begun using to avoid confusion with my father. Also: I am not sure if the MS is entirely plain about the double spaces—or more, if you think better—between sections of the chapters. A considerable pause is needed between these, and I do not care to use asterisks or any such device. But I imagine that you know more about that problem than I do.

Very sincerely yours,
John R. Dos Passos

To Rumsey Marvin

Madrid
[*December 31, 1919*]

Rummy—

Have you lost my address or—or have you taken vows of silence like a Trappist, or have you decided I'm not the sort of person one writes to, or what???

I haven't had a letter from you for so long that I swear I wont recognize your handwriting when I see it.

By the way, this seems to be the last day of the year. I am sitting in a rather pleasant little café, that dates, they say, from the time of Fernando Septimo, from the time of Goya. The old year has nearly run its course, a pretty sad specimen as years go. Though I suppose it is the fate of all years to enter in hope and die in despair.

Tonight I'm in one of the fits of crazy restlessness I get so often. I have been living a bovinely quiet life since that asinine illness laid me low, to the result that I am now entirely recovered and overflowing to the bursting point with all the inhibited desires of a lost autumn. The streets are full of people playing tambourines and zambombas, and in a little while the whole population of Madrid will eat twelve grapes between the twelve strokes of the clock, in order to have good luck in the new year.

Do let me hear from you—love

Jack

To Thomas P. Cope

[Madrid
January (?) 1920]

Dearest Tom—

I cant imagine why I haven't written you before. I have intended to time and time again, but I seem to be going though a period of the hustle complex with the result that I never have time to do anything.

Thanks for your offer of an asylum even though it be a bed that beareth me. I deny the allegation however—Day before yesterday I walked twenty five kilometers across country to prove it. From Aranjuez to Yepes, where there's a superb gold brown church of the early Renaissance, little cakes of almond paste that go by the coy name of melindres, and delicious white wine which we drank—lunching in the sun on a hillside—out of a most baroque bottle.

Your letter from Bermuda was delightful—also the description of your grandmother's library. How wonderful to have had an arctic explorer for an uncle. You know you chose rather well, when you picked out a family for yourself.

Why dont you send me a couple of yards of verse now and then? And what in Gods name do you paint? Why not try the front of your very respectable maternal mansion? A social revolution done on a grand scale might be rather fine—figures eight feet high and as many wide. People'ld come for miles to see it and you could tell them it was a new version of Washington crossing the Delaware or Pershing crossing the Channel or Foch crossing the Rhine or Kolchak crossing the Styx. No, but I do think it is important to do figures. But has the sculpting idea fallen through? I wish you wouldn't go to Germany yet—it is so begging the question; and what you need it seems to me—what we all need—is work. And when one is working hard it doesn't matter if one is in Brooklyn or Kamchatka.

The habit of work is so frightfully difficult to acquire. And puttering about is not work, though it is mistaken for it in America.

Whether in the end, it is really desirable to acquire the habit of work I often doubt—because once you have it, you have it for life.—Still you've got to sell your soul for something. He that would save his life shall lose it—

Fudge

Tom—I swear that when I write you the souls of all your damn quaker ancestors get into me and I start preaching sermons. I don't know why or how. Though its not for nothing that behind my mother lay a series of episcopal ministers . . .

The thing is I always get worried about everyone when they get into the power of their family, more so the humaner the family is.

I am writing this in a funny library place that goes by the name of the Ateneo and is abnormally full of literary-looking gentlemen, who busy themselves in heaps of books and make sad scholarly noises in their throats as they turn the pages. Still—there are many easily accessible books about protohistoric Iberians and Magdalenian archeology and the paintings of Luardi Carilla and other subjects—that notwithstanding the curious smell of erudition I find it a most convenient writing place.

But I must put off more till later—Do let me know all that goes on—and send me some Liberators and Dials if you can find them about.

Love

Dos

Remember me to your mother and sisters—

To Rumsey Marvin

Jan 2–1920——

Madrid

A day of sun and wind and scudding clouds.

Rummy—

Still, I swear, business, even with a Capital Big is not enough. Of course, everybody's got to scratch up a living and money for books and money for travelling, but before everything else, even if one never has a book in the world or travels farther than Dykman Street, one has got to have work to do. By work I mean construction, creation. One's character and thoughts and wishes are so damnably controlled by one's occupation. Delenda est Cartagum, as somebody or other used to begin his speeches and end them, no matter what he was talking about. I guess it must have been Cato.

The T.C.M. [Inspired by Dos, Marvin and two friends, C. D. Williams and Gale Kneeland, Jr., formed a group called the *Trois Cent Mots* their sophomore year at Yale. Their idea was to write 300 words a day to improve their style.] seems to me a splendid idea. Take the muse by the hair. If that young lady gets flighty and takes the habit of wandering, just tie her to the bed post. Anyway, writing, like everything else, is very largely a habit. And if you get in the habit of putting things down you are very likely, in the midst of much nonsense, to find unexpected pearls, to say nothing of rubies, carbuncles, garnets, tourmalines and pebbles. I wish you had sent me your story. Honestly your idea is excellent——It grasps the fundamental facts about learning things—that you have got to have gumption, encouragement and criticism. Think how much better it would be if one learnt everything that way instead of being prated at by dull and bored professors who've delivered the same lecture for twenty five years, so that now they don't even have to look at their notes——Why dont you found a paper, when once you get under way?

How about verse? Your verse had distinct possibilities. And dont forget, in verse and prose, that everybody has got to write his gueso of rubbish before he writes his page of literature.

Dont worry too much about style, let it come of its own accord. The only rule of style is to say things as briefly clearly and picturesquely as possible. But if one has to give up something it ought to be style rather than matter. If you cant say it fluently, say it anyway.

By the way—about Bolshevism: one has to remember that *all* that is published in the press is propaganda, that the Bolsheviki are the moderate social-revolutionaries, a political party, and the Soviets are a system of government based on the idea of "pure democracy" (—so called in the textbooks on gov't) that every man shall take direct part in the government of the country—which is arrived at by industrial representation through the heirarchy of soviets, and that much the same system would be in vogue in America—(geographical instead of industrial units) if Hamilton and the rest had taken the New England town-meeting as the unit of government instead of importing Montesquieu's ideas. It's silly to idealize things in Russia, but it is criminal to condemn them unheard. Anyway the attitude of condemning everything one does not understand is porcine.

As to atrocities, what do you think of General Dyer's little shooting match in India?

I cant understand the lack of gumption in Americans—I mean the ones who do think, who drift away into a condition of mild disapproval. Of course every country is full of people who dont think. Consciousness is a rare thing among featherless bipeds—but what puzzles and infuriates me is the strange flaccidness of the people that do think.

It's a thing I have never found anywhere else. Spaniards and Frenchmen of intelligence whom I know are tremendously awake, always doing a thousand things, throwing themselves vigorously into politics and archaeology and painting and music, as if they realized that we had a short time in the world and might as well make the best of it. But I know so many Americans, people of great talent and intellect, who are sunk continually in a faintly melancholy sloth. Charming people to be with, who talk wistfully of novels that may some day be written, of pictures that may some day be painted, of things to be done in archaeology, of going to Europe in the spring—

who drift along and watch with well-modulated dismay, the world going to barbarism about their ears.

Is there anything more damnable than lukewarmness?

Love
Jack

Bestwishes for the New Year to your mother and father and sister——

The Books haven't turned up yet—Thanks a lot for sending them——

To John Howard Lawson

[Madrid
January–February 1920]

Jack—I was enormously delighted to get your letter—How idiotic! What sins against the Holy Pigeon have we committed that we should both be laid up stiff as pokers in this year of grace? All I have accomplished has been a military novel which is all but finished and which I hate with a hate passing all hates hitherto hated. Spain remains joyously preposterous, but I—I have not been preposterous—I have been living a cabbage-like existence—

I am waiting in a café noisier than any other café on earth to go to a play called La Rosa del Maz—which I think is going to be dull.

The play was not exactly dull, but very sad and sweet: one expected everybody to turn into sugarcandy. A young gentleman had consumption and a young lady was sweetly sacrificial, and a second young gentleman sacrificed himself for the sad sweet young lady and it was all too sweet for words and ended by the sadsweet consumptive gentleman suddenly getting well and falling into the arms of the sad sweet sacrificial lady. The theatre in Madrid is rotten this winter—the acting always superb—but my God the plays—though they still remain on a faintly higher level than Broadway.

But, Jack, What has come from this unnatural coupling of yours? Another so called Baby's play?

About my movements. I am in a state—Spain is delectable, preposterous, decorative, everything—but in Spain is Madrid. It seems impossible to be in Spain without being in Madrid. I am bored with Madrid. I abominate Madrid . . . I have been, am and shall be in Madrid.

I am bored with everything. I seem unable to escape a regular three meals a day getup and go to bed existence. I have taken to going to a thing called an Ateneo where there is a library, where I write slowly and solemnly and heavily amid an atmosphere of literati. I do that every day . . . I dine at a little restaurant that boasts of being "style Duval". Outside the windows is a Dodo bird like the Dodo bird in Asolo and a live rooster that crows when the clock strikes.

My money is exhausting itself rapidly—I suffer from the limitations of space and time.

To illustrate: the other day we were jaunting in the province of Toledo. We came to a posada in a town named Orgaz—where we were taken for Comicos, as a troop of actors was due to appear—people kept asking us when we were going to start the performance: I was not amused. In the same posada was a maid named Anastasia and the wedding dance of a gentleman who had been engaged to one lady eight years and then had suddenly married someone else, and the patronia was named Diña Leona and looked it, had the tiniest whiskers I have ever seen in my life: I was not amused.

Like Knights on quests in Malory—I have fallen into a languor— The thing for you and Kate and the bambino to do is bring the potion.

I must have excitement. I must do something preposterous. Therefore America!

But I shall await your arrival patiently—I promise that—

Honestly though something must be done about me.

This business of convalescence is a porqueria—then period of moneylessness, another porqueria. Now I have money—in moderation—but I feel as if I were a shell—I am trussed up in a cocoon spun of my own ideas. The cure—America!

I'll probably be in Barcelona when you appear—or I may be sitting on the wharf in Bordeaux—or I may be in Paris, or I may be crazy—

Love
Dos

I shall send full instructions to Bordeaux as to where and why, with maps and diagrams so that you can find the tomb.

To Stewart Mitchell

Madrid
February 17, 1920

Dear Stewart. You will probably take this letter as the ultimate impudence of a congenital whippersnapper and cross me for ever off the list of the elect. I have enough faith in the spread of your Aukpinions to risk it.

I was desperately disappointed by the January *Dial*—which I had been looking forward to rather feverishly ever since the first rumors and rumblings.

It was so flat it might have been the Atlantic Monthly of the year 1889—or may be the Atlantic had life in those days.

Now, Auk dear, I perfectly realize that there were great difficulties to contend with and that it was impossible to please everybody—but I think that you owe it to your own integrity to impose yourself more. While you are running the magazine it ought to reek with Aukishness from cover to cover.

First from the purely practical side: You want people to read the *Dial* . . . Well look, the people who have read the *Dial* in the last year have read it because it expressed a distinct intellectual trend, that of the Chicago economic-social crowd, of John Dewey and Thorstein Veblen and the rest. In order that those people shall not stop reading it, they've got to be given something vigorous and definite that will arrest their imaginations and tickle their intellects if they have any.

I take it that you want to be literary, to embark on the grand vague sea of 100 per cent art.

Well I dont think it is possible to do that without exhibiting some definite trend, and I think that the only trend which will interest the sort of person who will read the *Dial* (school teachers, members of women's clubs, Greenwich villagers, thwarted literateurs and stenographers with romantic hopes) will be an attempt to exhibit or invent tendencies in American literature (of, for, & by Americans). Of course you scorn politics; therefore you must have sex, and carefully chosen literary novelties that will stimulate without startling.

In this number the Bourne thing, though dull, was worth publishing, though why did you not get in an article on Bourne? Who was wonderfully typical from the little I have heard of him of the best there is in Young Americans. There would have been a note to hang the whole number on

(All this is shockingly impudent, Auk. I realize it. But I am so totally detached from the world at present, that I think that my opinion—even in matters of detail—may have a value which it certainly wouldn't have if I were living in New York.)

But those sophomoric dribblings on Edith Wharton and Loeffler and that miserable snobbism of Symons about Thomas Hardy—how did they get in?

I must make an exception of Loeffler article, which from the purely practical point of view of interesting the audience is not at all bad.

Estlin's verse and the Sandburg poem and Estlin's drawings were certainly worth publishing.

But I cannot think of anything else in the number that means anything to the average moderately intelligent American. Gilbert Canaan I suppose is an attractive name. The story, you'll admit, was intrinsically asinine. And so many of the other things had the air of being stuck in to fill up. Of course the faint British perfume which pervades the whole may be an attraction, but it means that you go into the lists against the *English Review*—and I think most people will prefer the genuine London article to the American imitation.

But perhaps I am being desperately unfair. . . . I admit that my ideal of a magazine that shall be a lion to devour and a banner to lead the assault is impossible. For that very reason I have tried to judge this first number of the *Dial* from the practical point of view of securing an audience. And unless you give people juicier meat for their 35 cents I dont think you will.

And while you are out lionhunting, why neglect Amy and Dreiser and Masters and Mrs. Wharton? Even the *Seven Arts* succeeded better in expressing a tendency—and it was not able to secure its audience—though I admit that there was no little glory in its defeat.

To get away with a literary magazine at this moment in America, the *Seven Arts* will have to be gone one better, and more.

And Stewart you are certainly a vivider person and have greater intelligence than any of the seven artists. For Gods sake impose yourself—forget your nice manners, take off your coat, be willing to make an ass of yourself. Don't be a gentleman.

You have such a gorgeous chance. If you are willing to be a little reckless I think that—while money is supplied to buy printers ink and paper—you can impress yourself on chaotic unleavened America as no one has ever impressed himself before. The pot is coming to a boil. All depends on the moulds that are made now whether civilization or barbarism rules our continent and the world. But, you answer, that is not your business—art for art.

There has never been great art that did not beat with every beat of the life around it. If it is the most vivid expression of that life, how can it do otherwise?

And this moment is so on the brink of things. Overpopulation combined with a breakdown of food has wrecked the checks and balances of the industrialized world. In ten years we may be cavemen snatching the last bit of food from each others mouths amid the stinking ruins of our cities, or we may be slaving—antlike—in some utterly systematized world where the individual will be utterly crushed that the mob (or the princes) may live. Every written word should be thought of as possibly the last that humanity will ever write, every gesture of freedom the last before the shackles close definitely. And we who have worshipped freedom and writing as God—Shall we be annihilated by destiny filling up the precious printed pages with spacefillers?

The *Dial* is the one hope of all the people who, like you and I, want to express themselves freely and still remain Americans. Just think of the possibilities of it.

O I suppose I've been very silly—I certainly have expressed myself as blunderingly as a humming bee trying to get through a plate glass window.

But you will certainly realize that if I were not very fond of you, and that if I did not have great faith in your ability I should not have written this letter. You see I have been so long out of a literary atmosphere that I was really shocked and horrified beyond expression. We all of us, in our *Monthly* days, exhibited a little fire combined with much—O so much—perfumed smoke. I will not believe that the smoke has put out the fire—

For Gods sake send me a number of the *Dial* that will get me out of the dumps. And forgive me, Stewart.

Love
Dos

To Rumsey Marvin

[Madrid
March 1920]

Rummy—

Thanks ever so much for the Amy [Lowell]—She's always great fun and sometimes distinctly fine. Peter Middleton I have not read yet.

If you haven't read Amy you must—she's superbly lacking in solemnity and has a slightly "objet d'art" pictorial sense which is delightful and very much her own.

How is your famous three hundred word plan going? Why don't you send me some specimens I'll guarantee to rip them up the back for you.

I wish you'd been with me day before yesterday. We got up very early and took the train in the cold yellow dawn while the plain of Castile was still steaming with mist to Aranjuez—where Schiller's Don Carlos "die sonneyahre" etc happened—a redstone palace and gardens by the Tajo, that is jade green and glamorous with weirs. From there we walked up on to a great plateau where we inspected the church of a village called Ciruelos where it was with great difficulty that we escaped being given by the cura some of the earth that had been round the body of St. Raymond, founder of the knightly order of Calatrava. Then we walked on across the plain—green with sprouting wheat, blue with olive trees, with occasional vineyards full of the black stumps of the vines, until we saw a church tower rise out of the flat plain ahead of us. Gradually a roof rose up after the tower and, a long while later, other roofs and crenelated towers. Then after long walking we entered the gate of Yepes. In Yepes we found a beautiful rust brown church of the renaissance towering over the town the way the grain elevators tower over the towns on Lake Superior; also we found delicious white wine, tart as a winter's morning, little cakes of almond paste, that go coyly under the name of melindres de Yepes, a delicious concoction known as turrou, a great many beautiful wrought iron window-gratings, a retablo by a pupil of El Greco—and other joys. We lunched—lying in the sun on a little hill overlooking the garden patches and the town; and when we walked away, the town sank into the plain again as it had risen out of it until all we could see behind the silvery olive trees was the dark spire of the church. Then we climbed down from the mesa into the valley of the Tajo again and waited a long time rather sleepily, drinking aguardiente and water and eating the last of the melindres, for a train to take us back to Madrid.

I bet Orion doesnt show so bright across the common at New Haven as he did that night from the station platform of Castellejo.

And Rummy, when are you and I going to walk together to the moon and back?

Haveyouwritten any verse recently?

Remember me to your mother and father and give them my best wishes for the New Year.

Love

Jack

I'm sitting in this wretched library-place trying to write chapter four of the last lap of *Three Soldiers,* feeling about as fluent as an empty tea pot——

Embarquement pour Cythère
(After Watteau)

The mists have veiled the far end of the lake
This sullen amber afternoon;
Our island is quite hidden, and the peaks
Hang wanly as clouds above the ruddy haze.
Come, give your hand, that lies so limp,—
A nard-flower among the brown oak leaves;—
Put your hand in mine and let us leave
This bank where we have lain all the day long
Talking of old clear days that might have been.

See, in the boat the naked oarsman stands.
His eyes are fixed on us. There is a smile
In the full red bow of his young lips. Come
Let us walk faster; or do you fear to tear
That brocaded dress of apricot and green?
Love, there are silk cushions in the stern,
Of all rich colors, maroon and apple-green,
Crocus yellow, crimson, amber-grey . . .
We will lie and listen to the languid waves
Slap soft against the prow, and watch the boy
Slant his brown body to the long oarstroke.

But, love, we are more beautiful than he.
We have forgotten the greysick yearning nights,
We have brushed off the old cobwebs of desire
We stand in the flame of fulfillment naked, young,
Immortally young as the slender brown boy who waits
To row our boat to the island . . .

But, love, how slow,

How languid are your steps. Lean more on me;
I love to feel your cheek press my cheek hard . . .
But what is this bundle of worn brocades I press

So passionately to me? Old rags of the past,
Snippings of Juliet's dress, of Helena's
Scarfs of old paramours rotted in the grave
Ages and ages since. No lake but the ink
In the bottle that yawns at me from my littered desk
So you, too, were only a dream, love,
A bitter dream . . .

To Managing Director
George Allen & Unwin, Ltd.

c/o Credit Lyonnais
Barcelona
March 13 1920

Dear Sir,

I am not quite sure what you mean by a descriptive paragraph. I suppose it is the little puff that is used in advertizing. You probably know much better than I what would be suitable. However, it might be useful to say that the volume is made up out of notes written while I was an ambulance driver attached to the French army in the summer of 1917 and that I have tried to picture the state of mind of an American in his first contact with the war as well as the general moral atmosphere of the war at that moment. The notes were scratched down in dugouts and hospitals and were put in their present shape in the autumn of 1918, thinly disguised under a novelistic form.

If there is anything more I can give you in that direction, please let me know at once—c/o Credit Lyonnais Barcelona—

Very sincerely yours
John R. Dos Passos

To Rumsey Marvin

Gran Continental Café-Restaurant
Barcelona
14 de marzo de 1920

Rummy—a splendid bundle of miscellaneous literature from you was most enlivening. The doggerel's not half bad. The book review is excellent—a little too much the conventional book review, but excellent nevertheless. And the fire story is damned effective. Ça marche mon petit, ça marche. Rubberstamp words are still fairly frequent, and little ends of phrases stuck in without meaning. I'll illustrate later when I have the ms. to quote abominations from.

Your account of attempting a paper excites me much. It'll be wonderful fun. Write me all details.

Barcelona for a bomb city is singularly unexciting. Still I have hopes of discovering things about the singularly bitter and unrelieved class war that is desolating Catalan industry.

I'm crazy to see you. But I have not an idea in the world of where I shall be June 30th. I am in a moment of complete and desolating indecision. Half of me wants to go to America, half of me wants to hide in warm sun scorched towns, to sail in boats with lateen sails in harbors where the waves wash idly as if weighed down with blue and purple and crimson and orange and vermillion . . . and the economic monster licks his chops and sniffs outside my door.

Meanwhile I dont get my novel finished, which is a great aggravation.

I approve thoroughly of your walking plans, because the delightfulness of small French towns is only savored by walking in in the evening, and walking out in the morning, and the high beds of small French inns are superb places for exhausted legs, to say nothing of omelets eaten at little wooden tables in the sun washed down with un petit vin blanc as balm for tired spirits.

Barcelona is rather fun. I have a room overlooking the harbor, where I am wakened in the morning by the sound of winches and sirens and the clatter of rivetting hammers. And all day there is a smell of the holds of ships and tar and cordage and storehouses full of goods that have come across seas.

On the Rambla are piles of flowerstalls full of iris, white and purple and the pale lavender grey Florentine kind, fat pink peonies and yellow clamorous daffodils. Spring is on us pell mell. It's always rather terrifying—dont you think so?—the first rush of Spring. One wishes it would come more slowly, that one would have time to live up to it. It's such a dreadful challenge, the Spring.

The following are rather journalese than good Yankee dialect.
   "seething mass of flames"
   "the temperature was bitterly cold"
   "get wind of the affair"
   phrases in quotation marks like

" "in at the death"."
"exposed our situation"
"fire was raging"
"utterly"
——The trouble with such phrases is, as you see, that they are all ways of avoiding saying anything definite—and writing to be any good has, in my opinion got to be stripped naked. Like in good architecture, every inch must have something functional to do, must be an integral part of holding the building up. That doesn't cut out decoration at all, it just means that every bit of decoration must mean something. And yet it seems perfectly impossible to write things down as clearly as that, so sloppy our minds are; I find that I cut out easily a dozen words to a page the first time I read a thing over. You've seen the man who goes along a train in a station testing the wheels with a hammer—well every word on the page ought to be tested that way to see if it rings hollow, and if there is the slightest doubt—out with it.

Write me Morgan Harjes.

Au revoir
Jack

To John Howard Lawson

Barcelona
26–III [1920]

Jack—I have just met up with Kate and your sister—But really I feel rather desolated at not finding you. We must get rid of all this sickness business. What curious demon have you got in you? It all sounds rather like Rousseau's troubles. I am awfully anxious to hear the result of the Paris inquest. Of course you must feel wretchedly low. By God something must be done. What saint controls misplaced goiters? We must burn fat wax candles in chapels choking with incense. Gongs must be rung on hilltops. The rattles of medicine men must whir like locusts in a plague of Egypt.

I have had just enough of a taste of the feebleness of the flesh to know how frantic you must feel.

Write me at once whether you are staying in Paris or coming south. I'll meet you in Paris or anywhere you say in a week.

Don't you think if one could get somewhere where there was a great deal of sun and none of the stridence of cities the goitre-thing would go away?

If any carving is done, I'll come to Paris at once. Write me Credit Lyonnais here.

I am going over to Mallorca for a day or two—possibly I'll induce Kate and Adelaide to come with me.

But write me here at once what you will do.

Sun, air, green fields, blue water—swimming—baking on white beaches—All that I think is essential.

I am crazy to talk to you about many things. I hope to have the new novel "Three Soldiers" ready to read to you—and I want to hear millions of plays.

Kate says you are reading lots of spanish.

I've discovered some delightful poets.

Kate as always affects me as a superlative person.

Write at once or telegraph. I am rather anxious.

Love
Dos

To John Howard Lawson

[Barcelona]
April 8–[19]20

Jack: I wish I'd been with you to hold your hand and all that sort of thing, while your parts were being carved—by the way I'm not quite sure yet just what was carved. Everyone has preserved a tactful silence on that score, until I have come to picture unimaginable splittings, and shuddersome puncturings. No, I felt it was rather coarse of me to go to Mallorca and disport on the green at the crucial moment. Still your letters managed most excellently to give the impression that you weren't going to be split after all. But all this ill describes how crazy I am to see you.

No, by all means let it be Carcassonne—At twelve, noon, on top of the highest tower of the wall. Then we can journey, if need be in search of a nook, or nooks elsewhere. I would run up to Paris to fetch you if it were not that there is a spoke in my wheel. At this moment I possess four pesetas and a bad fifty centime piece (the remnant of money borrowed from Kate in Mallorca). At a certain bank, 1600 glittering pesetas await me, but somehow they are in the name of Carlos and not John, so that a bad beadyeyed bankclerk steadfastly refuses to let me have so much as a look at them. What's in a name? I moan distractedly. If the pesetas have not materialized Monday, the twelfth, I shall telegraph you to telegraph me enough to get to Carcassonne. I'm not doing it today as the bad beady eyed bank clerk swears he'll be able to give me my own dear pesetas Saturday; and the exchange, you know, is shocking.

Kate Adelaide and Co I saw off on the boat from Palma, bound for Alicante, Murcia, Granada, Seville and way stations.

But c'est entendu, is it not—At twelve noon, Wednesday the fourteenth, at the top most tower in the city wall of Carcassonne, or as near it as one can possibly get.

Telegraph me Credit Lyonnais here in Barcelona if there is any change in plans—

Love
Dos

To Managing Director
George Allen & Unwin, Ltd.

c/o Credit Lyonnais,
Barcelona
April 8–[19]20

Dear Sir,

I have gone through the proofs.

I am enclosing a dedication, and your advertisement, which seems excellently worded.

There remain the passages you suggest should be paraphrased. One I have cut out entirely, and the other, on p. 59, I think that you will agree is pretty innocuous. I admit that the "Old Boy" on page 71 may annoy some people, but I am very reluctant to cut it out, as it seems to me expressive. If you insist, however, it may be substituted by "You". Also I'd much rather have the "you"s addressed to the figure on the cross in small letters, but if you really feel it's your duty to capitalize them, go ahead.

Very sincerely yours
John R. Dos Passos

P.S. How would it be to drop the 1917 out of the title only keeping it on the title page, written under the One Man's Initiation, as I have indicated? But do as you like about it. As long as it appears somewhere, I dont mind how it is brought in.

To Managing Director
George Allen & Unwin, Ltd.

Marseilles
April 29 [*1920*]

Dear Sir,

I'm awfully sorry to have held up proceedings in this way. I had forgotten that the British public was so touchy about blasphemy.

Unfortunately I have not the M.S. with me so I cant be quite sure how the sentences read. Please omit entirely the three sentences. I think this can be done without adding anything, but if a sentence of bridging seems needed, put in anything brief and terse that seems suitable. The incident of the soldiers kicking the prop out from under the Cross will carry the idea. If you do not want to print that, please omit the entire scene. I am willing to have almost anything omitted, but I cannot consent to paraphrases.

Very sincerely yours
John R. Dos Passos

To Thomas P. Cope

Marseilles
April 29 [*1920*]

Tom, you old bum, you're a wonder! Just imagine your actually weighing anchor and setting out. For Gods sake keep me informed of all your motions as I shall be awfully anxious to hear where how and what you are. I half expect to see you turn up at one of the cafés on the harbor front here, a miraculous place, of inconceivable lowness where I am sure I have seen people of every race except possibly esquimaux.

I'm here with Jack Lawson, who's amusing himself wryly with complications of typhoid, (I) in the course of putting the finishing touches on that much delayed and much advertized novel.

Your gorgeous letter followed me from Madrid and nearly knocked me down, shivered my timbers, broke my shaft, blew out my pistonheads (or whatever you like) with excitement. It stank strong enough of deep sea pipes and bilge to make the hair curl on your chest, and made me feel a foureyed yellowbellied land lubber for fair.

Anything I do now will be but a pale imitation of your prowess. For I am also in a sort of a desperate mood. In fact I shall blow up and bust if I dont do something frightfully exciting very soon.

I sit with Jack drinking vermouth at the corner of the Cannebière. Sodom and Gomorrah, Bombay and Yokahama, Tiflis and Birmingham with a good sprinkling of Little Rock slouch by along the pavement. You cant beat Marseille.

We are going to Paris tomorrow, Jack to visit doctors, I to fulfill unprofitable destinies. I suppose its coming to the end of something you've been working on for ages that gives you this fin de siècle mood. I sigh dreadfully for draughts of Hyppocrene and bumpers full of the warm south, highly spiced and peppered. I've taken to wandering about with the fainthearted elegance of a God damned tourist. For my soul's sake turn up somewhere in tarpaulins with a Knock me down pipe and Shanghai me aboard a full rigged ship.

Write me where you are and what your plans are—to Morgan Harjes—

Really Tom you have my wholesale admiration

Love
Dos

Van's ship exploded on the way to Tananarive and had to go back to Hampton Roads. However he must be under weigh again by this time for the land of lima beans and fuzzyhaired queens.

Dudley's in Madrid translating Spanish novels.

By the way—why dont you send me some verse? The influence of nautical swearing should be interesting. I think—if you'd only untangle it and cut out latinized words a bit—your verse will come out of chaos into something damn fine. Let's see some.

To Rumsey Marvin

[Paris
May 1, 1920]

Rummy: if, as is most unlikely, you ever begin to lose interest in life, come to Marseille, walk down the Cannebière, along the harbor front, up through the garbage littered alleys where Corytho reigns, circle back through the city and come out in the full moonlight in the high platform of the church of the Magdalen, and if you dont feel interested in existence by that time, just give up hope and enter one of the respectable professions.

If there is a gateway to the gorgeous east it is that steel girder contraption that straddles the entrance to the harbor of Marseille.

People, filthy, grotesque, perfumed, low, purse proud, jolly, naive, yellow, white, black, chocolate colored, coffee colored, tobacco colored, green, brown, purple and spotted, every conceivable kind of person dressed in every conceivable kind of garment, uniforms, half uniforms, dress suits, bournouses, tunics, overalls, loincloths, cutaways, frock coats, of every color and in every stage of chicness and disrepair engaged in every conceivable sort of conversation, all moving back and forth, along the Cannebière and the water front. A wonderful feeling in the air that everyone has either just arrived from Tananarive or Patagonia or is just leaving for Singapore or the headwaters of the Blue Nile. And everyone eating, hating, loving, struggling, starving, fornicating——a bath in raw humanity.

O there is nowhere more epic than Marseille, nowhere bawdier, more farcical, jollier, wilder, more seething with humors. Talk about a barrel of monkeys!

May 1. Just-arrived in grey misty Paris, my Paris, full of memories. I *always* feel a curious bitterness when I come back to a place that has played an important part in my life. There is so much mockery in the sameness of things.

Haven't had a letter in a dog's age—Rummy.

Honestly I haven't an idea in the world where I'll be the end of June. Maybe in America. If I am anywhere near France I'll certainly see you and we'll jaunt about somewhere together. I am in the miserably restless moment of the end of the novel, and I may explode in a most unexpected direction. The other damn thing isn't out yet—

Lots of love
Jack

To Stewart Mitchell

Morgan Harjes—Paris
May 13 [*1920*]

Dearest of Auks—

I forgive you everything, even the stenog.—But for Gods sake let it be known, let it be shouted abroad, let it be screamed from the house-tops that I'll be damned to hell before I'm genial and genteel. So the pedlar hoists his sack on his back and seeks another street . . .

But Auk—I dont want business communications from you, even to the tune of thousand franc notes—(for which I offer due thanks); I'm interested in your immortal soul, not in your terrestrial typewriter.

By the way, before I forget it, have you received two articles one on Pio Baroja, one on Blanco Ibanez to put in your rotten old sheet? If you dont want them, send them back to poor Mack [Wright McCormick], whom I have suddenly converted into my literary executioner in America.

No, I think I'm coming back, if I can't find a way of going to China or Thibet. I'm sick of dangling on the margin of life. Though a pleasant margin it has been for me, adorned with gothic silhouettes and winebottles and tambourines. O if this literary existence were not so damn genial and genteel . . . Have you ever noticed the shrivelled souls of elderly literateurs?

Of course, if one had vices . . .

I am sitting in Dudley's very tiny room in the Hotel du Cardinal in a back street near St. Germain-des-Pres. Across the way a canary bird sings and someone practices dolefully as a lost faun on the piccolo.

—O c't musique! Puisqu'on nous fait avaler là? I hear an irate woman's voice below.

The room has a low ceiling and a big round mahogany table and a bed such as Manon and that sad solemn Chevalier made creak with the sentimental ecstasies of eighteenth century love . . .

What you say about taking what lies on the lap of the gods I agree to—only one can snatch it, can't one?

I'm sorry your book is still, and unmeritedly, refused. Why dont you publish a lot of verse in the Dial? Or dont you think it's genteel to step from off the editorial throne (would to God I could truthfully write thundering)

A silly little thing of mine is appearing in London (Allen & Unwin) after a long squabble about bad language. It ended in a compromise. I eliminated some disrespectful references to Jesus, and was allowed to keep several whores and one prophylaxis in return.

I'm just preparing to peddle the second great American novel—called Three Soldiers—or something of the sort. Wonderfully untimely, isn't it? Write me in your own fair hand, O Auk

Love
Dos

To Thomas P. Cope

En face du Pont Marie
comme autre fois
[Paris]
May 15 [*1920*]

Tom!

Honestly I approve of you highly. I keep thinking of you, and wishing I had the guts to do anything as violent and satisfactory.

Please write me long and detailed descriptions of everything.

Deering has turned up here. According to him you gave your avaricious skipper the sack and are looking for a threemaster to take you to Cathay and the Spice Islands. Also I am very anxious to have any details of the mechanics of declassing oneself. I had thought that my doughboy period would have done that for me for good and all; but, not a bit of it. I find myself bobbing up serenely again with all the mentality of the comfortably inane and dainty nostriled litterateur.

How about your verse? Are you producing fo'csle ballads, or Boiler Room Odes. The Lake Silver is—or rather was—I imagine, a rather tiny affair.

Hampton Roads is one of my old stamping grounds. There's a hotel in Norfolk where things to eat are glorious (comparatively). And the Cape Charles mosquitos—if you ever by ill luck got into the harbor they make their domain, will leave their memories.

Tom, your going to sea has had a distinct and probably fatal influence on my life.

Adiós
Dos

Dudley appeared a short time ago from Madrid. Mme Lecomte, Jeanette, Margot and André always talk about you. Perhaps you'll materialize. I'm going to England in a short time to peddle the triune doughboy—

To Thomas P. Cope

[London
June 1920]

Tom—

I've been hoping to have news of you—without much result. Are you halfway to Singapore aboard a fullrigged ship, or handling hawsers on a tugboat on the Susquehanna?

I am in London squabbling with my publishers. Verily of the making of books there is no end. The printers refuse to print *One Man's Initiation*—they say it's indecent! So more expurgations and changes must be made. The poor thing will be gelded for fair by the time it comes out. However, I am slightly consoled by the chance of an American edition, which seems to be solidifying. Literature's a silly business.

At present I have not the slightest reason for writing—its ages since I thought or experienced anything amusing or interesting. I have been suffering from an illusion of flatness for some time. Comes from lack of exercise I imagine—almost everything does. America has an unhallowed attraction for me—unless I can find something of unusual interest to do—to *do*—not to feel, see, think, hear; times come when one needs the illusion of action. Its only an illusion—a damn thin one—but I think you feel see think hear more sharply when you have it than when you are floating about swathed in the cottonwool of middle-class existence

To get rid of the cottonwool at all costs is the thing.

All these reflections are possibly due to the curious mental state one gets in when one finishes a work—*Three Soldiers* is irredeemably finished. I wish you were here to tell me what you thought of it.

Tom, when you get to be the Captain of the *Whinnying Wallaboo* you'll give me the job of crew of the captain's gig, wont you?

I must get out of the Doldrums of society,

Love—
Dos

In case you're hard up, cash this. I have about $600 or more in that bank so let me know at once if you need more—

To Thomas P. Cope

> [On board the *Espagne*
> *August 1920*]
>
> At sea six days West
> of the Azores—Sky like
> a robin's egg fringed
> with little clouds,
> sea blue with a curious
> pinkish mother of pearl
> sheen—

Dear Old Tom, you ancient mariner—I cant help writing you though I haven't an idea under heaven where to send this letter. I embarked on this palatial affair at St. Nazaire—It went first to Santander where I had a glimpse of a Spanish sunday, people going in carriages to the toros, sidewalks overlaid with little tables and beggars and blind musicians and bootblacks and the thick sunshine that seems to brush against your cheek like hot velvet. Then Coruña—and then twelve days sea towards Havana. The Azores were extraordinarily beautiful, buff and pale bright green with violet cliffs and vast plumed clouds piled above them. The water was a marvellous sapphire full of dolphins—What a wonderful curve they make when they leap clear of the water. There is something so sharp and breathtaking about it. How marvellous the sea must be on a boat that's not unpleasantly overcrowded with passengers. A passenger is an obnoxious object, be he ever so human and charming in another capacity.

Please write long letters—Your letters excite me tremendously. I have been awfully blue and disoriented for a dog's age—I have a sensation of sliding slowly and comfortably down ice on the slopes, without ever being able to grasp a handful of the real earth—Your letters are tufts of grass say—seaweed—! that I can catch hold of for a moment. I suppose I'll learn to live before I die—but there are times when I doubt it. I have an instinct—God knows where it comes from—to shrink from contacts. A sort of congenital cowardice—like that of the snail and his horns. Don't you think that snails may pass their lives wishing they knew what happened in the world after they had drawn back into their shells?

From Havana I go to New York to try to get a novel published—all these flowers blushing unseen are beginning to get on my nerves.

It's horrible how everyone is scattering—If you get to Paris, you will find Dudley—until October—living with his family at the Porte d'Asnières. 12 Rue Philibert Delorme—The Lawsons are all three in Paris, all four I mean.

Damn these floating palaces.

I'm tired of hearing that the Cuban lady at my table (who has a little dog like those Venetian courtesans have in Veronese and is that shape [refers to a sketch] and comes from Algiers and speaks Spanish with an Andalusian accent) sleeps alternately with the two fat gentlemen from Barcelona with whom I play shuffleboard for bottles of champagne, or that the French lady who dances so well applies a fresh pair of horns each day to her husband's forehead.

Last night we passed through Providence Channel and today we're full in the gulf stream between the Bahamas and the Florida coast. Tomorrow we will be in Havana and I shall take ship for New York.

Think of your plan of hiring or stealing or buying a ship and setting out. I'd be crazy to try it at any time. Van would probably give us a contract to carry beans from Madagascar to Nagasaki and back. Something must be contrived to transport us about the world without our having to suffer the ignominy of being passengers.

And I suspect that it will take a damn short time to get fed up with God's country—which now lies to the left of us still under the horizon.

I hardly know why I'm going back, except that there was no particular point in my staying in Europe—Christ—how the months fly—

Somebody is playing the Humoresque on the palatial piano in the palatial salon—In the steerage—which stinks I must admit to heaven—they play the gaéta. By sheer boredom and banality civilizations fall. The Humoresque has all the concentrated banality of those staid Roman gentlemen and ladies of decadent times who stand in proper rows on the tombs along the Appian way. Never mind—Warsaw has fallen—at least I suppose it has.

The other day we had some splendid waterspouts. Then, too, there have been gigantic porpoises and many playing fish.

Write all sorts of things. I'm crazy to hear your adventures.

Love
Dos

To Rumsey Marvin

Off the coast of Galicia
8/7/20

Dear Rummy—

On board a boat going to Habana—cloudy morning. Yesterday we were in Santander. It was Sunday afternoon, the town was wonderfully jolly, bands of music blind beggars, all the best people riding in limousines and carriages to the corrida, smell of beer and coffee and hot milk and roasted nuts and fire-crackers. After the extraordinary dullness of

St. Nazaire it was like stepping out of the door of a Methodist church into a five-ring-circus.

Write me to 214 Riverside Drive c/o Mrs James Riely Gordon—your doings after leaving Guisan. I think you'll find Italy wonderful, and you'll have a much better time when you are not being led round by the nose by a hired dry-nurse.

I have reams of paper the project of a play—Flaubert's correspondence and three fat black volumes by the Bless'd Frazer on the folklore of the Old Testament.

The boat is fancy, the food good, the people no duller than first class people always are. I have a luxurious cabin all to myself—and feel much like Heliogobalus. In fact there is something late Roman about large ocean liners.

I'll be awfully keen to hear about your wanderings—For gods sake remember that three score years and ten is a damn short time and see all you can, do all you can, eat all you can, drink all you can, think all you can. In Milan have a meal at Cova's and go to the most garlicky operas you can find. Also there's a very jolly marionette theatre, and a place, The Eden Theatre, where you can dine and watch an antiquated operette all at the same time. Dont miss Verona (San Geno), Padua (the Giotto Chapel and Donatello's horseman) or Venice. Bologna is lively—a mad city of writhing towers in orange and green—If, by any chance, you get interested in painting you must not miss Florence. And as for Rome—well you deserve to be tarred and feathered if you don't go there. Dine at the Palace of the Caesars(?) restaurant on the Esquiline go to Tivoli and Hadrian's villa and get very drunk on the wine of Frascati.

If Italy doesn't rush you off your feet make you forget your puritan ancestors and your business careers, I'll eat my shirt and vest.

Of course the lake region is probably very lovely. I once nearly froze to death at the end of the lake of Garda.

Write me all about it.

Love
Jack

To John Howard Lawson

214 Riverside Drive
[New York]
Sept. 12– [19]20

Jack—forgive me not having sent the 5000 sooner. I'll send it tomorrow by cable. It has taken time to disentangle pennies.

Floated up from Cuba on the Gulf Stream on a very delapidated boat—trip given over to the study and culture of the gin fizz. When the old thing docked at Brooklyn (with great difficulty as it's engines were aweary of this great world) the moment a gang plank was thrown down a great crowd of square jawed men with clubs piled aboard—prohibition officers—There was a marvellous amount of snooping about the dock—little men with sachels and hungry eyes called plaintively to those on the boat—have you any mail? and other cryptic phrases.

New York is rather funny—like a badly drawn cartoon—everybody looks and dresses like the Arrow-collarman. I've been amused, though glutted with relatives, eversince I've been here.

Plays I have not yet investigated, having seen only "The Bat" a bag of all the current melodrama tricks—very entertaining, to be sure, by Avery Hopkins and Rinehart, and an extraordinarily dull and ancient David Warfield play in Boston of which I've forgotten, thank God, the name. Everyone urges you to go to Lincoln & a certain play called The Bad Man.

Have seen the vague and shadowy Brandts and chatted with Mary Kirkpatrick who says she thinks your play will have to be bought back as she sees no chance of a production. The Brandts have carried on a long and rather obscure intrigue with both novels and the Knopf gang, which, to my relief, collapsed with the spewing forth of both MSS by Knopf. Rumor hath it that Monday there will be a signing of contracts for Jericho with Boney lieberwurst [Boni & Liveright]. But I think all will relapse into the mists again Mr. Brandt claims to have sat up until three in the morning reading 3 Soldiers and says it "ought" to be published.

But they are very vague, foggy misty, mysterious, mum.

I'm a goddam loafer. On the boat, instead of writing the play I wrote absurdities for the Dionysus novel which may be called Quest of the Core. However I feel murderously energetic, slit'em up and slash'em and blow'em up with T.N.T. so I—if I ever can find a place to lay my weary hind quarters—have hopes.

The Dial has a charming house with paradise bushes in the back yard on 13th Street, a lovely dark stenog named Sophia and some beautiful tall ice-tea glasses. They speak only French during office hours and are genteel, though I admit, delightful.

Griffin's in Provincetown, so I haven't seen him yet. John Mosher is about to retire to Albany to write a novel. He lives wonderfully from hand to mouth and gurgles and giggles and jerks himself about as delightfully as ever.

Everybody I meet is unspeakably unchanged.

Labor's belly up completely—The only hope is in the I.W.W. (which no one mentions even in a whisper) and in the Non Partisan league which has just captured the Dem. primaries in N. Dakota and I think in Montana, too

I'm going to make a sentimental journey to Virginia to weep over weed grown stamping-grounds. It's ghoulish the hatred of people who do work of any use and the interest in diseases. Everybody's running about having X rays taken of their teeth for fear of abcesses.

Love to Kate After all N.Y.'s damn jolly to look at. Babylon gone mad.

Dos

What about your troubles? Will you have to take another lining of quicksilver? Rotten luck—If you need moneys let me know. I'm either rather wealthy or penniless, I'm not sure which—

To John Howard Lawson

[214 Riverside Drive
New York
October 11, 1920]

Jack

Everything's belly-up. The acclamations with which Three Soldiers was first received by the Brandtine world freeze gradually. Leiberwurst, who promised to publish Jericho swearing by the Torah and the Talmud, has dropped it like a hot potato, and now, in a last passionate interlude over the telephone in Adelaide's studio Mrs Brandt —says that she thinks there's the making of a novel in the character of James Clough—but otherwise. . . . O ye Gods and mermaids and little puking fishes of the sea!

Last night I went to "Mecca" a dull pompous spectacle which interested me because of the fornicational goings on that were allowed on the stairs in a rather delightful badly costumed ballet by Fokine. People bellowed their lines like rundown phonographs and there were vast quantities of skinny undressed chorus men who were shriekingly funny. Also two camels, a donkey, goats, monkeys, and a comedy chinamen and his wife who just missed being very funny. General effect much like Scheherazade—in fact I thought several times it was Scheherazade.

Good performance of the Treasure—you know the Pinski play I've always chattered about—very good fun at the Theatre Guild.

Follies (Greenwich Village) mildly well costumed arty but relieved by a shriekingly funny and very raw man named Larry who dresses as a woman.

Have seen Berenice [Dewey, who with her husband Billy was a friend of Dos, Dudley Poore, and the Lawsons. She contributed verse to "F.P.A.'s" column in the New York *Herald Tribune*.] who gave me an impression of being off duty at the time. She Billy Adelaide & I dined at that dismal Greenwich Village Inn. She is very beautiful and on duty I imagine would quite overpower one.

The general impression one gets of the New York stage is dismal—the only hopeful sign I can see is its undressedness—and in the raw jokes that get by. Shall read the brass check.

The Freeman is a good paper. The Dial and I have little communication so there is no danger of their good manners being corrupted.

Dudley Field Malone is conducting a faint hearted Farmer Labor campaign. Harding will be elected by a large majority. One keeps meeting extraordinary people in all walks of life—mild little people who say with a worm will turn expression I'm going to vote for Debs—like little boys that say damn just because they're scared of the sound of it——

Write voluminously
If you get broke—cable—

Dos

Belly up   Belly up   Belly up
NEW YORK CONTINUES TO AMUSE!
Play's nearly finished—first draft—sounds to me like Percy Mackaye at his worst——!
Belly up   Belly up   Belly up

To Robert Hillyer (1895–1961), *a poet, who was a college friend of Dos'. Hillyer graduated from Harvard in 1917. An ambulance driver and later a lieutenant during World War I, he returned to Harvard in 1919 and taught there until 1944, afterward going to Kenyon College and the University of Delaware. He referred to himself as "a conservative and religious poet in a radical and blasphemous age."*

[213 E. 15th Street
New York
November 1920]

Bobby—

You are probably going to hate me. Please don't because I am very fond of you. The reverse of this is the result on me of Alchemy. Alas for the poor—penis-bereft, balls-bereft gentlemen of the illustrations

I'll explain. Two gentlemen a certain Levinson & a certain Malcolm Cowley waited on me in deputation one day saying I must review Alchemy for the Freeman. I was not anxious to do it—but I thought I would knock it more understandingly, and more sweetly perhaps than would a harsh outsider.

Anyway our definitions of poetry never did agree—so de gustibus non disputandum.

Thanks for the delightful letter

Who is Fru Christensen?

Tell me about the drama. Do you remember—I have been very enthusiastic over each of your dramatic essays. What eventually happened to the wonderful "Man Without a Visiting Card"?

The G.N. [Great Novel] still travels dolefully from publishing house to publishing house. Its younger brother "Three Soldiers" temporarily abodes with Mr. Huebsch. Rumor hath it that *perhaps* he will publish it. "One Man's Initiation" came out in the early fall in London. A lady wrote a long review in which abounded such phrases as "jaundiced pacifist", "crabbed internationalist"—making out that I was an enemy of England.

New York is silly and rather stupendous—I mean skies—buildings garbage cans. One drinks red ink in Italian dives and whiskey for tea. Its all rather like a badly drawn cartoon in the self-style funny section of a Sunday paper.

Plans! I have none, I wish you'ld take a house in the country and let me come to visit you. I have a hope of going towards the east in the middle of winter. Write me still 214 Riverside Drive c/o (My aunt) Mrs J. R. Gordon—as I am likely to move suddenly in almost any direction. Or we might get a yawl and sail the South Seas.

Why don't you take a vacation to Rome or some such sunny place? Dudley Poore & Jack Lawson are both there now. Perhaps I'll go through there on my way to Persia or Armenia or Abyssinia.

Did you see your mug in the Boston Transcript and a slobbery article by the fulsome negroid? I hope you duly vomited on reading it.

Write me about your play and about Copenhagen (scenery) and write me a fine polemic defense of Alchemy in heroic couplets.

What happened about the untying of Hymen's knot?

Love—You're a dear, Bobby and a poet in spite of all my venom—

Dos

To Thomas P. Cope

213 E. 15th Street
New York
[*November 2, 1920*]

I wonder where you are Tom. I've been in New York two months and I cant say I have accomplished anything. A few articles in the Freeman. The first draft of what I fear is an utterly futile play—and a certain amount of squabbling about Three Soldiers. The great Bogg.

Still New York is amusing. It has its hanging gardens of Babylon aspect. One talks to starving people on Park Benches. One eats eggplants squashed in oil of sesame in Syrian restaurants and drinks overmuch California chianti in the backs of Italian cafés. There are ferries and the Hudson and the palisades and in Stuyvesant Square the dry leaves murmur their deathrattle as softly as in the Luxembourg.

I see Canby Chambers and Esther Andrews occasionally.

One Man's Initiation is out in London—a measley little business.

Tomorrow Warren Harding is going to be elected president of these United States.

O for a bumper full of the warm south—for that I count on you Lofty—do they still call you that?

Really you cant imagine the old-maid-whose-grandnephew-has-gone-to-the-war-eagerness with which I read your letters.

I'm going to stick for three or four months more to the triste besogne of getting oneself published. Then? La vita commencia domani, domani, domani.

Best love
Dos

In a day or two I'm going to Cambridge for a week. I'll look up Oliver [Cope].

To John Howard Lawson

[213 East 15th Street
New York
November 2, 1920]

Jack, Grey purple heavy evening googles over the town like those thick sauces they pour over rice pudding. Little boys are tootling horns for Harding on 15th Street. Notwithstanding the horrible suspicion that that gentleman has 1/100000000 of negro blood—he is in process of being elected by a vast majority, at least so I suppose. Exercized my civic duty for the first time this morning by standing in line for a long while behind a number of overdressed ladies who would not give their ages—said they were over thirty, as if that werent obvious. Debs.

Last night went with Adelaide to what came near being a good production of what came near being a good play by O'Neill at the Provincetown players. "The Emperor Jones" about the negro emperor of a West India island who has to run for his life from his subjects and in diving through a dark wood sinks deeper and deeper into the slave-blackness of his race. Sees a man playing dice he has killed back in the States when he was a pullman porter, convicts, people buying and selling him, the hold of a slaveship and at last the Japanese dancer Itoro as a medicine man who feeds him to a crocodile and he's killed by his subjects. Its nearly all a monologue of the Emperor Brutus Jones—really superb—and played to perfection by a wonderful coon named Gilpin. The only trouble was they were so anxious to show off their in itself beautiful scenery that they let the audience lapse for fifteen minutes between each of the little scenes that made up the play and so lost the entire thing.

My other dramatic adventures (except the National Winter Garden Burlesque foot of Second Ave) have been unbelievable dreary.

But Jesus the alcohol. Prohibition will send the entire population of New York into D.T.'s if it continues. You go into a restaurant and innocently order clam bouillon and before you know it you are guzzling vitriolic cocktails out of a soup tureen. You order coffee and find yourself drinking red ink. You order tea and find its gin. There's no escaping drinks. The smallest wayside inns to which one wanders in New Jersey become before you've sat down, fountains and cataracts and niagaras of Canadian whiskey

Your Yugoslav epistle nearly gave me convulsions. No literary news. I'll get Gribble's play and send it.—Read your Indian Love. So good it deserves doing—dont you think so—

Love
Dos

To Rumsey Marvin

[Cambridge
November 1920(?)]
Dear Rummy—I've been trying hopelessly to work all morning—what a beastly bore writing is anyway—and at last a heavenly hurdygurdy-man has come under my window playing the Wearing of the Green and has utterly disrupted me. The same hurdygurdy man who made Cambridge hideous for me every spring with his wicked delicious pipings when I was an inmate of the wellknown institution.

Crimes of American Colleges

A. Inculcate snobbery, social climbing (about social climbing I could rave for hours) and a system of ideals, catchwords, morals for which I have no sympathy—but which hardly anyone escapes from getting saturated with, which I myself have taken a long time to recover from (am not so far recovered yet that I can boast about it)

B. The scholarly type: sycophants time servers, people who juggle the classics because they cant do anything else and secretly wish all the time they were insurance agents——O but I feel much too muddle-headed to argue this morning—What I suppose I meant was that I liked people simple, moderately direct in their emotions, moderately honest in their thoughts, moderately wide eyed and naive—and I find on the whole that the uncollegiate American usually comes much nearer to that than your goddamned nickel plated rubberized finished theory-fed socially climbing college grad.

As for an intellectual class it can go f—— itself. Its merely less picturesque and less warmhearted than the hoi polloi and a damnsight eagerer to climb on the band wagon in time of need. The war's the example. Why they had to run special trains to get the intellectuals to Washington they were in such a hurry to run to cover. And those that didn't went into the spy service.

Honest I dont mean to run down your Yale Renaissance or our Harvard Renaissance that died of acute pacifism early in the war—but I just doubt if it'll produce the goods—Phrases, heavily capitalized we have enough of in this type-ridden country. And I often wonder if the real advertizers and bondsellers aren't nearer the Kingdom of Heaven than the preachers teachers writers journalists and other riff-raff of the so-called spirit who merely sell phrases fads and snobbisms by the same method. I admit that American business is bunk, gigantic beautiful bunk But what I wonder is isn't American culture bunk too—and not so amusing.

I approve highly of your idea of segregating the intellectuals—in large well padded asylums—The only way for them to escape would be for each man to commit an act—a grimy fleshly bedrock act. Devil a few of them would ever reappear.

What do you mean by the masses—? People who work with their hands. As for ideas I wonder if they are anything more than the pale shadows of gestures. I wonder if most of the gestures aren't made by people who work with their hands.

As for Plato—I recently reread the Symposium and except for the skill of his style I think he's an utter windbag.

Why are toilers necessarily wretched and unhappy? Merde alors—

I'll be up sometime next week—I'll let you know when—And sure I'll eat steak & fries with you—

Yrs
Jack

To Eugene F. Saxton (1884–1943), *editor and publisher. Born and raised in Baltimore, Saxton began his book publishing career with a number of years at Doubleday, Page & Co. He had become editor of George H. Doran Co. when he first encountered Dos at the time of* Three Soldiers. *In 1925, taking Dos with him, Saxton moved to Harper & Bros. where he presided over the strong Harper lists of the next twenty years. His and Dos' personal friendship survived the publishing crisis occasioned by 1919.*

New York
[*March*(?) *1921*]

Dear Gene—

What's happened to the last chapter?—I've been advised of its sending but no whiff of it here—

About the cuts lets strike a bargain—If you people give me my Jesuses sonsofbitches etc.—I'll give you some alleviation in other quarters—That ought to be fair—

In the enclosed proofs you'll find concessions on galley 36—

on galley 63 I've already changed the passage in the former proofs

If you like some of the Jesuses can be spelt Jez'—but I dont want them cut out. I think it's very important to put down the American lingo as it is and I think that people will get accustomed to it very easily—no particularly messy hell was raised over Cummings' Enormous Room and that had everything except the two excommunicates.

As for Justice Ford—I think he's got to be *fought* and I consider cutting out a word giving aid and comfort to the enemy—

Freedom of the press does not mean compromise. It means publishing what Tom Dick and Harry damn please and letting people lump it if they dont like it—

Wrathily yours
John Dos Passos

P.S. I want my sonsofbitches especially

To Robert Hillyer

[New York
Spring 1921]

Robert—

Un peu de calme mon cher. The offending review will not be published.

You know perfectly well that I am fond of you and you have no right to get sore however clumsily I belabour you. I am awfully sorry that that silly criticism hurt you. Why should you hold your work so lightly as to deem it seared by the first blast of unfavorable criticism? Call it slander if you like.

After all one person's opinion is worth no more than any one else's. Why should you hold it unfriendliness on my part that our tastes in poetry differ?

Your invective was superb. Never Pope hurled juicier epithets at the head of blaspheming heresiarch.

But remember that one has to take ones friends bag and baggage— and if they are lumbering oafs like myself put up with many a dainty corn stepped on without malice, with much delicate dinner ware smashed in unseemly gesturing. In spite of everything I think you know that I like you—

Dos

To Rumsey Marvin

[On board S.S. *Mormugão*
March *1921*]

Dear Rummy—

At sea on the Portuguese boat Mormugão bound for Fayal Terceira Ponti Delegada in the Azores, Funchal on Madeira, Lisbon. Thence Paris London Constantinople and so east. I should certainly have run up to see you before leaving except that I departed suddenly on a dead run, la vie litteraire getting all at once too much for me— much the way people suddenly get seasick during the eight course oily Portuguese dinners on the good ship Mormugão nicknamed the Holy Roller.

Before leaving I did most that I had intended to do. Doran is publishing *Three Soldiers* in June—and *Rosinante to the Road Again* —a volume of essays about Spain and Spanish writing in the fall. And I have numerous openings for series of articles on the eastern situation.

And now I am on the sea—in the warm sopping air of the Middle Atlantic and extraordinarily content, and thanking my stars that I am no longer struggling to keep my head above water in the noisome angular whirlpool of New York—

Write me to Morgan Harjes—14 Place Vendôme Paris—as ever.

I still have a volume of Meredith's verse I have meant for months to send you—Shall send it from Lisbon. I seem to have seen so little of you last winter—So little of anybody I cared for . . . horrible how one gets cluttered up with business and indifferent people—all putrefaction to a decent existence.

Shall probably turn up in the Fall—What of Pittsburgh?

Love
Jack

[Paris
April–May 1921]

Dear old Rummy—Dont worry about your immortal soul—I swear that you have so much pep erdgeist fizzle splutter right-on-your toesness that it must come out one way or another—may take a hell of a long time but come out it will—

Send me your story—I'll beat the pants off it and send it back.

Dont you think Bruno is a very big cheese—I've always had a certain cult of him—That phrase of his excurbitor animis dormitantis (I've got the latin wrong but it means awakener of sleeping souls—) Fine red hot word *excurbitor*.

Have the finest room next to Mme Lecomte's—37 Quai d'Anjou—just above the tree tops with the Seine looking very small below under the pont Marie. Shall be here finishing *Rosinante to the Road Again* for a week or two—

Three soldiers has been put off till August—I'm scared to death that the publishers are getting cold feet—They say its on account of the binders' strike.

Wish you'ld been with Cummings & me last week on a pass in the Pyrenees—We got in snow up to our knees in the clouds so that we couldn't see a thing—and lost the way completely—Wonderful time—Slid off a summit into space over a lip of soft snow—of course there was something below—but we couldnt see it. Then scrambled down for hours with our tails full of snow among spruce trees. Then rained like sixty and we had to flounder across several enormous and swelling brooks—and at last we ended up in a fine little town named Bielle a hell of a distance from where we thought we were going. Going up everyone had told us it was impossible to cross at this season—so we felt awfully hair-on-the-chesty—like the famous mountaineers in the song—

Write me all about Pittsburgh and send me stuff you do—and do and do and do—flounder up to the neck in absurdity—What's the odds? And I swear that if you keep going—they'll have a hell of a hard time mummifying you into a tired business man—Only do do do Down with esthetes littérateurs poet-tasters-genteel dog-, picture-, life-fanciers! And it wont be so hard once you are out of the enervating air of college and correct clothing—Christ! the only thing those sons of bitches think of is whether their pants are pressed. And nobody gives a

damn after all—not even those very s's of b's——All of which you said
excellently in your letter——

Au revoir—
Jack

To John Farrar (1896–   ), *the publisher and author, whom Dos first
knew when Farrar was with George Doran. He went on to become a
director of Doubleday, Doran, then an editor and eventually chairman
of the board of Farrar and Rinehart, serving next in the same capacity
for Farrar, Straus and Giroux.*

37 Quai d'Anjou–Paris
[June 1921]

Dear John Farrar—

Here are the two last chapters of Rosinante—Hope they aren't too
g.d. rotten

Also a couple of pages which I should like prefixed to the essay on
Machado (Chap XI)—

That's that.

B.&K. [Brandt & Kirkpatrick] write that 3 Soldiers has been put
off till August— . . . I imagine you people know best when the lucky
day on the publisher's calendar is but still— . . . !

After unimaginable delays I expect to start east in a week.

About proofreading my stuff: would it be possible to do away with
italics except in the case of songs and quotations? So that Spanish and
other foreign words would not be overemphasized in the text. Also I'd
like 'dont' 'doesnt' 'cant' etc spelt without apostrophes—and the dash
used in conversation instead of quotes—: but I dont feel strongly
enough about any of these things to insist, if the honor of the house of
Doran is implicated in the continuance of the present system.

Anything happened about the verse?

Let me hear from you—c/o Morgan Harjes et Cie—14 Place Vendôme, Paris

How's your Sentimental Journey going?

Yours
John Dos Passos

Remember me to Mr. Saxton and Mr. Rinehart—

To Rumsey Marvin

[Paris–Venice
June–July 1921]

Hello Rumsey! Qu'est-ce que tu deviens? You must be sure to write often as so many letters get lost—I have been lingering about the flesh pots of Paris, hardly doing any work, trying to paint in guache, seeing many dawns,——I know too many amiable people here for the good of the Métier—Still I am leaving in four days for Constantinople. There's been a great deal of music here, new ballets: in fact my great thesis that Paris is dead has more or less fallen through.

I'm very keen to hear all about Pittsburgh.

Had a fine trip up from Lisbon through Spain with a whack at the Feria of Seville which was superb. Such wearing of white mantillas, such driving about in carriages—such dancing of Sevillanas with a solemn air in booths—and bullfights and ballerinas at the café—concert places in the evening. Then did a pass through the snow in the Pyrenees went to Carcassonne—and then a few days in London—England's beastly just at present everybody cross, everything grimy and closed up. At eleven in the evening London's like Broadway on a Sunday morning.

Have the finest room belonging to Jack Lawson on the Quai d'Anjou overlooking the Pont Marie—very high up so that I can see over the roofs opposite Montmartre and the Buttes Chaumont and almost everything else.

Thought of you at the place du Tertre t'other night.

I wrote you asking you please to send me your story, didn't I? *Stories!*

Venice

I must bundle this off to you somehow or Lord knows when it'll go. Stopping off here for a day or two en route for Constantinople. Fine jolly place—like Coney Island and a fancy novelty shop on Fifth Avenue mixed with a goodly proportion of Puccini and seasoned with a whiff of sea and saltmarshes.

Wonderfully good swimming on the Lido. I go over every afternoon. The rest of the time I look at the dull enormousness of Titian's and Veronese's and Tintoretto's religio-patriotic paintings and reaffirm

my warcries as to primitives and sanctissimo Giotto and the unbelievable Ucello—

Love
Jack

c/o American Red Cross
  Constantinople.

Buildings shoot rigid perpendiculars
latticed with windowgaps
into the slate sky.

Where the wind comes from
the ice crumbles
about the edges of green pools;
from the leaping of white thighs
comes a smooth and fleshly sound,
girls grip hands and dance
grey moss grows green under the beat
of feet of saffron
crocus-stained.

Where the wind comes from
purple windflowers sway
on the swelling verges of pools
naked girls grab hands and whirl
fling heads back stamp crimson feet.

Buildings shoot rigid perpendiculars
latticed with windowgaps
into the slate sky.

Garment-workers loaf in their overcoats
(stare at the gay breasts of pigeons
that strut and peck at dung in the gutters)
their fingers are bruised tugging needles
through fuzzy hot layers of cloth
thumbs roughened twirling waxed thread;
They smell of lunchrooms and burnt cloth;
the wind goes among them
detaching sweatsmells from underclothes
making muscles itch under overcoats
tweaking legs with inklings of dancetime.

Bums on the park-benches
spit and look upat the sky.
Garmentworkers in their overcoats
pile back into black gaps of doors.

Where the wind comes from
scarlet windflowers sway
on rippling verges of pools
sound of girls dancing
thud of vermillion feet.

Madison square march 5/21.

To Robert Hillyer

c/o American Red Cross
Constantinople
Venezia
July 3—[*19*]*21*

Dear old Robert—

Should have written you ages ago I swear, had I had your address. Have just bethought me that your publisher would probably forward letters.

Venice is a superb sort of a Super-Coney Island, full of music, spaghetti-tenors, bateaux-mouches, sunlight, Adriatic breezes and German tourists. It also at this moment is full of Cuthbert. Mitchell & Dudley Poore are probably coming down from Paris to send me off when I leave on the Orient Express some days from now.

I had hoped to see you in Paris, before leaving since there were persistent rumors about that you would appear there when the schools closed in Copenhagen: Where *are* you going?

Have just found your last letter, which unfortunately gives no address. Really we must send more traffic over the bridge. The tollgates are getting rusty. I wish I could see the alliterative Alexandrines. Feel a little in the sere and yellow and I'm sure a dose of alliterative Alexandrines would be a tonic to an enfeebled digestion.

Par delicatesse

j'ai perdu la vie.

My room looks over the Grand Canal. Little steamers keep tooting and starting for places and I run to the window to crane after them. Perhaps that will account for the extraordinary fragmentariness of this letter. I have few wits these days anyway.

Have you written any prose recently?

I am about to start working over the G.N. for the third time—then I suppose I shall publish it. I'll send it to you first to see if you still want to be it's dedicatee. That is: if Three Soldiers sells at all I'll have no trouble in publishing the G.N. If not, or if it sells as badly as poor little One Man's Init. (63 copies after 6 months & 23 of those accounted for)—the process of finding a publisher will have to be begun all over again. And uncertain as I feel now about my stuff, I should hardly have the heart to trouble.

Literature is a dirty occupation. Wish to God my father had apprenticed me to a cobbler.

O the old grindstone and one's poor nose sharpened with unsatisfaction.

Shall go swim at the Lido.

Love—do write

Dos

To Thomas P. Cope

Venice
July 5 [1921]

Arthur wrote me about how much he enjoyed meeting you.

Tom: Who on earth (I dont mean name but history) is your John Barlycorn popper? He sounds tiresome but vaguely instructive.

I see absolutely no reason why [John] Mosher should take it upon himself to tell poor little [William] Rollins he cant write. How can anybody tell what's in him. Christ, that amount of pain, neurotic as it is—should force something out of him. Yet I suppose its not necessarily those who suffer most joy and agony who express it. Poor kid. I wish he'd take to whoring or get married. Thats probably what's the matter with him.

Tell Mosher he's an old fraud and give him my love.

Venice is a sort of high-falutin Coney Island. Music in the morning, people feeding pigeons in front of St Maslas', spaghetti tenors yodling in barges on the Grand Canal—fine swimming and exhibition of legs of ladies of pleasure at the Lido, little boats chugging in every direction toodling and jingling, general bawdy brouhaha.

Have you ever tried using guache? Its much more fun than watercolor, thick and rather sandy in consistency. One can put enormous googles of it on the paper and get a pasty—pastry cook's icing—effect which is momentarily pleasing, but eventually rather nauseous.

Shall leave in a day or two for Constantinople in grand style on Orient Express.

Send me some of your verse now and then.

Address American Red Cross Constantinople.

Love to Canby Chambers and Esther Andrews (congratulations to the former for his Sat E.P. successes and to the latter for her ideal condition of joblessness.) You would weep to see Mme. Lecomte's. I think they are making money, though.

Dos

To John Howard Lawson

Pera Palace
[Constantinople]
July 20 [*1921*]

Jack!

There is a metro, a fine one runs up hill and has only two stations and is navigated by the simple method of being let down at the end of a string which is reeled in when it's pulled up again. Its cool and a good place for a quiet afternoon chat. It's known as Le Tunnel.

I landed—as might have been prognosticated in the lap of si vous voulez aller dans le luxe as the result of the frenzied clamor of all the other passengers on the Orient Express that there was no where else to go. And for once they seem to be right. I've only discovered a small half dozen hotels de Londres etc, all of which are brimming with decayed Russian generals and smaller vermin. So I remain in enormous spy-infested state in a room overlooking the Golden Horn and the suburb of Kassius Pasha, and the sacred dome of El Ayouli where the mantle of the prophet and the sword of Osman are kept.

A little while before I got here the British executed an enormous raid among the leading hotels and carried off bunches of alleged Bols, among them a lady who refused to dress on being knocked up as the British officer put it and was carried off nude. So the crise de logement is temporarily quelled.

Talk about whores bawds, concubines and others! The streets of Pera beat everything.

Theatrical entertainment consists of two funny gardens and a number of smaller joints where you eat dinner at about nine and at about ten appears the most shrieki set of vaudeville imaginable. You never know what is going to pop out at you, little ladies like in America dance the Moment Musicale in pink fluff, dilapidated French prima donnas sing arias from Lucia, Greek wrestlers do tumbling acts. Russian ladies shout hoarse comic bits in the best Swedish, gypsies dance really exciting thumping dances—in the audience vast quantities of officers of different allied armies roar about at little tables. Greek, French, Armenian, Polish and whatnot ladies unfold expensive charms for their benefit. Waited till midnight at Luna Park to see a Russian Company do la Belle Hélène which I'd last seen at the Eden in Milan.

Extraordinarily swollen moons red as wardrums rise up every night out of Asia.

According to everyone its quite easy to go everywhere, notwithstanding incidental wars—as might have been expected. Then too the railway to Tabrez out of Armenia is running once a week. Shall probably go in that direction before long.

Am glad I came.

Turkish cafés have the finest jazz-bands consisting of several elderly gentlemen in fezzes with lutes zithers and other outlandish stringed instruments, and usually one lady, who throw back their heads and sing in cheerful dischords, making a most satisfying noise a little like Alan's crying, a little like steam escaping from a radiator. I sit and drink mastic and listen to them by the hour.

Love to Kate—Alan—and everybody—

Where are you?

Dos

To Rumsey Marvin

Batum
Aug 7– [19]21

Dear Rummy—

You see—or rather you would see had you the somewhat doubtful fortune of being an inmate of the Piroscafo Aventino—me gnash my teeth tear my hair and console myself with strong waters and chapters of Montaigne and the reflections of Chinese sages for my ill luck— having up to now considered myself a fairly able picker of locks in passport barriers—or my ill skill (out with it) on this jaunt out of Constantinople. At Meboli there was not time to go ashore, and there were munitions and the Turks were afraid of spies, so on the Piroscafo Aventino I remained, at Samsoun the Turks were performing certain deportations of seditious christians which they did not want too closely looked in to—so I stuck all day cooped up on the Aventino. At Urdu, Kerasonde same story. And finally at Trebizonde, an unbelievably romantic town on a terraced promentory clewed into a great bulging hill which breaks into occasional purple cliffs where white stairways lead up to inexplicable monasteries—and in every direction huge cloudy capes jutting into the Black Sea—just as I was wheedling my way via the ship's doctor past the Kemalist guards, what should come on the horizon but a wretched Greek cruiser, decks trimmed for action, and throw everybody into such a panic that plus rien à faire. And le comble, the climax, the summit and jumping off place is that for lack of a visa I am held here on board of this same Piroscafo Aventino a full whole rich twenty four hours, while some extraordinary document is fabricated for me by the peoples commissars.

So here in the empty smoking room of the Piroscafo Aventino I sweat and bewail myself while beyond a rickety wharf and a few long guns lies bolshevism and Batum.

Great quantities of people are swimming round the wharves. Beyond, a green and deep blue harbor (pearlrock colors) edged by a strip of pale ochre sand, from which rise with a stupendous green swoop cluster after cluster of conical hills that end in the darkness of clouds and of the blue foothills of the Caucasus. Some mountains at least I suppose they must lead up to the Caucasus,—a fit torture place for the fire bringer.

A lot of little row boats go out seaward across the harbor with white awnings over them and people playing accordions and a twangy sort of guitar.

Tomorrow, by the grace of the peoples commissars of the Soviet Republic of Georgia temporarily occupied by the Red Army, starts a trip up to Tiflis Erivan, thence to Tabriz and Teheran.

But that is on the knees of an extraordinarily diverse collection of gods.

I'll write you from Teheran

Love
Jack

Saw Harry Hart before I left Paris—just for a minute.

To Rumsey Marvin

[Teheran
October 1921]

Dear Rummy—Like all knights squires scribes belted and spurred or merely carrying typewriters—I have fallen into a fever and then into a languor. In my fever I was succored, as is also proper, by a maiden— Her name was Shekher, which means sugar, and she had a mole on her forehead, the sign of beauty, and her eyebrows met in the middle, as according to the Persians do the eyebrows of the houris of Paradise. She was a Nestorian, and of vast proportions. Like Clementine, she wore herring boxes without topses, out of which towered vast elephantine ankles, and they were needed indeed to support the rest of that massy edifice. Shekher is chambermaid at the hotel de France. She brought me soups with eggs in them, which with the help of quinine eaten raw in great quantities and injected into my arms and legs, cured me of my fever in no time. As for the languor . . . it is as yet uncured. Its cause can hardly be the bright eyes and the three pearly teeth of Shekher. Launcelot fell into a languor and a fever and even went quite mad somewhere in a hermit's cell and his example was assiduously followed by all the Knights errant in the two Britannies— but that was over Queen Guinevere. Anyway I have been in a languor ever since I reached Teheran, and have skulked in my room at the Hotel de France, staring at my mute inglorious typewriter.

Persia is the home of strange diseases, physical and moral. At Tabriz one is seized by a special kind of diarrhea—at Mioneh there is a bedbug elsewhere unknown whose bite gives one a most individual fever—In Baghdad there are the bunions, dreadful eruptions that appear on one's nose or chin and remain for a year and wreck ones beauty for life, and there is no town so humble that it hasn't its particular kind of malaria. Dont think I mean to imply that Persia has nothing else to offer the wayfarer. There are carpets, sherbets, beards dyed crimson with henna, camels, brigands, plots, revolts, pomegranates, volcanos, processions, bazaars, pilos and many other things besides—but that is the impression one gets after drinking some few whiskies and sodas at the club at Khulikhak where the Europeans abide

Later

My languor was cured days ago, probably by a plot which the minister of war unhatched and which caused many of the dignitaries I had been chatting with vaguely over small cups of tea to be thrown into jail and others to seek a change of air in the mountains—Anyway things have quite looked up since I started this letter.

It is dusk and the hour of prayer and the air is full of the diffused chanting of hundreds of muezzins, that seems to come from everywhere and nowhere like larks' songs in a wheatfield.

Teheran is an amiable undramatic town with sparkling gutters and quiet treeshaded streets and huge gardens hidden behind mud walls and lots of dilapidated stucco porticoes. The bazaars are full of camels and splendid people in unbelievable costumes from all the ends of Asia. Fine pinkish ochre mountains rise up to the North and East and over them all Damavand, where the dirvs skulk amid the snows, stands tiptoe.

I am starting for Baghdad in a day or two. From there I shall try to cross the no man's land of the Syrian desert to Damascus. Still there's no saying where I'll land as voyages in these parts are of the most problematical. Everything's very uneasy, brigandage is an increasingly popular occupation, the roads are mostly myths and rivers have a way of suddenly appearing where never river was before. Despite these horrors one might add, people manage to move about with surprising ease. The real basic difficulty is that gasoline costs about three dollars a gallon and food for other more primitive means of locomotion about in proportion. My finances have long been up the flue, but I fear that this trip will blow them clean out of the chimney pot.

Any way it's very good fun and as to welt-politik highly oh highly instructive.

Incidentally I'm no more a journalist than I am a guinea pig and the sooner I go home and get to work writing and stop playing Richard Harding Davis the better. The good resolutions one forms in distant parts of the earth while waiting for money! The real time of

sack cloth and ashes is between the sending of a cable and the receipt
of a remittance—one always wonders whether the well isnt dry.

Morgan Harjes as ever—

Love

Jack

To Thomas P. Cope

Teheran—The tenth day
of Moharam in the year
of the Rabbit—
Hotel de France
[*October 1921*]

Dear Tom—

I have just come from seeing the processions of mourning for the
death of Hussein—vast quantities of people—black beating bared
breasts in time to a dirge in quick heady rhythm, great bloody crowds
in white slashing their heads with swords—rather terrific in the dust
and in the lashing sunlight, the reek of blood and the broken sound of
trumpets and the hoarse groaning cry of Hussein Hussein.

It seems that Hussein the most loved of the Imaums was killed by
Omar in a great battle in the desert on this day.

Extraordinary journey from Constantinople through Batum—
Georgia and Armenia and Adjerbaidjan—then by carriage here in the
company of a fine Persian doctor who made speeches advocating
progress and social democracy in every village and lanced boils and slit
ulcers and bandaged ribs and was a great connoisseur of watermelons.

Teheran is a delightful town full of watercourses and huge trees
and funny little pastry porticoes and great mud gates plastered with
pictures of battles and Shahs in tilework of a rather evil yellow and
green hue, overlooked by pink and yellow mountains and by the snow-
ribbed peak of Damavand, where the dirvs crouch in the rocky hollows
and cast malice out of the world—

Baghdad is my next objective—then Syria—Marseille—Paris—New
York—

Where are you?

Write me Morgan Harjes or to American Consul, Beirut Syria—
(before Oct 15) but that's silly it'll be months before you get this
letter—one forgets how far away this is—

Khuda 'afis—shimaum

Dos

To Robert Hillyer

Hotel de France
Teheran
[*October 1921*]
10th Moharam
Year Takhagoni-il

Robert! What ho?

I am afraid you have taken too seriously my notorious habit of blackguarding my friends, for it's ages since I heard from you. Be a sport and vouchsafe a little information as to your whereabouts, for 'tis a wide and scrawny world and singularly denuded of human inhabitants. And if the few who have possibilities of the laurel crown fall to quarrelling, we'd better all throw ourselves into the most convenient wells pointing for the last time desperate rear-ends at the sunlight. So be a good boy and write me an excellent and if possible intoxicated Hillyer epistle to Morgan Harjes-14 Place Vendôme Paris, so that I may find it simmering cheerfully where I next get mail.

I have just come from watching lugubrious processions mourning the death of the Imaum Hussein, endless crowds of men in black casting ashes on their heads and beating their breasts till the streets resound and slashing their foreheads with swords. Dust and burning sun and the reek of blood and the unfortunate rhythm of the songs, and occasional broken trumpet calls. For some reason it has given me idées noires.

I reached Teheran by a curious journey from Constantinople—by boat to Batum, then by a buggy Bolo express, very jolly, full of tea and Kavaritch and Ruskin conversation—to Tiflis. Thence on various box cars through Armenia where everyone was dying of cholera and typhus and starvation, and Adjerbaidjan to the Persian border. Then in an insane four-horse cab known as a phaeton across deserts and mountains and the fresh trails of nomad raiders, in the company of a Persian doctor who was a great judge of melons, to Teheran, where I recline in somewhat exhausted state at this funny little French hotel. Soon I am going on to Baghdad and then across, I dont know how, to Beirut and by boat towards France again.

I shall go back to America and settle somewhere for five years or ten or twenty and produce works of literature or take up chess or knitting.

As to my possibilities in word-mongering, I have never been deeper in the dumps. Things I write become every day more putrid.

As for the gorgeous east—

People dye their beards with henna and wear domed and enormous hats of felt, and robes of cinnamon color and parrot-green silk, and everyone constantly drinks tea out of tiny bulging glasses, and the roads are full of long striding camels, and broken down Fords hobbling on three cylinders. The wine is rich mahogany color and flavoured as dense as black walnuts. There is a drink called arak that is flavoured with berries and burns the guts and another sort that is healing and syrupy and smells of lemon blossoms.

Tell me about Denmark and Swedish punch.

The G.N. is being revamped for the "n"th time. When it appears it will be recognizable to neither God nor man and I fear totally illegible. Sic transit—

Imagine me in a flabby costume of pink silk, with a nose burned red like an over boiled beet and about my waist a great purple and green sash (to prevent diarrhea) stalking myopically about dim spice scented bazaars and dining with withered dignitaries in huge Reosepolis—Louis the Quinze—Wanamaker furnished halls. In Baghdad I shall wear a sunhelmet like a bully Britisher.

La chère est triste helas et j'ai lu tous les livres—

                                                          Love
                                                          Dos

To John Howard Lawson

                                                       Baghdad
                                                   Oct 23 [*1921*]

Dear Jack—Tumbled today into an extraordinarily dismal Anglo Indian establishment known by the romantic name of Hotel Maude —After the delightful eccentricity of Russia you cant imagine the drab of Anglo-India. Ghost of Haroun el Raschid! The shock of it is so great that I think I am preparing for a new fever. Amazing the temperatures one throws of an afternoon—amazing in suddenness of coming and going. Everybody has them and they seem to be the main thread of European—as of native (out fell word) existence in these parts. Am consoling myself by reading an excessively bad French translation of Euripides. But even under the academic diction of M. Louis Humbert of the Lycee Condorcet they are superb and extraordinarily present day actable.

Fine trip down out of Persia over the mountains on a bandy legged Ford—then in a wandering sleeper that carries me over the pancake flat plains of the Mespot to the city of Sir Percy Cox.

Nowhere have I seen East and West, so-called, mingle to worse advantage than in this dismal spot. Still it may all be mere humors—shake the malarial quinine bottle!

Now my great problem is how to get out of this God damn place—If possible I shall go overland to Syria—from Beirut—where (in shallah) my mail awaits me—to Marseille and then towards New York I suppose to find a quiet spot to write my million times delayed novel and revamp Fibbie.

As for travel it is a weariness of the flesh (malarial vapors!) and I'll have no more of it. Seabathing simple food and eight hours a day are all I require for long into the future.

You should see the main street of Baghdad, you should eat of the meals of the Hotel Maude. The East is an ashpile sprouting into shanty town—an ashpile out of which even the shards of blue porcelain have long been sifted and casted away, a shanty town full of third generation shanty dwellers who have no spirit in them. Of course there's the shell of it, iridescent as you like but dry dry and crumbling—People wear saffron bournouses and abas of cinnamon color and vests of parrot green silk and stride about with fringed turbans of black and white and long inlaid guns—Camels slouch single file across purple and rose colored deserts, and ancient Kings stare with blank eyes from the faces of burnt ochre cliffs. But I swear to God that Morris Flat is vernal animation compared to it.

Of course if you dig deep you find inexplicable things—But these aren't my diggings—and the great goggle-eyed banshee of malaria takes to me with more enthusiasm than I enjoy.

Still I have purged myself of my morgue. That was the main thing—I think now I'll be able to get to work with some sort of steadfastness—I think I've killed for five years the illusion of geography. I am very keen to get back into everybody's midst.

Love to Kate and everyone who is anyone who happens to be round—To all others silent damnation.

Malariously
Dos

To Rumsey Marvin

Baghdad
Nov. 5, [1921]

Dear Rummy—

It takes a most devilish amount of time to do anything out here. I've been two weeks in Baghdad trying to arrange to get into a caravan going to Damascus across the desert. And still everything is in a beautiful mist of Oriental vagueness. Meanwhile I sit on Tigris bank and eat potato chips and drink German Beer and pound out drearily on the corona articles on the politics of Persia. I'll be damned if I ever make a pretence at doing this job again. I'm no more good at it than a Persian cat at the Australian crawl. It's damn folly to try to do things one is not fitted for. I used to have a theory that anybody could do anything they had a mind to—but I retract it. Not exactly though—for the whole trouble with my selfstyled journalism is that I dont want to do it nearly as much as I want to do several other things at the moment. Anyway journalism is the business of fussing with bigbugs—and above anything on earth I detest bigbugs.

I'm rather beginning to look foreward to getting back to civilization. There are so damn few people to talk to out in this part of the world. One belongs automatically to the cast of bigbugs—which is desperate. O the Sahibbing!

It will be superb to get out on the sheer desert; where the Bedouins are more likely to put a load of buckshot into you than to call you Sahib or to invite you to official lunches—Between being Sahibbed and whiskey soda lunches there lies no intermediate ground.

Hurrah for democracy & the dairy lunch!

love
Jack

Out of the unquiet town
seep jagged barkings
lean broken cries
unimaginable silent writhing
of muscles taut against strangling
heavy fetters of darkness.

On the pool of moon light
clots and festers
a great scum
of wornout sound.

(Elagabalus Alexander
looked too long at the full moon;
hot blood drowned them
cold rivers drowned them.)

Float like pondflowers
on the dead face of darkness
cold stubs of lusts
names that glimmer ghostly
adrift on the slow tide
of old moons waned.

(Lais of Corinth that Holbein drew
drank the moon in a cup of wine;
with the flame of all her lovers' pain
she seared a sign on the tombs of the years.)

Out of the voiceless wrestle of the night
flesh rasping hash on flesh
a tune on a shrill pipe shimmers
a silver twisting wire tremulous
out of the twang of bowed strings
up like a rocket blurred in the fog
of loves curdled in the moon's glare;
staggering up like a rocket
into the steely starsharpened night
above the stagnant moonmarshes
the song throbs throbs soaring and dies.

(Semiramis Zenobia
lay too long in the moon's glare;
their yearning grew sere and they died
and the flesh of their empires died.)

On the pool of moonlight
clots and festers
a great scum
of wornout lives.

No sound but the panting unsatiated
breath that heaves under the huge pall
the livid moon has spread above the housetops.
I rest my chin on the windowledge
and wait.
There are hands about my throat.

Ah Bilkis Bilkis
where is the jangle of your camelbells?
Ah Bilkis when out of Saba
with lope of your sharpsmelling dromedaries
will you bring the unnameable strong wine
you press from the dazzle of the zenith sun
over the shining sands of your deserts
the wine you press there in Saba?
Bilkis your voice loud above the camelbells
white sword of noon to split the fog
Bilkis your strong small hands to tear
the hands from about my throat.
Ah Bilkis when out of Saba?

                                             Pera-Baghdad.

To Thomas P. Cope

                                                    Baghdad
                                          November 13 [*1921*]

Dear Tom—

I'm sitting on pins and needles in the worlds worst hotel. For three weeks I've been trying to get out of Baghdad. Every day the caravan has been about to leave in two days. First it was that there was a squabble between one of the sheikhs to whom safety money had been paid and his son, who demanded a share and said he'd plunder said caravan if he didn't get it. Then for another week, when that was arranged we waited through the sheer mercy of Allah. I couldn't discover any other reason. Now the camels have left town and wait while the bridge is repaired over the Euphrates, and I rot in the Hotel Maude and revile my typewriter. All this because I've been seized with an insane desire to go overland to Damascus a thing that is regarded in these parts with as much horror as a journey up Everest since the treaty of Levres pacified the Near East by setting everybody by the ears.

I wonder where you are Tom and what doing. Havent heard a word from anybody since I left Constantinople.

My plans are—Damascus Beirut Marseilles America and some retired and rusticflavored spot where I can settle for a year and a day and write continuously—not filthy little articles either. I've decided that this wandering about the world's hotels is a low form of existence. In shallah I shall give it up. If one's got to travel one should have the courage of ones convictions, take a staff and a begging bowl and a jar of hashish like a proper dervish and a fig for the city bred world. But this half-ass Cook's Miss Humphrey Ward manner of wandering is too low for words. If one hasn't any more imagination one should stay at home and learn accounting. Journalism is the stinkingest of compromises. One comes into contact with nobody but personages, chambermaids and drummers.

On the Tigris there are splendid boats called gurfas or something like that, baskets caulked with pitch and completely round. Baghdad has bazaars not to be sniffed at and infinite coffee shops and soda waterfactories and whiskey stores. Fords are more frequent than camels. To see turbaned Bedouin off the desert drinking gingerpop makes one think on the blessings of civilization—a town thoroughly instructive if not full of thrills (except in the movies: The Perils of our girl Reporters).

Tomorrow I shall go to visit the rooons of Babylon, possibly in the company of a Chicago Jewish gut-merchant who is my only crony in the hotel, a dismal little fat man with grey skin and a broad arrow-shaped nose.

By the way I have had a few doses of your malaria. In Teheran I won the admiration and respect of all present by suddenly producing a temperature of 105½, which I consider rather chic. The joke is that except for a few little spells I've been as healthy as an undug clam. I think the larvae are all drowned out in quinine by this time anyway. But I'll never take a mosquito into my confidence again.

Christ how tempus fugits! The moons race across the sky—they seem to swell and wane everytime faster. And I seem to accomplish less and less every week.

Am at present engaged in trying in an afternoon to learn enough Arabic to explain the mysteries of cookery to my camel driver, as no one in my caravan will speak any known language, except two problematical Jewesses from Aleppo who are said to be going—They may know French.

Au Revoir
Dos

To Robert Hillyer

Baghdad
Nov 20 1921

Dear Robert—

Have been spending a most dismal afternoon in the bar of that dismalest of hostelries, the Hotel Maude—reading Fibbie—and drinking whiskies and sodas, the most depressing of drinks. Christ what raw juvenilia!—and the joke from my point of view is, that after all the nasal upturnings at the early Hillyerian prose (not my nose, Robert) your chapters have undoubtedly much more *tone* than mine. They are certainly superior to anything I did while we were partners. There was a certain genuineness to their rose water: mine was mere vomitose eyewash. You must do something in that line someday.

I had an idea of salvaging certain parts of Fibbie—but I fear now it must all go—mere sub-structure—a pre Babylonian Babylon—on which please God and Sheitan something will be built someday.

This retirement into the wilderness was highly salutary. I have no conceit left. Mene mene tekel upharsin The enemy has broken in by every gate and the city is razed. The only hope is that these shivered ruins will make a good compact foundation—for what? I have no idea. Anyway there's not a cellar that's not been laid bare to the cold light of day and of solitary whiskies and sodas in the bar of the Hotel Maude.

I've been waiting for three Mortal weeks for a caravan in which I've hired a camel to make up its mind to start across the desert to Damascus. Every day some new excuse for delay has been found, squabbles among the desert sheikhs, bridges down, roads muddy and often the mere omnipotence of Allah. I'm crazy to sit in the desert at the door of my crimson slashed tent and sniff air unpolluted by gasoline and whiskey and see sunsets otherwise than across the military bridge and the Governmental Residence.

O Robert the years go by and the Thames is still unburnt and where are the monuments aere perennius that were to be set up in rows along the Hudson?

Write me Morgan Harjes 14 Place Vendôme, Paris

Love
Dos

To Rumsey Marvin

[In the Syrian Desert
December 8, 1921]

Dear Rummy—It's somewhere around the eighth of December. I sit
and shiver in a gaudy ten-sided crimson-lined tent that lets in the wind
and rain through every crevice—I am part of the caravan of one Ibn
Rawwaf, Agail, from Baghdad to Damascus and this is the fifth day
we have waited in the middle of the desert opposite the black tents of
the Delains while negotiations as to safety money dragged along with
one Ibn Khubain who was threatening to attack us and pull the very
fillings out of our teeth. I sport a large (comparatively) beard, a black
and white ishmak about my head and an aba of brown with a broad
white stripe. Its great sport, particularly as everyone swore it was impossible to get across overland to Syria. There never was a pleasanter
method of travelling than by camel. His long slouching walk sways
you sleepily; the caravan drifts west by almost imperceptible degrees.
You go eight or ten hours and then camp—marvellous writhing and
roaring and swaying of open mouths of camels against wintry desert
sunsets—Then everybody squats about campfires and drinks endless
tiny cups of the most delicious coffee I ever tasted coalblack and almost
as bitter as quinine—People are superb. I've never known such jolly
and admirable h.s's of b's as comprise this caravan. And the lank
Bedouin who are our friends and our foes are fine. I like them enormously. I have a camel named Malek—a harîm [old woman]—a most
sensitive animal. I've never seen anything so expressive of disgust and
distaste as the way she twitches her split lips on a rainy day. Also she
has bushy eyebrows that she wiggles when undecided whether to walk
or trot under the kicking of my heels. I have a silver studded saddle
and enormous saddlebags (full of a rather poor quality of canned
goods) with tassles of black, crimson and orange. Its great fun not
knowing the language and not having an interpreter; ones intercourse
with everybody is delightfully intimate and one has the advantage of
never having to take action; and having only the vaguest idea of what
is transpiring. Last night it was discovered to the horror of a delightful
man with a curly beard who brings me coffee and dates at intervals
while I sit in splendor in my tent that I was chatting amiably about the
weather with one of Ibn Khubain's merry men, who are out to cut our
throats, or at least our pursestrings, and feeding him cigarettes. He was

one of the nicest people I've struck, too, I was sorry to have him driven off.

No—its distinctly worth the month's rotting in Baghdad among the whisky and such of the Hotel Maude.

The unbelievable breadth and unexpectedness of everything——

Arabic is I think the most difficult language I ever came up against. The sounds are enormously diverse and difficult and the grammar is unbelievable. Anyway probably I would get along nearly as well with these fine people if I could talk to them in a less insane manner.

Insh'Allah—we get to Damascus in ten days. There I'll take the train to Beirut and make tracks towards civilization—or rather conversation, of which I am dreadfully in need—and then I must get to work on my poor languishing novel——I've been kicking round months longer than I intended as it is—

Love—
Jack

To Stewart Mitchell

[Enroute to Damascus]
December 10 [1921]

Auk—most reverend grave and noble Auk, if I haven't written you before it has not been that I haven't thought a great deal about you—

I am out in the middle of the Syrian desert in a crimson lined tent that bellies like a parachute in a mighty wind out of the west. Our caravan is slowly drifting towards Damascus, stopped by mud and the demands of divers sheikhs who hold us up for money. The desert is full of silver glints of water from last nights rain and pale sheen of new grass. Tomorrow, if Allah so wills, we mount our camels, throw to the breeze the tassels of our saddle bags and start out to try to reach Damascus in caravan. So far we have travelled five days and waited about, counting my preliminary stagnation in the bar of the Hotel Maude on Tigris bank, five weeks.

I have been very anxious to get back into the company of those few disreputable winebibbers whose company is worth bibbing in. Think, since I left you so hastily and brutally in Paris last June, I have had no conversation—Still, if I have tramped out of my system the beastly spleen that had me in its clutches it will have been worth while—I am afraid you took ill my not waiting for you as I certainly took ill your not following to Venice. Both were inevitable, I suppose, at least I know that in my case, there is no help for it if I am seized with the itch to go from a place. It's very silly but it's so. It did not mean—as you well know—that I did not desire your worshipful presence.

Now I am fed up with shoving my way about the face of the government-encumbered globe and shall be eager to settle somewhere where American is spoken and write three volume novels in quiet. And except for the Bedouin, who are great people, in all these days journeys I have not found a soul really companionable. Is it that my ardors are falling with my hairs or that in a generation only a few are turned out tuned to the same chords? More probably its sheer almighty accident.

Great excitement as a camel, about to die, has just been killed and is being dissected. To these people who cut meat once a twelvemonth it's a regular orgy—The wind is settling and the cairn away from the camp where I go to sit is full of little birds like larks—This caravan across the desert is the finest thing I ever did in my life. I only wish it were in company as charming as that in which I toured the wine shops of Touraine last spring.

By God we'll snatch many a similar jaunt from the envious weird sisters before you and I and Dudley turn up our respective toes to the last daisies.

Reading Martial and Juvenal (via Loeb) They do give one the meat and phlegm and semen of a generation, well salted too. I dont know if they stoke great creative fires, but to have nailed to eternity an epoch and a city and a landscape as they have is pretty much the aere perennius of which they were so confident. Probably its the Martial that has made me write you, though I have no address to send a letter to—I have been incommunicado since I left Stamboul—Martial's ideas of the desirable things are much like yours, included the seven (or is it eight?) suits of clothes that so raise Estlin's bile; and you know, Auk, you have a certain Roman Flavian pomp and sumptuousness about you.

Which reminds me that this rolling about the world doesn't speed me in the elaboration of my own little tin gods, of which the very shape is as yet undecided. So far the moulds have not produced anything particularly satisfactory, that is certain.

I look forward with extraordinary zest and watering of the mouth to fêtes and high triumphs and many bottles cracked when next we meet. Those dismal whiskies and sodas at the American Bar in Baghdad and the company of drunken gut-merchants of Armenian extraction have turned me against anything but wine, of which I have become—not having it—as much a worshipper as any Persian sufi.

One wonders if in America prohibition wont have the same effect among imaginative people as among the Persians, of turning wine into a mystery and a religion. When I think of Bourgueil . . .

I hope before many months to crack bottles with you, having come back less sad and less wise into the company of the illumined—

Love
Dos

Off the tents of the Delaim

THE GREAT DAYS

January 1922–December 1927

Late in December 1921, Dos' odyssey across the desert ended in Damascus, from whence he took a train to Beirut, where a large stack of mail awaited him. *Three Soldiers* was a success; the reviews and reports from Doran were exhilarating. The reviewer for *Atlantic,* for instance, although not wholly approving of "the propaganda and the pages of barrack pettinesses" which he thought made the book "curiously top-heavy," called it "a work of marked distinction. It is aesthetically honest and quite fearless." Heywood Broun in the *Bookman* wrote that "Nothing which has come out of the school of American realists has seemed to us so entirely honest. . . . It represents deep convictions and impressions eloquently expressed." There were those, of course, who disapproved. Coningsby Dawson's page one review for the *New York Times Book Review* of October 2 declared, "The book fails because of its unmanly intemperance both in language and in plot. The voice of righteousness is never once sounded; the only voice heard is the voice of complaint and petty recrimination." But Dawson's opinion was in the minority, and Henry Seidel Canby answered his criticisms when he passed the sort of judgment that made *Three Soldiers* one of the most important works to emerge from the experiences of World War I. "This is by no means a perfect book," he wrote for the *Literary Review,* "but it is a very engrossing one, a firsthand study, finely imagined and powerfully created. Its philosophy we may dismiss as incomplete; its conception of the free soul tortured, deadened, diseased by the circumstances of war, we cannot dismiss."

The critical praise was cause for relaxation, so before heading westward to the United States, Dos paused in Beirut for more than a week, enjoying the comforts of a plush hotel and answering the many letters he had received. Despite his complaints about America, he hankered to be "home," and after passing through France he was back in New York in February. He quickly settled down to writing. When New York got too hectic, he went to Cambridge to work on the manuscript for *Streets of Night* and—once again—*Seven Times Round the Walls of Jericho.* Nineteen twenty-two was a domestic year; Dos did not go back abroad but lived mostly in New York, sharing with Dudley Poore an apartment on Washington Square. The apartment belonged to

Elaine Orr, who was soon to be Cummings' first wife. Dos saw much of Cummings and her, Adelaide Lawson and her brother Jack, and met Scott and Zelda Fitzgerald, John Peale Bishop, Edmund Wilson, and Dawn Powell. He was trying his hand at painting, with some success. His room was large, almost empty of furniture, but with stacks of paintings along the walls. Dos had ripped his telephone from the wall in reaction against "the system," Dudley Poore remembered, and the only furnishings were a *bulle*—an eighteenth century Louis XV inlaid cabinet from his family—along with his cot.

That spring Dos, Marvin, Dudley Poore, and the later famous critic F. O. Mathiessen took a walk from Bryn Mawr out into the Pennsylvania Dutch country, which ended in Lancaster. Passing through the villages with names like Blue Balls, Love Mound, and Paradise, Dos observed the leaning wooden signpost at Intercourse and remarked to Marvin that he was sure the little town next to Bird-in-Hand had also been called Two-in-the-Bush. In June he, Marvin, and Marvin's college friend C. D. Williams took a night boat up to Saugerties for a walk in the Catskills, from which Dos had to rush away to get back to John Peale Bishop's wedding on the seventeenth in New York. The year was lively—friends, parties, good talk of art and literature—Dos thrived on them. Jocularly, perhaps in response to a wedding invitation, he scribbled a note to Bishop:

> Bishop!
> When the roll—
> boom boom!
> When the roll—
> boom boom
> When the roll is called
> Up yonder I'll be there
> Yrs,
> Dos Passos

Toward the end of the year he had eye trouble and later an attack of rheumatic fever, which would recur throughout his life. These illnesses made New York less appealing, and as 1923 came in, his thoughts had turned to Europe once more.

By mid-April he was in Florence, later going to Paris where he saw Gerald and Sara Murphy. In his book about the Murphys, *Living Well Is the Best Revenge,* Calvin Tomkins wrote that Dos with Gerald and Sara attended the rehearsals of Stravinsky's ballet *Les Noces* being staged by the Diaghilev company. Modern ballet intrigued Dos, and this was an opportunity to learn more about techniques and staging. The premiere was June 17; he remained abroad until the end of August, returning to New York in time to read the page proofs for *Streets of Night,* his much reworked novel first begun at Harvard, which was published November 9.

He also began *Manhattan Transfer*. "Haven't written a letter this fall to anyone," he wrote Marvin as 1923 ended. "Have been living a most hermit existence out at Rockaway Park practicing a new theory about my eyes—haven't worn glasses since Oct 24. and I think my sight has improved a little. . . . I'm going south to Savannah & New Orleans in a *little* while if I can scrape up some cash. . . . Deep in a new novel—everything else is the bunk."

By February 5, 1924, he was headed south, and on the eighth he sailed from Washington, D.C., for Savannah, then traveled on to New Orleans, where he was settled in by mid-February. He and Marvin tried to plan a walking trip for that spring, but Marvin, working as a journalist in North Carolina, couldn't find a time to suit Dos' vague plans, which included finishing a draft of *Manhattan Transfer,* travel to Russia or Mexico, and a cruise in the Mediterranean with Gerald Murphy, leaving from Marseilles about June 1.

While still in New Orleans, Dos met William McComb, who had worked with Marvin on a newspaper in Pittsburgh. The two saw a good deal of each other until Dos left. Much later he recalled that he might also have met William Faulkner then; if so it was but briefly. The writing of *Manhattan Transfer* was going well in New Orleans, so he stayed longer than he had first intended. Then in the spring he went to Florida and took a walking and hitchhiking trip, perhaps starting in Jacksonville, down to Key West before heading off for Europe.

He recounted in *The Best Times* that it was the summer of 1924 that he became a close friend of Ernest Hemingway, meeting him while in Paris—though they had met before as far back as Italy in the spring of 1918. The friendship was a curious one, because they were so different. Dos was shy and unathletic; Ernest, though sometimes shy, was often outspoken and intensely interested in demonstrating his courage and athletic prowess. But they had in common their devotion to writing. When they met in Paris each was attempting to develop a distinctive prose style, and it seems that as long as their friendship lasted, each lent some sort of spark to the other's creativity. Then too Dos admired Hemingway's brashness, his plain talk, his zest for life, and his sense of humor while it lasted, while Ernest admired Dos' learning and his modesty and appreciated Dos' clearly apparent respect for the younger author's ability.

During this and subsequent summer trips to Europe Dos saw a good deal of Hemingway, and also of friends like Donald Ogden Stewart, Gerald and Sara Murphy, and through them a host of artists and writers whom the Murphys brought together in Paris and at their beautiful Villa America in Cap d'Antibes. In August Dos, the Hemingways, and others of the Paris crowd of friends went to Pamplona for the fiesta of San Fermín. Though Dos recalled that most of the cast of characters were there, this was the year before the same fiesta upon which Hemingway based *The Sun Also Rises*. For Dos it was an amusing spectacle, and after it was over he headed off on a long walking tour in the Pyrenees with Captain "Chink" Smith and George O'Neil, two others of the fiesta party. The walk ended in Andorra after thirteen days, and from there Dos went back to Cap d'Antibes to work for a short while before heading to Paris.

By late October he had returned to New York to work on the last version of *Manhattan Transfer*, which he planned to deliver to Harper and Brothers by May 1925. Although he was deeply immersed in the novel, he had a real interest in an attempt to revive the *Masses*, which had been suppressed by the government in 1918. When the artist Maurice Becker wrote him early in 1925, he answered: "Dear Becker. Just received your announcement without the *pronunciamento* that somehow got left out. From the list of names I gather you are trying to start something like the old MASSES. If that's so I'm absolutely with you and would gladly do anything to help. The MASSES was the only magazine I ever had any use for. Let me know more about it. You can use my name anyway if it's any good to you."

The revived magazine became the *New Masses,* and Dos' association with it had much to do with his being thought a leading spokesman for the Communist left. But his interest was not so much in espousing any party line as it was in giving a voice to "the pacifist 'radical' tendency of the old Masses," as he put it in a letter much later to the historian Daniel Aaron. It is probably accurate to see Dos' concern for the *New Masses* as an early mark of his increasing activism in leftist movements, but one should remember that the *Masses* was an artistic, independently radical magazine, and these characteristics above all attracted Dos. The first issue of the *New Masses* seemed in the same grain as its predecessor. It listed him on the executive board along with, among others, Egmont Arends, Maurice Becker, Joseph Freeman, Mike Gold, Paxton Hibben, John Sloan, and Rex Stout. Its art—by such as William Gropper, Boardman Robinson, Maurice Becker, and Stuart Davis—was excellent; so was the writing, by authors like Babette Deutsch, Robinson Jeffers, William Carlos Williams, and Nathan Asch.

The winter of 1924–1925 was one of writing; only after completing his manuscript of the new novel and arguing for its integrity did he board the *Paris* in the late spring for Europe once more. One memorable event of that stay was the sailing trip he took with Gerald Murphy, which ended after a violent storm with their sloop, the *Picaflor,* being towed into Savona by a tug. As was his wont, Dos kept away from the States at the time a new novel was being published so he could avoid the usual round of interviews and other publicity affairs. Thus when *Manhattan Transfer* appeared in November, he was still in France, seeking some way to get to Morocco. He saw Hemingway frequently and tried to argue him out of publishing *The Torrents of Spring,* a biting satire of Sherwood Anderson's novel *Dark Laughter*.

By Christmas Dos had reached Morocco; he recalled a lonely time wandering around little villages. He took the trip partly to seek a climate that might quell incipient rheumatic fever, partly to write about the rebellion of Abd el Krim. But the prospect was discouraging; his heart was not in the project. He visited Marakesh, Magador, Kif, and was settled in Tangier when early in 1926 he received a cable from Jack Lawson urging him to join a new theatre group in New York. Presumably this was all the prodding he needed, so he hopped a mailplane from Tangier, and it bounced him to Cette, with stopovers at Alicante, Valencia, and Barcelona. He took a train to Paris; then in early March before heading to New York he spent a week with the Hemingways and the Murphys at Schruns in Austria. He tried his hand at skiing but found the best method of descent was sitting down, to the amusement of the others and the detriment of his pants.

So it was in late March or early April that he reached New York, in time to see a performance of his expressionistic play, *The Moon Is a Gong*—later retitled *The Garbage Man*—being performed at the

Cherry Lane Playhouse. This marked the real beginning of his connection with experimental drama and the New Playwrights Theatre, an eventful, emotionally enervating experience for him, particularly punctuated as it was by the culminating events of the Sacco and Vanzetti case.

His form of involvement in political causes was writing about them, so he went off on his own to Provincetown to work on a pamphlet for the defense of Sacco and Vanzetti, and when Rumsey Marvin wrote from Wilmington, North Carolina, asking about the possibilities of taking a walking tour along the coast of the Carolinas and Virginia, Dos responded that he was "chugging along under forced draft to get through in time. What about May?" He had secluded himself in a "little house in Provincetown" where "There's nobody here I know and I've lived absolutely alone with my work a volume of Casanova, an oil cookstove named Jiminy and a big toastburner named Gog and Magog."

What Dos was "chugging to get through" were the parts of *Orient Express*—his second reportage of travel—that had not previously been published, and a draft of *Facing the Chair: Story of the Americanization of Two Foreignborn Workmen*, which was his chief contribution to the effort to save Sacco and Vanzetti. During the spring or early summer of 1926 he nosed around North Plymouth and talked with the defense witnesses. Also he interviewed both accused anarchists, was impressed by them and sure of their innocence, and became the more thoroughly committed to their cause.

This work, and no doubt the problem of agreeing on a time, delayed the proposed walk with Marvin until late June. The two of them, C. D. Williams, then an assistant U.S. District Attorney in New York, and Hugh A. Leamy, associate editor of *Colliers,* met at Wrightsville Beach, North Carolina, to begin their jaunt. Their host there, Walter Williamson, sent them on their way with a half-gallon jug of corn liquor—"vintage" corn, Marvin recalled, it being roughly six weeks old. From Wrightsville Beach, the four took a bus to Morehead City and Beaufort, where they deposited their jug in the men's room of a hotel, only Leamy choosing to preserve some of the concoction in his canteen. From Beaufort they took a launch to Cape Lookout, spending their first night at the Coast Guard station. The next day they hiked along Core Bank to the Coast Guard station there; the third day, with the Coast Guard's help crossing the inlets, they reached Ocracoke. The sun baked them, no one else was around, so from time to time they would strip down and dive in the surf, then walk along until they had dried off. But even this system didn't keep them cool enough, so they decided they would trek from Ocracoke to Cape Hatteras by night.

Ocracoke was a delightful interlude. Several pretty girls enjoyed their company, they had beds to sleep in at Captain Bill Gaskill's hotel, and before leaving, fortified with the Captain's brew of Grape-Ola mixed with orange extract, they even had a rousing square dance. Revived, they headed off for Hatteras, only Leamy choosing to remain behind. He was not built for hiking, apparently, and some heavy doses of the vintage corn had done him in the previous days. Dos much later thought he remembered pushing Leamy in a wheelbarrow but confessed this might have been a dream.

The night walk to Cape Hatteras was startling, C. D. Williams recalled—a full moon, wild ponies running around on the bank, abandoned ships rotting away and creating grotesque shapes. The three got as far as Manteo, took a ship to Elizabeth City, North Carolina, then a train to Norfolk, Virginia, and then Richmond, where they explored Confederate memorials and gave out a playful interview to a Richmond paper, announcing that the next year they planned a trip to Asia. Dos chimed in that "There are [more] beautiful girls at Buxton [North Carolina] than any place in America," to which Marvin and Williams nodded assent. Why he said Buxton when they had square-danced at Ocracoke is not clear; but no matter, the whole trip had enlivened them all.

Dos was back in the northeast for the remainder of the summer, working with the Sacco and Vanzetti Defense Committee and the New Playwrights Theatre. For him, a little of that sort of involvement was enough, so to clear his head in November he left New York, visited his half brother James in Virginia, then began a walk down through the Blue Ridge and Allegheny mountains. He savored a swim in the mineral pools of Warm Springs after several days of long walks, then boarded a train in nearby Covington for Louisville, Kentucky, and points west as he aimed for Mexico City, where he arrived by mid-December.

Mexico—particularly away from Mexico City—was starkly beautiful. But for Dos the chief importance of this trip was the range of people he met—Gladwin Bland, a "retired wobbly" whose tales of the I.W.W. made him the source for Fenian McCreary, the "Mac" of *The 42nd*

Parallel; a young painter named Xavier Guerrero; and others whose radical theories touched off Dos' own growing political concern at that time. Coupled with the techniques of expressionism he had already tried out in *Manhattan Transfer* and *The Moon Is a Gong,* he had many of the ingredients to begin the *U.S.A.* trilogy.

He came back to New York for the spring months of 1927, plunged into work for the New Playwrights, and thought ahead to where he might go during the summer. Set designs and scenery painting pleased him, but he had no taste for the administration of the project, the constant search for funds, and the almost inevitable bickering among strong-willed, artistic personalities such as the other New Playwrights directors, Mike Gold, Francis Faragoh, Em Jo Basshe, and Lawson. He and Lawson remained close friends, but when later Basshe felt compelled to fire Ed Massey, Dos' friend who had directed *The Moon Is a Gong* and was directing Dos' second play, *Airways, Inc.,* he decided to resign. That, however, was early in 1929; in 1927 the newness of the drama experiment was more pleasure than pain. He was living back on Columbia Heights in a house where Hart Crane also was staying that spring, and the two had occasional dinners together. In May, just at the time of Lindbergh's landing in Paris, Dos, C. D. Williams, and Rumsey Marvin took a walk through the Catskills from Dover Plains, New York, down to Danbury, stopping to play croquet at Gaston Lachaise's house and meeting Crane there.

The spring and summer of 1927 were particularly active not only because of the theatre but because of the final efforts to reverse the death sentences for Sacco and Vanzetti. In June Dos took a short trip to the West Indies but was back by the beginning of July, and in the weeks before their executions in August, he worked as best he could for their cause, particularly directing an open letter to president Lowell of Harvard, which appeared in the *Nation* and several newspapers. And in the final days before the execution he served as a reporter for the *Daily Worker* to describe the various protest efforts. Once when police broke up the picketers in front of the Boston statehouse, Dos was swept up with others whom the police were arresting. He found himself in the paddy wagon next to Edna St. Vincent Millay, whose husband, Eugene Boissevain, quickly bailed them out.

The protests were of no avail. Sacco and Vanzetti died August 23, and Dos—like thousands of other Americans—felt deep disgust toward the nation's government. "Camera Eye 50" of *U.S.A.* recorded his bitterness at that time:

> they have clubbed us off the streets they are stronger they are rich they hire and fire the politicians the newspapereditors the old judges the small men with reputations the collegepresidents the wardheelers (listen businessmen collegepresidents judges America will not forget her betrayers) they hire the men with guns the uniforms the policecars the patrolwagons . . .
>
> we stand defeated America

With the deaths of Sacco and Vanzetti he moved as far to the left as he ever would; he took a more active interest in politics than before; and his stance was that of a fellow-traveler, though he never joined the Communist party and always had distinct doubts about it—about any regimented political group, for that matter.

To Thomas P. Cope

[Beirut
January 1922]

Hello Tom—

Beirut is a jolly little town with a number of Parisy jazz-palaces and a fine seafront and a smell of ships, and delicious fried foods— Came in via Boalbek from Esch Schom in company of a splendid South African travelling salesman—We viewed the ruins together— guidebook in hand and oh'd and ah'd where indicated. Hell of a lot stones piled up.

Missed Tadmor, on account of the Bedawi—had set my heart on seeing that stone pile on account of the hearty Zenobia. But one cup of coffee from the hand of Hasoon at the campfire of Djakem Er Rawwaf while the flames of the ruetha danced in one's eyes and the smoke stung one's nostrils was worth all the historic mornings on the bookshelves, and the sight of Ali staunching the blood from his mashed foot in the red embers pulverized all the marbles from Boston to Olympia— and the jolly ruffians who fought us carolling their wonderfully jaunty yodel as they rode to attack us, and the whistling of bullets across the flint strewn hills . . . The desert's gorgeous—the people in it are so damn fine. I didn't know the world contained such people—It's an excellent little pippin after all, the world is—When I got to Damascus even the year was new—

On my way home to find a quiet spot to finish my Streets of Night novel and do the final rewriting of Fibby—

See you soon—

My publishers must be geniuses for publicity. Really they deserve the goldenamelled urinal—They could probably make George Eliot go like hotcakes, or the Lamentations of Jeremiah—

tout à toi
Dos

To Eugene Saxton

Beirut—
Jan 7-[19]22

Dear Saxton,

Turned up in Damascus about a week ago after an amazing 39 days crossing the desert with a caravan from Baghdad—Superb. Found an enormous mail here, the first in five months—clotted with clippings about 3 Soldiers. There seem to have been a number of angoras captured. I doubt if Mr. Dawson's found his yet. Damn decent of Fred Nelson to remember me and stoke the fires in the Hartford Times. And you people, by the glimpses I've had, have been clanging the cymbals and beating the big bass drum loud enough to wake the very civil war veterans and make them call for their pensions. Shows what a well directed barrage of publicity can do.

I'm on my way home now to find a quiet place to finish my much delayed new novel—

As for photographs, I'll try to get some comic ones if you insist. How would one of those with a large head and little body at Coney Island do? Or must you have a camel in the background? How local must the color be? There were two stout and respectable dancing ladies with our caravan who would have done superbly but they've gone to Aleppo. No, but I'll try—anything'd be better than the horrid pieface I saw staring at me from those beastly clippings.

It will be fun to be back in the regions of copious food and drink and of enameled bathtubs. The (so called) Near East is in a rather scrawny state at present.

I'll probably have to make Marseilles via Port Said—then Paris London and the land that Liberty turned her back on—Morgan & Harjes will get me.

What are the chances of slipping back some of the expurgated scenes in another edition—if there is one? You dont know what qualms of conscience I have had about them. At any rate the French translation must be from the complete MS. Do you people or the Brandts handle translation? I wired the Brandts about it.

You people certainly have done well to push this novel over the top—granting it's gone over—Thanks a lot anyway.

Best wishes to John Farrar and Mr. Rinehart—

Yours

John Dos Passos

To Sherwood Anderson (1876–1941), *noted for his novels and short stories, particularly the collection* Winesburg, Ohio. *Never a close friend of Dos', they corresponded, however, and admired each other's work.*

Beirut
Jan 7–[19]22

Dear Sherwood Anderson—

Thanks a lot for your note. Since it seems to be a time for the passing of gold-embossed chamber pots let me blurt out that there's nobody in the country such a note means so much from as from you—The grammar is mixed but I hope you get what I mean—I hope we can drink another glass of beer together before long—like the one opposite Saint Germain des Près last summer

Yrs

John Dos Passos

To Robert Hillyer

Beirut—Syria
Jan 10 [*19*]*22*

Dear Robert,

On emerging from what was Arabia Felix a hundred times over (if
not geographically) I climbed down from my camel, Malek, took three
hot baths ate four full course dinners washed down by a great lovely
quart of pommard, and found my self confronted by America militant
in the shape of dirty press clippings, hornblowings, big drum beatings,
letters informing me I ought to be lynched or else elevated to the top of
the Flatiron Building and covered with sticky tinfoil—in the midst of
all that moist and stinking, ordure your letters and a couple from Jack
were the only havens of refuge.

At present I am bound for the U.S.A. having, bi Jasus, destroyed
the illusion of geography—No more retchings after Cook's tours, or
pinings to join the agile Mr. Neuman—in his Travel Talks—All of it is
bunk. When the final disgust seizes me I shall grow a great beard and
retire to the Nejd and have a great quantity of giggling wives in pink
nighties. Until that time comes I will content myself with the contemplation of the following truths. There's as bad wine to be drunk in
Tiflis as on Eleventh Street, the phonographs squawk as loud in
Baghdad as they do in Sioux City, and politics are no more comic in
Teheran than in Washington D.C. There's a fine suitable quotation out
of Ovid, but I dont know it—anyway one's hair falls as fast in
Kermanshaw as in Beverly Falls, and (what was Cuthbert's phrase
about the unique thrill of perfect beauty?) anyway that plum whatever
it is, we are as likely to pullout of the putty colored mush our thumbs
are irrevocably stuck into here as in New Bedford, or among the sages
that sit naked at the headwaters of the Brahmaputra.

Among other horrors is a contraption of mine in the middle of a
page in Vanity Fair that makes me think you are right in your diatribe
about color adjectives—I can imagine Ben Jonson's wrath when
confronted with "vermillion-tinted tambourines," say. You may be
right you old purist, but I doubt if you can reform me this late in the
game.

I'm now on my way home, as I said (curious word "home": I
wonder why I used it) and ought to be in North Atlantic waters early
in February—Oh we will have many a tipple if there is anything left to

tipple in Boston—together, and I'm keen to read your epic. I'm glad 5 Books is flourishing and the fact that the publishers are chilly about the new thing augurs well for its worth.

Do send me to Paris—Morgan Harjes—a copy of Armadas—I'm sure that those memorable events have been commemorated with the pomp they deserved—

Love
Dos

Tell Dudley he's a Kalbiby Kalb for not having written to me.

To Rumsey Marvin

Beirut, Syria
Jan 10– '22

Dear Rummy——

A great quantity of letters of yours sober letters, sad letters, drunk letters, gay letters, priggish letters, wise letters, comic letters, helped to make up for my five months of maillessness—Tumbled into Damascus the other day in the company of the Sayyid Mahomet on a grey stallion on a castrational saddle without stirrups—I have a vague idea I wrote you from there though—after thirty nine days of desert, ten of them cold as Christmas (it was) and very hungry for our food ran low and at the end we had nothing but rice and castawi—fried dates, delicious, one of the great elemental patriarchal foods. But the Arabs, the people I came over with, the Agail from the Nejel—Central Arabia, were the finest people I've ever known. I felt like kissing their feet I was so fussy and gawky beside them. I've never known people so intense, so well balanced, so gentle—I actually found myself crying after I had said goodby to them—

But now I've shaved off my beard and replaced the agal and ishmaq by a hat and sent my abaya to the wash and live at the best hotel in Beirut in the fattest most uninspired ease, and write letters in response to the little journalistic turds 3 Soldiers seems to have induced; envelopes full of them were waiting for me here—fragrant and foul.

But Rummy I must protest at this horrible Y man drug clerk attitude to girls or flappers or whatever one calls them that must be the mode at Yale just now—By Christ it may be funny in a highschool kid in his first long pants but it's a hideous grimace in someone who must have warmth and passion in him somewhere. God America's filthy.

Everything about sex is so hideously perverted it makes you shudder—
God I wish every college in America could be wiped off the face of the
earth. Beastly holes! Thank god prohibition isn't completely effective
in them anyway. Dont worry—Rummy you'll survive—You'll be great
as the chocolate king—no really, I love the idea—Forgive my silly
vehemence. I'm probably quite wrong—And my own existence vis à
vis women is so incomplete that I have no right to preach.

Shall turn up in the states soon

Beirut's a jolly little seaport sports an excellent jazz palace—where
there's one of the finest coal black niggers I ever saw who does a song
and dance, solemn as an undertaker. Been raining cats and dogs ever
since I got here—

Lots of love
Jack

To Stewart Mitchell

Beirut
Jan 15-'22

I should like your company, Auk—I sit on the terrace of the hotel
contemplating the dazzle of the sun on snowy Lebanon and the five
bootblacks of Beirut (Not that there are only five) The air is delicious
full of brine and vaguely chilly for the sun has not yet reached the
Hotel Bassoul.

The devil of it is I don't know your address—Which one of the
more civilized European states are you gracing with the pomp of your
presence? Dudley it comes out has returned to the vomit. A fat Christian lady has just passed under the terrace with an enormous basket of
narcissus on her head—white as gulls wings and very fragrant.

I am on my way to find some quiet nook where I can hear American spoken and fabricate some novels. The Gorgeous East has been in
fee long enough.

I emerged there from at Damascus about ten days ago, having left
the caravan of the Agail engaged in smuggling mysterious bales into
Syria on a windy hillside near the town of Imair. A few letters and
much garbage were the result of five months accumulation of mail
here in the consulate two cards from you have vague hints of Avignon
but further information I have not. Dudley does not deign to write. I

shall begin an inquest. Robert also, according to two jaunty notes, has returned to the Harvard vomit.

But perhaps I shall find you in Paris (I cant for the life of me remember the name of the street, but I know the house) In which case these vaporings are superfluous—

Love

Dos

To Rumsey Marvin

[Cambridge

March 1922]

Dear Rummy—

Sorry I cant get down to New Haven today. I think I'll be up here about a week more as I'm getting a lot of work done. At any rate I'll probably turn up some time next week—About speaking Rummy, you must let me off. I'll tell you why. If I speak somewhere people'll be sure to get wind of it and I wouldn't be able to refuse stoutly as I've done hitherto to shoot my face on any account. And anyway I can't do it, and dont want to learn. Tried to make a speech at a beastly dinner in New York and made a hideous mess of it.

I'm very keen to see you—but do let me creep in and out of New Haven unheralded and unsung. I'm all for the mute inglorious Milton stuff—and resent highly the attempts of Doran's publicity staff to turn me into a prize cow. That's what drove me away from New York to seek refuge in this fine little room up three flights on a back street that nobody knows here in Cambridge. Even here work is moving desperately slowly—but I find the mere sitting at a table all day in seclusion diversified by an occasional aria on the Corona delightful after the somewhat fevered galivantings of the past year. All I'm afraid of is that it'll go and get to be spring and wreck me.

Save me a wee drop o' gin—the "wine" & "gin" people feed one here are simply vomitose—infinitcly worse than New York—

love

Jack

To Theodore Stanton (1851–1925), *son of the feminist leader Elizabeth Cady Stanton, who was himself an author and had written about World War I.*

214 Riverside Drive
New York NY
[*April (?) 1922*]

Dear Mr Stanton,

I am asking my publishers to send you a copy of Three Soldiers and one of Rosinante to the Road Again, just out.

As for biographical notes: Graduated from Harvard 1916, served in Dick Norton's volunteer ambulance service in France, in the Red Cross Ambulance service on Monte Grappa in Italy and in the USArmy ambulance, have spent a good deal of time in France and Spain and have just returned from Persia and the Near East. White. Unmarried. 26.

As for France and the French: detest the literary tradition of the Academie as much as I admire the crosscurrents. Idolize Flaubert.

Thank you very much for taking the trouble to write to me.

Very sincerely yours,
John Dos Passos

By the way, Three Soldiers, is *not,* as people have tried to make out autobiography—

To John Peale Bishop (1892–1944), *a poet and essayist. A close friend of Edmund Wilson, he graduated from Princeton in 1917. When he returned from service in Europe during the First World War, he joined* Vanity Fair. *About the time Dos met him and Wilson, the latter two were publishing* Undertaker's Garland (*1922*), *a collection of verse and prose. He lived in France from 1924 to 1933, when he returned to America. Bishop was a retiring person, and much of his work was not published until after his death.*

3 Washington Square
N.Y.C.
[*Fall 1922*]

Dear Bishop—Got the same day nostalgia-inducing letters from both you and E.E.C. anent a certain party and jollification among the cauliflowers at which I wish I had reeled a third.

Thanks a lot for the Garland. I have sniffed with a good deal of delight the separate nosegays—I think I liked best The Death of a Dandy, The Madman's Funeral, and Emily in Hades & the Death of a Soldier. I wish you'd sweat more blood over the death of God—The title rather overbalances the poem as it is I think.

Talk about the classic tradition Mr Nock has been bleating after—he ought to get a whiff of it out of the Garland fit to take the back of his head off.

The Preface is damn fine—States the case simply & very well—The spirit of the whole business is fine and bubbling and explosive and grand-mannerous—Personally I'd have liked the style of the things more angular and corrosive, less in the round voluted copybook hand—but after all there is a certain splendor in the big bow wow style that you both manage to squeeze out of it at your best. The soldier things fit splendidly with the rest to my way of thinking. Anyway the failings are healthy calfish failings and the excellencies are of the sort that make damn good cornerstones for future building. Hell, I dont think I have the critical sense of a June bug—so forgive the foregoing ineptitudes—I think it's a very personable volume and I wish I could baptize it in your very excellent company in white wine and red—

Yours
John Dos Passos

Remember me to Margaret—How's Vienna? Do let me have news of your wanderings—

To John Peale Bishop

[3 Washington Square
New York
October 1922]

Dear Bishop—

I'd have written you sooner but my eyes have gone pop (like the weasel) and I've been resting them down in North Carolina in a place called Hickory Nut Gap.

I'd like to have been with you in Venice. Swimming at the Lido to a sound of brassbands is one of my ideas of the coasts of Heaven. And with Carpaccio entertaining?

Your letters make me distend my nostrils somewhat greedily to the waft off the fleshpots

Way down in Egyp' lan'

for although God's country is sure the place for me and far more

entertaining and rewarding as ashheaps and shoots of red hot ore are
rewarding yet I admit that I feel a creeping overme of a letcherous
desire to take my ease
                                        way down in Egyp land
the spirit is willing for wood alcohol and train wrecks and sunday
papers but the flesh craves sunlight and Côtes du Rhone
                                        way down in Egyp land.
Yow!—all of which means that I'm smoothing out my passport and
piling up my pennies for a couple of months galivant. So before the
winter is out we may crack a bottle together.

I dont see why those sons of a bitchin' reviewers knock the
Garland so. It's a damn good piece of work—I think they've probably
all had articles rejected by Vanity Fair. If A Huxley had done it aided
by the Hon. John Clinkingbottom they'd all bray approval, I bet you.

Last night Bunny Wilson and Elinor Wylie were reading your
new poem and I was allowed to listen in on it. Finest subject matter
imaginable. I wish there was more southern talk in it. The few intona-
tions I caught were very fine. And I thought it a little too Eliot—particularly the mannerism of using proper names of a baroque and
yiddish character. I felt it didn't exploit your own personal qualities
enough—The opening was fine and the business about the slaves being
whipped and the old woman lying among the faggots in the hearth her
hair in the ashes—

But the southern lingo is so fine for poetry. I feel it ought to be
given a free hand with the verse. All this may be rot—

My best to the missis

Yrs
Dos

To Robert Hillyer

[3 Washington Square
New York
Fall 1922]

Robert dearest chitterling

It's that I've been in Washington having my eyes polished and
down in North Carolina cooling ma fevered brow in the mountains.
That is why I haven't written you—I had rather a scare as the aforesaid
peepers were in a horrid state. Now they are moderately luminous, and
my novel's finished and I'm Queen of the May.

Yay for the Venice.

Tell Mr. Parisian the Armenian that I'm very busy and my eyes very bad and that I couldn't possibly write his booklet and that I rather despair of the use of booklets but that I wish him well—But I see you say to write him—

When are you coming to N.Y. I have a new and very comfortable couch which I would like to see dented by your honorable posteriors—I can feed you some delicious Marsala in a place on Prince Street—Do come down. Dudley is in the front Apt. in this house and also has couches and things—

What are you doing besides Harvarding the Freshmen?

Your health—

Dos

To F. Scott Fitzgerald (1896–1940), *the novelist, whom Dos first met in 1922 in New York and with whom he remained a good—if not intimate—friend until Fitzgerald's death.*

[New York
January 1923 (?)]

THE WHITNEY STUDIO CLUB
147 West 4th Street
INVITES YOU TO AN EXHIBITION OF
paintings by
John Dos Passos
and
Adelaide J. Lawson
and Sculpture by
Ruben Nakian

January third to January twenty-fourth
Open daily 11 A.M. to 11 P.M. Sundays 3 to 9 P.M.

[Dos Passos' note:]
Come and bring a lot of drunks

A desperate tea fight will be held at the Whitney S Club Friday afternoon Jan 5—Contestants are advised to wear masks and raincoats. Lost articles such as happy phrases, critical conundrums et al will be confiscated by the management. Rules: Catch as catch can. Any contestant looking at the pictures or mentioning the syllable art will be declared to have fouled and will be removed from the floor. Consolation prizes (listen to the cocktail shaker, listen to the cocktail shaker, listen to the cocktail shaker singing o'er her grave) will be administered. Follow the Green line It'll probably be a hellish bore—

Dos

To Robert Hillyer

[Midtown Hospital
231 East 57th St.
New York
February–March 1923]

Dear Robert it was delightful to get your letter. I have not been able to answer it as—for my sins or my lack of them, I don't know which, I've been in the clutches of a rheumatic fever or arthritis which has ruined me in every way, reduced me to an immovable painful vegetable. Still I'm much better now and I am promised that the cutting out of certain ingrown tonsils where the tenement house conditions among the streptococci, were just disgraceful, my dear, and as for their morals well . . . will put me on my feet again

It's all hellishly annoying as if it werent for this disease I'd be sailing towards Stromboli at this minute.

I'd love to come up to Pomfret [Connecticut] as soon as I can manage it—but I'm not going to make any plans to gang awry. When you come to New York I'll either still be in the Midtown Hospital 231 E 57th Street or I'll be recuperating at 110 Columbia Heights Bklyn. Write or wire a day or so ahead as I might possibly be sunning my wreckage on some beach or other.

After all after a thoroughgoing run of bad luck . . . merde, I sit here this accursed Sunday afternoon in a fuzzy hospital bathrobe looking out through a rusty flyscreen at the backyards and clotheslines and paradise bushes and I feel about as alive as an opened tomato can—La chère est triste hêlas et j'ai lu tous les livres—

Yours
Dos

X and XI
Sketches of Dudley Poore, spring
1918 (from Dos' sketchbook).

XII Dos (seated) and Rumsey Marvin on their walking
tour in the Auvergne, summer 1920.

XIII Edmund Wilson in the 1920's.

XIV   Dos in a photo taken in New Orleans, winter 1924.

XV Dos with Patrick Murphy on the Plage de la Garoupe,
Antibes, summer 1925.

XVI Honoria, Baoth, and Patrick Murphy presenting flowers to
their parents for their tenth wedding anniversary, December 30, 1925, in Antibes.

XVII One of the Murphys' picnics on the Plage de la Garoupe, Antibes, in the mid-1920's. Among the guests: Baroness Etiènne de Beaumont (in beaded swim-suit), Picasso (in dark hat), Sara Murphy (in white hat), Picasso's wife Olga (in dancing gown), and Picasso's mother (in black, seated with back to camera).

XVIII Skiing above Schruns, March 1926. *Left to right:* Hemingway, Fräulein Maria Glaser, Dos, Gerald Murphy.

XIX
Stewart Mitchell.

XX and XXI Dos in the mid-1920's.

XXII

Dos and Katy in Key West, spring 1928.
The man partly in the picture is the painter
Waldo Peirce.

XXIII   Dos (standing right) and Katy (seated left) with acquaintances
at Key West, spring 1928.

XXIV and XXV   Dos' watercolors of proposed sets for the New Playwrights Theatre, 1927–1929.

XXVI Katy aboard the Murphys' schooner *Weatherbird,* Antibes, circa 1932.

XXVII Ernest Hemingway in Montana, 1932.

XXVIII Letter sent to Patrick Murphy when he was sick with tuberculosis (Katy's writing, Dos' watercolor designs).

To Eugene Saxton

[Nerja, Spain
August 19, 1923]

Dear 'Gene—

At last the proofs appeared and I have duly mailed them. They came as third class mail, which is why they took so long—

The last chapter I will send off as soon as it appears—

As I'm sailing August 30 I ought to be in New York in time to see the page proofs

I hope reaching me at long distance this way hasn't caused you people too much worry and annoyance—

I've been spending a week in one of the sideshows they forgot to close up when the Eden Amusement Company boarded up its door for an indefinite closure. Places have no right to be so outrageously delightful as Nerja.

Best wishes to Mrs Saxton and the kids—

Yours,
John Dos Passos

By the way I promised Fitzgerald (F. Scott) I'd send him an advance copy of S. of N. Will you please forward one to him at Great Neck L.I. when convenient—

To Edmund Wilson (1895–1972), *America's outstanding literary critic, whom Dos met in New York in 1922. The two remained close always, although after the mid-1930's they agreed less and less about politics.*

[110 Columbia Heights
Brooklyn
January 12, 1924]

Dear Wilson—

I don't mean to unload that article on your head—Don't worry about it—I thought merely you might know somewhere it would be useful to stimulate interest in the poor Swedes.

How about conspiring to blow up the liberal weeklies? TNT cant be so very expensive in these quiet times. A bomb squad could be formed that would work incalculable good to humanity by a few well placed fuses. We could go disguised as Inflated Dragons of the K.K.K. and nobody would dare to object. Cant you see the headlines: "Burning Cross on Vesey Street" Patrolman Snuffs Fuses Saves Freeman—

Speaking of toilet paper—enclosed is a beautiful example of early
twentieth century silkfloss engraved roll type, used in the Kosher
columbaria at Rockaway Park. Model suitable for short lyrics—My best
to Mary Blair

Yrs

Dos

To Rumsey Marvin

510 Esplanade Avenue
Care Mrs Ordoñez
New Orleans
Feb. 17–[19]24

Hello Rummy

I'm all settled in a fine little room in the house of a little yellow
Central American woman with glasses. My bed is painted cobalt blue,
my walls are peeling apricot my ceiling is the color of raspberry ice—
and I'm working like a Trojan. The only inconvenience is that I'm
trying to economize and I'm rotten at it, and I have nobody to eat talk
or drink with. New Orleans is much more Creole than I had expected,
streets and streets of dilapidated houses with rusty elegant wrought
iron balconies, green and blue and pink and orange walls peeling in the
sun (at this moment its raining buckets)—You never tasted such food
as there is in divers old and expensive French restaurants—In fact the
whole place is thoroughly satisfactory and from the looks and odor of
the population reeking with liquor. The town is quite far under the
river that swells above its levees like a stream of molasses on a table. In
fact the question of how New Orleans got here in the first place is as
complicated as the famous question about the apple and the dumpling.
But here it is, full of noise and jingle and horseracing and crap shooting and whoring and bawdry.

Why dont you come down here when you get fired out of Salisbury? Incidentally I am pining for information about how and why
and what is Salisbury and the denizens thereof—My plans are now to
stay the month out here then go for a couple of weeks in the middle of
March to a place on Perdido Bay the Hibbens told me of, which is
cheap and desolate—What will you be doing about that time?

Except that I may be going to Russia in April or May—I shall be
interested in any high emprise in whatever direction or duration—so

for heaven's sake in the words of divine service Do good and Communicate

I'm sure some sort of extraordinary rampage can be concocted if we can only get together on it—

love
Jack

[New Orleans
March (?) 1924]

Dear Rummy—Forgive my not writing you but I've been working very hard. I sort of hoped you'ld turn up here. It's a fine town honestly. There's a regular Frankie and Johnny café called the Original Tripoli, full of vice niggermusic and rotten booze. There are streets and streets of scaling crumbling houses with broad wrought iron verandahs painted in Caribbean blues and greens. There's a square with a fine cathedral and wharves and ships galore and the air is full of the smell of molasses from the sugar refineries. There are levees along the Mississippi to walk on, Bayous leading into lake Pontchatrain. Winter scorched palms and palmettos everywhere—the streets are full of inconceivable old geezers in decrepit frockcoats, of tall negresses with green and magenta bandanas on their heads, of whores and racingmen and South Americans and Central Americans of all colors and shapes.

McComb and I dine together about every evening and he tells me extraordinary stories of newspaper life in Pittsburgh and Pennsylvania generally.

Oyez, if your job goes bing for any reason why dont you come down and walk down Florida with me. I think I'll go—in about two weeks or less—to Jacksonville and beat my way to Key West. What I'll do when I get to Key West is problematical—

Russia—I'm one of three people who the Kamerny Theatre in Moscow want to come and help them arrange productions for an American tour. If the arrangement doesnt fall through they will pay our way and feed and clothe us while in Moscow. So its not a chance to be missed if it comes through. I'll know in a month or so. If I dont go there I'm looking lustfully towards Mexico—Want to come?

Write me all about Goldsboro.

New Orleans suits me to a T. I don't know anybody so I live cheap and work continuously and spend the rest of the time doing voodoo on my eyes.

McComb is an awfully good chap. I'm very glad to have met him.

You must feel like a one man band in Goldsboro. Do you have to print the damn sheet too? You'll certainly be an expert on North Carolina and the tarheels. But I cant write anymore I must go out for my daily walk—

Write me here for the next week

Yrs
Jack

510 Esplanade Avenue
N.O. La
P.S. You never saw such good looking girls as this city produces.

To John Howard Lawson

[Antibes
August, 1924]

Dear Jack—

Numerous insane things have been happening. Russia's all off. Mr. Tearemoff has disappeared off the face of the earth. Its rumored that the Kamerny is being supplanted by a manager in Leningrad who uses steam shovels for actors and issues costumes to the spectators. I found myself I dont know how at a lot of bullfights in Pamplona at a ferocious fiesta with a lot of fake bohemians. Then I was walking up the spine of the Pyrenees thirteen days from Roncesvalles to Andorra in the company of a very comic English captain and a morose young man named George. Now I am working in a red plush room at the Murphy's place at Antibes where I'm being "entertained" as the New York Herald would say with great elegance and a great deal of gin fizz. Wonderfully good bathing. The Riviera in summer is a strange and rather exciting place. The people are very bastard and peculiar and the landscape is obstructed by villas full of artificial countesses under the influence of opium or spirits or spaniels. Has to be seen to be believed. Went to a curious fete at Cannes where the fishermen danced barefoot round the bandstand to the strains of Orpheus in Hades in a curiously hardboiled oversexed way. It's not at all like Marseilles.

Now I'm waiting for news of my millions from my aunt. I'm beginning to suspect that they are going to remain mythical. That'll be an awful mess.

Gosh, I hope you bought the castle on the Hudson. We can pay for it somehow. Though I suspect that there is something phoney about that man Freeman's option. An option always has a time limit. Probably he's getting a commission for selling it. Let me hear what you've done about it.

Here is les Esclaves—If you show it to the Theatre Guild dont let them snatch it and get the rights to it In fact it might be worth while for us to translate it mutually. Also Ed might want to do it in Boston. I'll write him that you have the MS if he wants to see it. I didnt make any arrangement with St Georges de Bonhelius who's a ridiculous little man, looks like his name but I assured him it wouldn't be mutilated. On rereading it seems to me everybit as good as ever.

Give my love to Esther and Sue and any other Melancholias that there may be about. Has Bedford Street come to an end?

Had a fine letter from Adelaide that seemed very gay—

Yours

Dos

To Rumsey Marvin

[Paris
September(?) *1924*]

Well Rummy Goldarn You—I was glad to get your letter.

Last spring McComb and I just about held funeral services over you. I wrote to all sorts of addresses and once telegraphed you to join me in Florida where I walked an extraordinary walk. He'd written you too and we just about decided that our little Rummy had turned up his toes to the everlasting daisies—

Met C D a month or so ago—he gave me your address and said you were alive and kicking—Unrest! Christ man, send me a package of calm.

Almost went to Russia, took a Kollossal and thirteen day walk instead along the top of the Pyrenees ending in a thunderstorm and a flood and a blind sliding down a gorge into Andorra at midnight. Then had some of the most marvellous swimming ever had at Antibes on the Mediterranean ate a great deal of choucroute in the rain under the dripping eaves of Strasbourg and drank riesling—muscat in rhomantick schlosses popeyed with weldschmerz and weibliche liebe until the cows came home.

Now I'm broke as a flounder flat as Humpty Dumpty, alimenting with bad Chinese and Czechoslovaque food at f 3.50 and haunting telegraph offices. C.D. said you were merry in love and comfortably fed in Wilmington—After all, even if the Thames doesn't catch fire. There's something so silly about running around the world like a dancing mouse. Discontent is just the seven year itch.

I mean one's energy is more likely to take monumental forms, perhaps—this is all through my hat—if you dont waste it in mere transportation and confetti like flickering unrest—wow—Toute même —I wish you were here tonight we'd go on a great bat at the Place du Tertre. Paris is sensual and melancholy in the warm rain, smells of faded lettuce and wilted women—write you bloated placeholder—

Dos

I did not write sooner because I didnt get your letters and wire until about a week late—

[110 Columbia Heights
Brooklyn
Winter 1925(?)]

Dear Rummy I waited a day or two to see if I could possibly manage a getaway—But it cant be done. I'm absolutely flat and I have an incredible amount of work yet to do on this novel which I have promised my publisher for May. So although I've got the pip and fatty degeneration of the essential organs I've got to stay here until I finish. It's hellish but for seventeen million reasons essential. So it probably will be May or June before I can come out of winter quarters in Brooklyn—and by that time you say you want to be back here in New York. It's all very exasperating—I'm darn sorry and if there were anything I could do I'd do it. The main thing is that I'll be a raving maniac if I dont get this goddamn piece of work off my chest immediately.

Still maybe you'll still be circulating about by summer—In that case I'll join forces with you somewhere—Before that I'm a dead letter, an unexpanded Japanese flower, an unopened can of beans, a coocoon, anything you like that's tied down pinned cribbed confined and uncomfortable

love
Jack

I dont think Mexico would be unpleasant in summer.
Have no idea how I would feed my face—Am and shall be broke

To Robert Hillyer

[On board S.S. *Paris*
Spring(?) *1925*]

Dear Robert—

Forgive me for not answering your letter. I was not in New York
that time—and for some reason letter writing has been impossible since
I've been sick. I'm stiff and very mediocre in health but my morale has
improved. I'm in the steerage on the Paris being transported eastward—Locomotion even under the most adverse conditions always
cheers me up. Still I wish I could have gone to help you plant trees in
Pomfret. I'll go up there as soon as I come back—if you'll have me.

New York last week was like being rolled naked in metal filings—
it took a great deal of aspirin to get me through smut talks with
Harper and his brother. Did you know that Kerist? was not blasphemous, but that Christ! was? And when a chaste vaudeville lady
spoke of "three a day", Harper and his brother, thought three men? I
ask you. Still my next novel, after the battle with the gelding-shears
was found to be not quite castrated, perhaps half a testicle remained on
the left side. So it was in a state of collapse and by pure reflex that I
landed sprawling on the Paris yesterday morning. Literature, Mr.
Hillyer, is a lousy trade.

And you ask me not to be angry when I write!

Well Herakles—Phoibos—Huppolutas I'll drink a (rheumatism
enhancing joint stiffening) draft of Chateau Yquem in your honor.
You'll notice the taste in your mouth one day eating a winesap in
Pomfret. If this keeps up I'll probably be being wheeled in a chair
when next you see me. Mort aux vaches! Sic semper tyrannis as the
governor of N.C. said to the governor of S.C. as they hurried to Warm
Springs to cure themselves of the gout—

Yrs
Dos

To John Howard Lawson

[On board S.S. *Paris*
Spring(?) *1925*]

I'm still uneasy about Nirvana—not exactly about its impressiveness
on the stage—it cant help but be enormously impressive—the people are
terribly real and eight or ten feet high—but there is something about it

that sticks in my gullet. Maybe I had preconceived notions about Nirvana—certainly your otherworld of El Greco saints impaled on bleeding chromos of St. Mary Alacoque (or whatever her name was) is very far from the soothing vacuum of the Buddhist Nirvana. The thing is one gets so caught up in the play that one rebels against its inferences as if one were one of the characters. I dont say that that isn't perfectly all right—but I think it will account for a great many people's alarm and confusion with regard to it.

Anyway actually produced on stage, the result may be quite different.

I think what worries me about it is that it not only paints the decay of art-science, but it gives the prophecy in the next step—and gives me a feeling of being hustled.

The S.S. Paris is excellent, full of very hearty people, miners and chinamen—The sea is fine, the wind northwest and I sleep like sixty.

Look I borrowed twenty bucks off Sue at the last minute. Will you please return them to her.

Did you hear that Harpers thought "three a day" meant three men a day. I ask you isn't it time somebody were shot off in a rocket. Also they thought "fanny" meant penis—Ecrasez l'infame—

Love
Dos

To John Howard Lawson

[Antibes
Summer 1925]

Dear Jack—The Guild as I have long suspected are the illegitimate offspring of female dogs. Pernicious anemia. I'm afraid that like Processional Nirvana will have to cool its heels a while until someone has the nerve to do it.

I'm as happy as a blue bird and twice as musical, having only the faintest traces of rheumatism, and free from the slightest literary itch. Nearly got thrown up on the mole at Savona in a wild storm. At the last moment when we were all ready to throw ourselves in the surf crying Mort aux vaches or Viva il fascio according to taste we were thrown a rope by a tug and hauled rather ignominiously into the harbor.

This real estate disease is really becoming serious. Suppose there's an earthquake. What will you and Ladle [Adelaide Lawson] do? One house is all very well—but a city block is distinctly exaggerating—I suppose it'll be the Woolworth building next.

Savona is a dead town—do you remember how swell it seemed in 1917—? It was communist and everybody has been killed by the fascisti or chased away. The most fantastically sinister place I've ever been in. We got into the fascist café and had drinks with the leading gunmen. An extraordinary set of thugs. All the time we were there not a soul in the allegro diurno except ourselves, no one in the restaurants, on the streets, around the harbor full of rotting steamers, except for the one café that was full of obscene roistering, overfed bruisers tossing down glasses of crème de menthe, and morbid looking school boys, sons of bankers, playing chess and drinking tea. The head of the black shirt squadron let us shake the hand that had that morning shaken hands with Mussolini at Parma.

Look about the Garbageman—tell the Lavatory people they can do it if they let Ed direct it. It'll get him down from Boston anyway. I'm tired of hearing about it. Also tell em to get busy on it right away.

Jesus there are some beautiful towns on the Italian Riviera—The people who built 'em really worked over the architecture. Porto Maurizio is all one great, superbly planned stage setting.

I won these postcards in a raffle on the Paris.

Still trying to get sent to Morocco where it seems Abd el Krim didn't shoot his prime minister out of a cannon after all. My best to everybody—

Dos

Postcard to E. E. Cummings

[Oran, Algeria
November 10, 1925]

Cummings—

Found a baby elephant engraved on the rocks near where the camel trail goes into Fignig. If it hadn't been part of a fifty ton boulder I'd bring him home to you. Monsieur le Colonel à la barbe fleurie says its neolithic. Bien à vous

Dos

To Rumsey Marvin

[Provincetown
April 1926]

Dear Rummy—thanks for an extraordinarily fine letter. I feel as if I'd been to Wilmington myself.

I never understood exactly why people get engaged—The only time I ever did the most disastrous things happened—but I feel that there's a great deal to be said for immediate matrimony always. If I once got started I'd probably have to become a mormon to cover my confusion. What I mean is that if he and she are crazy about each other it is sheer tempting God to stay apart, come what may. And if people arent crazy about each other being engaged wont help them. But my private life is such a disorganized menagerie of illfed desires that I'm no authority on Hymen—St. Paul had the last word anyway, when he said it was better to marry than burn.

Anyway I dont see why matrimony should interfere with Mexico or walking trips in the Andes or whatnot—I admit that most people use it as an anaesthetic—but it could be a stimulant.

Anyway we'll see how things are in the merry month of May— maybe we could get in a minor walkingtrip before your set of engagements.

Do write some more about Wilmington—

Yrs
Jack

[Louisville
December 1926]

Rummy—

I was awfully sorry not to get out to your place before leaving but I was so harried heckled and harassed by various trains of events that I couldn't get to see anybody. I've been wishing you were with me these last few days on my long solitary walk out from Staunton Virginia. I had three days of superb Indian Summer weather across the mountains, walked about twenty five miles a day, bathed in sulphur springs, ate a lot of corn bread—then it turned very grey and cold and sleety and I got on the train for Louisville in a little town called Covington—arrived in Louisville last night somewhat spavined and stiff and spent this morning in bed in the lap of luxury reading the Gideon's Bible.

Louisville is a grey sprawling redbrick dingy kind of place, full of darkies and jews. The Ohio flows tawny between the bridges under the sleety wind, the water looks dense and solider than the misty banks and the smudged blocks of buildings. Everything smells as if the chimney was on fire. I rather like it here. But I'm leaving tonight for St. Louis Dallas, San Antonio & Mexico—I'm damn sorry you're not along

Yrs
Jack

Address American Express City of Mexico Mex

Postcard to Edmund Wilson

[St. Louis
December 6, 1926]

When I was registering at the hotel in Staunton, Va. a man came up to me, winked his eye and said "I see you're a reading man . . . fond of good books . . . You get Bellamy's Looking Backwards", whereupon he disappeared. What would you do?

yrs Dos

To Rumsey Marvin

[Mexico City
December 1926–January 1927]

Say Rummy—I wish you'd come down with me—everything is pretty darn swell. Mexico City is a darn sight more interesting than I'd expected—Everything, people, air, food, drink, tobacco is of the first water—And everything is exciting and comical and full of drunkenness and fornication. I'm in Jalapa at this moment a most beautiful little town up in wooded flowery mountains. Just came up from Vera Cruz. Everything's so Goddamned pictorial it takes my breath away—Everybody carries a gun and people shoot each other if they dont like the way somebody balances a tooth pick—in spite of that life is very pleasant and calm, and people are very amiable.

Wonderful bathing and mint juleps in Vera Cruz. Here one dances the danzon and tango—The latter I cant manipulate but the danzon is a marvellous dance. And everything really is Indian—much more than I had expected—marvellous looking old Indian women in the markets, beautiful girls of a rich cinnamon color. They say there are places where people still shoot bears with bows and arrows and where the boas are so tame they act as watchdogs in the houses and rock the baby's cradle with their tails—

I hope your mother's all right. Do remember me to your mother and father and Judy.

Honestly for general merriment hospitality and liquor, Mexico's got Wilmington lashed to the mast—

Let me hear from you

Hoping to engineer great muleback trips soon—

Yrs
Dos

Remember me to Colonels C.D. & Leamy when you see them— Jalapa beats Ocracoke!

To John Howard Lawson

[Mexico
February(?) 1927]

Dear Jack—I wish somebody would enlighten me about these theatrical events. Just have a letter from you saying Loud Speaker opening March 2. Hurrah but I'd like very much to know what is up and where. I think I must have lost some letters; anyway I'm in complete darkness as to events in New York. I wish I felt like going back there—but I cant imagine what I'd do if I got back besides going to the opening of Loud Speaker—which will probably be a function in itself worth attending.

My play isn't finished and I cant seem to get any writing done And I am in a great state of mental and moral decay—despite the fact that everything down here is continuously enormously interesting.

But what's the cast? Who are the actors? Who's putting up the money? What is it called? I wrote Adelaide asking her for details but I haven't heard anything.

Ed's [Massey] a damn fool to continue puttering around the suburbs of Boston, but if he likes it I suppose its his look out.

Its amazing how long it takes letters to get down here Yours just received took ten days—So on second thoughts I'll send a wire—because if there is anything I could be useful in I'd just as soon appear—but I'm afraid its too late now to be of any use anyway So let me conclude this letter full of conundrums—which is an exact picture of the state of mind created by the juxtaposition of a gloomy individual with a fantastically brilliant day and a too large lunch too hot with chile washed down by too much beer, said lunch eaten in company with an exceedingly depressing A.F. of L. investigator of "conditions." talk about the Degradation of the Democratic Dogma.

Anyhow I'm as dumb as an ostrich that's had its feathers plucked and should be delighted to engage in any conceivable enterprise.

Yrs
Dos

To Robert Hillyer

[New York
Spring 1927]

Robert you old pater familias I would have written before but I couldn't think of what to say that would be most suitable for the perusal of expectant parents. Tried to find it in a correspondence book and in the little DONT WRITE TELEGRAPH booklet so kindly lent by the Western Union, but all I could find were congratulations on graduation. The little brats do linger so. I cant very well blame them for being reluctant, when I think of what they have in store. They have to wait so long for the more valuable things such as shadroe rum punch and fornication. Imagine having nothing but milk for a year or two, and having to go to school and take Government 1. My only suggestion is that you and Dorothy start reading Gibbon one starting at the beginning and the other at the end. When you meet in the middle something may have been discovered to have accidentally happened. I certainly will come up when you've a little recovered. Give Dorothy & the Unknown Stranger my best—I dont know about Port Jefferson—I go down there quite often when in New York—There's a chance I'll go to the West Indies in June and I've written asking about an island on the Maine coast but that may all fall through. If you went to P. Jefferson it certainly would be an added inducement to frequent it.

Love
Dos

To Ernest Hemingway (1898–1961), *the famous novelist, whom Dos first met when both were in Italy in the spring of 1918, then became a good friend of in 1924. These two very different men remained inti-*

mate until 1937, when arguments about the Spanish Civil War caused
a falling out that was never really patched up.

[New York
March 27, 1927]

For Christus' swoote sake Hem you old ostrich, Why didn't you wire
me that you wanted to go to Mexico. Geezus I hate mighthabeens—

I'm in deeper and deeper in the drahma every moment. I'm now
one of five directors of a little Otto Kahn-undernourished playhouse on
W.52nd street (near an excellent old fashion German saloon and beer-
swiggery) I do a lot of (against union rules) carrying about & painting
of scenery and switching on and off of lights which is very entertaining—but I dont feel its my life work, quite. Anyway it keeps me from
writing or worrying and I'm merry as a cricket. Why dont you come
out of those Parisian swamps, Hem—? I'm hoping to be able to go to
Mexico in May, again, but I'm not quite sure. Anyway New York is
getting to be just like Paris—only more exciting and really synthetic
gin isn't a damn bit worse than Anis Deloso—We even have Anthiel,
and Pound & Max Eastman are slated to arrive.

Honestly—Hem—I think that publication is the honestest and
easiest method of getting rid of bum writing—Unpublished stuff just
festers and you get to be like a horse that's pistol shy or whatever they
call it when they are wonderful horses but never can start a race. I'm
all for living by writing & making the best living possible out of what
one writes, but the thing is that one has got to have people to throw up
red flags (like Gammer's Goat) when one has produced a talented and
daintily-scented turd—which is the great danger with all us guys—Still
its better to do that than to get all full of romance and ingrown
literature like Pound   In Our Time was a goddamn good thing to
publish. So was The Sun Also. Its better to publish than burn as St.
Paul said.

Did Gerald & Sara go to Russia?

Let me know where you'll be in late May—I havent an idea myself
(if I can go back to Mexico) but I dont want to spend summer round
New York—Would even consider Spain Will have a hell of a lot of
work to do rewriting play.

Love to Pauline & Hadley when you write

Yrs
Dos

To Upton Sinclair (1878–1968), *the political novelist, whom Dos apparently first got to know when he was with the New Playwrights Theatre. They never became close friends, but each admired the other's ideas and work.*

New Playwrights Theatre Inc.
52nd Street Theatre
306 West 52nd Street
April 24th 1927

Dear Upton Sinclair,

Have you heard about the N.P.T.? We are trying to start a popular revolutionary theatre. This spring we have put on an experimental season of two plays, a play by Basshe about a negro religious revival, called Earth, and a political satire by John Lawson, Loudspeaker. Both plays raised considerable fuss, were righteously panned by the critics, and played to not entirely empty houses. Next we are planning a bang-up revolutionary season, revolutionary in social import, in direction, acting and scenery. We are only doing American plays. We want to open the theatre with Singing Jailbirds. Would you let us do it on the usual Dramatist's Guild contract? We are pretty hard up for cash, so we are not paying advances. On the other hand I think we can promise you a pretty good production—certainly a novel and experimental production.

Now about the play. I feel that considerable rearrangement of scenes, some cutting and possibly a little additional writing will be necessary to put across the superbly simple and fundamental drama of it. Would you mind if I undertook that? In the next mail I shall send you a synopsis and plan of the production. We would begin rehearsals about Sept 15 and open about Oct 15. We want to introduce a lot of singing and mass action into it. Could you send us some more wobbly songs? We need some gayer more satirical songs for contrast.

I hope you'll let us go ahead with the play as we are very enthusiastic about it. The thing is that for the novel type of production we are planning, we've got to have a pretty free hand with the text. We have not the slightest intention of denaturing it or taking away from any of its value as protest. Trust us for that.

Sincerely yours
John Dos Passos

To Upton Sinclair

> New Playwrights Theatre Inc.
> 52nd Street Theatre
> 306 West 52nd Street
> *May 1—[19]27*

Dear Upton Sinclair—

I wrote you to Pasadena, not noticing that you had moved to Long Beach, asking if we could do Singing Jailbirds as our first production next fall. The letter was probably forwarded to you.

These are, so far, rough plans for the production—

To open with a sort of tableau of the crowd milling round the jail, of a parade of strikers and cops busting it up—Then to go into the scene into the District Attorney's office—

We want to run in Act II scenes one and two of Act III ending the act on the nightmare scene of the abortion. Then run as a third and last act from Scene III (in the hole), the roadhouse scene running directly into the Hall of Hate scene, which would syncopate with Scene V (in the hole) and Scene I (IV) Keeping the whole play in one movement up to Red Adams' death—An intermission would let the audience down too much. We want to cut Scene IV (Act IV) for the same reason that it breaks up the mood too much—and why sugar the pill? We are trying to work up the musical end of it a great deal. Please let us know by return mail if we can go ahead on it and we'll send you a Dramatists' Guild Contract

> Sincerely yours
> John Dos Passos

To Upton Sinclair

> 110 Columbia Heights,
> Brooklyn, N.Y.
> *[May 1927]*

Dear Upton Sinclair,

I haven't thanked you yet for letting us do your play. We are thinking seriously of getting the skypilot to act in it as you suggest.

We havent the slightest objection to other productions by amateur groups—it's amazing to me that it hasn't been done already—although we'd rather not have any one do it near New York until say November.

We haven't definitely worked out the plan of production yet, and it would only be a very successful season that would send us on the road. I'll write Paul Spier a little later about our ideas of staging it. I havent read 'Hell' but shall as soon as I can lay hands on a copy.

I'll keep you in touch with what goes on.

About the Sacco-Vanzetti petition we'd gladly cooperate with you in anything; send us something and we'll sign on the dotted line. I'm pretty hopeless about getting any life out of that corpse the Author's League.

Yours sincerely,
John Dos Passos

Telegram to Edmund Wilson

Boston, Mass.
August 19, 1927

Edmund Wilson
Peaked Hill Bars C G Station Provincetown Mass Need picketters and speakers for last Saczetti protest staying here

Dos Passos

Postcard to Edmund Wilson

[Provincetown
September 19, 1927]

Dear Bunny—terribly sorry to have been rude about your kind invitation to a party at Provincetown—but you cant imagine how queerly your wire jangled my nerves—Jesus X Columbus—man didn't you realize that we were all virtually mad up in Boston—You try battering your head against a stone wall sometime—Let me know when you get back to N.Y.—and we'll have a dinner

Dos

To Ernest Hemingway

[New York
Fall 1927]

hem—Great to get your letter—So Papa Primo wont let his little innocents hear about the atrocities in the U.S.A. I'm not sure he's not right—Well its all over now and gone down in History—as far down as the public press can push it and hundreds of aviators have thrown themselves into the sea and everybody feels fine. . . . What about this goddamn human race anyway? I have finished my play and am busy doing sets for this so called theatre and I hope Tunney gets licked— You are in the mouths of all the village teafighters wherever one goes. If you came to New York and went to lunch at the Algonquin there'd be people tramping in the hall and police lines on 44th Street—Speaking of that cesspool it was damn decent of H. Broun to lose his job over Sacco-Vanzetti—dont you think so? Besides the guy delivered himself of four or five excellent sentences and was as firm in the path of prejudice as the feet of a Lowell ambling to a hanging etc.

Are you coming to New York or through it—? found a fine island on the Maine Coast with an empty village on it—Cranberry Island— I'm tied down until the theatre goes belly up or uptown—Were now on Cherry Lane & Commerce St. (God save us He wont)—I hope the communistas kick the asparagus out of the American Legion on the 19*th* which is tomorrow

Want to go to Russia and China—Let me hear where you'll be this winter—Don's going all Hollywood—maybe he's just off me.

Love to Pauline,

Yrs

Dos

"WE STAND DEFEATED AMERICA"

January 1928–December 1932

With the New Playwrights Theatre struggling to stay alive, Dos remained in New York through most of the winter, heading down in April to Key West to enjoy the company of Hemingway, the friends he had gathered around him, and perhaps meeting Katharine Smith, who at some point passed through on her way back from a trip to Mexico. She had been a friend of Hemingway's from his childhood days in Michigan and treated him rather like a younger brother. Dos, whenever it was he did meet her, was smitten, for in August 1929 they were married. Katy, more than four years older than Dos, was born October 26, 1891. She was a pretty, humorous woman, perhaps wittier than he, certainly just as deeply committed to friendships. She could make Dos feel at ease and her lively mind constantly charmed him. After her death in 1947, Dos' friend from Greenwich Village and Key West days, Canby Chambers, told him that Katy "always seemed to me so *alive.*" He remembered the two of them often playful, "calling each other names like 'Kingfish' and 'Possum,' " 'and he recalled to Dos that "after your marriage you brought her to see me in the American Hospital of Paris. She gave me pussy-willows. These were just right, like so many things about Katy." She too was a writer—of articles for women's magazines; with Edith Shay of a book about Cape Cod, *Down the Cape,* in 1936; and again with her of a novel, *The Private Adventure of Captain Shaw,* in 1945.

From Key West Dos wrote Stewart Mitchell that he was "sailing in early May with Russia more or less in view and not coming back till late in the fall." His reason for going to Russia, he said in *The Best Times,* was to study the theatre; but of course it was also to examine the socialist society which might offer an appealing alternative to the capitalistic system which had unjustly murdered Sacco and Vanzetti. By the first of June he was in France, by July 23 in Helsinki, after stopping off in Berlin for a few days, and by the end of July or early August he arrived in Leningrad.

He stayed in Russia all that fall; many aspects of the country he liked. He admired the people, and he ran into Dr. Horsley Gantt, an American who had been in Leningrad working under the guidance of Pavlov for seven years and would soon after return to the United States to set up a Pavlovian research laboratory at Johns Hopkins University. They liked each other immediately, and Gantt remained one of Dos' closest friends from then on. Dos traveled widely—he described his journeys in both *In All Countries* and *The Best Times*—and met actors, writers, and film directors like Pudovkin and Eisenstein, whose theories and camera work had an important effect on the technique of *U.S.A.* Gantt and he took a particularly memorable walking trip through part of the Caucasus Mountains, beginning near the town of Kasbek and ending after several days, numerous adventures, and a good deal of hunger in the town of Kutaisi. Dos then returned by himself to Moscow where there was much to see and to absorb. But, he liked to recall afterwards, even then he could not feel committed to Russian communism, and as his train pulled away from the Moscow station late that fall, he could not answer an actress friend who demanded of him, "Are you for us or against us?" He departed without responding.

The New Playwrights were into their final season when Dos got back to New York. His *Airways, Inc.* was to open the middle of February, 1929, so he immediately became occupied with preparations for it. The work was exasperating; it was at this time that Em Jo Basshe fired Ed Massey, Dos' good friend who was directing *Airways, Inc.* Dos stayed on, however, helping with his play and even putting up some of the money needed to keep it running a month. But after it closed, he resigned, explaining his reasons in a letter to the two directors with whom he remained most friendly, Jack Lawson and Francis Faragoh. If the actual experience had been painful, it had been instructive to him because he had developed further the techniques of expressionism which he incorporated in *U.S.A.*, and instructive to the general public because it had introduced new dramatic form and content. Summing up a piece entitled "Did the New Playwrights Theatre Fail?" which appeared in the *New Masses* the following August, he wrote:

> I think the New Playwrights Theatre failed, in the first place because authors are largely too preoccupied with their own works to make good producers and secondly because the problems involved were not seen clearly enough in the beginning. But the fact that it existed makes the next attempt in the same direction that much easier. One thing is certain: the time for half way measures in ideas or methods has gone, if indeed, it ever was.

When *Airways, Inc.* closed he could not wait to get away from New York. Hemingway had been urging him to come to Key West for some excellent fishing. Down he went, taking the chance to clear his brain of drama so he could be on with *The 42nd Parallel*. At least part of March and the first days of April he spent there. Hemingway's group was fun to be with—the Charles Thompsons, Waldo Peirce, and the local people like Bra Sanders, who became their fishing guide. But it was Katy Smith whom Dos really attended to. They had a glorious time that spring, fishing, poking around a Key West still largely unknown to tourists, and savoring good talk free of the ideologies that had so slanted conversations among the dramatists in New York. When Dos headed north in April, he and Katy had likely decided to get married later in the year. In any event, he settled down first to finish the new novel, writing Marvin on April 29 from Erwinna, Pennsylvania, that he was "living all alone with a small brindled kitten, . . . and working like a blue streak." Later that spring he went to Provincetown, then at the end of June headed to Otisco Lake, a summer resort near Syracuse, New York, to spend some time with Dudley Poore while on his way to Chicago and Michigan, where Katy was. He spent a few weeks with Poore, writing and taking long walks every afternoon, once going all the way around the lake, a distance of some twenty to twenty-five miles.

By July 26 he was in Chicago, for he wrote back to Poore that he was working in the newspaper files of a library there, no doubt digging up materials for the "Newsreels" of *The 42nd Parallel* and checking factual data for the biographies as well. Whether he had yet been to Michigan to see Katy again is not clear, but at any rate in early August they traveled together to Maine, where they were married in the little coastal village of Ellsworth. They took a short trip to Quebec, then settled down for a month near Wiscasset, Maine, Dos reading proof on the novel and thinking ahead to a European trip.

After most of the fall in Provincetown, they boarded the *Roussillon* on December 5—"sitting on the dock waiting for the Roussillon to sail," he wrote Stewart Mitchell that day. By mid-December they were in Paris, where they joined the Hemingways, saw much of the Fitzgeralds, toured some of the cafés with the French poet Blaise Cendrars, and planned a trip to Montana-Vernala near Sierre to be with the Murphys for Christmas. Then early in 1930 they headed for Schruns: "Swell trip from Sierre—Berne—Zurich Buchs—stopped in Feldkirch &

Bludenz due to bad connections but worth it—wish to hell you were along," he wrote Hemingway in January. Soon they headed back to France and spent a week with Cendrars at Montpazier, "in swellest country I ever saw in France and jesus the eats," he raved to Hemingway in another postcard, "wild duck, hare truffles pâté de foie—swell wine à volonté and prix du repas f 12. Cendrars is a hell of a good guy—off for Spain & I hope sunshine."

In March Katy and he took a small ship, the *Antonio Lopez,* from Cadiz and had a lazy voyage that took them to the Canary Islands, Mexico, and eventually to Havana, whence they went to Key West for more fishing with Hemingway. On the trip over Dos had been translating Cendrars' volume of poems, *Le Panama et Mes Sept Oncles,* which was published the following year. This was important work, he believed, as he explained in his foreword to the American edition:

> The poetry of Blaise Cendrars was part of the creative tidal wave that spread over the world from the Paris of before the last European war. Under various tags: futurism, cubism, vorticism, modernism, most of the best work in the arts in our time has been the direct product of this explosion, that had an influence in its sphere comparable with that of the October revolution in social organization and politics and the Einstein formula in physics. Cendrars and Apollinaire, poets, were on the first cubist barricades with the group that included Picasso, Modigliani, Marinetti, Chagall; that profoundly influenced Maiakovsky, Meyerhold, Eisenstein; whose ideas carom through Joyce, Gertrude Stein, T. S. Eliot (first published in Wyndham Lewis's "Blast"). The music of Stravinski and Prokofieff and Diageleff's Ballet hail from this same Paris already in the disintegration of victory, as do the windows of Saks Fifth Avenue, skyscraper furniture, the Lenin Memorial in Moscow, the paintings of Diego Rivera in Mexico City and the newritz styles of advertizing in American magazines.

It is an interesting document, reading like a roll call of the people who influenced him.

The summer of 1930 was spent in Provincetown, working on *1919.* Dos spoke out against what he termed "The monied reaction that is fast obliterating all trace of free institutions in America," when he wrote in August to the *New Republic* to raise money on behalf of the Emergency Committee for the Southern Political Prisoners. The committee was trying to defend six young people whom, Dos asserted, the state of Georgia was "trying to execute . . . under old insurrection laws passed during the civil war." He could never bring himself to become a practiced public speaker, but particularly during the 1930's he worked—as he did in this instance—for left-wing labor causes.

Hemingway was in Montana that fall, hunting at the L Bar T ranch of Lawrence Nordquist, near Cooke City. While Katy stayed with relatives, Dos went out, arriving at Billings on October 21. Though he was too nearsighted to be any good, he got a license to hunt elk and had a go—unsuccessfully—at downing one of the animals. They hunted and feasted until October 31, when with another friend, Floyd Allington, they packed into Hemingway's Ford roadster and headed for Billings. Near there at dusk the next night Hemingway, who was driving, was blinded by the lights of an oncoming car. He swerved; the Ford lurched off the road and flipped over. Allington and Dos climbed out, extracted Hemingway, who was pinned behind the wheel, and discovered his right arm was badly broken. They were able to get him to a hospital in Billings, and Dos telegraphed Pauline Hemingway in Arkansas. Later he drove the car to Columbus, Montana, for repairs, waited to meet Pauline's train, and then left only after the mangled arm was set and the incision sewn up, returning to Provincetown as the year ended.

From there he wrote Edmund Wilson, praising his piece "An Appeal to Progressives" in the *New Republic* when it appeared in January. He and Katy took a trip into Mexico in February, driving over from Jacksonville in a Model A Ford, but were back in Provincetown by April so he could continue work on *1919*. He finished the manuscript that spring and hoped for fall publication; however, Harper's for complex reasons turned down the book, and it was not until March 1932 that the volume came out with Harcourt, Brace.

The intriguing tale of Dos' break with Harper centered around the derogatory profile of J. P. Morgan, which was not altered when it appeared in the volume Harcourt, Brace published. A number of years before, the Harper company had been reorganized, a move involving refinancing, for which its president and editor of *Harper's Magazine,* Thomas B. Wells, had turned to Morgan. The loan had been negotiated with the house of Morgan through Thomas Lamont and was extended when Harper's finances were shaky. At the time the manuscript for *1919* appeared, the loan had been retired, but understandably the firm did not want to be in the position of attacking its benefactor. Dos, equally understandably, did not want to back down. Gene Saxton, who had brought Dos to Harper in 1923, was caught in the middle. Undoubtedly he argued for publication but was voted down. So Dos moved to Harcourt, Brace, though he and Saxton remained warm friends. After the episode, Wells—who by 1931 had retired from Harper but remained a stockholder and advisor to the firm—wrote Saxton from Paris about the affair, in a letter dated December 11, 1931:

> Dear Gene: While I am not posted as to what course you fellows have taken in the Dos Passos matter, I can imagine how you cursed me when my cable was received at the office. Sorry, I could not have taken any other position. It is difficult to be a business man and a gentleman at the same time as you have often heard me argue. But when the opportunity comes to be both, I think one ought to grasp it. If you have let the book go, we have probably sacrificed a good deal. Just how much I don't know. But we have played the game decently and have nothing to be ashamed of—and we have kept a good friend. If I had cabled "Splendid by all means publish", I could never have forgiven myself for that would have been "mucker ball" of the sort I don't want to learn how to play. As to the business man end of the argument, I think it is damn sound business to keep on terms of easy friendship with the world's strongest private banking house whose influence extends far more widely than any other among the banks of New York.
>
>   I am all for freedom of speech and uncontrolled publishing policy. Never in a single instance did Morgan try to control or influence us. He was far too wise for that and when he was bedevilled by our creditors he merely growled and told Lamont to see if something couldn't be done with the business. He could have called his loans any day (they were all demand notes) and then followed Morrow's advice & handed it over to Doubleday. His son could have done the same thing—and told me that unless I could do something—and quickly—that was what he *would* do. But he was too damn decent to force us & twice (I think) extended my option. And that's that. I know you hate the rich—like hell. I have an ardent dislike for almost all mankind. Don't get savage about this episode. That spoils your insides and reduces your liquor capacity. So cheer up & forgive me.

While Harper was struggling with this problem, Dos went with Theodore Dreiser and others to Harlan County, Kentucky, in the fall of 1931 to investigate the situation of the miners there. The conditions were abominable; Dreiser's committee worked hard to gather testimony, which Dos later put together, interspersed with his own narrative, in *Harlan Miners Speak*. The trip was instructive, and he went so far as to try to speak out on behalf of the miners. His long time friend Harold Weston recalled Dos, shy and disheveled, standing before an audience in Webster Hall in New York that fall and beginning, "Gosh, I don't know what to say." He gave a brief talk, but such was not his forte. Dos had some second thoughts about the way the Communist party manipulated people and situations to further its own ends, so when Earl Browder, head of the Communist Central Committee in New York, wanted him to return to Kentucky to stand trial for "criminal syndicalism," he refused. As early as 1932, deep in the depression and before Roosevelt's New Deal undertook reform, Dos was becoming less tolerant of the Communists' tactics, although he remained sympathetic to their concern for the laboring man.

On February 4, 1932, Dos and Katy left New York, first taking a ship to Havana, then staying with Hemingway for four days in Key West before sailing to Mexico. While in Key West he read Hemingway's manuscript of *Death in the Afternoon* and praised it in his next letter to Ernest, written as he and Katy prepared to leave their ship at Progreso. Probably while he was in Miami awaiting ship to Mexico he answered Malcolm Cowley's letter asking him what had happened to Mac, a key figure in *The 42nd Parallel* who never reappears, and also asking what Dos might say about the general trend of the work.

From Progreso they traveled through Guatemala, then visited Tehuantepec and Vera Cruz on their way to Mexico City. By the end of the first week in April, they had arrived in El Paso, from whence they took a train to Tucson, drove to the west coast, visiting Jack Lawson in Santa Monica, and then headed back for Provincetown, getting there by the end of the month. Hemingway had written a letter praising *1919* and offering some literary advice and had sent it to Mexico, but Dos didn't receive it until May in Provincetown. Ernest had high praise for the second volume, warning only against trying to make characters perfect, by which he meant trying to make them too much symbols and too little sweating, grunting humanity. And he wisely warned about being didactic—doing good—directly in the fiction. If, he concluded his advice, Dos could show life truly, then the good would follow. "A writer who writes straight is the architect of history," Dos declared in the introduction he wrote that June for the Modern Library edition of *Three Soldiers*. Just so, Hemingway was asserting, and Dos should not let himself be swayed by all the pressures

on him as a leading writer and a political activist. When Dos wrote the
introduction, he admitted that Hemingway's remarks were his inspiration.

That same April Edmund Wilson sent him a copy of a manifesto he,
Waldo Frank, and Lewis Mumford had written, in hopes that Theodore Dreiser, Sherwood Anderson, Robert Frost, Paul Green, Van
Wyck Brooks, Evelyn Scott, Edna St. Vincent Millay, and Dos would
sign. Dos agreed, although he did not like the "Thirteenth Street"
rhetoric and changed it some—the reference being to the Communist
party offices in New York. Where the draft spoke of "abolishing all
classes based on material wealth," he rephrased the statement to read,
"The producers"—by whom he meant the laborers—"must get control
of the machinery of production, as the necessary instrument for abolishing the power of money." The whole piece really did read like a
Party declaration. Perhaps the drafters realized this, because apparently
it never appeared.

For the *New Republic* he went to Chicago to cover the Republican
and Democratic conventions; he was fascinated by them. It was there,
observing Huey Long in action, that he got the idea for the character
Chuck Crawford in *Number One*. Certainly it was there that he got
his first exposure to Franklin Roosevelt, whose New Deal would
increasingly appeal to him as the 1930's progressed and he became more
disenchanted with the left wing. But that was later, and when the
November elections came around, he cast a vote for Foster and Ford,
the Communist party candidates for president and vice-president. That
was nothing but a protest, he recalled in *The Theme Is Freedom,* for
he "hadn't quite recovered from the plague on both your houses attitude toward the two conflicting systems."

It is worth examining his political position at this time, seemingly his
most left-wing period. Communists had every reason to believe he was
one of them. Granville Hicks, himself a Party member until disillu-
sioned by the Soviet-Nazi pact in 1939, when writing about "The
Politics of John Dos Passos" in 1950 for *Antioch Review,* asserted that
"no one had more influence on the leftward swing of the intellectuals
in the early '30's." Radicals saw what they wanted to in his work
which, hypercritical of American society, suited their needs. They
simply overlooked or reinterpreted his tendency toward liberalism and
individualism although he stated his position explicitly. For in the
New Republic in 1930 he had called himself "a middle-class liberal,

whether I like it or not," and he located himself politically as neither a member of the Communist party nor a pro-Capitalist. In 1932 he referred to himself as a "middleclass intellectual" and a " 'camp follower' of radical parties." To the question, "Do you believe that becoming a communist deepens an artist's work?" he answered, "I don't see how a novelist or historian could be a party member under present conditions."

So though he may have seemed committed to the radical left he was not. "It was somewhere during the early New Deal that I rejoined the United States," he wrote in *The Theme Is Freedom*. "I had seceded privately the night Sacco and Vanzetti were executed. It was not that I had rejoined the communists. . . . I wasn't joining anybody. I had seceded into my private conscience like Thoreau in Concord jail." Certainly seceding into his private conscience was more characteristic of him. He was not a "joiner" but a restless, shy loner, an artist more than a systemized political thinker. What seemed to some to be vacillation was his effort to find where he could stand among the political and economic ideas with which he sympathized.

To F. Scott Fitzgerald

[New York
April 1928]

Scott—will you and Zelda please sit down and write two mild little notes asking clemency. If that kid ought to be in jail we ought all to be there—Yrs Dos

[what follows is a typed letter Dos sent to numerous friends]

At the instigation of a certain George L. Darte, professional patriot linked up with various redbaiting organizations, the Daily Worker was prosecuted last summer for publishing a poem supposed to be obscene by David Gordon, a boy of eighteen, at present holding a scholarship of the Zona Gale Foundation at the University of Wisconsin. Gordon and the Daily Worker were found guilty of violating section 1141 of the Penal Law. David Gordon was sentenced to an indeterminate term at the City Reformatory. That means a possible term of three years. By the accident of being subject to the New York City parole law it was made possible to punish this boy to an extent far beyond the provisions of the penal law. Section 1141 sets a maximum penalty of one year but the Parole Law applicable to New York City alone authorizes the Commission to keep Gordon in jail as much as three years. Three years of the company of young criminals of every description, of beating by prison guards, a grim substitute for the college education he had earned by his obvious precocious talent as a writer. He is at present serving his term at the Reformatory. If you read the enclosed excerpts from the remarks of the judges you will understand the atmosphere of meanness and spite that surrounded the trial. The boy's real crime was that he was writing for a communist publication and that he was a Russian Jew. If this is the penalty for obscenity and disgust with America, most of our best writers should be in jail at this moment.

The important thing now is not to complain about fair play or freedom of speech, but to get him out. The length of the sentence is up to the Parole Board. A letter from you to the Parole Board, Municipal Building, New York City, will probably have considerable weight. Please write at once. Naturally a plea on the ground of the boy's youth will carry more with the Parole Board than abstract complaints about the obvious infringement on human rights involved in this case. The courts are always right. Even if you think it is a bad poem you must realize that the penalty is grotesquely disproportionate. Mr. Darte and his friends will do their best to keep Gordon in jail. They must be shown that there are enough men and women in New York with a sense of humanity and fair play to outweigh them.

Please send a copy of any letter you write to Gordon's attorney, Joseph R. Brodsky, 41 Union Square, New York City.

                                                    John Dos Passos

To Robert Hillyer
[Attached to typed copy of same letter sent to Fitzgerald and including a copy of David Gordon's poem.]

> [On board ship to Key West
> *April 1928*]

Dear Robert—

Just sending you these little enclosures to keep you up with the progress of liberty and the pursuit of happiness. You wont like the poem, but do you think it deserves three years in jail?—particularly as in the case of Maxwell Bodenheim, who had a good lawyer, the court ruled that the author was *not* liable. So do write just a little note (on fancy college stationery) asking the Parole Board for clemency. Zona Gale has been very decent about it and has written them that the University of Wisconsin was keeping his scholarship open. Unfortunately the copies of the rescript of the trial have given out, but you can take my word for it that two Irish Catholic Justices were as stinking as they could possibly be under the circumstances and neither the poor kid nor his rotten lawyer who gave away the case as lawyers usually do (I mean Joseph not CD Williams who took the case up later and is a good guy) had a chance to defend themselves.

Robert, I suppose its my own fault for never getting to Hartford that I never see you and have not yet laid eyes on the little Hillyer, but believe me that I have spent a year of great confusion and hard work and have never had a moment. The theatre and trying to write and private worries have almost driven me distracted—So you must forgive me for not writing and not showing hide nor hair. After all you might have looked me up. There's nothing like an accusation to draw a red herring across the path of guilt, as Daniel Webster said.

I'm off for Russia (I hope) early in May. At the moment I'm in a little jerkwater boat full of seasick passengers being conveyed (I hardly know why) to Key West.

Love to you and the missus and the little Hillyer—

As ever
Dos

To E. E. Cummings

[On the Volga River

September 1928]

Dear Cummings—Navigating the Volga with considerable success—
rapidly approaching Astrakhan, the capital of Caviar; things in these
parts are pretty darn swell—But we are coming to a dock—I must go
and work—The dock was only a section of the Autonomous German
Republic of the Volga full of watermelons. I live in great state on this
boat, breakfasting on tea and caviar at a little table on deck and continuing to drink tea for the rest of the day. When the boat stops I swim
and the rest of the time I worry over the Russian language and try to
converse about where one republic begins and another ends.

   The most interesting and lively people I met in Leningrad and
Moscow were the movie directors. They, as I suppose is natural, say
that the theatre is capoot. Eisenstein says that Meyerhold has ruined
the theatre by carrying each of his productions so far in a logical
direction that it is impossible to go further. Certainly the one Meyerhold show I've seen so far was damn fine (Roar China) but I dont see
that its the end of anything except perhaps Meyerhold's own energy.
Eisenstein is worried over the talking movies because he says he is
afraid they may become an art, and bring all the worst features of the
stage back on the silver screen. He thinks the first stages will be
all right and simply silly, but that then there will be a danger of
Moscow hating the talkies. Which is interesting, because they see
almost no American films here—and look upon them with great
admiration. Actors and directors make about $25 a week and think
they are lucky. I'm wondering what would happen to these people who
are all kids under thirty if they went to America. I've seen most of the
historical pictures and they are superb. Even the bum ones have
redeeming features in incidental photography. The great thing is that
they have little money for elaborate studio work and have to use actual
scenes and people and inventive photography. Eisenstein is for some
reason not a jew and looks like an ordinary German squarehead. He's
extremely gentil and a very interesting bird.

   Saw Pavlov's dogs in Leningrad. Incidentally all his work has been
on gland secretions other than the sexual and most of his work on the
physiology of the brain has been via the saliva glands of a dog where
he can measure the secretions. The whole thing is coming out in an
English translation this year (International Publishers) Everybody says

it'll annihilate Dr Watson (John) and make Freud look like 30 cents. Be that as it may. He hates the Soviet Government and roars against them in his lectures, and they give his laboratory more money every year, so everybody is happy. Talked to his wife. I imagine he really is a great man, nearly eighty with bushy whiskers and never missed a day in his laboratory all through the war and the revolution—

People are so hospitable here and so nice that its heartbreaking— and the breadth and emptiness of the country is magnificent.

My best to Anne—My address for a couple of months will be c/o VOKC, 6 Malaya Nitiskaya, Moscow
Let me know how long you will be in Paris—

Yrs
Dos

To Ernest Hemingway

[Botlikh, Russia
September 1928]

Dear Hem—

This is magnificent country—just crossed over from Sheshia into Daghestan. The Caucasus has been entirely neglected by Swiss hotel-keepers. The inhabitants dont eat fish, so the streams are full of trout (I havent seen one yet, but everybody swears its so). At present hung up in a little town named Botlikh while people haggle over the price of horses to take us on to the next place. The towns are little stone age villages and the country betweeen is wild as hell. In fact I'm having a swell time in Russia. Its nothing like anybody describes it. In the first place its easy to travel and rather cheap. Then there's a great deal of food, beer, vodka, wine and general gaity—Some people you meet are as optimistic as down town real estate agents—others are still Russian in the Dostoyevski sense but—things are certainly jollier and more varied than in the States though not so hectic. Everything is darned exciting. Before I got here I came down the Volga in great state— caviar for breakfast etc but here we live on pears and old bread and a Dutch cheese.

I'd love to have news of you and Pauline—Cant you drop a note to me care of BOKC, Malaya Nitiskaya 6 Moscow—How long are you going to be in the States? I'll be in Moscow through October—

Yrs
Dos

Postcard to Stewart Mitchell

[Moscow
October 1928]

Hello Mitchell (Arthur isn't getting my card this time) Leading a very
fine rather quiet life in Moscow, going to all theatres wrestling with
the language—walking round in misty October afternoons. Of course
I'm missing the elections and your speeches anent the political situation—Will it be prejudice or popery?

love—
Dos

To Dudley Poore

[Moscow
October 1928]

Dear Dudley—

An unfortunate man named Mr. Brown of Brown has been
writing me for years in an effort to trace you to your lair. Do take pity
on him and let him reprint the poems or have your picture as a
souvenir suspender button or whatever it is he wants. People who want
to publish poems should be encouraged; they are rare birds. I sent Mr.
Brown certain "facts" about you, such as that you went to Harvard,
graduated from the American Ambulance Field Service etc. Do you
mind? His letter seemed a bit frantic. The lack of your biography is
bitching his whole scheme. How the hell are you anyway and where?

I'm in Moscow, and I've been down the Volga from Yaroslav to
Astrakhan and had caviar for breakfast every morning and not seen a
single boatman, and I've been two weeks hard horseback riding across
Daghestan in the company of a 300 pound 6 foot American lady
journalist from the great open spaces of Mt. Ranier—god help us—and
I've scrambled a great deal about the Caucasus and spoke with people
of extremely various dialects and drunk magnificent Georgian wine—
and since then I've been going to the theatre every night in Moscow—
and I feel like a new man.

Honestly this country is enormously invigorating. Its not like
anything thats ever been said or written about it—the climate is unbelievable wet damp moist dank chilly muggy and detestable. Of course
there's been no sun—but the people are so hospitable and so swell—that
they quite make up for the lack of sleigh rides. The only trouble is that

they feed you an awful lot of rich cake which eventually accumulates on the liver and causes the bile to spread. Navigating the country by train is the best though. The cars are very large and very crowded and stop a long time at stations. There are three layers of bunks all filled with people fruit potatoes potted plants and baskets of babies—everybody eats continually and there's a great deal of scrambling for food at stations and everybody talks about everything under the sun, and I endeavor frantically to understand what people are saying. The Russian language is no joke. Under the strain of trying to learn it I've forced all the Spanish and most everything else out of my head and have managed to learn enough to make myself almost completely misunderstood wherever I go.

And the theatres are magnificent—Meyerhold's productions of The Wood (Ostrovski) and of Gogol's The Inspector General just clean knock your eye out. Are you ever going to be in New York? I'll be there after Christmas—Do let me hear from you c/o Gordon 214 Riverside Drive N.Y. Forgive me for writing Mr. Brown.

To Robert Hillyer

> [61 Washington Square South
> New York
> *January*(?) *1929*]

Dear Robert—

That was hellish luck our missing each other all round New York that way. Before I forget it, in case you find yourself in New York midyears, I live at 61 Washington Sq. South—I can be reached at New Playwrights Theatre—and afternoons at Grove St. Theatre, 22 Grove St. where we are rehearsing my little opus, God forgive it and us and all poor sailors out at sea on a night like this and fire and sleet and candlelight and Dr Campbell receive thy soul. Robert dont you ever write any plays—believe me there's nutten in it, kid—except worry and the loss of hair and hours and wishes causing dispepsia after midnight—

When the shooting's over about March first I might get up to Cambridge or somewhere—but I cant be sure—or maybe I'll be on my way to Maine a little later—Gawd Knows—

> Yours—
>
> Dos

Airways opens Feb. nineteenth but cant recommend it—If you did
happen to be in New York I'd have seats for you and you could help
comfort me with scotch or rye or applejack

My best to Dorothy and infant Hillyer

I'm well, not very happy, but energetic and hard boiled. Russia
was very invigorating—

To John Howard Lawson and Francis Edwards Faragoh (1895–1966),
*a dramatist and screenwriter, who with Dos was a director of the New
Playwrights Theatre. In 1934 Dos stayed with him in Hollywood,
where Faragoh had moved to write for film. He had to his credit the
screenplays for* Little Caesar, Frankenstein, My Friend Flicka, *and* Easy
Come, Easy Go, *among other films.*

[*New York*
March 1929]

Dear Francis,
Dear Jack,
excuse me but you'll have to read the same copy of this little gumdrop
as I havent any other. Have sent it to all the directors of the N
Peetoodle of odorous memory—

Yrs
Dos

I'm hereby resigning as a director of The New Playwrights
Theatre and feel that perhaps its worthwhile to sketch out my reasons.
First I want to say that the only reason for stopping the theatre now
will be the lack of interest or lack of gumption of its directors. Except
for the matter of money and organization the theatre is in a better
position than it ever has been. For the first time it has a reputation that
would mean money and audiences if properly exploited.

As I see it the trouble with this organization from the start has
been that the men who made it up have not been sure of their aims or
honest about them. Half the time we have been trying to found an
institution and the rest of the time trying to put over ourselves or each
other, and occasionally trying to knife each other in the back. I dont
think that this is anybody's fault; it is due to a typically New York
confusion of aims. The best thing to do is to dissolve the organization
and let the members of it paddle their own canoes.

But the fact remains that if any one is sincerely interested in trying to put over new unpopular, radical, revolutionary or even "good" plays in America the only way to do it is by the forming of an organization to do it. It's too big a job for anyone to do alone, and such plays are only feasible if presented in groups, in a theatre that has something like a repertory system. Such a theater can only be founded when the people who try to finally realize that cooperation is not an empty phrase, but a sane and businesslike method of attaining a certain fifty per cent of common aims. John Dos Passos

To Edmund Wilson

Over Sea Hotel
Key West, Florida
[*March 1929*]

Dear Bunny—

Was darned sorry not to see you before leaving New York as I should have liked very much to eat dinner with you and discuss the decay of the century—I'd have routed you out but was kept darn busy by my encounter with the Drama—Am down here licking my wounds, fishing, eating wild herons and turtle steak, drinking Spanish wine and Cuban rum and generally remaking the inner man. somewhat shattered by the encounter—Its a swell little jumping off place—the one spot in America desperately unprosperous—In the old days it was whaling but the whales went to the Antarctic, then it was sponges but the Greeks came and cleaned out all the sponges from under the noses of the Key Westers—Then they had the cigar rolling industry but that moved to Tampa. Then there was the boom and the overseas highway—but the boom was blown away in a hurricane and the county commissioner eloped with the funds so the overseas highway never got finished, so now the only industry is catching and shipping green turtles. The result is that life is agreeable calm and gently colored with Bacardi—the swimming is magnificent and you catch all sorts of iris colored finnies on the adjacent reefs, you broil them, basting them with a substance known as Old Sour and eat mightily well. Apart from that there's absolutely nothing to do, which is a blessing.

Have you read A Voyage to Pagany—W.C. Williams (in future to be known as Water Closet Williams)—Jesus and I used to think he was a good writer—gone the way of softening of the brain like Sherwood Anderson. God its terrible—or else I've lost the lovely youthful powers of "appreciation" and am getting old and crabbed—

I'm darned anxious to see your opus that they say is coming out in the American Caravan—

I think Waldo Frank's new book is pretty much shit too—and I used to think we were going to have writers in America—Are all the boys taking the King's shilling—have they all got paresis or what?

Drop me a line care Esther Andrews 72 Perry Street—saying where I can find you and I'll search you out in April sometime when I'm back in New York

Yours on the warpath
John Dos Passos

To Dudley Poore

[Chicago
July 26, 1929]

The sky is very pale here and the clouds very pearly over the lake and there's a dancehall on the Navy Pier and a fine little boat with a band on it that takes you up to Lincoln Park—Here its been raining and I hope some of that rain got as far east as Syracuse and fell on those unfortunate zinnias marigolds and cosmos marooned in that new bed—

So far as I can discover the speakeasy situation is none too good. fifty cents for a cup of indifferent dago red—but I havent had time to cover much ground yet. Swelter among the old newspaper files in the library Last night saw a fine old fashioned burlesque show The papers are full of bomb explosions but I cant seem to get with one of them

If any mail has accumulated would you forward it please care Dudley 242 E. Walton Place Chi, but just whatever is there when you get this letter as I may be moving soon and suddenly. Chicago is swell though—I bathe in the lake every afternoon and swelter in the library all day—

Give my love to your mother I wont write her a bread and butter letter, but explain to her what a good time I had at your diggings—I think I'd better send you this cheque—I probably can cash money here when I need it.

Yrs
Dos

How about the lady bug eggs?

To Rumsey Marvin

[Wiscasset, Maine]
August 21 [*1929*]

Dear Rummy—

Your telegram got relayed to me and I just got it. I'm terribly sorry not to have been able to go as I've been anxious to take a look at Gastonia etc. I've been busy getting married and drinking a certain Old Crow Bourbon whiskey in the Province of Quebec—Am settled for a month in a little red farmhouse near Wiscasset Maine—see you when I get back to New York in a month or so—my best to the tarheels.

Yrs
Jack

You must meet the lady when we get to the Big City

To Dudley Poore

Wiscasset-Maine
[*August 26, 1929*]

Dear Dudley—the tragedy of the cabbages is very sad. I'm afraid the garden will have to be fenced or else a woodchuck slaying dog with a thick neck and surly manners added to the household. Also its a shame that nothing better came of the zinnias in the new bed. I'm afraid that the elaborate screening that was given the soil removed whatever vitalizing shreds there might have been in it. I looked into all the works of Ellsworth Huntington in Chicago and found him and them thoroughly horrid. It's swell that the cucs did so well. I was afraid that the lack of rain would hit them pretty hard. I'm still looking for a climaturgical work that talks about the 42 Parallel and if possible Medicine Hat (about twenty years ago I remember Medicine Hat figured in all the weather reports) And time is passing as in a mad bad glad moment I told Mr. Harper & his Bro they could have this alleged novel in October—Kate Smith and I are living in a swell little red house in a region back of Wiscasset known as Birch Point, apple trees, swimming, Sheepscot river, hot rocks & cold water—thoroughly swell —swimming not far off and a sickly kitten half brother of the illfated Squeak named Nitwit—Due to a train of circumstances we found ourselves taking out a license for one dollar in Ellsworth Maine and submitting to the ministrations of a slightly used Unitarian minister. Nobody seems much the worse for it, though at the time it seemed as if the consequences would be fatal. Fortunately there appeared a splendid man with gold teeth all across his face named Mr. Mazurbie who fished a great quantity of Clear River Bourbon (and real Bourbon Whiskey) out of his lobster pots and everything has seemed much better since. Anyway its no worse than a bad cold. Al-Makari sounds magnificent. I'll lay hold of him the first chance I get—Do you by any chance know the words of *Cheyenne on my pony* or *Bury me not on the lone praire* or *Down on the Wabash* or *There's a broken heart for every light on Broadway* that Richard used to sing? *My mother was a lady* might do—I need them in my business. I enjoyed being in Chicago so much—excursion boats and people bathing on the lakeshore and toasting their backs and changing their clothes without being accosted by cops, and the Black Belt were very fine—much younger and less Jewish than New York—After all New York is just a stuffy ghetto on a gigantic scale, with all the hothouse interest of a ghetto but after all there's a limit to that sort of thing—My best to your mother & cousins Alvia & Lane and aunts

Yrs   Dos

To Eugene Saxton

[571 Commercial Street
Provincetown
May 1930]

Dear Gene—Had swell trip—Darn sorry to miss you and Martha in New York—and only by a day. We'll be in full operation at S. Truro [Massachusetts] when you get back—why dont you come out? I guess I'll need help on the cranberry crop because the book business surely wont feed us if this keeps up. Then there's always lobster pots—Have B. Cendrars' poems virtually finished (maybe in more senses than one) and working like mad on 1919.—You and Martha better have a good time while you can over there—we may all be selling needles next summer

Yrs—
Dos

Katy sends her best to you

To Rumsey Marvin

571 Commercial St.
P'town Mass
[*December 1930*]

Dear Rummy—Tremendously glad to get your letter—Have tried to get time to call you up each time I went through N.Y.—Next time we must get together—I want to hear all about the town clerk racket—Hope things are better with the pure flowers of southern womanhood—I think I'll have to give you a correspondence course in how to treat those girls—Just back from an attempted hunting trip in Wyoming which ended with Ford turning turtle and me (also the big game beasties) completely unhurt.—Why dont you come up to Provincetown some time We'll be here till Christmas at least—I'll be down to N.Y. for a day or two before then—and I will call up

love
Jack

Postcard to Edmund Wilson

[571 Commercial Street
Provincetown
December 27, 1930]

Say Bunny does anyone around the N.R. know where I could find the prison statistics of the United States? How many federal & state prisons, penitentiaries, reform schools etc and their population—insane rate mortality rate etc. If they are in hand could you get somebody to copy them down & send them up to me—Yrs

Dos

To Israel Bram (1883–1955), *a well known Philadelphia physician and endocrinologist, whose questionnaire regarding sleeping habits Dos was answering in this letter.*

[*1931*]

Dear Dr. Bram: Here are my answers to your questions about sleep.
1. I seem to make out perfectly well on seven or eight hours (from midnight or one to seven or eight o'clock in the morning). I've often done executive or physical work with much less sleep, but creative

work, such as writing, seems to require that amount in my case, though it seems to me that, as I get older (I'm 35) I can do creative work on less sleep than when I was in my twenties. On the other hand I dont think I have quite the physical powers after sleeping only three or four hours a night, that I had then. More than eight hours seems to clog my mind up, though occasionally I feel better physically after a long sleep.

2. Have no opinion on that as people vary so much in their habit; still, in my experience, too much sleep has a dulling effect on the nerves and brain.

3. I can go to sleep anywhere. My main trouble is keeping awake long enough to do the small amount of reading I stake out for after I've gone to bed.

4. I find that tea and coffee help me very little when I want to keep awake, have once or twice found that the very strong coffee you get in Spanish cafés tends to keep you awake if you drink too much of it.

5,6,7 At present I remember almost no dreams, though I tend to believe Freud's theory of the continuous quality of dreams. Occasionally events of the day reappear in them in distorted form, more often a distorted rehash of conversations just before bedtime goes through my head, particularly if the conversation was heated or if I was a little bit drunk. From the time I was very small up to the age of eighteen or nineteen I had continuous vivid dreams, sleeping and waking. But for a long time now my life has been too occupied with work, reading, conversation, exercise etc to give me any time for daydreaming, and dreams at night seem to have faded away in proportion. Probably that stuff goes into my work. I tend to regard sleep as an enemy, though I certainly enjoy it, because I find my waking working hours hopelessly too short for what I'd like to pack into them. After all we'll be a long time dead.

Sincerely yrs
John Dos Passos

To Edmund Wilson

[Provincetown
January 14(?), 1931]

Dear Bunny—

Just read your battlecry—I think it's splendid and very neatly oiled to slip past mental obstacles. I think the part about the position of the shibboleth experts particularly important—they—we?—really are in the position of people who are marching at the head of a parade entirely unconscious of the fact that the parade has turned down another street—A magnificent example is to compare [Hyacinthe Dubreuil's] 'Standards'—that interested me extraordinarily with Duhamel's ravings—the American intellectuals are entirely in the position of Duhamel (though we—looking at things from the same angle—cant quite see it) and what we need is a point of attack similar to—this bird Dubreuil's—a few simple human dogmas & actual experience. God damn it we dont any of us know what's going on right under our noses in technique of life and organization—The few writers who have a faint 13½ percent inkling stand out as wizards. Of course all the N.R. can do is stir things up and try to smoke out a few honest men who do know something about industrial life as she is lived. I hope Mr Soule wont pour too much oil on the waters next week. If you can keep up a series like this you really will have started something—though I'm beginning to think that every printed publication ought to be required by law to print at the bottom of each page:

NB. THIS IS ALL BULLSHIT

I mean there's such a gigantic tradition of hokum behind political phrasemaking that the antihokum phrases are about as poisonous as the hokum phrases— These reflections are the result of reading *Standards* which seems to me to express admirably the attitude of the person working at something towards the intellectual. Dont you think somebody ought to translate that book?— I haven't seen anything in English written by an actual worker that expressed the worker's attitude so well. Doc Walker's *Steel* is a good picture—but devoid of ideas (too soon out of college)—The ideas in Dubreuil's book are the kind that ought to be encouraged I think—I'd like to see the Daily Worker written in that language—instead of in clippings from Bukharin's scrapbasket—I think this question of language is pretty important— Maybe your article's a little too well oiled to stick at all—Of course if it hadn't been pretty well varnished it couldn't have appeared any-where—probably the thing to do is to reach a happy proportional medium between fact-words (like Dubreuil uses) and whoopee-words of which the N.R. is largely made up—and all editorials everywhere— Maybe its time the law stepped in with my new motto—

I dont mean that Dubreuil writes well—no I guess that's what I do mean—because his meaning is certainly clear—My father used to have a pet phrase asking people whether they got their ideas from experience or observation—the trouble with all our political economic writing and the reason maybe why it doesnt interest the ordinary guy who hasn't joined the fraternity of word-addicts is that it is made up right in the office and springs from neither experience or observation but from sheer intellectual whoopee—it really ought to be fought like drugs—Of course what I'm doing now is confusing the issue because if you wait until you've cleared up your vocabulary you'll never say anything and just remain stuttering on the pons asinorum like George Soule who cant ever make a definite pronouncement because the statistics arent all in yet.

I guess the trouble with me is I cant make up my mind to swallow political methods. Most of the time I think the IWW theory was right—Build a new society in the shell of the old—but practically all they did was go to jail. Anyway the extraordinary thing about Americans (as pointed out by Dubreuil) is that while they strain at a gnat of doctrine, they'll swallow an elephant of experiment—the first problem is to find a new phraseology that we'll be at home with to organize mentally what is really happening now—This is all very confused

See you before the 24th

Yrs
Dos

To Edmund Wilson

[On board ship to Jacksonville, Florida
February 23, 1931]

Dear Bunny—
Saw Scott in N.Y. he'd come over for his father's funeral—He was in damn good shape in spite of a miserable winter, worrying about Zelda etc. He seemed to have the situation pretty well in hand—he says its actual schizophrenia— this ballet stuff was part of it and persecution ideas about people. Scott and everybody trying to keep her from doing it—and that a great deal of the time she's in perfectly good shape and then something touches a spring and she's in the other personality. He seems to be going at it pretty darn sensibly—she's under the care of Forel and is beginning to realize that there is something the matter with her; that is the most important step towards a cure. He says that out of four people who go into schizophrenia one goes into complete

hopelessness, two recover enough to carry on ordinary life but remain eccentric and one is completely cured—He's certain that Zelda is no longer in danger of going absolutely and the question is how far she'll come back.

Scott seemed to me, although kind of worn, to have much less nonsense about him than other times I'd seen him. He's fundamentally a pretty solid proposition.

He greatly admired Axel's Tower [*Axel's Castle*]—which Katy is now reading and admiring. It's a swell day off the Virginia Capes— boat & people look exactly like the booklet "pleasure—trained senses seek relaxation on Florida's fashionable beaches" etc—People sit around in those droopy attitudes people always have in those travel booklets. Its splendid—Boat drops us at Jacksonville from which we continue by road to N.O., San Antonio, Monterey etc—Will keep you posted on conditions. Maybe you people will get down before we get back— we hope to have a little house somewhere we can park you in—Sorry as hell to have missed you in New York

Yrs
Dos

To Edmund Wilson

[Provincetown
July 15, 1931]

Dear Bunny—

Thanks for swell informative letter and postal card. Have been reading about Frank Keeney with great interest—Everything's calm in Provincetown—work swim eat mushrooms (that are very thick every where due to rainy season) and distill Smith's Simple—at the end of the week we are moving to Truro where we will follow the same avocations. I'm getting restless and anxious to take a leaf out of your book and do a little touring but cant do anything until I can get this incubus off my back. I'd like to see you all whooping over the plain on your cayuses—

Got a letter from Malcolm about a protest the N.R. is getting up about the slaughter of the 24 young literary people in China—wrote begging him that they do something more practical than protest about the barbarity of Chiang Cash Check—it was the British police that arrested them and turned them over to be executed even as Mr. Doak is

so fond of doing with foreign radicals in this country—and the place
for protest is parliament in England—their scalps ought to be hung
around Ramsay Macdonald's neck—certainly British pressure on the
chinks could have saved them—why couldn't the N.R. find the whole
dope about the British French and American exploiting forces in
China and who's really behind Nanking (not that private greed on the
part of Chinese warlords and business men isnt enough to account for
their actions—but its virtually certain that foreign interests are heavily
involved—loans—privileges—tax evasions etc.) This is particularly depressing as its a case where quick action—questions in Parliament—
rumpus in England etc might have saved the poor devils' lives—

Katy sends her best to the antichristical doctor and to Margaret &
Jimmy How about snake dances, the Whoopee Indians and all that?

Glad to hear you're coming to P'town.

Yrs
Dos

To Eugene Saxton

[Provincetown]
November, 1931

Dear Gene—

This certainly is a lousy break all round—but its no use worrying
any more about it. I've wired the Brandts to see what they can do
about getting somebody to take over the contract, and I imagine the
details of the transaction can be arranged without any particular difficulty. The main thing is speed—as I have a hunch there's something
fairly timely about the volume and that it ought to come out as soon as
possible. I'll be down in New York Saturday or Monday and maybe we
can have a drink together and talk about other things—Hell it's only a
book after all—

Yrs
Dos

An open letter

National Committee to Aid
Striking Miners Fighting
Starvation
New York City
January, 1932

Dear Friend:

Having just come back from a trip with the Dreiser Committee around Harlan County, Kentucky, and spoken to the miners and seen how they live, I can assure you that the name of this committee is no exaggeration.

The miners, their wives and children live in crumbling shacks, many of them clapboard, through whose cracks pour the lashing mountain winds, rain and snow. "We're not afraid of the wind", said a mother of five, "it's the loose boards in the walls".

A few crumbs of cornbread usually—a piece of salt pork occasion-ally—a few pinto beans for the more fortunate—this is their food. "Last summer we ate grass—this winter, I guess we'll eat snow", said another mother.

Wages? Aunt Molly Jackson, wife of a Straight Creek, Kentucky miner, said, "Better starve striking than starve working in the muck of a mine". If the men go on strike against these intolerable conditions, the slight local and Red Cross Relief being offered is entirely cut off and they are evicted from their houses. Then they face the entire armed force of the law, which in Kentucky, means vicious courts, jails, tear-gas-bombs, guns—manned by thugs known to have been "imported" especially for the miners.

Schools? Shoeless children are school-less children. Many lack even underwear. Thru the gray of any morning one can see a group of mourners behind a shack—a gash in the mountain-side, a little pine coffin lowered into the earth, and the earth close around the remains of a child that did not have a chance to live.

Can you give something to help bring food to the mouths of these freezing, starving children?

Gratefully
John Dos Passos
Chairman

To Ernest Hemingway

[Brooklyn
January 14, 1932]

Hem—it was swell to get letter—we ought to make K.W. about end of month—now going out for a few days with N. Atlantic fishing fleet—expect to vomit no end—Nineteen Nineteen put to bed—love to Pauline Damned anxious to see your bull book. Met Paul de Kruif who broke into tears at mention of your name and sobbed out a handsome bouquet anent you being only Amerikansky word fellow worth his pencil and ink "damnest sweetest writer" etc—and made me swear to transmit same—so here it is—

    Love to Pauline

Yrs
Dos

To Ernest Hemingway

[On board ship
February 1932]

Dear Hem—

    We certainly had a fine four days in Key West. Damn consoling to find you in such swell shape—well housed, catching sail fish, able to eat and drink. The boys dont seem to me to be holding up like I'd hoped on the whole—Never enjoyed anything more than the three days on the gulfstream—only it was rotten luck missing Pauline.

    The Bullfight book [*Death in the Afternoon*]—is absolutely the best thing can be done on the subject—I mean all the description and the dope—It seems to me an absolute model for how that sort of thing ought to be done—And all the accounts of individual fighters towns etc, are knockout. I'm only doubtful, like I said, about the parts where Old Hem straps on the longwhite whiskers and gives the boys the lowdown. I can stand the old lady—but I'm pretty doubtful as to whether the stuff about Waldo Frank (except the line about shooting an owl) is as good as it ought to be. God knows he ought to be deflated—or at least Virgin Spain—(why not put it on the book basis instead of the entire lecturer?) and that is certainly the place to do it. And then later when you take off the make up and assure the ladies and gents that its really only old Uncle Hem after all and give them the low down about writing and why you like to live in Key West etc.

I was pretty doubtful—Dont you think that's all secrets of the profession—like plaster of paris in a glove and oughtn't to be spilt to the vulgar? I may be wrong—but the volume is so hellishly good. (I'd say way ahead of anything of yours yet) and the language is so magnificently used—(why right there sitting in Bra's boat reading the typewritten pages I kept having the feeling I was reading a classic in the Bohn library like Rabelais or Harvey's Circulation of the Blood or something and that's a hell of a good way to feel about a book not even published yet) that it would be a shame to leave in any unnecessary tripe—damn it I think there's always enough tripe in anything even after you've cut out—and a book like that can stand losing some of the best passages—After all, a book ought to be judged by the author according to the excellence of the stuff cut out. But I may be packed with prunes with all this so for God's sake dont pay too much attention to it—the Books damn swell in any case—

We were laid low again by our typhoid and paratyphoid, but now better and getting ready to land at Progreso this afternoon. Say why dont you plan to come up to Provincetown or Truro in the spring before going out West? I'll have a small sailboat and it won't be so bad there—

Wish I was going down to Cuba with you—strafe the finnies and love to Pauline

Yrs
Dos

To Malcolm Cowley (1898–   ), *the author and critic, who knew Dos from the 1920's. It was during the years 1929–1940, when Cowley was literary editor of the* New Republic, *that Dos had most of his correspondence with him.*

[Miami Colonial Hotel
Miami
February 1932]

Dear Malcolm,

Mac stayed on in Mexico and died there some years ago of heart failure while playing hearts with a small party of friends. As for the general trend—gosh that is a poser—a blessed amnesia has set in about the whole business. I dont know if there's any solution—but there's a certain amount of statement of position in the later Camera Eyes. I think also—if I manage to pull it off—the later part of the book shows a certain crystalization (call it monopoly capitalism?) of society that didn't exist in the early part of 42nd Parallel (call it competitive capitalism?)—but as for the note of hope—gosh who knows?

Yrs
J.D.P.

To Eugene Saxton

c/o Wells Fargo Exp.
Mexico D.F.
[February 1932]

Dear Gene—

Had a magnificent trip down Arrived in fine shape somewhat groggy with scenery, bad roads, architecture and chile. Finest country in the world for motoring.

About that damn jacket. I dont suppose the original design is worth a hundred bucks to Mr. Harper or to his Boss. So lets make the best of it and go ahead as I've indicated. If you feel you must have a little piece of blurb in the upper right hand corner—make them think up something snappier. I'm sure that neither the words "new" or "novel" will ever break down anybody's sales resistance again.

Incidentally, Gene—my numerals weren't green; they were white —Oh well never mind about them. I want to use Nineteen-Nineteen— written out for the title page & at the tops of pages (if any)—It seems damn silly to make such a fuss about a lot of little things like that, but I think they are important, and I've heretofore been too damn careless about them—Even in the Cendrars book two fat misprints got by me, right in the introduction—

Anyway the color on your manufacturing dep't's jacket is good— I'll console myself with that.

You and Martha ought to come down here sometime and take a look at it—climate birds flowers churches indians all hornswoggling to look at—

Katy sends her best to both

Yrs
Dos

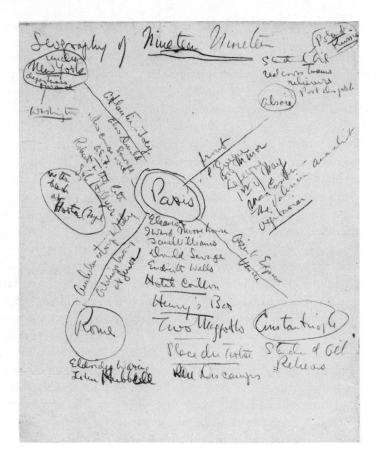

To Ernest Hemingway

[Guerrero, Mexico
March 1932]

Dont forget alleged indian love drama—ought to have spirituals in
it—tell me spirituals are what packs the box office—Why not chinee
spirituals?

Gosh Hem I wish I was there for the big termite season—Thanks a
hell of a lot for the newsclipping F.P.A. [Franklin P. Adams, a
columnist] must be sick or something—I'll send Mike the picture of
Trotski catching the snapper or rather having caught the snapper—and
as for Mr Cowley its like killing Chinamen—The United States of
Mexico are pretty swell and damn disunited—were in a place in
Guerrero where population alleged mountain woods full of leones
pumas Maybe you could get Uncle Gus to send his big game expedition down here. You ought to come anyway before the folk lore experts
wash the whole thing out. Fall duck shooting in Lake Chapala and
through Michoacan—its a damned extraordinary country anyway and
the landscape and sculpture (precolumbian)'ll knock your eye out.
Thanks very much for sending the mail—If any more drags in—our
address will be 571 Commercial Street—Provincetown Mass. Are jumping clear from here to N.Y. in a much too expensive Pullman—still on
the trail of the 4000 pesetas that Cenit alleges to have sent twice and
each time returned marked non compus or something of the sort.
Hope the big social life died down and Mahatma settled down to quiet
contemplation among his books and papers. I keep trying to be among
mine but they stink—The first story in this "El Feroz Cabecilla" is
damn good and the others are interesting—The guy who wrote them is
a darn good egg—ran away with Villa at the age of 13 and now has a
job on El Universal and a disagreeable half-English wife. They take
naturally to painting down here but their literature is pretty bum.
Normalcy setting in like mad politically. Looks like they'd soon be
back at the days of good Don Porfirio "when a white man could live in
the country." How soon are you gents leaving for Wyoming? Its the
rainy season down here but the weather's pretty darn fine, rains at
night. My best to Pauline

Yrs
Dos

Postcard to Edmund Wilson

[El Paso
April 7, 1932]

We're passing up the local horned toad Derby and speeding to the
coast—is it wise? is it right? What would you do? love to Margaret

Dos

They were men in those days [Reference to the postcard picture of the state penitentiary at Yuma, Arizona.]

Postcard to Edmund Wilson

[St. Louis
April 23, 1932]

There was a boy scout from Oak Park
Who went out with a girl after dark
He gagged her and drowned her
But all he said when they found her
Was "Judge we were just two young
  things out for a lark"

Postcard to Edmund Wilson

[St. Louis
April 23, 1932]

There was a young girl from Fort Riley
Who was very seductive and wiley
She said to an officer
"Don't be so stand-offish sir,"
But he only clicked his heels together
  shyly—

from Lyrics of the Middle West by Kate and Dan Parsons

To Ernest Hemingway

[Provincetown
May(?) 1932]

Dear Hem—
    Sure we adhere to the thesis of the 2nd session of the revery of the S.E.I.R. though we discern a distinct left deviation and subsection C14 of article 12 shows social-fascist tendencies that we hope to see stamped out. Havent got the letter and lit. advice (Jeez we're getting to heave lit. advice back and forth like regular wordfellows, but it cant be helped, once you're in the business) but damned anxious to read some and hope it will be sent back intact by Am. Express in Mexico City. Damn swell epistle and Katy and I laughed like fools over it, still laughing.

Hell yes, need advice bad. Any man who writes a trilogy needs advice (and a good physician)

Anxious to hear about the Cuban coast. Did we write you about the vast schools of swordfish and sailfish we saw in the Gulf of Tehuantepec?

A lot of the characters are climbing out of windows already and I'm barely under weigh on last tome. You're damn right, the Angel of Death is the novelist's only friend. Flu and machine guns will do the rest. Whole trouble with the opus is too many drawing room bitches—never again—it's like fairies getting into a bar—ruin it in no time.

F. Scott Fitzgerald's some topic. Hoped to see him on the coast; but he'd gone and everybody shook their heads about him out there—but they shake their heads about everybody out there. Saw Don [Stewart] who seemed more normal than most and in good shape—didn't sob on our shoulders about his ruined life and art and those beasts in the studios—enormous relief because everybody else did. There are a lot of thwarted subword fellows out there that are frightful.

We detrained at Tucson and bought us a very old Chrysler roadster—(wait till they hear that on union square) and drove to Yuma then to Santa Monica, back across the Mojave Desert to Flagstaff where we met a very decent guy named Jack O'Connor who teaches in a little college there and writes about Villa etc. Then through Santa Fé where even the garage men are fairies, wear riding breeches, and marcelled hair to Taos, a damn swell piece of country except for Mabel Dodge, through Western Kansas where it was blowing a three day gale from SE and worst dust I ever saw in my life to K.C. where we ate good beefsteak and saw an old friend of Kate's who'd seen you—U.P. man—Saint Louis, Cincinnati, Cumberland Md. Baltimore and so returned to base. Base in good shape Bill much better, dogs and cats O.K. now faced with prospect of labor—though feel like café life and pernod—It's very much like spring here and I'm scribbling in the vegetable garden—Wish you'd come up, damn it. Are you coming to N.Y. when you leave the island republic? Katy sends love—Love to Pauline

Yrs
Dos

To Edmund Wilson

P'town Mass.
[*May 1932*]

Dear Bunny—

Your note and Manifesto followed me back from the coast—Sure I'll subscribe to it—but I dont think it'll cause any bankers to jump out of fiftieth story windows—what are you going to do with it?—post it up on billboards? it might go well on toilet paper like ex-lax advertizing—or is it going to be laid on Mr. Hoover's breakfast table?—

I've taken the liberty of making some suggestions on the copy—it smells too strong of Thirteenth Street for my taste—

—I think the only useful function people like us can perform anyway is introduce a more native lingo into the business—and, Goddamn it, I havent enough confidence in the C.P. to give it a blanket endorsement. After all a manifesto is supposed to influence other people—I think the tendency of this, unless every touch of 13th Street is removed, is to merely put the tarbrush on the signers— Where's it going to be used—? after all that's the most important question—Drop me a line—I'll be down in New York in a couple of weeks

Yrs
Dos

To Ernest Hemingway

P'town,—Mass
[*June 7, 1932*]

Dear Hem—

Must have been the same sort of mixed schools of swordfish and sailfish we saw in the Gulf of Tehuantepec—you sure have been slaying the finny monsters—Habana must be damn swell that way too— wish to hell I'd been down with you—It sure makes me feel uneasy to hear you've been taking my advice about plucking some of the long white whiskers out of the end of Death in the Afternoon—I may be wrong as Seldes—A funny thing happened about that stuff I've been trying all week to write a preface to the 97 cent edition of "Three Soldiers"—and yesterday found it pouring out in fine shape—What do you think it was on rereading? Your remarks and the stuff about what you'd liked to have put in the book—and about the lit. game almost word for word—shows there must be something in it to have it stick in just a natural born preface—Say if you have an extra set of galleys of "D in the A" I'd like to read them over as I didnt read it all in Key West—due to lack of time and want to read it more slowly—Dont bother if its a nuisance—Am standing by to crown critics who may yap at it. It's the God damnedest best piece of writing that's seen the light for many a day on this continent—Am going to Chi to cover the conventions for N. Republic—never seen one—thought it might be funny to see—Will send the 200 bucks in a couple of weeks—1919 selling pretty feebly if at all

    love to Pauline—

Yrs
Dos

Let me know—where you go on your way west—Expect to be in Chicago last two weeks of this month—wont leave here till June 10 or so

To Katy Dos Passos (1891–1947)

c/o Rbt Morss Lovett
Hull House
Chicago
[June 17, 1932]

Opossum—how are you—? Do write at once air mail—I'm so anxious to hear how you are—I started this before the last session of the convention—but now its after and I'm wondering what in the dickens I can write about it. As a show it was rather well staged but the plot—well I cant say much for it. It was fine when all the little balloons came down from the ceiling when they nominated Hoover—If you want a gloomy street I tell you South Halstead is a gloomy street and Hull House may be full of peace on earth and goodwill to man, but its a gloomy place to flop if I ever saw one. Went around to a lot of rooms in the Congress hotel and never saw a drink, except at Heywood Broun's and he just pretended the bottle that was standing on the table was empty although I could see it was half full. Conventions aren't what they used to be. The high spot was when a highly imbecile ex-senator from Maryland, a certain Mr. France appeared on the platform and attempted to nominate Coolidge. He was hit on the jaw by Simeon Fess and removed by the cops instantly—And now I'm trying to write an article there are upwards of a thousand newspaper men in Chicago right at this moment all trying to be funny about the convention all sober as crutches—But in the end I was given a drink by a redheaded young man from Time—and here I am quietly absorbing a little drop of distillate—and looking at the long shadows of a summer afternoon creep unutterably sadly across S. Halstead Street and down the long shellraked side street opposite. I've got to write this junk now and think I'll go and sit on the municipal pier and think—

O possum I miss you—love you my

love
Dos

To Katy Dos Passos

[Chicago
June 20, 1932]

Sweetish little possum—

Its monotonous to say I miss you but I do—and wish I had a letter—had none yet—Have been making a tour with Lovett—went to a socialist Congress at Waukegan, to see Mrs Fairbank at Lake Geneva and now at the Lovett's at Lake Zurich—there's nothing so instructive as travel. Going to Detroit in a couple of days then back to Chi for the Democrats—Having a swell time and seeing all sorts of odd things—Be sure to write me your plans at once—and airmail—I'll light out home as soon as the Democrats stop convening—but of course I dont know when yet—If you're in New York I'll light out via New York—have hopes of finding a letter at Hull House tomorrow. Here I am in bed (and wish you were here too little buzzard) and just finished Conquistador which is certainly agreeable reading—skillful. I'd rather read it than lots of poetry but its not the real stuff. Hardly any is for that matter—Its all second or third generation—but darn good for Alexandria. You'll enjoy reading it. I did and would be able to read it once more—but now too sleepy—Goodnight, love—
Chi. Monday morning Oh possum at last I have a little note written on the seventeenth about the rain and the transplanting—fine picture of Mr Black and the fence. Mr. Black is extremely photogenique.

Oh possum are you going to New York or on the warpath? I need lots more letters. Will you forward any sensible looking mail? And write a couple.

Wish I was in Provincetown often—and with you all the time, but this is all very instructive and instruction is our aim. Chicago is certainly the place to hear the great heart of America beat—and it sure is beating out something. Nobody knows the code—I'm not at all sure that it isn't Braille to McKinley with Hoover. Mr Fairbank thinks It's Traylor and the Texas democrats. Meanwhile I'm going to see the new aquarium—they have a planetarium too out in the lake and the new exposition buildings look darn fine. Will call up Mr. Gunlack(?) today. There's a wonderful story about seven year locusts in the paper this morning which if it isn't bologny is hellishly interesting. Some bird at the U of Minnesota has discovered that locusts develop out of plain hoppers under crowded conditions. Raise hoppers in a cage where they are too crowded and instead of getting smaller, they get bigger, hungrier and fiercer and grow a yellow and black husk like a locust— A very alarming idea. Present my compliments to Miss Ruhl and Mr and Mrs Gorman P. Glaspell.

Yrs
Dos

Oh possum its absurd to miss anybody so much—

To Katy Dos Passos

[Hull-House
800 South Halsted Street
Chicago
June 25, 1932]

Oh possum I was so glad to find three letters from you on getting back to Chicago from Detroit—came on the night bus, an uncomfortable overcrowded but rather agreeable performance—Chicago is hot The Congress Hotel is crowded with sweaty democrats—Detroit was thoroughly interesting—gave me the impression that main street was reddening up—was full of good beer and cool northerly wind. Chicago has been dried up and seems to contain nothing but bad dago wine and needle beer Everybody says its going to be a great fight next week but I personally think its in the bag and however it comes out the referee will be for Sharkey who in this case is Roosevelt—but maybe not—of course Al Smith is an energetic person who has money behind him and its his last chance for the championship. Oh possum next week I'm coming scampering home—probably direct—via Boston—Having a

very good time with Lovett who's a hell of a good egg as I'd suspected
lots of love and kisses—Dos

To Fredricka Field, *editor of* The Golden Book

571 Commercial Street,
Provincetown, Mass.
November 29–[19]32

Dear Madam;

Thank you for your courtesy in sending me the last issue of your
magazine; however, I must point out that in quoting my very feeble
crack at the American Socialist Party, out of my replies to Calverton's
questionnaire, you twisted its meaning completely around. I dont see
how you can have failed to notice that what I intended was that the
Socialist Party was near beer in distinction to the Communist Party
(good 7½ pc). However much we may cavil at the Communists they
mean it when they say they are fighting for socialism, i.e. the cooperative commonwealth. Your note should have read "only hears thunder
on the extreme left". I should be much obliged if you could rectify this
error in some way.

Very sincerely yours
John Dos Passos

"PEELING THE ONION OF DOUBT"

January 1933–December 1936

Dos and Katy had spent most of the fall of 1932 in Provincetown, although they did take a trip in September to Percé, Quebec, staying at a "little farmhouse far out at sea," Katy wrote Stewart Mitchell's guardian.

In March 1933, Hemingway wrote from Key West, urging them to come down for some excellent fishing and also suggesting a trip to Spain, where they might search out locales and information for a movie they had talked of making about the Spanish Republic. But Dos was soon in no shape to travel anywhere. In Baltimore to be with Katy when she had her tonsils out, he was struck again with rheumatic fever in early April and entered the Johns Hopkins Hospital for treatment under the supervision of Horsley Gantt. Katy wrote Edmund Wilson about *"Black April 1933"*; only in May did Dos begin to mend. His friends quickly came to his aid; Hemingway sent him $1000, and the Murphys provided the cost of a trip to Villa America. He also got Harcourt, Brace to advance him $1000 for the trip to Spain and hoped further to "presell" some articles, so with Gantt's help at keeping hospital costs down, he could survive financially, but the enforced rest was boring, and massive doses of Proust—sent him by Edmund Wilson—did not help as much as he would have liked, though he did admit to becoming a "Prousty" after some reading.

It may seem strange that Dos and Katy did not have more money of their own. But his family inheritance brought him practically nothing, Katy's family was not wealthy, his books did not make large sums, and his and Katy's health problems were a drain on their finances. Dos' bouts of rheumatic fever usually sent him to a hospital, and afterward he would seek a warm, sunny climate to recuperate in. Katy had a number of miscarriages that required costly hospitalization. It was because of these reasons far more than because they were constant travelers that their finances were often shaky.

They sailed for Europe near the end of May, spending June in Antibes with the Murphys before traveling to Spain, where they centered their activities in Madrid but moved around the country while Dos collected materials for his articles on the second republic. He did not see much of Hemingway, who arrived in Spain the middle of

August, but they had some lunches together with Claude Bowers, an old friend then the ambassador. Dos also got to interview Manuel Azaña, the prime minister, and chatted with the Spanish philosopher Miguel Unamuno, whom he had known before.

He could not help feeling that the future bode ill for the socialists. He kept seeing "signs and portents," he wrote in *The Best Times*. In Santander, where at a mass socialist rally some white doves were released from a box to soar upward, symbolizing peace, they all tumbled down; and while the speaker addressed the crowd one bird thrashed around pathetically on the ground. And a little Fiat which he and Katy had bought to see the country was stolen from them in Madrid shortly before they were to leave in September. The police located the car after a few days, and Dos, again sick with rheumatic fever, wobbled over to the station where the car was residing, encased in chicken wire. The police were most solicitous; they understood he wanted to sell the car before he left Madrid; nonetheless there was nothing they could do because the car was needed as evidence when the thief was caught. After much fruitless discussion, he and Katy left on their train for Gibraltar, and their little Fiat still reposed, safe and absurd, enmeshed in chicken wire at the station. "The idiotic series of incidents," Dos ended *The Best Times*, "began to seem to me as illustrative of the human predicament as the misadventures of the Knight of the Doleful Countenance seemed to Unamuno." When next he would return to Spain four years later, it would be to witness Franco's relentless takeover of the country.

The end of September they sailed for home on the *Exchorda;* by mid-October Dos was settled down to work in Provincetown, putting together the materials for his next book of reportage, *In All Countries;* arranging for the publication of *Three Plays: The Garbage Man, Airways, Inc.,* and *Fortune Heights;* and continuing work on *The Big Money*.

Rheumatic fever still plagued him. He stayed north in the winter of 1934 long enough to do some reportage on Washington for the *New Republic,* then the end of February headed down to Key West, hoping the sun would bake out his maladies.

At about this time, along with other intellectuals, he signed an "Open Letter to the Communist Party," which protested against the manner in which the Communists had broken up a rally in Madison Square

Garden organized by the Socialist party. The Communists, the signers accused, had caused a riot by their strong-arm tactics, and the episode undermined the entire left-wing movement. The *New Masses,* in a piece entitled "To John Dos Passos," decried Dos' part in the open letter, but he responded that he had participated because to him the episode "indicated the growth of unintelligent fanaticism that . . . can only end in the division of the conscious elements of the exploited classes into important brawling sects. . . ." That the magazine should address him specifically is significant. Among the literati the Communists saw him as the most committed and bemoaned his presence in the company of vacillating intellectuals like Edmund Wilson, Lionel Trilling, and John Chamberlain. Only once thereafter this would he contribute to the *New Masses;* not that he felt openly hostile to the Communists in 1934, but, as he wrote at about that time to Philip Rahv, the editor of the *Partisan Review,* "they are down—they dont know it yet but they are."

Dos and Katy remained in Key West well into the spring, enjoying the time with their close friends, among them Hemingway, who had returned from an African safari in April. He talked Dos into going to Havana with him for the May Day celebration, but Dos could not remain long enough to witness the arrival late that month of Ernest's new boat, the *Pilar.* He and Katy returned to Provincetown before Dos headed out to Hollywood in July for a short stint working among the big money for the famous director, Josef von Sternberg.

Rheumatic fever, however, struck him soon after he got to California. Without Katy, who was in Columbia, Missouri, attending to details after her father's death, he spent a miserable four weeks convalescing, even though Francis Faragoh took him into his home at 1644 North Orange Grove Avenue. Katy arrived there toward the end of August; they remained in Hollywood until October, boarding a boat for Havana on the sixth and landing just after the middle of the month for a stay in the Hotel Ambos Mundos. Hemingway was there, fishing from the *Pilar* and full of the story about his exciting though unsuccessful attempt to harpoon a humpbacked whale.

Hollywood had been a bittersweet experience. He assured Jack Lawson that he had found it "enormously instructive," and it fired his imagination as he worked on *The Big Money.* But despite the excesses of Hollywood that he saw, he continued to withdraw from the Communist left and in his letters increasingly espoused some sort of revision of American democratic forms to defend against the threat of European fascism.

That fall he and Hemingway worked together to try to alleviate the situation of Luis Quintanilla, a Spanish artist jailed because of his political activities. They each produced an introduction to the program to accompany an exhibition of thirty-nine of Quintanilla's etchings at the Pierre Matisse Gallery in New York. Dos wrote:

> . . . Here are the back lots, the cheap whores, the beggars and boot-blacks, and the new business men greedy for power. . . .
>
> Staying at home it was natural that he should be a satirist; most of the best Spaniards have been satirists. There's a type of clear noontime logic in the Spanish blood that can only come out as satire. The sharp metal clearness of etching is particularly attractive to the eye and hand of a satirist. A satirist is a man who can't see filth, oppression, the complacency of the powerful, the degradation of the weak without crying out in disgust. A great satirist can turn disgust into violent explosive beauty. . . . Looking at his etchings it is hard to avoid drawing a parallel with Georg Grosz's early work in Germany. The political moment too is similar, a time of defeat of everything that gives men hope.
>
> For inventors of images and designs for the eye or the ear or that amalgam of feelings and sensations that writing appeals to defeat is sometimes better than victory. A good thing, too, because there's a great deal more of it. . . .
>
> . . . These etchings . . . are the statement of a grown-up man facing a bitter world in the sun at noon.

The statement, which after Hemingway's urging he sold to Arnold Gingrich for *Esquire,* is particularly revealing of Dos Passos' thoughts about his own work as well as Quintanilla's. He had attempted to write satire ever since his college days, and here, as with his statement about Georg Grosz's work written almost two years later, he was defining satire as he saw it. The introduction could as well have been to *U.S.A.* and no doubt was in his own mind.

Quintanilla's case got Malcolm Cowley in wrong with Dos. In mid-November 1934 he had written Cowley about the exhibition; Cowley, in turn, had put together a public "letter to the editor" from the personal note. Dos in his turn warned against making an appeal for funds or suggesting that an artistic success might influence the Spanish authorities. But the warning came too late, and the public letter, appearing in the November 28 *New Republic,* brought down Dos' wrath on Cowley. The latter, though bothered, kept calm and wrote back twelve days later:

> Naturally your letter of reproach—reproach is about the mildest word that could be used for it—has been bothering me ever since. After reading Hemingway's piece in the catalogue—it also mentioned the sixteen years sentence that was being demanded by the *Fiscal*—I think the only extra damage that could possibly have been done by printing the letter lay in the sentence about the possibility of getting better treatment for Quintanilla by organizing a protest in this country. On that subject you are a better judge than I am, but I don't think the Spanish government reads The New Republic. In the meantime, printing your note in the paper may help to get the signatures you want.

Dos' rancor was quickly soothed, but from time to time, when he was irritated against the "liberal weeklies" or anything else, he would get off some crack about Cowley.

In late November and early December Katy was in Boston for medical tests, probably to try to find a reason for her discouraging history of miscarriages. By December 3 she wrote the Murphys, "I'm all right now and quite lively again," and she reported that when they had seen Hemingway in Havana that fall he "was translated. . . . You remember how irascible and truculent (can't spell) he was before. Now he's just a big cage of canaries, looking fine, too—and followed around all the time by a crowd of Cuban zombies who think he is Hernan Cortez—He was sweet, but had a tendency to be an Oracle I thought and needs some best pal and severe critic to tear off those long white whiskers which he is wearing." She and Dos had other good moments with Ernest, but he wore those whiskers more and more, they thought, and he was less and less the "Old Hem" of the best times.

During this winter Dos thought a great deal about the Communists, Soviet Russia, and his own ideas concerning them, and he wrote Edmund Wilson several long letters which clearly reveal his shift toward United States democracy. He could more easily tolerate the tyrannies of American monopoly capitalism, he wrote from Jamaica, than he could the tyrannies of the Communist ideologues.

Back in Key West by the beginning of February 1935, he and Katy remained there until June. In March, while fishing with Hemingway, Dos heard the sad news that the Murphys' son Baoth was dead of mastoiditis. Both he and Katy wrote the Murphys the next day, but they could offer little real comfort.

The rest of the spring in Key West passed with few extraordinary events, except Hemingway's shooting himself accidently one day while he, Katy, Dos, and others were fishing from the *Pilar*. He was trying to kill a shark he had caught and gaffed alongside the boat, and when the gaff broke, his pistol discharged into both legs, just as Dos described it in a letter to Patrick Murphy, Gerald and Sara's son, who was in Saranac Lake for treatment of tuberculosis at the Trudeau Hospital. Healing, Hemingway was ready to fish again the next week around Bimini Key. Dos and Katy returned from there to Key West, Dos to rest from the residual effects of rheumatic fever that still lingered, and Katy to go to Baltimore for a brief hospitalization. Dos wrote her about his loneliness, amusing her with an episode in the adventure of a fox which apparently was a private joke between them and was a kind of satire of politics. When Hemingway in May related his version of an altercation between himself and Mike Strater, president of the Maine Tuna Club, Dos responded that it was "too damn bad about the President's Marlin."

At the end of April Malcolm Cowley had written inviting Dos to attend an International Congress of Writers for the Defense of Culture in Paris. He had only grudgingly written a piece already submitted to the American Writers' Congress that April and turned down the offer, in the same letter explaining why he had spoken out as forcefully against doctrinaire stances as he had. Cowley partly disagreed, and after he explained his reasons, Dos tried to clarify his beliefs: that the Communists could do nothing now but provoke oppression, and that a major problem was not one of left or right politics but of "worker-technician versus the bureaucrat." "No," answered Cowley in early June, "I think you are wrong about the Communists not being able to do anything except call down repression on themselves and others. . . . We have all got to hang together or we will hang separately."

Before heading to Provincetown, Katy and Dos went back over to Bimini. "It's a fantastic place," Katy wrote Gerald Murphy on June 20, "a crazy mixture of luxury, indigence, good liquor, bad food, heat, flies, land apathy and sea magnificence, social snoot, money, sport, big fish, big fishermen, and competitive passion. The big fishermen work over catching the big fish like Russians on a subway—they've got it all charted and organized and they're all out for records, and madly jealous of each other." She and Dos watched Ernest land a large tuna, an episode in part the basis for *The Old Man and the Sea*. Katy continued to Murphy:

> The fish are huge—a thousand pound tuna 800 pound sharks—600 pound marlin—We had the tuna on the line eight hours—Ernest finally brought him up, alive and almost landed when five sharks rushed him at once— They came like express trains and hit the fish like a planing mill—shearing off twenty-five and thirty pounds at a bite. Ernest shoots them with a machine gun, *rrr*—but it won't stop them—It's terrific to see the bullets ripping into them—the shark thrashing in blood and foam—the white bellies and fearful jaws—the pale cold eyes. I was really aghast but it's very exciting.

After visiting the Murphys in Saranac Lake, who were there to be with Patrick, Katy and Dos visited the MacLeishes in Conway, New Hampshire. Then he went on to Provincetown while she went to New York to try to sell some of her writing. After she returned, they settled into Provincetown until October, when they moved down to New York. They spent Christmas with the Murphys in Saranac Lake, trying to cheer up Patrick, of whom they were very fond. From time to time they sent him letters like the one describing Hemingway's shooting accident, or Katy would write an amusing note or bit of verse, and Dos would decorate the page with water color sketches.

> Dear Patrick,
> What can you say
> When it rains all day
> And only a duck
> Has any luck
> Except to record
> That we're very bored
> But respectfully yours
> The Chinese boors
> > Katy & Dos

went one verse, around which Dos painted ducks, the sun, and a Chinese couple, all holding umbrellas.

The first several months of 1936 were completely taken up with finishing *The Big Money* and then seeing it through page proofs. Thus until April they spent their time in Provincetown and New York; then, while he was still in the middle of reading proof, they took a short trip down to Key West and Havana, seeing Hemingway and afterward driving back up the east coast the latter half of May.

With *The Big Money* prepared for publication, Dos began a reading course he had set out for himself. He wanted to investigate American history, to dig into the country's past. This was, perhaps, his initial effort in a new direction; the first fruits would be the appearances of his introduction to *The Living Thoughts of Tom Paine* in 1940, and then in 1941 of *The Ground We Stand On: Some Examples from the History of a Political Creed*.

He could not help but be cheered by the prospects for *The Big Money*. Edmund Wilson wrote him in late July, praising it as a magnificent performance, and his editor "Cap" Pearce told him of an excellent advance sale. The novel appeared August 1, and in September Katy told Pauline Hemingway that the summer had been "a delirious roller-coaster kind of summer—all very up and down, fast yelling and out of control. . . ." She told of going on "a dandy trip to Maine with the Murphys and MacLeishes" and of plans to take in a round of State Fairs with the Murphys during the fall. When Dos heard of the chance of a second printing of *The Big Money,* he joked with Pearce that Harcourt, Brace was only running another printing of Hervey Allen's immensely popular historical novel *Anthony Adverse*.

Scott Fitzgerald—suffering from a cracked shoulder—wrote him in late September saying that the novel had had a tremendous effect on him. He found himself talking about the narratives as if he knew the characters personally. Dos, appreciating the note, responded, but spent his letter faulting Fitzgerald for the *Esquire* articles about his "crack-up."

And there were those who did not appreciate the book. Frank B. Copley, who had written a pedestrian biography of Frederick W. Taylor, complained vigorously to Dos, Harcourt, Brace, and the New York *Times* that Dos' facts were lifted straight from his book and that the picture of Taylor in *The Big Money* was defaming. It was a perplexing problem; what should an author do about acknowledging his sources? To Dos' letter "Cap" Pearce answered not to worry, but to check on any facts he might have doubt about. There the matter rested, apparently, although Dos did alter the biography slightly before putting it in *U.S.A.*

Although Dos fretted about sales and Harcourt, Brace's remaindering policies, *The Big Money* was in fact selling reasonably well, Pearce estimating in early November that the total sale then was 17,000 copies. Rarely were Dos' sales of "bestseller" proportions, but 17,000 copies was good news, and the excellent critical reception of the final volume of his trilogy must have made his efforts seem worthwhile.

To Ernest Hemingway
[*dictated to Katy Dos Passos*]

> The Johns Hopkins Hospital
> [Baltimore]
> *April 24, 1933*

Ay Compadre

Hope you are having luck with the finny monsters. Things are very bad in these parts. Brought Katy up here to have her tonsils out at cut rates and before I knew it was surrounded by medics and hog-tied in a little white bed under accusation of rheumatic fever and still have some of my term to serve—The only thing we could find out about rheumatic fever is that you can't have it in the tropics so you may see two thin and ghostly figures totter off the Ward Line any day, but can't tell about plans until I'm on my feet. Now can't even hold a pencil—Will let you know plans as soon as know plans but can't tell how long this damn thing will hang on—Hellishly painful—but that part better now—

> Dos

[Katy's note added]

Cuahtemoc (prominent Indian martyr) sank back then—and I step to the microphone. Oh Wemmedge it's awful. Pauline it's awful— But seems better today. Paws like boxing gloves for days—I'm writing you men (on writing machine.) M. Fish says he is working on Natural Enemies to finance a trip to Spain—Will write in proper hand (suo mano) as soon as gets use of it.

Who is Gingrich? says M. Fish? Explains situation lousy, work at standstill. Extreme irritability and feels trapped—How are you men? We send love

Your aff.
Katy

To Ernest Hemingway

Johns Hopkins Hospital
[Baltimore]
May 3 [*1933*]

Jesus Hem its mighty handsome of you to start raising that grand, but hold it for a while. Honestly I'll let you know if I need it. The thing is that if I get it off you I wont get it off our natural enemies, because its only when I'm broke that I start to chisel on them properly I've got a grand promised off Harcourt for the Spanish trip and am trying to make my agents presell some articles—also have nicked a lot of small sums off friends so that I'm able to pay my hospital bill and even the eventual medics—also Gantt is surrounding me with free medics and they are making the hospital cut rates also—so that way I'm really saving money being in here. Temperature cleared up yesterday for first time and feel pretty good—no pain for three or four days—This is a hellishly disagreeable disease, but is not chronic arthritis, in which I am damn lucky—according to the big boss medic here it always eventually leaves your carcase free (might be it leaves carcase enormously dilapidated) Only way known to avoid recurrence is to dodge under the tropic now and then

Gosh I'd like to be in Havana right now—must be damned instructive. Also I'd like to see a couple of your U boat marlins—I cant tell yet what I'll do when they let me out of this bed. How long will you stay in Habana? In any case I'd like to get to Spain maybe in time to take Katy to Pamplona. When are you sailing for Spain? Cant quite decide yet whether I can make it to Havana as I have many little jobs to do in libraries here before I sail—and getting sick has balled up all my plans for work—I'll write again in a couple of days when I'll be able to tell how fast I can get back on my feet. I sure would like to go through Havana while you're still there—and a touch of good sun and trade wind is just what I need

Been reading masses of Proust—you have to be awful sick and a little feverish to enjoy it—I think what people get is a cosy well to do feeling like a rich woman's appearance out that smells of flowers and lipstick and a little of gin and furniture polish—its surprizing how absolutely unarticulated his language is. You cant tell one sentence from the next. Half of the time I didnt know either where one began and another ended—because the punctuation is of the vaguest. He's not a hoax—but he's certainly no 'maitre'—Luck with the next monster.

Yrs
Dos

To Ernest Hemingway

[Johns Hopkins Hospital
Baltimore]
May 7 [1933]

Hi Hem—

Hope that chest didn't turn out to be anything—You said you were in bed. I'm anxious to know what your program is. Here's my situation—over fever etc and will be able to get up in a couple of days and get out of this damn hospital soon. But the sawbones claims, and he may be right, that I must lie around like a flounder for a month or six weeks after I get up—no exercise etc—this disease throws your heart and kidneys on the fritz—though all my innards are testing up O.K.— so I dont think I'll go to Havana—no use if I couldn't fish or anything—Damn shame because I sure wanted to see your Marlins— Gerald is sailing on 13th to Antibes and called up last week asking us to go with them—Damn handsome velvety offer We couldn't do that but might sail (Italian boat to Villefranche) later and lay up with them for a month or so—damn swell place to convalesce when you cant do anything—Then go to Spain and root around all summer. Dunque—when are you going to Spain and where? Jez I need a good trip after a damn disagreeable month Been lousy for Katy too—hanging around the hospital etc—and Baltimore's pretty flat as a recreation center

Be sure to drop a line

Got a letter from Bill seemed in very good shape—he's still trying to get a foothold in New York hell of a difficult business—

Damn it—I wanted to get a look at Havana—but what's the use if I couldnt go around or go boating or anything—

All my plans for work are frigged up for fair, too. Soon—we might sail the 20*th*—We'll certainly be here till tenth and then Hotel Lafayette N.Y.

How's Pauline? Esther says Bumby's turned into a giant fisherman—

Katy sends love to you both. Miss Tonsilectomy's picking up a little too—

Yrs
Dos

To Edmund Wilson

[Johns Hopkins Hospital
Baltimore
May 10, 1933]

Dr. E. Anti X Wilson
314 E. 53*rd* Street
New York City
Dear Sir and Dr.

Oh Doctor Wilson I have followed your advice religiously. I have applied hot and cold Proustian complexes to my extraverted limbs and joints, but Dear Sir and Dr., I get little or no relief. The phrases are so long and iridescent and the sentences hang out of the poultice in long slightly writhing threads. It is very hard to know where one begins and another ends. I often have to reel in on an idea for several hours to get it into a Kataplasm and then the essential virtue has run over into the next volume. And the individual words and phrases are quite lifeless and have little or no therapeutic value. The sentences escape me like strands of undercooked spaghetti—Oh Dr are you sure this is a first rate product you recommended. I have to take such large doses to get any reaction. Of course in retrospect I find it very narcotic and soothing. I lie in bed thinking of when I was sick with asthma at Balboa, oh but even when I used to go there to tea I thought those Guernantes people tiresome. I dont even like to remember them and as for M. de Charlus what kind of a gentleman is he? Oh Dr. are you sure? Perhaps the powders I have have deteriorated, though they are still in the original package with M. Gallimard's guarantee still legible. Oh Dr. I fear that if I dont get stronger medicine the disease will become chronic. In great distress sincerely I am your

Doshe Kalb

To Ernest Hemingway

> [Johns Hopkins Hospital
> Baltimore]
> *May 10* [*1933*]
> I'll be here another week

Say Hem I didnt want to cut into your African trip like that—Jesus that means fifty less jiggs on the safari. But its frankly an enormous convenience, particularly as I got 200 bucks off Gingrich that I'll have to return—I thought I could do a piece on Scottsboro for his front number—but I'm getting over this so damn slowly that I dont think I'll be able to do the necessary running around to get the material for it before I sail. The Italian boat doesnt sail till the 25*th* Gerald & Sara sail the 13*th* Katy's had to go to Provincetown to fix up her house to rent to summer boarders. I miss her. This damn disease is letting up gradually, but every four or five days I get a slight set back that holds things up. Jeez I'm beginning to feel what a hell of a lousy time you had in Billings.

I see Scott every two or three days—Zelda's better but its all hellishly precarious—Scott's in pretty good shape—aging up damn well—a hell of a lot less flighty than he used to be. He's certainly had no picnic these last years. He's finishing up that novel, the way he talks about it I wouldn't wonder if it was a knockout—

This disease is mild in my case and nobody ever dies of it but its one hellish nuisance—For gods sake let me know when you start to need all that jack back. Because it can be raised—I'm getting to be a damn nuisance to my friends & well wishers—love to Pauline

> Yrs
> Dos

To Edmund Wilson

> [Baltimore
> *May 16, 1933*]

Dear Bunny—

Thanks for the Conquerants. It gives you more idea of China than anything except perhaps some articles by Agnes Smedley. It gives me a nostalgia for the small world I grew up in where the Orient was all dark, and east of Suez instead of West of Frisco! Speaking of nostalgia I must confess I'm being had by Proust—after reading endless volumes

I find I can no longer do without it. And I must admit that the scene in the seaside whore house where M. de Charlus is looking for Morel and the scene in the café where he threatens to fight the duel, are as funny as Fielding. I can hardly wait for a friend of mine to get *La Prisonniere* out of the library for me. I'm afraid its introversion setting in. In fact I can feel a delicate mould of libido growing all through me, producing a pale fluorescence of tiny incests, tangled inferiorities, a light fuzz of thwarted desires, like you find when you open a rotten peach. By the time I get out of the hospital I'll be nothing but an old nostalgic brokendown Prousty.

Miss Loney Hearts starts out wonderfully. Its a damn shame the guy couldn't keep it up—I found all my interest dribbled away in the last few chapters and I finished it as dogeyed as if I'd been reading the New Yorker—It gets too damn smart, or maybe I'm just an old Prousty from the nineteen twenties, wanting my Galsworthy pap and my Lawrence gingersnap or a good dramfull of Evelyn Scott. Damn it I hope Cantwell's new book is good. I like to fall for very current literature.

Roosevelt continues a fascinating performer. He's no cripple; he's a sleek wire artist; see how delicately (just 24 hours after he'd sponsored it) he handed the red hot sales tax to Congress. The upshot of it is, that you and me and The Forgotten Man are going to get fucked plenty, but its almost a pleasure to be liquidated by such a bonny gentleman. And if he had false teeth and his eyes were a little further apart he'd be the spitting image of George Washington.

Hope to move the enfeebled and rapidly introverting carcase to New York towards the end of this week, weather permitting—

Yrs
Dos

To Ernest Hemingway

[Johns Hopkins Hospital
Baltimore
May 18, 1933]

Who the hell said I was getting out of here the tenth? Had a little setback, but now in fine shape—temperature subnormal, have been up, sat out in the hospital yard, etc, and it's pretty certain I can get out of here in a day or two. Damn silly business, I'm thoroughly ashamed of the old ancestral carcase for harboring such a disease. We're sailing for Antibes (Villefranche) the 25th—Conde Savoia—Gerald and Sara went and bought our tickets which was damn sweet of them—so we'll travel speziale in great style. This sickness has turned out to be a gigantic panhandling enterprise. The wily portugesee shakes down his friends. Damn lucky to be equipped with same. Anxious to hear your plans and news of Cuba. It must be damn interesting there.

Didn't Hitler roar sweetly as any sucking dove? And what about the slight of hand artist sitting in his wheelchair at the White House? Pretty Smooth.

I dont think there are going to be any wars or rumpuses for a while—only the slow extinction of the working stiffs and white collar grinds to a sound of lovely oratory. The peasant hunters and fishers'll be damn lucky if they dont get liquidated with the rest of us. If poor old Marx got out of his grave he certainly wouldn't know the working class. Only Wisconsin mars the lovely picture; thank God for the hayseed that discovered that you can throw a teargas bomb two ways.

I guess we'll enter Spain via Barcelona and mill around and leave in the fall for the U.S. by Vigo or Coruña, so as to see Santiago. Anxious to find out how much it costs to rent a Citroën or Peugeot or some little cheap coffeegrinder. A hell of a lot better to drive around than to go by train. I want to be a good while in Madrid, though it'll be hot. I'll have to be very quiet for a month, no moving around. After that I think I'll be back in the old form. What'll your Spanish address be? When sail? Love to Pauline

Yrs
Dos

To Ernest Hemingway

[On board ship to Europe
May 25, 1933]

Dear Hem

Damn Tootin we'll be in Spain, dead or alive. To attain that situation, haven't I just signed a contract to write a book (short book) about the Second Republic which will be burned by Hitler, pissed on in the Kremlin, used for toilet paper by the anarchist syndicalists, deplored by the Nation, branded by the New York Times, derided by the Daily Worker and left unread by the Great American Public. Being on a boat even a wop superdeluxe liner (just passed Flores—looked damn handsome—all green and plowed fields and waterfalls coming over the cliffs) has had a very therapeutic effect—Katy and I sleep twenty hours a day eata da spagett' the rest of the time—beginning to limber up in spite of the fact that it rains to beat hell night and day. I bet it'll be snowing at Antibes. Stuff like that always happens when the old valetudinarian goes out looking for the sun.

An "old buddy" of yours (frightful guy) named Captain Cohn came around to the Hotel when I was teetering around there waiting for the boat, stayed all afternoon, and claims he can sell any kind of used paper for gigantic sums, MS etc—Still he's just the kind of bull-shitter who could do it and may be useful—meanwhile your other buddy Captain Gingrich sent me back my two hundred again & $75 for drawing—asking for any type of used paper for his Rogers Peet Quarterly Sure I'll send him some—first time ever asked for used paper by an editor of a paying magazine Your buddies may come in very handy, Captain Hemingway. Jez I hope they wont be so upset by what they get that it wrecks the works. Maybe its new sources of income (other than sablazos a los amigos) rearing their ugly heads.

We'll be at Villa America, most of June—after that I'll let you know Spanish address—we'll probably go to your Hotel Biarritz in Madrid—Damn swell about the big marlin catch—we'll have to try the Gulf of Tehauntepec sometime. or off Cape Cod—big swordfish grounds off Block Island—love to Pauline

Yrs
Dos

To Theodore Dreiser (1871–1945), *the noted author of naturalistic fiction, whom Dos admired greatly. The two went to Harlan County, Kentucky, in 1931 to investigate labor conditions there. They kept in occasional contact afterward, always respecting each other's writing.*

[Hotel Alphonso
Madrid]
Sept 10. [*19*]*33*

Dear Dreiser,

I've been moving around a good deal and considerably hampered by my not having quite recovered from that damn rheumatic fever, so you must forgive me for not answering your very kind letter. I'd hoped to send you a piece before this, but although I have a lot of stuff in preparation, I have nothing ready yet;—inside of a couple of months I hope to be able to detach a short piece of some kind that will go in the Spectator. Sailing for home in a couple of weeks. World picture looks about as lousy as could be, doesn't it? If Franklin D. gets out 39 battleships to help the Americans save their dollars invested in Cuba, what about the poor gringos who invested their dollars at home in Iowa. It would be hard to get the battleships up the Mississippi, but they could always send those brave boys the marines with Admiral Swanson at their head to shoot up the bankers. And how about my dollars that are turning into fifty cent pieces right in my pocket now, and that have to buy my passage home, don't they deserve at least a navy tug?

Damn nice of you to have written

Sincerely yours
John Dos Passos

I read your preachment in Walter Winchell's column—I think you are right to give them a piece of your mind whenever any opportunity presents itself.

To Ernest Hemingway

571 Commercial Street
Provincetown Mass.
[October 1933]

Dear Hem—

Settling down to the old stand—have a hugeous amount of work to do—Thank Jinny for the 300 pesetas—we certainly needed them—will send a draft as soon as I get cheque from Captain Gingrich—How long will you be in Spain? How did the wild boars work out? Damned anxious to hear—also how things are going in Spain—from lousy to frightful, certainly looks like. Damn disappointed I couldn't see more of you gents, also get around Spain more—Summer was pretty much of a fracaso—was sick as hell in Gibraltar—but picked up on boat and now—weak but damn well—getting better every day—I think the disease is finally licked—Got myself looked over by an elderly Boston Medico, who seemed to think vital organs all o.k. and that it was just a question of time and rest. Let's hear from you from time to time when you're among the leos and the wildebeestes—

The U.S. is funny as hell under the Blue Eagle—but the chances are it wont be so funny after a while when the boys really start to clamp down—I've got to get to see a lot of stuff right away before they clamp down so tight nobody but Louis Bromfield'll be allowed to publish books—Things are certainly going to get worse—business already falling off—and Congress in Jan will be roaring and tearing for inflation—and these damn codes absolutely hogtie labor—leaving the boys running the monopolies in full control of the situation—of course Roosevelt is the cleverest politician turned out in many moons—but he cant sit on the lid indefinitely anymore than Azaña can—Please let me know if Azaña's really out or whether he is hovering in the background of Martinez Barrios—it certainly didn't take him long to deflate Lerroux—and I have a suspicion he'll be in again—men like Roosevelt and Azaña can keep up their slick wire walking as long as a majority of people manage to eat—but after that they have to give up the stage to more muscular and preposterous forms of hooey—

Speaking of Hooey—how's your friend Mr Bromfield's (our novelist laureate) return backscratching for Miss Stein. I haven't read the book yet as want to borrow instead of buy—

Katy's in splendid shape—sends love to all you gents—damn it I feel cheated out of those exterminated jabalís.

Yrs
Dos

To Malcolm Cowley

571 Commercial Street
Provincetown, Mass.
[February 4, 1934]

Dear Malcolm—

Forgive the messy manuscript—sending it just on the chance you might be interested in these two little squibs about Moscow and thereabouts—

Old Johnny Hopkins raised his gory head so I had to come back here and retire to bed for a couple of days instead of going to Washington—shall go before the first, however. I'm collecting the material for the other (atrocities) article by letter—but fear I'll be considerably delayed on it. This sickbed business is a damn nuisance—Will go straight on South from Washington and hang myself on a clothesline in the sun—

Yrs
Dos

I'll send the Washington stuff by mail from there—

To Malcolm Cowley

1401 Pine Street
Key West Fla
March 16 [1934]

Dear Malcolm,

Forgive the accursed delay in this list & book review of Bill Rollins whopping fine novel—but have been having horrible masses of proofs to read—unwisely hatching two volumes this spring (nonfiction)— Now settled and sunny in K.W. with nothing to do but burn my beak in the sun and listen to the coconuts fall on the asphalt—Say—if you people have any cheques round there—send them down here please and for God's sake make them as large as you can as I ruined myself running round Washington in 20 cent taxicabs in pursuit of Knowl- edge. My best to Bliven.

Yrs
Dos

To Edmund Wilson

1401 Pine Street
Key West Florida
[March 23, 1934]

Dear Bunny—

Thanks for that mass of N.M. enclosures—I had only seen their letter to me—I wrote them a short answer which they don't seem to have published—let me know if you see it. I dont intend to imply by it that the socialists arent bums too—I think it's very important not to add to the mass of inept rubbish on this subject—what is happening is that the whole Marxian radical movement is in a moment of intense disintegration—all people like us, who have no taste for political leadership or chewing the rag, can do, is to sit on the sidelines and try to put a word in now and then for the underdog or for the coöperative commonwealth or whatever—The Marxians have gotten into one of those hopeless situations like the French Huguenots in the years before St. Bartholomew, where everything they do helps the reaction—The Huguenots were right and so are the Marxians right—but I think we're fast getting into a situation where there'll be nothing left to do but go to the stake with as much dignity as we can muster—The only alternative is passionate unmarxian revival of AngloSaxon democracy or an industrial crisis helped by a collapse in the director's offices—That would be different from nazi socialism only in this way: that it would be a reaction towards old time Fourth of July democracy instead of towards feudalism—as we havent any feudalism in our blood I dont see very well how we can react towards feudal habits the way the heinies do.

How you can coordinate Fourth of July democracy with the present industrial-financial setup I dont see. Maybe Roosevelt is already as far as we can go in that direction But if you dont put your money on the Communists—it's no use putting it on anybody else until they've proved something—Wish you could come down here for a few days—

Yrs in Xst

Dos

To Charles A. Pearce (1906–1970), *whom Dos met when "Cap" was an editor at Harcourt, Brace. Pearce went on to found Duell, Sloan and Pearce, Inc., where he was editor in chief. Later he became executive editor of the Meredith Press and was also involved in other publishing ventures.*

[Key West
April 1934]

Dear Pearce—

The books came. The makeup and cover etc I liked—I suppose the jacket'll get by in a crowd. There's one thing we slipped up on—I say we because I should have caught it when you showed me the blurb—(The trouble is I'm constitutionally unable to read the damn things and just hold them in my hand and stare at them when my opinion is asked)—I mean referring to my lecturing . . . I never lecture—have only made speeches a few times in my life and consider lectures an extremely bum way of passing the time. I'm always getting offers of lecture dates and always write the people politely that it's not my line of work—so if they read that on the jacket they'll tend to think that I was lying. If you exhaust the present printing of jackets—perhaps it would be possible to cut that word out. I dont suppose it matters a hell of a lot, but it gives a very false picture of the life and habits of yr. humble servant.

I certainly hope this book wont be the flop Nineteen Nineteen was on the sales end. Getting in the red & need the money—and then you like to have the damn books read outside of an ever narrowing group of friends and wellwishers—

Yrs
JDP

To Ernest Hemingway

Hotel Hollywood Plaza
Hollywood, California
July 27 [1934]

Dear Hem—

That must have been quite a fish—wish I could get down—but I've just signed up to serve a term of five weeks in Hollywood teaching Spanish or something like that to Von Sternberg—I was in a sort of a gap in my work and thought I might as well take a stab at it, restoring my finances and taking a look at the world's great bullshit center— Flew across the continent in 22 hours—damned exciting to see the damn continent like that— filled two quart cartons full of vomit and felt a little groggy—also the look of this lousy suburb kind of gives me the sick—but its all very educational I suppose—

Was darn glad to hear that the boat had turned out so well—Are you taking that trip up to the west end of the island? Be sure to let me hear about it if you do. I wish I could be going on a good trip instead of undergoing this performance—but I need some of this stuff in my business and the best way to get it is to see it from the inside—but it doesn't look as if it was going to be as entertaining as I'd hoped. Katy's coming out in a couple of weeks and we'll go and see the worlds fair on the way back, but that probably wont be as entertaining as we'd hoped either—People you meet out here greet you with a nasty leer like the damned in Dante's Inferno—but I dont see what they have such meany consciences about—I'll probably learn in the next two or three weeks—Give Pauline my best.

Yrs
Dos

To Katy Dos Passos

[Hollywood]
[*August 1934*]

Oh Katy—it seems years since I left you and Patapoof at Fall River—
I'm now lying in bed (just a precautionary measure) as I fear a little
touch of the Chinese intermittent—Its not very funny around here—
but it is certainly worth seeing—I must be softening up through
affection and easy living and the luxuries of the imperial bed chamber—because I find myself feeling about Mr. Von S. and the Paramount a lot like a small boy who's just been sent to boarding school—
still I've almost ticked off a week already—I've spilt the milk and now
I've got to lap it up—so that's that. But I dont think I'll be found in
these parts soon again—

Have seen Don Stewart. He seems in fine shape although he
complains of the collapse of his internal organs. I'm in bed reading
Chekhov's letters and meditating on the ideas for a movie of Mr. Von
S. I'm fed by phony Russian waiters who bring up phoney Russian
food from the restaurant downstairs. That restaurant is funny; it looks
just like a place I used to go to in Constantinople years ago—except
that the pretty little Russian and Polish girls seem to have disappeared.
I suppose, if they survive, they put on those Hollywood faces. And the
music's not so good as it used to be. It's a curious place out here all
right.

I think I'll move over to Francis Faragoh's tomorrow or this
afternoon—I'll wire you the address—I'm treating the intermittent with
great care and respect and expect to be all right by tomorrow—

lots of love—I miss you so—prepare to be pretty bored out here—
but it wont be for long—love   Dos

Oh possum I suppose I'd have heard if you hadnt gotten back all
right from Fall River——

To Ernest Hemingway

Care Francis Faragoh
1644 No. Orange Grove Ave.
Hollywood California
Aug 20–[19]34

Hay Hem—

what are you up to? How is the cuban coast shaping up? Drop me
a line. What I did the minute I got out to this dump was put on a

small bout with the old rheumatic fever—In spite of statistics and the medicasters I seem to be getting over it, heart still o.k. also liver lights & kidneys—but weak as hell as I've been in bed nearly four weeks— Damn silly business. Everybody says I mustn't ever get another fit and prescribes tropics or Tucson Arizona. I've been writing my story for Mr. Von Sternberg all the time so its been a fairly profitable little illness—but never again This place is funny to see, but its no place for yrs truly—What are you doing this fall? I'm going to be back on an invalid status but active in a small way and trying to get some more sun on my carcase.

Katy just got out—she had a hell of a time—a couple of weeks at Columbia, Mo. with the temperature at 112 every day—Her father died and she got here to find me all tied up in knots surrounded by a long faced physician who was treating me for infectious arthritis and getting me considerably sick—So it hasn't been very hot for her—Also agreeable plans for fall boating on the cape more or less pooped—as I'll have to stay south for several months at least—anyway we'll pay our debts.

Say do you think £250 (free from tax) is a fair outright price for four novels published in England from Manhattan Transfer to the next one, outright sale of royalties to last five years from publication of next novel? Its a way of avoiding the gigantic English tax, but at the same time I suspect I'm getting gypped. Constable is the publisher. I said I'd think about it. What do you think?
Love to Pauline & Kids

Yrs
Dos

To Edmund Wilson

c/o Francis Faragoh
1644 No. Orange Grove Aveune
Hollywood
August 24—[19]34

Dear Bunny,

As it happens I've been stepping heavily on the orange juice and neglecting the sterling old Cape Cod characters—What I did on arriving at this remarkable burg via Ford trimotor somewhat gone with vomit, was to take one look at Mr. Von S. and that old smutstory by Pierre Louys, now happily dead, called La Femme et Le Pantin, and to dive into bed with an attack of rheumatic fever. And you say you dont believe in microbes. I was discovered in a local hotel being tended by a dreary group of fake Russian balalaika players by Francis Faragoh who very kindly dragged me off to his house where I've lain all the past month. In some way that I dont quite understand I am still collaborating with Mr. Von Stern and the walking ghost of Pierre Louys on this little drama of Spanish passion and still receive my salary. But frankly je ne suis pas heureux ici.

I've had considerable conversation with the medicasters and they claim I've got to remain in a tropical climate, or at least Tucson for some time I'm checking up on that but it may somewhat shuffle our future habits for this winter at any rate.

I've been so thoroughly in bed that I've seen nothing of Red raids or the Epic campaign. The odds are 2 to 1 in favor of Upton Sinclair getting the Democratic primaries, but everybody thinks the conservatives will gang up on him and elect Haight in November. However one should point out that three months ago the same everybody was poohpooing the Epic business. I think its easy to overestimate this sort of thing—at the same time its easy to underestimate it as the comrades do. U.S. is damn shrewd and in a curious way presents a real class issue—taking his point of cleavage at the $3000 proprietor—and he's getting exactly that vote. I dont suppose he will be elected, or that even if he was he would be able to establish his double standard society— However it must be handed to him that he has been the first radical to recognize the political importance of the double standard—(I mean the growing society for services T.V.A. etc along side of the society for exploitation.)

How are you keeping, Bunny? Gosh I wish you'd go down to Boston and see that corps of physicians Katy had lined up for you— Please hold this fifty for a year or so—We'll probably need it more later because this is my last emergence into the big money. Please take a turn at the Lahey Clinic—

Yrs
Dos

Poor Katy got here after a pretty gloomy period. It was 112° in Columbia, Mo. Her father died and everything was pretty bad. We are both beginning to perk up a bit now. Give our best to Niles and Betty—and to Arrie

Yrs
Dos

To Robert Cantwell (1908–   ), *the author of, among other books,*
Laugh and Lie Down *and* The Land of Plenty. *Dos and he admired
each other's work and, particularly during the 1930's, corresponded
about their mutual concern for American society.*

> care Faragoh
> 1644 No. Orange Grove Avenue
> Hollywood
> [*September 1934*]

Dear Cantwell,

Hell man, write it anyway. There'll always be places to publish
books—and it's always doubtful anywhere about publishing a book
that's any good. We'll probably see the time when people will have to
publish under an assumed name and then run like hell. That's what
old Voltaire used to do and it certainly didn't limit his output. The
racket's too easy now, that's why its all choked up with phonies.

I've taken so long fighting off this damned rheumatic fever attack
I shan't be able to get to Frisco at all. We had planned to buy a car and
to go out that way—but I'm not going to be able to go east all this
winter—the dope seems to be to stay in the tropics—so we are sailing
on the 6th of Oct for the Canal Zone and Havana. I'll probably hang
around there for awhile.

I'd love to see you if you should come by this way. Drop me a line
first

Frankly I dont see all this fatalism about fascism on the part of the
communists. If you mean repressive violence, sure, we've always had
that tougher than anywhere; if you mean Hearstian demagoguery,
sure—Hearst is handsome Adolph's schoolteacher—but fascism organized into the state I cant see—I dont think its in the breed—I think
you've got to have the feudal pattern in the social heritage to make it
stick—and that's one thing we haven't got. What turns out in Mussolini & Hitler in semifeudal Europe (Germany & Italy only date from
1870 as pseudomodern nations) in this country turns out in Al
Capone—Bilbo—Huey Long Upton Sinclair—Franklin D, the noblest
Roman of them all, Try to fit that group together into a fascist state. I
dont mean that the monopolies aren't going to run us, but I think
there's more life in the debris of democracy than the comrades do—; of
course they dont see it, working in industry, which is just where all
trace of democracy has been eliminated—but once you get outside of the
closed factory town you feel it—(that's why they have to keep those

towns closed up so damned tight—I bet you Stuttgart is a libertarian paradise compared to Wierton), and I think any movement towards ousting the bosses has got to mobilize that basic trend—Communism & Socialism now both run counter to it in most places—Petit bourgeois delusions, sure,—but delusions shared by so many millions. There are the same obstacles in the way of fascism that there are in the way of communism. Maybe the monopolists can overcome those obstacles— the reds, instead of giving them a clear field ought to try to get there first. I'd like to see 'em hang red ribbons on the liberty bell and take it away from the Chase National Bank—

Yrs
J Dos Passos

To C. A. Pearce

1644 North Orange Grove Avenue
Hollywood, California
September 18, 1934

Dear Cap Pearce,

Would you mind having a Three Plays sent to Julia Dorn, The International Union of the Revolutionary Theater, Suite 69, Petrovka 10, Moscow, U.S.S.R. I've been having another bout with the rheumatic fever, complicated by a short glimpse of Hollywood. Guess I'll have to stay some where in the tropics this winter. All this complicates matters so that all bets are off as to when I can have the manuscript of the last volume. I hope at least to be able to send you the title soon. If you people sold more books you wouldn't have me out in the red-light district like this, but coming to think of it I probably would have had to take a look at it anyway. It is interesting and not at all funny, but California, at least what I can gather over the radio lying in bed, is wonderful. Take care of yourself. My best to Messrs Harcourt and Brace.

Yours,
John Dos Passos

To Edmund Wilson

1644 No. Orange Grove Ave.
Hollywood Cal.
Sept 24 [1934]

Dear Bunny—

We were delighted to hear from Edie that you'd appeared in New York looking very fit. I certainly hope your distempers are definitely liquidated. Mine, as you suggested, have been frazzling out in a reluctant sort of way ever since that last paragon of old Viennese culture and I parted (on terms of mutual esteem) over the telephone. There was no reason for any burning of shirts;—I was merely in the position of Queen Marie endorsing a vanishing cream. It turns out that all the while a young man, whose name I believe is Nertz, was writing the real screen play behind the scenes. I'm darn sorry I wasnt able to stagger round the studios some more. It was interesting there though the horrid stalking of intangibles makes it more nerve-wracking, I imagine, than the average industrial plant.

I've greatly enjoyed reading your articles on Michelet and Renan— I haven't read Michelet since I was a kid and discovered some volumes of his history among a lot of blue paper Dumas books my father used to read to put him to sleep. I must say they kept me awake. I must read some more of him.

Since I've been in bed I've been reading a good deal of Veblen. He takes a good deal of reading. I admire his delicate surgeon's analysis more and more. In spite of the fact that everything he deals with is abstracted for classroom use, I shouldn't wonder if he were the only American economist whose work had any lasting value. His work is a sort of anthropological footnote to Marx. If you haven't read him recently you should read him—The Vested Interests or the Nature of Peace or Business Enterprise—(I think The Leisure Class is more or less of a side issue, though it will always be considered the type Veblen satire). Imperial Germany makes an excellent prelude to Hitler Over Europe [Henri] and The Berlin Diaries [Klotz]—before you finish the series you are working on now. There certainly seems to me to be more ammunition in his analysis than in any other for us, because he seems to have been the only man of genius who put his mind critically to work on American capitalism—Stuart Chase and Howard Scott got all their analysis directly from him. And certainly he's of an entirely different stature than the purely literary critics, like Van Wyck Brooks and Randolph Bourne who have the same beforethewar limitations. Its amazing how fresh his clinical picture remains.

Having been for a few weeks in the big money makes us feel strangely broke and parsimonious. Also we are faced with paying our debts—I dont think the big money is what it's cracked up to be—And now I've got the miserable sawbones to pay.

The Medical Profession has a theory you cant get or entertain rheumatic fever in the tropics. To try that out we are taking the Fruit Line boat from here to Panama and Havana on Oct 6. I'll hang around the Antilles all winter and see how I am—I haven't been a hundred percent since I had that outbreak in Baltimore eighteen months ago— and I want to find some method of throwing the business off if I have to get in clairvoyants and chiropractors—

Take care of yourself—Katy's been awfully thin and blue but is beginning to pick up a little. It's suddenly turned icy cold here with considerable rain. Katy sends her best.

Yrs
Dos

To Malcolm Cowley

1644 No. Orange Grove Ave.
Hollywood, Cal.
[October 1934]

Dear Malcolm—

The carcase is almost what the medical books call ambulant, and I've said good bye to Paramount, so I feel very much better. It's not exactly anything to be unhappy about (except when you find all the money going to pay back debts) but it's nothing to feel very good about either—it's like endorsing absorbine junior or Beauty Rest mattresses—Working in the movies as part of the technical staff would be more interesting but its a life work. I've been in bed ever since I got here talking to the studios over the phone and listening to Epic, Angelus Temple and the Christian Hebrew Synagogue on the air— California's a great place right now. You can look out the window and watch the profit system crumble.

Say, if you did anything with those remarks by Russ Fuller, he wants them signed (—if published with signature) Louis Fortunado as fears loss of job.

Say, it amazes me that nobody, in any of the organs of comment, has made the tieup between Sec Wallace's letter and the Ward Line disaster. The thing is that even if you were a three star imperialist you'd have to admit it that the mail subsidies have resulted in turning our steamship companies into rackets and that they are so badly run its amazing their boats ever make port. I happen to have had an interview with the bunch of four flushers that ran the Ward Line three or four years ago and if ever I smelt crooks (plain fingerprinted crooks) I smelt them in that crowd.

Dr Bach's address is Dr. D. J. Bach

Mollardgasse 69

Vienna VI

Mighty handsome of Bliven to write him.

I feel strongly about the shipping business because this disease is going to force me to spend a good deal of time in the tropics and I have to use their lousy boats—My best to Bliven & Betty Huling

Yrs

Dos

To F. Scott Fitzgerald

Hotel Ambos Mundos

Havana

Oct 19 [1934]

Dear Scott

Darn nice to hear from you. The trouble with me is I cant seem to throw off this damn rheumatic infection. We came round by boat to Havana and I shall have to hang out here or in Key West for a long time to come. The only dope about this disease seems to be that it is less severe in the tropics, so I'm going to try it out. The prospect is a long period of invalidism or something of the kind. Still I suppose it's not a bad way of getting a lot of work done. And there's a chance that I can get ambulant, as the medicasters put it, fairly soon. The old carcase seems pretty well pooped, but I havent quite lost hope of its getting on its feet again. California is very funny—I liked it fine out there—the screen writer is certainly a lamentable specimen. I didn't think the other people were so bad—racketeers, three card men etc rather funny to see for a while—

Old Hem is here pursuing marlin and latterly, humpbacked whales; he's in fine shape.

Katy's well, but its no fun for her suddenly to have to turn into a trained nurse—Sends love. How's yourself?

Drop me a line here—

Dos

To John Howard Lawson

[Havana(?)]
[*October (?) 1934*]

Dear Jack—

I think that Hollywood has been enormously instructive and greatly envy your experience there—all that cinema talk about integrity is the purest and most mouldy mahoula. And you may be right about the little dramas—damn sorry I didn't see them—It was damn handsome of the Group to make that hand out of the two grand. I wonder if a lot of their faults aren't just from New York neo-ghetto ignorance—the typical jewish New Yorkers seem to me more and more (I say Jewish because all cultured New Yorkers are jewish in mentality [A. Hitler please copy]) ignorant innocent and lacking in the sophistication of the average hired hand on a Georgia peanut farm—That makes them singularly illadapted to deal with the infantile-sophisticated, degenerate-energetic, vicious mentality of the epoch we are now entering—After all the whole New York jewish theatre guild, Damrosch, Otto Kahn Mike Gold culture (I mean jewish in the best sense) is an echo of the liberal mitteleuropa culture that has just bitten the dust with such a fearful crash in Europe—leaving people nothing but their feudal reflexes that take the form of Mussolini and Adolph Hitler. And you cant tell me that small groups of thugs can capture a continent unless the social organism they destroy has already collapsed from internal causes. Still the Groupies are young and might learn. What I'm trying to bring out is that we are now about to have to cope with the Georgia niggerraping peanut grower—The other thing is spent except in so far as (through Hollywood) it influences the simple sadisms and masochisms of the Georgia peanut grower. Erskine Caldwell overstates it, but not by a very high percentage. We have no feudal mechanisms to fall back on—we have nothing but desire under the cemetery elms, lynching bees, General Motors and the Ford car to fall back on when the irresistible reaction hits us. I dont think the groupies in their sheltered world understand these things. What I mean is that I'd rather have Red Square appear under the name of Bullet Proof Vest than 'Marching Song' or why not still go on calling it 'Red Square'—but it's important to remember that what's being carried on is a retreat—now a well conducted retreat is more valuable than a million gushy advances. What we're going to need now is dugouts, camouflaged trenches, trained snipers—just think back to 1919—May one in Paris Ville Lumière and figure out how much bigger the chance of socialism by revolution was then—Goddamn it if you're sailing on a rocky coast you've got to know whether the tide is running in or out—

I think all these rather confused remarks apply very much to the C.P.—the New York jewish leadership (me and Adolph just anti-semite buddies) seems to me to be indulging in a delirium of "you're bigger than I am, well hit me" tactics only equalled by the heresy manias of the early Christians as described by Gibbon—People who are on the right side seem to have a way of turning into bed bugs and lice—I didn't see Mike's remarks about you but I can imagine them. The result of this sort of thing is that people will hit them and knock their goddamn blocks off—I cant see that the whole Marxian-German socialist and Russian Jewish communist isnt frittering away into vicious and childish nonsense—If I thought there was anything in the Mustyite Am. Workers party I'd certainly be for it but I fear that they are just emasculated communists. The communists have at least a shrill vituperative heroism that you cant help admiring. I've been read-ing the Industrial Worker weekly with considerable pleasure—I still feel more in common with the wobbly line of talk than any other—and their clever absorption of technocracy data and their cheerful kidding of the comrats is a great relief after the humorless monotone of the Daily Worker—I think what's needed is a caustic testing of all the marxian premises in view of a psychology of defense (I dont say that maybe attack isn't the best defense) and an entirely refurbished view of people and events (such as the war furnished people of our generation fifteen years ago—

love to Sue

. . . just another old social fascist

Yrs
Dos

What I mean by harping on the jewish note is that I am just beginning to realize how much of New York rebellious mentality is a jewish European import and how it is dying out now that the sources have been bottled up. Now it's the creation of an american mentality or death—the dirty nationalist forms this will take will be the answer to a very real organic need—if we dont meet it, Dr. Wirt and the Silver Shirts will—

To Gerald (1888–1964) and Sara (1883–   ) Murphy, *whom Dos first knew in Paris in the 1920's, and with whom he remained on best terms all his life. The Murphys' kindnesses and flair for friendships with the likes of Picasso, Hemingway, the Fitzgeralds, and many other famous artists are recounted with great talent in Calvin Tomkin's* Living Well Is the Best Revenge.

> After Nov—10—about
> care Gen'l Delivery
> Key West Fla
> Hotel Ambos Mundos
> *Oct 30* [*1934*]

Dear Gerald—Sara—

We are most anxious to hear how and where you all are. Do drop us a line when you get a chance Havana is pleasanter than I have ever known it. We are in an agreeable Spanish hotel in two agreeable rooms with a view of the port and the Morro—not a tourist or a Havana blonde in sight. I'm beginning to pick up again and am now almost back to where I was last summer on the Weatherbird. I shant go north at all this winter—but shall try to toast myself in the sun and to take all possible measures to get this infection out of the system. It's a great pleasure to be on my feet again—

Hem's in wonderful shape, got a lot of dope about the marlin this summer, and discovered thirty six unlisted varieties of fish but had poor luck in size; they wouldn't come larger than 300 lbs.

This is certainly not the moment I would have chosen for navigating the Antilles but we are going to make the best of it. I'm going over to K.W. for a month while Katy goes north—then we'll get to some very hot island for six weeks or so, then, in the latter part of the winter, we thought we'd go and look you up in Tucson or wherever you've decided to nest in the injun country. By that time I ought to have a good deal of dope about curing the rheumatics—Are you & Sara going to be in New York before Christmas? Would like to know address.

Oh I wish you were all down here and everybody was well. We

could have some sessions again with the Camerones and the Marquis of Riscal, that splendid nobleman. Langostinos, no hay, but shrimp and stone crabs to a superlative degree. The cookery in Havana is magnificent as always—

People are still horribly poor down here and their main sport is still setting off small bombs in butchershops and lately in yachts and sailboats—but in the sun on the roof of the hotel it's very agreeable for us valitudinarians   love to all

Dos

To Edmund Wilson

Hotel Ambos Mundos
Nov 2 [1934]
Havana Cuba

Dear Bunny—

What the devil has happened about the Scottsboro case? From what I can make out from papers I get here the fat is in the fire for fair and one of those unfortunate nigs is bound to fry—Let me know if you can find out why the appeal wasn't filed in time—did the communists bolt Liebowitz or whatever his name is or did he bolt them or did the money run out? In any case its one of those situations from which nobody emerges with credit—and the poor devils of nigs are done for—

Looks like Uppie was slipping in California—obviously he didn't sell out—I guess nobody'll go around anymore saying they are out to abolish poverty—it's too patently kicking the props out from under the capitalist system—It makes a pretty bunch of two timing jellyfish out of Farley Roosevelt and Creel—swines I call 'em. AAA ought to pay mothers not to raise boys like that.

Have you seen the abracadabrating (to Mr Brooks Atkinson) work of O'Casey. Looks to me like another good man gone goofy. I tell you these are lean years for the selfstyled human race.

We're comfortable here in Havana—though the town is sunk, everything has petered down to Batista grabbing everything for the army and occasional epidemics of insane bombing on the part of the populace—still the weather's agreeable; the food is good I'm still pretty sickly but can totter onto the roof and take a little sun every day. Its a pretty dreary existence, but I'm getting a certain amount of work done and improving a little in health I think—Soon going to Key West for more of the same

Read with pleasure your Anatole France remarks (I doubt if he's worth that amount of space) At least nobody will ever have to bring him up again in our lifetime—and I hope that goes for Joseph Conrad too—Darned anxious to read to next part—

Take care of yourself

Yrs
Dos

To Malcolm Cowley

803 Waddell Avenue
Key West Fla
Nov 13 [*1934*]

Dear Malcolm,

Thanks for your note. I'm kind of recuping here—it's not just where I'd planned to be this winter—I hope in a couple of weeks to have a piece on that fellow Becker, the last of the Centralia people, who's still in Walla Walla—perhaps you'd publish it as an article or a communication. Then a little later I'll be having fragments of the last volume of this damned opus—just at the moment I'm trying to get the somewhat shattered carcase concentrated on its muttons again.

Say, Malcolm—on Nov 20*th* at the Pierre Matisse gallery on E. 57*th* Street there's going to be an exposition of etchings by Luis Quintanilla. I think he's a great etcher. He's a hell of a good guy and is at present in jail as a member of the Madrid revolutionary committee— the fiscal is trying to get a sentence of sixteen years—If you like the stuff, please try and get the boys to go to bat for it, articles and stuff like that. I'm hoping that if he's hailed as Spain's best etcher which he is—in the great line of Goya etc it may be possible to circulate a petition of some kind that might induce the Spanish gov't to go a little easy on him. And it might be an opening wedge for a general protest on the way they crushed the rebellion. Its not so very pretty to use Moorish troops, bombing planes and heavy artillery on your own people and towns—then of course they blamed all the damage on the revolutionaries—I'm not implying that the Asturian miners didn't raise a good deal of hell in Oviedo before the communist committee got control of the situation. Anyway Quintanilla's work is damn good and he's a wonderful guy and everybody ought to do everything they can to get him out

> Yrs
> Dos

To Robert Cantwell

> 803 Waddell Avenue
> Key West Fla
> address for all winter
> *Nov 14 [1934]*

Dear Cantwell—

My plans have been continually bitched by new little fits of this damn malady that is a hell of a thing to shake off. Came round by boat to Havana through Panama. Nice trip. Panama very funny, though I didn't see as much of it as I'd like on account of being in bed as usual—were a couple of weeks in Havana—too sickly to see much— then came over here where I'm building up and leading a quiet and solitary life, working. Havana's damn nice to look at due to the lack of tourists, enormously interesting too as a sort of social laboratory. It's like these machines they are going to put in the men's rooms so that the gents can find out if they have clap or diabetes—you put in a specimen and a little bell rings and zingo you register the disease. Just as present its suffering from the derechista wave unleashed by the failure of the United Front revolt in Spain. I dont pretend to have any idea of what the situation really is, or of the lineup of the parties or personalities. Your friend Mendieta seems to be just a dummy for Batista, who talks such a blue streak of such profound shit that its impossible to discover anything at all about him. I imagine he's a wily selfseeking bastard, burnt up with the cruder kind of ambition and playing all parties including Yankee imperialism. Then there are the terrorists who have enormous quantities of dynamite and dont care who they blow up or when. Cubans, I take it, are generally louses, though with those extraordinary exceptional cases of personal purity that are more common in Latin countries than among more northern people. And now there are the quajiro squatters taking to the hills to keep the army from taking their land. They'll probably mean busi- ness—That miserable island would be a wonderful place for a man to make a careful study of capitalist contradictions and revolutionary failures. It would take years to get the dope—

I'm sending this to California as I dont know any other address.
Let me know your plans as I expect to be in Havana again in December for a while before going to Puerto Rico or Barbados or Jamaica (if
jack holds out) for a month or so. The Hotel Ambos Mundos, calle
Obispo—is darn nice—Katy and I stayed there at $35 a week board &
lodging for the pair—swell food two rooms overlooking harbor—and
it's cheaper on the back—Tell the people there you know us.

Your project for a project-novel made me think immediately of
Uppie Sinclair's I Governor of California—If you feel blue about the
novel as natural history read Defoe. Natural history doesn't need to
make any apologies to anybody—The trouble is that most novelists are,
like Cubans, louses, and spend their time tickling the libido of ladies
after their menopause. That doesnt mean that agitational literature
isn't a good thing. Look at the success of the four gospels. There might
be a hell of a lot in a project novel—

If you are driving down this way—Key West is quiet as a cemetery—airy and sunny and has limited bathing—it's horribly dull but
has some agreeable features—its fine for the halfsick and for deep sea
fishing—

Luck with Filene—

Yrs
J. Dos Passos

To Edmund Wilson

803 Waddell Ave
Key West—Fla
[November 15, 1934]

Dear Bunny—

I eat up greedily all tales of the brightlights—as I'm getting a little
tired of being perpetually divorced therefrom. Did you see the O'Casey
drama?—it sounds pretty bad, but maybe not. If you happen to have
Joe Freeman's article or that book about the president I wish you'd
send them down. I'll return them. There are getting to be too many
people around named Hoover. I even met a man in Washington
named Calvin B. Hoover. I fear it portends the arrival of fascism.

Havana is now in the throes of a wave of right-mindedness, the
students are breaking up the furniture in clubrooms of the left wing
and throwing ink on the Riverastyle frescos. The terrorists seem to do

nothing but bomb old ladies in department stores or chinese laundry-
men so its hard to tell whether they've gone over to the parties of order
or not. I suspect they have.

Katy's at Edie's in N.Y. They'll go to P'town too—

Yrs
Dos

To Malcolm Cowley

[Key West
November 24, 1934]

Dear Malcolm—

If you print any letter from me dont put anything in about
Quintanilla's needing the jack—this isn't a plea for funds—(I dont
know whether I said he needed jack or not) or particularly dont say
anything about that an artistic success might influence Spanish Govt or
that son of a bitch Lerroux—that is definitely not for publication—
Maybe you could take a sentence out of my spiel in the catalogue—
Thanks for agitating around about it—

Yrs
Dos

To Malcolm Cowley

Key West Fla
Nov 25 [1934]

Dear Malcolm

Publishing my confidential letter to you was a great mistake. It has
just about ruined the effectiveness of what we were trying to do.
Having known you for years and thought of you as an honest and
trustworthy guy, I couldn't imagine that you could do anything so
stupid and—in its results, though not I suppose in its intent—so
treacherous. I was confidentially giving you the lowdown on the situation with the hope that you people might take the trouble to inform
yourselves about the matter I know how you boys in editorial chairs
feel about taking a risk—"maybe he's not a good artist, maybe he's not
a Kosher revolutionist"—but you must understand that there are times
when a buckpassing misstep like that can have very serious consequences. After all a man's life is all he's got. This isnt a literary game
played at café tables. If you werent willing to go to bat you should have

let the matter drop. The hell of it is that there's absolutely nothing you can do to patch the situation up that wont make matters worse. I shall know better than to expect anything from you another time.

What has happened in Quintanilla's case is this (and if you dont think my opinion of his etchings is worth anything go and look at them yourself): The situation in Spain is extraordinarily delicate, on the edge of a military dictatorship, in which case the chances are that the prisoners will be shot and no questions asked. The present government are scared to tackle the big boys, Azaña and Caballero, so they are taking the attitude that the Madrid committee of which Quintanilla is a member is *the* committee of the revolt. The Supreme Court has refused to take jurisdiction so that they will be tried by court martial, with the best possible sentence life imprisonment. It looks extremely black. That lousy letter of mine being published makes it very difficult for us to raise the kind of protest we were trying to raise in this country—

Another time try to remember that you yourself may someday be in a similar situation—where your life and liberty (its quite a different thing than just having your cush job at stake) will hang on sets of accidental circumstances of the same kind—and when you dont understand a situation, for God's sake, do nothing.

Yrs
John Dos Passos

To Theodore Dreiser

803 Waddell Avenue
Key West Fla
Nov 27—[19]34

Dear Dreiser,

I know that you are poisoned with petitions and protests—it is not signing them that I mind but the sense of their futility—but I am writing to see if you wont let us use your name on just one more. Ernest Hemingway and I are getting up a purely private petition to the Spanish government in the hope that they will go easy on our friend Luis Quintanilla, the painter, whose etchings I think are about the finest being done. He was arrested as a member of the Madrid Young Socialist committee in connection with the abortive revolt of last month, that was an effort to seize the government before the landowners, the catholics and the military got ahead of the Republican-Socialist Coalition. The civil courts have waived jurisdiction and the prisoners will be tried by courtmartial and will undoubtedly be sentenced to death or life imprisonment. The only chance is to appeal to the president and the members of the government who will ultimately decide the prisoners' fate, since they have the pardoning power: We have gotten up the enclosed petition, (which is for Spanish consumption as you'll notice by the wording) and are trying to get a few signatures of American and foreign writers and painters whose names would be recognized in Spain. Maybe you can get over to see the etchings. If you feel like signing it, would you mind returning it to me as soon as possible—How are you?

Yrs John Dos Passos

We want to get you and S. Lewis, Matisse, Thomas Mann and a few people of no definite political color.

To Edmund Wilson

803 Waddell Ave—
Key West Fla
[*December 1, 1934*]

Dear Bunny—Do you remember when you had all those books about Henry Ford? If they are still around the house I wonder if you'd make them up in a package to give Katy to bring down—(shall return same) or else could you tell her the titles of the couple of good ones and ask her to try to get some bookshop to advertize for them or to send round to the second hand stores. Damn sorry to bother you about it—but I'm somewhat out of touch with the library catalogues. When are you going west? When east? Did you see Quintanilla's etchings? I've finally broken off whatever relations I can ever be said to have had with our esteemed contemporary the Neuro [*New Republic*]—the yellow bastards published a private letter I wrote Malcolm about the situation of Q. etc—I suppose he thought it was unmasking Trotskyism or something—anyway nobody was going to get them to pull any chestnuts out of the fire. Louses I call 'em

Yrs
Dos

in haste—just going out fishing

To Malcolm Cowley

[Key West
December 1, 1934]

Dear Malcolm—

Thanks for your note. Hope you convinced the lady—Here is a copy of the piece which naturally I'd be delighted to have you use.

Say about Hemingway—he has his hunting license in the fact that nobody living can handle the damn language like he can. I dont think it's entirely because he's a good friend of mine that I'm beginning to get thoroughly sick of every little inkshitter who can get his stuff in a pink magazine shying bricks at him. If you are working in a trade it seems natural to admire and respect the craftsmen in that trade who really know their business. And working in a few Union Square phrases because they are the style doesnt make a man a good writer or a good party member. Wait till the style changes, you'll see all those little inkshitters or others just like them piping about home and country and the family like they always used to do. I suppose they are all sore at H. because they think he's in on the big money. If they had any professional feelings about the trade they'd be glad to see one of the boys making good. And for Christ's sake people aren't all black and white—or communist & fascist—When there's shooting going on you have to take sides I suppose though I'm not as sure of it as I was a few years ago—(I was always in the ambulance anyway). But I think that any movement that makes a practice of alienating men of ability is in bad hands. And you never want to forget that if a style sets one way, its sure to set the other way just as hard a little later—so that when the little inkshitters are on your side that's the time to start worrying and taking stock of your premises—"Intellectuals" are either great men or else just lice on the body politic—where the body politic goes they go—and any man who is really trying to dope things out directly from day to day—not accepting any ready made phrases without testing them—is sure to be in wrong with the inkshitters most of the time. And God damn it, you've got to admire that quality—the first rate quality—in people whether you agree with them or not

Yrs
Dos

To Malcolm Cowley

Key West Tuesday
[*December 12, 1934*]

Dear Malcolm—

Forgive me for lashing out at you so—it was largely my fault for
not explaining more carefully. But the situation is hellishly delicate and
Hemingway and I both feel we stepped too heavily on the revolution
business in our spiels for the catalogue. After all the aim in this business is to get the guy out and not to testify before the Lord. The
defense that is being followed, started by Largo Cabellero, seems to be
to deny everything—so any injudicious moves in foreign countries will
tend to upset the applecart completely. We (this is confidential) are
trying to get up a completely private petition of a few names they
might know to present to the members of the government—so there's
absolutely nothing that can help at present except boosting as an artist.
The etchings are selling pretty well in spite of the lukewarm press—
those bastardly critics probably thought Hemingway & I were trying to
clean up personally in some way. If anybody likes Quintanilla's work it
would be damn useful if they'd write him up—A woman named
Hoover from whom I imagine Newsweek & Time got their dope, is
around New York and could probably give information.

Forgive me for taking out my accumulated bitterness against the
liberal weeklies on you personally—I'm getting pretty crabbed in my
old age—also in spite of some twenty years spent in the continuous
cultivation of letters it's increasingly more difficult for me to make
myself understood either by writing or word of mouth. But I felt that
letter made a damn bad impression on each of the counts you mentioned—You may have noticed that the mission of that English lady
agent to Spain wasn't such a howling success

[Dos]

To Malcolm Cowley

[Key West
December 1934]

Dear Malcolm—

I wired you because I had a chance to publish that piece in Esquire
with a page of etchings—Hope it didn't ball up the situation for you.
Just one more remark and let's drop the business: all I wanted was to

make the suggestion that you people send somebody up to look at the etchings. I wrote a similar letter to the New Masses people who did as I asked and others seem to have gotten in touch with Newsweek & Time. My only justification for writing you so hotly—ordinarily I'd have stewed in silence—was old acquaintance etc—Having boiled over I have absolutely no feeling about it any more—and I hope you'll forget my plain speaking which was possibly addressed more to a mythical dummy in a swivel chair, whom we might call Mr. B. than to yourself. It's perhaps good for Mr. B. to know now and then, how we outsiders, newsstand buyers, hall bedroom writers—feel about him.

Yrs
Dos

To Edmund Wilson

[Key West]
Dec 23–[19]34

Dear Bunny—

The Γιγαντομαχία Σούθ ῞Αλστηδ Στείτ [Gigantomachia of South Halsted Street] is a very fine thing. Thanks also for the great box of books. Henry's [Henry Ford] goat certainly ought to be in there somewhere. As soon as I've finished the Veblen life I'll return it, as you might want to look at it; it's almost unreadable—Mr. Dorfman spends his time and mine with long dull pharaphrases of all Veblen's books—but it does contain a certain amount of matter that cant be found anywhere else.

The Engels letters are very good reading. They certainly let fresh air into the subject. The one they published in International Lit. enlivened the whole issue.

What are you doing about your further study of Marx etc? I gather, reading Engels—I should like to strongly advise you to read all Veblen has to say about Marxism. *The Place of Science in Mod. Civ.* has I think some articles on Marxism that I found very illuminating— Also the *Theory of Business Enterprise* is a sort of later corollary to *Das Capital*—I think the argument is completed in *The Vested Interests.* I'd look over them all if I were you.

Have you read [William Henry] Chamberlin's Russia's Iron Age? When I was in Moscow he seemed to me to be the straightest and best informed of the foreign newspapermen I met there. The book is damned informative—though of little eventual value, because Chamberlin has no broad basis for his slants only the little chickenshit middle class attitudes of a bright student in a girl's college—But in point of fact—if you can disassociate the fact from the eye of the beholder—I find everything I saw, or heard from Gantt and others—confirms his worst suspicions. This business about Kirov looks very very bad to me. In fact it has completely destroyed my benefit-of-the-doubt attitude towards the Stalinists—It seems to be another convolution of the self destructive tendency that began with the Trotski-Stalin row. From now on events in Russia have no more interest—except as a terrible example —for world socialism—if you take socialism to mean the educative or constructive tendency rather than politics. The thing has gone into its Napoleonic stage and the progressive tendencies in the Soviet Government have definitely gone under before the self-protective tendencies. The horrid law of human affairs by which any government must eventually become involved in power for itself, killing for the pleasure of it, self perpetuation for its own sake, has gone into effect. That doesn't mean that before that happened, enormous things were not accomplished, things that it will take the rest of the world a century to absorb—If that is true, it would be mere mealymouthedness to say I hope it isnt, because I'm pretty well convinced it is true—all the orthodox communists overhere can do is lead their followers up a blind alley and obediently dissolve when the next war begins. I certainly dont think anything can be gained by denouncing them or publicizing the situation in any way—but I think that those who are more interested in getting at realities than being on the right side, should keep the situation pretty thoroughly in mind in elaborating theories or laying down ground work for writings.

Naturally I agreed with Sidney Hook in his plea for democracy in the soviets—but Mr. Hook did not tell us how to get it in the soviets or anywhere else. Surely Mr. Hook doesn't think that the lack of democracy in Russia is due to anybody's wickedness—I suppose you could make out a case for Slavic atavism as Chamberlin does—but that seems to me to be a sort of afterthefact explanation that would be no help to people trying to avoid the same pitfall another time. Meanwhile I think we should be very careful not to damage any latent spores of democracy that there still may be in the local American soil. After all the characteristic institutions of the Anglo Saxon nations survived feudalism and Tudor absolutism (not that they ever completely existed, but

they've been and still are in the background of the minds of Englishmen and Americans and Australians) and there's no reason why they
shouldn't survive monopoly capitalism—

How about the Indian dances? Take care of yourself—I hear
Thomas Wolfe has withdrawn his epic supernovel to rewrite it with a
Marxian slant—I must confess I didn't think that superannuated dodo
Mencken was so far wrong in his mouthings—

Did you?

Yrs
Dos

It would be funny if I ended up an Anglo Saxon chauvinist—Did you
ever read my father's Anglo Saxon Century? We are now getting to
the age when papa's shoes yawn wide.

To Edmund Wilson

Dunn's River House
Ocho Rios P.O.
St. Ann
Jamaica, B.W.I.
[January 1935]

Dear Bunny—

Jamaica is wonderful to look at and smell when you're away from
any human habitation—but the condition humaine here presents a
dreary, and not comic as you'd expect, similacrum of British society in
blackface—The climate is wonderful and so are the fireflies and the
little chameleons and the hummingbirds, but I certainly shant be sorry
to leave this terrestrial paradise. We almost kissed a large party of cruise
passengers with rattles, beads, little bottles of rum, souvenir baskets etc
that poured into Charley's Bar where we were having a drink today;
they looked so much more lively than the local prunefaced mulattos—
what a miserable race. That dreary woman who used to attend on
Rosalind was a regular wife of Bath compared to most of them.

I certainly would be with the American orthodox against the
Adamics and Stolbergs and even possibly against the ingenious Mr.
Hook—more for what they do than for what they say, which is getting
to be increasingly vicious rubbish—but I think the time has passed to
be with any of the Marxist parties—the whole thing has entered the
realm of metaphysical and religious discussion—What I said about the

new terror (even if they were "guilty", no government is in good shape
that has to keep on massacring its people. Suppose when that curious
little wop Zangara took a potshot at Franklin D. the U.S. Secret service
had massacred a hundred miscellaneous people, some because they
were wops, others because they were anarchists and others because they
had stomach trouble, what would all us reds be saying?) I've been
rather startled in talking to various Cubans of radical educations, one a
negro, to see how instantly they repudiated the whole Stalinist business.
Whether the Stalinist performances are intellectually justifiable or not,
they are alienating the working class movement of the world. What's
the use of losing your "chains" if you get a firing squad instead?—The
Sahr vote shows horribly the state of the European popular mind—
Some entirely new attack on the problem of human freedom under
monopolized industry has got to be worked out—if the coming period
of wars and dictatorships gives anybody a chance to work anything
out—that's why it seems to me that backing the American communists
is like suddenly coming out for the anabaptists or the abolitionists—I
cant see that the Trotskyites are any better—because they've definitely
lost the popular pulse—for Muste to join them seems to me to be
political suicide. About Russia I should have said not politically useful
rather than politically interesting—I suspect that a vast variety of
things are going on in Russia under the iron mask of the Kremlin, but
I dont think that any of them are of use to us in this country—if our
aims are freedom and the minimum of oppression—because they are
working out various forms of organization that our great conjunctions
are also working out in a very similar way. While those forms were
headed towards workers' democracy they were enormously interesting
but since they seem to have turned away from that (the decline of the
Soviets the absence of the secret ballot—disappearance of factory
committees and of the Workers and Peasants' Inspection) I personally
would prefer the despotism of Henry Ford, the United Fruit and
Standard Oil than that of Earl Browder and Amster and Mike Gold
and Bob Minor and I think most nonintellectual producers feel the
same way. By Anglo Saxon Insititutions I mean the almost obliterated
traditions of trial by jury common law etc—they dont count for much
all the time, but they do constitute a habit more or less implanted in
Western Europeans outside of Russians—Just compare our civil war
with the Russian civil war—compare the treatment—the runaround if
you like, an American citizen gets in Washington, applying for

information at the pension office say, and the treatment a Soviet citizen gets from a bureau in Moscow where he has to transact some kind of business. After all its by things like that not by the allurements of doctrine that the average American makes his choices in styles of government—granting that he's in a position to make any choices at all. My enthusiastic feelings, personally, about the U.S.S.R. have been on a continual decline since the early days. The steps are the Kronstadt rebellions, the Massacres by Bela Kun in the Crimea, the persecution of the S.R.'s, the N.E.P., the Trotsky expulsion, the abolition of factory committees, and last the liquidating of the Kulaks and the Workers and Peasants Inspection—which leaves the Kremlin absolutely supreme. I dont know why I should blurt all this out except that since I've been laid up I've been clarifying my ideas about what I would be willing to be shot for and frankly I dont find the Kremlin among the items.

This dismal progression leaves me exactly where I started in 1917 when I embarked on the S.S. Chicago to see the world in the uniform of Mssrs Norton Harjes—The Industrial Worker I still read with a certain pleasure—but gosh I should think the events in Germany—Austria and Spain would give pause to the most hardshell Marxian. Intellectual theories and hypotheses dont have to be a success, but political parties do—and I cant see any reason for giving the impression of trying to induce others to engage in forlorn hopes one wouldn't go in for oneself.

By all means go to Moscow—and try to cope with Russian—German will be a great help—be sure to let me know in time to send names and addresses of some of the people I knew and liked there. We'll be back in Key West soon. I'm feeling extraordinarily well—I hardly like to say it—Katy's lively and rosy and sends her best—

Yrs
Dos

Of course I've overstated the case against the Kremlin—but I'm now at last convinced that means cant be disassociated from ends and that massacre only creates more massacre and oppression more oppression and means become ends—its the sort of thing you have to grow up and look around for a number of years to see—possibly it's the beginning of adult ossification—but I dont really think so.

To Robert Cantwell

Dunn's River House
St. Ann Jamaica, B.W.I.
Jan 25–[*19*]35

Dear Cantwell,

Naturally I was kidding about Uppie's campaigns documents—still the attempt to reproduce peoples actions as they were being so inordinately painful, it makes me shudder to think of how difficult it would be to produce people and actions on paper as they might hypothetically be. It would probably be a question of lighting. Still I think it would be dangerous for anyone who is trying for objective reality (I cant think of good writing in any other way than as reality, though I'd hate to have to define what I mean by the term) to start with any such rubber stamp as "Fascism" even in the fringe of his mind. It's the sort of thing general staffs such as you bring up are always doing and localing down on; trying to fight the Argonne by the rules of Gettysburg. That's the great danger of sectarian opinions, they always accept the formulas of past events as useful for the measurement of future events and they never are, if you have high standards of accuracy. And it's the high standards of accuracy that make for useful work—There are always plenty of Comrade Hicks to evolve formulas out of old scaffoldings thrown down when any real job is finished.

I thought you pulled off what you intended pretty thoroughly in the *Land of Plenty*—I agree with you that it might have been even more useful if it had been possible to indicate more ramifications into the mass of the population of the continent—but it was certainly better to leave the strings untied than to gum them together with obsolete labels out of Daily Worker editorials.

Since I've been laid up in bed (incidently I'm very much picked up—I dont know if it's the influence of the tropics or the wearing out of the disease) I've been worrying a great deal about the communist veneer of phrases that is being slicked over so many people who get their talk from New York and I can see less and less to be encouraged in in it. I happened the other day to read Gorki's introduction to a book [*Henry Ford—America's Don Quixote*] by a man named Lochner about the Ford Peace Ship, written (in 1924 I think) in Gorki's Jesus Christ-Island of Capri period, and it brought a lot of things to a

head in my mind. It seems to me that that was the time for a man to
be a communist (when Gorki was out Christing among the brown-
eyed girls) and that all this literary Gorkyism we have now is an ex
post facto performance, more of an afterglow than a daybreak. I've
tried for years to stomach it, because I believe (as much as I believed
any set of abstract words, which isn't much) in the things the Gorkies
claimed to be striving for, but now I've suddenly become immune to
the whole vocabulary—I shall have to see people in action for it again
to believe it. You had the good luck to see some of the San Francisco
strike, but I haven't seen anything for a long time—fortunately a writer
who's any good can piece a great deal out of a few odd fragments of
events, but he certainly cant do anything with faiths hopes ideals and
mindclosing labels. I'm unloading this social fascism or what not on
you because I thought I detected in your article on Henry James in the
NR a slight touch of communist holier than thouishness—it's curious,
and I may have imagined it, because it was reading your Laugh & Lie
Down that reawakened a long dead interest in Henry James in me—
it's something I've been guilty of myself therefore I'm particularly well-
qualified—as a repentant sinner—to point it out in others. I mean that
it's just as silly for a professional writer to allow himself the luxury of
the attitude of a factory hand, as it is for him to pretend to be a
bankpresident—thats the great difficulty in producing working class
writers—a writer as such is just that, if writing is his full time work,
and pretending to be something else produces all kinds of hypocrisy
and mealymouthedness à la Gorki. It doesnt matter if he worked for
years in a slaughterhouse—when he gives that up to write a book—he
has to sit a desk so many hours a day and lead what is essentially a
middleclass life. Of course that life is getting to be more like that of a
factory hand all the time—as skill disappears from industry—but I dont
have to tell you that it's still damn different—The writer works out of
what he's picked up in his past life—his present attitudes can light it
but once they begin to change it, the work is no good. A man writes to
be damned and not to be saved.

But this is getting complicated—and is more or less out of order.
Excuse it. But I dont see why old Mr. Filene is any worse hypocrite
than a man like Gorki or André Gide—I didnt mean to condemn
Gorki as a writer in these remarks, or even as a man, merely to point

out that time produces strange changes. The main pleasure in surviving is that you begin to notice them—

Yrs
J Dos Passos

We'll be in Key West from the first of February on—Best of luck with Mr. Filene—

To Edmund Wilson

1924 Sidenberg Avenue
Key West Fla
Feb 5 [*1935*]

But Bunny it's not the possibility of Stalinism in the U.S. that's worrying me, it's the fact that the Stalinist C.P. seems doomed to fail and to bring down with it all the humanitarian tendencies I personally believe in—all the while acting as a mould on which its obverse the fascist mentality is made—and this recent massacre is certainly a sign of Stalinism's weakness and not of its strength. None of that has anything to do with Marx's work—but it certainly does influence one's attitude towards a given political party. I've felt all along that the Communists were valuable as agitators as the abolitionists were before the Civil War—but now I'm not so happy about it. Damn it I wish I knew more about the history of the reformation. I've been trying to wade through Carlyle's Cromwell but Carlyle manages to obscure everything so that even Cromwell's letters and speeches which are good reading, didn't make much sense to me. Do you know any good books about the period i.e. books that have the letters & documents of the time? I can understand how the Walkers are happy with Trotski; its much easier for economically disinterested people to be with the outs than with the ins. By the way I think you misinterpreted my remarks about Marxians —I mean the political groups and not the enormously valuable body of ideas aspirations, humane rebellions etc. It's the behind the lines war psychology that is so lousy—you must remember those great and glorious days of hun hating—well the economically disinterested intellectuals who wallow in communist hatreds are just exhibiting the same sort of disease—things I read in the New Masses give me the impression of expressing nothing but the same kind of middle class neurosis. I've never met working people or front line soldiers who talked or felt that way—though of course you sometimes meet a real butcher &

sadist—but that's quite different and more interesting than verbal sadism—though I suppose the best thing to do with congenital killers is to kill them as quickly as possible—they are very rare. I've only met one or two in my life.

Tell Malcolm to excuse my outburst of savagery in his direction—I honestly was not writing to him personally so much as to the New Republic that is a continual irritation—a paper in a position to be so useful and frittering it all away in jobholder sluggishness. But damn it, if people dont act straight in small things how are they going to act when a really important issue comes up. Incidentally the Quintanilla campaign has been more or less of a success. They've moved him into the fancy cell Juan March had fixed for himself and the rumor is that they'll let him off with six months. If he gets out it'll be due to Hem's rapid & subtle work—after all isn't it better to get guys out of jail than to be on the right side?

I'm anxious to read your stuff about Marx and Engels—very good tie up with the romantic generation of poets—I wish I knew Heine—I guess I'll have to read some Deutsch, if I ever get out of this accursed novel.

That reminds me I've got to get back to work—if Franklin D would arrange a 48 hour day I'd be perfectly happy—

Tell Malcolm (or better imply it, otherwise it'll make him sore) I know he's a good guy—

Yrs
Dos

If you take Christianity, the Renaissance, the Enlightenment, the Romantic individualist revolt, the scientific spirit,—a man's a man for all of that etc out of Socialism—what have you? Hell you might as well have Hearst-Hitler, except for the momentary pleasure of seeing those bastards bite the dust.

By the way—I dont agree with you that a hundred years ago was a better time than now—they had the great advantage that everything was technically less cluttered and simpler—but dont you think that perhaps in every time the landscape seems somewhat obstructed by human lice for those who view it? We have more information to go on, more technical ability to carry ideas out and ought to produce a whale of a lot of stuff—if I was a European I wouldn't think so, but here we still have a margin to operate on—

To Gerald and Sara Murphy

Dear Gerald and Sara—

You've been so brave through all this horrible time that it seems hard to write that you must go on and be brave. We admire and love you and wish so there were something we could do to make you feel just a little better. Perhaps later we will be able to cheer you up a little—just now we feel its too frightfully hard for anyone to bear— perhaps it can be a slight too slight consolation to feel that you have friends who feel what you feel—even if dimly and far away—and that you play a large part in their thoughts and feelings. And we want you to go on living bravely and looking around at the world in spite of everything—I wish I could have said goodby to Baoth. Trying to think of some kind of cheerful word to end a letter with I cant find any—

love
Dos

To Edmund Wilson

Dear Bunny—

It was certainly handsome of you to send me the Trotski pamphlet. Do you want it back? The old man, as you say the Walkers call him, certainly keeps his head—and a damn clear head it is. If it wouldn't be too much trouble, before you go to Russia, I'd love to see a copy of your new play. I'll try to get Clarendon this summer. Have you Wilder's or Tom Boyd's novels—if they are around and you have no use for them I'd be enormously grateful if you managed to put them in the mail—but dont worry about any of these demands if you are too busy—as you most certainly are. I gathered from a letter of Dawn's to Esther Andrews that you failed to be panicked by MacLeish. I found it exciting to read but couldn't see that it was about much, mostly about Jack Lawson's Success Story—I suspect. The little dedication, however, seemed rather good after I'd gotten over trying to fit it into "Urn burial".

Katy and I are both in pretty good shape—with considerable yen for the bright lights of the north countree—I'm afraid you'll be gone by the time we get north though—I spend my time struggling painfully with my damned narratives. Writing seems to get harder every year and every year it seems to get harder to write anything that gives me even an illusory pleasure when I read it over.

I finally consented, against my better judgement, to put my name down on the Writers Congress roster. I'm going to try to write them a little preachment about liberty of conscience or freedom of inwit or something of the sort that I hope will queer me with the world savers so thoroughly that they'll leave me alone for a while. I frankly cant see anything in this middleclass communism of the literati but a racket. I dont think Mr. Strachey looks very pretty either. —and all the time the real guys are being framed and jailed in all parts of the country—God damn it, nobody has any right to say anything publicly or write anything that he isn't willing to go to bat for.

How are you going with your Marx stuff? Are you going to bring out any more of it before going to Russia? For God's sake take your time about it—one or two clearly thought out and clearly expressed paragraphs by a bird who knows what his words mean, are worth more than all the debates in Cooper Union and Mecca Temple laid end on end. People haven't any right to make a living out of politics—It's selling stock in a corpse-factory. Take care of yourself and let me know when you are leaving—

Yrs
Dos

To Stewart Mitchell

[Key West
March 27, 1935]

Dear Stewart—

It was a great pleasure to get your letters preprandial and post-prandial, and the telegram from the festive diners. I wish I could have been there. Key West is pleasant enough but I'm thoroughly sick of my career as a valetudinarian. Much better, but the question is whether I'll sicken when I go north—anyway I can always handle the disease, I think, by ducking back into the tropics.

We have an agreeable house here, bathe every day in the briny and occasionally go fishing out on the Gulf Stream, a magnificent and mysterious phenomenon, always changing and always present like a range of mountains—So you see I can hardly be said to be fretting myself against the ungodly—What frets me is the increasing difficulty and complication of the business of writing. I find it harder all the time to get anything on paper that I can read without wanting to vomit. I keep kidding myself with false hopes of turning over a new leaf when I've finished the book I'm involved in now, and entering a region where simple declarative sentences, composed only of Anglo-Saxon words, will flow easily and daily from the pen. By that time, by the time I have learned to write I suppose I'll be so gaga that it wont matter what I write or how I write it. Such is the career that I, without having ever exactly planned it, find myself helplessly engaged in.

As for the state of the nation, I cant say that I share your pleasure at the spectacle of Franklin D smilingly going over the falls in his wheelchair, though I must say that his method of whiting the sepulchre with fair phrases and handouts is more agreeable than the Hitler-Mussolini style of capitalist consolidation—; but when, as the local barber puts it, the last greenback has been picked off the moneytree— wont we be up shit creek worse than ever, with hired men of Hearst or Long or Coughlin goosing us with machineguns?

Key West is bankrupt and has been taken over by the F.E.R.A. and is an astonishingly interesting thing to see. The processes of liquidation of the ordinary citizen all appear enlarged here as in a microscope. The set up of pauperism on the one hand, relief racketeering (do you remember the Red Cross in the war?) with the consolidation of wealth and power in two or three hands, is all enormously visible here. Although many of the officials are well meaning enough personally, and many of the relief measures seem sane and necessary on the face of them, the result is that what was a town of small owners and independent fishermen and bootleggers is rapidly becoming a poor farm. Its all very comic tragic and useful to me in my business if I can keep out of jail long enough to write about it. But that also is part of the profession of which I find myself an unwilling member—Katy joins me in love—we must see each other this summer.

Yrs
Dos

To Edmund Wilson

[Key West
April 2, 1935]

Dear Bunny—

Dawn writes that you are thinking of taking a motorcycle to
Soviet Russia. I think it would be an enormous help—get you out of
literary society and VOKS etc—and you'd run into the more up to date
and sporting element. I'm sure youd have no other trouble than bad
roads—People are enormously hospitable and mad about mechanical
devices of that sort. Be sure to take a good waterproof outfit—it rains
all the time—waterproof shoes—a good warmish raincoat, woolen
socks and even one of those English waterproof suits—you know that
greenish material that's red inside—If you're going through England
you can get it there much cheaper than here where its only to be found
at Abercrombie and Fitch. Honestly you'll find it an enormous comfort—The climate until you get south of Moscow is incredibly dreary.
The country right to the Volga is a continuation of that gloomy
leaden-skied plain that runs from the North Sea through Germany and
Poland—If you've ever been to Leipzig you know what its like. With
your German and a Hugo's Russian Grammar you can go anywhere
without much language trouble. Be sure to take waterproof shoes &
wool socks and a couple of sweaters.

In Leningrad try to see my friend Valentine Stenich (I dont know
his address) who translates my stuff. He knows English well and is a
darned interesting guy—Also go out to see Tchukhovsky the old pre-
revolutionary critic and ex-friend of Gorki—I think that VOKS can
give you their addresses—though I found VOKS a collection of arrant
shits everywhere.

In Moscow Sergei Dinamov at the International Literature office is
a straight organization man but a nice fellow. He's usually to be found
at Kuznetzki 12—Look up too Sergei Alymov at Stolyeshankov-9-
apartment 12 and tell him to introduce you to Vishnevsky—whom
I've never met but who sounds like a nice fellow from his letters. Get
Dinamov to get hold of Fadeev and Lebidinsky who both talk German—I stayed with Fadeev and his wife when I was in Moscow and
liked them very much—Go round to the Kamerny Theatre and present
my compliments to Tairov and Mme Koonen—they might do one of
your plays—They are very agreeable—I'll write them & Dinamov and

Alymov that you are coming. The reason I'd like to insist on your looking these birds up is that the danger is in Moscow that you'll only meet the official greeters or else the American colony—Its damned hard to break out of that ring and only the most independent people who are sure of their positions dare talk freely to foreigners even about the most trivial things. Someone else who might be interesting to see is Limacharsky's first wife. She used to live in Limacharsky's old apartment in the Kremlin. Tell her I sent you and remember dining with her.

Ask Dinamov if it would be possible for me to send you an authorization to spend some of my roubles if you get hard up—You could pay me later in Guggenheim gold. Ask him if it can be arranged and how. I think I have a bank account there.

Would you like me to get you some letters to scientists from Horsley Gantt? Write me right away and I'll ask him for them.

Another person you ought to see is Pudovkin—I think you can arrange to see him fairly easily—Also I found Trauberg of the Leningrad Movy Company very nice to talk to He's a friend of Stenich's. Eisenstein is an interesting bird but I suspect he's getting pretty difficult. But Im sure Pudovkin & Trauberg would remember me.

For Moscow Ritz you ought to see that woman who lived with Mayakowski—I cant remember the bitch's name. Also Ivy Litvinovna is said to be very entertaining. If you want to take trips try to go with Narcompovrs instead of Intourist— people will tell you it's impossible—but I did it for no money and very pleasantly—Anna Louise Strong of the Moscow News—to whom present my respects—can arrange many things if she wants to. Dont believe anything anybody tells you in English or French—there are more lies and more hushdope in Moscow—just as there's more of everything else—than in any other capital in the world. Thats why German is a good language to go on—its damn hard to lie in German.

Yours for the Motochyklysteschki Critik!

Zdorovia

Dos

To Patrick Murphy (1920–1937), *the youngest son of Gerald and Sara, who died of tuberculosis at Saranac Lake, New York, after fighting the disease for eight years.*

[Key West
April 1935]

Dear Patrick—

Well we started out to Bimini but we didn't get very far. About five miles outside of American Shoal we ran into an enormous school of dolphins. Immediately everybody was hooked into great big dolphins (about 20 lbs) that looked very silvery as they jumped. When you get them near the boat their fins look bright blue and they have peacock colored spots on them. Then when you bring them up out of the water they turn green and yellow and finally die a greyish yellow. We'd been catching dolphins for about ten minutes when two huge sharks appeared—a deep sea kind of shark with a tail like a mackerel shark and very large tails and fins. In Cuba they call them galanos, but I dont know what their name is actually in English—anyway they were mean looking customers. Mike Strater got one on his light rod and Ernest got his in first (he'd previously popped two lines·and the shark had the hooks and leaders hanging from his maw—but they didn't seem to discourage him) and shot him once with a rifle. Then they gaffed him with a very heavy gaff and were holding him up out of the water for me to photograph with the movie camera when an odd thing happened. Ernest had out his small colt automatic (.22) and was just going to finish the shark off with a final shot to get his hooks and leaders back when the shark went into a tremendous spiral convulsion and broke the pole of the gaff. The broken piece hit the pistol which went off. We didn't hear the shot on account of the great snapping noise the gaff made breaking. The bullet (a softnosed lead bullet) hit the brass edging of the boat's rail and splattered into both calves of Ernest's legs. Fortunately the wounds were not very bad, but we thought it was wiser to turn back to get a doctor to dress them. So we are not in Bimini yet. As soon as we finish taking the movie reel we'll send it up. I think it shows the gaff breaking. I hope it came out all right but I'm afraid it wont be very good because it's the first time I've ever tried to use a movie camera. Give everybody my love and Katy's

We'll take a lot of reels and send them up as we take them.
You be good and dont kick the covers off too often

love
Dos

To Malcolm Cowley

[Key West
May 1935]

Dear Malcolm—

It's damn handsome of the defenders of culture to offer—and thank their representatives very cordially for it—to pay my fare to Paris. I cant possibly go on account of this disease that still hangs around like a partially divorced wife ready to raise cain every minute and because I'm very busy working. I'm very sorry that piece got to the congress late—I was sure I'd allowed enough air mail time. If you can put your hands on it, would you mind sending it back to me? I havent a copy of the exact version I sent up. I'd like to go over it anyway before publication. How are you planning to publish the record?—in a pamphlet or something like that? The form of that piece depends a good deal on where it comes out—as I knew the comrades would have the floor most of the time I stated the other side of the case a little more forcibly than I would have if it was to have been read in an assembly of bankers say—

Thanks for writing

Yrs
Dos

To Katy Dos Passos

[Key West
May 4, 1935]

Katy—here are a couple of letters came for you—I tell you it's quiet here. The paper has just come—I took a nap after lunch after a dip at the navy yard and now its three thirty of a hot but airy afternoon and I'm writing my opossum Went to the Jacksons to dinner last night—with Canby and mint juleps—very much picked up—struggled with my work all morning without getting much of anywhere and writing and wondering and wishing I had that opossum here or was up there.

Damn it I'm sick of these diseases. Oh possum it wasn't the paper it was the mail with two cards and a letter—The weather is lovely, hot and airy—oh I hope you didn't have any trouble getting into Baltimore so late last night—The house is quiet and tidy. I played the little Stravinsky pieces and drank a glass of vermouth before my lunch. I'm just on the edge of finishing my Anderson narrative. Think I'll go to the movies tonight Oh Katy now if you were only here we could really have a good time—oh hurry and come back—

The Mexican news is very confused. It seems that during the dinner groups of angry peons began to gather in the square outside the hotel with reclamaciones on account of loss of chickens—The fox—at least a party said to resemble him strangely—slipped out after the dessert and while the politicos were ordering up champagne and, wearing a serape and a large straw hat made a stirring speech to the inditos on the right of the small chicken raiser. There was immediately found a Sindicato agrarista of male chicken raisers with the slogan of Three hens and a rooster for every honest tiller of the soil and Death to large scale chicken farmers. The politicos got wind of it in the hotel and a light tiroteo followed, fortunately without doing any harm. A difficult situation was averted by the fox's immediately organizing cockfights between the various groups in the course of which considerable money changed hands. The situation cleared up with a good deal of drinking and it was morning before the last chicken fanciers had gone home—Then the hotel keeper appeared with the bill for the banquete which the politicos had neglected to pay. The fox tried to explain that the hotel keeper ought to charge it all up to advertizing and publicity but the hotel keeper wouldnt listen to reason and threatened to attach the fox's car. The fox's friend retired into the persimmon tree suffering from shock—Oh Katy it was handsome to send the cards and the letter—now crazy for Baltimore news—love you so much too much— Solitary A.

To Edmund Wilson

[Key West
May 8, 1935]

Dear Bunny—

I'd already written Gorki—it would be interesting for you to get to see the old walrus—I told him you were the A 1. lit critic etc and maybe he'll have the Huzzar band out to meet Edmund Axel Wilson—I'm sure you'll have no trouble. If you do, Gorki is the man to get hold of—he is alleged to have the ear of the Kremlin more than anybody. I once got an old lady out of jail for somebody by cabling him. I've never met him. Present him with my most dissembled compliments.

Bon boyage   Dos

To Ernest Hemingway

Sunday
[Key West
May 1935]

Dear Hem—Here's your five bucks. It's sure worth it—for a couple of weeks it looked as if I might get that tenspot—but now I think there's little chance of it—

Too damn bad about the President's Marlin—it was surely a husky one by its picture. Maybe by this time you have another.

Katy came back feeling fine—and according to Dr. Richardson completely o.k. internally. Its very lucky she went up there to Baltimore because situation demanded very skillful handling and I think got it—also high type of hospitalization at cut rate and the medico refused to charge—wants an autographed book—We feel very good about the whole thing.

Pauline & Mex and Gigi are fine. It's pleasant here and not too hot yet, but we certainly miss you around these diggings. A little art colony phony has appeared and covering the walls of Josie's with phony murals—Maybe they're good—We live in a mural age, a Cowley Age an age of Bohemianism and shit and of writers congresses. Expect to wake up any morning now and find Gilden Flump affixing murals to wall of our bedroom. How about the mural situation in Bimini—? Next year the wave will have reached there.

Damn busy or would have written sooner. Had a swell time on trip and in Bimini and damned ashamed of having pooped out—Still I'm planning to wind up the whole disease situation pretty soon.

Katy reports Gerald working all day at Mark Cross. Sara pretty frightfully miserable, but leading her regular life—but Patrick holding his own. The Ingelbaums, about whom I take back everything,

induced Laurasson Brown to take the case, Patrick's being moved to
Saranac this week—it may be hopeless, but it certainly looks as if he
were getting a better chance for his life. Katy says the idea of going to
Saranac has cheered him up a great deal already. Katy saw Ada and
Workers' Laureate MacLeish in New York and reports them in fine
shape.

I hope we can get out to Bimini for a week on our way north—in
June maybe—ya veremos.

Esther left here in fine shape—looking better than I've seen her—
much pepped up by Bimini trip.

Give 'em hell Custer—

Yr
Dos

Give old Bread and Saca my best.

To Robert Cantwell

[Key West
May 1935]

Dear Cantwell—

I wish you'd sent that letter—After all letters are largely written to
get things out of your system. I plagued all my friends with arguments
and hypotheses all winter and now feel much better—like after a
good dose of castor oil. If you still have the letter do send it along.
Anyway its only occasionally that you want to go in for naked ideas
and formulas . . . the work in hand is always more interesting and
pleasanter—after all I've now gone into a completely new state of mind
about it—I can read Mike Gold on Dreiser without nausea and probably could read Dreiser on Mike Gold with the same equanimity.
Maybe its the result of going to considerable pains to write up a thing
for the Writer's Congress and then sending it there too late to have it
read—anyway I can now contentedly paddle my own canoe and to hell
wid 'em—I enjoy paddling my canoe—it's my business, I make a fair
sort of a living by it, I do it the best I can, I think—and to hell wid 'em.
You cant do better than your best, your best, maybe is none too good,
but worrying and formularizing wont help it and politely and sincerely
begging their pardons, to hell wid 'em.

Hope to be in New York in June. I'm going to see how long I can stay in the north without sickening. If I sicken back to the tropics I'll have to go—

Take care of yourself. I'm sure you'll feel better when you get Lincoln S. Filene off your chest—

Yrs

J Dos Passos

To Malcolm Cowley

[Key West
May 28, 1935]

Dear Malcolm—

I'm through with writing these lousy statements. I cant make myself clear. What I meant to imply was that the issue right now is the classic liberties and that the fight has got to be made on them. The reason I see no other ground is that I dont believe the Communist movement is capable of doing anything but provoke oppression and I no longer believe that the end justifies the means—means and ends have got to be one—I also wanted to bring up the important problem of the worker-technician versus the bureaucrat which exists on both sides of the political fences. I dont think the situation is improving in this country—the comrades are just parroting Russian changes of mood and opinion, which shows their impotence up more than ever. Of course the classic liberties are all relative—but so's t.b. That doesn't change the fact that some people die of it and others are well.

Haven't anything for the Neuro right now, but may have later— Book pretty lousy, thank you but at least accumulating pages which are after all the eventual aim of a literary composition—Hope to hit New York on 2½ cylinders in June—

Yrs
Dos

To Rumsey Marvin

Miami Colonial Hotel
Miami, Florida
June 19—[*1935*]

Dear Rummy—

I was damn glad to hear from you and damn sorry about your taste and smell buds—did the bastardly physician cut the nerve—?

What a hell of a note—maybe he just mangled it and it'll gradually regenerate itself. In any case he ought to have his face punched in.

We've just come over from fishing for a week in Bimini—where at last yrs truly got enough sun on the carcase. Driving north tomorrow to try a new medico—it may be I never had rheumatic fever at all. Anyway I'm going to try a few more horse-doctors, crystalgazers, etc before I retire to Rio de Janeiro or some such place. America's getting more interesting to me every day, so I certainly dont want to pull out until they run me out. I'm knocking on wood as I write that right now I'm in first class shape though a little out of shape from too little walking etc. Sure we'll stop at your club and see how the young banker-politico is making out.

About publicity (personally I'm a Garbo) you are quite right. Mr. Kubik the Provincetown hermit said the best thing about it when I found him and Fat Francis mysteriously drunk in our little barn at Truro and asked them what the devil they were doing there. Mr. Kubik replied rather vaguely that he was accustomed to publicity. He said when he was a boy he'd won a race rowing a flatbottomed boat on the Connecticut River at Hartford. "When a man's been in the public eye it makes it hard afterwards". And now what's happened to Mr. Kubik? He's given up being a hermit and has allowed himself to be dressed up like a pilgrim father and rings a bell advertizing the best shore dinner in Provincetown. I saw his picture in the sunday supplement.

No I havent any ghost. That Becker piece sounded a little funny to me too, I thought there was a touch of the scoutmaster about it. I think it came from trying to convince the reader that Becker oughtn't to be in jail (wasn't a damn fool to stay there when he could be paroled)—I dont know. I worked like hell over it, but there was always something wrong about it. Writing protests that mean anything is a difficult business and if they dont mean something very special they are worse than useless.

I bet you are getting to know considerable about Larchmont and Mamaroneck—Mr. Banker-Politico

Take care of yourself—see you soon I hope—Katy joins me in love—

Yrs
Jack

So sorry to hear that Hugh Leamy died. I hadn't heard anything about it. What a darn shame—

To Ernest Hemingway

[571 Commercial Street
Provincetown
July 23 (?), 1935]

Hay Hem—

I'm up in Conway at A. MacLeish's on way to Cape—wondering if you're still in Bimini. Glad that the stuff got there in good shape— What's the tuna and marlin situation now? Cant get used to not having the Bimini (clear as gin) water to swim in. Just spent a couple of days at Saranac with Murphys—Patrick after having been very bad indeed ever since he got up there—seems to have taken a turn for the better—but he looks terribly small and thin. Still it must be better for him than New York. They are on Middle Saranac Lake—a handsome northwoods lake—somewhat trampled by Guggenheims and Unter-meyers and speedboats—but it has the advantage of being in the State Park so that it has less camps and possibly more bass and Whitefish than most such places—Sara very thin and pretty and in better shape than I'd expected—Gerald I like better and admire more than ever before—spends all his time on Mark Cross and the Fifth Avenue Association—gives him something to use his brains on—he's like he was years ago when he was painting—I certainly hope he sticks to it—there's nothing like economic pressure.

Personally my economic pressure is at the top of the dial and I'm getting considerable work done—health seems ok., am trying a new system—anyway have a hunch that the infection or what not is, well maybe weakening a little. Had a gigantic cold (contracted I believe from Mr. William B. Leeds) without any rheumatics after it. Taking a few shots of various kinds—anyway to hell with it. Hope to send you gents some jack soon—but so far cant seem to sell anything. You and Pauline were certainly lifesavers last winter—it must have been a bloody bore continually operating the breechesbuoy—Anyway I think that period is over. Anyway too goddamn busy finishing this lousy superannuated hypertrophied hellinvented novel to get diseased for a while or to worry about the tottering debtstructure.

Lots of love to Pauline—Damn it I hope you've got a big one by this time. No money in this teacher business—take care of yourselves—

Dos

To Edmund Wilson

571 Commercial Street
Provincetown Mass
July 29 [1935]

Dear Bunny—

I have been intending for a couple of months to send you off a small bulletin on the state of the nation—but moving around and a great deal of alleged literary work have kept me from doing it. Katy and I are now established in our ancestral halls and damn glad of it— Provincetown is fine—more nickelodeonish than ever and absolutely free of what Mrs Standwood calls the better type of tenant—in fact she says she's been showing houses to people who aren't desirable at all without inducing them to rent. Niles and Betty are here in good shape—It's cold as blazes, like October and quite empty of people we know. The Walkers have been up here for a couple of days having Theatre Union board meetings in Wellfleet. They are in fine shape and very Trotskyish.

It certainly was a pleasure to get to New York. We spent a couple of very hot weeks there with great pleasure. Saw Ethel Merman before she closed in *Everything Goes.* I think she's immense. Wasnt so convinced by the plays of Odets outside of Waiting for Lefty. He certainly has an ear for dialogue and a knack for stage nifties, but I dont see that he has anything else. *"Awake and Sing"* is *"Another Language"* interspersed with bad Lawson. This country—you feel it in New York—is suddenly getting cheerful again—there's a sort of frivolity about everything that goes on—may be Mr Roosevelt's boom will really come across the counter this fall. It's a great pleasure to be able to navigate around and drink beer in bars and that sort of thing again— You get the feeling that perhaps Franklin D.'s frivolity is catching—the investigations in Congress have been taking on an air of innocent merriment—of course it'll get very boring like Gilbert and Sullivan when you get too much of it—as if everybody was playing charades. Or the pleasure of having the carcase in fair shape may be making me imagine the sort of Trianon atmosphere. Maybe it's a prewar manifestation. Anyway the New York Times is really delirious reading every morning. I dont suppose any good will come of this state of mind.

So glad you were able to tap the roubles and that you are having a good time among the Sovietskis. I'd like to get another look at it soon—but I cant do anything until I've put this last volume to bed with the printer—gosh it's slow work. Must get back to it right now. Give my best to the various characters I used to know around Moscow. I hear you are living in Duranty's apartment—remember me to him—do drop a line—as we are very anxious for a full account of your travels. How is the Marx Engels Institute? How do you find that straw colored vodka that has oakleaves on the bottle?

When are you coming back to these fantastic shores? I'm sure looking forward to hearing about things you've seen

Katy sends her best.

Yrs

Dos

Gosh that clipping about the opera gave me pause. Well the more the merrier and the sky's the limit. Gosh a lot of water's gone under the bridge since October.

How are you getting on with the Russian language?

To Katy Dos Passos

Sunday evening
[Provincetown
August 5, 1935]

Oh Katy here I am established in the hall—it's raw and grey outside and inside its very quiet and smells terribly of puppies. I'm at work at the big desk and already want to go where the opossum is. Just about to step out to take Pouf for a walk as dusk is coming on.

Mary Morris has everything organized but it'll be many a day before we get the smell of pups out of the house.

Met Tiger on the Fall River Boat on his way home from Cuba—seems in fine shape liked Cuba but bored he said.

The Horners met him in Yarmouth with their little poodle—dont you think that there are getting to be too many poodles?—and swept us up to the Cape.

Now its getting dark and I want to stop working and where is the opossum to play with?

love
Dos

To Katy Dos Passos

[Provincetown
August 1935]

Sweetest and missedest opossum—Oh Katy please come home Wednesday—havent seen the Count yet but will see him this noon The Lawsons came Sunday—Jack & Sue and Adelaide and Esther and had a fine time with them—Esther's coming back next week to collect Mrs Cat—Everybody was in fine form—we drove all around this end of the Cape—ate a great many steamed clams and scallops and drank up all the whiskey gin and beer in the house. They left for Wilton yesterday afternoon.

I'll wire you as soon as I see the Count if he wants to drive down tomorrow—if not I'll meet you at Yarmouth Thursday—because I dont think you can take Pata pouf on the bus—Oh how are you Katy? Not a peep since the disappearing act—(that I'm so tired of) that took place Saturday—It seems so long since you were here—not only seems but is and I have a funny feeling of what am I doing here without the opossum—Maybe I'll get a letter today. After this maybe we can go back and forth together—oh please let's—

Love
aquatic solitariest nose on the
grindstonest A.

To Ernest Hemingway

Provincetown Mass.
Sept 20, [1935]

Gosh Hem—
You have all the luck with hurricanes—that was a damn fine piece in the Daily Worker. It must be fine in Key West now with all communications cut off. What are you people up to? How are you? Drop us a line We'll be here until about Oct 1. then in New York for a couple of months—then I dont know where—the rheumatics are abating—have little fits but on a very picayune scale—Have a sawbones

who claims he can fix the whole thing up, but I havent tried his system yet.

Had hoped you people were coming north—from Sara's last letter we gather that Patrick is definitely improving up at Saranac—Working pretty conscientiously but this job is endless—love to Pauline

Yrs
Dos

Did Gingrich fade out on you on the Hurricane piece? I'd like to know—

To Ernest Hemingway

[On board Fall River ship
February 7, 1936]

Gosh Hem—

this novel business is an awful business. Why the hell did I ever get mixed up in it? I'm in perfectly good shape this winter for the first time in years—but I can feel the old warmish blood running off into ink—the most completely lousy feeling I've ever felt—has disease lashed to the mast. What will be left will be a sort of mummy in a fatter version of Rameses II as exhibited in the museum in Cairo. And even at that the fornicating business wont get itself finished.

Just preparing to go to bed on the Fall River boat—hell's own amount of ice in this Sound—

Gosh I certainly would enjoy to spend a day out on the Gulf Stream—not that the winter hasn't been damn swell—being in New York and walking around the streets and everything—but now a little sunlight and seabreezes would fit in very well. It's a case for sunburn; feel very fungoid after all this time in New York. Christ so fagged I cant even write a letter—Away to Cape for a breath of (cold) air Love to Pauline and saludos to Mex & the Irish Yid. Feel worse than Scott but no Grand Canyon—

Yrs
Dos

Soon take hell of big cockeyed trip—but Christ it's hard to get any money for anything or to get any bastard to publish anything—

To Katy Dos Passos

> [On board Fall River ship
> *March 22, 1936*]

Oh Katy here I am on the Fall River Boat (the Plymouth) and the band is playing *Dinner for one please James*. The Plymouth is empty and rather dreary and I've just eaten a muttonchop and am on my way to bed. It's dreadful not having any opossum to play with, but I hope to find a very lively one when I get back. Had my hair cut, have read Time and the Work Telegram and have virtually exhausted the possibilities of the S.S. Plymouth, which was always a rather dreary vessel. Still except for the terrible lack of opossum I'm rather glad I came—there's nothing like a little change of air.

Oh Katy please cross crossings carefully and keep your toes and fingers covered so that we can get through this gloomy period

> lots of love
> yr wandering A

To Ernest Hemingway

> [Provincetown]
> *May 31st '36*

Say Hem—finally read that story in Esquire and was much bucked up by it. You certainly have Madrid down cold—It made me feel as if I was there and just about to go down to the Cafe du Puerto Rico to have coffee and read the papers in the morning. Did the marlins keep on getting bigger? Don't feel as if I'd been down to see you at all, was so buried in galleys and whenever I did stick my head out everything seemed so unaccustomedly goofy. Drop me a line to 571 Commercial Street—Provincetown—about your habits—I'm sending another case of stitt champagne to Bernie Pappy for you hope it gets there before you leave for Bimini. I'm still mucking around with these damn proofs—pages now—Christ I'll be glad to be quit of the whole business; it's gotten to be a kind of a quicksand—What I need's a gigantic trip of some kind on muleback or on foot—Just at the moment we've gotten into a snarl with our housing up here and have to hang around and get it in shape—The climate is damn pleasant up here now—have only the slightest rheumatic fits—Love to Pauline and to the Mexican Mouse—Hope to send you that money soon—

> Yrs
> Dos

To Edmund Wilson

[Provincetown
June 27, 1936]

Dear Bunny—

I've just finished the two Democracies [Wilson's *Travels in Two Democracies*]. It gets better and better as you read it. In all the Russian part after Moscow (no right from the moment you get on the boat) I got that feeling of permanent pleasure I dont often get reading contemporary stuff. It made me think of Thoreau and, for some reason, of Sterne—You hit a fine tone of eighteenth centuryish equanimity—. It sure does pay to put down what happens just as it does happen—I'm not at all sure that it isnt all anybody can do that's of any permanent use in a literary way. Though actually to do that is just as difficult an imaginative process as anything else. Its pleasant to read something you really enjoy for a change. I hated to finish it.

Provincetown is agreeable in a goofy sort of a way—more and halfwitteder looking tourists appear every year. Everything's almost too silly now. This is a difficult time to find anywhere to live—The process of corruption of the country by the city is going on so fast. When everything is finally one big suburb I dont suppose it'll be so bad. What are you up to?

Yrs
Dos

To Ernest Hemingway

Provincetown, Mass.
July *10* [*1936*]

Hey Hem,

What the hell happened to your little chocolate friend Joey Louis? Matrimony? Dope? Disease? Or is Hitler right? Jesus the powers of Nordic bullshit or whatever sure are having a good summer Haile Selassie—Anthony Eden, Joe Louis—and old man Baldwin seems to be receiving the count right at the moment.

That crossing must have been the most rugged yet. I read about the storm. Damn good you had all that practice with big seas fishing outside of Havana. A thing like that changes the shit all right—You'll probably be as sweet as a sucking dove for a year or more. The sort of

thing a man cant get out of reading or even the highest speculator price
ringside seats.

I'm not doing a damn thing—reading Capt John Smith and
Moult's Relation and stuff like that (Smith, or whoever wrote it for
him, is a damned amusing writer), weeding the garden and doing a
little smalltime sailing in the harbor—It's all right here if you stay on
the water.

Gerald and Sara drove up for a day. They are in fine shape—have
just discovered that you can have a good time on the American Continent and that it's fun riding around in a car. We went up there over
the fourth—Sara has fixed up a new camp on a different lake—God its
gloomy on those Adirondack lakes. Patrick certainly seems better: can
get down to the dock and fish for perch—they roll his bed down its
pepped him up a lot.

Somebody said you'd spend July over on Cat Cay—Ought to be
damned nice. I should think it'hd get rather crowded with important
fishermen around those little docks—I'm beginning to feel restless as
hell. Want to see a little of the world—but I'd like to finish this damn
course of reading—Gosh I'm a lousy reader—when do people get time
to read all that stuff? And it takes so damn long and half the time
you're wondering whether you are getting anything out of it or not.
Maybe I'm trying too long doses. I've got a list of stuff that covers 30
pages of a notebook and more turns up all the time. And I keep
thinking maybe I ought to be nosing around in France and Spain. Hell
of difficult thing to do, read.

Best to Pauline & from Katy—Say hello to the Mexican Mouse—
We'll soon have tuna here if you leave any in the water

Yrs
Dos

To Ernest Hemingway

[Provincetown
August 1936]

Say Hem—

Have you heard anything about Quintanilla? I picked up a rumor
that he'd been shot by Fascist gunmen, but may not be true—Civilization seems to be going in for one of its richer phases of butchery. When
you said a thousand years of fascism you said something. When they've

properly massacred the Spaniards they'll start on the French. You'd better hurry up and buy those clothes and go to England, the old leo's losing a good many teeth these days—and there may not be any after a while. Things are certainly about as goddam frightful as they could be in Europe—

Feel too lousy to do anything How are you and Pauline? How's Wyoming

Yrs
Dos

To Upton Sinclair

Truro, Mass.
September 2 '36

Dear Upton—

I'd rather some day if you ever get the time have you read three novels in one volume, as I hope to bring them out, and tell me whether you still think the method is too confusing. Anyway I'm off on another tack now and the four way conveyor system is temporarily shelved. My address is always 571 Commercial Street, Provincetown Mass. Take care of yourself. I'll be delighted to have Coöp

Yrs
Dos

To C. A. Pearce

Truro Mass
Sept 22 [1936]
damned rainy

Dear Cap—What's all this nonsense about another printing? Are you sure you aren't binding up some lost sheets of Anthony Adverse behind that jacket. If this keeps up we'll be garnering in the mortgages with the October apples—Its probably some other book. It'll be a long time before it makes any difference to me yet, but my creditors must be rubbing their hands. Who said you couldn't sell books?

But what I'm writing for is to ask you what the error was that I was talking about changing. A complete amnesia that would be more interesting to a psychoanalyst than it is to me has come over me about that damn work. Have any other errata turned up?

Yrs
Dos

To F. Scott Fitzgerald

Truro—Mass
[*September 1936*]

Why Scott—

   you poor miserable bastard it was damn handsome of you to write
to me. Had just heard about your shoulder and was on the edge of
writing when I got your letter. Must be damned painful and annoying.
Let us know how you are. Katy sends love and condolences. We often
talk about you and wish we could get to see you.

   I've been wanting to see you, naturally, to argue about your
Esquire articles—Christ man how do you find time in the middle of
the general conflagration to worry about all that stuff? If you dont
want to do stuff on your own why not get a reporting job somewhere.
After all not many people write as well as you do. Here you've gone
and spent forty years in perfecting an elegant and complicated piece of
machinery (tool I was going to say) and the next forty years is the
time to use it—or as long as the murderous forces of history will let
you. God damn it I feel frightful myself—I have that false Etruscan
feeling for sitting on my tail at home while etcetera etcetera is on the
March to Rome—but I have two things laid out I want to finish up
and I'm trying to take a course in American history and most of the
time the course of world events seems so frightful that I feel absolutely
paralyzed—and the feeling that I've got to hurry to get stuff out before
the big boys close down on us. We're living in one of the damnedest
tragic moments in history—if you want to go to pieces I think its
absolutely o.k. but I think you ought to write a first rate novel about it
(and you probably will) instead of spilling it in little pieces for Arnold
Gingrich—and anyway, in pieces or not, I wish I could get an hours'
talk with you now and then, Scott and damn sorry about the shoulder—Forgive the locker room peptalk—

Yrs
Dos

To C. A. Pearce

[Truro, Massachusetts
October 1936]

Dear Cap,

Just as I was closing up this unusually dresssuited epistle to you it occurred to me that it might be a good moment to bring up something that I've been brooding about for some time. I dont at all like the idea of your remaindering "In All Countries". I dont think it's the way to handle my particular type of work. I know that the whole present day habit of the book business is highpressure selling and quick turnover, but I think that you ought to go back, for part of your list, at least, to bofoa de woa salesmethods.

Suppose you have an author, Nathaniel Twinklebottom, say, whose work seems to have some permanent value. Instead of looking for El Dorado on a speculative basis with each book of his you publish and then having the officeboy sweep it out from under the desks six months later, I think your aim ought to be to build up a slow basic sale from all his works. To do that you have to begin from the ground up by convincing the booksellers that it's to their advantage to be a little less hysterical about their business, and alongside of the big wows of the moment, to keep the past works of a certain number of writers in stock instead of only their overpublicized novelties. Then, if somebody comes in to ask for the next novel by Nathaniel Twinklebottom before its printed, instead of trying to sell him *Eyeless in Gaza,* the clerk could sell him some of Nat's past works, an early volume of poems or essays. That's the way it used to be in the good old days, and that's the way it ought to be now. Such a system would give a muchneeded stability to the book business and from the point of view of the craft of writing and criticism would remove some of the hectic flybynight shell game air that the whole business is getting. You'll answer that the booksalesmen wont do it, that the department stores are too involved in the system of quick turnover of novelties, and that it's against the spirit of the times. That's all true, but somebody's going to change all those things and there's no reason why you and Nathaniel Twinklebottom shouldn't be the ones to do it.

Coming back to my own work, and the fact that I have to make a living out of it, I feel very strongly that is how it ought to be handled. I can think of fifteen or twenty American writers whose work ought to be handled in the same way. Once the industrial setup is straightened up, you'll find the critics settling down to saner ways. After all the critic's only a sort of barker outside of the publication's advertizing tent. Somebody's got to start bringing the bookselling and publishing business back to sanity, and it seems to me that Harcourt Brace is the firm to do it. I dont see why it shouldn't be possible to combine the two things. But the present setup is absurd both for the point of view of the writer and the reader. There are about fifty books of considerable importance published in the last fifteen years that it's absolutely impossible to buy a copy of in a bookstore. Even books a year or two old are impossible to get hold of without advertizing in the secondhand market. Obviously this situation cant be changed overnight, but I very strongly feel that it's time the progressive publishers started to work on some scheme for stabilizing the business. After all the "backlog" was the whole capital of a publishing house in the old days.

Pass these suggestions on to Mssrs Harcourt and Brace, will you? I'd like to know what they think of them. You are all certainly putting on a big show in connection with the B.M. [*The Big Money*].

Yrs
Dos

To C. A. Pearce

Truro, Mass.
Oct 10, [*19*]*36*

Dear Cap,

Here's what I know about Mr. Frank B. Copley, the biographer. Several years ago when the Taylor piece in a little longer form was published in Esquire, he wrote me a bumbling sort of letter claiming that all the material in my piece came from his biography, an official and very dumb one, of Taylor. At the same time he remarked that the facts were all accurate and suggested I ought to give him some sort of credit. Accordingly I got Gingrich to put a little note in the next number saying that a certain amount of the material came from Copley's work. I also told him I'd give him some sort of credit in the book. Then I promptly forgot Mr Frank B. Copley, the biographer, until I received a riproaring epistle from him demanding that I retract the lies in the piece about Taylor. One other point;—when I first wrote him, thinking he was enquiring in good faith about sources, I sent him the list I then had of various material about Taylor in English and French. He retorted that all these articles had been drawn from his book, too, so I think he may be a little bit hipped.

I get the impression from his letter that he's trying to trap me into quoting his own book back at him so as to have material for a nuisance suit. I dont think he'd have any real ground for legal action, as there are no quotations from the book, and the facts (he now claims they are untrue) are certainly not of a copyrightable nature.

I'm enclosing his letter and shant answer it until I hear from you. He could probably be appeased by the publication of a note giving credit to his lousy biography.

I'd hate to take the time to do it, but I could if I had to get the bibliography up again, and I'm sure it would turn out that Mr Copley was not the only source of material about Taylor. The general atmosphere of it I got from Taylor's own works.

Also it is obvious to anybody reading the piece that there is no intention to blacken the character of a very remarkable man or of his family. What makes me suspicious of Mr Frank B. Copley, the biographer, is that his letters to me when the piece came out in Esquire sang quite a different tune. Unfortunately I didn't keep them. I remember definitely that I asked him at the time whether the piece seemed accurate and he replied that it did, comparing it favorably to a chapter on Taylor in a Viennese novel of which I have forgotten the name that came out at the same time, that he claimed was inaccurate. If you people think its wise I'll merely write Mr Copley that I'm sorry I forgot him and that if he insists I'll publish a note in the next edition of the book similar to the one printed in Esquire, to the effect that some of the facts used came from his biography. The trouble is that if I did that I ought to publish a complete bibliography of the sources of the material used in the whole book, which would be nonsensical. It was a mistake I guess to give him his little note in Esquire in the first place.

Let me know what the more experienced opinion of H and B is on the subject.

Yrs
Dos

To Ernest Hemingway

Truro Mass
[*October 1936*]

Gosh Hem—it sounds pretty swell up there in the grizzlie belt. I cant get out there this year—wish to hell I could no money the B.M. is selling very moderately—but it'll have to sell a hell of a lot more to do me any good. We've gone and increased our standard of living and somethings got to be done about it. Seems like the more money you make the further off you are from balancing up the books. Maybe the combined volume will sell. What worries me about making a living at this lousy trade is that books have less and less permanent sale—One book a year makes a million dollars and everything else drags out an existence on the shelves, is remaindered and forgotten—If people keep on using books at all by the end of this century they sure will have a time weeding out the few sound bits of meat among the garbage—

Anyway even if I had any money I'd have to stick to this asinine pamphlet I'm trying to write. I read and read and if I keep up I ought to be able to get a college degree—God damn it, to try to use your mind is difficult painful & hazardous—no wonder so few people do it.

If I can ever get through this I'll have to take a lot of trips. I didn't want to go ahead on my trips until I'd gotten a little better educated in history and stuff. Result missed going to Spain—Things happen too damn fast these days—I've had a stagnant kind of summer—guess I ought to have taken my reading to the wars with me. The wars is a fine place to get a lot of reading done—

Everything I hear from Spain sounds pretty goddamn horrible— but things are always different if you see them—

Gosh I hope you get to go. Carlo Tresca has a theory that the British are encouraging a semi anarchist state in Catalonia and that the fascists wont try to recapture it—dividing up the Peninsula three ways—Gosh I hope you get to go—Even a week in Barcelona would be worth while.—Paris must be damn curious too—

I wish we could ever get to see you gents. Let me know if you go through N.Y. in November—or somewhere else would be better—I dont want to go to New York again for a hundred and one years—

love to Pauline

Gosh we're getting the good October weather & it's mighty agreeable

Yrs
Dos

CHOSEN COUNTRY

January 1937–December 1946

Nineteen thirty-seven began happily; Dos received a letter dated January 6 informing him of election to the National Institute of Arts and Letters in the Department of Literature. Into March he was busy in New York, trying to raise money for a film about Spain before leaving, as he wired Stewart Mitchell, to take "a view of Europe's ruins." Hemingway showed up in New York in February and, Dos later told Carlos Baker, joined him, Archibald MacLeish, and Lillian Hellman in a corporation they named Contemporary Historians. Having engaged a Dutch director, Joris Ivens, for the film—to be called *The Spanish Earth*—they worked on plans to fund and distribute it once it was completed. This episode contributed to the rupture in Dos' and Hemingway's friendship that would soon occur. Dos told Baker that from the start Hemingway wanted to concentrate on the military picture in Spain; Dos thought the rest of the world should be shown the suffering of the people.

The rift occurred after Dos got to Spain the latter half of March. Along with friends like the writer Josephine Herbst he went to Madrid once he and Katy had arrived in Europe. From the Hotel Florida they ventured out to observe the warfare, and Dos and Hemingway still argued about what should be the focus of their film. Disagreement about that, however, was only one cause of their quarrel. Hemingway, thriving in his role as war correspondent extraordinaire, became increasingly intolerant of other people's ideas—or simply, of other people. The most important matter was the case of José Robles, Dos' close friend from his earliest days in Spain. Robles had fought with the Loyalists until arrested late in 1936. Dos, trying to find out the reasons, was first assured that all was well, but he soon found out that Robles had been executed by the Communists as a Fascist spy. The truth of the matter never became clear. He believed that the Communists killed Robles for being unfriendly to their ulterior motives in the war. Robles' family thought he was framed by the Anarchists. Hemingway, predisposed to believe whatever the Loyalists and their Communist allies asserted, accepted their version. According to Harold Weston, while Dos was being thwarted at every turn when he tried to find out what had happened, Hemingway came to him to say that if he did not clear out, there would be trouble. To Dos, this seemed a sort of betrayal on Hemingway's part.

Dos stayed in Spain through much of April, doing work on the film, writing about the situation, and going to Valencia to try to protest Robles' murder through the American ambassador. It is not clear exactly when he next saw Hemingway, but it seems likely that the time was between the tenth and fifteenth of May, as both were in Paris on their way back from Spain. And it seems likely that this was the time when Dos, with Katy, told Ernest that he was going back to the United States to tell the truth about what was going on. As William L. White, editor of the Emporia *Gazette,* remembers Dos' account, Hemingway responded, "You do that and the New York reviewers will kill you. They will demolish you forever." Katy fired back, "Why Ernest I never heard anything so despicably opportunistic in my life!" The altercation might have occurred later, but all evidence indicates that the two saw little of each other after the spring of 1937; Dos Passos' "Farewell to Europe" would appear in July, and a year later Hemingway in writing would criticize what he considered Dos' naïveté about Spain. The point is their friendship had ended. Dos could no longer tolerate what he saw as Communist subversion of left-wing movements. Hemingway, only recently politicized and much absorbed in the courageous fight of the Loyalists, could not believe Dos Passos' charges, nor could he accept the challenge to what he considered his superior knowledge of the subject, and he chose to ignore Dos' own familiarity with Spain and her people.

"Farewell to Europe" appeared in *Common Sense.* Dos was renouncing his close ties with Europe, turning his back once and for all on any primary allegiance to that continent or to political creeds that seemed to him to be of European origin. Neither England nor France, he believed, was going to further the democratic idea; and in Spain a struggle existed "between the Marxist concept of the totalitarian state, and the Anarchist concept of individual liberty." He turned toward the United States; in that country and its governmental systems was the answer to what he had been searching for since his Harvard days. The Atlantic Ocean, he thought, was "broad enough to protect us against air raids, but it can't protect us against the infectious formulas for slavery that are preparing in Europe on every side." If the United States would shun European ideologies, she was in a position to work out her own problems. Dos recognized "our class war" and "our giant bureaucratic machines for antihuman power," but he still felt his country was closer to being correct than were the European nations. He declared, "Not all the fascist-headed newspaper owners in the country, nor the Chambers of Commerce, nor the armies of hired gunthugs of the great industries can change the fact that we have the Roundhead Revolution in our heritage and the Bill of Rights and the fact that democracy has been able, under Jefferson, Jackson, and Lincoln, and perhaps a fourth time (it's too soon to know yet) under Franklin Roosevelt, to curb powerful ruling groups."

Back from Europe, he had immediately gotten down to work, not only on reportage about Spain, but on a new novel, and he began to pepper Harcourt, Brace with suggestions for ways of marketing his writing. The publishers were not initially interested in a trilogy, but he and his agent, Bernice Baumgarten, convinced them it was worthwhile. "The title for the complete novel will be *U.S.A.,*" he announced to Cap Pearce in the middle of the summer. "The more I think of it the more essential it seems, both as a money making proposition and from the point of view of the work itself, to bring it out. A year from this fall is the latest possible date."

He did not write much to his friends about the dismal scene in Spain. To Marvin he commented only that he had "had a very instructive trip abroad—in fact rather too instructive. Spain is a pretty grim place right now." In August, when Stewart Mitchell wrote him about a fight between Max Eastman and Hemingway that had made the papers, Dos responded, "Damn silly that fisticuffs for the press—in fact makes you vomit," which was about as close as he ever came to evincing his distaste for Hemingway's antics.

As 1937 drew to a close, Dos was hard at work, reading proof for *U.S.A.,* which would appear in April, and writing *Adventures of a Young Man.* And in December he published in *Common Sense* an answer to those who had criticized what he had written since returning from Spain. In "The Communist Party and the War Spirit," he explained that, while "the declared aims of the Bolsheviks were . . . admirable," the problem was "whether the dictatorship method didn't make these aims impossible to obtain." He continued, "In my opinion the one hope for the future of the type of western civilization which furnishes the frame of our lives is that the system of popular government based on individual liberty be not allowed to break down." When the Communists lent their support to the Spanish Loyalist troops, it "was life itself. . . . The Communists took to Spain their organizing skill, their will to rule," but they also took "their blind intolerance." The result was an attitude of "Whoever is not with us is against us" which destroyed the possibility of building up a viable, independent popular base against Fascism. Having taken this position, he had now become as much anathema to the Communists as before he had been their literary hero. But the statement was well reasoned, and most of all, it re-emphasized what had always been foremost in his thinking: individual liberty.

Nineteen thirty-eight was an American year. Thinking as he now did about the situation in Europe, Dos sought to know his own country better. He continued his program of readings in early United States history. After seeing *U.S.A.* through to publication and preparing *Journeys Between Wars,* he and Katy set off on a trip that took them through Alabama to New Orleans before heading up the Mississippi delta to Cairo, Illinois, whence they headed east, settling in at the Warm Springs Inn, in Warm Springs, Virginia, by mid-March. They returned to Provincetown in April, and this, except for a cruise in the Mediterranean during July and part of August, was home base for the rest of the year. At some point, Dos did see Hemingway in New York at the Murphys' apartment. Dudley Poore remembered that Gerald Murphy told him of the incident. The two writers went out on the balcony to talk; after a time Dos came in and said to Gerald, "You think for a long time you have a friend, and then you haven't." That was, apparently, all he said, but clearly the two had been arguing more about Spain, Ernest had turned on Dos, and their relationship was sundered further.

During all this Dos also worked on *Adventures of a Young Man* which, if literarily one of his less important works, would nonetheless be a dramatic statement of his new stance. He finished a first draft with the notation "Provincetown Jan 27 '39 3:30 PM" and in a statement included with a draft of the novel wrote, "Adventures of a Young Man is the first of a series of contemporary portraits in the shape of stories. Glenn Spotswood has been raised in the tradition of American idealism. He suffers from a congenital sense of right and wrong. He grows up alone in the world of the twenties and thirties. He has a tough time." To say the least, Glenn has a tough time. Not surprisingly the book ends with his death in Spain, shot by Fascist gunners, but sent to that death by the Communists.

The novel was not well received by the critics, and its appearance in June 1939, marked the beginning of the decline of Dos' literary reputation. It would be easy—and unfair—to dismiss the critics, saying that they were simply reacting to his changed political stance. Certainly many of them disagreed with his turn against the Communists, but the novel lacked the exciting techniques of *U.S.A.;* and, because of the intensity of the thematic statement and the involvement with Glenn, it is hard to recognize the satire Dos intended. To be effective, satire requires a sense of distance between the narrator and the narrative, and this seems to be lacking in *Adventures of a Young Man,* even though Dos asserted to Edmund Wilson that he was trying to be "extraverted."

He and Katy did not venture out of the country at all in 1939, though again that spring they traveled west—"We've been cruising around West Texas," he wrote Stewart Mitchell the end of April, "very blood heating country hot as hinges of hell in fact but damn fine place to live—nothing is more encouraging than travelling round the U.S." With the situation in Europe worsening and their own finances precarious, they stayed put in Provincetown much of 1939 and 1940, and Dos went on educating himself in American history for his historical narratives. Because they were not away as much, they saw more of their friends, wrote fewer letters, and those they did write were often no more than brief notes.

The historical work took Dos to Virginia in 1940. In February he told Stewart Mitchell that he and Katy were in Alexandria for a month while he worked in the library and tried to arrange to get back the farmland Aunt Mamie Gordon held in trust. In June he wrote that "We're about to get back part of my father's Westmoreland County farm," something which pleased him doubly because of his increasingly fond memories of his family and his rapidly growing interest in Thomas Jefferson country. He and Katy went back to "T.J. country" again in October, poking around among Jefferson's architectural achievements, admiring the man more and more.

The Ground We Stand On was published August 29, 1941. By the time it appeared Dos was deep in further research on the colonial and revolutionary periods in the United States. He and Katy had vacationed in April and part of May in St. Augustine, Florida; then in October he went to England to survey the wartime scene. For *Harper's* he wrote of his impressions: respect for the Britishers' dogged determination, and a guarded optimism that out of all the carnage a more egalitarian society might emerge, despite the pessimism H. G. Wells voiced when Dos visited him. When the United States declared war against the axis powers in December, he was back in Provincetown, and no doubt he began to think what he could best do to help the war effort.

What he undertook was reportage on wartime America, and he began traveling around the country in the spring of 1942. During March and April he was in Arkansas and Texas, "making a last little tour of investigation in connection with some work," he wrote Rumsey Marvin from San Antonio in early April. While most of the summer was spent in Provincetown, that fall he traveled around the northeast. In December he told the Murphys, "I'm about in the middle of my New England tour." From this came the first of his "People at War" series that appeared in *Harper's* throughout 1943. "Downeasters Building Ships" he dated "Portland, Maine, December, 1942" when it appeared as "Yankee Mechanics" in *State of the Nation*. After Christmas in Provincetown he and Katy headed south, spending part of January and February in Washington before heading to New Orleans.

While he was traveling, Houghton Mifflin, his new publishers, brought out *Number One* in March 1943. The thinly disguised portrait of Huey Long sold well; Dos was pleased with the publisher's efforts to market his novel, which by June 15 had sold 17,197 copies in the U.S. This and the press of writing for the *Harper's* series buoyed him up.

From New Orleans they passed through Texas down into Mexico, then came back up through Texas again as they headed east. After a short stay in Provincetown, Dos headed back to Washington in June, staying with his friend Gardner Jackson, nicknamed "Pat," while he gathered material for further pieces in the "People at War" series.

Summer they spent in Provincetown before Dos left for more investigations. Early September found him in the mining regions around Pittsburgh; in October he headed west to do the last articles for *Harper's*. The trip took him from Washington to Columbus, Ohio; Chicago for a week; Coon Rapids, Iowa, where he became a good friend of his host Roswell Garst; then on to Minneapolis; Jamestown, North Dakota; Butte, Montana; and finally to the far west, Seattle and Portland. As he traveled he wrote his articles to meet *Harper's* deadlines. Katy's letters about their pets and about the people around

Provincetown amused him; while he enjoyed the country, he could not wait to return to his "possum," however. By early December he was back in Provincetown, where he settled down for much of 1944 before heading out to the Pacific the very last part of November. *State of the Nation,* though a compilation of previously published articles, took time to revise and put together before its appearance in July. He also worked when he could on a biography of Jefferson, a long, laborious task he would not finish until 1954. And the farm in Virginia occupied him. Though he had taken over his portion of the land in 1940, it was not his free and clear until 1944, after C. D. Williams brought suit against Aunt Mamie Gordon, her daughter, and her son-in-law in order to clear the title to the land and obtain a portion of the money which, it turned out, was owed Dos. "The great Virginia lawsuit came to a head last week in the Federal Court with a victory for our side," he wrote Robert Hillyer on April 3, "but like military victories it leaves the mopping up to be done. . . . Anyway it's a relief to have it over as it took an unconscionable amount of work and time from things that are I hope more important." It was a relief too because it eased the financial burden some. Dos and Katy during these years continued to be strapped for money, having to borrow from friends to cover debts, and at one point in 1944 going so far as to hock a ring of Katy's, which Dos later retrieved. The problem was not that they lived high, but their writing did not produce a large income, they were trying to manage more than one house on the Cape and could not seem to make them pay, and they were generous, for example caring for a boy of Provincetown friends for some length of time.

Dos' voyage as a war correspondent into the Pacific theatre of operations was to get a picture of the activities behind the front lines. He started out from San Francisco December 9, passed through Honolulu the next day, then spent Christmas on Kwajalein, one of the Marshall Islands. He jotted on a slip of paper in one of his notebooks a list of the places he visited:

> Hawaii
> Marshalls
> Marianas
> Ulithi
> Guerrilas
> Manila

> Guadalcanal
> New Caledonia
> Air Force   New Guinea
> Australia

His dispatches from the Pacific, which appeared in *Life,* later made up a part of *Tour of Duty,* his next book of reportage.

By mid-April he returned to the United States, spent the summer in Provincetown, then set off early in October on the second part of his "tour of duty," an investigation of war-shattered Europe.

The scene was bleak, as he repeatedly asserted to Katy. France showed signs of pulling herself together, but he felt a gloomy pall hung over Germany and Austria, and after a short time there he could not wait to get out. The destruction of the country was only part of what discouraged him. The political scene was the real worry. Utterly opposed to Communism, he foresaw nothing but trouble as the United States tried in his opinion to accommodate the Russians. "Who sups with the devil," he wrote in his Berlin notebook, "must need a long spoon—it is time Americans got it through their heads that Democracy & Dictatorship cant coöperate—not that democracy is perfect or that Russian dictatorship is perfect." The United States, after winning the war, seemed to him to be losing the peace.

Voyaging home aboard the aircraft carrier *Croatan* in mid-December, he reflected upon what he had seen and jotted down in a notebook:

> when you think of the things we've done so well in this war—the brilliant planning of supply—the Philippines campaign the Normandy landings it does seem that somebody could work out a plan of action in Europe and Asia—all we need to do to have the whole world with us is practice what we preach we have the force to back it up—

Back from Europe, he proceeded to report his impressions in a series of articles for *Life* during the first months of 1946. "Americans Are Losing the Victory in Europe" was the title of one appearing early in January that summed up his opinion as the United States headed toward the cold war.

Once he had finished the reports for *Life,* there was the matter of putting them together for *Tour of Duty* to attend to. But this was no major task, apparently, so he and Katy took off in March for a driving trip around the country. "We've been taking a vacation," he wrote

Stewart Mitchell on April 4, "doing no work and driving like fury around the country—got as far as the Rio Grande valley where the oranges and grapefruit were in bloom and a mountain full of huisache blossoms up above Monterrey." They returned to Provincetown, but work on the house on their farmland at Spence's Point continued—it was a convenient place to be while Dos worked in Charlottesville, where Jefferson's papers resided at the University of Virginia. October 7th he wrote Gerald Murphy from Hague, a little village near Spence's Point: "May sleep in our house any night now," and nine days later he told Sara, "We are actually sleeping in the house." Provincetown was still home base, but Virginia was becoming a second home.

To Ernest Hemingway

[Hotel Lafayette
New York]
Jan—9th [*1937*]

Dear Hem—

For God's sake drop me a line to the Hotel Lafayette—letting know when you hit this lousy town—we'll probably be here part of next week and a little while after—next week if we're not here we'll be in Provincetown Sure would like to see you—Pulling out for a short trip somewhere and then hope to get over to Spain & Paris for a few days—if there's any of it left. Sore, broke, and damn sick of everything. Living in the latter Roman Empire's not such fun. I'd rather read about it in Gibbon.

Damn sorry about not being able to pay you back any dough but this lousy novel hasn't made any—and have had to catch up on more pressing debts—I dont know if its the fault of the publisher or whether the stuff is just unsalable by nature—it sells moderately, but not on a money basis.

It was darn nice talking to you gents over the phone—can't say I wish you'd been up there because things are pretty horrible. Gerald and Sara both behaving so well in their separate ways that it's heartbreaking.

Take care of yourselves and my best to the Mexican Mouse—

Yrs
Dos

Hope Pauline's coming—Saw so darn little of her last time.

To Stewart Mitchell

Provincetown, Mass.
[*January 22, 1937*]

Dear Stewart—

Forgive my not sending back your books—Bentley's very interesting but he reads exceeding slow. Also please forgive my not sending back the fifty bucks—I'll have it for you, I hope, inside of a week. Money's been gigantically tight for me this winter. Anything I manage to scrape up goes into the maw of several large debts that follow me like sharks. However we hope to sell one of our houses soon and that will give us cash at least temporarily. If I dont get back through Boston before pulling out for a trip I'll ship you the Rev. Bentley—carefully packed—by parcel post—but perhaps we can get through Boston for an evening.

Had an evening with Cummings a couple of weeks ago. He seems well and lively though his politics are more tory than you could imagine. Why do poets nearly always become violent reactionaries in middle life? Harcourt Brace is publishing a Collected Poems which shows remarkably good sense on their part. We wished you had been with us.

I'm just on the edge of calling you up on the telephone to see if you have a copy of Orient Express you could lend me. I'm looking for a quotation from it to use on the catalogue of a show of watercolors. If I cant find one in Provincetown, I'll have boomed at you over the wires before you get this letter—Wish we could have a leisurely dinner together soon.

Katy joins me in love

Yrs
Dos

To Edmund Wilson

[Provincetown
February 6, 1937]

Dear Bunny—

Your smoking out of deVoto was great—

I've been trying to read The Flowering of New England. I've rarely read a book I disliked so much—there's a kind of female enthusiasm in it I find disgusting. What the devil is it about? Did you ever read Bazalgette's Thoreau? In spite of manifest inaccuracies it seems to me to do the same sort of thing much better. Looks to me like Brooks was going to be god's gift to the women's clubs—

Hope to see you next week—At the Lafayette Tuesday or Wednesday

Yrs
Dos

To Robert Hillyer

Cunard White Star
R.M.S. "Berengaria"
[*March 1937*]

Dear Robert—

Have hoped to see you the last few times I've been in Boston—but I'm never there for more than a few hours and the times I've called you up you've always been out—

We're headed for a little trip around Europe but hope to be back in May—wont you take the trip you planned one year with the small Hillyer and come across the bay to see us?—We'll be back in June. Katy has been urging me to produce you again ever since we spent such a pleasant evening with you in your black velvet jacket—so you must come.

I have a sort of hope of going through Amsterdam and dragging old Van out of his consulate for a drink.

Do come over and see us next summer; why its so difficult for me to spend a few hours in Boston I cant exactly explain—but I never get anywhere without being in a considerable rush; I'm always overdue on so much work—Provincetown is the only place where I'm not in that state of rush. I hope we'll have a boat and can take you sailing—

My best to Dorothy

Yrs
Dos

To Alexander Woollcott (1887–1943), *a journalist and essayist, whom*
Dos knew as an acquaintance. Woollcott was drama critic for the
New York Times *from 1914–1922, and later (1925–1928) for the* World.
He did some acting and was known for his idiosyncratic wit.

> Cunard White Star
> R.M.S. "Berengaria"
> [*March 1937*]

Dear Woollcott—

Received your handsome check but didn't have time to call you up
as was in a great scramble to get on the boat—passport visas etc—What
I think I'd better do with the check is the following: Malraux says that
there's an immediate need for X-ray plates and anaesthetics in Valencia
and Madrid—In Paris I'll find out what agency—French or Spanish
Government is most likely to send a shipment immediately and shall
turn the money over to them—so that inside of two weeks it ought to
be taking the form of whatever surcease from pain anaesthetics can
give. Malraux says that the situation in the hospitals is terrific—so the
money really will mean something immediately—

We've been asleep ever since we got on the boat but we're sending
a note to your friend and shall ask her to have a glass of Gerald's very
good sherry with us.

Thanks so much—Hope to see you in the spring sometime—if
they'll still be having some when we get back to New York

> Yrs
> John Dos Passos

To American Committee to Aid Spanish Democracy
Medical Committee

> [On board R.M.S. *Berengaria*
> *March 1937*]

Gentlemen,

Somebody in connection with one of the Spanish committees has
been using my name in ways I never authorized that have caused me
grave inconvenience and threatened what little usefulness I may have as
a reporter—so let me ask you in future not to use my name in anyway
that I dont specifically authorize by letter, and please to remove it from
all letterheads and lists of sponsors etc.

> Sincerely yrs
> John Dos Passos

To F. Scott Fitzgerald

On Board RMS Berengaria Eastbound
March 7 [*1937*]

Why Scott you big bum you made it all up. It was a great pleasure to
see you. You know I'm always restless and had some damn fool thing
to do that was on my mind, a date of some kind, I've forgotten what it
was. But I'd a damn sight rather see you drunk than a lot of people
sober. But there's nothing in explanations either way—just let me say
that Katy and I are both damn fond of you and that we think about
you a lot and that we wish like all hell you could find some happy way
of getting that magnificent working apparatus of yours to work
darkening paper, which is its business. Our address until May will be
American Express, Paris, after that Provincetown—Do drop us a line
to let us know how you are getting on. I'm anxious to take a final look
at Europe—but I'd hate to stay away from the U.S. long these days.
Things seem a darn sight more live and kicking there than anywhere
else in the world—my main pleasure now is just driving around the
roads and looking at the damned American continent—

Yrs
Dos

To Edmund Wilson

[On board the Southampton Paquebot
March 9, 1937]

Dear Bunny—

Was darn sorry to get through New York without seeing you but
was in a terrific jam with passports etc. Some halfwit in connection
with one of the committees gave out a story that Hemingway and I
were going to combat in Spain that gave me endless trouble with the
State Department. I'm absolutely completely and irrevocably through
with all committees, protests, nonpaying magazines, relievers and
uplifters whether I agree with them or not. That whole business has
gotten to be a smalltime racket supporting a group of bureaucrats like
Associated Charities. Their ends are not my ends, their methods are
asinine when they aren't actually damaging to the causes they pretend
to serve and to hell with 'em.

Finally worked my way through "The Flowering of"—certainly
there are valuable suggestions and occasional traces of a superb skele-

ton idea, but its all so overgrown with marshmallow that I dont see how it can ever be a very useful book. A great relief to turn to Parrington—who really makes sense and writes pretty well for a college professor.

Was disappointed not to go to Mexico, but the chance of taking a little tour of Europe once I found a way of paying for it by doing some work for Fortune—getting up some material for them that I wont have to write—was not to be turned down at this moment. The greatest stream of people seems to be pouring across the Rio Bravo, I suppose attracted consciously or unconsciously by the new volcano, the Walkers—Solow—Bill Smith, the Waugh's—It'll be like the great days of Whitfield the preacher. It certainly would be worth going down to see the show—but I think that show will last longer than the European show. Take care of yourself and drop us a line to American Express, Rue Scribe, Paris—

Yrs
Dos

Katy sends love

To E. E. Cummings

[Provincetown
August 23, 1937]

Hello Cummings—Rumor in the remarkably pleasant shape of Morry Werner hot footing it out of the Public Library informed me that you pulled out of New York for an ape farm near London just about as we pulled in after various much too instructive travels among the civil wars. He also furnished me with an I hope not entirely fictitious address of yours in the Shade of the Exposition Unique mondiale et planetaire. Then at Bunny's we all listened to your—for shame Franklin D. Cummings—record, which incidentally is remarkably good and ought to have a very good effect on people who are about to read the volume Harcourt Brace is bringing out. By people sir I refer to the American people, 130 million of them. All of which caused Katy to accuse me of never fetching out Cummings, and me to regret that there was no Cummings to fetch out on this side of the water—As more and more old friends pass into the adult stage—singularly disagreeable among all the primates including man—they become more old and less friends. No less a person than Michael Loyola Gold accused me in print of not passing into that stage, but of remaining alas in a state of bourgeoisie unreconstructed and unliquidated adolescence—and here's heartily hoping that you are also still more nearly approximating the playfulness of the young rather than the savagery of the old gorilla— How's yourself, Cummings? How about dropping into a mailbox a postal card describing habitat and general environmental features.

I'm in my ivory tower—a damn tall one which I'm hoping to fireproof against incendiary bombs—and damn cosy there. It takes a little trip out to the firing line now and then to make you appreciate its excellence—firing line, hell, chain gang is more like it—anyway the sawdust trail is not for me. How do you like Paris this year? I suddenly got a rush of liking it again and the French. When things are thoroughly lousy the French get damn good. They seemed to me this time much more like they used to be in the war—chipper, lively, and even generous with their money—If you see Leger give him Katy's and my best—he was damn nice when we were in Paris.

Never enjoyed the cape so much as this summer—plenty saltwater small boat sailing small time vegetable garden.

Katy joins me in
Love to Marion & to yourself

Yrs
Dos

To Edmund Wilson

[Provincetown
August 24, 1937]

Dear Bunny—

How are you keeping? How about coming up here for a few days during the fall? Dont you need a little dip in the sea?

Here's a medical survey of Soviet Russia that I think is fairly well balanced. I wonder if, maybe, now that the Marxists have been liquidated, the U.S.S.R. wont go into a period of peace and prosperity—the days of the Good Czar Shtalin—The rise in the birthrate—if authentic, might indicate an increased enthusiasm in the people—or just slum conditions—Anyway the short account of the 1932 famine is one of the best I've read—

Have you read Beal's book [*Proletarian Journey*]—? Fred Beal of Gastonia strikes It's thoroughly worth reading—shows you what an honest not over-intelligent textile worker gets into when he puts his life in the hands of the C.P. Beal is such a typical fellow that his adventures have a good deal of importance I think—

Here's Bingham's little pamphlet too, which I very largely agree with

Yrs
Dos

To C. A. Pearce

Labor Day
571 Commercial Street
Provincetown Mass
[*September 1937*]

Dear Cap

Thanks for your note & the Stuart Chase outline. Be sure to send me the book when it comes out—sounds like a damned important vulgarization of a set of ideas that are in great need of being spread around Stuart Chase is a mighty useful guy that way.

I'm anxious to see your dummies for U.S.A. I'm also anxious to get together with you and Mr. H & Mr B and talk over a five year plan of publications. I'm also trying to get together a few suggestions for advertizing and publicity—because I thoroughly understand that it's useless to pick flaws without countering with some kind of suggestion.

My stuff about the Spanish Civil War will probably amount to about 75 typewritten pages. Can you think of any profitable way that it could be brought out?

Also; what do you think of republishing Orient Express and some of the stuff from In All Countries in one book of travel sketches?

Also; is your idea of bringing out a volume of the biographies entirely discarded?

You see I'm not going to give you people any rest until we hit on a method of handling my work that is logical and cumulative.

Cant give any definite assurances about this short (at least I hope its going to be short) novel, yet. Hope to be able to unfold an entire plan by early Oct or late this month when I'll probably get down to the big city for a day or two.

Yrs
Dos

Another suggestion to put into your pipe—how about bringing out the Spanish material from the long defunct Rosinante—and the essay from In All Countries and the new stuff in a volume? It would make a logical sequence—

To Stewart Mitchell

Provincetown Mass
Sept 27 [*1937*]

Dear Stewart—

Thanks enormously for that fifty—shall repay instantly—we suddenly found ourselves broke and suffering with bank overdraft—I ought to be old enough by this time to organize my finances a little more sensibly. The trouble is that we live higher than we can earn—if we didn't our living would be meagre indeed—so life is a continual race with the sheriff. Fortunately we think of ourselves as continuously on the edge of a big killing of some kind—and in the meantime we are a burden on our friends. See you in Boston I hope—we had to scoot home to revamp our bank account this time. Dont forget that there's always bed board and whiskey sour out on the cape if you should want a change from Boston—There wont be any trains after October 1—but possibly improved bus connections—The NY NH and H is gradually giving up the business of being a railroad.

Katy joins me in love—we greatly enjoyed your visit and wish you would come more often—

Yrs
Dos

Spent the night with Cummings at Silver Lake—He was looking well and seemed cheerful and lively.

To C. A. Pearce

Provincetown Mass
Sept 28 [*1937*]

Dear Cap—

I'll be down in New York for a day or two next week—hope to bring a suggestion for the jacket of U.S.A. I wont have the preface done, but I'll do it as soon as I can—in the next couple of weeks—I'll also bring the Spanish stuff—possibly minus its tailpiece—so that we can talk about it.

I think if we can polish off U.S.A. and a possible reprint of travel stuff as early as possible we'll be in a position to go ahead on a short novel which will be a completely new departure—(it may turn out to be a series) next fall—What I'd like to see is all my past stuff that still seems to me to have any interest served up in available form for people who might happen to want to read it—We'll talk the whole thing over next week; I think I'm now far enough away from the stuff in question to be able to look at the merchandizing problem from the viewpoint say of an advertizing agency—

Yrs
Dos

To Arthur Davison Ficke (1883–1945), *author of numerous volumes of poetry, the best known of which is* Sonnets of a Portrait Painter.

571 Commercial Street
Provincetown, Mass.
[September 29, 1937]

Dear Arthur;

The annoying thing about Esquire is that the bastards will publish almost anything but that they absolutely wont pay—I've managed to raise the ante to $250 but cant get any higher—Hemingway I believe gets $500 (all this please under the capacious brim of the fellow wordfellow's hat)—but they will use stuff that other editors cant stomach—and that's all I know about them. Their regular price is $100 for anything—they are getting so rich that maybe they could be induced to see the publicity value of paying big prices—but I doubt it. I know Carl Brandt has been making impassioned speeches to Gingrich on the subject—the sweatshop tradition of the suit and pants business from which they sprang is too strong—and they can get the stuff for the price they pay.

Damn nice to hear from you—and best of luck with any price raising operations. I'd keep on hammering at them

Yrs
Dos

To John Howard Lawson

Provincetown
Nov 4 [1937]

Dear Jack—

Dawn and I went together to see Processional last week. It's amazing how well it holds up. The production is excellent—although the sets are a little on the gunnysack side—The general tone is much less brilliant and cute than that of the Guild production and the wisecrack side of the play doesnt get over so well, but it seemed to me that the underlying struggle got over much better. It seemed to me damned stirring and it certainly stirred up the audience—the fact that it got a bad press from the left, is to my way of thinking merely one more proof of the left's complete ossification. Hope to see it again next time Im in New York—the musical score is excellent—in tone with the general charcoal drawing effect of the production. I've been trying to make out why it stirred me more than Marching Song—which has the materials of a much more important play in it. I think it has something to do with the fact that the rapid cartoon style is much more consistent in Processional—and I think must be an integral part of your way of thinking. In Marching Song it tends to bog down and become soggy in places—a little over serious. The brashness and freedom from preoccupations of Processional is what gives it its great punch, although a great deal of your work has been better since then—it hasn't had the surface consistency that seems to be so important in a play. It's too bad you cant see it—it might almost be worth the expense of a trip east to see it. Its terms are the terms of Broadway and for some reason ring truer than the Theatre Union terms of Marching Song—The reason is that the American Left theatre, not yet having come into existence, has no terms of its own and is continually wobbling between Broadway the Jewish art theatre and the Russian movies. Seeing Processional made me feel that you ought to sit down and write about a dozen more plays in rapid succession to build up your personal theatrical idiom—There's no left to lean on anymore, only a few discordant individuals swirling around in the suction as the water runs out of the basin that's the kind of people who write valuable plays—the tonic effect of despair etc getting the adrenal glands to work—I was very much pepped up by seeing it and feel a certain vague interest in the theatre—which for a long time has caused me only disgust—reawaking. That proves that its a good play—love to Sue

Yrs

Dos

Gosh thanks for the $200—it was like a heavy shower in a drouth—instantly soaked up by the thirsty soil—but it relieved the tension a little—the sheriff and the banker are temporarily out of the living room——

To John Howard Lawson

[Provincetown
Fall 1937]

Dear Jack—

You must have patience with the unbelievers—the real difference
between your attitude and mine about politics is that you think that
the end justifies the means and I think that all you have in politics is
the means; ends are always illusory. I think that Anglo-Saxon democracy is the best political method of which we have any and I'm for or
against movements in so far as they seem to me to be consistent with
its survival. To survive its got to keep on evolving. I have come to
believe that the CP is fundamentally opposed to our democracy as I see
it and that marxism, though an important basis for the unborn
sociological sciences, if held as a dogma, is a reactionary force and an
impediment to progress. Fascism is nothing but marxism inside out
and is of course a worse impediment—but the old argument about
giving aid and comfort to the enemy is rubbish: free thought cant
possibly give aid and comfort to fascism But we've had this all out
before and it is not arguable—except in matters of detail. Naturally
that position was reached after considerable travel. I now think that
foreign liberals and radicals were very wrong not to protest against the
Russian terror all down the line. There's just a chance that continual
criticism from their friends might have influenced the bolsheviks and
made them realize the extreme danger to their cause of the terror
machine, which has now, in my opinion, eaten up everything good in
the revolution. What we have in the U.S.S.R. is a new form of society
but I dont think it shows any sign of being a superior frame for the
individual human than the poor old U.S.A. And waving the fascist
spook at me isn't going to make me think any different.

On the other hand you are perfectly right in saying that the
unbelievers must have patience with the believers. What I had to point
out is the fundamental difference in aim. The fact that my particular
slant in thought has few adherents at present, doesn't make it any less
valid in my opinion. So there we are—

Perhaps there still exist some small segments of life that dont have
to be classangled. Frankly I'm in favor of enlarging those segments as
much as possible. And opposing political opinions dont necessarily
involve moral turpitude—

Speaking of moral turpitude—if it should come about that you got the job of writing on a hypothetical movie of Charley Anderson, I certainly shouldn't be opposed to it—a sale is a sale is a sale—In fact now that the whole matter has been aired I think we could face the prospect almost cheerfully. I think its always a good idea to put the worst foot forward when engaging on any common enterprize. I wrote you still somewhat smarting from certain other adventures of a movie nature in which politics and the silver screen played a somewhat double and hardly (to me) satisfactory game. In this case there'd be money in it to sweeten the draft—blessed H'wood.

Say for Christ's sake remember that in all my querulous complaints and crossings of unreached and probably nonexistent bridges—there's no question of my admiration for your ability as the slinger of the dramatical word. Hell I'd be able to like and admire a writer of ability even if he were a fascist. Once we grant a complete difference in aim—everything clears up—Is Sue in H'wood—love to her and Jeffry and Mandy—and write a play to undermine the republic during the winter months—you big tchekist.

Yrs
Dos

Damn sorry to have to call for the 200—I'd thought you were rolling in gold—I'm pretty broke—but might be able to return it in a month or so—if my wicked reformist libertarian enterprizes bring me any profit.

To Sherwood Anderson

[New York
February 1938]

Dear Sherwood—

It was damn nice of you to write and I'm damn glad you liked the article. What worries me about the bastardly communists is that they seem to me to be spreading around—(and they certainly are skillful organizers) ideas that now that they've thrown overboard all their social revolutionary aims—are purely fascist. If we all have to go into an army I'd rather go into the U.S. army—I know what that's like. I dont know Mr. Stalin's army from the inside—but it seems kind of creepy to a spectator. They've certainly got the literary boys eating out of their hands. Maybe there was something in the ivory towers after all.

We'll be at the Lafayette until the middle of Feb. Call up if you come
to New York—

Yrs

Dos

To William H. Bond (1915–   ), *who was a graduate student work-
ing on a long paper for a course in literary criticism when he wrote
Dos. Bond went on to become librarian of the Houghton Library at
Harvard.*

Warm Springs Inn
Warm Springs
Bath County, Virginia
March 26, 1938

Dear Mr. Bond—

Thank you for your nice letter. Your remark about Whitman is
very much to the point. I read him a great deal as a kid and I rather
imagine that a great deal of the original slant of my work comes from
that vein in the American tradition. Anyway, I'm sure it's more likely
to stem from Whitman (and perhaps Veblen) than from Marx, whom
I read late and not as completely as I should like. The Marxist critics
are just finding out, with considerable chagrin, that my stuff isnt
Marxist. I should think that anybody with half an eye would have
noticed that in the first place—

Very sincerely yrs
John Dos Passos

To Upton Sinclair

Warm Springs Inn—Warm Springs
Bath County, Virginia
[April 1938]

Dear Upton—

I think your letter to [Eugene] Lyons in the New Masses was an
excellent statement of what we might call the American Socialist point
of view. My main reservation would be that I have come to think,
especially since my trip to Spain, that civil liberties must be protected at
every stage of every political movement that is going to have good
results—at whatever costs—we've got to invent a democratic way of
waging war. In Spain I am sure that the introduction of G.P.U. meth-

ods by the communists did as much harm as their tank men, pilots and experienced military men did good. The trouble with an all powerful secret police in the hands of fanatics, or of anybody, is that once it gets started there's no stopping it until it has corrupted the whole body politic—I'm afraid that that's what's happening in Russia. At the same time the great achievements of the revolution will be no more swept away by the Russian Terror than the achievements of the French Revolution were swept away by their Terror and by the Napoleonic period.

As far as this country goes, I feel more and more that the Communists are introducing the fascist mentality that has made Europe a nightmare (After all its the Bolsheviki that invented all of Hitler's and Mussolini's tricks—) and I'm very much afraid that its the reactionaries that will profit by them. So I've come to think that the communists in this country are a pestiferous nuisance—Stalinist and Trotskyite alike— and that for the time being the best thing people like us can do is keep out of their clutches—Thats why a sane piece of writing like yours is such a pleasure to find in the hysterical pages of the New Masses—

Yrs
John Dos Passos

By the way, much of Lyons' book [*Assignment in Utopia*] is factually correct—in my experience—but he's a man without real intellectual breadth—The part about the lives of foreign correspondents in Moscow is very valuable. I dont think his conclusions are of much importance.

To Helen Taylor (1906–   ), *who was advertising and publicity director at Harcourt, Brace when Dos wrote her. She later worked for other publishers, retiring in 1968 from the Viking Press, where she was a senior editor.*

[Provincetown
April 1938]

Dear Helen Taylor—

Forgive me for continuing to make your life miserable. Believe me it's not that I've suddenly gotten a case of authoritis at my time of life, as Dorothy Parker used to say, but it's the wolves. You may have met them. I used to think they were friends of mine of long standing, and always kept a few in the basement, but now they are showing a rather nasty spirit, hardly spirits—man like, particularly those from the Home

Leasers Foreclosure organization. Journeys has been reviewed all over
the place, and I'm wondering if maybe you people couldn't be induced
to sell a few copies. It seems to me a much easier proposition than
U.S.A., but naturally people have to be given an inkling of what's in it.
For Christ sake can that stuff about twenty years of travel—not even
the sturdiest bookbuyer will stand up under it and bookbuyers are as
feeble as lettuce plants with the wilt this season. What interests people
this spring is European politics. I'm sure; all you have to do is to listen
to the radio—

In the NeuroP from which I cut out this ad (in which somebody
has miscapitalized my name; the Dos is part of the hinder part of the
name the way my father & I have always spelt it) there are a few
sentences from Josephson's review that give the general idea. I'm sure
that the "foremost literary" stuff scares as many people off as it attracts.
After all the proof of what I say is in the fact that in spite of being as
much talked about etc as any books in the country people aren't buying
the damn things in any appreciable quantities. I hate to nag, but I dont
think that the game needs to be given up as hopeless yet. I cant see why
Journeys isnt as saleable as Personal History or The Way of a Trans-
gressor—theres less "personality" but more varied kinds of things.
Ordinarily I wouldn't worry because I think that in the long run on
the cheap edition people will buy it, but its those wolves that are
nagging me and that's why I'm nagging you—

   Take care of yourself

                                                              Yrs
                                                   John Dos Passos

To Upton Sinclair

                                                   571 Commercial Street
                                                      Provincetown Mass
                                                      May 20—[19]38

Dear Upton—

   Thanks so much for The Flivver King. I read it through at one
gulp without a single drop in interest. Its one of your clearest, simplest
and most moving narratives. You are inside Ford and his workers and
the Detroiters all at the same time. I dont follow the critics much, so I
didn't know about their boycott until afterwards. I think it was mostly
due to stupidity. Its hard to get it into us outsiders' heads that a novel is

something that comes between boards in a colored jacket presented by an advertizer and priced at $3.00 or $2.50 to most of the people in the trade. They never think of writing as something unpackaged that has been going on for a long time, even before the Book of the Month Club was started. The Flivver King seems to me to be one of your very best pieces and one of the few important things written recently in America. I think the readers will think so too—

Yrs
John Dos Passos

To C. A. Pearce

New York
June 27–[19]38

Dear Cap—

This is to introduce Sam Baron, whom I met in Spain last year when he was correspondent of the Socialist Call there. He had some rather peculiar adventures in that capacity that he has put down in a narrative of his trip, with a general picture of the Civil War situation. His account of the veiled dictatorship of the C.P. on the Loyalist side seems to me so important that I have offered to write a foreword for the book.

Two sides of the Spanish story have been put before the public. Sam Baron's account gives the third side. It seems to me essential that the American public have a chance to get at the full truth of what is going on in Europe, so I think somebody ought to get this book out right away. Naturally its up to you people to judge whether you see your way clear to do it. There's a chance that this perfectly simple and sincere account of an American socialist's adventures might arouse the same sort of interest that Lyons' book on Russia did. It will annoy the communists and give a certain amount of ammunition to the Catholics, but I think that the facts are always worth taking risks to get out.

Yrs
Dos

By the way, the time element will count for a good deal, so I wonder if you could give him a quick decision on this thing. My foreword will be ready in two weeks

To Robert Hillyer

Provincetown Mass
[*September 10, 1938*]

Dear Robert—

We were delighted to get your letter but darn sorry to hear about the dropsy. But Robert you cant and mustn't have dropsy in spite of its Elizabethan sound. We must get you some powdered unicorn's horn or the bladder of an Abyssinian crocodile—Are you sure your doctor is right about it—? The thing to do is to search around until you find a physician who recommends at least light wines and beers. After all they had me condemned to the unalcoholic tropics and to all sorts of strange diets—and I seem to be thriving with the help of an occasional turkish bath in any latitude.

Being sick is a damned annoyance and I'm heartily sorry. Come up and convalesce here for a few days—We'll be here, with occasional interruptions all the fall.

We spent two months—I mean one month—the climate was so uneventful it seemed like two—being gently wafted around Sicily on the schooner belonging to a friend of ours. It would have been dandy if it hadn't been that instead of Italy you now have Mussolini-land—I dont see how our fascist friends can like it so much there—why should you like to live among people that make you despise the human race? The miserable wops look much poorer than twenty years ago, they are more fawning and thievish and beggary—their bread is adulterated, their spaghetti is bad and their clothes are ragged and they look scared to death. France, that decadent democracy, seemed full of life and vigor; people actually laugh there.

We're in fine shape except for a pestiferous lack of money that seems to threaten to become chronic. God damn it I'm sick of being always broke.

The boat is still running. Why couldn't Dorothy drive you up during Sept.?

Katy joins me in love to you both

Yrs
Dos

To Bernard Knollenberg (1892–   ), *an historian and lawyer. In addition to his career as a lawyer and administrator in the federal government, Knollenberg has written, among other titles,* Washington and the Revolution: a Re-Appraisal, Origins of the American Revolution, *and* George Washington: The Virginia Period.

571 Commercial Street
Provincetown, Mass.
Sept 18—[19]38

Dear Mr Knollenberg,

My tardy answering of your very nice note is due (apart from original sin) to my having been away from home and without mail most of the summer. I'm still plugging at Sam Adams etc. It seems to be taking the form of a series of historical footnotes—John Lilburne—Milton and Roger Williams, Defoe, Sam Adams, H. H. Breckenridge, and the Whiskey Rebellion, Jefferson's foreign travels etc The idea is to trace the descent of the "great" tradition of libertarian ideas in this country and to try to indicate where the American tradition breaks off from the British. Christ only knows when I'll get it finished—

Do you ever drive down the Cape? If you do during the fall look us up, please. I'd like a little more talk about that period.

Sincerely yrs—
John Dos Passos

To Sherwood Anderson

Provincetown, Mass.
May 19 [1939]

Dear Sherwood—

It was darn nice to hear from you—If I get into New York during June I'll certainly call you up—It seems to me that all those highsounding organizations have pretty well outlived their usefulness—if they ever had any. And I think some of them tend to encourage individuals to stick their heads out at times when nothing is to be gained by sticking their heads out. At bottom I think most of them are the tools of the Communist Party in its strange and devious and, it seems to me at least, thoroughly disastrous policy—I certainly think your letter to Romain Rolland is very reasonable. I think I'll write him in the same vein—Its so long since I've read any of their releases, because they discourage me so, that I haven't any idea what position we hold on the letterhead

Yrs
Dos

To Edmund Wilson

P'town—
May 20 [*1939*]

Dear Bunny—

How much longer will you be in New York ie: in Stamford—
Drop me a card will you? Hope to go down there for a couple of days
and would hate to miss you by an hour—I'm in a deadspot with regard
to that novel at present—and dont know whether I agree with your
criticism or not—I'm sure you are right about the inadequacy of the
straight naturalistic method—but in this case it seemed the only way to
do it. I'll look it over again a few months from now—I rather envy you
going to Chicago—I have to settle down to my reading. I'm a little
reluctant to settle down anywhere. I seem to have a better time away
from the eastern seaboard at present—I think the King and queen of
England are casting a terrible forepall of boredom over the continent.
Christ, I hope we can react to it. We might all stay that way—

Yrs
Dos

To Edmund Wilson

[Provincetown
June 27, 1939]

Dear Bunny—

I've been thinking about what you said about Adventures of a
Young Man being too extroverted and have seen the same plaint in less
intelligible form in various wellwishing reviews. I haven't had a chance
to reread the book, but what I'm wondering is whether you are giving
the behavioristic method the credit of being a method—After all its
the method I've been trying to elaborate these many years—with what
success is another question! By behavioristic method I mean the
method of generating the insides of the characters by external description—Defoe does it supremely and its more or less the method of
english novels up to the romantic school, as of Cervantes and Quevedo
and Petronius and Apuleius—Now whether I've ever succeeded in
doing that is another thing—but to ask me to be "less extroverted" is
like asking Joyce to be less "introverted" and less pedantic—Pedantry
and introversion are the materials he builds his work out of.

Do you think there's anything in this notion or is it just a piece of cheeze?

Love to Mary and young Mr. Wilson.

Yrs
Dos

To Katy Dos Passos

[Provincetown
Summer 1939(?)]

Oh Katy, it certainly isnt very nice here without the opossum—I work and work and get very little done and the house is very gloomy—(in spite of seeing various people around) and I sure do wish I was where you are—I hadnt planned to be so disappointed when I got your wire saying you weren't coming till Friday. But to be here alone with all these dreadful houses and the bills pouring in is certainly not much fun, and I have to work afternoons to get anything done at all and that glooms me up, because I dont get any running or walks. A daily swim is about as far as I get. Haven't gotten over to get the boat fixed up as havent wanted to spend money. 200 bucks appeared from Rummy Marvin which I thought I'd deposit in your bank to pay bills with. Oh Katy please let's not run up any more or buy any more houses, I've always lived successfully from hand to mouth without the slightest worry, but I cant combine that with unpaid bills and financial operations

Forgive these gloomy reflexions. They are induced by a summons from Days to pay a coal bill I never heard of. I'll wait till you come, if you really are coming Friday. Otherwise I'll send Marvins check to New York and pay up. We dont have to appear in court before the 27th so there's considerable time—but possum we just cant continue leaving unpaid bills around like this. Honestly its a mania with you not to pay bills. Let's clean it up. I feel as depressed and lethargic as an old Provincetowner.

But Katy if you should come Friday I'd feel much better—and the two hundred bucks will pay all the more pressing bills so dont worry— But it's just horrid here without you I love you so

miserable mournful all out of shape and
always hanging crepe—solitary A.

To Josephine Herbst (1897–1969), *the novelist, whom Dos had known from the twenties, and with whom he observed the Civil War in Madrid. Her trilogy*—Pity Is Not Enough, The Executioner Waits, *and* Rope of Gold—*is in its anticapitalist theme and something of its techniques like* U.S.A.

[Provincetown
Summer(?) 1939]

Dear Josie—

Darn glad to hear from you—forgive me for being such a stinking poor correspondent. Thanks for the books—I dont know when people get time to read books I dont seem to do anything else except write eat walk and drink and I cant even get through the books I have to read for my work—Frankly I'm pretty sick of books.

Jez I bet South America's a mess—I'd love to go there but not to write about—Mighty handsome of you not to have written about it. There ought to be a series of medals struck off for people who refrain from writing about subjects they dont understand—we wouldn't need many. My a lot of things people and ideas are going down the drain; even thats better than the ones like the editors of the New Republic who refuse to go down the drain no matter how often one pulls the chain, but just bob drearily in the porcelain receptacle—

Best luck and hope to see you soon—shall always remember how human you looked and acted at the old Florida that morning—amid many depressing circumstances that was one thing that made me feel good—

Take care of yourself

Yrs
Dos

To James T. Farrell [1904–   ], *the novelist, most noted for his trilogy about* Studs Lonigan. *Farrell's naturalistic bent likens his fiction to Dos'; the two admired each other, and Farrell in later years was more favorable toward Dos' fiction than were most critics.*

571 Commercial St.
Provincetown, Mass.
[*Summer 1939*]

Dear Jim Farrell,

Harcourt Brace sent me the proofs of your Mercury article. It's a damn good article and said a lot of things that needed to be said, and well. Anyway the spectacle of a writer coming to the defense of a contemporary is rare enough to be notable.

Criticism is in a lousy mess in this country. The corruption of the Left seems to have infected everything. So damn few people have any standards that the bureaucratic racketeer organizations have everything their own way. Naturally the last thing the racketeers want is discussion—and who'd pay them to discuss.

I think the universal revulsion against the Adventures is based on something a little deeper than partisan feeling. It's very [fringes of the page burned here]—they'll read any kind of spinach about okies or Eskimos or even perfectly straight stuff about the "proletariat", whatever that is, but they start to get sore when the stuff hits them too close. Adventures is about the world from which most of the reviewers come—the Jewish-liberal college humanitarian stratum of our society. I think that's why even the anti Stalinists echo the same cry—and I've heard it from people who are entirely sympathetic with my work in general. I think they are wrong and have a certain amount of confidence in the book although I well know that opinions about your own work are worth damn little.

What you say about my characters and their way of talking and smelling [page burned here]

I think you have one of the few real character making knacks on the market—your people have the real promethean spark and seem to me to get better from book to book. Incidentally I kind of envy (purely from the point of view of literary material) your having been raised a Catholic. The Holy Church is sure in a state of rot unseemly in so old and maidenly an institution—I wish I knew enough about it from the inside to write about it.

Wish I sometimes got to have a talk with you—

Yrs

J. Dos Passos

To Dwight Macdonald (1906–   ), *journalist and critic, who was an
editor of the* Partisan Review *when Dos corresponded with him about
the Robles affair in 1939. As a Trotskyite in those years, Macdonald
was likely to have been sympathetic to Dos' stance.*

[Provincetown
July 1939]

Dear Dwight Macdonald—

Here's a copy of a letter I sent the New Republic. I rather under-
played the stupid way in which Del Vayo lied to me about the manner
of Robles death. After all people act in big things the way they do in
small; my talks with him about this business certainly didn't increase
my confidence in that paladin of the workers of hand and brain. If
some American wellwishers hadn't started raising a yammer about the
matter in Madrid, I should have been able to get at the facts at that
time, I'm sure, although Robles death had had the intended effect of
making people very chary of talking about the "Mexicans" as the
Russians were familiarly known. After my American friends started to
give tongue I decided that it was useless to stay longer in Spain and
that my being there might be dangerous to the people I was associating
with. I've just learned of a funny incident that more or less bears out
this contention. Barea, the telephone and cable censor in Madrid for the
foreign press, who certainly seemed orthodox to me, got into trouble
with the C.P. and was thrown out of his job sometime after I left
Spain, and in fact escaped from the country with considerable difficulty. When the C.P. agents raided his room they found some Tausch-
nitz volumes I'd autographed for him and carried them off as evidence
of Trotskyism (or whatever he was being charged with) It would all
be comic in any other context. The whole story of the Spanish Earth is
excessively comic, but it's too long and complicated to tell. The way it
was gradually made to appear as if all I'd done in connection with the
two movies was sabotage them was a masterpiece of the peculiar mass
formation tactics of our friends the comrats. Anyway thanks for
writing—

Yrs
J. Dos Passos

To the editors of the New Republic

Provincetown, Mass.

[*July 1939*]

The Editors of the New Republic
Dear Sirs:

I did not intend to publish any account of the death of my old friend José Robles Pazos (the fact that he had once translated a book of mine, and well, was merely incidental; we had been friends since my first trip to Spain in 1916) until I had collected more information and possible documentary evidence from survivors of the Spanish Civil War, but the reference to him in Mr. Malcolm Cowley's review of my last book makes it necessary for me to request you to print the following as yet incomplete outline of the events that led up to his death. As I do not possess the grounds of certitude of your reviewer and his informants, I can only offer my facts tentatively and say that to the best of my belief they are accurate.

José Robles was a member of a family of monarchical and generally reactionary sympathies in politics; his brother was an army officer in the entourage of Alfonso of Bourbon when he was king; one of the reasons why he preferred to live in America (he taught Spanish Literature at Johns Hopkins University in Baltimore) was his disagreement on social and political questions with his family. He was in Spain on his vacation when Franco's revolt broke out, and stayed there, although he had ample opportunity to leave, because he felt it his duty to work for the republican cause. As he knew some Russian he was given a job in the Ministry of War and soon found himself in close contact with the Russian advisers and experts who arrived at the same time as the first shipment of munitions. He became a figure of some importance, ranked as lieutenant-colonel, although he refused to wear a uniform saying that he was a mere civilian. In the fall of '36 friends warned him that he had made powerful enemies and had better leave the country. He decided to stay. He was arrested soon after in Valencia and held by the extralegal police under conditions of great secrecy and executed in February or March of the following year.

It must have been about the time of his death that I arrived in Spain to do some work in connection with the film *The Spanish Earth,* in which we were trying to tell the story of the civil war. His wife, whom I saw in Valencia, asked me to make inquiries to relieve her terrible uncertainty. Her idea was that as I was known to have gone to some trouble to get the cause of the Spanish Republic fairly presented in the United States, government officials would tell me frankly why Robles was being held and what the charges were against him. It might have been the same day that Liston Oak, a onetime member of the American Communist Party who held a job with the propaganda department in Valencia, broke the news to José Robles' son, Francisco Robles Villegas, a seventeen year old boy working as a translator in the censorship office, that his father was dead. At the same time officials were telling me that the charges against José Robles were not serious and that he was in no danger. Mr. Del Vayo, then foreign minister, professed ignorance and chagrin when I talked to him about the case, and promised to find out the details. The general impression that the higherups in Valencia tried to give was that if Robles were dead he had been kidnapped and shot by anarchist "uncontrollables." They gave the same impression to members of the U.S. embassy staff who inquired about his fate.

It was not until I reached Madrid that I got definite information from the then chief of the republican counterespionage service that Robles had been executed by a "special section" (which I gathered was under control of the Communist Party). He added that in his opinion the execution had been a mistake and that it was too bad. Spaniards I talked to closer to the Communist Party took the attitude that Robles had been shot as an example to other officials because he had been overheard indiscreetly discussing military plans in a café. The "fascist spy" theory seems to be the fabrication of romantic American Communist sympathizers. I certainly did not hear it from any Spaniard.

Anybody who knew Spaniards of any stripe before the civil war will remember that they tended to carry personal independence to talk and manners to the extreme. It is only too likely that Robles, like many others who were conscious of their own sincerity of purpose, laid himself open to a frameup. For one thing, he had several interviews with his brother, who was held prisoner in Madrid, to try to induce him to join the loyalist army. My impression is that the frameup in his case was pushed to the point of execution because Russian secret agents felt that Robles knew too much about the relations between the Spanish war ministry and the Kremlin and was not, from their very special point of view, politically reliable. As always in such cases, personal enmities and social feuds probably contributed.

On my way back through Valencia, as his wife was penniless, I tried to get documentary evidence of his death from republican officials so that she could collect his American life insurance. In spite of Mr. Del Vayo's repeated assurances that he would have a death certificate sent her, it never appeared. Nor was it possible to get hold of any record of the indictment or trials before the "special section."

As the insurance has not yet been paid I am sure that Mr. Cowley will understand that any evidence he may have in his possession as to how José Robles met his death that he or his informants may have will be of great use to his wife and daughter, and I hope he will be good enough to communicate it to me. His son was captured fighting in the republican militia in the last months of the war and as there has been no news of him for some time we are very much afraid that he died or was killed in one of Franco's concentration camps.

Of course this is only one story among thousands in the vast butchery that was the Spanish civil war, but it gives us a glimpse into the bloody tangle of ruined lives that underlay the hurray for our side aspects. Understanding the personal histories of a few of the men women and children really involved would I think free our minds somewhat from the black is black and white is white obsessions of partisanship.

Sincerely yours,
John Dos Passos

To Dwight Macdonald

[Provincetown
July 1939]

Dear Dwight Macdonald—

Thanks for your letter. The N.R. say they'll print my communication—All I wanted to straighten out was Robles' case. I dont think anything could be gained by arguing with Malcolm Cowley about my mental processes or what influenced them. He has a right to make what deductions he cares to—on the other hand, it should be obvious to any intelligent observer that his deductions are all wet.

Yrs
John Dos Passos

To Stewart Mitchell

Provincetown,
Jan 10–1940

Dear Stewart—

    Darn glad to get your letter; I thought I detected a note of vigorous convalescence in it. Once an event has happened there's nothing we can do but take it, and the less praise or blame we dish out to those we like or have liked the better, I think. People have some mighty tough rows to hoe.

    I'm getting near the end of my Roger Williams essay. I've been corresponding with Mr. Brockemier, who has sent me some excellent clues. When its finished I'm going to ask you to read it, if you dont mind, and enter any protests you think of on style, facts, dates or interpretations. Would you mind? In it I'm branching off into, for me, unfamiliar paths and the whole business may be rubbish. Hope to see you in Boston towards the end of the week. A propos, have you got three hundred dollars loose in your bank I could borrow for about a week? If so would you send me a check special delivery? And by borrow I mean *borrow;* because I'm on the edge of considerable (temporary alas,) affluence, having managed to recover my War Risk Insurance from my aunt who was "keeping" it for me. It'll be payable to the tune of ten thousand dollars next January and meanwhile I can borrow on it at a low rate of interest—meanwhile ie: while we await loan from Washington we are flat here and haunted by the pale faces of bill collectors, cant borrow from the bank here because its full of our notes and mortgages. Have to send two hundred to New York Friday to save a batch of holograph (if thats what you call it) from the clutches of a bookshop where I hope to sell it for considerably more. So far the year has been full of financial alarums and excursions but the general tone of our finances is surprising firm If its not convenient— drop me a line and I'll try to get an advance from the Guggenheims on my felony—that has been my main support this year—

    Hope to see you soon—and hope fervently to stop borrowing— have great plans for financial reconstruction and rehabilitation—Katy sends her love—

Yrs
Dos

We drank the champagne the next to the last day of '39 with Charlie and Adelaide Walker, the Wilsons and the Shays—wished you were there. Everybody had plenty; nobody had too much.

To Max Eastman (1883–1969), *a poet, essayist, and editor, whom Dos first saw, apparently, when Eastman was speaking at a Socialist Party rally in New York during the spring of 1917. He was one of the founders of the* Masses, *and along with Floyd Dell, Art Young, and John Reed was tried for sedition by the United States government because of his stated opposition to World War I. He founded the* Liberator, *became interested in Soviet Russia and went so far as to join the Communist party. In 1923 that ended; afterward, like Dos, he became increasingly opposed to Stalinism and Communism.*

Provincetown Mass
Nov 14—[19]40

Dear Max—

Thanks for your book [probably *Marxism, Is It Science?*]. I know some of the material and am looking forward to reading the new part—You've done more than anybody to keep the subject alive for Americans, and to make some sense of it. The danger is that we'll be thrown off the valuable part of Marx by the religious fanatics and by the college professors who mainly verbalize on the subject. I think your slant on it is just right—though I'd like to see it linked up more with practical politics,—by politics meaning the art of inducing people to behave in groups with the least bloodshed and destruction—

Take care of yourself

Yrs
Dos

To Edmund Wilson

P'town—Friday
[*Fall(?) 1940*]

Dear Bunny,

Your corrections are excellent. About Ralph's alexandrines—I have a notion that he did write real alexandrines—but I cant find my note about it or the reference to him in the *Dunciad* so for the time being I'm changing it to heroic couplets as you suggest. He undoubtedly wrote them too. I'll eventually look the matter up.

The volume will probably be called *The Ground We Stand On*, with some sort of subtitle such as The Establishment of an American

Bent, and deals, as you suggest with the divergence of an American from a late English Tradition, both branching from the main stem of English thought and culture, according to this thesis, definitely shattered by the ruin of the Commonwealth. The Commonwealth spirit survived in New England in ossified form, while the country gentleman republicanism of the seventeenth century that was such an important fact of the Commonwealth survived in Low Church Virginia— The two traditions fused again in the American Revolution. Meanwhile Britain became an oligarchic empire in which the ruins of the commonwealth were encysted in a sort of ghetto—from which a continual stream of men fled to America, highly energized by the pressure (types as various as Tom Paine & Samuel Insull) The cowardly and increasing provincialism of American thought after the Civil War managed to obscure the fact that the major branch of the great Anglo Saxon tradition had already taken root in America. That's very schematic, but is roughly the theme. As I want to present a fairly rounded picture of the fragments of lives and events I deal with I cant rub that in much—but I hope some such inkling will remain in the mind of the reader—The volume will deal with Roger Williams and his time (the rise and fall of English republicanism) with the rise of the eighteenth century businessman, Jefferson's reaction to Europe and England, the career of a typical American citizen of the world: Joel Barlow ending with the check of squirarchical ideas in America on the collapse of Hamilton's bid for power.

Tell Mr. New Republic 2 cents a word is a damn gyp—but seeing it's you we'll let it go. They used to pay 2½.

So you think we ought to picket H. & B? Better sue than stew— But I certainly think its a damn dirty trick—I haven't seen many papers, but none of them had any ad of The Finland Station. If they didn't want to do their best by a hell of an important book they ought to have had the decency to let you turn it over to some other publisher. Have you thought of trying to get Max Perkins say to take the book over lock stock and barrel—That might be suggested as a settlement if you bring suit—because it would be no use bringing a case like that to trial unless you absolutely have the goods on them and could get damages—Anyway it might blast their bloody complacency.

Hope to see you next week—

Yrs
Dos

XXIX Dos and Katy, circa 1940.

XXX

Dos as a war correspondent in the
Pacific, spring 1945.

XXXI

Dos, Betty, and Lucy on the front
steps of the house at Spence's Point,
circa 1957.

XXXII
Dos and Betty in the garden at
Spence's Point, August 1964.

XXXIII
Lucy and Dos on the beach at
Spence's Point, August 1964.

XXXIV Spence's Point, Easter 1966. *Left to right:* Christopher, Dos, Lucy, Rumsey Marvin, and Betty.

XXXV Dos with Beniamino Segre, president of the National Academy of Lynxes, after receiving the Antonio Feltrinelli prize for fiction, Rome, November 14, 1967.

Katy joins me in love to all of you—

To hell with deceitful publishers and magazines that pay 2 cents a word—What we need is a good 5 cent weekly.

To Edmund Wilson

[Provincetown
January(?) 1941]

Dear Bunny—I felt very badly about Scott's death. I was fond of him and had great respect and admiration for him. He died just at the wrong moment in his career. I am sure his next book would have been good. It was impossible for him to be anything but a writer. Unfortunately I'm so pressed for time I can only write you a hasty paragraph. I'll try to make amends to Scott's memory some time later when I can take the leisure to read over all he wrote—love to Mary

Yrs
Dos

To Alexander Woollcott

571 Commercial Street
Provincetown Mass
June 26–1941

Dear Alec Woollcott—

We certainly did a pretty good job keeping off the subject of Jefferson's architecture at Conway. Next time we might try wigwagging from different hills on a foggy night. Anyway it was nice seeing you.

I'm mailing you today bound proofs of The Ground We Stand On—with a couple of places marked. What I had in mind after talking to Gerald who had talked to you, possibly about something totally different, was a volume of photographs of all Jefferson's work that is extant with an amplification of the passages indicated as text. The only thing that exists about Jefferson as an architect at present is Fiske Kimball's very limited edition of the drawings in the Coolidge Collection in Boston. We could possibly include a few reproductions of Jefferson's drawings. Is that anything like what you had in mind?

Drop me a line when you get a chance—Naturally if your eye should chance to roam over any of the rest of the book I'd be delighted to know whether it interests you or not—It seems to be turning out to be a sort of general introductory spading up of the historical garden preparatory to a life of Jefferson I've rashly contracted to attempt.

Katy sends her best. If you should ever find yourself on Cape Cod for gosh sakes let us know so that we can broil you a lobster—

Yrs

J. Dos Passos

By the way I think T.J. the best architect we ever had in this country.

Are you by any chance related to the Oliver and Alexander Woollcott—sons of a governor of Connecticut, who were friends of Joel Barlow's at Yale in 1778?

To Alexander Woollcott

571 Commercial Street
Provincetown Mass
July 7—1941

Dear Woollcott—

As I get older I find myself more and more appalled by the difficulty of communication among us unfeathered bipeds (here's another). "In re" (I sometimes get a grisly entertainment out of such phrases, but you are right that I shouldn't inflict them on others) the photographs of Jefferson's buildings; I must have dreamed the whole business. There must have been something in your attitude or past remarks that made it seem not unplausible that you should not be uninterested in such a project—But lets forget the whole business—and no hard feelings—

Sincerely yours
John Dos Passos

To John Wilstach (1892–1951), *a journalist and author, who apparently wrote Dos asking what work Scott Fitzgerald was doing when he died.*

[Provincetown
February 8, 1942]

Dear Mr. Wilstach,

Part of the work Fitzgerald was doing was 'The Last Tycoon'—if it had been finished it would have been one of the greatest American novels—even unfinished I wonder if it wont have a great deal of influence—I have a hunch it may turn out to be one of those fragments that have an influence out of all proportion Its attitude of moral aloofness is unique for one thing—

Sincerely yrs
John Dos Passos

To Carl H. Milam (1884–1963), *who was at the time Dos wrote him executive secretary of the American Library Association.*

571 Commercial Street
Provincetown, Mass.
December 1 1942

Dear Sir;

While I quite understand the difficulties the American Library Association had to face in getting up a list of books to send in sheets to England, please allow me to add my name to the growing list of those who were profoundly disconcerted by the omission of Farrell's "Studs Lonigan." The book is well known and much admired in England and I'm afraid that leaving it off the list gotten together under the caption of "Interpreting the United States" will give the British the very unfortunate impression that we are trying to give them a doctored picture of our literature and of our society. I know that they have their top shelf at Moody's just as we have a number of tightly organized minority groups working night and day to set Mrs. Grundy back on her throne, but I hate to see these considerations destroying the excellent record the American Library Association has built up in the last few years of broadmindedness and real enthusiasm for good writing.

Is there any chance that the matter might be reconsidered?

Very sincerely yours,
John Dos Passos

To Robert Hillyer

c/o General Delivery
New Orleans, La
Feb 24 [1943]

Hello Robert, how are you? I've been running around over the landscape like crazy and still dont feel very much the wiser. I haven't even managed to change my climate very perceptibly. There's a fine Latin quotation on that subject I'd save up to have engraved on my tombstone if I could ever remember it.

Feeling somewhat stumped this morning in a dreary hotel room made me think of your doctrine of immoveability. Here I am working my head off writing articles for a miserable rag of a miserly magazine just to get myself a trip, and this is one of the times when I complain about my drug. My this is a big untidy soulstirring country we live in. I feel myself continually tortured by curiosity about it. And curiosity is one of those diseases that grows on the meat it feeds upon—as William Shakespeare (who it turns out was a man named Dyer) might have said. Anyway I wish you were here to go out with me to have a beer and a plate of Bon Secour oysters—I'm tired of trying to fish the brains of the local inhabitants—who have it must be admitted—very small oyster like cerebral cortexes—

Take care of yourself Robert—please do. See you in the spring

Yrs
Dos

To Robert Hillyer

Laredo, Texas
March 24—1943

Dear Robert—

This is one of the world's jumping off places but the weather today is so beautiful—thin cold desert wind and thin cold desert sunshine—that it seems quite wonderful. I was delighted to get your letter. Have you ever tried, speaking of nervous depressions, thiamine chloride, that is vitamin B_1? For some reason I never heard of doctors recommending it but I've found that ten mg.s a day really had an effect times when I've been afflicted with gloom, foreboding, nervous gas, financial tension, and other ills. We've fed it to a friend of Katy's who was fit to be tied with excellent results. Do try it if you havent so far. The assorted vitamins dont have the same effect at all. It must be at least 10 mgs of B_1—It would be worth taking 20 mgs to be sure. It cant hurt you and its not very expensive. The brands vary greatly in excellence so be sure to get it made up by a first rate drughouse.

I'm delighted you like Number One.—I've been hoping it would seem funny to people. Nothing ever seems to seem funny to the critics. Those little Mifflins have been working like Trojans trying to oil the public oesophagus for it, but I hardly know yet whether it'll be sweetly swallowed or sourly regurgitated. Nobody ever tried to get anybody to read a book of mine before so it'll be interesting to see what happens.

Certainly we'll eat breakfast on the terrace at Pomfret and on our bulkhead in Provincetown where we'll all have to go fishing for our dinners—See you in May. Katy joins me in love to both of you

Yrs

Dos

To Katy Dos Passos

Washington, D.C.

[*June 23, 1943*]

My much missed Katy sweet possum—

Wow its hot rather delightfully hot in Washington D.C. I'm continuing my round—much as described above [on the letterhead, which states that his hotel, the Continental, is within a mile of the Capitol, House and Senate office buildings, Library of Congress, Union Station, Smithsonian and National Museums, White House, Treasury, Washington Monument and the theatrical and shopping district]— would be having quite a good time if it weren't that I'm already dreading having to write about it. Never appreciated the pleasures of a shaylike life on the cool green sea breezy empty cape. There are too many people in this man's country, too many all in one place—I've just been in the Pentagon and came away immensely depressed. How are we going to run the world if we cant do any better with the Pentagon. Just dipped into a shower and now off to the Statler to meet a man in the bar and then to Pat's for dinner afterwards to Milo Perkins and so to bed at Pats. I'll stay there hereafter under their hospitable roof. Hope to find a little possum letter there. Didn't we have fun gardening? Wasnt the swimming delightful? Wont we enjoy the sailing?

Now I must run

love

deliberape

To Katy Dos Passos

Pittsburgh

[*September 4, 1943*]

Katy Opossum—

Its immensely muggy in downtown Pittsburgh. The soot falls gently over everything like warm black snow. The rivers flow sluggishly under the bridges to make the Ohio. The location is so sensational the geography shows through the immense confusion of construction. I'm getting organized. I've been very busy seeing people except this afternoon something fell through and I was suddenly all alone in a beastly stuffy little box of a room, without benefit of opossum, in a city where I didn't know anybody, where my existence seemed aimless and transitory. I went to two movies in rapid succession but got very little relief. I went to a wop restaurant and ate a plate of white spaghetti and two glasses of wine but got very little relief and now I am back in my room that opens on an airless shaft in the bowels of a mournful hotel. In rapid succession I've spent hours with a judge a lawyer an Irish priest, the famous Pat Fagan who's only recently been unhorsed as boss of the United Mine Workers in the section—a Roosevelt man done in by John L. Lewis—and various other characters—especially an odd little Slovene ex-miner whom I'm going out to see tomorrow at a place that rejoices in the euphonious name of Herminie—but meanwhile the days press on, the deadlines get closer and closer and I wonder in an ingrape sort of way if I'm not making a monkey of myself dragging my carcass around the country this way. I rather envy Pusse's sitting in his office and staring at his blank wall—or Shay kept for a pet or Hackett checking his street cars.

But mostly I suffer most acute possumlack in the straw at breakfast, in the evenings. I bet it's lovely in P'town. I hope you are having a good time and getting your work done. Katy I miss you every minute—love

Desolape

Sunday I got to Herminie—Monday on a tour with an O.P.A. investigator—Tuesday Uniontown—Wednesday Washington——

To Katy Dos Passos

Coon Rapids [Iowa]
Nov 1 [*1943*]

Katy Opossum—disappointed at not finding a little possum communication—hoping one will come in during the day—Tonight I go out to Minneapolis and Jamestown North Dakota. I'll be there till the fourth. It's wonderful here. Nobody thinks of anything but corn—not corn liquor but hybrid corn (100 bu. to the acre) standing pale and gaunt in immense fields rising in ranks over the rolling hills. I'll call up from Jamestown—just to see how you are. It would be great fun if you were here. The Garsts are an immense busy noisy cheerful talkative clan all very tall and rich and healthy and doing all their own work—Across the road from where they live is a sort of Ritz where 1200 hogs sows and little piglets live in considerable style. The weather is still incredibly fine, sunny, just under freezing. I wish you were here. Do try to catch me with an airmail letter to Jamestown North Dakota, general delivery. Would feel fine if I didn't have a rather grewsome deadline Nov. 10—May sit down and do the article in Jamestown. I bet it'll be chilly up there—

lots of love—
Western investigape

To Katy Dos Passos

[On board the North Coast
Limited, traveling west]
Sat. Nov 6 [*1943*]

Katy—Picked up and remailed the contract before leaving Jamestown and also two most delightful letters—which I've just been rereading over a frugal supper—frugal because I'd eaten an immense steak for lunch. Jamestown was full of most delightful people, had a little trouble with students from the inevitable small college who kept producing copies of U.S.A. at the most embarrassing moments when I was trying to talk to farmers or the local presbyterian minister. It's rather a relief to be comfortably settled on the train and out of the snowstorm that's advancing handily from the west. Supposed to get into Seattle Monday morning. We are just leaving Bismarck, N.D., an hour and a half late, soon to cross Missouri River into mountain time. The story about the shark is terrific. Do you suppose it's sunspots. Indeed the demoniac possession of Goody Poodle is a grievous thing. Have you tried praying with her? Poor little possum, just as we feared spending all her time caring for invalid Shay. I'd loved to have seen that unfortunate Russian beset by the shark. I havent noticed any revolt of the animal kingdom in these parts. People seem to have stored up enough shotgun shells to keep it in order and serve it up in the form of game, not that I've managed to eat any, but everywhere I'm told that if I stay over another day I'll be fed a game supper. So far have been running too fast—I must trot that possum in the west right away. It does get very pleasant in these parts.

I'm still struggling with that Colonel, I hope to get him under control on the train tomorrow and mail him from Seattle.

In spite of what everybody tells you about hijeous conditions, the sleepers are comfortable, the diner is excellent. There's beer in the lounge. There's a little animation among the military and naval passengers and some harmonizing, but I dont find anything to complain of. Well I'm getting towards the zenith of my trip and soon will be hurrying home to meet my sweet possum and my very unsweet bills. How about poor Bluestocking? I hear she's leaving soon. Will she still be there when I get home?

Do give my love to Susan and tell her I'm so sorry. I wish she could be gotten away from Hubert.

My those were cute letters. I'll write Chauncey apologizing for having given him away. I had no idea so many people read Harper's—
so much lonesome love
entrained sleepy meditape

To Katy Dos Passos

Portland Oregon
Friday Nov 12—[1943]

Oh my sweet smallpossum—Left Seattle without getting any mail because the P.O. was closed Armistice Day—no mail here. Oh I hope you are all right. Ill send a night letter demanding an answer tonight— I wish you were here My the Northwest is interesting—the climate is a little like Europe damp and chilly—The one thing we needed to complete the variety of this country. It really is different—the air and light are different. Came in last night from Seattle on the plane—lovely moonlight flight—with a somewhat intoxicated sailor man from the Solomons—a bombadier on a bomber, and a young man who was completing his first trip around the world—by coming home to Portland. You get more feeling of the Pacific war here than anywhere I've been. Everybody says the Alcan highway is absolutely no good and that it's the Canadian Railroads that are blocking the building of a really first rate road over the route that's been surveyed ever since old Harriman's time. In Seattle, too, you are suddenly very close to Russia. I've about decided not to try to take in Southern California but to come back from San Francisco around this way again and back over one of the northern railroads. I'll be about saturated with material by the time

I've been around San Francisco a little. I'm not quite certain yet—because it's a little shorter coming back by Los Angeles—but a little easier to get transportation this way. How are you getting on with your work—? How is poor Bluestocking? Will she still be there when I get back? It's fun barging around but I miss you so much and also I'm a little uneasy about creditors, the situation on the farm etc. I wonder what these rumors mean about the imminent collapse of Germany. The crop is certainly thick—We've got to work to stabilize our situation down in Virginia—selling what we want to sell—before somebody steps in with measures to halt the boom in land—Its already getting out of hand in the Dakotas. Values have risen fifty percent in six months there.

I notice that the young men coming back from the theatres wish each other a short war—in no uncertain terms when they say goodby.

These regions are, as Janway said, very Willkieish It looks as if the only people who could reelect Franklin D was the old guard republicans. Undoubtedly what they are trying to do is to get all the state delegations pledged to favorite sons and then trot out MacArthur to the tune of the Star Spangled Banner. It may work. Though I should think Franklin D. could stop that sort of thing by giving MacArthur a job in the cast he couldnt possibly resign—Franklin D. still has a fifty fifty chance I think—Now I must run off to be about my business—

love
busy investigape

"Soon we go home"

Delicious crabs on this
coast—write right
away Airmail to
General Delivery—
    San Francisco to
catch me there—I'll probably go on down
there Sunday or Monday

so much love
solitarape

I'm staying in a seedy old hotel by McKim Mead & White rather pleasant, and cheap. People seem to eat well in Portland: in Seattle everything was so crowded it was hard to eat at all.

To Robert Hillyer

Provincetown
Dec 26 [1943]

Dear Robert—

It was delightful of you to call up so promptly—we had gotten into a panic due to overdrafts in each of our accounts and nonarrival of some checks that were due me. At the last moment a check arrived and the day was saved. This sort of thing always happens to us at Christmas time. We have come to visualize Overdraft as a dreary sort of a character in a long old fashioned nightgown with a quill behind his ear and a ledger under his arm who suddenly starts getting into bed with you in the middle of the night. His feet are clammy. His B.O. is thoroughly disagreeable. He has a long pendulous nose with a drop perpetually suspended from the end of it. In a world whose people get more like hyenas every day it was particularly heartwarming to have you call up with your century neatly packed for relief. I may have to call on you yet but I think I can navigate now until I can drag in a little more money. All in all its a miracle that I've been able to walk this tightrope so far—Take good care of yourself—

Yrs
Dos

To Robert Hillyer

Provincetown, Mass.
January 21—1944

Dear Robert—

Have you still got that little century loose in the bank? I'd love to borrow it for about three weeks if it doesn't cause you too much inconvenience. When are you going West? I'd love to see you before you go. This damn book still holds me chained to my desk. What a hideous profession. I've been dragging along all winter in a can't get any money till I finish the book, cant finish the book until I get some money dilemma. Money is the root of considerable discomfort in my life, though hardly of all evil. Is there any chance of your coming out here on the train for a little Hillyer weekend before you go? We can feed you well. It's rather pleasant here this winter. In fact it would be delightful if this book didn't drive me like a jockey his aging race horse on the the last lap—

Drop us a line,

Yrs
Dos

To Max Eastman

Provincetown,
April 12—1944

Dear Max—

I read the New Leader with the greatest interest—but the last few years I've been too damn broke, to be brutally frank, to do unpaid articles. Furthermore I've worked out a rule for myself to go on no letter heads unless I am actually working in the organization. Tell the New Leaderites that as soon as I manage to write them an article I'll be delighted to have them list me as a contributor, and that I'm very much honored by their request. I wish I got to see you now and then. Next time I'm in New York I'll see if I cant catch you in some time.

All sorts of good wishes,

Yrs
John Dos Passos

Your last article in the N.L. made most extraordinarily good good sense, I thought.

To Robert Hillyer

[Provincetown,
October 1944]

Dear Robert—

We certainly shall look you up soon—have been intending to for a hell of a time—I dont think there's much Hillyer in [Richard Ellsworth] Savage [in *U.S.A.*] (except for the story of the late General Hillyer that you probably noticed I cribbed from your career and some peace conference courier stories). When you start making up people for a book you cant help taking incidents and traits from the lives of your friends and your own—but that's very different from trying to do a portrait of somebody you know. I dont know just how you'd go about that. People have a mania for finding themselves or their acquaintances in novels. I've had several letters from people I never heard of claiming that episodes from their lives had been used in my books—and, it turns out that there's a New York newspaper man named Ward Moorehouse who's out to slay me. It's a hell of a business—

Yrs
Dos

To Robert Hillyer

Provincetown Mass
Nov. 3—1944

Dear Robert—

It serves you right for departing from your resolution not to read your friends' books. But really you've got it wrong. Savage was a synthetic character as all the characters in my novels are. In developing him a few little touches of Hillyer may have crept in. In fact I think I put in some of your inimitable stories about the late General Hillyer in Tours. But there was never any intention of producing a portrait or a caricature of my friend Robert Hillyer. You've written novels yourself and you know how you start out with a few notions and anecdotes about somebody you know and then other scraps of the lives of other people get in and a large slice of your own life and then if you are lucky the mash begins to ferment and becomes something quite different. I haven't a copy of Nineteen Nineteen here, but I dont think there's any trace of Downes in any of it. I think there were traces of Downes in a character in Manhattan Transfer. And how could your father have gotten in when I never knew him and I dont think ever heard you speak of him? Gosh Robert you must not let yourself be affected by the literary gossipmongers who are always lifting the skirts of literature and peeping under and giggling and tittering about something that isn't there at all. This work was done about fifteen years ago and it's hard for me to remember back. But it never occurred to me then, of that I am sure, that the faint traces of Hillyer around the French part of Savage's career would bring forth anything but a laugh and a few lightnings from you if you did read them.

You know perfectly well that I've always liked and admired you. I'm very sorry that you have felt for a moment embarrassed or misprized on account of that miserable lay figure. It was never my intention.

If you want an affidavit from me that Savage was an imaginary figure and that any resemblances to anybody in the heavens above or the earth beneath or the waters under the earth was purely accidental, I'll gladly give it. But I think the way to treat prying and nosy budding novelists is to slap them down or better to laugh them off.

You live in a dimension so different, so much ampler, so much uglier and so much lovelier than any character in any book, just by being alive, that even if someone tried to make up a portrait of you I dont see why you should be affected by it because it simply wouldnt be you.

Anyway it will be much better to talk about this by word of mouth than on paper. I hope to get to see you next week. Meanwhile please forgive the friend for the transgressions of the novelist.

Take care of yourself Robert and dont forget that our novels and schoolrooms arent all of our lives and that we've managed to like each other in a different plane of our lives for thirty years or so. I for one intend to go on liking you.

Katy sends her love.

Yours as ever

Dos

To Lovell Thompson (1902–   ), *who while vice president and then executive vice president of Houghton Mifflin was one of Dos' editors. When Thompson retired from Houghton Mifflin, he established Gambit, Incorporated, of which he is the managing director.*

care Gerald Murphy,
131 E 66th Street,
New York N.Y.
Nov 11 1944

Dear Lovell,

We greatly enjoyed our night in Ipswich. Our only complaint was that we didn't see enough of the smaller Thompsons. We must get them all to Provincetown in the spring and turn them loose on the harbor.

I duly turned over the signed contracts to Paul and the letter on movie rights. If H M Co gets out a check this week please send it to me at above address.

That snowbank of yours has kept me worried. The flaw in it I think is that the process isn't continuous. From your end it works all right but the gap comes in the bookstore. The more I think about it the more certain I become that the only people who get to buy my books are those who really fight for them. They are very rarely in the windows or on display. The bookstores tend to wait until there's a demand to reorder. There's still more sales resistance at the bookstore level than there is at the customer level.

Is there any way that you could check on these hunches? I hate to nag but I have the feeling that nature is being allowed to take its course in the normal routine way in the case of "State of the Nation" as it was in the case of "Number One." From the publishers point of view it is so much the easiest thing to do. The reason I keep on nagging is that I feel that you really are interested in this particular problem.

I feel that Houghton Mifflin has done an excellent routine job (better than routine on the advertizing matter) in these two books, but looking at the record the results are very little better than were the results of Harcourt Brace's very inert routine. Now we can either sink back into the damn fatalistic snowbank or we can try to dope out the flaw in the process. Experiment is so much more fun than routine that I cant believe you wont find yourself, in spite of publishing tradition, thinking up some new dodges.

For the purposes of this argument we have to take for granted that the books are of permanent value and interest to the inhabitants of these states. Particularly about "State of the Nation" I feel that you are taking it for granted that the book has only temporary interest. I cant argue about that. All I can do is refer you to the people who write as if they liked that part of my work better than any other part and to the fact that "Orient Express" is still selling in England after nearly 20 years.

If Jonathan Cape can sell "Orient Express" to a lot of bloody limejuicers I dont see why you cant go on selling "State of the Nation" to decent Americans for 40 years

The only concrete suggestion I have is my still untested notion about doing the sort of publicity about the book that Amy Vanderbilt would like to have done about the miserable author. It means working out a new technique. But hell Lovell that's what you are sitting in that office looking out at those starlings all day for.

Yrs as ever,
Dos

To Katy Dos Passos

[Kwajalein(?)]
December 31 [1944]

Poor Forty four this is his last day. I'm back in (look up the Marshall Islands on the map) Have been hopping around like a flea among the atolls. We got as far south as Apamama a few miles north of the Equator in the Gilberts. That's the palm fringed island with white beaches and a mottled green lagoon of the storybooks. Abeiang where old Hiram Bingham started his missionary operations looked even more beautiful but we only saw it from the air. At Tarawa I just missed meeting Dr Cass's son Kenneth who was in there in a boat of some kind. The pilot of our plane met him at the officers' club but by the time I'd been routed out from the other side of the island where I was being regaled with Old Granddad by a lawyer from Pittsburgh he had gone. The pilot said he seemed in fine shape and a very nice kid. Call up the Casses if you get a chance and tell them I ran across his tracks.

You cant imagine the transportation by air and boat there is in these parts. The minute we land on an atoll it begins to look like La Guardia Field. We bring in distillators to distill seawater. We attack the flies and the rats. We oil for mosquitos. We level everything off and establish a city dump. The result isnt picturesque but it's eminently practical so that in the central Pacific at least the islands become extraordinarily healthy. Meanwhile in the places where we are not life goes on as it did a long time ago. The brown Micronesians fish and sail their magnificent outrigger canoes and fatten somewhat on the overflow of our canned goods. I havent had time to go fishing yet or to get a sail in a canoe, but I still have hopes.

This has been a busy week. In the evenings I wonder how you are what you are doing whether you are still in P'town. Oh Katy please be careful crossing streets, driving the car, running up and down stairs. Not too nocturnal, please. Remember the fate of somebody's relatives. I guess this is where Forty Four makes his bow. He's been very happy in his keeper. So much love. Next letter from '45 who they say is alas also a literape——

To Katy Dos Passos

> At sea on a battleship
> *January 23* [*1945*]

Smallest and sweetest of opossums, I seem to be at sea on a battleship
headed to throw some shells into Iwo Jima. It's wonderful aboard here.
Excellent company. Good food. Clean towels. Hot showers. The only
trouble is, as poor Julie used to say, It is too much machinery. The
whole great mammoth is so packed with machinery and men in blue
dungarees curled up in every crevice that I cant find my way around.
When there is an alert I am supposed to get to my battle station or
lookout, a place called Sky Control. The trouble is that there immediately ensues a situation in which all doors and hatches are closed and
you find yourself climbing up the outside, up the wrong ladder to a
place where you hadnt ought to be. Then you are given earplugs a
helmet a Mae West life belt asbestos gloves, mask hood and God
knows what all into which you are supposed to climb. It's very confusing. I fumble and stumble around like a centipede in skiboots.

Feel in splendid health and spirits even if I find it increasing
difficult to get anything on paper that makes the slightest sense. If I
knew just where you were, just how you were right at this moment all
I'd have to worry me would be the fact that I'm not there too. Oh Katy
we mustn't do too much of this kind of thing separately. But I wouldn't
have missed this particular trip for anything in the world.

Think occasionally, but cheerfully, with fur wellcurled and best
bib and tucker on of your poor wandering and absent, crazy about his
possum investigatory

> affectionape.

To Katy Dos Passos

> [Kwajalein(?)]
> *Jan 29* [*1945*]
> time goes by

Katy. O how are you? Here I am but my mail is in Guam and I dont
know when I'll get it. Try sending a couple of letters care CINCPAC
PRO (Advanced Base), Fleet Post office San Francisco Cal. They
might get to me sooner. I'm sitting on my bed in a Quonset hut on the
breezy side of the island. My battleship went up and did its small piece
of business and was very noisy about it and now I'm back

It's absolutely amazing to think that we only landed here recently. Every feature of a miniature portable America . . . Movie Theatre, Refrigerators, distillers for fresh water, generators for electricity, baseball field, stores, bar and beergarden has been set up under the monotonous palms. There's not a fly or a mosquito. It's an odd little aseptic civilization we set up but it certainly works. The shape of it has been pretty well crystallized by now. It's the navy's contribution to life ashore. I'm looking forward to getting to the Phillipines to see where the army version is any different. The shape of the day may be standardized but the people you meet in the course of its certainly arent. You get a constant review of everything we've got in the way of characters.

The military and naval situation in these parts seems almost too good to be true. If my letters seem a little formal its that I find I more and more write them with the censor in mind. I've got to be off now. Shall write some more this evening . . . So much love A.

The wind blows—The surf roars—You get very wet out in small boats—I miss you

love again
navigape

To Gerald and Sara Murphy

Phillipines,
February 21 1945

Dear Gerald and Sara,

How are you all? I'd have written sooner but this little vacation I'm taking seems to keep me most amazingly busy. Particularly now that I'm cabling stuff instead of just noting it down for future reference. Today I'm taking a little rest in a ruined sugar plantation set among big trees draped with Bougainvillea and an immense growth of philodendron. There are immense wallowing carabao with big black buffalo horns and the tiny dusty underfed people drive little painted up twowheel carts a little like the tartanas in Valencia. The horses are amazingly tiny, hardly bigger than the widow poodle. The burning and pillaging and murdering of the retreating Nips has left the civilians in a heartbreaking plight. Popeyed correspondents keep sending off horrible atrocity stories. The surprizing thing about them is that they tend to be understated rather than exaggerated. This is the grimmest I've seen since South Russia way back in '21.

It's perfectly absurd but in spite of the constant aeroplane hopping, jeep and truck driving and the heat and the dust and the mud and the general carnage I seem to remain in raging health. I attribute it entirely to Saras vitamins which I religiously crunch every morning Lots of love

Dos

Isnt it time for Sara to go southish? I wish you were both here today. It's a delicious hot summer day out in the Press's country retreat.

Katy said Gerald had a bad throat. I do hope that's mended now. Dont you think you ought to take each other somewhere for a short bake in the sun.

To Katy Dos Passos

[Australia]
March 8 [1945]

Katy. Mailed you a letter but forgot to say I promised young Dr Cahan, whom I met on a plane coasting these solitudes, I'd write you to tell Barbara to tell G. Lawrence to tell his wife that I'd seen him that he's well and a very pleasant fellow, attached to a very pleasant troop carrier outfit. Now its the Ninth—overcast day—mountains full of scraps of clouds. Damp and almost cool. Last night I got a proper look at the Colonel's pets. They are not squirrels at all but little flying opossums. Their fur is very rich and soft and they have large liquid eyes—They are hopelessly nocturnal Their ears are very much like those of an American opossum. They make me feel very homesick.

Now I'm in Australia and I think it's Sunday March 11—after an incredible flight across the great Granje Range in Dutch New Guinea we flew up a canyon that ended in an immense cave, then we flipped over the ridge and saw a sort of immense blowhole in the mountain in the bottom of which the river runs—a subterranean river like in "King Solomon's Mines"—As soon as you get over the ridge there's a type of cultivation, terraces up the hillsides and walled villages with oval cocoon shaped houses—and drained gardens in regular rows raised from the beds of ponds—a little like Xochimilco, down in the wet part of the valley. Tall naked brownish people brandish their spears at the plane as it buzzes the villages. There are what look like very long-legged pigs and an animal that might be a goat. A man throws a spear at us and probably thinks he's scared this strange bird off as we zoom up the valley. Then we thread our way down an immensely deep canyon full of waterfalls with terraced fields and villages up in the high precipices. And then suddenly all signs of civilization stop and we are out of the mountains headed south over the swamps and winding sluggish rivers of Southern New Guinea. It was *all* very blood heating. Torres Strait is shallow so that you can see the bottom almost all the way over. That's why New Guinea has the same type of mammals as Australia—used to be joined up—Then there was the York Peninsula of Northern Australia all opening with clouds and rough flying down the high blue coast of Queensland and we got in last night in a hot stuffy town named_____. Ate supper with some appetite (hadn't eaten all day) and went out to drink elegant australian beer with the funny little local ladies who speak an almost indecipherable cockney, at the officers club. It was like a little town in some out of the way part of Florida, only more ramshackle, and the people as quaint and stubby a collection of old cockney characters as you ever imagined. This morning we set off without any breakfast as usual (travelling by bomber you never get any meals) and flew through very turbulent rainy weather down to_____where I now am taking my ease in a large hotel room with bath and hot and cold running water—and streetcars go by outside and there's not a trace of burning and bombing and its Sunday and there's no possible way of getting a drink. I feel a little dizzy and fearfully sleepy after what's something like a thirty eight hundred mile hop from the Philippines. The Col. who brought me on this little jaunt runs the troop transport service. He's a Mormon from Salt Lake City, an old airline pilot who was a lawyer in his spare time and who went out to the Philippines just before Pearl Harbor to superintend the building of airfields. He's an extraordinary fellow about 50 absolutely tireless, never eats or sleeps, pilots his bombers all day and does business all night. He has a pair of wallabies being held for him at the Brisbane Zoo until he can get them home to California. He it was who owned the flying opossums back in Hollandia. But alas there's no opossum flying with the solitary   aviape

To Edmund Wilson

P'town
May 18—1945

Dear Bunny—

How are you? I'm burned up with curiosity to know what you are doing, what you are discovering and how you are getting on. Do drop us a line.

I got back from the broad reaches of the Pacific about a month ago, my behind sore from travelling in bucket seats and somewhat dizzy from the airplane rides, but very much cheered and stimulated. I understand why the people who dont have to do the fighting and rotting in rear bases enjoy war so much. Saw more attractive and interesting people in the space of a few months than I'd seen in years and came back with considerable confidence in the ability of younger and less important Americans to cope with the terrific problems that face us everywhere. We dont know how to do many things but the things we do know how to do we do so damn well. Taken up in detail things are not at all discouraging. Even MacArthur seems to know his business. But now when I get back and see more of the overall political picture, I feel appalled again. World War II seems to be hurriedly merging into World War III and, as usual we are betraying our friends and feeding up our enemies. But why go into that? You are seeing more of that than I.

It was so long since I'd seen masses of young men that I'd forgotten how much pleasanter men of between twenty and thirty were to be around with than older men. It isnt so true of women. When I was in my twenties I thought the grown adults I ran into were a disaster and now I know I was right. But that's not here nor there.

We miss you horribly on the Cape—Nobody left here at all not even last summers old drunks and nitwits. In the course of my investigations I may get to England etc later in the summer for a while— Let me know where you are—

Yours
Dos

To Edmund Wilson

Provincetown Mass
July 19—1945

Dear Bunny,

Had dinner with Rosalind and Jeany and Floyd Clymer at your house last night. The girls are cute as bug's ears and Rosalind has grown up to be a perfect peach. We missed the Laird of Money Hill very much. Your letter from Rome arrived. I envy you your travels there. Europe is in the dark ages I guess. I dont quite understand your remark about "faith" in socialism. Socialism is something we've got, so it looks to me, like railroads and air conditioning and cancer. It's quite outside the realm of faith. Faith I take it is the unreasoned fringe of belief. I still retain unreasoned belief in individual liberty. As I see it the problem is how to apply it to the various forms of socialism the world suffers from. What worries me about European socialists is that they dont seem to have advanced beyond the bureaucratic state of mind. We have enough examples of bureaucratic controls in things like the O.P.A. I dont see any very different mentality among the labor party people in England. We seem to be heading towards monolithic bureaucratic social systems whether they are based on force as in Russia or on persuasion and apathy as in England and the United States. I cant see anything very appetizing about the prospect—though I suppose its no use crying over spilt liberties.

I wonder what they are cooking in Potsdam over Mr. Truman's liver and onions. Any chance of your poking your nose into France and Germany before coming home?

There's still a chance that the United States may pull something out of the hat—some liveable variation of the deadly pattern—I dont see that any other people have the surplus energy or wealth left to afford such luxuries. We are somewhat in the situation of England after the Napoleonic wars. We may produce something analagous to the British reform bill at home—if we manage our own affairs well enough at home. No great sign of it on the horizon now, god knows.

Take care of yourself—hope to see you on the Cape in early September. I'm just reading your Fitzgerald's Crack Up. Another of your first rate editing jobs. I was surprised how well those articles read that annoyed me so in Esquire. They turn out to be a very much more reasoned and deliberate piece of work than I'd suspected. In their setting I find them quite admirable.

Yrs
Dos

By the way I dont think people have explored enough in recent years the possibilities of our banal American arbiter-government notion—government as the referee among warring monopolies, cartels, trade unions etc. I'm beginning to think I'd prefer to live under it than under monolithic socialism even of the most benign cast.

To Katy Dos Passos

Hotel Scribe Paris
Friday Oct 12 [1945]

Katy Here I am in a dreary little room that has another bed in it that would be much more cheerful if it contained an opossum but it doesnt. The weather is beautiful—Paris looks almost frighteningly unchanged. I was taken around to a salon run by an old lame lady back of the Palais Bourbon where the people all looked as if they'd been left over from Proust and talked like the Second Empire.

I'm busy setting up my trip to Germany which will I imagine be more interesting Here in people's faces, in the papers, in the advertizing of plays and concerts you get the feeling that it's just plus ça change plus c'est la même chose only drearier and deadlier.

Evening: I've just come in from walking on the Boulevard and I dont know that it is drearier and deadlier—the vast card board hats the women wear and the coiffures—they must take days to do. The puffed up hair on top—the ranks of little curls climbing in steps from the forehead to a peak at the back of the head—really they give the place a weird mediaeval flavor thats fully in tune with the times we live in. Just saw a rather bad film about François Villon—but at least it had none of the Hollywood moral turpitude. It was gotten up by people who had some notion of human decency. I imagine Paris will take a lot of looking at these days—more than I will have time for.

Went to a press conference to see what De Gaulle looks like. He's not quite so tall as his pictures show and he has a sort of elephant snout, not disagreeable—some where I've seen an early French portrait of a Duc de Guise who had that same look—He talks remarkably well in a rather professorial manner—he has two voices the Sorbonne voice

and the père de famille Henry Quartre—bonne soupe kind of voice—
There's more to him than we had been led to believe I think—something sly and old fashioned French—They say that seventy five percent
of everything is going into the army—that he's going to build up to a
million men. Food, starting up industry, reconstruction all come after
that. God knows he may be right. There may be nothing else to do.
Anyway he's different than I imagined him.

Certainly the French are doing a wonderful job sweating dollars
out of the Americans at 50 francs to a dollar. The real value of the
franc must be two or three times less than that. When they've gotten
all they can this way they'll devaluate the franc in time for the tourist
trade. Katy how I miss you, now I'm creeping into my damp and
lonely straw.

Here at the hotel the restaurant cooks up US Army ration for the
correspondents and they certainly do a very good job of it. We pay
thirteen francs for a meal that would cost a hundred in a legal restaurant where you have to give ration coupons or a thousand or more in a
black market joint. I havent visited any of them yet. How people who
are still getting wages of three or four thousand francs a month live I
cant imagine.

Its particularly maddening to see other men with theirs—often
neat in uniform—that possum would have looked awfully cute in
uniform. Still I'll be back before you can say Jack Robinson—Remember the ladies of Paris and comb your fur very carefully night and
morning—

so much love
solitary investigape

To Katy Dos Passos

Biarritz [France]
Oct 22 [*1945*]

Katy—Arrived in Biarritz yesterday after a delightful ride down from
Paris in a jeep. Wonderful weather—the autumn countryside was very
beautiful. Except for Orleans which was badly smashed up we saw
very little war damage. The country looks empty and sad but I suspect
that things are picking up. Spent a night in Simoges, ate a wonderful
lunch, with the same paté de foie gras we ate on the way to see
Cendrars at Montpazier that time, at Périgeux. Spent the next night in

Bordeaux. Arrived here yesterday and now waiting for a delayed plane to take me back to Paris. Biarritz is all turned into a G.I. University and is most amazing. The gambling casino is an American style library. It's all been set up in two months—and is likely to be dismantled in another two months. America in France is much weirder than America in the Pacific. In spite of what everybody says I have a notion that the French are pulling themselves together in their own peculiar way. Everything is on the verge of collapse, but things dont collapse.

Oh Katy my sweetest opossum how are you? I hope to find a letter when I get back to Paris—I wish you were here except that transportation is very much of a hop skip and jump affair and it would be very difficult to get around à deux. Here I have a wonderful room in the palais Napoleon III built for the Empress Eugenie—when I look westward out over the bay of Biscay I can almost imagine I can see the Provincetown monument and a small opussum scuttling briskly about in its shadow. Separation is horrid.

Driving along I looked longingly at old churches and buildings but didn't have time to look around very much. There's an awful lot of France left. I havent much appetite for Europe at present. I want to be home—that's about the size of it.

Write me about your poor friend Mrs Shay's ankle—Give her my love. Katy I miss you every hour on the hour—and twice as often in the straw.

love

investigape

To Katy Dos Passos

Wiesbaden [Germany]

Oct 30—[*1945*]

after supper

Katy my sweetest opossum—The weather oddly enough remains delightful—I just got back here to the gloomy Grünewald Hotel to find no mail. Oh dear I had hoped for just one letter. I wonder where its going. I've only had one since I left. I've been down in the funniest little corner of Hessen—around Fritzlar and Ziegenhain—where people still wear funny peasant costumes and have faces like andirons. All this section of Germany is much more unchanged than I'd expected. I suppose what carries Europe through its wars is that the original village economy has never quite broken down and there's a trace of it always there to keep people going when the large scale economy collapses.

Now I've got to start writing an article. I'm awfully sick of this sort of thing but I am beginning to get onto the home stretch.

Downstairs in the dining room I got to talking just now to two young men from the Education and Information branch. They were talking about the Soviet Union just as I used to talk about it in 1919. Surely something has happened since then. I got feeling quite dizzy (incidentally professional morning and night dizzy spells seem to be abating). I just dont understand what people mean when they talk about how we are defaming the Russians. But the propaganda is still flowing strong. Talking to the victims is very discouraging.

Here is all the brutality of war and army life without the enlivening element of danger that gives it what poetry it has. It's very gloomy making. I knew I was letting myself in for something when I came over here. Will be home soon with a flea in my ear. Oh Katy I miss you. Are you writing?

Your loving desolape

To Katy Dos Passos

Nuremberg
Nov 3 [1945]

Katy sweetest of opossums I wish I were where you are. This has been a wasted day. Spent the morning fussing and fuming about transportation to Munich and the afternoon waiting at the airport for a plane that never came. My how many hours I've spent waiting at airports in the last year. They were much pleasanter out in the Pacific where everything was smooth and new. Here everything is cluttered with the ruins of Europe. Nuremberg is particularly horrible. Most of the city is a waste of charred and broken buildings. The buildings that survive and that are occupied by the army have a dreary shopworn air. PWs are always sweeping and sprinkling but nothing is ever very clean. Misery sweats out of the stained and grimy walls. The Nuremberg Palace of Justice where the Nazi leaders will be tried, is particularly grizzly in spite of the mild Washington air of many of the civilians from the D. of J. and other institutions who roam around as if it were the Pentagon. No wonder everybody hates it in Europe and talks hysterically about getting out of the army. There's a sort of mood you could cut with a knife. It all had to be seen smelt and heard—but I certainly will be ready to come home when I've waded through the work I have to do. I ought to be doing it now instead of chatting with my opossum—Tomorrow I start out to Munich by jeep and hope to find some mail there—or at least a tiny telegram. Like everything else the mail service seems to have gone to pieces. Katy I love you I miss you and I really count the days before I can start home.

Fortunately the probability seems to be that the Nuremberg trials will start on Nov 20 as scheduled. I'll hang around for a week or so and then start the struggle for a priority on some sort of westward bound craft—

This press camp is in a weird "Schloss" built by members of the Faber pencil family its full of naked ladies in ghastly white stone, hideous stairways inlaid with various marbles gold chairs of horrid design chandeliers that are about to fall on your head—murals—festoons of what Bunny so aptly called pukids—German schrecklichkeit at its worst. The vast rooms have had the furniture taken out and are filled with rows of cots where the swarms of correspondents about to arrive will sleep. In the main gate there's a wonderful pair of chinese lions but they are in the minority. Now I must stop—so much love

exacerbape

To Katy Dos Passos

[Bad Wiessee, Bavaria
November 4, 1945]

Katy   It's Sunday, nov 4, and I've just arrived in a place on a lake in Bavaria called Bad Wiessee. It was a cold drive in a jeep in the raw befogged afternoon. The ruins of Munich, largely because the mad King of Bavaria filled the place with columns, make a nobler showing than Nuremberg or Frankfurt, but it's pretty depressing. Here we are up in the Bavarian foothills in an unfoughtover region full of green meadows and cows and little piles of wellrotted manure that the local inhabitants are spreading over their pastureland . . . and I wish I were doing it too. I'm hungry and lonely and pleasantly situated in a plain little white room very delightful after that dreadful Schloss and I wish I had my opossum there.

Everything is different than where I was in Hessia. The houses are plastered white with carved wood upper stories like Schruns but broader, with a less highpitched roof. Now its Monday morning and the sun has risen over a lake through the mist and now I've absolutely got to sit down and work. In the morning light the place turns out to be a dullish little German resort—but its wonderful to see a place that's totally undamaged. At the dock four little sail boats are tethered patiently waiting for somebody to sail them

My program seems to be the following—I stay here through Thursday—Then drive into Vienna where I'll spend about a week, then back to Nuremberg for the opening of the Nazi trial on the twentieth. I'll stay there a few days with a dash for Berlin in there somewhere and then start for home.

I've only had one sweet little possum letter since I left. I wonder where they have gone. Still have hopes that some of them will catch up with me before I leave here. Oh Katy please thrive. How's Frenchy. I'm so afraid that Bluestocking wont let her in the house.

Darling I miss you—

misanthrape

P.S. I dont like it over here. Not us nor the squareheads nor nobody.

To Katy Dos Passos

Bad Wiessee [Bavaria]
Nov 8 [1945]

Oh Katy how are you. I sent a second cable through Calhoun at Life but still no reply. I'm sure they've snarled up my mail and messages at USFET in Frankfurt. I keep telling myself that if there were any bad news it would have reached me—but its hard to go so long without a word from my small and most valuable opossum. Are you still in Provincetown? Did you get the furniture down to Virginia?

It's a raw misty morning. The clouds hide the mountains and hang in a fringe across the little towns on the opposite side of the lake. There are a few large black ducks scooting around among the reeds outside my window. Tomorrow I set off for Vienna in a jeep. It'll be a long cold ride I've got my article about half finished—maybe a little more than half. It will be a relief to get that off my desk. I wish I could shake off the gloom. Mini pills dont help. People coming back from Budapest say that life is fantastic and gay there in spite of everything—but I'm not going to take the time to go there. Berlin and Vienna will be enough. I feel as if I had taken on more than I could absorb already. It looks as if the Nuremberg trial would be postponed until after the first of the year. It will open on the 20th and the defendants will be granted more time to prepare their cases. I'll take in the opening, if I can get in, then rush up to Berlin and back to Paris and light out for home. Getting home will be a problem but I imagine I can get myself squeezed onto a ship of some kind. I've put in a request for December 1.

From Vienna I'll be able to cable you direct and perhaps get an answer while I'm there. I cant tell you how shut off from the world you feel in Europe. Everything seems to be crumbling and festering. Now I have to go out and see some more m.q. setups—

so much love
desperape

To Katy Dos Passos

Nuremberg
Nov 22 [1945]
—a cold raw day

Katy sweet opossum
Two more November letters appeared—You speak of a disorder. Oh dear I do hope the opossum is thriving—I'm afraid she's being kept up all hours by callers—Dont put any confidence in that wicked old Dr. Antix It's time the keeper came home. Just have Berlin to tick off—I dont think I'll even try to go to London—I have had about as much of the ETO as I can absorb already—

Robert Jackson's opening for the prosecution yesterday I thought magnificent. A few more speeches like that and the poor old ship of state thats been wallowing rudderless in the trough of the sea will be back on its course. He really is making an effort to make some sense out of what without him would be an act of vengeance. His delivery was amazingly without pomp or self-importance—He might very well be a first rate man. There was a moment when the Nazis in the prisoners dock seemed to see themselves for the first time as the world sees them. I'll never forget the look of horror and terror that came over their faces when Jackson read the orders for the massacre of the Jews. Either they had not known what documents were in our possession or something like remorse swept over them for a few minutes. Jackson represented the USA as I like to see it represented. He was reasonable practical and full of a homey kind of dignity. The Nazis are a strange crew. Hess really looks like a man with some disease of the brain—Streicher and Funk are monstrosities but the rest of them look like men of considerable intellectual brilliance. I had a very good seat and was able to see them very well. Goering's a weird character. He still seems to think he can laugh it all off. I'm getting off an article to Life today—I wonder if they'll print it. Anyway I begin to see daylight and possumlight ahead. Please Katy take good care of yourself—and where's Frenchy. You are staying on in Provincetown caring for the sick and wounded. No October letters have come in at all. I wonder where they are—Maybe resting quietly in Paris—the army's in such a state of deliquescence that nothing works right.

This afternoon I'm driving over to Frankfurt hoping there to find some way of getting transported to Berlin.

Poor Bob Benchley. I'm so sorry he's dead.

Katy go right back to bed and dont get up till I come. Please thrive for the sake of your loving distracted distraught and hardworking

affectionape

To Katy Dos Passos

[Berlin]
Monday
November 26 [1945]
and my it's cold and raw

Oh Katy—how are you today—Finally worked my way up to Berlin after a chapter of automotive collapses. One car burned out a bearing in a place called Northeim—from there I made my way by British lorries—and very nice the people were—into Berlin where I tumbled into the Press Camp more dead than alive. Slept warmly and well after a dinner of real roast beef and woke up to find myself in Seelindorf—one of the most grewsome little projections you ever saw—a perfect Scarsdale bomb torn and war grimed—there the press occupies a group of dilapidated millionaire nests around a lake—The cold and stagnant sky of Northern Europe presses down on you from above cutting out all light and warmth—all around are the dreary imaginings of some Berlin realtor of the twenties among which the miserable inhabitants with blue lips and hollow eyes drag their little boats of wood or slog about under shapeless bundles of things they've taken out of the house to sell to get a little more of something to eat. A cold dank hell. Now I'm sitting in the Time Office where its warm but where a radio goes all day The architects of gloom and misery around here have done a better job than in Vienna. They had more to work with in the first place. In the middle of this wilderness the army is busy melting away—

At the end of this week I dash to Paris to try to get myself on a homeward bound ship—Now I'm going over to try to find Joe Maloney—

so much love—
hastily
affectionape

It's begun to snow and its much pleasanter—Joe Maloney went home about a month ago it turns out—I wish the same could be said of yours truly—

To Katy Dos Passos

Paris
Dec 3 [*1945*]

Katy darling—I've just discovered that I can sail on the Croatan, a small converted carrier, tomorrow morning from Le Havre—so I'm off—the night train having just pulled in from Frankfurt this morning Found three sweet little possum letters from late October—oh Katy please be well and flourishing till I get home so much love

affectionape navigape

Should be in around Dec 11 in New York—say 12th—Could you be there with a room and some civilian clothes—I'll call up suddenly—

Oh Katy drive carefully—come by train if the roads are bad—dont walk under ladders be very careful on the stairs—

excruciape

To Upton Sinclair

Provincetown Mass
December 30—1945

Dear Upton,

I got back to find your very fine letter waiting for me on my desk—(I've been in Germany for 2 months). On foreign rights we seem from your account to be just about in the same boat. I too have had dealings with Horch. I've seen him a couple of times and think highly of him. He's an Austrian émigré who had some connection with the theatre in Vienna. He's a literate and intelligent fellow and I think as upright as people come these days. How effective his agents in various countries are I dont know—but he is certainly the best thing I've turned up for sometime. No my sour character was a man named Barna who operates in Brazil and with whom the very reputable firm of Brandt and Brandt got tied up at one time to everybody's loss and confusion.

Have you discovered any way of getting royalties from the Soviet Union? Talking to a little Ukrainian schoolteacher in Vienna I was surprised to learn that my books—or some of them were still being printed there. Yours, of course, are. There's immense hunger for books all over Europe—and if the currency situations ever clear up so that publishers can get paper to print on there will be quite a market for American stuff.

Never felt so much sadder and wiser in my life as after this trip to Europe. Maybe the Russians are right and man is vile and can only be ruled by terror—but I still refuse to believe that everything the West has stood for since the first of the Forefathers tumbled out of their leaky boats to do their washing on this beach I'm looking out at as I write must go on the ash heap. My god the tide runs strong against us.

Hope to see you one of these days

Yrs
Dos

CENTURY'S EBB

January 1946–September 1970

San Simignano

Turner

Tour of Duty appeared in August 1946; in the first months of 1947 Dos worked on the Jefferson biography, but his major effort was the third book about the Spotswood family, to be entitled *The Grand Design,* which together with *Adventures of a Young Man* and *Number One* would constitute the trilogy *District of Columbia.* Until July 1947 he worked on the novel; then that month he and Katy went to England to see the effects of Clement Attlee's labor government. Not surprisingly Dos did not like what he found. "Britain's Dim Dictatorship" was the title of one article he wrote for *Life* afterwards; "The Failure of Marxism" was the second.

Back in Provincetown by the end of August, he and Katy had settled down when tragedy struck. Late in the afternoon of Friday, September 12, they set out for Old Lyme, Connecticut, where they planned to spend the night at the Bee and Thistle Inn on their way to visit C. D. Williams and his wife in Norfolk, Connecticut. Driving through Wareham, Massachusetts, Dos was blinded by the afternoon sun and did not see a truck which had pulled off to the side of the road. They crashed into it, shearing off the top of the car and practically decapitating Katy. She died immediately; Dos was hospitalized by the loss of his right eye and by several small injuries, but his physical pain was relatively minor.

It took courage to bear his grief as he did. His loneliness was immense; only by filling the days with work could he keep from becoming overwrought by what had happened. His friends did what they could to help. Lloyd and Marion Lowndes drove him to Virginia for a short while; he stayed with Stewart Mitchell in Boston; then after his injuries healed and his "new luminary"—a glass eye—was fitted, he headed west where he spent several weeks with Roswell Garst in Iowa while he researched his next piece for *Life,* "Revolution on the Farm."

In November Edmund Wilson wrote Dos a kind, thoughtful letter about Katy. To Wilson, recalling her brought her into focus as at the center of what had been "the great days" for his whole group. Katy's death and the burial ceremony put that time in perspective, and remembering her gave the era a meaning he rarely thought of.

. . . Katy had been from a phase now far past somehow at the center
of it as a principal of imagination and intelligence and beauty and charm
—so that her death and the little hilltop cemetery seemed to give the
whole thing a kind of dignity such as I did not ordinarily grant it.
Everybody seemed much older, both from strain and from losing Katy,
who had always remained so young. We had all been getting old together, and it was already, I say, a whole life behind us, with many
things that we could never have again.

The worst thing is that really clever and sensitive women are very
hard to replace, and that, once you are over forty, you find you can't
bear the idea of living in the country or travelling with even attractive
and amiable ones of the kind that you can't really talk to. Katy must have
been a wonderful companion—I had the impression that you were never
bored with her, and that—rather shy with most other people—she must
have been inexhaustibly entertaining with you and inexhaustible in her
gift of investing life with something that the statistics don't add up to
but that is one of the only reasons why one would like to see life continue
on this planet.

Dos returned to New York by mid-November and settled in with
the Lowndes at Snedens Landing in Palisades. It was there he received
a telegram from Van Wyck Brooks notifying him of his election to the
American Academy of Arts and Letters. Brooks, Sinclair Lewis,
Deems Taylor, Edna St. Vincent Millay, Carl Sandburg, and Eugene
O'Neill had nominated him. His election was announced at the
Academy's annual meeting on November 25, and he became the fifth
occupant of Chair 14, following Teddy Roosevelt, Maurice Francis
Egan, Henry Hadley, and Willa Cather. This was a fine honor, but
Katy was gone, and for the time nothing could stem his loneliness, "the
archipelagos of remorse and boundless continents of grief," he called it
when in January 1948 he answered Edmund Wilson's letter.

In February 1948 he went to Haiti. Dawn Powell arrived early in
March; together they were amused by the local scenes. Dos had to
return to New York by the middle of March "for the final settlement
of the Virginia business," he told Sara Murphy. This referred to a
division of the land he and his half-brother Louis had agreed upon.
After the settlement, Dos held on to 1,800 acres, but because he chose
the waterfront land, which was valued at a higher figure than Louis'
portion, he had to mortgage his part for $21,500, which he did through
a local doctor. In the early 1950's he was able to sell Cherry Grove
Farm, a piece of land not contiguous with the rest, and pay off the

mortgage. Then in 1954 he laid out lots along the shore of the Potomac and subsequently sold several at $3,500 each.

The spring and summer of 1948 were largely taken up with finishing *The Grand Design,* published January 3, 1949. Only after completing that did he leave the northeast again, first attempting to renew an old friendship by visiting Hemingway in Havana, then traveling to Brazil and Argentina to investigate two countries of the continent in which he would take a great interest during the rest of his life. "Pioneers in Brazil," the first product of his labors, appeared in *Life* that December; "Visit to Evita," an article about Evita Peron, wife of the Argentinian dictator, in April 1949.

Dos spent Christmas of 1948 in Washington, D.C., then was back at Snedens Landing by the first of the year, putting together his South American materials and also making plans for his next bit of reportage, a series of articles about General Mills which the company had commissioned him to do for its employee magazine, *Modern Millwheel.* He worked with Abbott Washburn, who was at that time Director of Public Services, and the series appeared from January through July, 1950. Before undertaking the research for "The General," Dos headed to Cuba for about a month in February and March. If one can take his novel *The Great Days* partly as an account of what he did there, he attempted to gather information about the political situation but could find no publisher interested in handling the report. Returning to the United States, he visited Atlanta as he began his investigations for General Mills, then after returning to Snedens Landing he headed west in May to observe other areas of the huge wheat operations.

Through the Lowndes he had met Elizabeth Holdridge in 1948. They had seen each other once before at the Lowndes in 1938 when both were married, but Elizabeth and her husband were out of the country much of the time, and they had not met since. Her first husband had been killed in an automobile accident in 1946, leaving a son Christopher, whom they called Kiffy. A handsome, dignified woman behind whose reserve lies a lively wit, she and Dos had similar interests in the land, in literature, and in the adventure of travel. They were married August 6, 1949, at Ridgecrest Farm, in Baltimore County, Maryland.

Immediately thereafter they headed for Spence's Point, which would be home henceforth. Then after a trip to Europe in September they found that farming life quickly filled their time and thrived on it. "We are planted down here among the weeds with no neighbors but the crows and the wild geese and an occasional swan," Dos wrote Stewart Mitchell as the year ended. He could have added that he felt content and settled for the first time after two lonely, painful years. And when a daughter, Lucy Hamlin, was born May 15, 1950, he was a proud and eager father for the first time at age fifty-four.

Dos' new life did not lessen his pace of production. *The Prospect Before Us,* an attempt to analyze the contemporary scene and an espousal of a sort of Jeffersonian liberalism, appeared October 1950; at the same time he was at work on the novel *Chosen Country.*

He missed conversation with his literary friends at Spence's Point, so he intensified his correspondence with Edmund Wilson. The two had a running conversation by mail throughout the next years, turning to literature and politics. Dos commented on what he was reading; in 1950 he was disappointed by Hemingway's novel *Across the River and Into the Trees.* As before, Wilson and Dos discussed Dos' fiction; in December 1951 the subject was *Chosen Country,* just published.

These were the years when more people began to ask him questions about himself and his contemporaries, as critical and biographical studies of Fitzgerald, Hemingway, and other writers accumulated. When Myra Champion, Librarian of the Pack Memorial Library in Asheville, North Carolina, asked about Thomas Wolfe, for example, Dos wrote a kindly, insightful response.

This was the era of the McCarthy hearings. Dos, now adamantly opposed to Communism, initially approved of what the government's loyalty program was trying to accomplish. But more and more McCarthy's techniques annoyed him, so when in early 1953 he issued a statement to the House Committee on Un-American Activities defending Horsley Gantt's loyalty, it was apparent that he thought the committee's challenge of Gantt as absurd as the concept of loyalty was important. He could be on occasion an apologist for McCarthyism, but he believed, he told Gantt, that finally it had done more harm than good.

Dos and Betty's life had to follow a regular pattern. They were seriously trying to farm the land, which required their presence, and with two children in the family he and she could not travel as extensively as had been his wont. But there was plenty to keep them scrambling; "This has been a hellish year," he wrote Rumsey Marvin in

October 1953. "Drouth crop failures, financial setbacks of all kinds, but were all alive and kicking and in good health—Lucy's enormous—Kiffy's boarding at Gilman School in Baltimore—and Betty's taking up weaving." They decided the best arrangement would be to take a small place in Baltimore, where they could stay during the weeks in the winter months while Kiffy went to school and Dos did his research and writing at the Enoch Pratt Free Library or the Peabody Library and sometimes in later years at the Eisenhower Library at Johns Hopkins University. Baltimore for the week days, Spence's Point on weekends became the routine until Dos' death.

Amidst this he continued to write prolifically; *The Head and Heart of Thomas Jefferson* appeared in January 1954; and *Most Likely to Succeed,* a satiric novel incorporating his New Playwrights and Hollywood experiences, that September. He was pleased to have written about Jefferson, but as he told Robert Hillyer after the book had been out for some time, he was disappointed because "the damn thing is selling flaccidly and it took a hell of a lot of irreplaceable time and money to construct. You know, the feeling of shoving your work down a rat hole."

To bolster his finances he took to lecturing on occasion, in October and November 1954, for example, traveling west to Eugene, Oregon, to talk. He had never before been fond of public speaking, nor was he now, but the pay was good, and he could indulge his love of travel, even if the life was somewhat arduous. Travel was easier too, now that Lucy was no longer a baby. They had been spending some time in the summers in Wiscasset, and in 1955 a month in Wellfleet, Massachusetts, but in 1956 they journeyed through Colorado, Utah, and Wyoming—"a magnificent trip," he wrote his cousins the Brodnax Camerons in mid-August, "a lake in the Colorado Rockies. Mesa Verde, across the desert to Salt Lake city duly swam in lake. Now freezing at Jackson Hole."

The work which he found most demanding was an historical narrative, *The Men Who Made the Nation,* published in February 1957. Betty recollected that it took at least twice as long as Dos had expected, and before it appeared, they had to borrow money four times from a local bank. But perhaps the more significant volume to appear at that time was *The Theme Is Freedom,* which appeared in March 1956. Dos collected his essays going as far back as the earliest written in the

1920's; putting them in chronological order he attempted to show, from what he had said all along, that it was always—and precisely—individual liberties which he had espoused.

Nineteen fifty-seven was the year in which he was awarded the Gold Medal for Fiction from the National Institute of Arts and Letters. The ceremony was May 22; years later when Joseph Blotner, writing a biography of William Faulkner, asked Dos some questions, he told of the amusing scene at the presentation. Faulkner and he had sat through seemingly interminable talk, so when their time came, Faulkner put aside his speech, thrust the medal at Dos, and said, "Nobody deserved it more or had to wait for it longer." Dos' acceptance speech was not so abrupt; he talked about his writing, and particularly about satire. In response to those who found his work embittered he remarked:

> I wonder if any of you have ever noticed that it is sometimes those who find most pleasure and amusement in their fellow man, and have most hope in his goodness, who get the reputation of being his most carping critics. Maybe it is that the satirist is so full of the possibilities of humankind in general, that he tends to draw a dark and garish picture when he tries to depict people as they are at any particular moment. The satirist is usually a pretty unpopular fellow. The only time he attains even fleeting popularity is when his works can be used by some political faction as a stick to beat the brains out of their opponents. Satirical writing is by definition unpopular writing. Its aim is to prod people into thinking. Thinking hurts.

The statement might not have changed anyone's mind, but once more he went on record as attempting to satirize in his fiction.

For two weeks in September Dos was in Japan for a literary festival with John Hersey, John Steinbeck, and Ralph Ellison. Then, after taking his family to Mexico for a month in November, he settled back into his regular pattern of work. Even with the interruptions, he had accomplished a good deal of writing, particularly finishing the manuscript for *The Great Days,* a novel in which he wrote about Katy's death, his own sense of failure, and of the United States' failure to capitalize on her moment of greatest power at the end of World War II. The central character, Roland Lancaster, is terribly depressed and equates his own "defeat" with what he believes to be a defeat for the country. The last item Dos wrote for *The Great Days* is an expression of his mood revealed in the novel:

> When he shall hear
> His loved ones story whispered in his ear,
>   woe woe will be the cry
> No quiet murmur like the tremulous wail
> of the love bird the querulous nightingale
>   Finished copying
> Three in the morning—went into
>   quiet kitchen and jumped out of the window
>   to his death

Roland's failure and half attempt at suicide in Cuba, the death of his first wife described in a flashback, and the country's failure all combine in the novel to create the mood expressed in the five lines of poetry and the prose note added to them. This bitter time had passed for Dos, but the novel was a necessary writing out of it.

Doing the series for *Harper's* on wartime America and then traveling about the country for General Mills, he had learned something about labor and the unions. Early in 1958 he looked into this subject again. *Reader's Digest* asked him to do a piece which he entitled "What Union Members Have Been Writing Senator McClellan." The senator headed the Senate Select Committee on Improper Activities in the Labor or Management Field. Robert Kennedy, at that time working as counsel for the committee, permitted Dos to use the files. Dos, finding a letter from Edward Grant Taylor, a union member who had written to the Senate group, contacted him. Taylor in response wrote at great length describing his struggles with corrupt labor and management people. The article appeared in September 1958. Dos also made use of his researches for his next work of fiction, *Midcentury,* in which the theme of labor corruption is central and the situations he had learned about form some of the novel's episodes.

Once he had finished this research, he, Betty, and Lucy packed up and headed to Brazil for six weeks during July and August 1958. The trip was not just for pleasure; Dos collected information which would later be of use in articles and in *Brazil on the Move,* a book of reportage. Back from South America he had to be hard at work immediately, preparing *Prospects of a Golden Age,* an historical narrative which appeared in November 1959. Then too he was trying to complete *Midcentury* and finally, to work ahead on a narrative about Woodrow Wilson, entitled *Mr. Wilson's War,* to be published in November 1962.

In 1956 he had signed an agreement to "organize a venture with

respect to 'U.S.A.' for motion picture and related purposes. . . ."
Although efforts were made to adapt *U.S.A.* for films, nothing came of
this, but in 1959, with Paul Shyre, Dos adapted the trilogy for a stage
reading. Late that year it began a successful run at the Hotel Martinique. He also proved himself to be an inventor. With Gene Towne,
who had earlier been involved in the attempts to adapt *U.S.A.,* he had
thought up a "bubble gun." The idea was amusing; some attempts
were made to market it, but Dos told an interviewer from the
Washington *Post,* "About all I got out of that idiotic bubble-gun was
lunch with a man known as the 'bubble king.' "

The next years were as busy as ever. Dos continued his remarkable
pace of writing. After he argued with Houghton Mifflin about the
company's method of having a committee recommendation from
several young people, *Midcentury* appeared in February 1961 and
became a best-seller for a time; the book about Wilson came out the
next year, *Brazil on the Move* in September 1963, *Thomas Jefferson—
The Making of a President* in August 1964, as well as *Occasions and
Protests,* a collection of essays, that October. He fitted in three weeks in
February 1963 as writer-in-residence at the University of Virginia. And
summers allowed him travel. In 1960 there was a trip to Spain, France,
and Italy; Spain again in 1961; South America in 1962; Canada and out
to Wyoming in 1963; San Francisco, and later a tour through Alaska,
in 1964.

When in May 1965 Dos received the Alumni Seal Prize from Choate
School, he commented:

> Sometimes I wonder whether in this sort of citation in the orders of
> the day one shouldn't perhaps list some of the brickbats, too; the spite-
> ful reviews, the pained expostulations, the angry letters of disappointed
> readers, the people who were once your friends who cross the street to
> avoid you. . . . Writing is and I guess it ought to be one of the hazard-
> ous professions. . . .
>
> The first thing a man—striving to come of age in any period of human
> history—has to do is to choose for himself what is true and what is not
> true, what is real and what is not real in the picture of society established
> for him by his elders. . . . Today every avenue of the senses is con-
> tinually assailed not only by the siren voices of the hucksters singing
> "Cigars, cigarettes, tiparillos" but by the subtly deluding propaganda of
> all the groups of men that seek power. In the search for truth there are
> no secret formulae that can be handed down from one generation to

another. Truth I believe is absolute. Some things are true and some false. You have to find it.

What he said here was in part an extension of what he had written Edmund Wilson in their exchanges that centered around Wilson's protest, *The Cold War and the Income Tax: A Protest.* As Dos had told him, he'd come to believe that right and wrong " represent something definite in the human make up." Right and wrong he had come to define for himself and had expressed in books like *Adventures of a Young Man, Number One,* and those that had followed. If he sounded dogmatic, he had not meant to, because, as he told the students at Choate, although he believed truth to be absolute, there are no secret formulae for finding it. Each generation has to find truth by searching among the welter of information assailing us all.

In June 1965 Dos had a scare from a "heart fit," as he described it the next February to Rumsey Marvin. "I scared everybody to death early one morning in June," he wrote, "when we were visiting our old friends the Givens on Cape Cod, by having a seizure of gasping and heaves. A local medico appeared with an injection which stopped it instantly. . . . I'm a little more careful than I used to be about early to bed etc and tend to malinger on snowshovelling and things like that, but otherwise feel fine." He added that the damage from his old bouts with rheumatic fever might be catching up with him, but concluded, "Anyway it waited till I was headed for threescore and ten. Everything is gravy anyway after the last Jan 14."

The seizure did not slow down his writing or his travel. *Shackles of Power: Three Jeffersonian Decades* came out in March 1966. The same year he organized a selection of writings entitled *World in a Glass: A View of Our Century,* that appeared in November. He published his memoir, *The Best Times,* that same month. Edmund Wilson wrote him about it, doubting the complete accuracy of some of the narrative. But Dos was quite sure of his facts, even of the tale about Scott and Zelda lobbing tomatoes at the Murphys' guests during a party in Antibes. The summer of 1965 the family flew west to show Lucy some colleges; then they went to the Boyer Ranch in Wyoming. In March 1966 they took a trip to Yucatan, and then traveled to Brazil during July and August. The following July and August Dos, Betty, and Lucy visited Portugal, particularly because he was now engaged in writing a history of the country, *The Portugal Story,* which would be published in April 1969. Then in November 1967 he and Betty flew to Rome, where he received the $32,000 Antonio Feltrinelli Prize for fiction. He had almost refused it, for when he received a letter from Edmund Wilson telling him of the award and giving the amount in lira, he had figured it out to be $3,200, not too much more than the cost of the trip for him and Betty. But because Lucy and Betty knew he had never been strong with figures, they rechecked and realized the sum was $32,000.

With Lucy at Occidental College in Los Angeles, her parents headed to Florida in February 1968. They visited Dudley Poore at Summerland Key; Poore remembered Dos striding up to his house with a basket full of the makings of drinks, and his fascination with a heron named Mike. From there Dos and Betty went to California in March; then they traveled in the Midwest during the summer, visiting the Garsts in Coon Rapids and the Marvins at Walloon Lake, Michigan, before heading east to Wiscasset and thence down to Spence's Point. After a fall in Westmoreland, they flew to Easter Island in January, 1969, explored the Chilean lakes, then passed through Buenos Aires. Travel still excited him; with great relish he described the eventful trip to Lucy. Though they returned to Virginia, Dos went to Florida in May to watch the Apollo 10 moonshot from Cape Kennedy.

The event stirred him. The United States Information Service commissioned him to write about it; and he declared, "Mankind was on the threshold of a new beginning." In every person who watched the flight was "the need to know, the smouldering spirit of adventure," and he took heart at this "fresh assertion of man's spirit" amidst the hideous spectacles of the twentieth century.

Although Dos continued to work—his projects were a short book about Easter Island and the completion of what he called the "Thirteenth Chronicle," later entitled *Century's Ebb*—his heart bothered him more and more. In October he had to check in for tests and medication at Johns Hopkins. Though he was allowed to go to Spence's Point, he had to return to the hospital in January. After a stay there, he and Betty traveled to Tucson, Arizona, for the month of March. He was very weak upon his arrival, needing a wheelchair at the airport. The time was hard for Betty, but he improved and was able to be up and even working some in his garden when they returned to Westmoreland in April. He kept up his wide friendships as well, joking with Edmund Wilson about his heart troubles, agreeing with William L. White to nominate William Buckley for the Century Club in New

York, offering Horsley Gantt his ideas on Gantt's editorial, "B.F. Skinner and his Contingencies," that appeared later in *Conditional Reflex,* and enjoying a weekend in June with his cousin Lois Hazell and a mutual friend, Manoel Cardoza. But in July he had to go back to Johns Hopkins, staying in Baltimore until the end of the month before going to Head Tide, Maine.

The trip back down to Baltimore the end of August was long and painful. Dos was feeling worse but had hopes that another visit to Hopkins would revive him. He was in the hospital for a time, then seemed well enough to move to the small apartment at Cross Keys Village in Baltimore which he and Betty now kept. The evening of September 27 he visited the Brodnax Camerons but was very quiet and clearly not comfortable. The next morning, Betty stepped out to get a paper, leaving Dos seated in the apartment. When she returned, she found him fallen forward on the floor. She called Horsley Gantt, who immediately came over from his home nearby, but there was nothing to be done. Dos had died quickly from the heart failure, still, Gantt recalled, with the inquiring, interested look on his face that typified him throughout his life.

After services in Baltimore and Westmoreland, Dos was buried in the Yeocomico Church cemetery, a short distance from Spence's Point, October 7, 1970.

To the editor
The New York Times *Book Review Section*

Key West, Florida
March 15 1947

Dear Sir,

There appeared in your paper on March 9 a review by Mr Lawrence Lee of Mr Godfrey Blunden's A ROOM ON THE ROUTE which dealt with that absolutely first rate novel in such misleading terms that I cant help calling your attention to it. I had read the book already or assuredly I should never have read it at all, so well calculated was the review to dampen the interest of even a fairly close student of the Soviet Union.

I imagine that you are not aware of the fact that there has existed in the New York press for a number of years now an invisible censorship of all books dealing frankly and seriously with Russian life and especially of books which do not fit into the pattern of thinking which our enthusiasts for the Kremlin regime have learned from the subtle and diligent propaganda fostered by the Communist Party in this country. I dont mean to imply that you personally share the enthusiasm of these people for each and every aspect of Soviet life or that you dont feel your responsibility as the editor of one of the important literary organs in the country, but I do feel that the time has come to make a particular effort to impress upon every American in a position of authority the need for an open mind and for continually fresh evaluations in relation to every topic that deals with the Soviet Union. For quite long enough now the country has been flooded with propaganda from the dominant party in Russia. It is time we heard from the under dog. And by under dog I dont mean the political dissidents, I mean the great tortured majority of the Russian people.

John Dos Passos

To Robert Hillyer

Boston Mass.
Sept 19 [1947]

Dear Robert,

Thanks so much for your sweet letter. This is so much the worst thing thats ever happened to me that its hard not just to sit in a chair and snivel. Fortunately I have a great deal of work on hand and the good old sheriff right around the corner so I'll have to stir my stumps. The eye business is nothing—I've got a wonderful little hunchbacky physician whos already preparing a new one wired for sound and equipped with radar and a monacle—

Thanks for your kindest of invitations. I'll give you a ring when I'm in New York—

Yrs as ever
Dos

To Edmund Wilson

> c/o Roswell Garst
> Coon Rapids, Iowa
> *Oct 29—[1947]*

Dear Bunny,

I got hold of the last section of Sartre's article in Temps Modernes —He is developing a splendid style for the journalism of ideas. The weakness underlying his political thinking as I see it is this: he has not confronted the basic verity—(at least so it is coming to seem to me) that socialism is a new system of exploitation of man by man very much more total and without any of the loopholes that capitalism allows—through which the individual can escape and lead a life of comparative freedom and dignity. Until it meets that dilemma all social thinking continues to tread on the quicksand of later day liberalism. If you still have the early numbers Id like to borrow them as soon as I have a stable address—In that connection I read over half of Democratic Vistas the other night and found it much more based on realities than Sartre. Today no man can base his political thinking on Marx any more than he can base his Geological and Anthropological thinking on Darwin—That doesnt mean that seen through the relativity of a philosophy of history—supposing one possessed such a valuable eyeglass—Marx and Darwin aren't still useful citizens

By the way I'm carrying around the six volumes of Toynbee and I must say I find Vol 1, though full of pedantries and odd quirks, very good fun.

Love to Rosalind and Elena

> Yrs as ever
> Dos

To Van Wyck Brooks (1886–1963), *well known as a critic and biographer. As an admirer of Dos' work, he had a hand in getting Dos elected to the American Academy of Arts and Letters in 1947.*

> c/o Lloyd Lowndes
> Snedens Landing
> Palisades, N.Y.
> *November 24 [1947]*

Dear Brooks,

Thanks for your very nice telegram which was read to me over the phone. Unfortunately I'm still suffering from the backlash of my accident and shan't be able to be present. Enclosed is the only photograph I have. Possibly the New York office of Houghton Mifflin has some glossy prints. The list of books in Who's Who is I think correct and up to date. Please express to the electing members my sincere appreciation of their very handsome gesture. Hoping to meet you again one of these days—

Very cordially yours,
John Dos Passos

To William Rose Benét (1886–1950), *a poet and novelist, who was the older brother of Stephen Vincent Benét. William had known Dos from New York days in the twenties; it was as a member of the National Institute of Arts and Letters that he wrote Dos in 1948.*

c/o Lloyd Lowndes
Palisades, N.Y.
Jan 12 1948

Dear Bill,

I'm not signing the card you sent on the resolution about the Thomas committee's performances one way or the other, because, although I think that the right of congressional committees to ask people to reveal their political affiliations is a matter that can be argued both ways, I feel that the adherents and zombies of Mr. Stalin's communist party have managed to pull wool over everybody's eyes. The Thomas Committee, although they certainly spotted the right people, were very inept in their handling of the situation. The propaganda for communism as a social system that the embattled screenwriters were accused of spreading was of course perfectly harmless but what nobody pointed out was that they were not spreading propaganda for a social system they believed in. They were—in some cases consciously and in other cases unconsciously—just as much part of Stalin's machine for world conquest as if they were working out of one of the propaganda bureaus in Moscow and their aim was to capture the movie industry for Moscow purposes and especially to keep out any writers who they suspected of working honestly from an American point of view. The obligation of party members not to admit that they are party members even if they want to unless—they have special permission—makes it very difficult to deal with their operations, which are not subversive in the old sense of being revolutionary but in the new sense of preparing the machinery for a communist conquest such as that of Yugoslavia or Bulgaria. In my opinion the Thomas Committee's work although clumsy was necessary and has ventilated a very unhealthy situation. If there were some way of getting something like the above into your resolution I'd be for it. Of course I endorse completely your approval of the Truman Committee on Civil Rights—

How are you anyway, Bill?

Yrs ever
Dos
(John Dos Passos)

To Robert Hillyer

c/o Lloyd Lowndes
Palisades N.Y.
Jan 13 '48

Dear Robert,

Thanks for your kindest of letters. Actually my eye situation isn't bad. I have no trouble reading or writing. The field of vision is limited but the left eye has pulled itself together and will do. I'm leading a parasitic life with some friends of long standing up here at Snedens Landing, but the arctic winter makes transportation rather a problem. I get into New York once or twice a week and shall try to call you in Greenwich if I ever get a moment. Various little projects keep me busy when I'm in town and out here I do nothing but work. The problem of what to do when not at work has been solved for a while by Toynbee's voluminous volumes. The fact that I have so much unfinished business in the writing line is the only thing that gives life any plausibility at the moment, so here I am at last a helpless inkshitter—I do want to see you. I'll be calling up after the 20*th*.

Yrs ever
Dos

To Edmund Wilson

c/o Lloyd Lowndes,
Palisades, N.Y.
January 27—1948

Dear Bunny,

I've thought a great deal about your letter. The thing that has struck me most is the fact that I had been able to live fifty two years without really envisaging the existence of these archipelagos of remorse and boundless continents of grief. I had thought myself fairly well versed in the miseries of life. Suddenly I find I had been completely ignorant of all these things. It makes you wonder how much else there is that you dont know about. I have had the kindest letters from all sorts of people, many of them people I've never met, who all have evidently their pilots licenses in those regions One reason people are so kind to you at such a time is that everybody understands about it. Thinking back to my feelings when Margaret died:—Though I didn't know her well, I was particularly fond of her and I had been fond of you since a day many many years ago when you turned a modest summersault while waiting for an elevator in an office building—I forget which—in New York;—and felt her loss keenly but I never for a moment imagined what I now know you were going through. We live and learn.

What do you think of Truman Capote? There's certainly talent there. I find Merle Miller pretty glib out of O'Hara out of Fitzgerald, but I find myself reading Capote with real interest.

Drop me a line about Elena's health etc from time to time. Care G. Murphy 131 E 66*th* Street New York N.Y. I'm going down to Nassau for a week or so with the Marquands next month and might very well go over to see Phyllis and Eben when they get established at Port-au-Prince.

This is certainly a formidable winter.

Yrs ever
Dos

Love to Elena

To Edmund Wilson

Hotel Oloffson
Port-au-Prince Haiti
March 2 '48

Dear Bunny,

Most delighted to get your letter and to know that little Helen arrived and that everything is working out. Congratulations. And give Elena my love. I'm very anxious to see the infant. Also got a letter from Dawn saying she had just talked to you on the phone. She seems to be arriving here at the end of the week.

Haiti's the oddest damn place I ever saw. The houses they were building up to a few years ago in Port-au-Prince were the cutest little cuckooclock scrollsaw contraptions. Its a different world. Not so different. Had dinner last night with Selden Rodman and his very short little wife and a large dark handsome middleaged Haitian business man who had a little Hunter College type of blonde for a wife. Rodman and a very tall American who seemed to have had some connections with Princeton and said he'd won an Atlantic Monthly prize, were dressed in sooty batik shorts. The young man wore a gold button in one ear. The only party who made much sense was the Haitian who was an automobile dealer and quite a sound fellow, very much like any good agent in the states. Primitive art has reared its ugly head, dans ces parages fomented by a man named DeWitt Peters and the local boys seem to enjoy hugely selling to American tourists. They use automobile enamel and strangely enough some of them paint quite well. Nobody ever stops telling about voodoo, Zombies, possessions, Baron Samedi etc C'est à dormir debout. Dawn will be a great help.

By the way Capote really is worth reading—he just left here but nobody knows enough French to get proper satisfaction out of his name. I also read Wilder's Caesar, with enjoyment, but I didn't feel it added much to the other accounts. Catullus was lamentable. In fact I dont feel its one of T.W.'s really best efforts.

It's too hot to take up your political arguments today. I certainly stirred up a hornet's nest that time. My only supporters seem to come from Saskatchewan—where the local paper said everything I intended to say only better. Naturally I promptly lost the clipping. I dont see why people are so freshly horrified each time because its the same line I've been pursuing since The Ground We Stand On to the effect that its political methods and not political aims that count. I think you are all just blinded by prejudice—but whoever's to blame its obvious that the international picture is going from worse to worser—Cant wait to break a bottle of champagne over popper and mommers heads—

Yrs
Dos

To Lloyd (1901–1968) and Marion (1906–   ) Lowndes, *longtime friends of Dos', with whom he lived at Snedens Landing for a period after Katy's death. Dos came to know Marion when he visited her*

mother, his good friend Susan Smith, in Wiscasset, Maine, around the
time of Sacco's and Vanzetti's executions.

Warsaw [Virginia]—Sunday Night
[*August 1948(?)*]

Dear Lloyd & Diddy,

The poor old house at Spence's Point looks very lonely for the
Lowndeses. There's not a jellyfish at jellyfish beach, tell Susan, but the
swimming is unusually delicious. Susan and Tania are much missed on
the shore and the lack of apsos [Lhasa apso, a small breed of dog
originally from Tibet] is appalling.

We had a big day: interviewed prospective tenants, a man named
Smith with Gramps and a brood of children and a nice bright wife and
a tractor and hens, geese, ducks, four sheep and five milk cows. They
yearn for a great hog lot and may be hooked. The miraculous draught
of fishes continues. The country lawyers are now in it, have discovered
a statute of 1680 forbidding anybody except a resident of the county to
haul seine on the county's beaches. The boys from Northumberland
retaliated by a terrific ordinance against fishing on Sunday—It's a regular gold rush—1000 boxes at $16 a box caught off Albany at the mouth
of Nomini creek. The great catch off Spence's Point the night Walter
got back is already legendary. He got six hundred dollars for that
nights fishing rights. To return to our big day: We drove the cattle
back into a permanent pasture. Wrestling with a calf Walter got a
fearful splinter in his thumb. Wrestling with the splinter he spied a
hawk and promptly shot it. Thumb further damaged by hawk's talons
in its death throes. After a little shooting at porpoises we met a
carpenter and decided to shingle the Hominy Hall house with asbestos
shingles. Also to build a privy a henhouse and to dig a well—all on
hardhead money. Then had a long session of bargaining with Mr.
Garrett of Lynch's Point about a land swap. Eaten by mosquitos and so
home to Warsaw.

Andrew Garland got his truck run into. "Wasn't in it" was how he
described the incident.

There are still soft shell crabs. You all ought to be here right now.
Love to Susan.

Yrs ever
Dos

My the house was left sparkling Thank you.

To Sara Murphy

Havana
Sept 8—[19]48

Dear Sara—

Got in just in time for the Despedida de Hemingway which is described inimitably in the enclosed—The old Monster was much better than the sour Mr. Juarez (who wasn't invited) implies, had his weight down and seemed in splendid fettle. The trouble with the party was not the champagne which was excellent but the fact that the steamer, which was Polish, kept forgetting to leave. First it was 10:30, then 12:00 noon and then when I had to tear myself away to go about my business 4 p.m. The good old Monster kept ordering up more giggle-water with the results that are described within. Love to Gerald: the briefcase travels marvellously.

Yrs ever
Dos

[Dos included an amusing clipping from a local paper which reads:

Ernest Hemingway, United States author and in an exceptionally large way, left Havana for Europe yesterday on the "Jagiello". Some said he is going to Italy They all gave him a farewell however as though he quit Havana. Many have been here with him long. The inseparable ones, as Juan Dunabeita, skipper or chief officer for a ship. C. G. Echevarria, one more in that capacity and career, he of the "Atlantico", and others would keep him company for ever if left to them. Bakques, and particularly such people as mentioned, team up with him because he is one American that can match them in their mother tongue and in their acts including bridge and the jai-alai. And he can almost outbid them in travels by sea, which is their game, by land and by air. When it comes to drinks, few can reach his level. Mr. Hemingway in the past war took risks for his country and for the Allies. He had an accident in London, nearly died, stayed in the hospital, and again reincorporated to live in full swing. He makes news wherever he goes, as he will now, and as he did in Africa, in Asia and all abouts. His books sell by the thousands, so it was "For Whom the Bell Tolls", which turned out the more in his profit for the picture. The only thing he gets out of them is money, and that serves to keep him going and well. His yacht here Pilar II is one of his precious relics, a relic in his absence, for the yacht moves much while he is on it, even as he is heavy, if only in the sense of size and weight. Friends were with him till the ship parted from the docks. They all wish him well and back him up to that extent. Julio Hidalgo, the pilot gave him his send-off aboard ship. It was his turn to put ship and him on trail out. They hugged each other till they next be together shortly again. Mr. Hemingway owns home and piece of property, or resort, at San Francisco de Paula near Havana.]

To Sara Murphy

> c/o Time Inc.
> Avenida Presidente Roque Saenz Peña 567
> Buenos Aires, Argentina
> *Nov 7 [1948]*
> good lord how the time goes

Dear Sara—

Now it is B.A.—a large synthetic city that looks very much like the Paris of the Parc Monceau region—Everybody looks well fed and well shod and rather stuffy. People on the street have a rather disagreeable expression on their faces like Chicago without the humor. The steaks are sensational but the rest of the cookery is done with linseed and cotton seed oil and pretty quelquonque. Huge German style restaurants full of people getting red in the face over gigantic slabs of prime beef—No matter how hot it is nobody is allowed to take off his jacket on the street. Even little children have to wear neck ties to get into the moving picture theatres. And all this dominated by the extraordinary figures of Mr. & Mrs Peron.

Sara it was sweet of you to send the flowers to Truro. I cant yet find words to write. After a year the void is as deep as ever. The only thing is to keep busy.

I cant wait to see the raised cottage in the course of transformation—there's still a lot of work to be done before I can start home

Love to Gerald & Honoria—

> Yrs ever
> Dos

To Abbott Washburn (1915–   ), *who was managing the Department of Public Services for General Mills, Inc., when Dos met him. Washburn soon thereafter went to work for Dwight Eisenhower's campaign for president, later becoming a deputy director of the U.S.*

Information Agency. He continues to work in public relations for the government and in private business.

[Snedens Landing
Palisades, New York]
April 14 1949

Dear Abbott,

Jim Selvedge turned out to be a very interesting person indeed. I spent several days with him in Atlanta and in Johnson City and got a pretty good notion of the operations and personel of the Southeastern Division.

The next thing I think I had better do is spend about a week in Buffalo. Whom should I get in touch with there? Apart from the regular organization, I need to get hold of somebody who is not "brass" but who is well enough acquainted to get me around to talk to people who work in the various operations, outside of working hours. Jim Selvedge and Wallace Calvert arranged for me to get taken out fishing by an assortment of people who worked in the mill at Johnson City and besides spending a pleasant day I found it was much easier to get people talking than on the company premises. The problem is to find someone who could go around with me to see people in Buffalo who didn't represent the company too much in the minds of the rank and file.

The rest of the trip depends a little on the schedule of the wheat inspectors. I'd like to get a day with one of the people who inspects the crop without having to go too far out of the way for him. After Buffalo I'll have to come back East for a few days, starting out about the second week in May to take in Kankakee (is the plant operating there yet?) Keokuk, Minneapolis and whatever seems necessary further West. When do the Texas and Oklahoma wheat crops start to move? If they start soon enough perhaps I should take them in on the way west. Would there be enough of interest at the Detroit experimental farm to warrant a detour?

The story is forming up something like this:
1. Buying the wheat
2. The Flour Business
3. By products, present and future

and incorporated in there somewhere will be a sort of social analysis such as Kinsey made before he got down to the gory details of his

report. I sort of begin to see the organization dividing into a financial
statesphere, a class of managers, a class of salesmen, and, somewhat out
of touch with the rest, the people who do the physical work: but that's
all subject to correction. It's a hell of an interesting scene.

Maybe you could wire me the names of people to get in touch with
in Buffalo Monday or call me Tuesday morning 19th at Piermont N.Y.
751j. I may have to go to Boston for a day or so Wednesday and would
go right on to Buffalo from there.

To Upton Sinclair

Snedens Landing
Palisades, N.Y.
May 4, 1949

Dear Upton,

The other day when I was having a chat with George Counts of
Teacher's College, at Columbia, he showed me your statement in reply
to Fadeev's ravings. It was very well put I thought and it made me feel
very good to know that you had come out against the grewsomely
efficient aggressors who control the Kremlin and from that fortress two-
thirds of the world. We who believe in the democratic process have got
our backs against the wall for fair. It had never occurred to me to
doubt which side you were on, but it was with a great sense of relief
that I saw it down in black and white.

How are you anyway? Hard at work I know. All sorts of good
wishes,

Dos

To Ernest Hemingway

Snedens Landing,
Palisades, New York,
June 23, 1949

Well Hem you old salamander. Imagine skiing. I havent tried since I
was a corporal. I'll write a certain Mme Hebert to turn over what
should be the equivalent of $900 to M. Charles Ritz, that is if she and
an agent named Chambrun havent shot it all at Monte Carlo. If that
works I'll try to feed him out a little more later. I've taken up farming
and find it much more fun than other ways of running into debt. You
ought to see me with the angus cattle I own jointly with a gigantic

negro cattle dealer named Lloyd Thompson. This was a farm of my fathers down in Westmoreland County Virginia which I got back with the help of the law when other members of the family had cut off the timber and sold off the beach and otherwise despoiled and denuded it.

So I go and write articles about how well they farm in Iowa, and use the proceeds for a tractor and barns. If I ever manage to get any quail back I'll ask you over to shoot me some one of these falls. Please condole with Mary on her leg and give that charming young lady my love.

Yrs Ever,
Dos

Damn nice to get a letter: write again.

To Sara Murphy

Address in August
c/o W. R. Griffith
Warsaw, Va.
Wiscasset [Maine]
[July 25, 1949]

Dear Sara,

It was sweet seeing old friends on the Cape but its still too painful there. I had to go to do some things—Tell Gerald I put those lines—"How to keep . . . from vanishing away" on the little tablet, on the back. Wiscasset seems deliciously remote after the crowded Cape. Lloyd and Diddy and I spent a large part of suppertime last night wishing you and Gerald were here. I'll be through New York for a second next week on my way to Maryland—where Betty Holdridge and I are going to get married privately in a cornfield and then hurry down to Spence's Point to go to work on the farming and house organization there. I've gotten tangled up with an event in Venice in mid September similar to the one Gerald packed me off to years ago in England. We'll be back October 1 and eager to receive a brace of Murphies in those rural solitudes along the Potomac—Anyway I'm hoping to see you in New York or Snedens on my way through—

love
Dos

To Lloyd and Marion Lowndes

Westmoreland Va
Feb 23rd '50

Dear Lloyd and Diddy,

Thanks very much for the volumes fished out of the garage. How are you anyway? The weather continues spring like with wintry interludes—cherry & plum in bloom—doves coo in the pines in the early morning, peepers peep round the edges of the marshes. We have six calves, all bulls; one cow died calving. It gives this year no heifers. Sign of war people used to say. We wish we saw more Lowndeses, but allowing for the distance from friends, Spence's Point stands up very well as a winter habitation. Yesterday we celebrated Washington's (and Betty's) birthday by going to Williamsburg. Hence the paper dolls for Susan to whom all kinds of love. Kiffy was indignant because he wanted us to hold a birthday party and invite all his little friends. The house is inhabited by some remarkable mice, last night they not only ate the cheese and dragged the traps out into the middle of the floor in Mr. Madison's room, but they carried one trap off completely. Where? Mystery.

How are Gerald and Sara and the other Snedens denizens? Drop us a tiny line

Betty joins me in love

Yrs ever
Dos

To Stewart Mitchell

307 Thornhill Road
Baltimore 12 Md
May 21–'50

Dear Stewart—

How are you anyway? I feel I didn't see you at all the last time I was in Boston separated as we were by a sea of publishers cocktails. Fond as I am of the Thompsons I find those half-business half-social events very trying. My mind was full of the advance I needed to extort and before I had come to you had gone off into the night.

This is to announce the arrival of a tiny squalling leaky little character named Lucy Hamlin Dos Passos, whom I hope you will meet one of these days. Tell Arthur and give him my best—and drop me a line We continue on in Baltimore for a few weeks until the little chit is cleared by the pediatrician and then we'll resume our rustic existence among the weeds of Westmoreland.

Are you by any chance going to be in New York during the next couple of weeks. I'll probably be there for a few days as soon as this household gets back into its normal tenor—

Yrs ever,
Dos

To Edmund Wilson

Westmoreland Va
July 19 '50

Dear Bunny,

I read The Little Blue Light on the train back to Baltimore and it sure did give me the gooseflesh—as grewsome as "1984"—These days I rather tend to rate literary work by the square inches of gooseflesh it brings out on the carcase. Judith is a true bitch—hardest thing in the world to do a proper bitch—I was a little doubtful about the long long speeches of the opening of act one, but now I think they are all right. You never quite know where it is that you realize that you are in for a very bad time. I've always been frightened by blue hydrangeas, and now more so than ever. I came upon a lawnful of them in Kinsale yesterday afternoon and almost ran the car into a hydrant from pure terror. Ellis is a blood chiller too—the real Alger Hiss. I think its a hell of a good job all through. Ahasuerus will be hard to handle, but maybe not. The first time I read his final speech I wished it were in heroic couplets—but on rereading I wasnt sure. I hope Charles Addams is going to do the set.

Hemingway's story [*Across the River and Into the Trees*] (the parts I read) brought out the goosepimples in a different way. How can a man in his senses leave such bullshit on the page? Everybody—at least speaking for myself I know I do—writes acres of bullshit but people usually cross it out—It made me wonder whether I really did get all my bullshit into the wastebasket in time. I was discouraged by reading The Cocktail Party too—What a meager and spiritless work— Intruder in the Dust made me feel better and The Little Blue Light gave me the works. I think you've hit the real macabre.

I had a fine lunch with Dawn Friday and we wished for you—
Give my love to Elena and Rosalind—Are little Helen's eyes still so
blue? We dont quite know what little Lucy's going to develop in the
way of eyes and hair—steely gray and brown I guess—she seems fat
and well—

Yrs ever

Dos

To Edmund Wilson

Westmoreland, Va

August 1 [1950]

Dear Bunny,

I've barely started La Mort dans l'Ame. I find it a little hard to
read novels while I'm novelizing myself—but I'll work at it. Most of
my reading is still in the direction of those Jefferson essays that have so
long hung fire. I dont know Leonov—Moravia I nibbled on a little
last fall. It's pretty glib—but I find both Moravia and Sartre less
uninteresting than Steinbeck—though Steinbeck really has talent.
What did you think of Intruder in the Dust? I was very much set up
by it. It's such a pleasure to find an American writer that passes middle
age without going to pot.

I've only read two of Malraux's Musée Imaginaire essays—didn't
know about the Goya book—Where did you get it? He's really a first
rater. I suspect that these essays are the best things written about the
art of painting for some time. They seem to me to far outclass Elie
Faure and Berenson and stuff like that. They really sum up a period
that seems to have reached stagnation and death in Picasso's dove of
peace. I must order the Goya thing. Where do you order your French
books? I find Brentano fearfully sluggish. Where did you get your
Genêt? Sartre showed me some pages in Paris years ago which
impressed me very much but the books were introuvable when I was
in Paris last fall.

Our summer has been rendered nightmarish by building operations that drag on and on becoming daily more expensive—Lucy is fat
and flourishing. We rather miss drinking companions though we have
dug up a few—but farming operations and building keep us horribly
busy.

When is the play coming on? Best of luck with it and love to all of
you—

Yrs ever

Dos

Have you seen a volume of somewhat Frenchified poems by a
young Jamaican (I dont know of what color) named Louis Simpson—? If you haven't I'll put them in an envelope. They are at least
highly readable. I see little recent verse that I can ever read.

To Edmund Wilson

Westmoreland, Va.
Sept 19—[*19*]*50*

Dear Bunny,

Hope we'll coincide in New York another time. I'm tied up with
an endless chapter and with all the exasperating complications of
trying to build a wing—(much needed for young fry) on the house
and with the resulting pillage of the farm and woodlands to find the
cash to pay the bills. Let me know if Clurman or The Theatre Guild
came through—You may still have to try to get a London production
first—those New York characters are timid as hares and always want
to bet on a sure thing.

Thanks for the information. I'll write Schoenhof—I find Brentano
useless except for current books. Where would one write Sartre?

Did you read the Kon Tiki expedition? Its not a literary work but
the subject is—as Katy's father used to put it—blood heating. It's quite
well written by the way and the sort of book I always enjoy. I'll send
you Simpson when I can find it. If I get a chance next time Im in
Washington I'll call up Philo Marcelin—is he the one I met in Haiti or
the brother?

The evidence seems to point, by the way against Jefferson's having
had any mulatto children—The mulatto children of Monticello so the
overseer (I've forgotten his name and cant put my hand on the reference) wrote in a little book he published in Kentucky soon after
Jefferson's death—were the offspring of some other members of the
family—though T. J. treated them, as he did Dabney Carr's children—
almost as his own. I'll have to make an expedition into that curious
region of the private life of plantation owners—before I wind up my

Jefferson operations—The whole subject is confused by a number of forged letters—one purporting to be from T. J. to G. Washington inviting him to come and see a pretty mulatto girl I remember being shown as a boy down here as a smut item. Most of the children plantation owners had by negro women were lumped with the other slaves—but sometimes special provision was made for them—The whole subject is veiled in reticence and distorted by political slander in the letters of the period, so that right now I don't know what to believe. The whole attitude of people of English culture towards their half breed children seems to have been incredibly brutal and revolting—quite different from the more normal human behavior of people of French and Spanish and Portuguese culture who tended to esteem their half breed children in proportion to their whiteness but still treated them as humble members of the family. Maybe I'd better look up the references in Black Odyssey—which I havent read.

This is the root of the problem in this Jefferson work that keeps stymying me—There are situations I can imagine quite easily but others I haven't collected enough data on to be able to visualize—I'm only trying to visualize a few events, naturally, but I keep running out of useful data—and the historians seem to spend their time obscuring rather than bringing to light the sort of thing that would be useful to me in my operations. Wanted a Kinsey report on Virginia circa 1750.

Love to Elena and Helen and Rosalind even among the Mifflins—

Yrs ever
Dos

To Marion Lowndes

Westmoreland, Va.
December 31–1950

Dear Diddy—

You ought to see Lucy in the little red dressing gown. She wears it in the morning and looks very cute standing up in her crib in it, even if she is yelling her head off—my what lungs. She's entered the smeary zweibach period and takes a few steps. Another great sight was Kiffy in the coonskin cap wielding a wonder sword and an enormous round metal shield his Uncle Larry made for him in his shop (We are in the

Arthurian stage and he's endlessly building armor). I too wear my fireman's gloves to wrestle with the fireboards. Christmas was rather tumultuous. Kiffy and the little Carden boys all fell down the dumbwaiter, mashing Kif's hand. Bob Carden and I rushed him to Dr. Griffiths's—There Bob was met by the news that the field back of house was on fire. By nightfall, however, everybody was eating rather over done turkey. No bones broken. Fire out due to timely arrival of the new fire engine from Kinsale. God what a year we face. Here's luck and we need it

Love and thanks to all of you

Yrs ever

Dos

Betty wants to know Susan's birthdate—Jan 8 She's hoping to finish that dressing gown for her by then. Please salute the apsos. I'm sure Fari doesnt like the idea of the communists invading her fatherland.

To Edmund Wilson

Westmoreland, Va.
July 6 1951

Dear Bunny,

Thanks for letting me see the Sat. Rev. article. I immediately felt my pulse and wondered about my blood pressure, and rate of alcoholic intake. It all seems normal but you never can tell. I'll have my urine cast at the first opportunity. I have had no call from the mortician, not yet. Ruel sounds dandy. I felt considerable interest in T. R.'s writings when I worked him up for the piece in U.S.A.—I imagine he was at his best in his letters. It's hard to imagine today a public man who had a private life—private interests, enthusiasms etc. Our presidents have been getting to be synthetic monsters, the work of a hundred ghostwriters and press agents so that it is getting harder and harder to discover the line between the man and the institution. Did T. R. write his own speeches, or is that too much to hope? There was a good deal of Hemingway about him. The strenuous life still subsists as part of our mythical world, I suppose as a late phosphorescent afterglow from the real life of the frontier—I'll have to read his letters.

I've just reread (in connection with my Jefferson operations)

Gibbon's autobiography What a complete picture you get of himself and his father. I'd forgotten it was so interesting

Lucy gabbles a great deal, but no words yet. We are wondering what she'll say when she gets beyond the da-da-da ma-ma-ma stage. These syllables seem to apply to almost anything, the cat, a stray visitor, a cap pistol.

Our best to Elena—

Yrs ever
Dos

To Edmund Wilson

Westmoreland, Va.
Sept 15 [19]51

Bunny,

How are you all doing? I hope you and Elena recovered promptly from your colds. It was a disappointment not to see more of you during our short delirious period on the Cape. Life down here is interesting and highly exacting but it is sadly lacking in conversation. Recently I've been reading about various Scottish characters in the mid-eighteenth century; largely through Lord Kames' letters and the memoirs of an entertaining clergyman named Alexander Carlyle. Hume and Robertson and Reid and Adam Smith seem to have managed to differ about fundamental matters without bitterness and to have entertained each other at various meeting places with hairsplitting and claret and sharpened each others wits no end. I always found the Dr. Johnson legend rather repulsive, but while that eminent bore was booming at the Thrales, the Scotch seem to have been really using their heads. In the last few years conversation has entirely disappeared from my life and I'm beginning to miss it. It has been a period, generally I suppose, of intellectual blight. There must be young men coming up whose minds arent cast in the dreary mould of Corliss Lamont but I swear I dont run into them. I'm now entirely committed to the termination of this Jefferson operation and I'm finding it a hell of a lot of work, with only the prospect of another goddam book to shove down the goddam rathole.

There's no use mentioning the fact that I'll be in New York for a day or two at the end of next week (Thurs? Fri. Sat.) because it always turns out that we are there at different times. I'll call up the

New Yorker on the chance—so leave an address if you are there My Helen was cute. Betty joins me in best to both of you—

Yrs ever
Dos

Ruel looked fine.

To Ernest Hemingway

Spence's Point
Westmoreland, Virginia
October 23, 1951

Dear Hem,

It's hard to think of Pauline gone, though she died suddenly and quickly, the way we would all like to die. I was very fond of her. Lord it seems longer than half a lifetime ago, when I first met the dark-haired Pfeiffer girls with you in Paris. October's a month when everything seems far away and long ago.

How are you and Mary? We are all in pretty good shape to tell the truth. Lucy is a bossy young woman of a year and a half and my stepson, Kiffy, is almost as cute as the Mexican mouse.

I have a letter from a thesis writer from Bradley University whatever that is wanting me to answer a questionnaire about your early life. Being historically minded I usually send these characters what dates etc I can remember; or do you want me to tell him to make up his own dates? Meanwhile I'll keep his self addressed envelope until I hear from you. What's your news anyway?

Best to Mary.

Yrs ever,
Dos

To Myra Champion (1905–   ), *a librarian, and the curator of the Thomas Wolfe Collection, Pack Memorial Library, Asheville, North Carolina.*

Westmoreland, Va
November 22 '51

Dear Miss Champion,

Unfortunately I only met Thomas Wolfe once, at Max Perkins' for dinner. We walked around New York streets afterwards and wound up drinking coffee in a little room far east somewhere. I forget what we talked about. As Hemingway said it was like being with a gigantic baby. There was a mild ferocity about his attitude that was very appealing. He was just the man to walk about the streets with, appreciative. I took a great liking to him and regretted afterwards that we never met again. Still there was something frustrating about him, perhaps it was the sense you had that this very great talent would never come to maturity.

Yrs
John Dos Passos

To Edmund Wilson

Westmoreland Va
Dec 13–[19]51

Dear Bunny—

So sorry about Helen. How is she getting along?

I was very much enlivened by your remarks on the book. I find the concomitanta of publication more and more depressing, to tell the truth, the ego damnation spelling itself out with more and more force with each successive volume. I think of them, in more cheerful moments, as the little crosses and sticks in somebody's private dog, cat and pet rabbit burial ground—Anyway to hell with it.

What will happen to the New Yorker now that Ross is dead?

Let us hear how Helen is getting on.

Lucy's quite the young woman.

Love to Elena,

Yrs ever
Dos

I think you're right. It looks as if I had Jay reading Ulysses in '21—still it's in the mists of memory.

About the communists I think I'm correct. Looking back at my experience with the committee in Boston, the complete pattern of communist behavior was already there. I was too full of adolescent hoopla to pay attention to it.—But except for the Italian names I dont think the Sabatini case bears much resemblance to the Sacco-Vanzetti case. I certainly didn't intend it to.

To Edmund Wilson

Weekday address: 552 Chateau Avenue, Baltimore 12, Md.
                    (Hopkins 9854)
Weekends:

Westmoreland, Va
September 14 '52.
(Hague 2674)

Dear Bunny,

I envy you your Civil War readings. I'll be glad to get out of the Eighteenth Century, though it looks so different to me now than it did when I went in that I cant complain of monotony. The more I think of the Hemingway sea story the better I like it. The lions on the beach are the old master at his best. But the boy (I mean the boy in the story) is a vacuum, and an envious competitor might complain that the whole operation is a little too shrewdly calculated. The only thing the critics like is something they've seen before. He's betting on a sure thing. Hell, more power to him. A very successful coup: but faulty as it was, the Venice book (in spite of the phoney countess) interested me more. It may be that my recollections of his Cuban-fishermen-with-marlin stories, as told in the old days, a little took the edge off it. I liked it better the way he used to tell it.

I too was attracted by Stevenson at first; the more I read his speeches the better I like Eisenhower's. I'm afraid he'll turn out a subtle bleeding heart, weak where Roosevelt was strong. If you want a continuation of the rule of Roosevelt's epigones, he's the man to vote for for Big Brother. Damn it I wish the candidates would wipe that smile off their faces. I dont see much to smile about as I look out on the world.

Love to Elena. Was my puppet-tableau still there when you arrived? I thought it rather good.

Yrs ever,
Dos

Statement prepared for the House Un-American
Activities Committee

New York
January 22, 1953

JOHN R. DOS PASSOS, being duly sworn, deposes and says:

I. I reside at Westmoreland, Virginia. The purpose of this affidavit
is to contribute the information which I have attesting to the loyalty of
Dr. William Horsley Gantt in connection with security proceedings
involving his employment by the United States.

II. My own qualifications. As this affidavit not only states facts but
also draws conclusions, I shall first briefly state my own qualifications
to express opinions on the subjects of Communist sympathy and
loyalty to the United States.

I am a writer. I was born in the United States in 1896. My father
was a well-known New York lawyer. I received a good education and
graduated from Harvard College, Cambridge Mass., in 1916. Filled
with enthusiasm for the Allied cause, I volunteered for ambulance
service with the French Army and, after the entry of the United States
into World War I, I joined the American Army. After the War I felt a
great sense of disappointment in the results achieved after so many
sacrifices, a disappointment of which I wrote in a novel entitled "Three
Soldiers." Partly because of this disappointment, partly because of the
youthful intellectual's desire for change for the sake of change, and
partly because of its humanitarian pretensions, in the mid-1920's I became interested in the Soviet experiment. This interest led me to visit
the Soviet Union in 1928. During this visit I first met Dr. Gantt. As I
later develop, Dr. Gantt realistically described Soviet life in practice.
This description made me appraise the Soviet system more validly and
created in my mind a skepticism about it. This skepticism deepened as
time went on and the ruthlessness of Stalin became more apparent.
However, I suspended final judgment. In 1936 the Spanish Civil
War broke out. It seemed to me important at that time to preserve the
Spanish Republic, not because of any sympathy for Communism but
because of my anxiety about the success of Fascism. I endeavored to
assist the Republic and for that purpose in 1937 went to that part of
Spain controlled by the Republican Government. My observations in
Spain brought about my complete disillusionment with Communism
and the Soviet Union. The Soviet Government operated in Spain a

series of "extra legal tribunals," more accurately described as murder gangs, who put to death without mercy all whom they could reach and who stood in the way of Communists. Subsequently they smeared their victims' reputations. I became satisfied that a victory for the Republic would mean a triumph for Communism and withdrew from Spain. Subsequently I described this situation in fictional form in a novel entitled "The Adventures of a Young Man." By this time I was thoroughly convinced that foreign ideologies were no substitute for the American system. I set forth this view in a series of essays entitled "The Ground We Stand On." Making frequent trips to Washington, I also became aware of the Communist infiltration of agencies of the United States Government and of our media of communication and expression (such as the radio). I described this infiltration in fictional form in a novel entitled "The Grand Design." This novel may have made some contribution to preparing public opinion for the loyalty program. My reflections on the subject of government have persuaded me that decentralization of power, i.e., the opposite of the Soviet system, is highly important. I express this view in a book entitled "The Head and Heart of Thomas Jefferson," about to be published.

As I am a writer the evolution of my thinking is well known in literary circles and has been frequently mentioned in print by book reviewers and other critics. I have paid a certain penalty for my change in attitude because a leftist approach is rather predominant among leading book reviewers; the comment on my books tends to be distinctly less enthusiastic than in my earlier days, and characteristics formerly hailed as virtues have become faults.

My experience has however enabled me to determine with confidence whether or not a given person or a given point of view shows Communist sympathy. I know very well the turns in the party line for thirty years, and I know what talk and action during that period has denoted the party member, the fellow-traveler, the Communist sympathizer, the deluded but innocent liberal, and the non-political patriotic American respectively.

III. I first met Dr. Gantt in Leningrad in the summer of 1928 and we have been friends ever since. Having gone to Russia as a young doctor on a mission of famine relief with the Hoover Commission, he had become interested in the work of the great Russian physiologist, the inventor of the study of conditioned reflexes, Professor Pavlov, and had returned to Leningrad after he finished his relief work, to study in Pavlov's laboratory.

At the time I met him Dr. Gantt was at work on the translation of Pavlov's books into English. Since then he has pioneered conditioned reflex work in America and become the most eminent interpreter of Pavlovian methods to the western world.

Soon after I met Dr. Gantt we took a walking trip together. Our conversations gave me every opportunity to learn his attitude towards Soviet Communism. His attitude at that time was very much more critical than mine. Dr. Gantt's attitude, a rather common one among scientists, was that political theories and political movements were out of his field; but he viewed the Soviet life around him highly objectively and appraised it with a robust common sense which he brought with him out of the old fashioned red schoolhouse where he learned his letters up in the foothills of Nelson County, Virginia.

This critical attitude had been sharpened by daily experience with the passionate hostility which his teacher Pavlov felt towards the Soviet government.

Efforts have been made since by Soviet propagandists to make it appear that Pavlov was a supporter of their system, but, as letters of his still extant can prove, he was very much opposed to it. As the son of an orthodox priest of the Russian church he protested frequently against the persecution of religious people and of churchmen and their families. It was only because Lenin considered Pavlov's scientific work of great importance and because of his unique reputation as an early winner of the Nobel prize and as the greatest European physiologist of his time that he was given freedom to continue his researches under the Soviet regime. Though he was not allowed to move his laboratory out of Russia his work was subsidized by the government and he was allowed to say and write things which from anyone else would have meant prison or death. Of course Pavlov's statements were not allowed to go further than the walls of his laboratory.

Since Dr. Gantt's return to the United States in the early 1930's, I have seen him frequently, especially since 1949, in which year I made my residence at Westmoreland, Virginia. I have also spent a great deal of time in Baltimore where Dr. Gantt has worked for many years since around 1930. Our conversations have almost always included some discussion of Pavlov's attitude towards the Communist delusion and Dr. Gantt's own attitude towards it and, in the twenty-five years that have gone by since our first meeting, the development of world Communism and the Soviet Empire. These conversations, confirmed by Dr. Gantt's writings to which I later refer, enable me to say without the slightest reservation that the idea of Dr. Gantt's being a party to or a dupe of the Communist conspiracy in this country is absolutely ludicrous. He is thoroughly aware of the cruelties and deceptions of the Soviet regime, and in fact has made that point of view clear not only to me but to the scientific world.

Anyone who cares to document himself on Dr. Gantt's viewpoint need only look up his excellent History of Russian Medicine or the very considerable number of articles and monographs he has published dealing with science in the Soviet Union. In this connection it is well to remember that Dr. Gantt was the first man to deal with the falsification of vital statistics in the Soviet Union and the first man to publish an account of the enforced famine which inaugurated Stalin's Five Year Plans. It is absolutely incredible that anyone in any degree associated with the Communist movement would have published such articles. It was the revelation of facts which the Communists and their dupes were desperately anxious to suppress. On account of his knowledge of the language and of Russian science in general his writings have offered students in this country a mine of objective information on things Russian.

Though naturally I can only speak as a layman, it is my impression that his development of the Pavlovian research into conditioned reflexes in his laboratory at the Johns Hopkins Medical School has resulted in some scientific achievements of a very high order. It is hardly credible that the authorities in charge of security should be so ill informed as to deprive the conditioned reflex work at the Veteran's Hospital at Perry Point of the service of the top man in this particular field because they have discovered that during the period of the Russian alliance he allowed his name to be used in behalf of war relief or spoke before organizations for Soviet American friendship which were endorsed at the time, we mustn't forget, by most of the high officials of the administration in Washington.

To sum up, I must repeat that, having known Dr. Gantt intimately over a quarter of a century, and having talked with him on innumerable occasions about Russian Communism and the operations of the Communist conspirators in this country, I can declare he has never sympathized with Communism and that the use of his name, if it has been so used for the purpose of Communist propaganda, must have been without his knowledge or intention.

To Stewart Mitchell

> 552 Chateau Avenue
> Baltimore Md
> *January 31 '53*

Dear Stewart,

Acting as Miss Lucy's secretary let me say she thanks you for her note. If you should be journeying to Washington to present your views to the administration (I often wonder why they dont ask for mine; I have a great many) do stop off—if it were a weekend and no blizzard or icestorm we could drive you down to the Northern Neck. I'd like you to meet the young woman; she'll be three in May, and I was recently favored by the Heinz Co. with a box of pickles on my 57th birthday. A truly delicate attention. Fugit Fugit—

> Yrs ever
> Dos

To Van Wyck Brooks

> Westmoreland, Va.
> *November 14—1953*

Dear Brooks,

I shall be very pleased to be a member of a committee to award a gold medal to Ernest Hemingway. He certainly is, as you say the logical choice.

> cordially,
> John Dos Passos

To Edmund Wilson

> [Westmoreland
> *December 19, 1953*]

> Irascible BUNNY
> Strives to be funny
> His CHRISTMAS cheer
> Is spiked with a jeer.

His misunderstanding of current events
Makes him keep landing
    the wrong side of the fence.
    and a HAPPY NEW YEAR,
       damn yr eyes,
       Bon Voyage—
              Dos

He says he's the Talcottville squire
But the facts will prove him a liar
He don't plow he dont harrow
He dont push no wheel barrow
He juss sets and holds forth by the fire

To Max Eastman

          Spence's Point
          Westmoreland. Va.
          Christmas Day 1953

Dear Max,

I enjoyed your Christmas sermon. Work, indeed, is the only cure for melancholy. I'd been intending to write you all fall to tell you how pleased I was that you liked the Jefferson book. One of the bitterest things about growing older is the sense of solitude that hedges you about. Old friends harden into fanatics and stop liking you because they dont like the things you say. Sometimes I feel as if I were working down at the bottom of a well . . . Anyway it was damned heartwarming to know that somebody understood what I was trying to do.

I got your phone number from the Cummingses, and tried to call you to say How do you do, or as you put it to find out what you'd been learning, but there was no answer. Perhaps you would drop it on a card into the mail. I'll try again when I'm in New York in the middle of January for the obsequies of the Jefferson book.

My health is pretty rugged. I have a farm (unmortgaged) a cordial wife, and a very cute small daughter so I have no reason to complain, but I must admit that the growing sense of isolation blues me up at times.

All sort of good wishes to you and yours.

          Cordially,
          Dos

To Upton Sinclair

Westmoreland, Va.
April 20 [*1954*(?)]

Dear Upton,
    Thanks very much for your book. I'll read it as soon as I get out
from under a very exacting piece of work I'm at present involved in. I
thoroughly sympathize with the way you are making clear to the
world that when we used to talk about socialism in this country we
didnt mean what Malenkov means—

Yrs ever
John Dos Passos

To Edmund Wilson

Westmoreland, Va.
June 11 '54

Dear Bunny,
    Delighted to have news of you. You are behind the times. I was
admitted to the 155*th* Street Immortals a number of years ago but had
never been there before. Too bad you weren't present to hear the
ritualistic castigation of Joe McCarthy by every speaker. No decent
man will rise to his feet now without a few lashes at the whipping boy.
What curious times we live in. They serve excellent free bourbon on
155*th* Street. Have you read Gruzenko's book. It's about the fall of
Gorki and is really a very interesting novel though written with a meat
axe. It's pretty heartening that even in the secret police there should
still be a Russian capable of writing such a book. It may be rather a
literary curiosity than a first rate novel, but the Russian scene is presented angrily and vividly and it's fascinating to see the power of the
old nineteenth century traditions even rescrambled in Soviet style and
dipped in the quiet Don. I'm afraid I shant be in New York again for
some months. I wish you could come down here. I'd love to spend an
evening with you somewhere even at the risk of being beaten about the
head and ears with the "raw head and bloody bones" of that dreadful
senator from Wisconsin. Dont you think maybe somebody might start
thinking of something else?
    What do you think of your friend Eisenhower now—re Oppen-
heimer?

Love to Elena. Lucy's four and big as a house—Betty sends her best to all of you—Kiffy's fine.

Yrs ever

Dos

To Edmund Wilson

Hotel Multnomah
Portland 4, Oregon
Nov 6 '54

Dear Bunny,

I'm particularly distressed not to have seen you in your biblical student suit. If you think of it jot down on a card when your article on the Dead Sea scrolls is coming out. I missed your piece on Genesis. If you should have a reprint or something kicking around, send it to me. I'd like to read it and can't find it in any of the back New Yorkers we have in the house.

I was certainly pleased that you found a few things to laugh at in Most Likely. Such criticisms as I saw took it with depressing seriousness.

Betty and the children were delighted with your visit.

Lecturing I find a highly depressing occupation It almost, but not quite, takes away the pleasure of travelling round the country. This stint is almost over. I certainly shan't do it again unless I absolutely have to. Though "you must never say to the fountain etc" Making a living seems to get harder every year.

About "most likely"—: I did try to introduce more goys but they all went Jewish as fast as I got them down on the page.

Feel it's too long since I've seen you. I'll be in New York for a week in the middle of January So drop me a card with your address— We'll be hoping for a weekend with you and Elena at Spence's Point in the spring—

Yrs ever

Dos

To Van Wyck Brooks

> 552 Chateau Avenue
> Baltimore, 12, Maryland
> *November 3, 1955*

Dear Brooks:

Forgive me for taking so long to answer your note. I was in a great spate of work on a manuscript I had to get to the printer by November 1st and just piled my mail in the drawer. I explained to Miss Geffen that I can't write a tribute to Thomas Mann because I think he was an old bastard. I don't like German novels anyway. I guess he'd rate with Galsworthy and Hugh Walpole at that. Anyway somebody else can do him more justice. Hope to see you one of these days.

> All sorts of good wishes,
> Dos

To Robert Hillyer

> 552 Chateau
> Baltimore 12 Md.
> *April 29* [*1956*]

Dear Robert,

How are you? I'm almost dead from working around the clock to finish a gigantic historical narrative.

This is to ask your advice. The University of Virginia is setting up a writer in residence scheme and has asked me to be it next winter. I'm tempted by anything that looks like a meal ticket these days—but am floored by the fact that they have asked me to suggest a figure for the pay. What is the top sum other universities pay for operations of this sort? Thought you might know.

As soon as I get out of these particular woods I hope to get to see you—All good wishes to Jeanne.

> Yrs ever
> Dos

To Edmund Wilson

Spence's Point
Westmoreland, Va.
Oct 14 '56

Dear Bunny,

You old boulevardier.

We, on the contrary, were very much delighted with our trip to Colorado last summer. I even found the crowds of tourists in the Yellowstone agreeable, all from the sticks, scrawny hill people or industrial workers mostly, most of them quite different from the Main Streeters I'd expected to find. What I do miss, living in the country as I do, is finding anybody to talk to—in the old republic of letters sort of way. Though I work continually I have almost ceased to think of myself as a literary gent. I catch myself seeing in the mirror an unsuccessful farm operator or mismanager of timber deals. On New York I agree with you. I enjoy two days there but after that I find it absolutely unpracticable. Lack of money has usually driven me off by that time anyway.

I'd like to go to Europe one more time to see painting and architecture but the thought of sitting in a café gives me the jittering jeebies. I'd feel like a movie extra.

Its delightful to think of you in the role of aficionado egging on the rabbis and the jesuits and the bearded and beardless scholars to fresh combats. I just read you in Commentary. Carrying out the role of uncircumcized rabbi very well, I thought.

We are all in pretty good shape I've just finished a narrative of the early republic for a collection edited by (you'll laugh) Lewis Gannett. Maybe if people think he wrote the book instead of me they may buy it. Kiffy's almost six feet and a football player. Lucy's awfully tall for her age: she's in second grade at the local public school and seems to be learning to read and write in spite of all the teachers can do. It's a beautiful October day and I feel restless as hell—

Our best to Elena

Yrs ever
Dos

To Stewart Mitchell

Spence's Point
Westmoreland, Va
October 15, 1956

Dear Stewart,

Your brochure arrived while I was still in the hurlyburly of getting a book ready for the press. I read it out in Colorado in August and since then I've been completely employed getting up an article on Stevenson—which might amuse you—I'll try to send you a copy. I just reread your Labour Landslide. It rereads well. It's a very cogent and amusing little piece. Much more cogent than appears on the surface. The Great Auk at his best I would say. Thank you very much.

Following Adlai Stevenson—and he is not at all an unattractive figure—on a day's campaigning in New York and one in the Jerseys I was overwhelmed by a feeling of the futility of the process. Just compare it with the World's Series—that miracle of organized skills and mass appeal that was going on at the same time. Even if Stevenson had been as good a statesman as the Yankees and Dodgers are baseball players, nothing would have been accomplished. Whoever wins the election, the sovereign people are going to have very little influence on its results, if any. The only influence I can see is a degradation of the politicians who have to keep their already flabby minds to an imaginary lowest common denominator. The gears of self government just dont mesh into the machinery of government. Even so I'm not ready to 'curse God and die.' That doesn't mean that they cant be made to mesh. The necessary formula would be a miraculous discovery, but if a way could be found to get the best minds to work on the problem instead of the worst, why should it be more difficult than the miraculous procession of formulae that brought about nuclear fission and nuclear fusion?

Of course its much easier to throw up the sponge with Justice Holmes and say "God damn them all"—but where would physics be if Newton had had that attitude towards his everlasting apple, or Einstein towards his long pages of mathematical symbols? (which I certainly dont understand, I hope you do).

Anyway I wish I saw you more often—

Yrs ever,
Dos

To John Farrar

Westmoreland, Virginia
February 9, 1957

Dear John,

How perfectly ridiculous. It never occurred to me—at the time or later—to consider you in the faintest way responsible for the "Bowdlerizing" of Three Soldiers. I made the decision myself to let G. Doran have his way. I've occasionally regretted it and occasionally not regretted it. So please tell anybody who teases you about it, from me, that he's a god damn liar.

Yrs ever
Dos

I'll read the Austrian book when it comes and if I can find a moment

To Sara Murphy

Westmoreland, Va.
Sept 2 '57

Dear Sara,

It was a disappointment to have to pour through the West side Parkway without hailing you and Gerald but babies are inexorable. Lucy stood the trip magnificently. You would have been proud of your god daughter. She tossed articles out of the car with great good spirits. Her appetite was excellent. Her elimination constant. She stood the trip better, indeed, than her unfortunate parents who were shaky by the time they reached Baltimore and reduced to a jelly when they finally crawled out of the car at Spence's Point. Anyway, here we are, settling down into a temperature of ninety in the shade and faced again with all the problems of trying to make a living out of a savage piece of wilderness. Still, it's magnificent too. The garden is unbelievably rank, the deep freeze has been stuffed with vittles out of the bay, the cattle are calm, the crops look good; we only wish there was some chance of your affronting those grim three hundred and sixty miles of truck traffic and dogstands. May be after the first frost—

Do write from time to time and let us know how the grand child thrives.

Yrs ever,
Dos

Betty sends love

To Charles Norman (1904–   ), *the author of many books, who contacted Dos while writing* The Magic Maker: E. E. Cummings.

Westmoreland, Virginia
September 29 1957

Dear Mr. Norman,

If I have any records of the Lawrence Gomme business I wouldn't know where to look for them. My recollection is that I induced my father John R. Dos Passos, the lawyer, to put up $750 to guarantee the printing costs. I've forgotten who edited the volume but I think it was Stewart Mitchell. His recollection of these matters I find reliable. Why dont you write him at the Massachusetts Historical Society? I was away, first in Spain and then, after my father's death, in the Norton-Harjes Ambulance in France.

Coming back to your earlier letter, let's see what I can remember about my Monthly days. Cummings' extraordinary verbal effervescence, the oldfashioned Cambridge household on Irving Street where his father presided at the head of the long table . . . I've cherished my recollection of it as a link with the Jameses and all the generations of old New Englanders back to Emerson and Thoreau . . . Italian restaurants and cheap Italian wine in Boston . . . Cummings improvising on the piano for the edification of his admiring family. Dr Cummings booming from the pulpit—was it the Arlington Street church? or did I hear him preach there on some special occasion?

Although I was an enthusiastic pacifist I wanted to get into the ambulance service to see what the war was like. There hadn't been any great wars for some time. The attraction was enormous. My eyes were so myopic that it was the only way I could get anywhere near action. Another motive was that I had a horror of serving in the army . . . a good many other young men of my generation felt the same way. Everybody's idea was to get into the war without getting into the army. Later, after I'd seen the front lines a little, I felt quite differently. In fact I went to a great deal of trouble to get into the army after the volunteer services were disbanded and I've always been glad I did. It was the most valuable part of my education during those years.

You had better check with him but I imagine that was the first time EEC came into contact with Rimbaud and Verlaine and Apollinaire. Did he read Barbusse's Le Feu? I know I did an immense amount of reading of French poets at that time, also Italian futurists, etc.

Gilbert and EEC and I (was there somebody else? I dont remember) had had one of our long bibulous and conversational dinners and were walking, maybe noisily, through one of the dark little streets near the Place St Michel when Cummings decided to take a leak in a corner. As I remember it he was set upon by a whole phalanx of gendarmes who carried him off to a poste de police. We followed protesting. I tried to get in to argue with the authorities in what I considered my very best French and was thrown out bodily a number of times. C. did some funny drawings of this scene. Gilbert went off to call up his acquaintance Paul Morand who, as a fellow littérateur—he was fairly highly placed at the Quai d'Orsay—had Cummings sprung sometime before morning . . . it was an idiotic but fairly comic incident and much laughed over by all our friends.

Best wishes with your project.

Cordially,
John Dos Passos

To Robert Hillyer

Westmoreland, Va.
November 8 '57

Dear Robert,

I did look in one container but found such a tangle that I couldn't look further. Someday I'll nerve myself for the ordeal—I know there are Hillyer letters, but where? Autumn has been magnificent. We never had finer chrysanthemums—It's been complicated for me by the fact that I spent nine days in Japan in September, finished off a novel, concluded an article and now Betty and Lucy and I are going to Mexico for a bare month. We'll probably all be in Baltimore after Jan 1. Then perhaps we can start visiting back and forth again.

I'm going to miss old Mitchell. I was fond of him.

Delighted to hear you and Jeanne are in fine fettle again—love to both of you—

Yrs ever
Dos

To Edward Grant Taylor, *who had been in the Rubber Workers
Union and had tried to fight the corruption he saw at the local level.
After some urging, Taylor wrote Dos at least two long letters describing the union situation as he saw it, and Dos used some of what he was
told in the narrative about Terry Bryant in* Midcentury.

3911 Canterbury Road
Baltimore, 18, Md.
3/30/58

Dear Mr Taylor,

Mr [Robert] Kennedy turned your letter of March 22 over to me.
I'm hoping that you will reconsider to the point of seeing if we cant
arrange to have an hours chat somewhere, at some place and time that
will be convenient for you.

Let me explain what I'm trying to do.

When the Readers Digest asked me to do an article for them on
the letters from the rank and file of working people that come into the
Select Committee, Mr Kennedy consented if I would promise not to
mention names or to describe situations so that they could be identified.
The idea is to try to give the reading public a picture of the dreadful
situation the working man finds himself in, caught between the mill-
stones of predatory management and predatory labor.

Your letters I found particularly interesting because some fifteen
years ago I wrote an article for *Life* about the Rubber Workers, interviewed Buckmaster etc. At that time it seemed to me one of the best
run unions in the country.

The situation you found yourself in is so typical of that of the
honest and conscientious fellow trying to work in the Labor movement, and your letters told the story so clearly that I'd like to hear a
little more about it. Also I'd like to get your ideas about what can be
done to remedy the situation.

I really think, although I quite understand that it's painful for you
to look back on what was obviously a mighty difficult period in your
life, that you would be doing a public service in cooperating with me
in my effort to get the story into print. The fact that I already have a
little background on the Rubber Workers—I know how mistaken a
journalist's or outsider's view can be in a situation like this—would
make anything you told me particularly useful.

You say you still have faith that someday each individual American will have the protection he's entitled to. So have I. The first thing we need to do is to publicize the individual American's plight.

The general public is absolutely ignorant of the state of affairs your letters told of. I didnt read all the hundred thousand in the committee's file but read enough to feel that something had to be said and quickly.

Thousands and thousands of them wrote in such terror of their lives they didnt dare sign their names. Many of them even tried to disguise their handwriting.

If you do decide to consent to an hour's talk somewhere, let me know where Jamestown is in relation to New York or Trenton, and what time of day, and what day of the week would be convenient for you.

Cordially yours,
John Dos Passos

To Arthur Schlesinger, Jr. (1917–   ), the noted historian, with whom Dos apparently had an exchange about some historical matters. Schlesinger does not recall exactly what.

[Baltimore]
13 April 1958

Dear Arthur:

Just got your note from Barbados. I am returning your books with thanks.

The McClellan is interesting, with its alternations of querulousness and smugness, and such remarks as that Halleck is a *"bien mauvais sujet,* not a gentleman." It gives me a clearer idea of McClellan's personality than I had ever had in reading about him.

As for the Plan B presented by the Japanese, it doesn't seem to me that Langer and Gleason make out a very good case for our summary rejection of it: see page 880. Nor can I see that the intercepted telegram from Tokyo ought seriously to have affected the situation. (Of course, I start with the assumption that we had no business worrying about China.) I have just received, by the way, two pamphlets containing blasts by Harry Elmer Barnes. I am not well-posted enough to argue all the points he raises but I am in general sympathy with his point of view. (I haven't read the book of yours—*The Vital Center*—that he scolds you about.) It seems to me that there is a myth of the war and our position vis-à-vis the rest of the world which has been swallowing us up in an alarming way. Actually, we are disliked and feared by the rest of the world just as Napoleon, and England and Germany have been. At the same time, we have worked up a self-justificatory fantasy about the nobility of our actions and aims. I agree with Barnes that the self-righteousness, the bogus moral principle of Dulles—exhibited in his *New Statesman* reply to Russell—is a kind of thing that was begun under Roosevelt, and I am afraid it is true that McCarthy is an outgrowth of the Roosevelt administration, too. (If you haven't seen and and want to see these pamphlets of Barnes's, I'll have copies sent you, but I imagine you know all about his point of view.)

The point is that, whether one approves or not of the present activities of the United States, one ought, I think, to recognize that we are really an expanding power unit, and that all our idealism is eyewash. Of course there are many who actually believe that we stand for "the free world" and that American institutions are preferable to those of other countries; but, whether or not these beliefs can be defended, they have not been the cause of our farflung adventures, and I think that what they have been based on has been rather going by the board as we have been getting more bureaucratic and monolithic.

I have just looked up, in this general connection, your old article in the *Partisan Review* on the causes of the Civil War. I agree, of course, that the historian must have a moral point of view, but it ought to be his own, not that of the participants in the events he is describing. The contentions of the "revisionists" you criticize seem to me aside from the point—which is that the Civil War was simply—like the Mexican War—a consolidation within this continent of the big North American power unit. The Abolitionists were fanatical about slavery, but this moral issue, again, was merely something, like Hitler's atrocities, that was useful for propaganda. Neither Sherman nor McClellan regarded the freeing of the slaves as one of the aims of the war, and Garrison, on the other hand, was all for having the North secede from the wicked South. Allen Nevins in his history of the war takes a view somewhat similar to this, but the difference between him and me is that Nevins enthusiastically approves of everything the U.S. has done since in the way of intervention and expansion.

Let's talk more about this when I see you again.

[Dos]

To Edmund Wilson

3911 Canterbury Road,
Baltimore 18, Md.
4/ 19/ 58

Dear Bunny,

It was a great pleasure to hear from you. I've been missing your conversation and have been too busy with the ratrace of trying to write articles to support the family, as well as continuing my own operations on the side, to write letters. You may be right. Perhaps I should have expatiated on Ro Lancaster's opinions. I tried to, but it seemed so corny that I cut it all out. Unfortunately, unless I start doing a George Moore and rewriting all my old books, that's water over the dam. Next time we'll try harder.

By the way I dont think I ever did go along with Franklin Roosevelt's Dr Win-the-War as I did with his Dr New Deal in its early stages. I remember going to listen to Willkie in 1940 in the hope of finding anything but me-tooism and then voting for Roosevelt as the lesser of the two evils. My interest in the results of wartime organization, (in The State of the Nation) was a little different. The Great Days represents something of the inevitable disillusionment with that enthusiasm for airfields and labor-management committees and floating bases and amphibious landings. I still think we have something better to teach the world than the Russians have. The essential thing is the politics of balance and moderation. Compare our handling of Puerto Rico with the Russian handling of Hungary . . . But I have to catch a train. Hope to get through New York while you are there.

Yrs ever
Dos

Postcard to E. E. Cummings

[New York
August 15, 1958]

My I enjoyed learning you hate Gide—Hope he's in hell.

Love to Marion
Dos

To Van Wyck Brooks

Westmoreland, Va.
12/23/58

Dear Van Wyck,

We spent six weeks in Brazil last summer and I penetrated enough into the language of my grandfather to conclude that there was some hellishly good writing being done by Brazilians. It's too bad the Nat. Acad. etc has no Brazilians on its honorary list. Elizabeth Bishop is presenting their leading historian Octavia Tasquinio de Souza and I'd like to sponsor Gilberto Freyre and Erico Verissimo—Verissimo is their Sinclair Lewis and Freyre is, I think, one of the few first rate extant sociologists—I hate to apply such a boring label to a man who writes with fire and lyricism. Maybe you have read "Casa Grande e Senzala." I'm sure you would like it if you did. It was translated by Sam Putnam (I dont know how well) under the title of "Master and Slave"—

Would you mind seconding them?

Needless to say the election of a few Brazilians would be very valuable public-relations-wise in a country for which—as a relapsed Portuguese—I feel real affection.

A very merry Christmas to you both—

We'll be a little more accessible after Jan 4—at 4 Longwood Road Roland Park, Baltimore 10—(Westmoreland is always my address—) Any chance of you coming this way?

Yrs ever
Dos

To Mark Schorer (1908–   ), *a well known author and critic, who wrote to Dos as he was preparing his monumental biography,* Sinclair Lewis: An American Life.

Westmoreland, Va.
2/18/59

Dear Mr Schorer,

Being a very impatient young man in those days, I'm afraid I underestimated Sinclair Lewis. Dropped *Main Street* half way through, was only mildly amused by *Babbitt*. It all seemed journalistic, not the aere perennius I was looking for.

From a few conversations, spread out over a long term of years, with the strange hagridden man, I can remember my feeling of respect for him. In spite of his obsession with everything connotated by the word 'celebrity', fatal to so many good American intellects I had more regard for him every time I met him.

As a sort of folk hero of the time he is a marvelous person to write about. I envy you your job.

Cordially,
John Dos Passos

To Daniel Aaron (1912–   ), *now a professor at Harvard, who was doing research for his book,* Writers on the Left, *when he corresponded with Dos.*

Westmoreland, Virginia
April 9, 1959

Dear Mr. Aaron,

Joe Freeman is right. There were several Communists on the first editorial board but it was several years before Mike Gold and the CP took over. Egmont Arends was the first Editor, I think, and he was very far from a Communist. The idea as I remember was to revive the pacifist "radical" tendency on the old Masses, suppressed during the war. I think if you could go through a complete file you would be able to trace the gradual hardening of the CP line. Have you read my "The Theme Is Freedom" (Dodd, Mead)? You'll find a tolerably accurate retrospective picture there of my state of mind in the early twenties. That fellow Hicks has a most extraordinary aptitude for getting things wrong.

I'm rather hard to reach, as I live deep down in Tidewater, but I'll be glad to answer any further questions you may have. Have you read Joe Freeman's books?

Best regards,

John Dos Passos

To E. E. Cummings

Westmoreland, Va.
July 8 1959

Dear Cummings,

Thanks very much. I hope this finds you at Silver Lake and in perfect health. If we can manage it we'll try a little jaunt to the eastward in August—Maybe we can spend a night at Silver Lake and run up the hill for a chat. How are the bats? Lucy wants to know.

There's one more Brazilian I want to put in line for an honorary membership—he's a very gentil little red faced man with gray hair and a capacity for looking wise and agreeable without emitting a word in any language. My Portuguese has made, I fear little progress from the days of the Mormugão though I work on various volumes with a dictionary from time to time. What I'm getting around to is would you second this character too? After all we can't get any stupider people than we've already got on the roster, no matter how hard we try. Just mail it back if you don't feel like appearing as an authority on Brazilian history. After all you know more about it than Malcolm the Cow—just sui generis—if you get what I mean. Lucy, Betty, Kiffy all join me in best wishes—and to Marion.

love
Dos

To Cabell Greet (1901–   ), *a teacher at Barnard College for many years, whose particular interest is linguistics.*

Westmoreland, Va.
Oct 18 '59

Dear Cabell Greet,

My lord what a lot of ghosts your letter raised. I certainly hope we can meet at the Century someday. Unfortunately I'm in New York very little and mostly in connection with accumulated publisher business of one sort or another—that leaves me almost no time to see friends. We live in a deep and rural section of the Northern Neck. Lucy is only nine but she's a young woman with her own ideas. Maybe she'll turn out a borderer, a dweller in no man's land like me.

I'm pretty shy of personal appearances but occasionally—as in Colorado—I'm tempted by curiosity to hear what the students have to say. If I should get stuck in New York on a Thursday afternoon I'll remember your kind invitation

All good wishes

Dos
(John Dos Passos)

To Van Wyck Brooks

1821 Sulgrave Ave.
Baltimore 9 Md.
Oct 23rd [*1959(?)*]

Dear Van Wyck,

I'm still trying to get a couple of Brazilians into the Hon. Academy. Would you mind resigning these two nominations? I dropped off de Souza because nobody ever heard of him. They didn't even spell his name right on the printed list. And you ask why we are unpopular in Latin America. Verissimo's little book on Mexico has just been translated if you want to take a peek at it.

Hope to see you during this winter.

Yrs ever
Dos

Who else would sign these nominations? Cummings is abroad and I can't think of any names.

To Robert Hillyer

Westmoreland, Va.
Nov. 24 1959

Dear Robert,

I was most delighted to hear from you but distressed about the medical report. I'd been hoping to get you and Jeanne down here, but it looks now as if Mohamet would have to go to the mountain. The trouble is time. Every year there seem to be less hours in the day. I'm trying to finish a long documentary narrative in the (modified) manner of U.S.A.—I'm distracted by a stage version—or at least a "theatre in the round" version—of some of the U.S.A. material that is now running in the Hotel Martinique—of all places—in New York, and I'm threatened by a contract for another book for Doubleday's historical series—I've more or less retired from farming, thank God, having sold my interest in the cattle—but lumbering and "forest practices" take up, and delightfully, a good deal of time.

The fall has been delicious. Lucy's nine. Kiffy, my stepson, is a freshman at Randolph-Macon. The wild swans are anchored off our shore, ducks flying, hunters prowling, venison in the deep freeze. Darn it I wish we could get you and Jeanne down for Thanksgiving Dinner.

Anyway I'll try to pay a social call before the school year ends—
Betty joins me in best to Jeanne and yourself

Affectionately,

Dos

To Lovell Thompson

Westmoreland, Virginia

March 13 '60

Or would it be simpler, and saving of headaches, hypertension and cholesterol if Houghton Mifflin said No right now?

Dear Lovell,

The final rewriting of a book is a much too hazardous enterprise to entrust to a committee. There's not much sense in making recommendations at this stage of the game, because the things your editorial people liked or disliked may appear in a totally different light or may not appear at all in the final version. I had hoped that Houghton Mifflin would be sufficiently intrigued by the first few pages to say "Yes we'll take a real stab at it."

By the way: ON FINDING YOUR PLACE IN THE WORLD is only the title of the first section.

It looks as if the possibility of fall publication was pretty well bushed. If I should send you a final typescript fairly in April would you have to take two or three weeks mulling it over. Even then I'm afraid the general operation will turn out to be too delicately cantilevered to be susceptible of much change. As you know I'm always fairly amenable to suggestions about details.

Your final typescript wont be exactly what a publisher would want. It probably wont even be what I would want. It will only be the best I can do at the time. That is my responsibility.

What will be the latest deadline for fall publication

Yrs ever,

Dos

To Robert Hillyer

Westmoreland, Va.
May 18 '60

Dear Robert,
I'm so sorry I cant come to your dinner Damn it I'd love to see you Unless Mr. K. starts a war over Berlin (oh Christ what Eisenhower ineptitude. Let's have no more presidential diplomacy) Lucy and Betty and I are sailing for Italy June 11 for six weeks—Will you be in Europe next winter? How idiotic this retirement business is. Write

Affectionately
Dos

To Lovell Thompson

1821 Sulgrave Ave,
Baltimore 9 Maryland
1/20/61

Dear Lovell,
From my examination of the NY interviewers, I'd say we'd have to prepare for a mixed reception, but this time it will be mixed, rather than universal repudiation. I was appalled by the young man they sent up from Newsweek. He hadn't read the book and was still looking for McCarthyites under the bed. I'm afraid there wont be any chance of Betty's getting as far as Boston. Lucy's school etc.
Beware the calends of March.

Yrs ever,
Dos

Postcard to Sara Murphy

[Bailén, Spain
August 1961]

Sara—
Until I read of his [Ernest Hemingway's] poor death I didn't realize how fond I'd been of the old Monster of Mt. Kisco. In Madrid I found myself in places I'd been with him. Helas. We are spending the night in a little dump in Bailén as hot as Virginia
Love to G.

Dos

To Edmund Wilson

1821 Sulgrave Ave
Baltimore 9 Maryland
May 21 1962

Dear Bunny,

I certainly had a good time reading Patriotic Gore—As you probably have noticed there has been an infantile block in my mind on that whole period which has kept me from being even decently informed about it. Your book supplied the education. With The Shock of Recognition it furnishes a remarkably clear picture of American thought in the 19*th* century. It helps clear up the confusion (to my way of thinking) that has resulted from Van Wyck's well meant efforts and from the weird hodge podge of dramatics—melodramatics I associate with Bruce Catton—I liked your ending on Justice Holmes—who has always been an indigestible figure to me. His cynicism finds an echo in Mark Twain of the Mysterious Stranger and the gentlemanly pessimism of the Adamses. Its always maddened me. Those men produced a vacuum in American thought which no one has yet been able to fill.

I was disappointed not to hear from you when you were in these parts. Hoped you might stop by. When are you going to Talcottville?

We'll be here till June 6 except for a long weekend in New York June 1–5 (New Weston probably)

love to Elena & Helen
Yrs ever
Dos

To Edmund Wilson

Spence's Point
[Westmoreland, Virginia]
Dec 24 '63

Bunny,

It was delightful hearing from you. I'm writing Doubleday to send you a Brazil on the Move. Your Protest aroused my patriotic gore to the point of causing me to sound off in the pages of National Review I hope you wont find it offensive. I hold up your hands on some rather important points. What a strange and grewsome business was the shooting of Kennedy. The response from the mass misinformers has been to me more grewsome than the nasty crime itself.

Lucy demanded a subscription to the New Yorker for Christmas so we'll be thumbing through it hopeful of reports on Canada Hungary and maybe the land of the new franc—

Yrs as ever

Dos

To Edmund Wilson

1821 Sulgrave Avenue,
Baltimore 9 Md
Feb 6 1964

Dear Bunny,

I dont agree with a word of it; and besides, your reputation as a Trotskyite wrecker has caught up with you, you are known to have associated with the anti-party group and show every sign of becoming a running dog of Hungarian exceptionalism.

Pax.

By Lucy's request we now subscribe to the New Yorker, and I am looking forward to reading your piece on the Canadians. I got the same impression when we spent a couple of weeks on Lake Massawippi a number of years ago. It's very heartening that there suddenly seems to be cerebration going on north of the border. I shall be very much interested to hear what Hungary is like. I understand you've been studying the language. Comrade Khrushchev's tanks and machinegunfire may have been "stimulating" to the younger generation in Hungary but isnt it a rather drastic way to arouse people from feudalism? Certainly Hungary and Rumania do seem to be working their way out of the Marxist jail. I shall await the details with a great deal of interest. It would be amusing if it turned out that the Eastern European countries were the first to recover from the spell of nineteenth century socialism. The fact that so much that is human has survived the massacres, the purges, the brainwashings is generally encouraging about the human race.

Let me know if you change your address. Love to Elena.

Yrs ever,

Dos

What is the name of the book about the Rosenberg case?

To Edmund Wilson

> 1821 Sulgrave Avenue
> Baltimore 9 Md
> *April 18 1964*

Dear Bunny,

To continue this argument profitably we would have to agree on a certain number of premises. With a straight Marxist, I'd have no trouble doing that, but in this in between world—between for and against—I find myself bogged.

You complain of my use of "right" and "wrong". As a result of the somewhat varied experiences of a longish life I've come to believe—with Jefferson and the eighteenth century people—that these terms represent something definite in the human makeup—part of the equipment for survival built up over generations. We really arent talking the same language. Apart from that some of your strictures have a certain validity. "There's no fool like an old fool" etc. I'm getting more and more leary of shooting my face in public—when I have to I usually read selections from various books—but once a year or so I have to stand up and be counted.

Anyway best of luck among the Magyars—I'd love to know when your European pieces will appear in the New Yorker—

I guess I'll send this to Wellfleet. My best to Elena—

> Yours ever
> Dos

To Edmund Wilson

> 1821 Sulgrave Ave
> Baltimore 9 Md.
> *Oct 3 1964*

Dear Bunny,

The time has probably come to admit that two moderately reasonable people can reach diametrically opposite conclusions from the same set of facts. It has been amusing to follow, during this period, the great embargo row in Jefferson's second administration. Timothy Pickering was absolutely convinced that President Jefferson was being managed directly by Napoleon Bonaparte, which of course was absolutely false; and Jefferson and his friends held similar delusions though better founded ones about the activities of the federalists.

What are you doing in Middletown? Corrupting the relapsed Methodists at Wesleyan? Have you given up your place in Cambridge? Had hoped to see you there when I read to the jumping Jesuits at Boston U. on October *22nd*

Our best to all of you—

Yrs ever

Dos

To Edmund Wilson

Westmoreland, Virginia 22577
December 3 1966

proof correction in your letter. the offending periodical is called National Review not the National Weekly—I'm glad you follow it with such assiduity

Bunny,

I could swear I'd seen you set off from someplace for Red Bank on a red motorcyle. Anyway its a good story. Maybe it was just a dinner of the Society of Magicians you went to, but I thought they'd made you an honorary member. My apologies.

It may have been about Whitehead you discoursed on in the surf, but we did have a conversation about Henry James about that time or how would you have known how much he bored me. It's a scene I've always remembered with pleasure. I'm sure I'm right about the tomatoes at Antibes, because Gerald and Sara told me the story soon after it happened. The vegetable garden was just below the terrace where you dined at Villa America and Sara's old Italian gardener had grown some particularly fine tomatoes that year, trained up on little stakes. The damage to the tomatoes, the gardener's distress etc, were part of the Fitzgeralds' crime. I believe Archie did go out and either socked or threatened to sock Scott. A horrid scene.

Thanks for the proof corrections. I'll take advantage of them before there's another printing if I can.

By the way have you read "African Genesis" and "The Territorial Imperative" by Robert Ardrey? I'm recommending them to those who suffer from stubborn cases of the Liberal Syndrome.

I'll try to find you if I'm in New York in January. Meanwhile a Joyeux Noël and best wishes to Elena and Helen in which Lucy and Betty join.

yrs ever   Dos

To Rumsey Marvin

1821 Sulgrave Avenue,
Baltimore, Md 21209
March 13 '67

Dear Rummy,

Forgive me for taking so long. I've been struggling with a recalcitrant chapter and letting mail collect in a box on my table.

I know the date was July and I'm pretty sure it was 1926. The summer of '28 I was in the Soviet Union. You left out the booming of the surf, the marvelous great holly trees on Ocracoke Island and that curious little settlement named Plymouth where the people spoke such a quaint dialect. I've since heard it described as a sort of Cockney, but I dont remember it's hitting us that way. We decided it was all pretty Elizabethan. I'm pretty sure that Captain Bill Gaskin's deadly brew was spiked with Lemon Extract. I remember that you and CD [Williams] and I were pretty leary of it because we'd read alarming reports of what it could do to you. Did I dream it or did we transport Hugh Leamy in a wheelbarrow next morning? I have a distinct recollection of pushing him in a wheelbarrow hoping he'd sober up enough to come along. He was a charming fellow drunk or sober.

A couple of days ago I did a reading at NC State at Raleigh and Harry Hayden's friend, whose name has slipped my mind for the moment, turned up to ask me to write something. He's going to write me more in detail. Let me know what more details CD remembers.

Thanks for the Patches. Love to B.

Yrs ever   Jack

To Lovell Thompson

Westmoreland Va 22577
March 30 1967

Dear Lovell,

It is certainly good news that you managed such an excellent deal with NAL [New American Library] for the next USA paperbacks. I'm hoping that they will gradually take on a few more reprints— District of Columbia maybe—or some outofprint items, if they find USA and THE BEST TIMES do well.

Carol [Brandt] says you would like to have a notion of what the

"Thirteenth Chronicle" will consist of. Well the central story seems to be still "The Later Life and Deplorable Opinions of Jay Pignatelli." Interwoven with that are several stories; a young Greek business man; a character who turns out to be a cross between Eddy Gilbert and Bobby Baker who ends up in Brazil; an Iowa seed corn magnate. The final part will be about the building of one of these new from the ground up cities—like Columbia, Md. Of course it may develop entirely differently, but that's the way it looks now from the notes and scattered semicompleted bits. Before I can start pulling it all together I'll have to get the Portuguese off my chest. I hope to get them pretty well licked by the end of the year.

Spring at last is appearing in these parts, though we had to drive clear down to Charleston to find it. The robins have gone through. Have they turned up in Boston yet?

Yrs ever—Dos

To Edmund Wilson

1821 Sulgrave Ave.
Baltimore Md 21209
April 12—1967

Dear Bunny,

It was nice of you to be the messenger of good tidings. Twenty million lira, when you boil it down, isn't such a hell of a lot, but—as the man said—it's better than a poke in the eye with a burnt stick. I'll drop a line to Professor Praz. His name has become legend in our family since we drove him down to the Northern Neck (at your suggestion) years and years ago. Lucy and Kiffy were both small and Betty had the habit of stuffing them with buns to keep them quiet on the road. This time it was jelly doughnuts and they started tossing them around the station wagon. They just missed a couple of direct hits on the shiny black hair in the nape of the professor's neck. As luck would have it we had a flat tire as soon as we started; there was construction on the road and I made a desperate effort to take a short cut which turned out endless. It turned darker and darker. The trip took four hours. As the country got grimmer and grimmer; no lights anywhere; he seemed to be thinking we were taking him to be murdered in some lonely wood. Happy ending: when we arrived at Spence's Point our friends the Whites, who had come for the weekend, had fires going, drinks on the table, wine ready for dinner. "It eesen't possible" he cried out.

I envy you your trip to Israel. Love to Elena and bon voyage.

Yrs ever,
Dos

I'll read Thornton Wilder's book.

To Lucy Dos Passos (1950–   )

Walloon Lake
Petoskey, Michigan
August 2 1968

Gros Lapin,

It was certainly a relief to get your cable from Belo and a postcard from Recife. We get to moping if we dont hear from you every week or so. It got to the point where I wrote Ellen Geld asking her to start, telephonically, dragging the harbor for you. Just called up Martha who was all set up from receiving a postal card. Her brother Tom is better and home. She says she's worn out trying to feed Kiffy, who is in good shape and reporting regularly at Potomac.

We had a wonderful time with Bob Garst in Coon Rapids. Everything is transformed. He says there wont be money in corn and soy beans for years. He's transformed his whole operation into a cow and calf herd (expects beef prices to hold up for a few years). Of course this is separate from the hybrid seed corn business, which is bigger than ever. To me the most astonishing thing to discover was that the uptodate breeders for beef now cross with dairy cattle. When we were trying to raise Angus that was considered the unforgiveable sin. You remember the enormous Charolais cattle we saw in São Paulo. Well, since it's expensive to import bulls on account of the quarantine against hoof and mouth disease he crosses Charolais with Herefords by artificial insemination and he expects to cross again with two enormous breeds of Swiss, getting calves (fed on corncobs, molasses and urea), added to a forage sorghum he grows on land interdicted to corn by the government program. He expects to raise 1100 lb calves in nine months and sell them to the finishers. Tell the Gelds when you see them I'm writing them more at length about the operation. I'm sure they know about it but it was all news to me.

Be sure to remember us to Marília and her family and to present our affectionate salutations to Doctor Israel.

Love,
Pa

To William L. White (1900–   ), *the son of William Allen White and, like his father, editor of the Emporia (Kansas)* Gazette *and author of many books. White and his wife Kathrine met Dos in New York in the thirties, from then on keeping in touch with him.*

Wiscasset Maine
8/8/68

Dear Bill,
    Your note made me wish I'd gone to Miami—but I'm all tied up with a last (?) contemporary chronicle and decided to pass up the folk dances this year. So I try to look at it on T.V. Was it as boring as the liberal commentators said it was? Where will you be in October?
    Love to Kathrine—

Yours ever,
Dos

To Lucy Dos Passos

Spence's Point
[Westmoreland, Virginia]
October 3 [1968]

Gros Lapin,
    September came to an end without a drop of rain. In spite of the drouth your parsley came up nicely, a model of proper seed planting. As I remember l'Ile des Pingouins is the book of Anatole France that amused me most. He's a light weight, but particularly in French, an entertaining writer of the old school. I'm delighted you are doing a lot of sketching. Maybe you ought just to buy a cheap bookcase one of these days, still bricks and boards do very well.
    Sure I'll comment on the new college generation. "Better educated" is a positive good. "Sophisticated" I dont think much of. Discoverers and inventors are usually unsophisticated people. Well as long as Oxy doesnt end up another Antioch I wont feel too worried. "Liberal" as you know has become a term of abuse with me. All of the phrases that

had meaning fifty years ago and are now decayed and rotten are going out with the tide. I sincerely hope that Mr. George Wallace isnt going to lead the reaction. People are going to face up to the fact that there is a great deal more evil than good in the human character and that the monster has to be kept under control. This leads back to religion. People cant do without it . . . except Goethe who set up Art in its place. End of Comment.

I think I wrote you that we saw Tito Leite in New York. We invited him down here but he has not shown. I hope they dont turn off the Mexico City Olympics. It would be uma atroz decepção for the Leite family.

The swimming remains delicious.

Love   Pa

To Lucy Dos Passos

Santiago de Chile
Jan 20 '69

Great Rabbit,

We found your letter of Jan 12 as soon as we reached the hotel. It must have been highly distressing when the computers produced C's instead of A's—we found the A in biology particularly notable.

The long flight down wore us out; then we spent one night dangling around a plane—old fashioned four motor very comfortable—that couldn't leave on account of bad weather on Easter Island. For some reason they always leave at 2:30 a.m., which is always changed to 3:30. Anyway next night we made it and arrived on Easter Island at 8:30, their time.

The statues were much more interesting in the stone than in photographs more varied. The whole strange prehistory unrolls as you ride around—in bumpy pickups over rocky roads of stony dust—first the fantastic efforts to carve out and move the statues to their locations on the great megalithic platforms—then after some social upheaval the equally strenuous efforts to knock them all down.

The present day Easter Islanders are not nearly as scrubby as they looked in the pictures. Handsome bright and somehow they keep themselves and their children moderately well dressed—Great supplies of underground water have recently been discovered. We were there for Father Sebastian's funeral—whom we met in New York and who died in New Orleans on the way home. Another landmark in the island's history—we came away feeling we had lived there for years. One of the most interesting places we have ever been—love   Pa

We'll be here until Jan 28 I think descensando etc.

Postcard to Marion Lowndes

Temuco Chile
1/29/69

Diddy How was India? Easter Island was immense. We find ourselves suffering a nostalgia for the great statues, the rock carvings the mysteries such as how did tutora reed (which only grows on Lake Titicaca) get there—and the people—We saw much too little of them— They are smart civil and interesting. They still do an immense amount of wood and stone carving—in fact nobody really knows which of the sculptures which keep appearing are really antique or produced yesterday. The wood carvers work free hand with little adzes singing to the guitar and drinking wine (when they can get it) as they work. The funeral of Father Sebastian, with the whole congregation singing the service in Spanish & Polynesian was really moving—When the time came to leave we hated to go

love
Dos   Betty

To Lucy Dos Passos

Buenos Aires
Argentina
2/12/69

Saturday Feb 15 we fly to Porto Allegre to
see the Verissimos—then Iguassu, then São
Paulo, Rio and so home

Great Rabbit,

2 letters arrived—one direct to Astra and one through Westmoreland. Don't worry I'm over my crud. It was violent while it lasted— undoubtedly caused by an Easter Island Aku-aku—A young Chilean geologist disappeared completely a few months ago—horse equipment and all must have fallen off the rim of one of the craters into the sea and no trace found. We wished for you so much fishing on the Rio

Tolten that runs out of Lake Villarrica into the sea—Brown trout and rainbow and what they called landlocked salmon but they seemed to me just oversized rainbows. Each day we caught enough for lunch and then for supper. One man in a boat rowed down through the rapids— They were worth the trip in themselves to say nothing of the views of Villarrica volcano. What they called a picnic was a marvelous business—the boatmen are first rate cooks and roast a whole leg of lamb (almost as good as Wyoming lamb) over a huge fire. While the lamb is roasting they cook up the trout all washed down with a bottle of first rate Chilean white wine. The camping places incredibly romantic— Robin Hood's dens and an immense variety of unknown to us birds— that we've forgotten the names of—although the boatmen spelled them out patiently

love
Pa

To Lucy Dos Passos

Westmoreland, Virginia 22577
March 8 1969

Gros Lapin,
     Your little note of March 3 arrived yesterday. We've talked to Kiffy on the phone. Did medium well on exams, but passed. Next time you write let us know your chronology. My understanding is that spring vacation is from March 15 to 23 and that you'll need a check for the Treasurer: Occidental College ($995.00?) on March 24 Is that right? Where is the Hiking Club going in Baja? I'll be envious. Everything is confusing in Brazil. One great opponent of the regime, Julio Mesquita the owner-editor of Estado de São Paulo agreed with general Portela that the Castro-Chinese incented subversive situation was very dangerous. There have been numerous attempts to blow up the building, which contains both my favorite Hotel Jaragua and the newspaper. The Estado is protected by a private army with the consent of the government. Mesquita pointed out a khaki-clad thug with a submachine gun with some pride when I went to see him. Daily political bank robberies and attempted robberies continue in São Paulo. Most people point out that a great many government measures do more harm than good, by driving young people into the revolutionary camp.

Censorship is erratic. One newspaper gets by with an article while another gets closed down for the same statements. Rumors are wild. The day we arrived in Rio a fellow from the US Embassy had just heard—on good authority—that Chico Buarte had died in prison from ill treatment at the hands of the police. Next day we heard that he was living quietly in Rome, having been smuggled out with the consent of the authorities. He wrote a song about camaradajem very unpopular with the military. Carlos Lacerda has lost his civil rights and was supposed to be exiled in Europe, but the last thing we heard before leaving Rio—from Tito Leite—was that he was on the way home, with the tacit consent of the military

I must go back to my Easter Island article. We are driving up to Baltimore this afternoon, because the radio announces a big snow and sleet storm for tomorrow. Maybe it will be like your California earthquake.

Love
Pa

Tito and Lowndes sent love and so did the Gelds and their friends in São Paulo the Hayes.

To William L. White

Westmoreland, Va 22577
April 7 1969

Dear Bill,

I've intended to write so often about Report on the Asians that maybe I actually did get a note off making this all redundant. I've always enjoyed your reports, but this one seems to me particularly good. You actually made me want to go to India and the Vietnam part is refreshing after all the hysterics. I should have liked a little advice to Mr. Nixon on what the hell to do about it. I particularly liked the report on Mao's China. All through you strike a reasonable kind of a man on the street tone that I find soothing and stimulating after the psychedelic ravings of our juniors.

We'll try to find you in New York on Wednesday.

Love to Kathrine.

Yrs Ever
Dos

Thanks so much for sending it to us. The Digest to my amazment, bought the Easter Island piece. We must tell you about it.

To Joseph Blotner (1923–   ), *a teacher and writer, who corresponded with Dos while he was preparing his biography of William Faulkner.*

Westmoreland, Virginia 22577
October 7 [19]69

Dear Mr. Blotner,

There's just a chance that I was introduced to Faulkner for a moment in New Orleans sometime in the mid twenties winter 1924? by either Sherwood Anderson or Lyle Saxon. My first real conversation with him was at the Hotel Algonquin. I might have gone there with Don Stewart. It was one of those drunken evenings with all sorts of characters popping in and out of bedrooms. Mrs. Faulkner was there, looking very deep Mississippi and thoroughly unperturbed. I remember wondering how she stood all these goings on. There were certainly other meetings but I dont remember them clearly. Then we met at that Jefferson Society Lecture and at the National Academy on the occasion of the gold medal. Neither Faulkner nor I were ever happy in these stuffed shirt surroundings. At lunch Faulkner sat next to my wife and she earned what seemed to be his undying gratitude by giving him her wine. The waiter must have thought she had great capacity because her glass was always empty, she doesn't drink wine. The proceedings were boring to a degree. I could see Faulkner bubbling like a teakettle about to boil over on the seat in front of me on the platform. The Americans were longwinded enough but Salvador de Madariaga (a gentleman whom I have much esteemed in many ways)—produced an incredibly long dissertation on Leonardo's Saint Anne. Reproductions were passed around the hall so that we wouldn't miss an allusion. (My private hunch is that it was an old doctor's thesis that he'd produced for some study of aesthetics at the Sorbonne or somewhere many years ago). I hate aesthetics and if Faulkner listened at all he didn't like what he heard. When finally after a good deal more wordage we finally got to our little act . . . Faulkner abandoned what he had been planning to say, shoved the medal into my hand and said "Nobody ever deserved it more or had to wait for it longer."

The business about indebtedness I dont go for. I read Pylon with great pleasure about the time it came out, but I swear I dont think

Faulkner was indebted to my work in any way. At certain times styles and methods are in the air, as contagious as the common cold. In that way we were all indebted to each other.

All good wishes,
John Dos Passos

To Edmund Wilson

Westmoreland Va 22577
April 25 1970

Dear Bunny
I shall be delighted to become a member of the Cape Cod chapter of the Exalted Order of Digitalis Users (though I understand Charlie cant tolerate the friendly drug) Hygroton, digoxin and allopurinal; these three I do obeisance to every morning. I'm not sure that I can blame Easter Island for all of my troubles though I did come away with an Aku-aku in the form of a violent throat infection which almost strangled me when I was trying to swallow a piece of turkey in the garden of the U.S. Embassy in Santiago de Chile. Anyway I had a damned unpleasant winter, lost some forty pounds and emerged from "The Good Samaritan" convalescent hospital sadder and wiser.
Lucy, who is forging ahead with her plans for Landscape Architecture, will have a job at the Arnold Arboretum this summer so we'll be lurking around the Boston area in August and might possibly get out to the Cape. Would love to see you all.
Betty joins me in all of the best to you and Elena—

Yrs ever
Dos

Doubleday is bringing out my narrative of Easter Island combined with long quotes from the first European visitors much illustrated— (the photographs are the cause of the delay)—next winter. You shall have one as soon as the volumes are ready.

To William L. White

Westmoreland Va 22577
May 12 1970

Dear Bill,
Please dont get riled up at Bill Buckley. You know the overextended life he leads. I'm afraid he'll wear himself out too soon Anyway

I shant send in any letter until I hear from him. If he doesnt want to fight the liberals who seem to have taken charge of the Century Club it's all right by me. The more I hear about them the more I feel like resigning—There are better ways of spending $150, particularly as I visit the place about once a year—

I wish we could see you but I dont suppose you could find a couple or three days to drive down to Virginia

Love to Kathrine

Yrs ever
Dos

To Lucy Dos Passos

Westmoreland Va 22577
May 23 1970

It's hot here too (80° to 90°)
Manoel Cardoza is driving Lois [Hazell]
down for the night and the Lafourcades,
a couple we met in Chile, are coming to
lunch. Lois & I will call in the morning

Sweet Rabbit,

Last Saturday's letter was a pleasure. The birthday party must have been great fun. The Irani feast sounds wonderful. Dill we have but I've never known how to use turmeric. Rice with dates and lentils must have been good. Maybe you'll reproduce it for your doddering old parents one of these days. (I feel a little doddering this morning because our best cherry tree collapsed last night. No wind or rain, but it's a total loss. Rotted at the root. I feel I should have done something to save it but I dont know what. Since the other tree decided not to bear this year, it means no cherry pies.)

Ever since seeing the documentary "Woodstock" I blame everything on TV. What we are suffering from is the generation weaned and raised on TV. I think one reason you find the orientals, Mexicans etc so much more amusing than the poor palefaced WASP's is that they didn't spend those countless hours staring at TV. They learned to play as children. The abuse of narcotics stems in part from an effort to get back into the old TV coma. Woodstock is worth seeing. I'd like to know how it hits you. To me it was endlessly depressing. Sociologically interesting, yes. To my way of thinking none of the music had any life (except for a few familiar African rhythms). No invention or originality. The best numbers were old Beatles tunes. All these half naked people, young and not so young rejoicing in the fact that there were two hundred thousand of them there. At any time in my life if I'd taken a young lady out to the Catskills, I'd have wanted a little privacy. I should think they would have been ashamed to show their under-developed muscles. Nobody, except the construction workers who put up the stand, looked as if they had done a decent days work, plain physical labor, in their lives.

It seemed to me that, instead of sobbing about how bad the system is, the people of your generation should be trying to develop themselves, physically and mentally and morally into decent human beings.

You are perfectly right this is the time for people of sense and discrimination to try to channel all this energy into something that will help to build a better society. Among the pure satanic evil that has come to the surface there is some good. The pathetic thing about the great wellintentioned mass of college and highschool students is that they have been so badly educated they have no knowledge or under-standing of the complications of the world we live in and they have been so conditioned and prejudiced by generations of ill-taught teachers that they refuse to see a fact when they are confronted with one. Ask one of your revolutionary friends if he ever heard of Kronstadt?

I'm all for dematerialising, but its not an easy task. The Soviet Union has been working on it back-handedly for fifty years but the struggle for material possessions is more desperate now in the USSR than in any of the "capitalist" countries. My perennial advice to Marxist young men is go get a job in Moscow and see how you like it.

I suspect that you are wrong in playing down suburbia, even Glen Burnie. For years some of my friends dreamed of trying to make American cities into organic centers as Paris and Madrid and Rome were in the period of World War I. The trend is all the other way in Europe and America.

I liked your paragraph about chlorophyll.

There's nothing new about working for the pure pleasure of it. That's been the motivation of first class people from the beginning of time.

You are right about the American culture we have never yet dis-covered.

I read every word of your letter with pleasure and agree with more of it than you think; still I feel it is tragic that the young people have allowed themselves to be led by their elders into this hysteria about Cambodia*—it's the first rational military step taken in the whole war, and whether you agree with him or not President Nixon deserves acclaim instead of obloquy for having had the courage to try it in face of overwhelming Communist-inspired propaganda campaign modeled on the campaign that had its first success among the French at the time of Dienbienphu and Algeria. If Nixon fails it is just this generation that is raising such cain that will have to bear the brunt of the results. I'll be in my grave re-entering the carbon cycle. Aside: I still believe, in that connection, there is more to life than just chemistry.

                                                                love
                                                                Pa
*naturally there is room for rational differences of opinion on the whole subject. I've always wanted the United States to be a neutral country like Switzerland

To Horsley Gantt (1893–   ), *whom Dos met in Russia in 1928 when Gantt was doing research at Pavlov's laboratories in Petrograd. He returned to the United States in 1929 to set up a Pavlovian Laboratory at Johns Hopkins University. Gantt has been a leader in the study of neurophysiology and neurotic behavior in animals and human beings. Since retiring from Johns Hopkins he has continued his work at the Veterans' Administration Hospital, Perry Point, Maryland. Gantt has authored several books and many articles about his field and edits the journal* Conditional Reflex.

                                                    Westmoreland Va 22577
                                                          June 21 1970

Dear Horsley,
    This piece is outstanding.
    If Skinner aspired to be a writer he certainly achieved his ambition. He writes dangerously well. I suppose what he meant was he wanted to be a novelist. Certainly the novelistic aspects of Walden II dont hold up to Walden I.
    You treat, what seems to me his grave fault of superficiality, very tenderly. After all he is a good friend. I remember him as a charming fellow to talk to.

When I see you I must get you to explain "Skinner's Box."

From page 5 on I agree with you thoroughly. It seems to me that what has happened is that the entire ideology that springs from John Locke and the French encyclopaedists has reached maturity and died. Ideas have their lifespan like natural organisms. To my mind the importance of Pavlov rests chiefly on his dedication to objective reporting which left him no time to fuss with fashionable ideologies.

I would say that in later life Bertrand Russell became an intolerant materialist. I dont know much about modern astrophysics but my impression is that Russells cosmogony has been completely demolished. What about the hypothetical universes made necessary by modern mathematics?

What you say about Darwin is very much to the point.

From page 12 on you enter into a most eloquent description of what I might call the religion of a scientist. These are some of the finest pages you have ever written.

We'll talk about this later

On page 11a let me point out that "tenent" should be tenet. It is an English usage of the latin TENET (he holds) The Oxford Dict. does give one sixteenth century case of tenent being used for tenet but I suspect that was a misprint.

I would say the review was just about ready for the printer.

See you Friday or Saturday.

Yrs ever,

Dos

To Lois Hazell (1896–   ), *a cousin of Dos on his mother's side, who knew him from their childhoods in Washington, D.C. She remembers him for his kindness to her—at Annisquam during the summer of 1910 he gave her his entire box of lead soldiers. Once after Dos had been visiting his cousins for several days he said, "Goodbye, I am walking down to Mexico to meet a friend on a mountain," and off he went.*

Westmoreland Va 22577
June 24 1970

Dear Lois,

Thanks so much for this second collection of photographs. It was a good weekend and these commemorate it splendidly. I'm returning this young fellow's letter from Vienna. There have been thousands like it. Its amazing that these strange deluded people of the colleges dont catch up about what it's really like in their ideal republic. It will be interesting to hear what Manoel has to say. He's attending some sort of international historians gathering this summer in Moscow. The dreary thing about the situation is that we know all about it already. Any international visitor is sealed off from the Russians. The two great successes of the Communist system seem to be subversion and repression.

Sometimes I cant help rejoicing in the fact that I'm not likely to live much longer—

love
Jack

Betty says hello. Lucy is established at her job in the Arnold Arboretum. That is her mailing address Arnold Arboretum Jamaica Plain Mass 02130. She has an apartment at 215 Commonwealth Ave Boston Mass 02116

To Harold and Faith Weston. *Harold (1894–1972) had known Dos from their days at Harvard, but they had not been particularly close. Then in 1921 John Farrar, who had the manuscript for* Three Soldiers, *told Weston that Dos wanted to take a trip to the Near East. Weston had been in Persia, so he wrote Dos; their correspondence continued, and they became good friends, Dos always remaining interested in Weston's art.*

Westmoreland Va 22577
June 25 [*1970*]

Dear Harold and Faith,

It was delightful to hear from you. I'd been intending to write for months. After a very unpleasant winter in and out of Johns Hopkins and a convalescent place known as the Good Samaritan I got out to Tucson Arizona and was very much set up by the climate etc. Charlie Walker—another heart patient—was thoroughly established there and we had a very good time with the Walkers and my dear friends and cousins the Camerons. The male Cameron, Brodnax, was there for respiratory reasons. Anyway I came back much refreshed and have been thriving down at Spence's Point until about three weeks ago when various little symptoms started to appear. Congestive heart failure is an uphill battle which you are sure to lose in the end. I'd be sunk if I weren't able to keep working. I've put to bed a book—delayed—that came out of our last delightful adventure: the trip to Easter Island—January 1969 and I'm putting the finishing touches on a last forlorn Chronicle of Despair. The rank criminal idiocy of the younger generation in this country is more than I can swallow.

Ever since receiving your letter we have played with the idea of stopping off at St Huberts on our way to Maine. We have rented a little house in Wiscasset Maine (or rather at Head Tide up the Sheepscot)

Your arthritis has undoubtedly been painful and frustrating. Old age is no circus. We heard in Tucson of arthritic sufferers being relieved by the intensely dry climate. My theory still is that any kind of action is better than none

We'll be starting north, if the old carcase holds out, in late July. If we can possibly work in St Huberts we'll let you know. Do want to see you both—Betty sends her love to the pair of you—particularly to Faith. She now understands that these medical embroglios are harder on the wife than they are on the protagonist.

Yrs Ever
Dos

To Harold Weston

3B Hamill Rd
Cross Keys Village
Baltimore Md 21210
July 10 1970

Dear Harold,

So nice to get your letter of July 5. I've had what I hope is a small set back. This heart business is tricky. My doctor hopes to have me straightened out in a couple of weeks, but you never know, meanwhile we are holed up in our perfectly comfortable apartment here. The Northern Neck is too hot for me at this season of the year—we may be able to make St Huberts going North or coming south. I agree with you that it is important for old friends to see each other at this stage

Yrs ever and love to Faith
Dos

To the Committee on Admissions
The Century Association

Westmoreland, Virginia 22577
July 17, 1970

Gentlemen:—

Since wit and conversational powers are, as I understand it, qualifications for membership in the Century Association I can't imagine anyone better qualified for membership than Bill Buckley. Since the grand old days of Bob Benchley no one has appeared in the publishing world so full of high spirits and sheer animal warmth. No one held Bob Benchley's occasional political acts against him. There are probably a few mighty men still around old enough to remember them. I hope you will remember that when you are inviting someone to join the Century you are not inviting a bundle of current notions but an entire man with his past behind him and his future before him.

Cordial regards
John Dos Passos

Notes to Chapter Narratives

"A HOTEL CHILDHOOD" *JANUARY 14, 1896–JUNE 1917*
P. 4 *The Best Times* (New York, 1966), p. 22.
P. 6 *The Best Times*, p. 8.
P. 7 *The Best Times*, p. 15.
P. 8 *The Best Times*, p. 15.
P. 10 *The Best Times*, p. 25.

ONE MAN'S INITIATION *JUNE 1917–AUGUST 1918*
P. 84 *The Best Times* (New York, 1966), p. 70.

"WE STAND DEFEATED AMERICA" *JANUARY 1928–
DECEMBER 1932*
P. 378 *Panama or the Adventures of My Seven Uncles* (New York
    and London, 1931), pp. vii-viii.
P. 382 *The Theme Is Freedom* (New York, 1956), p. 103.
P. 382 Granville Hicks, "The Politics of John Dos Passos," *Antioch
    Review, X* (March 1950), 92.
PP. 382–383 " 'a middle-class liberal' ": "Back to Red Hysteria," *New
    Republic,* LXIII (July 2, 1930), 169.
P. 383 "he located himself politically . . .": "Wanted: An Ivy Lee for
    Liberals," *New Republic,* LXIII (August 13, 1930), 371–372.
P. 383 " 'I don't see how . . .' ": Quoted in Martin Kallich, "John Dos
    Passos Fellow-Traveler: A Dossier with Commentary," *Twen-
    tieth Century Literature,* I (January 1956), 181.

"PEELING THE ONION OF DOUBT"
JANUARY 1933–DECEMBER 1936
P. 418 " 'signs and portents' ": *The Best Times* (New York, 1966),
    p. 227.
P. 418 " 'idiotic series of incidents' ": *The Best Times,* p. 229.
P. 419 " 'To John Dos Passos' ": Quoted in Daniel Aaron, *Writers on
    the Left* (New York, 1965), p. 363.
P. 420 " '. . . Here are the back lots . . .' ": "Facing a Bitter World. A
    Portfolio of Etchings," *Esquire, III* (February 1935), 25.

CHOSEN COUNTRY *JANUARY 1937–DECEMBER 1946*

P. 496 " 'You do that . . .' ": Letter to the editor, December 30, 1970.

P. 497 "Farewell to Europe," *Common Sense,* VI (July 1937), 10–11.

P. 498 "The Communist Party and the War Spirit," *Common Sense,* VI (December 1937), 11–14.

P. 498 " 'Adventures of a Young Man is the first . . .' ": MS at Alderman Library, University of Virginia.

P. 502 " 'Who sups with the devil . . .' ": Alderman Library, University of Virginia.

CENTURY'S EBB *JANUARY 1946–SEPTEMBER 1970*

P. 572 "Acceptance by John Dos Passos," *Proceedings of the American Academy of Arts and Letters,* second series, no. 8 (New York, 1958), p. 193.

P. 573 " 'When he shall hear . . .' ": MS at Alderman Library, University of Virginia.

P. 574 " 'About all I got . . .' ": Washington *Post,* July 16, 1959, p. B1.

PP. 574–575 " 'Sometimes I wonder' ": MS in the Choate School Files.

P. 576 "On the Way to the Moon Shot," *National Review,* XXIII (February 9, 1971), 135–136.

INDEX

Note: The index below is a listing of people and places that figure significantly in this volume and of all the titles of Dos Passos' works. Works other than his are indexed according to author; thus when "Satyricon" appears in the text on page 252, a reference to Petronius is listed in the index. In addition, references to various political ideologies are included.